Fifth Edition

Counseling

Theory and Process

James C. Hansen
Robert H. Rossberg
Stanley H. Cramer
All of State University of New York at Buffalo

Allyn and Bacon
Boston • London • Toronto • Sydney • Tokyo • Singapore

Series Editor: Ray Short
Series Editorial Assistant: Christine M. Shaw
Production Administrator: Annette Joseph
Production Coordinator: Holly Crawford
Cover Administrator: Linda K. Dickinson
Manufacturing Buyer: Louise Richardson

Copyright © 1994, 1986, 1982, 1977, 1972 by Allyn and Bacon
A Division of Simon & Schuster, Inc.
160 Gould Street
Needham Heights, MA 02194

The fourth edition of this book was written by James C. Hansen, Richard R. Stevic, and Richard W. Warner, Jr.

Library of Congress Cataloging-in-Publication Data
Hansen, James C.
   Counseling : theory and process / James C. Hansen, Robert
Rossberg, Stanley H. Cramer. — 5th ed.
      p.   cm.
   Includes bibliographical references and indexes.
   ISBN 0-205-14819-0
   1. Counseling.   I. Rossberg, Robert H.   II. Cramer, Stanley H.
   III. Title.
BF637.C6H36 1993
158′.3—dc20   92-42153
                                                                                       CIP

Printed in the United States of America

10 9 8 7 6 5 4 3 2 1   98 97 96 95 94 93

Text Credits: Pages 279–280 from "The Hidden Minority: Issues and Challenges in Working with Lesbians and Gay Men" by R. Fassinger, 1991, *The Counseling Psychologist, 19,* pp. 170–171. Copyright 1991 by Sage Publications. Reprinted by permission of Sage Publications, Inc.

Continued on page 404

Brief Contents

Contents

PART II   *Counseling Process   189*

Preface

Counseling is a process that helps people learn about themselves, their environment, and ways to handle their roles and relationships. Although individuals seek counseling because they are experiencing problems, counseling is not necessarily remedial. The counselor may assist an individual with the decision-making process in educational and vocational matters as well as with resolving interpersonal concerns. Counseling is an applied field in which the counselor uses behavioral knowledge to help the client. Theory is helpful in understanding the development of behavior patterns, the manner and extent of undesirable behavior, and the development of procedures for changing client behavior.

This book is in its fifth edition. The acceptance of the earlier editions endorses the importance of the counselor developing a personal approach in counseling. Most counselors begin modeling the theoretical approach that is most comfortable for them and then evolve a personal systematic eclectic approach. This book reviews numerous prominent theories and then presents the general counseling process that allows counselors to add techniques and procedures consistent with their approach. Each edition has incorporated suggestions from counselors and counselor trainers. We endeavor to provide up-to-date literature and research and yet retain a place for the classic material.

The purpose of this book is to provide a base from which students aspiring to be counselors or counselors working in the field can build a personal theory of counseling, ideally a theory that will guide their own practice. We realize that no one book can do justice to all the theories in the field of counseling. Our goal is not to present an exhaustive treatment of each theory, but rather to provide the tools and general background to enable an individual to build his or her own counseling theory. To achieve this goal, we begin in Chapter 1, with a general discussion of theory and theory development. The next nine chapters are an overview of the contributions to counseling from various theoretical positions. Chapters 2 through 4 are devoted to psychoanalytic theory, derivatives of psychoanalytic thought, and ego counseling. Chapters 5 through 7 are focused on humanistic approaches to counseling theory: self-theory, existential approaches, and the Gestalt approach to counseling. The behavioral therapy, cognitive-behavioral, and rational-emotive approaches are discussed in the remaining chapters on theory. Chapter

11 assesses the present status of counseling theory and compares the various theoretical approaches.

From the theoretical base presented in Part I, the second part of the book moves to the process of counseling. The section begins with a chapter describing counseling as a relationship between counselor and client and examining the dimensions that occur in that relationship. In Chapter 13 the focus is on the stages in the counseling process. In Chapter 14 we examine the social factors in the relationship. Chapter 15 presents concepts related to the diagnostic and treatment planning processes in counseling. The next three chapters are concerned with specific topics in counseling: decision making, use of tests in counseling, and career counseling. In the final chapter, we discuss ethics, legalities, and values that may confront a counselor during the counseling process. Case material is presented to illustrate the counseling process. Obviously, a professor's use of tape recordings and films as illustrations is an excellent way to make counseling come alive.

Although this is the fifth edition of the book, there are two new authors: Robert Rossberg and Stanley Cramer. We feel grateful to Richard Stevic and Richard Warner for the foundation they developed for the book. Many of the theory chapters continue to show the work of Dick Warner. With new authors come new ideas and changes in material. In the first part of the book a specific chapter on Adler was modified to include the concepts of Karen Horney and Harry Stack Sullivan. Chapters on transactional analysis and reality therapy were discontinued and replaced by chapters on existential and cognitive-behavioral approaches to counseling. In the second part of the book, most of the same topics are present, but have been updated and rewritten. The chapter on initiating counseling was discontinued, and much of that material is covered in the chapter on the stages in the counseling process. A new chapter focuses on the social factors that impact on the counseling relationship. This chapter covers such topics as counselor-client characteristics and multicultural and gender issues. The last four chapters are completely new material on the topics of decision making; testing and counseling; career counseling; and the place of ethics, values, and legalities in counseling.

We have drawn the material in this book from the theories and research of many writers in the field of counseling. We also acknowledge the stimulation of our colleagues and students as an important contribution to the completion of the book.

Part I

Counseling Theory

The major premise of this book is that counselors must understand both the why and the how of counseling. A counselor who has knowledge of one but not the other is not sufficiently prepared to be of service. Therefore we focus in this text on both the theory (why) and the process (how) of counseling.

Each counselor should develop a personal theory of counseling. In most cases this personal theory will be eclectic, a systematic combination of bits and pieces from several existing theories. There is evidence that this systematic eclecticism is increasingly necessary and useful. Garfield and Kurtz (1977) in reporting the views of 154 clinicians indicated that no single current theory applies adequately to the many kinds of clients seen in counseling and therapy. In view of this, our aim is to help the reader build a personal systematic approach.

Corsini and Wedding (1989) note that counseling and psychotherapy are an art and that "all good therapists are eclectic." They applaud the rise of "formal eclecticism" as a sign of the maturation of the counseling art. At the same time, they note that the development of eclecticism "does not mean that [counselors] do not follow a particular theory or use specific methods associated with particular approaches to therapy." Our goal is to help the reader determine a reasonable congruence between his or her beliefs and values and those of a particular segment of theories in order to evolve a workable, personal systematic approach.

This process begins with an examination of the current thinking within the profession; therefore, Part I presents theories that are currently receiving the most attention by counselors today. Each chapter describes the theoretical background and examines actual counseling procedures advocated by an approach. The second part of the book examines the general concepts and methods through which theories are translated into the counseling process.

Part I begins with a chapter devoted to the process of developing a personal counseling theory. It provides a system that will facilitate the development of a systematic personal theory as the reader moves through the text and subsequent training.

Our presentation of theories begins with analytic approaches and then proceeds through approaches that have moved further and further away from Freudian influence. Few approaches to counseling or therapy have not been influenced in some way by Freudian psychoanalytic theory. Freud's theories have affected the work of psychiatrists, psychologists, counselors, social workers, and others involved in the helping professions. Major Freudian concepts are briefly presented as a necessary background to Chapters 3 and 4. These chapters focus on derivations from Freud, including the ideas of Adler, Sullivan, and Horney and ego counseling. Chapter 4 examines ego-analytic approaches to counseling. Although in many respects there is only a slight distinction between psychoanalytic theory and ego-analytic theory, the difference makes the latter approach more appropriate to counseling.

Chapters 5 and 6 discuss two approaches that represent clear breaks with Freudian thought and its philosophical underpinnings. These two chapters present the humanist views of the self-theorists led by Carl R. Rogers and the existentialist views of writers such as Rollo May. Many of the proponents of these viewpoints share a belief in the capacity of individuals to be self-directing and, ultimately, self-actualizing. Another viewpoint, which shares this basic belief system but differs markedly in concept and technique, is the Gestalt view of Fritz Perls, presented in Chapter 7.

The remaining chapters in this section dealing with theory derive their impetus from the complex of ideas that are generally considered under the rubric of behavioral approaches to counseling. They are attempts to place some emphasis on counseling as a special type of learning situation. Chapter 8 describes the broad range of classical behavioral approaches to counseling. Although there are many differences among those who refer to themselves as behaviorists, all share a belief in the use of the laws of learning to bring about behavioral change. This chapter focuses on the basic laws of learning adhered to by most classical behaviorists and on how many of these laws are translated into specific counseling techniques.

Chapters 9 and 10 consider counseling from a rational point of view predicated on the assumption that while counseling is a learning process with cognitive and affective elements, these approaches place more faith in human capacity for reasoned thought and conscious control than do the classical behaviorists. The ideas of Aaron T. Beck, D. H. Meichenbaum, and Albert Ellis are considered.

Advocates of the theories presented in Chapters 2 through 10 are continually modifying and updating their approaches; the theories are not final products. The reader who is interested in any of these approaches is encouraged to go beyond the basic information presented here to read original material.

Chapter 11, the final chapter in Part I, compares the material presented in Chapters 2 through 10 to provide the reader with a framework for developing a personal situation vis-à-vis counseling as well as a starting point for the material on the counseling process presented in Part II. As people approach counselors in their search for help in the solution of human problems, counselors have constantly searched themselves and their own beliefs for insights into the human condition. This is an endless search with continuing modifications of personal positions. These chapters are a modest beginning of that process.

Chapter 1

Toward a Personal Theory of Counseling

The profession of counseling, begun by Frank Parsons in the early 1900s, experienced tremendous growth in the 1960s, a modest but profound change in direction during the 1970s, and has moved into the 1980s and 1990s striving to retain what has been of value while being responsive to new needs. In the 1960s, an influx of federal funds into programs for the preparation and training of counselors created not only more counselors but also more and generally better programs. New social programs in the 1970s broadened the work setting of counselors. The changing populations and social needs of the 1980s and 1990s have further increased the demand for competent professional counselors. Highly competent counselors are now found in such diverse settings as schools, colleges, drug and alcohol abuse centers, insurance and family counseling centers, career and employment settings, churches, and mental health agencies.

Each counselor, regardless of the setting, must develop a personal counseling model as a framework for operating in his or her particular specialty area. This model must be consistent with the counselor's beliefs and values. The model not only provides a foundation for practice but also informs ethical decision making. Counselors are constantly called upon to make judgments and choices based on their models of practice. This becomes the theoretical formulation upon which most practical action rests. This chapter is designed to help develop that process by providing a framework for integrating theory and process into a personal theory of counseling. It may help provide a way of looking at the world of counseling that will increase the possibilities that the choices we make are understood in terms of our motives and that we are aware of what we are likely to see of the world and how we are likely to respond.

Counseling: What Is It?

As Tyler (1969) points out, *counseling* is a word that everyone seems to understand, but it is quite apparent that no two people understand it in exactly the same way. The rapid growth of the profession has confused the issue of what counseling means. Part of the confusion may also stem from the fact that counseling as we know it had its beginnings in related but separate fields.

An Interdisciplinary Background

Counseling is an applied social science with an interdisciplinary base composed of psychology, sociology, cultural anthropology, education, economics, and philosophy (Glanz, 1974). Each of these disciplines has made and continues to make its own unique contribution to counseling. From psychology we learn about human growth and development; sociology provides insight into social structure and institutions; anthropology helps us understand the importance of culture; and from economics we learn about the dynamics involved in the world of work. For readers who wish to investigate how each of these disciplines has affected the base of knowledge on which counseling rests, Hansen's *Explorations in Sociology and Counseling* (1969) is an excellent source. In addition, Raoull Naroll's *The Moral Order: An Introduction to the Human Situation* (1983) provides an anthropological and socioeconomic appraisal of the human situation across cultures, as well as a comparative examination of personal and family problems across a wide cultural sample.

The purpose of counseling makes clear why such varied disciplines have influenced the profession. The purpose of counseling is to provide for the individual's optimum development and well-being, but the individual functions in a social context, not in isolation. If counselors are to enhance the well-being of the individual, they must understand as many as possible of the factors that affect people; they must adopt an interdisciplinary approach. Such an approach is a product both of our past and of the current demands made by the people we serve.

Counseling, like most professions, has gone through a developmental process since its inception in the areas of vocational and educational guidance. Frank Parsons, generally regarded as the founder of the guidance and counseling movement, was primarily interested in developing a system for matching individuals with appropriate occupations. Counseling from his perspective was seen as a process whereby data was gathered about the individual and about occupations, then the two were matched for the best fit.

A second group of pioneers was led by the work of Brewer and Davis. Brewer was troubled that schools were concerned chiefly with translating knowledge and did not relate this knowledge to the world that students would enter. In Brewer's view, education should provide guidance for young people in how to live. Davis was instrumental in developing the concept of educational guidance as moral guidance or guidance for living. These developments broadened the scope of counseling activities beyond concern with a prospective occupation; counseling came to include the total life of the individual.

Related to Davis's concept of guidance for living were the developments taking place as a result of a book by Clifford Beers. In 1908, Beers published the book *The Mind That*

Found Itself, which called attention to the problem of mental illness in the United States. Coupled with the emergence of the field of psychoanalysis, Beers's work led to increased interest in both the concept of mental illness and the methods for helping those afflicted. This movement promoted rapid expansion in psychiatry and clinical psychology. Many people in these fields referred to what they were doing as *counseling.* Those in education most often referred to the process as *life adjustment,* defined as "that which better equips all American youth to live democratically with satisfaction to themselves and profit to society as home members, workers and citizens" (U.S. Office of Education, 1950, p. 1). Both groups regarded counseling as a means of helping people adjust to themselves and society. This position contributed to the notion that counseling should help people understand themselves in relation to the world.

In the early 1950s there was an increasing emphasis in psychology on developmental tasks. Havighurst defines these as tasks that arise "at or about a certain period in the life of an individual, successful achievement of which leads to his happiness and to success with later tasks, while failure leads to unhappiness in the individual, disapproval by society, and difficulty with later tasks" (1952, p. 2). The role of counseling in this process was to facilitate individual movement along the developmental path. Counseling services extended over a long period and focused on enhancing a person's inherent ability to move toward maturity. This was in sharp contrast to the crisis-intervention approach implied by the emphasis on adjustment being advocated by those more clinically oriented.

Related to the developmental approach was an emphasis on counseling as an aid in decision making. This approach held that counseling was necessary only when individuals needed help in making decisions.

In the following decade, counseling evolved in two sometimes conflicting directions. In 1958, passage of the National Defense Education Act (NDEA) put counseling under pressure to meet national work force needs. The purpose of NDEA was to recruit more young people into science, and counselors were trained to channel bright students in that direction. At the same time other pressure was developing for counseling to serve as an agent for social reconstruction. This approach recognized that many of the difficulties a person had were derived from the inadequacies of the society. Counseling was perceived, then, as a means of righting these wrongs.

There has also been strong pressure on the profession to recommit itself to career development counseling. This pressure emanates from the career education movement. "Few concepts introduced into the policy circles of American education have ever been met with such instant acclaim as career education" (Hoyt, Evans, Malkin, & Mangum, 1972, p. 1). This movement is largely a response to the problems created by a rapidly changing, complex society. Herr (1974) suggests, "As societies become developed (industrial) the concomitant magnitude of opportunities poses a 'burden of decision' for the young and displaced" (p. ix).

During the 1970s and early 1980s, counselors, as a distinct professional group, became an important element within the broad field of mental health. Counselors are now providing a variety of therapeutic services to a wide range of clients, including those with alcohol and drug problems, those with marital and family problems, adolescents, those with disabilities, and those who are occupationally displaced. Counselor training programs responding to these new demands on the professional counselor have also changed drastically over this period. Counselors now being trained represent a radical departure from the traditional educational counselor.

In the 1990s, counselors and counseling psychologists, in particular, have entered the realm of private practice, a development that needs to be watched carefully since it has the potential of separating theory from practice. In addition, counseling psychologists have moved into roles that deal with prevention, attend to problems of geriatric populations, and respond to needs in industrial settings.

This broad examination of the major influences on the development of counseling implies the existence of rather simplistic, separate models. Helping someone select an occupation or the appropriate educational courses might appear to be a relatively easy task. If, however, counseling is defined as a process concerned with an individual's optimum development and well-being, both personally and in relation to the larger society, the task involves the synthesis of a complex model that comes close to encompassing all the emphases discussed. The evolution of the definition of counseling has involved additions rather than substitutions. Far more important, the development of counseling has involved growth not simply in the number of emphases but also in the scope of preparation required and services provided.

Counseling versus Psychotherapy

A second source of confusion about what counseling is stems from the attempt to differentiate counseling from psychotherapy and counselors from clinical psychologists. This has been particularly true where counselors and psychologists have functioned in the same or similar work settings. Most counseling authorities regard psychotherapy and counseling as a continuum of services. According to Brammer and Shostrom (1977), counseling is largely concerned with the so-called normal individual and is characterized by terms such as *conscious awareness, problem solving, educative, supportive,* and *situational;* psychotherapy, on the other hand, is concerned with *reconstruction, depth emphasis, analysis,* and *focusing on the unconscious* and especially on *neurotic* and *emotional problems.* The authors suggest that counseling and psychotherapy are terms that are generally used interchangeably.

A special committee report of the American Psychological Association (APA) suggests that counseling involves helping individuals plan for a productive role in their social environments. "Whether the person being helped with such planning is sick or well, abnormal or normal, is really irrelevant. The focus is on assets, skills, strengths, and possibilities for further development. Personality difficulties are dealt with only when they constitute obstacles to the individual's forward progress" (APA, 1961, p. 6). Unlike the Brammer and Shostrom continuum, the focus of the APA continuum is not the individual *but the manner in which the counselor and psychotherapist work with their respective clients.* These are only two examples of many attempts to differentiate the two professions.

Let us concede that counseling and psychotherapy are related ways of helping people in need and that they exist along a continuum. Both exist because our complex technological society has placed many demands on individuals, demands that involve the roles they are expected to fulfill in society. In some cases the transition from the demands of one role to the demands of another causes intrapersonal difficulties: the individual experiences internal value conflicts. In other cases, the difficulty arises from the nature of the roles themselves; the individual has difficulty assuming a particular role. The continuum is discernible in these two interrelated but somewhat different problem areas. At one end are intrapersonal conflicts; at the other are conflicts that involve role definitions.

This continuum, shown in Figure 1-1, illustrates that an individual's difficulty may occur in the development of personality, in the destruction of the personality through role demands, in role transition, in role choice, in conflicts among roles, or in contradictions between values and role expectations (Perry, 1955). In these cases, either psychotherapy or counseling can be useful.

Given this dimension of the continuum, it is clear that problems vary in intensity and are often related. However, an individual can have very serious role problems without any intrapersonal disturbance. Likewise, an intense intrapersonal conflict can exist independently of role demands. In large part, a person's ability to deal with any problems that arise from the role conflict is related to the degree of intrapersonal conflict: Someone who is experiencing intense intrapersonal difficulties will be unable to deal with any role-related concerns. Thus, the type of assistance that can best serve a particular individual is related to the degree to which that person suffers from some internal disturbance. We can assume that the smaller the degree of internal disturbance, the better able the individual will be to deal with difficulties surrounding his or her role. In effect, someone with minimal internal disturbance will be more apt to respond to shorter-term, direct guidance (Perry, 1955).

Although everyone needs to understand her or his personality, people with minimal internal conflicts require no complete restructuring of personality in order to deal with problems of role. Restructuring personality is not necessary in order to make a vocational choice or to deal with a marital problem. In contrast, those with an intense intrapersonal conflict will be unable to deal with problems created by role. These people require an intense therapeutic relationship over an extended period, an experience designed to restructure the personality.

As the sample situation in Figure 1-2 indicates, most psychotherapy occurs in the area of intrapersonal conflict of high intensity. The counselor works at the other end of that continuum with people who are more likely to respond to short-term, more direct kinds of learning experiences. The difference, then, is that counseling works toward helping people to understand and develop their personality in relation to specific role problems; psychotherapy aims at reorganization of the personality through interaction with a therapist.

FIGURE 1-1   Counseling-Psychotherapy Continuum

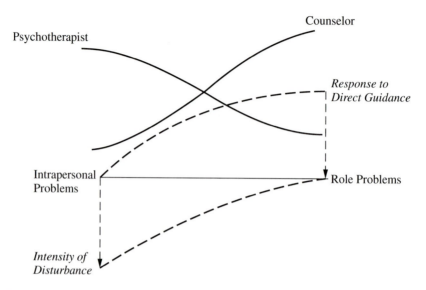

**FIGURE 1-2   A Sample Situation on an Intrapersonal/Role Problem
Continuum**

Counseling, then, as we define it, is "a therapeutic and growth process through which individuals are helped to define goals, make decisions, and solve problems related to personal-social, educational and career concerns. Specialized counseling provides assistance with concerns related to physical and social rehabilitation, employment, mental health, substance abuse, marital and family problems, human sexuality, religious and value choices, career development, and other concerns" (Warner, 1980, p. 2). Counseling does not attempt to restructure personality but to develop what already exists. It is chiefly concerned with individuals' adjustments to themselves, to significant others in their lives, and to the cultural environment in which they find themselves.

Theory

What Is a Theory?

We can now examine the role of theory in counseling. As each of us finds all too often, our memories are not infallible. Confronted with vast arrays of information, we need a framework for organizing that information. Solving a problem, even with a great deal of applicable information, is almost impossible without a plan or model. A theory provides such a model. It is a structure on which information necessary to the solution of a problem can be organized. This framework enables us to assign various kinds of data to their proper places and to develop a sense of the relationship between each piece of data. Wolman (1973) defines a theory as a system composed "of empirical data derived from observation and/or experimentation, and of their interpretation" (p. 333). Thus, a theory grows out of a systematic analysis of past events.

According to Stefflre and Matheny (1968), a theory is a model that the theorist uses to blend the reality of experiences with ideas about plausible explanations for these experiences. The theorist attempts to make sense out of life through constructing a framework that permits a logical and reasonable explanation of events. A theory, then, is an explanation of events on which future courses of action can be based.

Thus, a theory provides a standard by which to measure progress toward a desired outcome. This view assumes that a theory should influence the approach to a problem. If it does not, the theory is useless (Polster & Polster, 1973). To function without theory is to operate without placing events in some order and thus to function meaninglessly. Those who claim they can operate without theory generally hold some vague and implicit assumptions about the nature of events; in reality they are working from a theoretical frame of reference. The danger of this approach is that an implicit or hidden theory is subject to the interjection of personal biases into the interpretation of experience. To state a theory in explicit terms runs the risk of dogmatism, but it also minimizes the intrusion of bias.

In summary, a theory is an explanation for events that can be tested by events; it is useful only to the extent that it influences behavior; and it is better stated explicitly than held implicitly.

How Does a Theory Develop?

If a theory is a structure, we must assume it is based on several smaller pieces of information. In building a theory about human behavior, we begin by examining current theories on the topic. Then we attempt to verify those theories through observation. In attempting to understand why a child is often absent from school, for example, we might first offer several reasons based on what has been written about children's behavior in school. To authenticate these explanations, we observe the child. If we note that the child is absent every time a math test is scheduled, we might infer a relationship between the two events. If we observe these events for some time, our inferences may become a hypothesis: The child is afraid of failure. At this point we have made a statement about what we believe to be the relationship between the two events. If we observe the behavior of this child in several situations, we are likely to see several kinds of events and may make several additional inferences about the relationship among these events. We may observe that this child does come to school to take tests in other subjects. Further, we may see that the math teacher is extremely intolerant of students who fail, whereas the other teachers are much more tolerant and encouraging. As many of these events are observed and several inferences are made, a series of separate but related hypotheses may emerge. These related hypotheses are the bases for a theory about the child's behavior. Thus, in this example, as in all theory development, we started with existing possible explanations, observed actual events, and made inferences about the relationship between these events. Over time these inferences became hypotheses; assumptions about the relation of these hypotheses followed; the structure for a minitheory was formed. If we observed many children and began to combine all the minitheories, we would be developing a theory about one facet of children's behavior.

In line with this procedure, this text is designed to help in building a personal theory of counseling. Part I, which examines current theories, is designed to provide a general framework for understanding human behavior. Part II, which focuses on the actual process of counseling, should help develop counseling strategies that fit a general framework. As you read and discuss each chapter in Part I, you should begin observing human behavior, ideally in a setting similar to one in which you work as a counselor. As you move through Part II, you should begin to try different process strategies in a supervised setting. Our hope is that as you finish the text, you will have developed a tentative approach to counseling.

The process does not end there. A theory is not a law. A theory is always in the process of being formulated; it is not static or stable. With new observations of events, new inferences and hypotheses may develop that will affect the basic structure of theory. A theory is only a provisional formulation of a position or interpretation, subject to some form of verification and testing and followed by reformulation (Williamson, 1965). A theory is based on observations of events, but continuing observations are necessary, either to verify assumptions and hypotheses or to generate new hypotheses when the original ones cannot be verified.

A theory, then, is a framework of inferences and hypotheses made about the plausible relationships between a series of events. But a theory is generated by people in a certain culture at a particular time. As Stefflre and Matheny (1968) pointed out, a theory is derived from bases that are personal, historical, sociological, and philosophical. Seldom is it truly scientific; both the individual theorist's personal needs and societal needs tend to dictate which questions are asked and which answers are acceptable.

Personal Need

The element of personal need is present in both the adoption and construction of a theory. Shoben (1962b) suggests that it is our own psychological need structure, not what research tells us, that dictates what theory we will adopt as our own. Thus, both the theory builder and the person selecting a theory should look closely at their needs to determine their reasons for choosing one theory instead of another. In this process it is essential to examine one's basic personal philosophy about human nature and human development.

Philosophy

To some degree, the prevailing philosophy of the time or of the place where the theorist works or where the theory is to be applied dictates the kind of theory that is used or developed. It is, in part, philosophy that defines goals for people. Philosophy defines what the good life is or what the acceptable answers are. These definitions change with place and time. Hence, a theory that is developed or used at a particular time tends to reflect the dominant philosophy of the time.

Historical Period

The development of theory is also tied to the period in which it is developed. A theory too far ahead of its time is nearly useless because it does not fit contemporary requirements;

its answers to problems are unlikely to be considered plausible. History is full of examples of theorists who were far ahead of their times and thus found few people who would even listen to them, let alone try to implement their theories. The early troubles of men like Freud and Rogers are examples of this phenomenon.

Cultural and Racial Framework

Similarly, sociological and cultural elements affect the development of theory. U.S. society is based on order, yet at the same time promotes the concept of people's unique individuality. We strive to find order in all things so that we can understand events and behaviors, but we also want to feel that each person has some freedom of choice. Thus, we try to blend these two sometimes contradictory feelings in the development of most of our personality theories. Recently, for example, many writers in counseling have been discussing an approach called humanistic behaviorism. These writers are attempting to blend two seemingly divergent views.

The reason such divergent efforts exist at the present time is that we are becoming increasingly aware of the need to test our theories in the realm of populations far more diverse than when the theories were originally formulated. How sensitive are our ideas to the rapidly changing populations of the United States? How do these theories take into account the various implications of our increasing sensitivity to the role of race, gender, and conflicting social values?

For example, in a reference cited earlier, Naroll (1983) pointed out that in a relatively small area surrounding Gallup, New Mexico, there are five diverse communities (the Ramah Navajo, the Zuni, a Spanish-American village, a Mormon town, and a group of farmers—homesteaders or Texans). These groups represent widely divergent cultures and hold significantly different values and perceptions of the world. Historically, their roots are quite different and their goals and objectives are quite divergent. In some cases their folkways and mores are in conflict. To further complicate the picture, these cultures represent four separate languages: English, Spanish, Zuni, and Navajo.

A counselor functioning in the environs of Gallup, New Mexico, would have to be prepared to deal with this diversity. And this is reflected in New York, California, Colorado, and in dozens of other locales. How shall we educate counselors to cope with these cultural issues? How shall we interpret and apply our theories in this context?

The issue we have been discussing and the example used do not even begin to address the issue of racial diversity in this country. We need to become more familiar with ethnocentric viewpoints and incorporate their adherents into our educational frame of reference. We need to emphasize the increasingly interracial nature of our society, which incorporates not only increasing numbers of African Americans but also a burgeoning Hispanic subculture and a rapidly growing Asian population. All these developments have major implications for theory.

Applicability

In the United States the prevailing concern is with what works. We are generally not interested in theories that dwell in the past; we are concerned with what is happening now. As a pragmatic people, we expect our theories to relate to and give plausible reasons for events and behaviors occurring in today's world.

In summary, theories do not grow in isolation. Because so many factors influence theory development, they are rarely completely scientific. They are in fact a product of their time and place. To understand why certain theories are developed and used, we must know something about the personal needs of the theorists and of those who adopt the theory for use. We can understand the development of a theory better if we understand the context in which the theory was developed. This does not necessarily mean that the theory is tied to the period in which it was developed. A good theory is always evolving; it is receptive to the formulation of new hypotheses based on observations of new events.

In our discussion of theory, we have dealt with the general concept apart from any one discipline. Shertzer and Stone (1974) describe the four major functions of theory.

1. A theory synthesizes a particular body of knowledge. It brings together a body of related knowledge and, in shorthand fashion, attempts to organize the separate findings into a meaningful and useful whole.
2. A theory increases the understanding about a particular body of knowledge. It attempts to order data and to demonstrate the pieces of the puzzle that are the most important.
3. A theory provides tools for making predictions. Like a diagram, it depicts various points and what may be expected to occur at these points. For the practitioner it acts as a guide to pathways that are possible and what may result from following certain routes. It points out the relationship between means and ends.
4. A theory encourages further research in the area. It makes no difference whether the theory is proved correct or incorrect; its importance is that it stimulates further investigations into the phenomena with which it is concerned. Thus, a theory is always in the process of becoming. As new research evidence is accumulated the theory is substantiated, revised, or simply rejected. (pp. 236–237)

Theory in Counseling

What do we mean when we talk about counseling theory or theories? Where do these theories come from? How are they developed? Of what value are they to the practitioner? How does a counselor decide which of the vast array of theories to adopt? How does one counselor develop a personal theory of counseling?

A counseling theory is a tentative model on which plans of action are developed. This model enables counselors to distinguish normal or rational behavior from what is abnormal or irrational. A counseling theory also provides a frame of reference for understanding the possible causes of behavior that are typical and damaging to the client. For a client having problems with say, interpersonal relationships, this frame of reference enables the counselor to understand the possible causes of such difficulty.

This is not to say that the counselor will have a definitive set of answers for each problem that clients present, or that all clients with similar problems will share identical explanations for their behavior. Nevertheless, a theory does enable the counselor to make some assumptions about the general causes of such behavior. If, for example, the counselor concludes that the client's interpersonal difficulties are caused by some events in early childhood, the counselor may try to help the client gain insight into how these events are affecting present behavior, and through this process the counselor will assume that the client's behavior will be changed. On the other hand, the counselor may view the client's problem as the result of learning inappropriate responses to the situation and will try to help the client learn more appropriate ways of behaving. In either case the counselor makes assumptions about the causes of the behavior and, based on those assumptions, tries to help the client. "What we listen for here and respond to . . . depends in part on us as persons and part on our orientation, that is on a theory which has made particular assumptions about the causes of problems and the methods of treatment" (Schwebel, 1962, p. 328).

Some counselors maintain that theory has no place in their practice. Whether the counselor's theory is implicit or explicit, however, some theory does exist. As soon as a counselor begins to confer with a client, he or she begins to construct a mental picture of the individual. The counselor gathers data that is placed on some mental framework or schema. This picture is the basis upon which the counselor acts. A counselor who operates with an implicit theory is operating without being aware of why she or he is doing what it is he or she is doing. Without asking what is happening, without some model for action or some assumptions about counseling, it is likely that the counselor will do the client more harm than good.

Counseling theories provide a means of organizing what people have learned about the process of counseling. They are designed to serve as guides to indicate possible causes of a client's difficulties, alternative courses of action, and the desired counselor behavior in the counseling process. The theories themselves grow out of concepts of human nature and what people should be, and out of assumptions about how behavior is changed in the desired directions.

We also need to be open to new ways of looking at theory and new paradigms for theory and research. Hoshmand and Tsor (1989) suggest changing the philosophical base of our approach to theory building to include approaches from alternate frameworks including the "naturalist-ethnographic," the phenomenological, and the cybernetic. This might allow us to suspend our value-laden judgments and possibly emerge from the domination of the reductive-positive conceptions of research and theory. Perhaps these alternative approaches will lead to new theories or, at least, to significant alterations of the old ones.

The Basis of Counseling Theory: Personality Development

A counseling theory needs to be based on, or in some way derived from, a theory of personality. Counselors must have some knowledge of the manner and means of person-ality development from infancy through adulthood (Williamson, 1965). Not only must they have some knowledge of the development of the normal personality, but they must also understand how nonadaptive behavior develops. Only when they understand the development of adaptive and nonadaptive behavior can counselors hope to formulate ways to help their clients. A counselor's understanding of how these developments take place in people will largely determine which theory of personality he or she adopts. A counselor who views human behavior as basically causally determined will counsel from one perspective; while one who believes that people basically possess free choice will counsel from a completely different frame of reference.

Behavior Change

Counseling is a process designed to bring about changes in both attitudes and behaviors; therefore a counseling theory must incorporate a concept of how human behavior is changed. Even though theorists may argue over whether the behavior change follows an attitude change or whether the behavior change is followed by a change in attitude, they all agree that behavior change is the ultimate goal of the process. There are, of course, also different views as to how this change is brought about, but all theoretical positions include a procedure for affecting change.

Goals

Counseling theory must also include an idea of what are both intermediate and long-term goals of counseling. Each client being different will mean that each counseling case will involve a different set of intermediate goals. The intermediate goal for most counseling, will, however, be essentially the same: enabling the client to lead a happy, rewarding, responsible life. To this end, every society develops methods for attempting to change undesirable behaviors and for encouraging desired ones. That is, society attempts to determine what the "good life" is, and a good counseling theory includes similar notions. In essence, it creates a hierarchy of values toward which the counseling process is aimed.

Role of the Counselor

Last, but certainly not the least important, a counseling theory must include notions about the counselor's appropriate role. The theoretical frame of reference will determine, for example, how much control of the interview the counselor will undertake, how much faith to put in testing and other diagnostic devices, and the extent to which he or she uses directive techniques and interpretive statements. Perhaps most important, the theory will define the counselor's position on the utilization of specific techniques.

Counseling theory must be based on knowledge of human development and personality. From these a counseling theory must derive notions about human nature and how individuals learn. Because counseling is an applied field, the task of counselors and counseling theory is to define how behavior change is brought about and, more important, how this change is brought about in the counseling context. Because the counselor's role or behavior in counseling is in large part influenced by theoretical orientation, each counselor needs to evolve his or her own particular theory.

Theory and Practice

One of the criteria of a good theory is that it be useful, yet many practicing and prospective counselors seem to question the efficacy of applying theory in their day-to-day work.

The reason may be that many of the presently constructed theories of counseling are not useful; it may be that many of our theories are only descriptive, providing no real plans for action; or it may be that counselors simply have not understood the theories as presented. Whatever the reason, the time has arrived when counseling from no frame of reference will not satisfy those whom we serve.

Counselors must ask some very pertinent questions of themselves. First, What is the basic purpose of what I am doing? Once they have determined the answer, they need to ask: What are the means of reaching those goals, and how are these means different from what other people do? In determining these means, they need to know what assumptions they are making about human nature and its development. Kehas writes, "How do we build knowledge and test it if not by inquiring systematically into experience, making some generalizations about it, and then testing those generalizations to see if our explanations are accurate and help us understand what is happening. Surely we need to know in order to do" (1972, p. 1).

Brammer and Shostrom (1977) indicate that a counselor who does not have a solid foundation in the current thinking and research in the field, as well as a solid personal counseling theory, is only applying cookbook techniques to help clients solve their problems. "Without [an explicit] theoretical orientation . . . action is vulnerable to oversimplified and glib initiativeness—even mimicry—and to use of the gimmick" (Polster & Polster, 1973, p. 3). When a theory is explicit, a counselor has a better opportunity to test and evolve a personal theory based on experiences and some systematic personal research efforts.

If we can accept the suggestion of John Dewey (1939) that creative and reflective thinking is essentially a matter of seeing events and concepts in a unique or new pattern, then we can make the next assumption that every counselor has the potential for developing a personal counseling theory. The logical place to begin is with a theory that has made some assumptions about the nature of counseling and been submitted to some empirical testing. This theory can then be subjected to counseling experience, and out of this process should grow new hypotheses and assumptions or verification of the previously held assumptions. The original theory is helpful to the extent that it provides the counselor with a base from which to explore her or his world and an opportunity to develop a tentative personal theory, which in turn gives meaning and direction to his or her counseling.

Most great theorists, among them Freud and Rogers, were first of all great therapists, and their theories evolved from their practices. These theorists, like those who have followed, continuously revised their theories on the basis of new findings. In essence, a theory is practical because of, not in spite of, its heuristic nature. It enables the counselor to make systematic observations about counseling experiences; it encourages the combination of various concepts; and it helps the counselor to predict, to evaluate performance, and to improve outcomes (Brammer & Shostrom, 1977).

Figure 1-3 illustrates a systems approach to conceptualizing the relationship between theory and practice and to developing a personal theory of counseling. The figure demonstrates the relationship between theory and practice; they are components of a system. Any successful system has built-in feedback mechanisms that permit it to adjust itself. The system shown in Figure 1-3 contains feedback loops from counseling practice and client outcomes to observations of human behavior, indicating that theory should have a

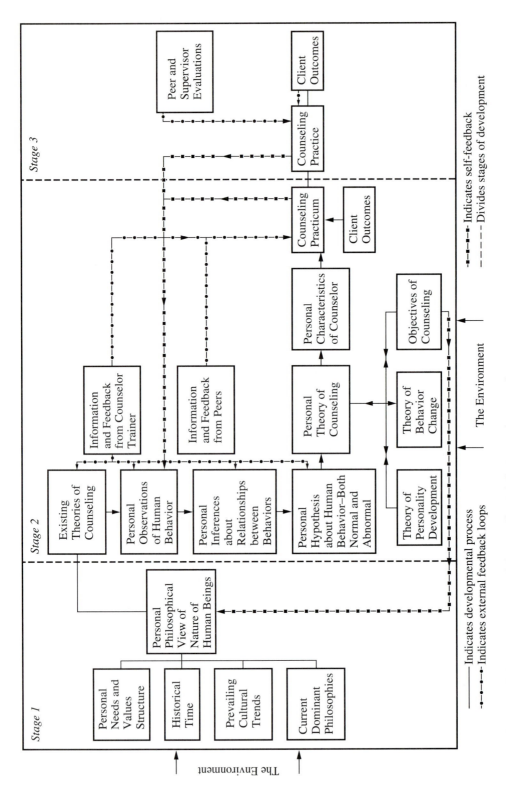

FIGURE 1-3 Building a Theory of Counseling: A Systems Approach

direct bearing on practice. The feedback of counseling practice and client outcomes into the system permits a theory to be modified by practice.

Most important, the system shown in Figure 1-3 demonstrates the process of personal theory building. It moves from abstract ideas through observations to actual practice and back again. The first stage represents developmental processes that occur in prospective counselors prior to entering a counseling program. Because it is going to affect their attitude to existing counseling theories, a necessary first step is to examine their philosophical view of people.

The second stage is roughly equivalent to the training process of a prospective counselor. This text is designed to facilitate movement through this stage; Part I covers the first step, examining existing counseling theories at an abstract level. The trainees then evaluate these data through their own observations of human behavior. These observations lead to inferences about relationships between events and then to general hypotheses about human behavior. All the data then begin to crystallize into a primary or basic theory of counseling, a theory that now contains concepts about how personality develops, how it can be changed, and what the objectives of counseling should be. Part II, which focuses on process, is designed to help develop specific counseling skills within the framework of personal characteristics and the personal approach to counseling. Ideally, as trainees move through the material in Part II they have an opportunity through a prepracticum or practicum to try various approaches and to receive feedback about their efforts, both from those conducting the training and from peers who are also going through the process. This feedback permits continual modification honing, refining, and updating of approaches to counseling.

The third stage represents the professional counseling process. In this stage the most important feedback comes from what happens to clients, but the counselor should also continue to seek feedback from peers and supervisors. This information flows back into the system and helps the counselor modify and update the whole system.

The process outlined in Figure 1-3 is really a subsystem of the world in which we live. As such, it is affected by events in that larger world. What is most vital to each counselor is the encouragement to develop a theory that is explicitly formulated, regularly evaluated, and subsequently subjected to modification (Ford & Urban, 1963).

Rotter (1954) summarizes the principal values of theories. He suggests that theories serve as the basis for constructing new instruments and methods as well as for testing old methods. In addition, they (1) provide a means of evaluating counseling techniques and ideas and problems in counseling practice, (2) provide encouragement for the development of consistent assumptions, and (3) act as an aid to the counselor in recognizing and resolving contradictions in the theory and inconsistencies between theories and practice. We need to know what it is we are about. A systematic theory helps us know that

Summary

In this chapter we have discussed what counseling is and how it differs from psychotherapy. We concluded that counseling is chiefly concerned with the individual's adjustment to self, significant others, and the cultural environment in which he or she lives. Next we considered how theory is developed, why it is developed, the necessary ingredients for a good theory, and the functions it can serve. Third, we discussed what counseling theory means and how the theory should relate to actual practice. Counseling theory provides a structure from which the counselor can work in meaningful ways; by itself, counseling theory has no meaning. Finally, we discussed the need for counselors to develop their own theory of counseling, based on a study of present theory, but modified and developed through their own counseling experiences and research. To begin this process, we now turn to an examination of some contributions to counseling theory.

References

American Psychological Association (1961). *The current status on counseling psychology: A report of a special committee of the division 17 of the counseling psychology.* Washington, DC.

Brammer, Lawrence M., & Shostrom, Everett L. (1968). *Therapeutic psychology* (2nd ed.). Englewood Cliffs, NJ: Prentice-Hall.

Brammer, Lawrence M., & Shostrom, Everett L. (1977). *Therapeutic psychology* (3rd ed.). Englewood Cliffs, NJ.: Prentice-Hall.

Corsini, Raymond J., & Wedding, Danny (1989). *Current psychotherapies* (4th ed.). Itasca, IL: F. E. Peacock.

Creative inquiry (1959, November 21). John Dewey Centennial, *Saturday Review, 42,* pp. 22–23.

Dewey, John. (1939). Intelligence in the Modern World. New York: Modern Library.

English, Horace B., & English, Ava Champney (1958). *A comprehensive dictionary of psychological and psychiatric terms.* New York: McKay.

Ford, D. H., & Urban, H. B. (1963). *Systems of psychotherapy: A comparative study.* New York: John Wiley and Sons.

Garfield, S. L., & Kurtz, R. (1977). A study of eclectic views. *Journal of Consulting and Clinical Psychology, 45,* 78–83.

Glanz, E. G. (1974). *Guidance foundations, principles and techniques* (2nd ed.). Boston: Allyn and Bacon.

Hansen, D. A. (1969). *Explorations in sociology and counseling.* New York: Houghton Mifflin.

Havighurst, R. J. (1952). *Developmental tasks and education* (2nd ed.). New York: Longman's Green.

Herr, E. L (ed.) (1974). *Vocational guidance and human development.* Boston: Houghton Mifflin.

Hoshmand, Lisa, & Tsor, L. S. (1989, January). Alternate research paradigms: A review and teaching proposal. *The Counseling Psychologist 17*(1), 3–80.

Hoyt, K. B., Evans, R. N., Malkin, E. F., & Mangum, G. L. (1972). *Career education: What it is and how to do it.* Salt Lake City: Olympus.

Kehas, C. D. (1972). What research says about counselor role. *Focus on Guidance, 4*(9), 1–10.

Miller, C. H. (1961). *Foundations of guidance. New York: Harper & Row.*

Naroll, Raoull (1983). *The moral order: An introduction to the human situation.* Beverly Hills: Sage.

Patterson, C. H. (1966). *Theories of counseling and psychotherapy.* New York: Harper & Row.

Perry, William G. (1955, November 7). The finding of the commission in counseling and guidance on the relation of psychotherapy and counseling. *Annals of New York Academy of Sciences, 63,* 396–407.

Polster, E., & Polster, M. (1973). *Gestalt therapy integrated: Contours of theory and practice.* New York: Brunner/Mazel.

Rotter, J. B. (1954). *Social learning and clinical psychology.* Englewood Cliffs, NJ: Prentice-Hall.

Schwebel, Milton (1962, December). Some missing links in counseling theory and research. *Personnel and Guidance Journal 41,* 328.

Shertzer, B., & Stone, S. C. (1971). *Fundamentals of guidance* (2nd ed.). Boston: Houghton Mifflin.

Shertzer, B., & Stone, S. C. (1974). *Fundamentals of counseling* (2nd ed.). Boston: Houghton Mifflin.

Shoben, Edward J., Jr. (1953). New frontiers in theory. *Personnel and Guidance Journal 32,* 80–83.

Shoben, Edward J., Jr. (1962a). The counselor's theory of a personal trait. *Personnel and Guidance Journal, 40,* 617–621.

Shoben, Edward J., Jr. (1962b, Fall). Guidance: Remedial function or social reconstruction? *Harvard Educational Review, 32,* 431–443.

Stefflre, Buford (ed.) (1965). *Theories of counseling.* New York: McGraw-Hill.

Stefflre, Buford, & Matheny, Kenneth (eds.) (1968). *The function of counseling theory.* Guidance Monograph Series, Boston: Houghton Mifflin.

Strupp, H. H. (1958, January). The psychotherapist's contribution to the treatment process. *Behavioral Science, 3,* 34–67.

Sundland, D. M., & Barker, E. N. (1962, June). The orientation of psychotherapists. *Journal of Consulting Psychology, 26,* 201–212.

Tyler, Leona (1969). *The work of the counselor* (3rd ed.). New York: Appleton-Century-Crofts.

U.S. Office of Education (1950). *Report on the national conference on life adjustment.* Washington, DC.

Vance, Forrest L., & Volsky, Theodore C., Jr. (1962). Counseling and psychotherapy: Split personalities or Siamese twins. *American Psychologist 17,* 565–570.

Wallach, M. S., & Strupp, H. H. (1964, April). Dimensions of psychotherapists' activity. *Journal of Consulting Psychology, 28,* 120–125.

Warner, R. W., Jr. (1980). *Individual counseling.* Atlanta, GA: Georgia Department of Education.

Williamson, E. G. (1965). *Vocational counseling: Some historical, philosophical and theoretical perspectives.* New York: McGraw-Hill.

Wolberg, Lewis R. (1954). *The technique of psychotherapy.* New York: Grune and Stratton.

Wolman, Benjamin B. (1973). *Dictionary of behavioral science.* New York: Van Nostrand Reinhold.

Chapter **2**

Classical Psychoanalytic Theory

Sigmund Freud (1856–1939), the founder of classic psychoanalytic theory, was primarily a practitioner of what became known to the world as *psychoanalysis.* Freud was born in Moravia on May 6, 1856. Despite mixed personal feelings, Freud entered the University of Vienna in 1873 at the age of 17. It took him three years longer than normal to finish his degree, which he did in 1881.

Ernest Jones (1953) reports in his monumental biography of Freud that it was probably Goethe's essay on nature that determined Freud's choice of a career in medicine. The characterization of the warm, nurturing mother nature may have contributed to Freud's early romantic notions of the world. He was undoubtedly also influenced by the scientific discoveries that were revealed during his early life (Hall, 1953). Darwin's *Origin of Species,* published when Freud was a child, Fechner's creation of the science of psychology, Mendel's contribution to genetics, Pasteur and Koch's revelations about the germ theory of disease, all had an influence on young Freud.

Freud studied for some time under the neurologist Jean-Martin Charcot in Paris, but it was his work with Josef Breuer and the case of Anna O that really launched his career. Together they published what was Freud's first work, *Studies of Hysteria* (1957). It would be impossible in the space available here to chronicle a career that was so active and so long. Freud died in England in 1939, and he was an active therapist, theorist, and writer to the very end. He established not only a model theory of personality and therapy, but also a model for the development of theory in therapy. He was a practitioner whose careful observations of his patients led to his formulations, not an armchair thinker who sat on the sidelines. Out of his therapy work Freud came to believe that an individual's behavior is determined by both interpersonal and intrapsychic factors; he called this assumption *psychic determinism.* Human beings, in Freud's view, are not masters of their own destinies; rather, their behaviors are driven by the need to gratify basic biological needs and instincts. Behavior is not random but is determined by past experiences. In this context, behavior is *lawful* and *connected*.

"What was Freud?" asked Calvin Hall (1953). He was by turns physician, psychiatrist, psychoanalyst, psychologist, philosopher, and critic. "He was a genius," and he was "one of the few men in history who possessed a universal mind. Like Shakespeare and Goethe and Leonardo da Vinci, whatever Freud touched he illuminated. He was a very wise man" (Hall, 1953, p. 21).

Levels of Awareness

One of the earliest conceptualizations developed by Freud (1935) was his belief that three different levels of awareness act to influence personality development: the conscious, the preconscious, and the unconscious. At the conscious level we can only be aware of a very limited part of our environment at any one time. A particular thought, idea, or feeling may occupy the conscious for only a limited time, but while it is there, we are unaware of other stimuli around us. The person who focuses attention on a particular task while an array of events is occurring around her or him is an example of this phenomenon.

The second level of awareness described by Freud is the preconscious. Many ideas or thoughts, though not a part of the conscious, can be brought to the conscious level. When we are asked to recall a past meeting or event, we are calling into consciousness some ideas or events in the preconscious.

The third level of awareness is the *unconscious*. In Freud's view, this is the most important portion of the mind because it largely determines human behavior. We are not aware of the mental activities that occur in this part of the mind, nor can we bring them to the conscious level. In fact, we unknowingly resist doing so. The traditional example is the man who hates his mother yet is unaware that he has these feelings. In psychoanalytic theory, the importance of these unconscious feelings is that they constantly strive to become conscious, and the individual must expend energy to keep them in the unconscious. Thus, Freud regarded people as being in a constant state of internal conflict of which they are not aware.

Structure of Personality

In his later work, Freud retained the concept of the conscious, preconscious, and unconscious in his view of the individual as composed of three subsystems: the id, ego, and superego. These three elements interact to such a great extent that it is difficult to measure their separate effects on behavior. One subsystem seldom operates independently from the other two; rather, a person's behavior should be considered the result of interaction among the three.

Id

Freud regarded the id as the original system of the personality. In the classic psychoanalytic sense, a newborn infant is all id. The id consists of the constitution of the infant—all the infant brings into the world. It is the source of a fixed reservoir of sexual energy, which Freud referred to as *libido*.

Within the domain of the id Freud included human instincts, the two most important of which are sex and aggression. The basic function of the id is to maintain the organism in a comfortable, or low-tension, state. Thus, when an infant is hungry and demands to be fed, the id seeks immediate gratification of hunger in order to return the organism to a comfortable state.

Freud believed that this "pleasure principle" governs the id into adult life. Most of the id processes occur at an unconscious level and influence overt behavior without the person being aware of that influence. In the example of the man who hates his mother, we can see the id in operation. His feeling toward his mother may affect his relationships with other women although he may be unaware of this influence on his behavior. Generally, id impulses come into consciousness only when the ego is in a weakened state.

Ego

Unlike the id, the ego is not present at birth but develops from the id as the individual interacts with the environment. Its function is to develop muscular and sensory control of the body and to sort out and understand the outer world. In the early stages of development, the infant cannot distinguish among objects, which is the primary reason a hungry baby will put anything it touches into its mouth. At this stage of development, there is no sense of the reality of the world, and the infant must learn to discriminate between mental images and objective reality. In this process the infant soon learns that forming a mental image will not satisfy a need; as a result the infant is forced to begin to differentiate self from the outer world, learning to find something there that matches the internal image. This matching process is called *identification* and is the process that separates the ego from the id. It is one of the most important concepts in psychoanalytic theory for it is important in the development of both the ego and the superego.

Thus, the primary function of the id is to satisfy the needs of the organism without regard to external realities. The ego develops out of the id because of the organism's need to deal with those realities. The object of the ego is to mediate between the pleasure principle, by which the id operates, and the outer world. The ego, then, operates on the reality principle and attempts to contain the discharge of energy until there is an appropriate external object to satisfy the need. In the example of the hungry child, the development of the ego alters behavior. As the infant learns to identify objects in the outer world that will satisfy hunger, the infant ceases putting everything into his or her mouth. The ego, then, functions as the executive of the individual's personality.

Superego

Not surprisingly, the earliest objects in the external world that satisfy the infant's needs are parents, but early in development the child also learns that these important others are likely to look with disfavor on direct expressions of his or her impulses. The parents act as disciplinary agents, and through a process of rewards and punishments of varying degrees, the child learns what is acceptable behavior and what is not. As this process continues through the child's early development, the superego not only adopts the parents' values and customs but also incorporates the accepted values, traditions, and customs of the society.

The superego is a form of individual internal control. When a child's behavior is appropriate even when no one else is there to watch, the superego has emerged. In Freud's view, the superego is made up of two subsystems: the conscience and the ego-ideal. The conscience represents things the individual would like to be. Both of these subsystems often come into conflict with the id impulses.

The superego is a built-in control mechanism whose principal function is to control the primitive impulses of the id, which would not lead to accepted behavior. Control occurs largely in the unconscious part of the mind, not in the individual's awareness. The superego represents what is ideal within the individual; it strives for perfection.

In Freud's view the dynamics of personality center on the interaction among the id, ego, and superego. He described psychoanalytic theory as "a dynamic conception which reduces mental life to the interplay of reciprocally urging and checking forces" (1950, p. 107). The id, operating on the pleasure principle, constantly seeks gratification of needs, while the energies of the ego and superego operate both to meet the needs of the individual and to hold in check some of the impulses of the id. The ego must not only interact with the real world, but also be able to mediate between the id and the superego. An individual dominated by the id will tend to be impulsive; a person dominated by the superego will be overly moralistic. The function of the ego is to keep the individual from these two extremes. The actual form or pattern or interaction among the three subsystems is a product of the individual's development through the psychosexual stages. We now turn to the process of development through these stages.

Psychosexual Stages of Development

Freud contended that an individual's personality is basically formed during the first five years of life, as the individual attempts to learn new ways of reducing tension that emanates from four basic sources: physiological growth processes, frustrations, conflicts, and threats (Hall & Lindzey, 1957). Much of the latter three are products of the growth process of the individual.

In Freud's view, the development of personality, including the various defense mechanisms the individual uses, is largely dependent on the course of her or his psychosexual development. Much of this development occurs during the first five years of life, after which there is a period of relative calm for six years. Then, during adolescence the process becomes very active once again. Another of Freud's major assumptions is that at any point in a person's development, one body area predominates as a source of pleasure. In normal development a person moves through an orderly sequence in which one body area gives way to another; the order of this sequence is the same for everyone. The third major assumption is that failure to complete this normal sequence will result in serious personality problems.

Pregenital Stages

Freud labeled the first three stages of development the pregenital stages. These are the oral, anal, and phallic stages.

Oral

Freud believed that the infant sucks not just to take in food but also because sucking produces a pleasurable sensation. This stage of development usually lasts through the first year of life, during which the relationship with the mother is extremely important. As the infant identifies with the mother, it turns from self-love or narcissism to love of others. Freud contended that there are two dangers at this stage of development. If the infant's relationship with the mother becomes too comfortable, the child becomes too dependent and will fixate at this stage, resulting in an overly dependent personality in adult life. At the other extreme, the child who experiences a great deal of anxiety in interaction with its mother may feel insecure, and this insecurity will continue into adult life.

Anal

During the second year of life the source of pleasure shifts to the anal zone of the child's body. During this stage the manner in which toilet training is conducted is extremely important. A child who is dealt with very strictly during this stage may develop into a very retentive personality type. A person who is cruel, obstinate, or stingy is said to have been fixated at the anal stage. During this stage the child first attempts to achieve control over him- or herself and others.

Phallic

From age three to five or six the child is in the phallic stage of development. This stage often produces maladaptive behavior later in life. Freud asserted that during this period the child receives pleasure chiefly through self-manipulation. As the importance of the genital area increases, several psychological developments may occur: castration anxiety, penis envy, and the famous Oedipus complex.

Castration anxiety arises from a boy's fear that he may lose his penis. His parents, in an attempt to stop him from masturbating, may make him fear the loss of his penis, particularly if he has an opportunity to see a girl, who does not have a penis. He may conclude that he will be punished just as she has been punished. Similarly, a girl may develop penis envy when she observes her lack of a penis. She may feel that hers has been removed because of some wrongful act on her part. In either case, Freud asserted that serious problems of personality development are attributable to these developments.

The last development during the phallic stage is what Freud called the Oedipus or Electra complex. Briefly, the Oedipus complex involves the boy's desire to possess his mother and remove his father from the scene. The Electra complex is the desire of the girl to possess her father and remove her mother from the scene. Because this relationship cannot be consummated, resolution of this conflict is extremely important for later personality development. The child must abandon the parent object and become sexually motivated toward others. Subsequent attitudes toward people of the opposite sex and toward those in authority are largely determined by the individual's success in working out the Oedipal complex. This is accomplished largely through the child's identifying with the parent of the same sex; then, through the processes of incorporation and sublimation, the child is able to redirect his or her libidinal energies.

Latency Stage

In Freud's view, from the end of the fifth or sixth year of life until puberty the child is in a stage of latency during which the child spends time developing skills with no sexual implications.

Genital Stage

The first three stages of development can be characterized as narcissistic; during the genital stage, self-love begins to change into love of others. With the beginning of puberty the child enters a stage that normally culminates in mature heterosexual behavior; the individual is transformed from a self-loving individual into a socialized adult. In this ultimate stage of development, the normal individual does not get pleasure from oral, anal, or autoerotic activities and is not affected by castration anxiety or an unresolved Oedipus or Electra complex. Rather, the greatest pleasure comes from a relationship with a member of the opposite sex.

Defense Mechanisms

Each stage of psychosexual development is fraught with potential for producing frustrations, conflicts, and threats. Freud believed that individuals deal with these tensions through identification, displacement, and other defense mechanisms.

One of the most important roles of the ego is to deal with events that arouse anxiety within the individual. The ego may approach this problem by realistic problem solving, or it may attempt to deny, falsify, or otherwise distort reality. If the ego approaches the problem realistically, the individual's personality stands to be enhanced; however, if the alternate choice is made, the development of personality is impeded. Although Freud classified identification, displacement, and sublimation as defense mechanisms, these three arc realistic problem-solving procedures and differ substantially from other defense mechanisms, which tend to deny, falsify, or distort reality and which operate in the unconscious. Although defense mechanisms may operate effectively for a time, the more they are used, the more rigid the individual's personality becomes.

In the early stages of development, the threats to the self that create anxiety are external. An example is people who are physically larger and who have complete control over the child, such as parents. As the superego develops, threats to the self can also occur from within: An individual's fears that the id impulses will assume control can result in great anxiety. The defense mechanisms develop to cope with both internal and external threats. They occur primarily at the unconscious level.

Identification

In an earlier section, identification was mentioned as a process whereby the ego and superego develop. That process is extended later in life to include functions much like imitation: The individual, in an attempt to reach a certain goal (such as reduction of tension), incorporates the characteristics of another person into her or his own personality. Most of this occurs at the unconscious level and consists in trial and error; that is, if the behavior taken on reduces the tension, the individual retains the behavior. If the new behavior is not successful in reducing tension, the individual discards it. Although parents are the first and usually the most important people with whom the individual identifies, the adult personality is the result of numerous identifications made throughout development

Displacement

One uniquely human characteristic is the ability to transfer the object of psychological energy from one object to another. If an object that served to reduce tension is no longer available or loses some of its power, another object can and will take its place. This process of redirecting energy from one object to another is called displacement. The development of personality depends to a great extent on this process of energy displacement or object substitution: Because the new object is not likely to satisfy the need for tension reduction as well as the original object did, the individual is constantly seeking new and better methods of reducing tension. Displacement accounts for constant human striving and the variability of our behavior.

Freud felt that the most significant form of displacement in the development of civilization is sublimation. Sublimation is the process whereby the individual modifies the expression of a primitive impulse to conform with behavior that is socially acceptable. Sublimations usually take the form of channeling aggressive or sexual energy into intellectual, humanitarian, cultural, and artistic pursuits. Hence, as an individual matures, she or he sublimates or displaces energy in ways that not only yield personal satisfaction but also contribute to the larger society.

Repression

One of the earliest concepts developed by Freud is that of repression. Repression is the act of forcing from consciousness an impulse that causes anxiety. The individual attempts to do away with the impulse by refusing to acknowledge its existence. An individual experiencing repression may not see an object that is in plain sight, or the repression may actually have a physical effect: A man afraid of the sexual impulse may become impotent. Although repression is necessary for normal personality development and occurs to some extent in everyone, some people become overly dependent on repression as a defense. Such people tend to withdraw from contacts with the world and generally are tense and rigid in personality. In such individuals the superego is said to predominate over the ego; the ego has lost some of its controlling power to the superego.

To deal with a repressed impulse, an individual must believe that the impulse no longer constitutes a danger. A child who represses sexual impulses during adolescence may find that her or his adult ego can cope with these impulses, and the repression will cease. In many cases, however, the individual never learns that a repression is no longer necessary.

Projection

Anxiety that originates externally is easier to deal with than anxiety that comes from the id impulses. Hence, if an individual can attribute anxiety to an object in the external world, he or she is likely to feel some relief. This defense is called projection. It consists, first, in not recognizing a characteristic within oneself and, second, in attributing the same characteristic to another person. Instead of saying, "I hate my sister," the individual using projection says, "My sister hates me." Projection is a favorite defense among those who try to enhance their self-esteem. The individual attempts to make her- or himself look good and at the same time to downgrade others.

Reaction-Formation

When an individual has an impulse that produces anxiety, the ego may attempt to deal with the impulse by concentrating upon the direct opposite. If an individual feels hate for someone else, the ego may attempt to deal with the hate impulses by showing great outward signs of love toward that person. This form of defense is called reaction-formation. Extreme forms of any behavior such as a phobia usually can be attributed to reaction-formation.

Fixation

In Freud's view, normal personality development occurs through a series of well-defined stages of psychosexual development. Moving from one stage to the next involves many frustrations and anxieties. If this anxiety becomes too great, the normal pattern of psychological growth halts at least temporarily because the individual is afraid to move on to the next stage. He or she experiences fixation. In such cases the individual does not want to give up a behavior pattern that has been satisfying to adopt new behaviors that might not provide the necessary satisfaction.

Regression

Similar to the defense of fixation is the mechanism known as regression: A person may revert to an earlier phase of development instead of moving forward to another stage. This usually occurs when the individual is faced with a severe threat. A little child may revert to infant behavior in a situation in which he or she feels threatened by a loss of love. An adult may withdraw from heterosexual activities because she or he feels inadequate, and through withdrawal from these activities avoids the situation that causes the anxiety. It is generally held that an individual who regresses returns to a stage of development at which he or she was once comfortable.

Occurrences of either regression or fixation are relative in degree. Fixation at a particular stage of development is rarely complete; likewise, regression to an earlier stage of development is rarely total.

In summary, Freud believed that individual personality develops as a result of two major factors: maturation by moving through a natural growth pattern and learning to overcome tension and anxiety that result from conflicts, frustration, and threats by utilizing identification, displacement, and the defense mechanisms. All these processes rechannel the original impulses into more accessible and acceptable sources or objects. This development of personality occurs in an orderly manner and is related to the areas of the body from which the individual derives pleasure. Finally, the Freudian model of personality is a dynamic one, in which the constant interaction of the id, ego, and superego determines the way in which the personality develops. Freud saw good mental health as a product of the balance among the id, ego, and superego.

Abnormal Personality Development

Classic psychoanalytic theories view the causes of abnormal personality as rooted within the individual: The internal equilibrium has been disturbed and is out of balance. The two possible causes of this imbalance are (1) ineffective dynamics among the ego, id, and superego and (2) inappropriate childhood learning. In the first case the ego for some reason has failed in its role as executor of the organism. Instead of serving an integrative function, the ego allows the individual to overuse the defense mechanisms. This overuse, primarily of repression, begins in early childhood. The child uses repression to deal with impulses that cause anxiety, pushing them into the unconscious. There they remain, only to arise at later stages of development to cause increased difficulty. If the ego had been able to deal with these impulses when they first developed, the potential for a healthy personality would have been increased.

A second cause of the development of maladaptive behavior is childhood learning. Freud believed that behavior is acquired either to reduce psychological energy so that it will be socially acceptable or to control drives that might produce pleasure but would be accompanied by severe penalties. Hence, most of these learned behaviors are products of an approach-avoidance situation: There is internal motivation to engage in the behavior, but external forces inhibit it. Such a conflict can produce problems such as anxiety neurosis, obsessive-compulsive behavior, or schizophrenia.

In Freud's view, the nature of a neurosis is determined largely by early learning experiences, the defense mechanisms the person has used against tension, and the stage of psychosexual development which the person has fixated or to which he or she has regressed. After attempting to cope with a situation and failing, the person resorts to regression to satisfy her or his needs. This regression brings forth earlier anxieties and tensions that have been repressed. Neurotic behavior develops in the attempt to deal with this tension. This behavior requires increasing amounts of energy to deal with the anxiety;

hence, the individual has less and less energy for dealing with the realities of the world. A vicious cycle has been established.

Goals of Therapy

The major goal of psychoanalytic method is to bring to awareness the repressed impulses that are causing anxiety. These are the impulses of the id with which the ego has been unable to deal successfully. In therapy people receive a chance to face situations with which they have been unable to cope. The therapist establishes a nonthreatening context in which the client learns to express thoughts and feelings without fear of being condemned. This freedom allows the individual to explore the appropriateness or inappropriateness of current behavior and to consider new behaviors.

Freud himself described psychoanalytic treatment as a "re-education in overcoming resistance" (Freud, 1904/1950). It was a method designed to bring what was unconscious to the level of conscious awareness. "Psychoanalytic treatment certainly makes great demands upon the patient as well as upon the physician. From the patient it requires perfect sincerity—a sacrifice in itself; it absorbs time and is therefore also costly; for the physician it is not less time-absorbing, and the technique which he must study is fairly laborious" (Freud, 1904/1950, p. 257).

For Freud the basic goal of treatment was to create a situation where it was possible for the patient or client to engage in those behaviors that would lead to the development of insight into the motives which drive his or her behavior. To accomplish this the analyst maintains a basically neutral stance, avoids either-or thinking, and attempts to be helpful and analytical. In short the analyst maintains an "analytic attitude" and the patient remains committed to the process (Schafer, 1983).

Techniques in Therapy

The basic techniques used in therapy are free association, transference, and interpretation. Because traditional psychoanalysis is seldom used by counselors, discussion of the techniques will be brief and highly simplified.

Free association is simply the practice of letting—indeed, making—clients verbalize whatever is on their mind. Although this sounds simple, it is most difficult to get clients to engage in this behavior. Trying to verbalize everything that comes into one's mind is generally a socially discouraged behavior.

The transference phenomenon is quite complex. It consists of the individual's directing emotional feelings toward the therapist as though the therapist were the original object that caused the feelings. This process enables the client to work through the original conflict.

The therapist uses interpretation to help the individual intellectualize and to replace superego functions with ego functions. Thus, interpretation is designed to bring the patient step-by-step back to the world of reality. The therapist may base interpretations on material presented by the client in free association, from dream analysis, or from transference.

Summary

Psychoanalysis has had a fundamental influence on the understanding of general human behavior. While it fails to provide us with a comprehensive theory of human behavior, it has led to insights into the relationship of art and literature to human behavior. It has stimulated a rich literature in artistic and literary criticism from a new perspective.

Psychoanalysis has provided a new perspective for the examination of social organizations and structures including religion. It has stimulated the growth of particular lines of research in child development and education (Arlow, 1989).

The work of Freud and his colleagues is credited with the origin of the so-called "talking cure," which is at the heart of psychoanalytic technique. Classical psychoanalysis has influenced a variety of approaches to counseling and psychotherapy particularly the derivations of psychotherapy discussed in Chapter 3 and the ego-analytic approach presented in Chapter 4.

The entire psychodynamic movement in counseling and psychotherapy has roots in classical psychoanalytic theory. While the traditional approach to this area of practice is not directly applicable to the practice of counselors, the influences are all-pervasive in the field of practice.

References

Arlow, Jacob A. (1989). Psychoanalysis. In Raymond J. Corsini and Danny Wedding, *Current Psychotherapies* (4th ed.). Itasca, IL: F. E. Peacock.

Breuer, J., & Freud, S. (1957). *Studies of hysteria.* New York: Basic Books. (Reprint of Vol. XI of Standard Edition).

Ford, D. H., & Urban, H. B. (1967). *Systems of psychotherapy. A comparative study.* New York: John Wiley and Sons.

Freud, S. (1950). Psychogenic visual disturbance according to psychoanalytical conceptions. In *Collected Papers* (Vol. 2). London: Hogarth Press. (Original work published 1910)

Freud, S. (1935). *A general introduction to psychoanalysis.* New York: Liveright.

Freud, S. (1950). On psychotherapy. In Joan Rivere (Trans.), *Collected Papers* (Vol. 1). London: Hogarth Press. (Original work published 1904).

Hall, C. (1953). *The life and work of Sigmund Freud* (Vol. 1). New York: Basic Books.

Hall, C. S., & Lindzey, G. (1957). *Theories of personality.* New York: John Wiley and Sons.

Jones, E. (1953). *The life and work of Sigmund Freud* (Vol. 1). New York: Basic Books.

Schafer, R. (1983). *The analytic attitude.* New York: Basic Books.

C h a p t e r **3**

Derivatives of Psychoanalytic Thought

In the long history of psychotherapy, a variety of approaches and interventions prevailed before the modern era. In ancient times, in both Eastern and Western societies magic ritual and mythical concepts prevailed (Ehrenwald, 1976). Some societies sought salvation through renunciation of religion and of its accoutrements. However, religion prevailed as the dominant psychotherapeutic force including the use of the healing miracles of the Bible. Strong belief and faith prevail to this day. Witness the power of Christian Science, a healing doctrine that has held sway for over 100 years. For a time, the force of hypnotism and suggestion was a powerful influence on the process of intervention in the search for reduction of mental discomfort.

In the late eighteenth and early nineteenth centuries, the influence of Freud melded mental health concerns with the scientific method. He brought his basic methodological training in science to the issue of mental health and mental illness. While others were first to observe some of the same phenomena and to utilize a similar uncovering methodology, Freud was the first to systematically integrate his findings into a coherent theory of personology (Ehrenwald, 1976). "His discoveries have been likened to those of Copernicus or Galileo in the field of physical science. . . . He based his theories—and his new method of treatment—upon painstaking observation and therapeutic experimentation in case after case" (Ehrenwald, 1976, p. 272).

Freud's scientific worldview has often been described as congruent with those of Hobbes and Darwin. It essentially depicts society as an undifferentiated collection of individuals living in isolation, competing for the survival of the fittest. The natural emotion of this mass is anger and hostility, and the occasional bonding together of the species into apparently orderly groups for the purposes of self-protection is done largely unwillingly and at a high cost to individual autonomy (Brown, 1964). Freud's conceptions depicted human beings as living in carefully constructed ivory towers outside which they hung their works of art and other signs of skill within the scientific community. But to Freud's discerning mind the "ivory towers conceal the inner stinking cave by the entrance of which they ruthlessly trade physical needs or personal relationships for private gain, returning to the innermost recesses to enjoy them without interference" (Brown, 1964, p. 14).

It is not surprising that with such a dour worldview, several of those closest to Freud would ultimately differ with him. The spread of the psychoanalytic movement from the First International Psychoanalytic Congress throughout Europe and indeed throughout the Western world was accomplished in a relatively short period of time. Institutes were established in London, Vienna, and Budapest. The New York Institute was opened in 1931 and the Chicago Institute in 1932 (Brown, 1964).

By the end of the first quarter of a century of its existence, psychoanalysis had spawned a variety of dissidents or developers of divergent viewpoints which challenged both Freud's worldview and his scientific interpretation of human behavior and the etiology of mental illness. The important thing to note about the dissidents or the derivatives as we prefer to call them is that they were regarded by Freud and his loyalists as resisting truth. Theodore Reik reports that "every critic appeared as a moral hypocrite, every honest and serious judgment was considered a resistance. In this atmosphere it was inevitable that those who disagreed with him left the movement not at all with the tacit agreement to differ but rather in an aura of heavy disapproval and the sort of invective that was once heaped upon the heads of heretics in the ages of Belief" (Brown, 1964, p. 37).

In this chapter, we examine the work of three of those who differed from Freud and went on to formulate partially original and unique viewpoints. We examine the work of Alfred Adler, Karen Horney, and Harry Stack Sullivan, the derivatives having the most relevant ideas to share with modern counselors. We also examine briefly the activities of modern psychodynamic counselors and theorists. In Chapter 4 we will present further refinement of psychoanalytic doctrine with an analysis of ego counseling. Our selection of Adler, Sullivan, and Horney was based on their interest and concern with the impact of culture and interpersonal relationships as a major influence on human behavior and problems of mental health.

The Individual Psychology of Alfred Adler

Alfred Adler, though often thought of as a student of Freud, was more of a colleague. Younger than Freud by 14 years, he was already a practicing physician when he joined Freud and others to form the Vienna Psychoanalytic Society. Prior to joining Freud, Adler had gradually shifted his medical practice to the specialized area of neurology. During the early 1900s, Adler began to develop some of his own ideas, which evolved out of his direct work with clients in psychoanalysis. By 1911, these ideas had developed to the point that he broke with Freud and the Vienna Psychoanalytic Society.

In 1926, Adler came to the United States for the first of what came to be yearly visits. From 1932 until he died, he was a professor at the State University of New York (Sahakian, 1976). Adler's development of what became known as individual psychology "had an immediate influence on people outside the analytic professions: on teachers, doctors, criminologists, and the man in the street" (Munroe, 1955, p. 355). This probably was because Adler's concepts were both less shocking and easier to accept and understand than Freud's (Munroe, 1955). After his death, Adler's influence seemed to diminish. In 1955 Munroe wrote in her book *Schools of Psychoanalytic Thought,* "Adlerian theory is no longer vivid" (p. 355). She did add in a footnote that she had been told a renaissance was beginning and that statement proved true. In the last 20 years individual psychology has experienced a rebirth. Individual psychology societies today are believed to number more than 20,000 lay and professional members (Allen, 1971). Dinkmeyer, Pew, and Dinkmeyer (1979) list over 60 different settings where an individual can receive some form of training in Adlerian-based principles. Other approaches to therapy have incorporated many of the concepts originally developed by Adler. According to Ellenberger, "It would not be easy to find another author from which so much has been borrowed from all sides without acknowledgment than Alfred Adler" (1970, p. 645). Given this renewed, widespread influence, let us examine the thinking that generated it.

Theory of Personality Development

Structure of Personality

Adler's split with Freud centered on Freud's theory that humans are social beings driven by aggressive and sexual drives. Adler came to believe that the individual is not driven solely to satisfy personal pleasure but is also motivated by a sense of social responsibility and a need to achieve. "This socioteleological approach implies that people are primarily social beings motivated by social forces and striving to achieve goals" (Corey, 1981, p. 162). Unfortunately, Adler's basic concepts have often been misunderstood. Basically, his concept of need to achieve amounts to a common humanistic notion that "the individual is engaged in the striving for self-realization, in contributing to his fellowman, in making the world a better place to live" (Mosak & Dreikurs, 1973, p. 40).

Adler saw each individual as a consistent and unified entity striving toward a chosen life goal. Each individual chooses a goal and develops unique, characteristic ways of attempting to reach it. Adler believed that the way to understand an individual is to find out what her or his goal is, then to determine the life-style the individual has developed to reach it.

The Adlerian position emphasizes the interaction of the environment, heredity, and the individual as the determinants of behavior. Thus, a heavy emphasis is placed on the importance of the family environment particularly during the early years of an individual's life. Adler contends that the individual's perception of events, not the events themselves, determines behavior. An objective event in an individual's life—a physical deficiency, a broken home, or an intolerable teacher influences the individual's responses only indirectly. The actual event may affect the likelihood that a particular behavior will develop but in itself does not determine behavior. Most important is how an individual perceives and interprets such events. There are innumerable ways of perceiving any given event. Adler refers to these individual perceptions as fictions and emphasizes that they are not to be confused with reality. Nevertheless, each individual behaves as though the fictions are reality. This is a holistic and phenomenological rather than deterministic view of personality and behavior. It is also a clear shift from the "musical" or sickness model of Freud to a developmental or growth-oriented approach to personality, behavior, and therapy. The Freudian approach looks for what has gone wrong in the hopes of making a correction, while the Adlerian approach looks for what is right to make it stronger. Both seek the same goal but attack it from different ends of the continuum. Adler's theory is that in addition to creating fictions of real events, each individual develops a personal fictional goal as part of an effort to overcome his or her inherent weaknesses in relation to the world. The attainment of this fictional goal represents overcoming this inherent weakness and securing ultimate happiness. Just as the individual's interpretations of events are fictions, so the goal he or she chooses is a fiction, which in reality is unattainable. In Adler's view, this fictional goal serves as the unifying force for each individual; all individual behavior is directed toward the accomplishment of the chosen goal and is an operating force in day-to-day behavior. "[The individual] will continuously interpret the daily happenings of life in the perspective of his fictional goal" (Bischof, 1970, p. 181). Adler referred to this pattern of the individual's behavior as his life-style.

Life-Style

Adler felt that if an individual is to achieve superiority, she or he must live in accordance with her or his unique behavior pattern or life-style. This life-style is a product of the person's inner, self-driven, and determined direction of behavior and of his or her environment, which influences the direction the inner self will take (Bischof, 1970). "Schematically the life-style may be seen as a syllogism: "I am . . . The world is . . . Therefore . . ." (Allen, 1971, p. 5). What follows the *therefore* dictates what the individual will do with his life. Adler believed that everyone goes through this process of judging the status of self and the status of the world and, based on those perceived judgments, begins to form a pattern of behavior that becomes the life-style.

Social Interest

Adler also emphasized the importance of the social context of human behavior. He believed that individuals are born with an interest in other humans. Like other drives, social interests need contact to be activated, but in this case the activation is automatic (Bischof, 1970). The child's interactions, first within the family and then with others, establish certain conditions for the types of behaviors that may develop (Ansbacher & Ansbacher, 1956). All human behavior is interaction with other beings. "For this reason, we can presume one basic desire in all human beings; the desire to belong, which Adler called 'social interest'" (Dreikurs, 1961, p. 60). Hence, whatever a person does is done in relation to a social group. Consequently, Adler believed, the only way to study human behavior effectively is within the social context. For this reason Adler considered his theory of human behavior a social psychology (Ansbacher & Ansbacher, 1956). To understand how these concepts affect the development of the individual we need to examine Adler's sequence of personality development.

Personality Development

Adler believed that most of what an individual becomes in adult life is formed during the first four or five years of existence and is largely the product of the interactions within the family unit. During this time the child develops a notion of self, a pattern of behavior, and a life-style and begins to select a life goal, the attainment of which represents all that is good and toward which all behavior will be directed.

Adler believed that every individual is born with a feeling of inferiority. The infant is helpless in its environment. Even if it is born perfectly developed and normal, it is completely dependent on others. Almost everything it perceives is bigger and more competent. An additional burden exists if the infant has a physical defect. Adler believed that the infant soon perceives this inferiority and that this results in an uncomfortable internal state. This feeling is extended through early childhood as the child continually confronts his or her inability to be self-sufficient and people who can play ball, tie shoes, button shirts, and the like better than she or he. This process is normal, inevitable, and occurs in everyone to some degree. Adler asserted that this basic feeling of inferiority is the ultimate driving force of humans. The child, perceiving his or her inferiority, begins to try to find ways to reduce the uncomfortable feelings caused by this subjective evaluation of self. The direct consequence of this feeling of inferiority is a striving for superiority. This concept should not be confused with a drive toward social eminence or leadership. Rather, it is a basic drive within each individual to master the environment. This force, Adler contended, causes a person always to be moving forward and improving his or her situation. "All our functions follow its direction. They strive for conquest, security, increase, either in the right or in the wrong direction. The impetus from minus to plus never ends. The urge from below to above never ceases" (Adler, 1930, p. 398). Essentially, each individual has two types of goals: immediate and long-term (life goal). Immediate goals are related to the life or long-term goals and are easily observed in day-to-day interaction. The long-term goals reflect private inner logic and the individual's basic outlook on life (Dreikurs, 1957).

The child, in a search for ways of dealing with a world in which he or she feels inferior, first creates some internal order by using an inherent capacity to attend to certain events in the environment and then interpreting these events. In effect, the child builds a world of perceptions about events. This process involves active participation. Adler did not believe that people are simply blank screens on which life experiences are drawn. Rather, an individual's perceptions of experience are affected by internal expectations. Thus, someone suffering from paranoia will perceive even the most favorable intentions from others as somewhat hostile. This concept is much like what we commonly refer to as the self-fulfilling prophecy. A person who expects hostility will probably behave in ways that will generate hostility. Throughout childhood the individual develops an increasing number of these perceptions, and they become habitual as well as interrelated. Soon the child has an organized picture of his or her world, a picture that is partly accurate and partly inaccurate. Some of these perceptions, or fictions, involve further objectives, the attainment of which will allow the child to value herself or himself as superior, removing the unpleasant feelings created by the feelings of inferiority.

In conjunction with the fictional goal, the child's innate social interest is also developed. In Adler's view, favorable conditions in the child's early interactions with family members encourage this social interest (Dreikurs, 1957). Because these responses are developed in conjunction with other behaviors, striving for superiority becomes fused with social interests. In this way the child becomes a social being, seeking to attain her or his goal in ways that will also benefit others. One of the best ways to overcome the uncomfortable feeling created by feelings of inferiority is to believe that one is contributing to the welfare of others and is therefore valuable (Ansbacher & Ansbacher, 1956).

As the child matures, he or she begins to focus on one particular goal, which serves as the organizing element for all personal behavior. The child projects this goal in the belief that its attainment will overcome all obstacles and bring perfect security. This unique goal determines the individual's interests, the situations that summon involvement, and the kinds of behaviors he or she is most likely to develop.

Once the child has selected a goal to work toward and established habitual patterns of behavior designed to reach it, she or he has developed a life-style, the most comprehensive level of behavior. The individual's life-style dictates all that is considered his or her personality: "It is the whole that commands the parts" (Hall & Lindzey, 1957, p. 123). Everyone has the same ultimate goal of superiority, but the objective and the manner of seeking it are unique. In this way Adler accounted for human individuality.

The development of life-style conforms with the three basic tenets of Adlerian psychology: self-determination, teleology, and holism (Dreikurs, 1971). Adlerians hold that individuals determine their own behavior; external events do not. They also believe that the chosen behavior is goal directed; it is purposeful, not random. Finally, unlike Freud, they believe that individuals cannot be subdivided into parts; people behave holistically. Adlerians, then, perceive individuals as self-controlled people who move toward their chosen goal as unified wholes.

This life-style, once formed, rarely undergoes change, but the specific behaviors an individual uses to bring about the desired end often change as situations demand. For example, a young child may use whining behavior to achieve a certain goal, but later in life finds that whining no longer works and so changes behaviors, perhaps asking for things in a favorable way. The goals have not changed, only the means used to achieve them. Once the individual has selected a life goal and developed a life-style to achieve that goal, it is very difficult, and even painful, to change it. She or he may change elements within the system, but is reluctant to abandon the system itself.

In Adler's view, people's life-styles have developed by about the age of five years. From that time on, their personality retains the same basic form and dictates everything they do (Ansbacher & Ansbacher, 1956). Adler believed, however, that people are not fully aware of their life-style: They cannot explain it to themselves because much of it has been formed before they developed the ability to symbolize events through language. This explains not only why people do not understand all of their behavior, but also why their patterns of behavior remain relatively unchanged throughout life. It is difficult for people to change their behavior if they cannot verbalize it. This is one of the prime reasons why people who are experiencing difficulty need someone else to explain their life-style to them.

In summary, Adler viewed personality development in terms of the child's struggle to remove him- or herself from a position of inferiority to a place of superiority. To accomplish this task, the child forms fictions as a means of bringing some sense of order out of the environment. Part of these fictions are goals toward which the individual moves in order to remove a feeling of inferiority. Gradually the individual selects one goal around which he or she organizes behavior and fuses this with an innate social interest to form a unique life-style. At this point the primary personality of the individual develops.

This primary personality may undergo minor changes during the person's lifetime, but its basic form remains stable.

We now consider what happens within this normal progression to account for abnormal behavior.

Abnormal Development

Adherents of Adlerian principles reject the belief that people are "mentally sick." "No behavior is irrational if we understand the point of view of the person and his or her peculiar situation as he or she sees it" (Dinkmeyer, Pew, & Dinkmeyer, 1979, p. 37). Nonetheless people do behave in ways that are maladaptive. In Adler's view, the initial cause of such behavior is a heightened sense of inferiority developed early in life. In an attempt to deal with the overwhelming tension created by these feelings, individuals develop inappropriate patterns of behavior to compensate for the inferiority. Proponents of Adler assert that the three main reasons an individual develops increased feelings of inferiority are being born with a physical or mental defect, being pampered by parents, and being subjected to neglect.

Physical and Mental Defects

Adler believed that children who are born physically defective do not necessarily develop increased feelings of inferiority. The original, organic inferiority does, however, play a central role in development. Some individuals never overcome their feelings of inferiority and develop failure life-styles. Others somehow compensate for their physical defects and achieve normal life patterns. Still others may overcompensate; these and the people who have adopted failure life-styles are more apt to develop abnormal patterns of behavior.

Mental defects are much more difficult to overcome than physical ones. Compensation is difficult in a world that relies on and gives the highest esteem to brain power. This, Adlerians claim, is the reason for more maladaptive behavior in those who are mentally defective than in those with a physical defect (Bischof, 1970).

For a child born with either a physical or mental defect, the important factor is not the defect itself. It is the child's reaction to the event and the reactions of others that influence the path of development. If the child's reaction is positive, development may follow a normal course. If, on the other hand, the child and those around him or her react to the defect as a serious liability, the probability of abnormal development increases.

Defects in Childrearing

Adler also stressed that abnormal or maladaptive behavior is often a product of environmental forces, generally parental behaviors, acting upon the young child. He felt that a child who is pampered and constantly cared for will come to see himself or herself as lacking self-sufficiency, which increases feelings of inferiority. A child who is given no opportunity to try things and to experience her or his own successes and failures will not develop autonomy and self-control. Such a child is likely to become egocentric, seeking a sense of superiority by taking from others. In Adler's view, this is the personality development most harmful to both the individual and society.

Similarly, the child who is neglected is not likely to develop normally. The neglected child, given no direction, must rely completely on trial and error in order to learn; even when the child achieves some minimal success, the parents provide no reward for accomplishment. As a result the individual develops a lackadaisical life-style that brings neither personal satisfaction nor happiness to others (Bischof, 1970). Such a person causes society less harm than the pampered child but is just as harmful to himself or herself.

Once the individual has developed an unusual amount of tension because of increased feelings of inferiority, the likelihood of subsequent abnormal behavior increases. One form this behavior takes is an overstriving for superiority. In an attempt to deal with tension, the individual establishes an extremely high fictional goal, and the behavior for reaching that goal will probably be extremely rigid. Adler likened it to seeking a godlike state of perfection.

Another result of intense feelings of inferiority is inadequate development of social interest. The child who is pampered, neglected, or in some way treated as different is not likely to have human encounters that encourage expectations of satisfactory interactions with others. This leads the child to conclude that cooperation with others in pursuit of her or his goals is unlikely to prove fruitful (Ansbacher & Ansbacher, 1956). As a result the child selects objectives designed to satisfy personal needs without any consideration of common objectives that may also serve others. Developing selfish goals and behavior in turn affects the amount of interaction he or she has with others. Although Adler did not elaborate this concept, he believed that the individual who develops abnormally has a lower activity level than that of a normal person.

In Adler's view, then, abnormal behavior development is the result of the same factors that account for normal personality development. The differences lie with the abnormally high feelings of inferiority created within the individual and the subsequent development of inappropriate patterns of behavior in the attempt to deal with the heightened tension.

As an Approach to Counseling

According to Mosak (1958), faith, hope, and love are central concepts in the counseling process. Following Adler's socioteleological model, Adlerian counseling deals with the whole person—"one's physical, emotional-interpersonal, intellectual, and spiritual aspects as they interact within the unity of the self" (Garfinkle, Massey, & Mendell, 1980, p. 63). Dreikurs (1967) explains that this kind of counseling does "not attempt primarily to change behavior patterns or remove symptoms. If a patient improves his behavior and finds it profitable at the time, without changing his basic premises, then we do not consider that as a therapeutic success. We are trying to change goals, concepts, and notions" (p. 79).

This may seem a rather global goal, but Adler considered the development of abnormal behavior to be directly related to the individual's feeling of inferiority. The more specific goals involve taking the client back along his or her developmental path in an attempt to restructure that development and help the client understand his or her life-style and current social situation. The first of these goals is to help the individual reduce the negative evaluation of self, feelings of inferiority. The second is to help the client correct his or her perceptions of events and, at the same time, develop a new set of objectives toward which to direct behavior. The final goal is to redevelop the individual's inherent social interest with his accompanying social interaction. Adler felt that this last step was crucial, for "not belonging is the worst contingency that man can experience; it is worse than death" (Dreikurs, 1957, p. 173). If the goal of increasing social interest and participation is not reached, the rest of the process is largely wasted (Ansbacher & Ansbacher, 1956).

The Process of Counseling

Adler was one of the first to recognize the importance of the relationship between counselor and client. He believed that the counseling situation establishes an "interpersonal relationship in which the client's lifestyle can become apparent" (Garfinkle et al., 1980, p. 63). In his view, therapy is essentially a social relationship, and the whole process of counseling is a process of socialization. The client's problems are largely a result of lack of socialization, and counseling can be a powerful tool in redeveloping this process. Counseling has this potential largely because of the social interaction between the counselor and the client. For many clients this relationship is unique; it is the first time they do not have to be afraid in a situation with someone else. Given a permissive and warm atmosphere by the counselor, the client feels accepted and able to describe to the counselor the social-psychological environment in which he or she grew up. Adler stressed that the life-style of individuals could only be understood when these early life conditions were known and understood (Mosak, 1958).

Sonstegard and Dreikurs (1973) contend that a counselor's sincerity is of paramount importance in establishing a client's feeling of trust. In addition, the counselor must be an objective and attentive listener who can communicate a liking and concern for the client. The counselor must also be able to remain patient, even in the face of hostility and resistance. In Adler's view, the client should never in any way be offended by the counselor. Thus, the counselor must be able to state things in a manner acceptable to the client. This last ability is extremely important, for it is the counselor, not the client, who will develop an understanding of what is causing the difficulty. If the counselor cannot communicate this understanding in ways that the client will accept, the latter will never come to understanding her or his own behavior and its logical consequences. And if there is no understanding by the client, there will be no change in behavior.

Adler also believed that it is important in the counseling process to treat the client as a responsible individual. The counselor must communicate that it is the client's responsibility to act and that from acting in a responsible way, he or she can expect success. Moreover, Dreikurs (1961) points out, the counselor needs to maintain the human quality in interaction with the client; anything that detracts from the spontaneous nature of the relationship can only harm the counseling process.

In Adler's view, once the proper relationship has been established, counseling proceeds through three stages. In the first stage the counselor strives to develop an understanding of the client's goals and life-style. Once this analysis is completed, the counselor tries to interpret the client's behavior to her or him. In effect, the counselor explains the individual to himself or herself. Central to this process is helping the client understand the goal of his or her behavior and how that goal determines disturbing attitudes, thoughts, and behavior. Once this understanding is achieved, the client will be able to select new goals, which in turn will result in new behaviors. Finally, Adlerian counselors believe in the importance of developing the client's social interest. They see the therapist's role as similar to that of a mother. The therapist gives the client the experience of a loving contact with another human being and then helps her or him to transfer this heightened social interest to positive feelings toward others. Ultimately this would bring the client's private goals in line with goals of the larger society and give him or her confidence that any problem can be solved in cooperation with others. Adler assumed that going through this process would change the client's behavior. This was the real test of counseling for Adler: An individual cannot develop a true understanding of self without a subsequent change in behavior. If there is no change, then there has been no self-understanding, and the counseling has not been successful.

More often than not counselors who use an Adlerian approach rely heavily on group procedures. Thus many of the specific techniques discussed in the literature are designed for a group setting. Dreikurs (1961) outlines four stages of Adlerian group counseling, which can also be used as a guide for a counselor working in an individual setting. The stages are (1) the establishment of the counseling relationship, (2) analysis of life-style, (3) development of client insight, and (4) behavior change.

Having discussed the establishment of the client-counselor relationship, we can now turn our attention to the specific techniques that fall under the last three of Dreikurs's stages.

Techniques of Counseling

Adler elaborated few specific techniques to be used in counseling. This may account for the relatively infrequent use of his therapy system for many years, in contrast with the widespread use of many of his concepts. Others such as Dreikurs, however, have recently developed Adler's concepts into specific techniques.

From Adler's perspective, the most important task of therapy is for the counselor to develop an understanding of the client's life-style. To come to that understanding, the counselor must first examine the client's current behavior by asking the client to describe events in his or her current existence and his or her reactions to them. At the same time, the counselor must observe the behavior of the client within the counseling situation. The permissive atmosphere is designed not only to enhance social interaction but also to permit the client to behave in an open fashion. In this way the counselor can gain firsthand knowledge of the client's behavior patterns. Once the current situation is understood, the counselor tries to understand the individual's entire life-style.

Adler identified two general techniques to be used by the counselor during this analysis stage: empathy and intuitive guessing. The counselor needs empathy to understand the feelings that are guiding the client's behavior. Intuitive guessing is the ability to interpret the client's mind. Dreikurs (1961) refers to this technique as finding the "hidden reason" for a client's behavior. These techniques keep the counselor from having to rely entirely on the self-reports of the client, who is unable to verbalize all the reasons for her or his behavior (Ford & Urban, 1963).

Gushurst (1971) specifies four things the counselor must know in order to develop an understanding of life-styles. First, the counselor must be aware of the factors that Adlerians believe have a significant influence on personality: organic inferiority, pampering, and neglect. Second, the counselor must be able to recognize patterns of behavior, to infer, from the presence of two or more specific behavioral traits that certain related aspects of behavior are likely to be there also. For example, the counselor can expect that the pampered child will use a variety of behaviors to get things from others. Third, the counselor must be able to compare patterns within the client's family constellation to determine areas of similarity and difference. Finally, the counselor must be able to interpret the material accurately so that the client will understand her or his life-style and its logical outcomes.

One of the first steps in this process is to have the client describe his or her family constellation, listing all family members, with particular emphasis on siblings. The client is then asked to describe each family member, to rate each one on several dimensions (such as intelligence, temper, femininity, being spoiled), to describe differences and similarities in family members (such as who is most different from or similar to the client; who played together). These data are used to establish what factors exist in the individual's environment and may be contributing to certain patterns of behavior. By examining this constellation, the counselor can begin to understand the unique interactions between individuals that may have affected the client's life-style. This particular technique is receiving increasing attention in the field of counseling, particularly at the elementary school level. Counselors are increasingly turning to observations in both home and school settings in order to understand the causes of a child's difficulty.

Dreikurs, a student of Adler, believes it is possible to distinguish between counseling and psychotherapy at this point. Dreikurs believes there is no need to analyze the entire life-style in order to provide vocational counseling, marriage counseling, and child guidance. Instead, these problems can be solved by an examination and understanding of current behavior. To solve a problem in marriage, for example, it is not necessary to explore the complete life-style of each individual but to change the two partners' erroneous behaviors toward each other (1961).

Early Recollections

To understand the complete life-style, the counselor must engage the client in a discussion of early recollections. Adler believed that memory is biased and that the individual remembers only events that have meaning in his or her current life-style. Hence, if the counselor can understand which events have formed the basis for the client's life-style, she or he will be in a position to present a new understanding of these events to the client.

Early recollections are specific events that the client remembers from childhood, preferably before the age of ten. They are things that the client can recall clearly, not only the incidents but also the feelings that went with them (Gushurst, 1971). These recollections are good indicators of current attitudes and desires. According to Mosak (1958), the counselor interprets these early recollections in terms of both themes and specific details; characters who appear should not be treated as specific individuals, but as prototypes. The specific character may represent men in general, authority figures, and the like. The counselor brings the various themes of the early recollections together to understand their unity and pattern in terms of the client's life-style (Nikelly & Verger, 1971). All the material from the early recollections can provide the counselor with a picture of how the client sees herself or himself and other people and of the client's life-style in general.

Interpretation

Once the counselor has come to understand the client's life-style through analysis of family constellation and early recollections, she or he needs to interpret this understanding to the client in such a manner that the client will accept the information. In general, this is a process of pointing out the "basic mistakes" in the client's approach to life. Adler never said exactly how this was to be done, only that the counselor must be flexible and use whatever methods he or she feels will develop new understanding in the client.

In Adler's view, once clients have developed a new understanding of their behavior, that behavior will change. Dreikurs (1961) believes the counselor can enhance this process by providing encouragement. In large part, this encouragement consists in helping clients understand that they are causing their own difficulties and are responsible for improving the situation. This awareness of power over self tends to free individuals. Once clients realize they can exert control over the direction and quality of their life, counseling can terminate.

Adlerian Consultation

One major area of development in the Adlerian movement is in consultation procedures for parents and teachers. Bernice Grunwald, a public school teacher and member of the Alfred Adler Institute of Chicago, suggests that if all children were brought to realize that every class in school is a working–problem-solving unit, with every individual responsible for his or her own behavior, many problems in schools would not exist. Grunwald believes this kind of realization is possible only if the teacher believes it, too, and is willing to learn group dynamics and procedures (1971). It is safe to say that parents, too, might benefit from approaching the home as a working–problem-solving unit and their children as responsible partners in it. To establish this kind of environment, parents and teachers often need specific training. The counselor is often in a position to offer such consultative services.

One Adlerian-based approach to consultation with parents and teachers has been developed by Dinkmeyer (1971). Dinkmeyer, long associated with the Alfred Adler Institute of Chicago and the field of elementary counseling, refers to his procedures as "C" groups. The psychological foundations for these groups are as follows:

1. Behavior is holistic and can be understood only in terms of unity.
2. Behavior is significant only in relation to the consequences it produces.

3. An individual's behavior as a social being can be understood only in terms of its social context.
4. Individual motivation is best understood through observation of how the individual seeks to be recognized.
5. Behavior of individuals is goal directed.
6. A feeling of belonging is basic to human existence.
7. Behavior can be understood only in terms of the internal frame of reference of the individual.

These seven principles are directly related to Adlerian concepts of human growth and development. Dinkmeyer's "C" group is a way of teaching Adler's principles and the means of implementing them in the home and school. The approach is based on creating environments in which children are encouraged, not discouraged, and where they learn both that they are responsible for their own behaviors and how those behaviors affect others. The actual procedures used to train teachers and parents are discussed in Dinkmeyer and Carlson's *Consulting: Facilitating Human Potential and Change Processes* and in Dinkmeyer's *Raising a Responsible Child.*

The Essential Culturist: Karen Horney

Karen Horney started her professional career closely affiliated with Freud. Certainly if one takes a broad view of Sigmund Freud's influence, she would be considered within the scope of his influence. Horney's training in Germany was in classical psychoanalysis. Her break with orthodoxy came shortly after she arrived in the United States in the mid-1930s. She herself considered her theories "corrective" of Freud rather than as deviations. However, she broke with Freud in a number of fundamental issues, the most important of which was her rejection of both his instinct theory and his conception of the structural theory of the mind (id, ego, and superego) (Harper, 1959).

"The underlying determining principle for human behavior, according to Horney, is not Freud's instincts of sex and aggression, but the need for security" (Harper, 1959, p. 63). The latter stems from the nature of culture and the pressure exerted in individuals by the society wherein we live. Horney takes Freud to task for disregarding cultural factors in the development of the individual and in the creation of the individual's problems. In her landmark work, *The Neurotic Personality of Our Times* (1937), she noted that "Freud's disregard of cultural factors not only lends to false generalizations, but to a large extent blocks an understanding of the real forces which motivate our attitudes and actions" (Ehrenwald, 1976, p. 324). It is the perception of the world as a potentially dangerous, hostile, and unforgiving place that creates basic anxiety in the individual. It is this anxiety that lends an individual to develop various coping strategies. Individuals develop these strategies to cope with their sense of isolation and hopelessness. Their needs are very likely to be irrational and become part of a neurotic attempt to solve their personal problems. Horney identifies ten such needs that essentially fall under three categories, namely, *moving toward people, moving away from people,* and *moving against people* (Ehrenwald, 1976; Harper, 1959).

These ten broad categories break down into the following neurotic needs (Harper, 1959):

1. A need for affection and approval
2. A need for a life partner who will provide guidance and direction
3. A need to circumscribe one's life and keep it within narrow borders
4. A basic need for power
5. A basic need to use and exploit others
6. A need for prestige
7. A need to be personally admired
8. A need for achievement
9. A need for independence and freedom from the help of others
10. A need for "perfection and unassailability"

Some of these needs bear the influence of Alfred Adler and some the influence of Harry Stack Sullivan. However, her conception of the normal-neurotic continuum is unique. Horney agrees that the very nature of existence gives rise to fears. The determination of whether a response is normal or neurotic depends largely on the manner with which the individual deals with fears. We all experience fears; they are unavoidable in everyday life. The normal individual, Horney contends, is able to function in his or her culture despite the fears. The normal person is able to respond to the possibilities in his or her culture. "He does not suffer more than is unavoidable in his culture" (Ehrenwald, 1976, p. 326). Horney observes that "the neurotic, however, not only shares the fears common to all individuals in a culture, but because of conditions in his individual life—he also has fears which in quantity or quality deviate from those of the cultural pattern" (Ehrenwald, 1976, p. 326).

Intervention and Treatment

Horney's approach to treatment is much more direct and confrontive than the approach of classical analysis. It is a "sitting up" therapy with the focus on the present reality of the patient. The object of the therapist is to provide help in facing the disturbed self-image of the patient and in helping the patient face the real self. The relationship between the therapist and the client is very much a part of this process. Interpretation and confrontation are very much a part of the therapist's repertoire. What is integrated frequently revolves around the patient's idiosyncratic and/or neurotic drives. What is confronted is sometimes the manifestation of those neurotic behaviors within the therapeutic relationship. The therapist also provides help to the patient in combatting the idealized self-image, which frequently includes many of the neurotic needs of the individual. Confrontation frequently involves "Putting the patient therapeutically through this 'disillusioning process' and thus working the obstructive forces" (Harper, 1959, p. 65). The latter process aids the patient in mobilizing his or her constructive forces in order to facilitate self-growth. In their conceptualization of the treatment process, Horneyian therapists and counselors often present themselves as direct and confrontive in the service of restructuring the possibilities of self-growth.

The Proponent of Interpersonal Relationship Theory: Harry Stack Sullivan

Harry Stack Sullivan, born in upper New York state was an early pioneer in cultural and interpersonal influences on human behavior. He was a disciple of Adolph Meyer, the psychologist, and of William Alanson White. He founded the Washington School of Psychiatry and deviated from orthodox psychoanalytic thought because of his emphasis on interpersonal relationships as having more importance than an individual's drives or instincts. For Sullivan, the self is formed by the unique pattern of interpersonal relationships experienced by the individual. "An excess of 'depreciatory' attitudes (on the part of others) results in similar attitudes of the child toward himself as well as toward others. It is one of the major sources of anxiety. Conversely, loving attitudes communicated to him by emotional antagonism in empathy make the child capable of love, fellowship and good social adjustment in general" (Ehrenwald, 1976, p. 305).

Sullivan's approach to the understanding of behavior and personality had a decidedly humanist cast to it. He implied, but never specifically stated, the uniqueness of human beings in a biopsychological sense. He tended to respond to this uniqueness in his observation of behavior and in his intervention stance. He once remarked "In most general terms, we are all much more simply human than otherwise, be we happy and successful, contented and detached, miserable and mentally disordered, or whatever" (Bauer, 1990, p. 251). This humanistic orientation is not surprising considering the seminal influence on him of William Alanson White, who represented a broad humanist trend in his philosophy and teaching.

His concern with conceptualizing human behavior was complex. His interests led him to consider what went on between two people as well as what went on within the individual self. More than that, he was aware of the complex baggage that we bring with us to interpersonal situations so that his conceptions included complex configurations of the past and present both interpersonally and intrapersonally. This could also include previous experiences with similar individuals, "dream" or fantasy figures, and wishes along with the reality of the experience. Sullivan characterized the notion of such personifications occurring, at least partly, in fantasy, as "parataxic distortion." This tends to occur in all interpersonal situations and, as we shall see, became a major focus of the therapeutic intervention. With this strong emphasis on interpersonal relationships, Sullivan conceived of psychiatry as "The study of processes that involve or go on between people. The field of psychiatry is the field of interpersonal relations, under any and all circumstances in which these relations exist. It was seen that a *personality* can never be isolated from the complex interpersonal relations in which the person lives and has his being. . . ." (Ehrenwald, 1976, p. 305).

This concept became the keystone of Sullivan's conceptions. Everything he wrote and observed about personality development and intervention was seen in this cultural and interpersonal context. Human behavior, he thought, was engaged in two major activities, namely, the pursuit of satisfactions and the pursuit of security (Brown, 1964). Satisfactions according to Sullivan include meeting the drives and needs for basic physical fulfillment such as food, drink, rest, and sexual fulfillment. Beyond this, the pursuit of satisfactions include the need to reduce loneliness through the physical need for touch and comfort from another.

The pursuit of security, on the other hand, has a cultural basis and relates to being able to conform to the approved patterns of behavior that culture teaches us are right and "good" and to avoid those behaviors that culture teaches us are wrong and hence "bad." Anxiety, in part, is the failure to attain security. However, anxiety may have a physical or psychosomatic component to it in the form of a failure to attain satisfactions.

"The process of becoming a human being is, in Sullivanian terms, the process of socialization" (Harper, 1959, p. 67). This socialization is conveyed to the developing infant through that most important individual in this environment, "the mothering one" (Brown, 1964; Harper, 1959). Evolving as a personification of the self are three conceptions of "me": "good me," the construction and experiences of security; "bad one," the framing of those experiences that reflect anxiety; and the "not me," experiences too dreadful to remain in the awareness of the individual which usually manifest themselves in psychosis or nightmarish behavior.

Sullivan was greatly interested in the developmental process and conceptualized a hierarchy of development more complex than that of Freud. It was rooted deeply in the cultural experiences of the individual and couched in those terms. It also brought the individual to the edge of adulthood and so extended developmental concerns in psychoanalytic thought beyond the first half dozen years. Sullivan's "epochs" are as follows (Harper, 1959, p. 69):

1. Infancy: from birth to articulate speech
2. Childhood: from speech to play
3. Juvenile era: companionship to peer development
4. Preadolescence: from chum to genital sexuality; the entrance of the opposite sex
5. Early adolescence: interpersonal and genital interests
6. Late adolescence: from lust to love

The earlier goals of the pursuit of satisfactions and security remain the same throughout development but, obviously, manifest themselves differently at different stages. They are symbolized and incorporated differentially given the cultural-biological interplay at each level of development.

Sullivan's conceptions led him to characterize individuals according to their prevalent modes of interpersonal relationships. Some of the categories listed below are no longer relevant to current psychiatric and psychological classification but are useful from a historical perspective. They include the following categories (Harper, 1959):

1. Non-integrative: lacking any strong social responsibility, psychopathic
2. Self-absorbed: wishful thinking
3. Incorrigible: essentially hostile
4. Negativistic: attention-getters
5. Stammerers
6. Ambition-ridden: driven to power
7. Inadequate: dependent, in need of protection

8. Homosexual: an adjustment to anxiety

9. Chronic adolescent: perpetually immature

Some of these categories are still useful in thinking about interpersonal patterns of behavior. Others are, for all practical purposes, obsolete and inoperative, such as the stammerers and the homosexual. Nevertheless, it is interesting to note that Sullivan viewed the behavior as responses to anxiety, rather than as problems in and of themselves.

Sullivan's Approach to Intervention

Sullivan's concept of "the psychiatrist's participant observation in the treatment process is highly original" (Ehrenwald, 1976, p. 312). His motives of intervention were much more activist than those of Freud and in his clinical work he was much closer to Horney. He believed in dealing with the *parataxic distortions* in the historical interpersonal relations of the client and related those to disturbances in relationships in the patient's current life both outside and inside the therapeutic interview. He admonished the therapist that the desired stance in an interview was engaged observation. The therapist is a participant in the interpersonal process but is also able to listen to and observe objectively all that is transpiring in the patients' communications. Sullivan characterized the psychiatric process as having four stages. These include the *inception* (allowing the patient to develop ideas, observing the patient), the *reconnaissance* (collecting data through intense interrogation), *detailed inquiry* (testing hypotheses), and *termination* (interpreting and ending) (Harper, 1959).

Sullivan believed in the transmission of meaning in the therapeutic relationship. He believed in being as real as he could be in order to support the patient during those periods of distress resulting from attacks on early distortions and dissociations. Sullivan also believed that successful relationships later in the individual's life could help alter negative distortions, particularly if the successful relationship was with a new mothering one.

While Sullivan himself was frequently the target of criticisms because of his difficult writing style and because of alleged problems in his personal life, his emphasis on interpersonal relationships, a strong cultural context, and a humanist approach to understanding human behavior has had a strong influence on many theoreticians.

Modern Psychodynamic Derivatives

Among the most significant derivations from classical analytic approaches to treatment are the developments in ego counseling and in brief dynamic psychotherapy. These will be dealt with in Chapter 4. At this point we need to point out that psychoanalytic technique or at least psychodynamic principles are still operative in the work of some practitioners who would classify themselves as direct descendants of Freud and not as derivatives or deviationists and certainly not as ego psychologists.

Karl Menninger is a case in point. In his textbook *Theory of Psychoanalytic Technique* (Menninger & Holtzman, 1973), he indicates quite clearly that all of the basic psychoanalytic constructs are still quite operative. Even though the nature of the consulting room may have changed and even though the focus may be on a more problem-oriented approach to treatment, the basic principles of psychoanalysis as outlined in Chapter 2 remain at the core of his theory.

The constructs of transference, countertransference, transference neurosis, regression, resistance, and interpretation still apply. The manifestations of countertransference still need to be dealt with in the therapeutic context The treatment mode is still dominated by the two-party transaction between patient and therapist with each contributing something to the two-party contract. "A sufferer petitions a therapist for help and as the object of the latter's professional efforts, assumes the obligations of a client or patient" (Menninger & Holtzman, 1973, p. 16). The exchange is usually money for service. The therapist gives his professional service to the patient in return for money. The patient agrees to the terms of the contract re time and working conditions. The contract becomes an essential part of the therapeutic relationship. All these issues, the nature of the services, time of meetings, frequency of meetings, money that is paid, the role of relatives, are all part of the contract but also are part of the therapeutic exchange (Menninger & Holtzman, 1973).

The loyalists to Freud, persist in the use and application of his method. They reject efforts at reform and revision as "vague and inarticulated" (Menninger & Holtzman, 1973, p. 187). Menninger goes on to point out that "none of the new therapies in our view, direct their efforts to the kind of internal psychological investigation that psychoanalysis calls for" (p. 189). Our point in this brief section is that there remain in practice some devotees to classical psychoanalytic methodology who practice this approach in its unadulterated or shorter forms and who believe that for some problems and some issues, no other therapy is appropriate. Moreover, many of these individuals are committed to keeping the methodology alive as a continuation of the search for new knowledge within the framework of psychoanalytic thought.

Summary

We have examined a few of the major derivatives from classical psychoanalytic thought. In particular we have presented the individual psychology of Alfred Adler, the cultural view of Karen Horney, and the interpersonal relations approach of Harry Stack Sullivan. We have looked at each in terms of conceptions of personality development, evolution of maladaptive behavior, and intervention approaches. We have pointed out departures from the classical psychoanalytic model. Finally, we have presented a brief look at currently functioning psychoanalytic practitioners.

References

Adler, A. (1930). Individual psychology. In C. Murchison (Ed.), *Psychologies of 1930.* Worcester, MA: Clark University Press.

Allen, J. W. (1971). The individual psychology of Alfred Adler: An item of history and a promise of a revolution. *The Counseling Psychologist, 3*(1), 3–24.

Ansbacher, H., & Ansbacher, R. (1956). *The individual psychology of Alfred Adler.* New York: Basic Books.

Bauer, G. (1990). *Wit and wisdom in dynamic psychotherapy.* Northvale, NJ: Jason Aronson.

Bischof, L. J. (1970). *Interpreting personality theories* (2nd ed.). New York: Harper & Row.

Brown, J. A. C. (1964). *Freud and the Post-Freudians.* Middlesex, England: Penguin.

Corey, G. (1981). *Theory and practice of group counseling.* Monterey, CA: Brooks/Cole.

Dinkmeyer, D. (1971). The "C" group: Integrating knowledge and experience to change behavior an Adlerian approach to consultation. *The Counseling Psychologist, 3*(1), 63–72.

Dinkmeyer, D. (1973). *Raising a responsible child. Practical steps to successful family relationships.* New York: Simon and Schuster.

Dinkmeyer, D., & Carlson, J. (1973). *Consulting: Facilitating human potential and change processes.* Columbus, OH: Charles E. Merrill.

Dinkmeyer, D. C., Pew, W. L., & Dinkmeyer, D. C. (1979). *Adlerian counseling & psychotherapy.* Monterey, CA: Brooks/Cole.

Dreikurs, R. (1957). Group psychotherapy from the point of view of Adlerian psychology. *International Journal of Group Psychotherapy, 7,* 363–75.

Dreikurs, R. (1961). The Adlerian approach to therapy. In M. I. Stein (Ed.), *Contemporary psychotherapies.* New York: The Free Press.

Dreikurs, R. (1967). *Psychodynamics, psychotherapy, and counseling.* Chicago: Alfred Adler Institute.

Dreikurs, R. (1971). *Social equality. The challenge of today.* Chicago: Henry Regnery.

Ehrenwald, J. (1976). *The history of psychotherapy.* New York: Jason Aronson.

Ellenberger, H. F. (1970). *Discovery of the unconscious. The history and evolution of dynamic psychiatry.* New York: Basic Books.

Ford, D. H., & Urban, H. B. (1963). *Systems of psychotherapy: A comparative study.* New York: John Wiley and Sons.

Garfinkle, M. I., Massey, E., & Mendell, W. M. (1980). Two cases in Adlerian child therapy. In Gary S. Belkin (Ed.), *Contemporary psychotherapies.* Chicago: Rand McNally.

Grunwald, B. (1971). Strategies for behavior change in schools. *The Counseling Psychologist, 3*(1), 55–57.

Gushurst, R. S. (1971). The techniques, utility, and validity of life style analysis. *The Counseling Psychologist, 3*(1), 30–40.

Hall, C. S., & Lindzey, G. (1957). *Theories of personality.* New York: John Wiley and Sons.

Harper, R. A. (1959). *Psychoanalysis and Psychotherapy: 36 Systems.* Englewood Cliffs, NJ: Prentice-Hall.

Horney, K. (1937). *The Neurotic Personality of Our Times.* London: Routledge, Kegan Paul.

Menninger, K. A., & Holtzman, P. S. (1973). *Theory of psychoanalytic technique* (2nd ed.). New York: Basic Books.

Mosak, H. (1958). Early recollections as a projective technique. *Journal of Projective Techniques, 22,* 302–311.

Mosak, H., & Dreikurs, R. (1973). Adlerian psychotherapy. In R. Corsini (Ed.), *Current psychotherapies.* Itasca, IL: F. E. Peacock.

Munroe, R. I. (1955). *Schools of psychoanalytic thought: An exposition, critique, and attempt at integration.* New York: Dryden Press.

Nikelly, A. G., & Verger, D. (1971). Early recollections. In A. G. Nikelly (Ed.), *Techniques for behavior change.* Springfield, IL: Charles C. Thomas.

Sahakian, W. S. (Ed.). (1976). *Psychotherapy and counseling techniques in intervention,* (2nd ed.). Chicago: Rand McNally.

Sonstegard, U, & Dreikurs, R. (1973). The Adlerian approach to group counseling of children. In M. M. Ohlsen (Ed.), *Counseling children in groups.* New York: Holt, Rinehart and Winston.

C h a p t e r **4**

Ego Counseling:
A Psychodynamic Approach

In our earlier discussions of the work of Alfred Adler and Harry Stack Sullivan, we pointed out the importance of the ego for both of these theorists in the development of their work. "Among Freud's followers, Adler became spokesman for the primacy of the ego over drives" (Loevinger, 1976, p. 8). In some ways, his break with Freud, once the primacy of the ego or self, gave rise to a new emphasis in modern psychoanalytic thought, namely, the evolution of ego psychology and the ultimate development of ego counseling, an essentially psychodynamic approach. The ego psychologists argue that the ego has a life of its own rather than evolving from drives and conflicts between the id and the social world. Like Adler, contemporary ego psychologists place more emphasis on the social aspects of ego development as contrasted with a more narrow psychological source of energy.

As ego psychology evolved, much emphasis was placed on the mediating role of the ego. In this role the ego provides the impetus to integrate new learning, to monitor decision making, and to regulate adaptation to the external world (Mackey, 1985). The ego is not separated from unconscious sources of behavior since it also is the repository for the defense system.

In its role as decision maker or "executive," the ego is concerned with "cognitive mastery, emotional sensitivity, reality testing and object relations" (Mackey, 1985, p. 46). Much of the executive role of the ego is concerned with understanding the environment in relation to the self, with developing consciously controlled affective responses to others and with evaluating and testing the external world.

The ego, through its adoptive role is also concerned with the relationship of the self to the external world. In this context adaptive behavior is directed toward the external world "in more conscious, rational, task-oriented, and problem-solving modes" (Mackey, 1985, p. 46).

It is in its defensive mode that the ego turns around and is concerned with protecting the integrity of the self from both externally perceived threats and from internal and

53

unconscious assaults on the integrity of the self. All three aspects of the ego work in harmony with other aspects. This "inter-systemic equilibrium of ego systems" is at the heart of the integrating and mediating function of the ego and is the primary focus of the work of the ego counselors (Mackey, 1985, p. 49).

There are a large number of individuals who could be included under the umbrella of ego counseling, but much of what is contained in this chapter is based on the work of Edwin Bordin. Bordin's approach to counseling is a psychodynamic approach, which synthesizes the concepts of Freudian thought with the concepts of Rank and other neo-Freudians. Bordin received his Ph.D. degree from Ohio State University in 1942, after having completed earlier work at Temple University. He immediately went to work as a practitioner in the counseling center at the University of Minnesota. After a short stay at Washington State University from 1946 until 1948, he joined the staff of the University of Michigan where he was chief of the Counseling Division of the Bureau of Psychological Services. It was out of his work in these counseling centers that he developed a psychodynamic approach that goes beyond the limits of classical psychoanalytic thought.

Even under the common umbrella of ego analysis there is a great variety of thought. The basic concepts are, however, an extension of psychoanalytic thought, with major emphasis on the functions of the ego. According to Hartmann, "Ego psychology represents a more balanced consideration of the biological and the social and cultural aspects of human behavior" (1967, pp. 158–159). Ego-analytic counselors are concerned "with the ego as organization—with ego-strength" (Hummel, 1962, p. 464). The ego is not viewed as dependent on the impulses of the id; rather, it is viewed as a partially rational entity that is largely responsible for an individual's intellectual and social accomplishments. The ego has its own source of energy, apart from the id, and its own motives, interests, and objectives. It develops independently from the drives of the id and, once developed, resists being reattached to the id (Hartmann, 1967).

Ego-analytic counselors believe that there is a distinct difference between clinical patients and essentially normal individuals who are experiencing problems in living. They contend that because most of Freud's ideas were based on work with the abnormal personality, the validity of his assumptions about normal behavior is doubtful. Ego analysts also believe the antecedents of behavior are more complex and varied than the simple instinctual drives expounded in classic psychoanalytic theory. In their view, people are also influenced by the events with which they come in contact.

Hartmann, one of the leading exponents of ego-analytic theory, believes learning plays a role in the development of the individual. In his view, the ego is composed of inherited ego characteristics, instinctual drives, and the influences of external reality (1964). This balanced approach has led to "an improved understanding of man's relations to his environment, and to the most significant part of it, his fellowmen" (Hartmann, 1967, p. 158). Ford and Urban (1967) have pointed out that, essentially, the ego analysts have developed Freudian psychoanalytic theory into a broader, more adequate theory of psychology. The ego analysts, though not making major revisions in classical psychoanalytic theory, give more importance to the effects of environmental events and learned responses. Although they acknowledge the importance of situational events, they are equally concerned with the role played by the psychological energy of the ego.

The ego-analytic position is deterministic, but it is much less so than classical Freudian thoughts. While admitting that behavior is greatly influenced by unconscious drives and needs, they also believe that people have the ability to develop an understanding of these drives and needs. This understanding permits them to develop some control over their own behavior, perhaps a kind of self-determinism.

Theory of Personality

In their view an individual is born with the capacity to respond to different kinds of stimuli, only some of which can be attributed to innate energy. In early infancy the individual responds instinctually to satisfy such needs as hunger. These response patterns soon lose dominance as the individual begins to develop response patterns for his or her environment. Most adult behavior is related not to instinct but to the manner in which an individual responds to events. Ego analysts have devoted most of their studies to the learned behaviors of the individual. As described by Brammer and Shostrom (1977), ego psychology is concerned with the adaptive functions of individuals and places a priority on the utilization of cognitive functions in the control of behavior.

Stages of Development

Freud conceived of personality development as a sequence of psychosexual stages. The ego-analytic position regards personality as the product of a wider variety of factors over a longer period. Erikson's (1963) eight stages of ego development are probably the best example of this view. The first four stages of psychosocial development are roughly equivalent to Freud's first four. In line with the belief that the ego, in the form of conscious thought, becomes more important as the individual matures, the first four stages are dominated by unconscious drives, the last four by conscious thought processes.

In each of Erikson's stages of psychosocial development, there are critical periods through which an individual must pass. As Table 4-1 illustrates, success or failure at these critical points produces opposite effects on the personality. Failure at any one stage jeopardizes, but does not preclude, full development at the later stages. Success at these critical points demonstrates that an individual's ego "is strong enough to integrate the timetable of the organism with the structure of social institutions" (Erikson, 1963, p. 246).

Erikson warns against the assumption that the sense of trust or identity "is an achievement, secured once and for all at a given state. . . . The assumption that on each stage a goodness is achieved which is impervious to new inner conflicts and to changing conditions is, I believe, a projection on child development of that success ideology which can so dangerously pervade our private and public daydreams and can make us inept in a heightened struggle for a meaningful existence in a new, industrial era of history" (1963, pp. 273–274).

In effect, the ego is always in a state of evolution and open to both forward and backward change through the stages. Furthermore, at each stage the question is not one of either/or. A child does not develop trust to the exclusion of mistrust; rather, it is hoped that individuals will develop a reasonable balance between the two dimensions so that

TABLE 4-1   Erikson's Psychosocial Stages of Development

	Success		Failure
I. Early infancy (birth to one year)	Trust Child received affection and need satisfaction.	vs.	Mistrust Child abused or neglected.
II. Later infancy (one to three years)	Autonomy Child encouraged to develop self-control and is provided respect by parents.	vs.	Shame and Doubt Child made to feel inadequate and not worthy of respect.
III. Early childhood (four to five years)	Initiative Child encouraged to use imagination and test reality on his own.	vs.	Guilt Child made to feel guilty for his fantasies, which are often sex-related. Reality testing is discouraged.
IV. Middle Childhood (six to eleven years)	Industry Child has developed sense of duty and accomplishment.	vs.	Inferiority Child does not value accomplishment. Exhibits sense of failure.
V. Puberty and Adolescence (12 to 20)	Ego Identity Individual has now developed a sense of self-concept, a sense of what he is not, can do, and cannot do.	vs.	Role Confusion Individual has no real sense of being. Confused about himself and his relation to the world.
VI. Early Adulthood	Intimacy Individual has ability to form close relationships.	vs.	Isolation Individual remains apart from others. May even be antagonistic toward them.
VII. Middle Adulthood	Generativity Time of productivity in work and family.	vs.	Stagnation Time of nonproductivity and wandering. No real accomplishments in any area.
VIII. Late Adulthood	Integrity Approaches state of self-actualization.	vs.	Despair Loss of faith in self and others. Fearful of approaching death.

they will trust those things they should and mistrust those things they should. Keeping in mind the importance of this balance, we can turn to how it is maintained through the individual's developmental process.

Process of Personality Development

Of initial importance in the development of the ego is the infant's relationship with his or her mother. Through this relationship the infant begins to develop a sense of ego and non-ego, a concept of what is self and what is outside of self, that is the environment. If the child is frustrated in this relationship, then further development of the ego may be impaired because the infant is mistrustful of those things that are outside the self. If, as is usually the case, this relationship is good, then the individual's trust and interest in things that are outside the self are increased and the chances for further normal development of the ego are enhanced. This, then, is the beginning stage for the development of the ego functions. It is important to remember that, according to the ego analysts, the ego develops from its own energy source and thus is not dependent upon energy from the id, which is what the classic psychoanalytic model says.

With the development of an awareness of ego and non-ego in a nonfrustrating atmosphere, the child begins to explore the outer world. Trial-and-error learning first appears during this period as the individual attempts different types of coping behavior for the situations that arise in the child's environment. Hartmann (1964) places great importance on this period, for during this stage of development physical maturity allows the child to manipulate things within the environment as well as the self. This development, in turn, causes the child to come in contact with more stimulation to which responses must be learned. The ego analyst's contention is that most of an individual's behaviors are consciously focused toward specific objectives. Hartmann (1961) contends that the individual derives pleasure or satisfaction not only from fulfilling innate drives, but also from developing mastery over problems presented by the environment. The child learning to manipulate a particular toy receives satisfaction, not of some inner need, but of the desire for success in accomplishing a particular task. As Ford and Urban (1967) have indicated, it is this attention to behavior initiated through thoughtful, conscious planning that separates the ego analysts from the classical psychoanalysts. The ego analysts acknowledge that some behavior is caused by events of which the individual is not aware, but they also maintain that most behavior is caused by events in the individual's environment.

One of the most important events in the development of the normal ego is the development of communication skills that allow the child to deal in abstractions. The child learns to differentiate between the symbol for apple and the apple itself by learning that the latter will satisfy the need for food but the symbol will not. Development of this skill allows the child to think about events without actually experiencing them. Hence, the individual can imaginatively experience a trip to the moon without actually facing the dangers of such a trip.

The development of language skills also increases the individual's ability to differentiate among objects within her or his environment by formulating abstractions. According to King and Neal (1968), the child now has the power to understand that being bitten by one dog does not mean that all dogs will bite, and thereby avoids the overgeneralization that all dogs are bad. If the individual cannot make such an abstraction after being bitten by a dog, he or she will fear all dogs.

Equally important is development of the ability to delay termination or satisfaction of some behavior elicitor. As Erikson (1946) points out, it is the individual's ability to retain habitual patterns of behavior to bring satisfaction that provides entity. In the face of deprivation of satisfaction, the individual must be able to recall times when satisfaction occurred after a similar period of deprivation and, following that, learn to anticipate a future event that will lead to satisfaction. This calls for the development of control over one's drives. The individual who continually seeks immediate gratification of needs will be constantly subjected to situations that cause tension and anxiety.

One of the major influences on the development of the ego and its functions is the significant others with whom the individual comes in contact. According to Hartmann (1964), the child learns from these others certain methods for coping with and solving problems. Fromm (1947) suggested that personality develops through the process of relating oneself to the world, by acquiring and assimilating things from the world in order to satisfy needs and by relationships with other people. Fromm called this process of identification with other people in the environment the *socialization process.* It begins with the childrearing practices of the parents and then is extended to others with whom the child interacts. This process plays a dominant role in the development of the individual's life-style in that it provides the individual with a pattern of behaviors that will allow him or her to operate within the society (Fromm, 1947).

Thus, the ego analysts tend not to emphasize the negative effects of society on the individual as Freud did but acknowledge the equal importance of its positive effects. This emphasis on the importance of the society in shaping behavior allows the ego analysts to be more optimistic about the individual's potential for modifying behavior later in life. They accept the premise that the basic patterns of behavior are established during the first six years of life, but they regard them as only a base on which new behaviors are built throughout life. The key to the development of normal personality is the ability to develop new patterns of behavior or modify old ones to cope with new demands. Kubie (1958) points out that the development of a normal personality requires that the individual be flexible. This flexibility confers the freedom to learn through experience; the ability to listen, evaluate, reason, feel, and adapt to changing internal and external demands; the freedom to respond to rewards and punishments; and the ability to recognize achievement of satisfaction. A person lacking this flexibility will cease to develop or will regress to earlier patterns of behavior in the hierarchy. Either way, she or he can then be said to be behaving abnormally.

Ego-analytic theory believes that people, through conscious effort, learn new patterns of behavior. From an ever-expanding repertoire, individuals are able to select ways of behaving that are appropriate to each situation. Such individuals are not subject solely to behavior elicitors outside their awareness but are instead active agents in choosing and directing personal behavior. These behaviors, used often enough, become automatic and do not require conscious thought. For instance, a child learning the complicated behavior pattern of hitting a thrown ball with a racket must at first think about what he or she is doing. With an increasing proficiency, however, the child no longer gives conscious thought to all the procedures required but perhaps instead to where to hit the ball. This, too, with repetition becomes an automatic behavior. According to Ford and Urban (1967), these patterns or systems of behavior may become quite independent of the original reason for their existence. A behavior originally used to respond to a physiological need may subsequently be used to respond to an event unrelated to the original need. In this situation the ego has made an active choice of behavior to teach a particular goal. This is just one way in which the ego functions in an active, adaptive fashion. The following section deals with those functions in more detail.

Ego Functions

Ego analysts tend to view the functions of the ego in a broad, positive manner. In the traditional analytic view, ego functions involve the use of repression, projection, and other Freudian defense mechanisms that emphasize protective or regressive behavior. In the ego-analytic view, the ego functions are employed to cope with the environment through the use of reasoning and conscious thought processes. The analytic processes look to the past, the ego-analytic ones to the future. According to Kroeber (1964), the defensive functions of the ego are dominated by rigidity and the distortion of present reality, whereas the conscious coping functions of the ego are dominated by the reality of the situation and are flexible. The ego-analytic approach emphasizes the individual's ability to deal with the environment and personal needs positively instead of defensively.

The three categories of ego functions established by Kroeber (1964) are impulse economics, cognitive function, and controlling functions.

Impulse Economics

Impulse economics is the ability to control impulses and channel them into acceptable and usable behavior. In classic psychoanalytic theory, the individual deals with impulses by displacement, repression, or reaction-formation. The latter two processes amount to denying the impulse; displacement involves finding another outlet for it. Even in displacement, however, the ego is being reactive. If, instead of these behaviors, an individual chooses to deal with impulses in a more positive way, she or he will cope with the impulse by redirecting its expression or by delaying satisfaction of the impulse until a more appropriate time. Functioning thus, the ego is being active and positive, not reactive. An example is a young couple who delay sexual gratification with each other until marriage because they believe it is the right action to take.

Cognitive Function

Like impulse economics, the cognitive function of the ego can be used either defensively or positively. A person who uses the cognitive function negatively distorts reality through such mechanisms as intellectualization and rationalization. In contrast, a person who chooses to deal with his or her feelings copes with the situation by developing objectivity. In this instance the individual is exercising the ability to analyze the situation and logically think through a solution (Kroeber, 1964).

Controlling Functions

The controlling functions of the ego allow the individual to develop ability to concentrate on the current task without being affected by personal feelings. They permit the development of flexible behavior rather than regression to past behaviors. They also promote awareness of others' feelings. On the other hand, an individual using the controlling functions in a defensive manner will ascribe her or his feelings to others, will regress to earlier patterns of behavior when confronted by a difficult situation, and will simply deny awareness of feelings that are painful.

There are two keys to the ego analysts' view of personality development and use of the ego functions. One is the importance they assign to people's ability to respond to external situations. The other is the exercise of conscious control in responding to behavior elicitors. In the ego analysts' view, people often direct their behavior through active cognition and may respond either in a rigid, defensive manner or in a more positive, coping manner. The ego analysts regard personality as a structure, or pattern, of behaviors interrelated with a network of independent systems. Some of these patterns are developed in response to innate psychological needs. As individuals mature, they develop more and more of these patterns through conscious thought processes in response to new situations.

The Development of Abnormal Behavior

Ego analysts contend that abnormal behavior results from a breakdown in the normal ego functions. In an individual with a normal pattern of behavior, the ego functions establish patterns of behavior that cope successfully with the demands of environmental experience. The behaviors are increasingly under the conscious, thoughtful control of the individual and these patterns develop into a network of behaviors that constitute the person's life-style. When a situation or a series of events causes the individual to lose this self-control, the result is a behavioral breakdown. That is, when an individual is threatened or overwhelmed by a situation and behavior moves from conscious control to unconscious control, the potential exists for a behavioral disorder (Rapaport, 1958). This occurs, the ego analysts believe, when the ego functions have not been strong enough to cope with the demands of the particular situation and the ego functions surrender control of behavior to the id. In their view, this breakdown in the ego functions generally results from inadequate ego development during some phase of the psychosocial stages of development. A breakdown in one of the ego functions, however, or the ego's failure to exert control in a particular kind of situation, does not necessarily indicate a total breakdown of the ego. Some behavior patterns may continue to operate normally. Because all patterns of behavior are interrelated, however, it is necessary to understand the whole system of behaviors (Hartmann, 1953). The malfunction of one pattern of behavior in response to a particular situation is related to the function of the entire system. In battle, for example, one person will react to the stress abnormally, while another will not. Individual differences in reacting to stress reflect the different patterns of stable behavior that the individuals have developed.

What causes an individual to lose control over his or her behavior? What renders the ego unable to deal with situations that it handled adequately earlier? According to Rapaport (1958), a particular pattern of behavior can be maintained only as long as the behavior receives some reward. For example, a child who has developed a basic trust in individuals (Erikson's first stage) will interact with others in a trusting and open fashion. This pattern of behavior will continue as long as it is rewarded by others. If, however, at some period the trusting behavior consistently encounters rejection or hostility from others, the trusting behavior will begin to disappear; the ego loses its ability to behave in a trusting fashion. This loss is the germination of maladaptive behavior, for now the individual, even when presented with a situation calling for trust, will be unable to respond, because the behavior has been eliminated. As Erikson stated, the fact that the ego learns the appropriate behavior at one stage does not mean that the behavior is permanent. Individual behaviors are continually modified through encounters with the problems of existence (Erikson, 1963).

Abnormal patterns of behavior, then, develop when the individual loses the capacity to respond appropriately. This may happen because previously adequate behavior has not been reinforced and the pattern of behavior is no longer usable. An extreme example is a sustained period of stimulation deprivation such as the U.S. hostages experienced in Iran. A second cause of abnormal behavior is the inadequacy of current patterns of behavior to meet the demands of a situation: The individual loses control because the ego has not developed sufficiently to cope in an appropriate way. Rapaport (1958) cited the emergence of puberty as an example of a new situation for which a person may not have built an adequate pattern of behavior. In this case the sexual urge will dominate until the individual has learned patterns of behavior that will bring the sexual urge under conscious control.

In the ego-analytic view, then, abnormal behavior does not reflect a total failure of the ego but a breakdown in a particular pattern of behavior. The normal individual has an ego that is flexible and capable of changing with the demands of the environment as well as the demands of internal drives; the abnormal individual has patterns of behavior that are inflexible to the demands of the environment or to internal demands.

The ego analysts attribute more conscious control of behavior to the individual than do the Freudians. The ego analysts also attribute more power to external events in eliciting and affecting individual behavior. In their view the behavior, and indeed the personality, of the individual are affected not only by early childhood experiences, as in the Freudian view, but also by environment and the subsequent strength of ego functions as they develop throughout life.

The Goals of Counseling

Bordin (1955) believes that counseling was designed for individuals who are essentially well integrated and organized, while therapy was designed to focus on modifying the personality structure of the individual. Thus, the goals of ego counseling are, in a sense, more limited than those of classic psychoanalytic therapy. Ego counselors attempt to help clients with one or two specific ego defects that are causing difficulty. According to Kroeber (1964), counselors do not view clients in terms of their defense mechanisms but instead attempt to help them divert their energy from maladaptive to adaptive behavior. Ego counselors, then, look for specific maladaptive ego functions within the individual, not for unconscious evidence of a traumatic event in infancy. Ego counselors try to help clients see and understand their maladaptive behavior and, then, to help build new ego functions that are more adaptive. The chief goal is to help each individual develop what Erikson (1963) might call a sense of ego integrity, such that the individual is better able to cope with developmental tasks related to interpersonal and interpsychic problems.

The Counseling Process

Ego counseling focuses on normal and conscious characteristics rather than on uncon-scious motivations or internal causes of behavior. To this end the counseling relationship is reality- and present-oriented. The emphasis is on the cognitive rather than the conative domain. This does not mean that during counseling certain material that the client has repressed will not be brought out and dealt with, nor that strong affective feelings are not expressed in ego counseling. What it does mean is that the ego counselor tends to be more concerned with today's behaviors than with past ones. The goal is to help the client with today's situation, not yesterday's.

In discussing the prime concerns of the ego counselor, Hartmann (1961) emphasizes the need to understand the whole behavior system of the client, both habitual behavior patterns that are functioning normally and those that are functioning abnormally. The counselor must strive to understand both parts of the ego: those that are strong, and those that are weak and unable to cope with either innate needs or the demands of the individ-ual's environment. The ego counselor acknowledges that innate needs or drives may cause discomfort and thus abnormal behavior. The emphasis, however, is on the situational threats that cause the individual to deal ineffectively with such events. The counselor attempts to help the client understand in what respect his or her behavior is not functional and what the client can do to change.

Ego counseling, then, is generally much less intense and of shorter duration than psychoanalytic therapy or other forms of intense interpsychic therapy. Although both counseling and psychotherapy are concerned with personality, the ego counselor is not concerned with reshaping the whole personality. As Bordin points out, "Personality is dealt with only as it bears on the decision or problem situation and the client is not encouraged to go much further afield" (1955, p. 336). In Hummel's view, "It seems foreign to the concept of a counseling process intended to further normal (ego) develop-ment, to commit this process to extensive efforts at personality reorganization" (1962, p. 466). The counselor's tasks are to keep the specific goals of counseling in mind and to direct the counselor relationship so that its emphasis is on the current problem. Conse-quently, "the counselor influences the counseling deliberations as early as his assessment of a counselee warrants, so that a gradual focus is made on a set of counselee constructs with relation to some [significant] role or relationship in reality" (Hummel, 1962, p. 469). The counselor accomplishes this task by giving selective attention to the client and by defining the counseling relationship. The emphasis of counseling is on rational thought processes and on the cognitive dimensions of the relationship.

In essence, then, the counselor, not the client, controls the nature of the relationship. This control, however, is not mechanistic. The counselor must be warm and spontaneous, and the client must perceive the counselor as someone not only professionally competent but also concerned with the client and willing to make some commitment. This requires that the counselor be a good and objective listener. A counselor must communicate both acceptance and a willingness to help; at the same time the counselor must maintain an objective frame of reference in order to help. Without this objectivity, the counselor's own need pattern may intrude itself. If a counselor responds to a client by suggesting solutions that have worked for herself or himself, it is likely that the counselor has become too involved to be effective. On the other hand, as Bordin (1955) points out, some involvement is necessary; it is difficult to understand the feelings of others without relying to some extent on personal emotional experience. The important concern is not to let those emotional experiences interfere with meeting the needs of the client. According to Hummel (1962), the ego counselor is aware of the power of the relationship, but also aware that not only feelings, but also facts, alternatives, and decisions must be examined and resolved.

The counseling relationship, then, is one in which one individual, the client, comes to another, the counselor, seeking help with a problem. The counselor is a professionally trained individual who should be able to give this aid. For counseling to be effective, both people must be committed to solving the particular concern. A solution is best accomplished in an atmosphere of mutual trust, understanding, and acceptance. The counselor, by virtue of professional training, is responsible for controlling the relationship so that the client can achieve optimum growth. The emphasis of the counseling process is upon helping the client understand how her or his behavior in certain situations has been maladaptive, and then helping the client develop new patterns of behavior that are adaptive.

Because ego counseling is concerned with relatively normal individuals who function adequately in most situations but are troubled by specific concerns, the duration of counseling is relatively short, usually five to six sessions. "We are assuming that a relatively well-integrated person can make use of a brief counseling experience to set in motion a learning process that carries far beyond the relationship itself" (Bordin, 1955, p. 334). By the end of the counseling period, the client should feel capable of dealing effectively with new situations as he or she encounters them. The counseling process is best ended on a positive note, so that when new difficulties arise, the individual will not feel the need for a counselor. The goal is for the client to feel self-sufficient so when a new crisis arrives he or she will not feel dependent on the counselor.

Techniques of Ego Counseling

The techniques used in ego counseling are not a set of prescribed, inflexible methods. They are a set of preferred attitudes and strategies for the counselor to use while respecting the client's right to be an individual (Hummel, 1962).

Initial Behavior of Counselor

The process of counseling begins when a client comes to the counselor seeking assistance with a problem. In the initial stages of counseling it is the responsibility of the counselor to try to develop an understanding of the client and to tell the client the rules by which they will operate. In this respect ego counseling resembles other theoretical approaches. Bordin (1955) emphasizes that the counselor must allow as much freedom to the client as possible in these early stages. Given this freedom, the client can express her or his concerns, which in turn will enable the counselor to define the task before them. In ego counseling it is essentially the counselor who defines the task after careful attention to what the client has presented. As Bordin (1955) indicates, the inexperienced counselor is often not patient enough to listen carefully and completely to the client before defining the problem area or task.

Control of Process

Once the client and counselor have established a relationship that permits them to define the client's difficulty, it is the responsibility of the counselor, as the professionally trained person in the relationship, to maintain a focus on the task. The counseling is designed to build the ego strength of the individual, but the expertise of the counselor facilitates the process. The counselor selects the aspects of the individual's problem to work on and keeps the relationship focused on this goal. "The counselor does this by selective responsiveness and by helping the client to establish greater intellectual control over other conflicting responses" (Bordin, 1955, p. 340). The counselor discourages wide digressions, in the belief that the best course is to work on one concern at a time. Once that concern is resolved, investigation of another area of concern is appropriate.

The counselor also guides the relationship by controlling the cognitive and conative dimensions of the client's expressions. The cognitive dimension refers to overt behaviors or expressions; the conative dimension refers to the individual's emotions. The aim of the counselor is to keep a balance between the two dimensions. Counseling cannot be geared only to the expression of emotion, because most client problems also have a cognitive or reality component. Nor can counseling be geared only to the cognitive aspects of the problem while ignoring the client's feelings about the problem. The ego counselor strives for a balance between the dimensions by not letting the client communicate in one dimension to the exclusion of the other.

Control of Ambiguity in the Relationship

The counselor's use of ambiguity is another technique designed to facilitate the counseling process. Ambiguity, or lack of structure within a particular situation, is necessary in counseling so that a client does not feel compelled by the situation to behave or respond in prescribed ways. In general, the counselor should strive to establish a highly ambiguous situation in the early stages of counseling so that the client will feel free to express herself or himself. The counselor must define some areas of the relationship, such as what topics are appropriate and what the limits are on the client-counselor relationship, but the counselor should keep in mind that the more defined the relationship, the less ambiguous the situation. Nondirective techniques, which involve little talking by the counselor, increase the ambiguity of the relationship; directive techniques, in which the counselor takes the lead in the interaction process, decrease ambiguity.

It is important that the degree of ambiguity offered be appropriate to the client's problem. Generally, the more cognitive the problem, the less ambiguity needed. Bordin (1955) suggests three specific purposes for the use of ambiguity in the counseling relationship. First, an ambiguous counseling context provides a background against which the feelings of the client can be contrasted. Second, ambiguity elicits responses from the client that represent unique aspects of his or her personality. Third, the eliciting of these responses facilitates the development of transference through projection. Transference enables the counselor to understand the reasons for the client's behavior. Thus, ambiguity facilitates the process whereby the counselor comes to understand the personality of the client and the accompanying behavioral patterns, both those that are appropriate and those that are inappropriate.

The inexperienced counselor often will present a very ambiguous situation to a client without realizing its implications. This may leave the client with so few guidelines that he or she becomes uncomfortable with the process and quickly terminates, or it may act to encourage a very intense relationship that the client may not be equipped to handle.

Transference

Although ego analysts acknowledge that transference may occur in counseling, they do not ascribe the importance to it that Freud did. Hummel (1962), for example, contends that for most clients the use of transference is unnecessary and is, in fact, inappropriate for those who are relatively free of crippling neurotic defenses. In the classic sense, transference occurs when the client displaces feelings from previous situations onto the therapist; the therapist becomes a substitute figure for a person from the client's past.

Watkins provides a more helpful description of transference: "The transference experience . . . [is] a rather special expressional set that predisposes the client to perceive and act-react toward situations and people in a somewhat decided way. Consequently, the counselor enters a relationship—be it of an impersonal, friendly, or therapeutic nature—with a fixed bent in perceptions and feelings" (1983, p. 206). Such fixed perceptions can cause individuals difficulty in their everyday lives and may become manifest in the counseling relationship thereby affecting the interaction between the client and the counselor. Thus, it is our view that counselors must be aware of this possibility and sensitive to ways to utilize the transference phenomena. Watkins (1983) provides a potentially useful model for understanding five general forms that transference might take in counseling and the appropriate way for a counselor to respond to each of these forms. An abbreviated form of the model is shown in Table 4-2.

Countertransference

This consists of the counselor's projections onto the client. Frequently, countertransference is counterproductive to the therapeutic process and must be controlled. Examples of countertransference include the counselor repeatedly experiencing erotic feelings toward the client, encouraging the client's dependency on the counselor, seeking and obtaining satisfaction from client praise, overinvolvement in any number of ways with the client including arguing, being overly critical, or even sadistic. Any behavior in which the counselor's needs interfere with the constructive pursuit of the therapeutic process may be manifestations of countertransference. Those behaviors should be dealt with by the counselor either in supervision, consultation with a peer, or in a case conference. Failure to resolve persistent countertransference behavior probably requires the referral of the client.

TABLE 4-2   Client Perceptions and Counselor Responses

Client views counselor	Counselor responds by
1. as ideal. Client sees counselor as perfect individual who does everything just right.	1. focusing on client's false expectations of a counselor and accompanying self-negating behaviors.
2. as seer. This is the old notion of counselor as expert who has all the right answers.	2. focusing on client's apparent need for the correct answer, for advice.
3. as nurturer. Client wishes to be dependent on someone stronger, to be cared for, soothed.	3. focusing on client's need for a dependent status or position, his or her unwillingness to take responsibility for self.
4. as frustrator. Even though client has come to counseling the counselor is viewed as the enemy, someone who will block what the client wants.	4. focusing on building trust in the relationship.
5. as nonentity. Very close to the notion of a therapist as a blank screen.	5. focusing on establishing contact with client—as individual with feelings.

Having examined the negative aspects of this phenomenon, we should also point out that countertransference also carries the positive force and energy that enables the counselor to help the client. As Menninger notes "in the words of Annie Reich, 'Countertransference is [not only an unsuitable feature but also] a necessary prerequisite of analysis. If it does not exist, the necessary talent and interest is lacking. But it has to remain shadowy and in the background.' It is a part of the interrelationship" (Menninger, 1973, p. 82).

Diagnosis and Interpretation

The counselor's control of the dimensions of the counseling relationship facilitates the client's self-exploration, which in turn enables the counselor to achieve a full understanding of the client. Based on understanding, the counselor makes a tentative diagnosis of the problem. Although this diagnosis should not be imposed on the client, the counselor is responsible for defining the problem, sharing the diagnosis with the client, and helping him or her to understand it fully. The primary technique for helping the client achieve this understanding is interpretation. The counselor uses interpretation to help the client crystallize thoughts or feelings, to compare conflicting ideas, and to point out the defense mechanisms that are being misused. Through interpretation, the counselor attempts to put what the client has said into a more understandable perspective so that the latter can see the reasons for her or his behavior or feelings. "The counselor introduces new meanings into the discourse as one who is trying not to convert the counselee, but to join him in a mutual effort at comprehension" (Hummel, 1962, p. 475). Even though the counselor is the acknowledged expert, she or he must take care not to impose an interpretation or diagnosis on the client or to use interpretation too early in the process. In either case the client may resist the interpretation by establishing defense mechanisms even more firmly.

Thus, the timing of the interpretation is extremely important, and the counselor must be aware of the client's readiness to deal with it. Only when the client is ready will the interpretation be meaningful and help the client to develop both an intellectual and emotional understanding of his or her behavior. Once this understanding has been achieved the client is ready to assume normal growth through the building of new ego functions.

Building New Ego Functions

Once the client fully understands the problem, counseling can focus on the development of new behaviors—new more comprehensive and flexible ego functions. This part of the process may be very cognitive in nature; the counselor may actually instruct the individual in the proper way to behave, utilizing a role rehearsal technique in which the client practices new behaviors within the safe confines of the counseling office before trying them in a real situation. The counselor may also assign homework in which the client must try some new behaviors to strengthen the ego so that it can function more appropriately in the situations that are causing difficulty.

Short-Term Psychodynamic Intervention

One of the developments in the modern application of ego psychology has been the emergence of short-term approaches to counseling and psychotherapy. Predicated on the assumption of building on the client's strength, the short-term brief or time limited approaches assume the existence of a relatively intact ego and work to reinforce strengths already in place. The technique is essentially to identify areas of client distress, within a circumscribed set of goals and then, enhance the client's existing competence by selective reinforcement, providing help to the ego in solving the problem.

Bauer and Kobos note that "short term psychodynamic psychotherapy is challenging and gratifying work. . . . Carefully selected patients respond well to the treatment format" (1987, p. 9). The approach is most effective in those circumstances when the counselor evaluates the client as being able to learn how to solve emotional problems, to respond well to the proffered therapeutic alliance, and to maintain the focus of the treatment (Bauer & Kobos, 1987).

While the approach was originally offered to patients in crisis, the widespread success of the technique of brief therapy or counseling has broadened its scope considerably in the past two or three decades (Malan, 1976). With careful selection of clients and the application of ego counseling concepts in a brief or time limited format, the short-term approach has been widely adopted in mental health centers, counseling centers and venues that do not have the luxury of extended, open-ended treatment formats.

If the client is reasonably intelligent, able to maintain at least one meaningful relationship, demonstrates the ability to relate well with the counselor, seems motivated to work hard, and can define a specific problem area to work on, he or she is probably an excellent candidate for brief intervention (Malan, 1976).

Some practitioners in this field add the dimension of **time** to their concerns. Mann points out that "whatever differences there may exist among the various kinds of short forms of psychotherapy, or among their proponents, the factor common to all is the obvious and distinct limitation of **time**" (Mann, 1973, p. 9). Mann suggests that adding a time limit to the treatment process helps define the expectations of termination and focuses the client on the need for problem resolution in a circumscribed framework (Mann, 1973). Obviously, only individuals with reasonably intact egos who can meet the criteria outlined above are likely to be able to deal with the added pressure of a specific time limit.

Summary

The ego counselor's principal techniques are methods for controlling the counseling relationship. These consist chiefly in balancing the cognitive-conative dimension and in controlling the amount of ambiguity offered to the client. Within this context the counselor comes to understand the client's problems from the expressions and behaviors the latter exhibits in the counseling relationship. These behaviors and expressions are often elicited through the use of modified or moderate transference phenomena. Once the counselor understands the client's difficulty, he or she attempts to bring the client to that understanding through the use of interpretative statements, taking into account the client's readiness to accept the interpretation. Once the client understands the problem, the counselor and client can begin to discuss, and then practice, new modes of behaving.

Hummel (1962, pp. 479–480) outlines a series of steps that a typical ego counselor and client might follow. The client's problem in this example is academic study.

1. The counselor first helps the client examine feelings about his or her life, performance in school, and other school-related tasks.
2. The counselor encourages the client to project herself or himself into the future, to discuss career and life goals. The counselor then attempts to get the client to see some relationship between present behavior and future goals.
3. The counselor attempts to discuss with the client obstacles to the client's reaching those goals and how these obstacles might be removed.
4. As the discussion of obstacles continues, the counselor, through interpretation and reflection, attempts to get the client to examine herself or himself and external circumstances. In addition, the counselor attempts to get the client to see the interrelated nature of his or her feelings and behaviors.
5. Finally, the counselor helps the client establish a revised set of intentions in relation to academic study, and then, if possible, to rehearse new behaviors. The rehearsal involves getting the client to envision how she or he will behave in various hypothetical situations, such as setting up a study schedule.

In effect, the purpose of ego counseling is to produce changes not only in specific behavior—in the example, better grades—but also in "the complex of meanings and organizing principles which guide the counselee in his transactions within the sector of academic study" (Hummel, 1962, p. 479).

Although ego counseling is based largely on classic psychoanalytic theory, ego counselors believe that ego functions control or account for more of individual behavior than the psychoanalysts indicate. They attribute a large part of a person's behavior to conscious control. Hence, they tend to give more credit to the role of environment in a person's development and subsequent behavior. Ego counseling is also much more concerned with relatively normal individuals and with helping these develop stronger, more fully functioning egos, instead of placing emphasis on the abnormal and complete personality reorganization.

Ego counseling is designed to help individuals develop the coping aspects of the personality. It is designed to help people cope with the realities of the world through building ego functions. As Grossman (1964) points out, ego counseling is concerned with getting the ego to the point that it can deal with problems in the real world, while helping the individual to eliminate the defense mechanisms that hinder interaction with the real world. Finally, we have pointed out the natural extension of ego-counseling principles to short-term psychodynamic and/or brief approaches to counseling and psychotherapy.

References

Bauer, G. P., & Kobos, J. C. (1987). *Brief therapy: Short-term psychodynamic intervention.* Northvale, NJ: Jason Aronson.

Bordin, E. S. (1955). *Psychological Counseling.* New York: Appleton-Century-Crofts.

Brammer, L. M., & Shostrom, E. L. (1977). *Therapeutic psychology: Fundamentals of counseling and psychotherapy* (3rd ed.). Englewood Cliffs, NJ: Prentice-Hall.

Erikson, E. H. (1946). Ego development and historical change. In *The psychoanalytic study of the child* (Vol. 2). New York: International Universities Press.

Erikson, E. H. (1963). *Youth: Change and challenge.* New York: Basic Books.

Ford, D. H., & Urban, H. B. (1967). *Systems of psychotherapy: A comparative study.* New York: John Wiley and Sons.

Fromm, E. (1947). *Man for himself.* New York: Rinehart.

Grossman, D. (1964). Ego activating approaches to psychotherapy. *Psychoanalytic Review, 51,* 65–68.

Hartmann, H. (1953). Contribution to the metapsychology of schizophrenia. In *The psychoanalytic study of the child* (Vol. 8). New York: International Universities Press.

Hartmann, H. (1961). The mutual influence in the development of ego and id. *Psychoanalytic Quarterly, 20,* 31–43.

Hartmann, H. (1964). Essays on ego psychology. New York: International Universities Press.

Hartmann, H. (1967). Psychoanalysis as a scientific theory. In T. Millon (Ed.), *Theories of psychopathology.* Philadelphia: W. B. Saunders.

Hummel, R. C. (1962). Ego-counseling in guidance: Concept and method. *Harvard Educational Review, 32,* 461–482.

King, P. T., & Neal, R. (1968). *Ego-psychology in counseling.* Boston: Houghton Mifflin.

Kroeber, T. C. (1964). The coping functions of the ego-mechanisms. In R. W. White (Ed.), *The study of lives.* New York: Atherton Press.

Kubie, L. (1958). *The neurotic distortion of the creative process.* Manhattan, KS: University of Kansas Press.

Loevinger, J. (1976). *Ego development.* San Francisco: Jossey Bass.

Mackey, R. A. (1985). *Ego psychology and clinical practice.* New York: Gardner Press.

Malan, D. H. (1976). *The frontier of brief psychotherapy.* New York: Plenum.

Mann, J. (1973). *Time limited psychotherapy.* Cambridge: Harvard University Press.

Menninger, K. A., & Holzman, P. (1973). *Theory of psychoanalytic technique.* New York: Basic Books.

Rapaport, D. (1951). *The organization and pathology of thought.* New York: Columbia University Press.

Rapaport, D. (1958). The theory of ego autonomy: A generalization. *Bulletin of Menninger Clinic, 22,* 23–35.

Watkins, C. E., Jr. (1983, December). Transference phenomenon in the counseling situation. *The Personnel and Guidance Journal,* 206–210.

C h a p t e r 5

Self-Theory

The concept of self-realization is traceable to Aristotle's doctrine of the need of each individual to realize his or her own *telos* or goal (Friedman, 1984). Since that time the concept of self-realization has evolved through various iterations in philosophies as diverse as humanism, mysticism, vitalism, pragmatism, psychologism, and existentialism. "The concept of self-realization lies at the heart of Sartre's 'project'; of Heidegger's realization of one's ownmost, not-to-be outstripped, nonrelational possibility; of John Dewey's ethics of personality; and of the thought of such varied psychologists and psychoanalysts as Rollo May, Carl Rogers, Medard Boss, Erich Fromm, Karen Horney and Abraham Maslow" (Friedman, 1984, p. 57).

While all of the aforementioned psychologists appear, in one form or another, in this book we want to concentrate at this point on Carl Rogers. His entire professional life was devoted to understanding how people communicate with each other and the process of describing that communication. In a career that spanned parts of seven decades, from the mid-1920s until his death in 1987, Rogers influenced most of the practicing psychologists of the twentieth century. His pioneering efforts in recording and publishing transcripts of psychotherapy, helped to demystify the entire process. His development of a program of research to evaluate the outcome of his counseling and psychotherapy and the relation of those outcomes to the process of psychotherapy was original. He authored 16 books and 200 professional articles and research studies. He is one of the most often cited contributors to the psychological literature, and, along with Freud, he influenced the spread of ideas about counseling and psychotherapy involved in the practice of psychology (Kirschenbaum & Henderson, 1989).

His development of the system of nondirective counseling was a direct protest to the perceived authority-based, medical-model approaches to treatment. He approached the condition of human distress from a completely different philosophical viewpoint from that which preceded him. He believed that the individual has within himself vast resources for self-understanding, for altering his self-concept, his attitudes, and his self-directed behavior—and "these resources can be tapped only if a definable climate of facilitative psychological attitudes can be provided" (Rogers, 1980, p. 49). This was the essence of the nondirective approach to intervention which ultimately evolved into a developed theory of personality called self-theory.

Carl Rogers was always open to new experiences. He developed his approach to human communication based upon his personal experiences. Beginning with his own studies at the University of Wisconsin, Union Theological Seminar, and Columbia University, he developed a theory of counseling that has had a deep, controversial, and important influence on the field. His seminal book *Counseling and Psychotherapy* (1942) provides the basic ideas of his approach and establishes his desire for evaluative research to be part of the counseling process. A mark of this theoretical approach is its commitment to ongoing evaluation, which is expected to lead to new understandings about the counseling relationship. In this way the client-centered approach is always evolving and, it is hoped, improving.

Throughout the 50 or so years since his original work, Rogers's writings and activities suggest some changes in his position. He used his approach as a way to look at all kinds of concerns and situations including education (*Freedom to Learn,* 1969), marriage (*On Becoming Partners: Marriage and Its Alternatives,* 1972), and groups in counseling (*Carl Rogers on Encounter Groups,* 1970). In his view, theory is "a fallible, changing attempt to construct a network of gossamer threads which will contain the solid facts—a stimulus to further creative thinking" (1959, p. 191). His idea that the theory should be questioned and tested and his willingness to do it probably account for the impact and popularity of client-centered therapy. His work, *A Way of Being* (1980), integrates his thinking over the past half century.

Background

Rogers's early involvement as a therapist in clinics such as the Child Guidance Center in Rochester, New York, led him to question the commonly accepted approaches to psychotherapy, mainly Freudian in nature. His experiences led him to thinking about a different approach to counseling. At Ohio State University he was able to work with graduate students and test his ideas in clinical psychology. During his tenure at Ohio State, he wrote *Counseling and Psychotherapy* (1942) in which he presented his approach to his professional colleagues.

After leaving Ohio State, he moved to the University of Chicago where he organized a counseling center. Through his experiences and research at both Ohio State and Chicago, he further developed his client-centered therapy approach. In 1951, he published the book *Client-Centered Therapy,* which includes the theoretical formulations of the nature of therapy as well as a tentative theory of personality. In 1957, he moved to the University of Wisconsin where he continued his therapeutic activities as well as his research efforts. During this period, he extended his practice to include work with hospitalized schizophrenics.

After leaving Wisconsin, he was associated with several special groups in California. His work at the Western Behavioral Science Center and the Center for Studies of the Person represents another phase in his continued involvement in the development, application, and evaluation of the client-centered approach. While his work represents, in part, a synthesis of the ideas (theories) of others, Snygg, Combs, and Rank prominent among them, his major hypothesis comes from his own experiences and research efforts honed down through interaction with other therapists—some friendly, and some not so friendly, to his position.

Rogers states "that if I subtracted from my work the learnings I have gained from deep relationships with my clients and group participants I would be nothing" (1974, p. 120). His ideas have been expressed for public scrutiny and intensive study. Many therapists have adopted the approach, and some have been involved in further extensions of the basic theory. In sum, Rogers's theories have withstood the test of time and are a viable theoretical approach to psychotherapy and counseling.

Theory of Personality

Although there is a theory of personality from which client-centered counselors work, it is not a central focus of Rogers's work. "Although a theory of personality has developed from our experience in . . . therapy, it is quite clear to anyone closely associated with the orientation, that this is not our central focus" (1959, p. 194). For the purposes of this discussion, however, we believe that a presentation of his notions of personality, its development, and the nature of normal as well as abnormal behavior will be helpful to the reader.

Some of the key concepts are that people are positively motivated, rational, socialized, and can largely determine their own destiny. Rogers asserts that "the individual has the capacity to guide, regulate, and control himself providing . . . that certain definable conditions exist. Only in the absence of these conditions, and not in any basic sense, is it necessary to provide external control and regulation of the individual" (1959, p. 221). When the person is part of a reasonable and positive living situation, he or she will grow and mature along constructive lines and be relatively free from internal anxiety.

According to Rogers, people have the capacity to experience maladjustment. Furthermore, they have the capacity and the tendency to move away from maladjustment toward a state of psychological adjustment. This tendency, which will be released in relationships that have therapeutic characteristics, is called *self-actualization.* The therapist, through his or her interaction with the client, provides the environment to liberate this already existing capacity from within the person.

The Structure of Personality

There are three essential ingredients in the structure of personality according to Rogers: the organism, the phenomenal field, and the self.

The Organism
The organism, or the total individual, is a well-organized system in which change in one part may affect other portions of the organism. The actions or reactions of the organism

are as a total entity and are aimed at satisfying the needs that the person (organism) has. The organism's one basic drive is the need to become actualized: "the urge to expand, extend, develop, mature" (Rogers, 1961, p. 351). The person's desire is to develop and to be free of external controls, to be his or her own governing body.

The organism receives messages and has experiences. At times some of these are helpful for maintaining actualization; others tend to be negative. The organism sorts the messages and experiences and moves toward those that facilitate attaining self-actualization.

Essentially, the organism becomes a trustworthy guide to behavior. The total organism, including consciousness, leads to the individual being fully functioning; he or she feels right, and the resultant behavior is satisfying. The organism, as a complex computer, processes data and moves the individual toward behavior. Since data are sometimes incomplete or unavailable, the resultant behavior may be unsatisfactory. The organism, however, can use this unsatisfactory result as feedback to gain new knowledge and to behave in a more self-actualized way.

Phenomenal Field

The experiences that provide data for the organism exist in the phenomenal field. This is a constantly changing world of experience with the individual at the center (Rogers, 1951). The phenomenal field includes external as well as internal experiences. It is the events in the phenomenal field, consciously perceived by the individual, that are important. Whatever others may believe is reality is not important. What is important is what the individual perceives. This is his or her reality, a reality upon which the person bases his or her actions.

The Self

The self in client-centered therapy is the organized but differentiated portion of a person's perceptions of the I or me. The self is the center around which personality evolves. It is affected by the interaction of the self (I or me) with others. Interaction and the resultant integration of values and other aspects of life have an effect upon the self as well as the behavior of the individual.

Some distortion of these factors may occur. The self, however, strives to maintain the organism's consistency of behavior as well as its own consistency. Those experiences that are consistent are integrated. Those that are inconsistent are perceived as threats. (This sometimes causes anxiety.) Overall, the self is always in process; it grows and changes as a result of interaction with the phenomenal field.

Synthesis

A central concept of Rogers's theory is that the personality is always in a state of development. The organism, the phenomenal field, and the self interact and produce changes, as a person strives toward self-actualization. In addition, Rogers suggests that behavior is goal directed to use the environment and to control a person's place in the environment. Behavior is innately good and does not need to be under external control. A person is capable of a "balanced, realistic, self-enhancing, other-enhancing behavior" (Rogers, 1961, p. 105).

Reality is what a person perceives as a result of his or her experience. This perception of reality affects the choice of response. A person will respond actively to events based on his or her perceptions of reality and through a thought process. Humans are active, not passive.

Rogers sees personality as the product of continuing interaction among the organism, the phenomenal field, and the self. Basically people are good and given normal conditions for development will move toward self-actualization and be responsible for their own actions.

Personality Development

Organismic Valuing Process

Each person is born with a tendency toward actualization, which some identify as the master motive. Infants perceive experiences as reality. From the outset an infant's behavior is goal directed, focused on the need to satisfy the organism as it interacts with the phenomenal field. The infant behaves as an organized whole and exists in an environment of its own creation. It is only possible to understand the infant from its internal frame of reference.

The interaction of an infant with his or her perceived reality is as a unit, a totality. The infant begins to evaluate experiences as to whether they meet the need for self-actualization. Those that meet the need are seen as positive. Those that do not are perceived as negative. This process has been labelled the *organismic valuing process*. It is "an on-going process in which values are never fixed or rigid but experiences are being accurately symbolized and continually and freshly valued in terms of the satisfactions organismically experienced" (Meuller & Keller, 1973, p. 137).

This process, which continues throughout life, starts another process of differentiation whereby a person pays closer attention to positively valued experiences and incorporates those into the self. He or she tends to avoid those experiences that are negatively valued, keeping them from becoming part of the organism. The key is whether the experience maintains its actualizing tendency. If yes, the experience is good; if not, the experience is bad.

Positive Regard from Others

With the development and awareness of self comes the need for positive regard from others. As the infant interacts with the environment, specifically those who are significant to him or her, this awareness of his or her own experiences is differentiated from the phenomenal field and is the beginning of the self. At this point the individual begins to move from an internal locus of evaluation (Is what I am experiencing satisfying my needs?) to a need for positive regard. This can only be provided by other people. The need for positive regard from significant others is of particular importance (Meador & Rogers, 1973). In a somewhat behavioristic manner, the child receives positive responses and warmth when he or she does certain things. At the same time anger, rejection, or other negative factors follow behaviors that others do not seem to value. Since the need for positive regard from significant others is a necessary part of development, the infant tends to repeat those behaviors that elicit positive responses and avoid those behaviors that elicit negative responses. In so doing the evaluative process begins to move from Am I happy with myself? to Are other people happy with me? This self-evaluation continues to lead to behaviors that are valued by others. Thus, positive regard from others replaces the internal locus of evaluation as a basis for behaving.

Self-Regard

The next step in the process is for the infant to develop self-regard: a learned sense of self based upon his or her perception of the regard received from others (Meador & Rogers, 1973). Behavior is now judged as good or bad on the basis of what others value, with less regard given to what is personally satisfying. He or she now has two processes for selecting behavior: the internal innate organismic valuing system and the externally produced values of others. Obviously, if an individual's behavior becomes dominated by the need to please others with little or no regard to what is innately satisfying, a problem may exist in that the organism must always decide whether the behavior is good or bad from another point of view. A person then likes or dislikes himself or herself not on the basis of internal feelings and values but upon the evaluations of others. The person's locus of evaluation for all behaviors is totally external to himself or herself. As we will see later, this is often a reason for a person to seek therapy.

Development of Conditions of Worth

A person now finds that he or she cannot value himself or herself in a positive way unless he or she behaves in terms of these introjected values, regardless of the potential for the behavior to be innately satisfying. When experiences that have previously been valued positively do not engender positive regard from others, the person tends to avoid or deny the experiences. This has been termed *conditions of worth*. The person begins to attach positive value to some experiences that before were innately satisfying the organism. On the other hand, he or she assigns negative value to some experiences that were and/or are satisfying.

In this case, the person has not received unconditional positive regard. To restore the organism to its former state, the individual must receive only unconditional positive regard. This would eliminate or halt the development of conditions of worth and lead to uncondi- tional self-regard, congruence, and the need for positive regard and self-regard with organismic evaluation, and the maintenance of psychological adjustment (Rogers, 1961).

Proper Conditions of Normal Development

The person who receives constant unconditional positive regard from significant others in his or her environment will develop a healthy personality according to Rogers. The person experiences positive evaluation from others, which is satisfying even though some of his or her behaviors may not be acceptable. No conditions of worth need develop under these circumstances. The organismic valuing system and his or her needs for self-regard and positive regard are congruent. Thus the person begins to behave in ways that bring positive results and are personally satisfying. These behaviors will be accepted and valued by the larger society, and in this way people become socialized and well adjusted (Rogers, 1959).

In Rogers's view, people who are given the proper conditions for growth will develop into fully functioning individuals. Under these conditions, people will be open to all their experiences and will have no need to apply defensive mechanisms. They will be aware of all their experiences and will be able to symbolize them accurately. The organismic valuing process will determine behavior, and people will be in a continual state of change as they have new experiences. They will be able to deal with new situations in creative and adaptive ways because there is no need to distort or deny awareness of any experiences. As socially effective people they "will live with others in the maximum possible harmony because of the rewarding character of reciprocal positive regard" (Rogers, 1951, p. 234). Rogers does not describe such people as "well adjusted" but as "fully functioning," to imply a continuing process instead of a static state. "The fully functioning person would be a person-in-process, a person continually changing and becoming. Thus, his specific behavior cannot in any way be described in advance. The only statement which can be made is that the behaviors would be adequately adaptive to each new situation, and that the person would continually be in a process of self-actualization" (p. 234).

Characteristics of a Fully Functioning Person

The above discussion suggests that several important factors are related to the development of a normal personality. This notion has been translated by some into a concept called the fully functioning person.

Each person possesses an inherent tendency toward self-actualization. This means a person can symbolize experiences accurately, but it also means he or she needs positive regard from significant others as well as positive self-regard. When these conditions are met to a maximum degree, the person is fully functioning.

1. He or she is open to experiences. The person is not defensive or inhibited about any experience. He or she receives stimuli and processes these without distorting them. He or she thus experiences whatever is presented to the organism without selectivity or without being hampered by self-conscious awareness.
2. He or she lives in an existential mode. Each moment brings a newness to life. The person participates in the experience without needing to have complete control of the experience. He or she cannot predict what will be done in advance of the behavior. This openness becomes a major personality trait or characteristic.
3. He or she trusts the organism as a guide to satisfying the behavior. The person is able to behave by experiencing "feeling right" and gains a natural satisfaction in the behavior. The person trusts the organism to be wiser than conscious reactions alone. The resulting behavior may not be perfect, the organism is not infallible, but there are feedback mechanisms, again uncluttered by distortion and external valuing, that provide corrective measures, that is, the behavior is altered to be more satisfying.

Development of Maladaptive Behavior

In the normal developmental process there is a need for positive self-regard. As suggested earlier, this is often related to regard, positive or negative, from others. Whenever these conditions of worth, the external locus of evaluation, are incongruent with the innate organismic valuing system, the person tends to distort or deny awareness of those experiences that do not provide satisfaction. Self-experiences that are inconsistent with these conditions are excluded from the self or are inaccurately included. This creates the possibility for incongruence between the self and the organism's experience. Incongruity leads to vulnerability and maladjustment. The person's behavior will either be inadequate to meet his or her needs or will stop altogether. Since the needs are not being met or the person feels badly about what is happening, he or she tends to withdraw and is no longer a fully functioning person. Rather, the person is tentative, unsure, reactive, and not trusting. The person finds that in trying to please two masters neither is happy. The person is confused because at times the organismic valuing process controls behavior, while at other times the introjected conditions of worth are the controlling factor.

Characteristics of the Maladaptive Personality: The Non-Fully Functioning Person

In the same way that there are personality characteristics of people who are fully functioning as a result of the proper interaction of organism, phenomenal field, and self, so there are certain noticeable characteristics of those who fail in this process. Some of these are estrangement, incongruous behavior, anxiety, and defense mechanisms.

Estrangement

The conditions described above, that of the person who strives hard for the positive regard of others, is called *estrangement*. "[Man] has not been true to himself, to his own organismic valuing of experience, but for the sake of preserving the positive regard of others has now come to falsify some of the values he experiences and to perceive them only in terms based upon their value to others" (Rogers, 1959, p. 226). This process begins early in life and is affected by the differences between the child's need and the needs of the parents and significant others. The child cries when the parents want him or her to be quiet. The child shows interest in sexual matters. This embarrasses the parents. Soon the child is behaving on the basis of these external reactions. This leads to incongruity between self; experience estrangement occurs; and the potential maladaption begins.

Incongruity of Behavior

This incongruity between self and experience often leads to conflicts in behavior. Those behaviors that occur as a result of conditions of worth tend to maintain and enhance experiences that are not part of the self. The self responds by distorting or denying these behaviors. A person's actions become inconsistent. Sometimes the person will act because it is innately satisfying to the organism. At other times, the same behavior will be distorted or will not occur because the person reasons the behavior is inappropriate. Not only is this behavior confusing to the people in his or her life but the person is also confused and anxious.

Anxiety

Anxiety is a state that the person experiences but may not know or acknowledge the cause. It is a state of incongruence when the self and the experience of the person are approaching symbolization in awareness. Potential symbolization is important because the person will begin to perceive the threat to his or her existing concepts of self and is likely to reject the threats and to defend against the incongruities. Often very common defense mechanisms are brought into play, and the person denies the threat or places the responsibility for his or her inaction or inappropriate action on others. The anxiety caused by the incongruities of self and experience is threatening. The person defends himself or herself in a number of ways but most importantly is moving toward potential maladjusted behavior that may be a reason for seeking outside assistance in the form of counseling or therapy.

Defense Mechanisms (Coping Methods)

Defense mechanisms keep the person's perceptions of experiences consistent with the self-structure. This occurs through selective perception, or distortion of the experience, or through a process of denial that keeps the experience from the person's awareness. But since neither the actual behavior that causes the anxiety or threat to the self, nor the conditions that lead to distortion or denial have changed, the person adopts an inflexible and maladaptive pattern of behaving. He or she becomes more rigid in behaving as the perceptions of self-experience continue to be distorted. The person cannot be fully functioning because most experiences are not assimilated into the structure of the self. He or she is not able to experience life on the necessary existential basis.

Almost everyone uses defense mechanisms to protect him- or herself, and, in most cases, the person is able to function satisfactorily. When the inconsistency between concept of self and experience, however, goes beyond the normal range, a person is faced with inconsistencies that cannot be denied or distorted; the defense mechanisms will not be enough to cope with the situation. A person's reaction is one of heightened anxiety that relates to the perceived degree of threat to the self.

In this state, the person begins to behave unpredictably. His or her behavior is not only unpredictable to others but also to him- or herself. For example, the person may react in a hostile way to others in a particular social situation. Something that occurs triggers a negative response, one that is perhaps out of place within this situation. The same situation, however, at another time will evoke socially acceptable behavior that had previously been integrated into the self.

In general, a person who experiences this tends to be in a constant state of anxiety or tension. Behavior becomes rigid as a result of inaccurate perceptions or experience. The person is unable to adopt new behavior for dealing with new situations. New experiences are no longer assimilated into the self-structure. The person begins to misjudge many situations and to avoid any new experiences. At the same time, while they are anxious, they are not aware of this lack of behavior or maladaptive behavior since they are denying the experience or, at least, distorting it to fit their self-concept. The person's behavior is not only unpredictable but often irrational. The person feels he or she has lost control of at least his or her own behavior. The end result is dysfunction or maladaptive behavior with the accompanying downward cycle leading to ever greater problems. This then becomes the concern for which counseling may be necessary. Self-theorists, client-centered counselors, provide a specific way of helping people return to fully functioning, self-actualizing people.

The Goals of Counseling

Before examining the process that might be used, it is valuable to examine the goals of client-centered counseling. One of the most important aspects of this approach to counseling is that the client must establish the goals. This becomes essential since it allows and encourages the client to move toward the ultimate goal of self-actualization. If the therapist sets the goals, it would perpetuate the problem that has led to the need for assistance. The person must organize life's experiences to meet the needs of any external locus of control.

Rogers's belief is that people, under the proper circumstances, can develop goals and can regulate their behavior. And, if the conditions are properly provided, the behavior will be positive and socially acceptable. It may take some time for this to occur, but the goal of the therapist is to establish an atmosphere or environment in counseling that will allow the innate actualization process to take place. The client will change the locus of evaluation from outside of himself or herself to an inner locus and thereby resume a normal development pattern.

In a more specific sense, the goal of client-centered therapy is to help the client reinstitute the process of self-actualization by removing the obstacles to this process and the need for the client to use defenses or maladaptive behavior for his or her existence. One objective is to help the client free himself or herself from those behaviors that inhibit the innate tendency of self-actualization. The client is helped to develop his or her own resources and use these to reach his or her potential (Boy & Pine, 1963). It is expected that, given the proper situation, the client will establish individualized goals. In essence, client-counseling is a process that allows the individual to use already existing personal strengths, inner forces, to gain new insights into the interrelationship of experience and self. Once this occurs the individual's behavior will become more positive and actualized because the obstacles that hinder this have been removed.

In the client-centered view, the complete goals of counseling have not been accomplished when the person leaves counseling; only the patterns for future change have been established. The obstacles to growth have been removed and new ways of perceiving experiences established so that the individual can proceed toward self-actualization. Rogers did not believe the counseling experience, "no matter how uplifting, to be an end in itself, but finds its significance primarily in the influence it has on later behavior. . . . " (1970, p. 70).

The Counseling Process

Based upon the above information concerning the fully functioning and the maladaptive individual, the process of client-centered counseling takes the form of an if-then postulation. If certain conditions exist, then a definable process of growth and change will occur. The conditions that are normally associated with the "if" part of the equation are created by the counselor within the counseling relationship. Six of these have been postulated by Rogers as being necessary and sufficient. All must be present in the counseling relationship, and if they are present, they are sufficient to lead to change. (There have been some suggestions over the past decade or so that there are other conditions that will enhance the process, which suggests that the original six are not, in fact, sufficient.)

Rogers's Conditions for Counseling

We shall examine the original six conditions as the basis of the presentation of this counseling approach. We note again that the theory states that if the conditions exist, or are provided, change will occur in the client. If they do not exist, change may not occur.

Psychological Contact

The first condition for individual counseling normally listed suggests that there must be psychological contact between the two persons. In order for the contact to be a reality, it must make a difference in the experiential field of the other person. This can be a minimal difference, but it does express the need for the two individuals to be somewhat serious about the encounter.

Minimum State of Anxiety

A second condition for this approach is that the client must be in at least a minimum state of anxiety, or be vulnerable, and/or experiencing problems of incongruence between self-concept and behavior. The greater the degree of anxiety about this incongruity, the greater the possibility of change occurring. The individual who experiences enough discomfort will be more likely to want to change and to work at accomplishing this change.

Counselor Genuineness

The third condition relates to the counselor's functioning in the relationship. The counselor must be congruent within the relationship. He or she must be (1) an integrated person whose concept of self allows him or her to be aware of his or her behaviors and (2) someone who permits an accurate awareness in experiencing these behaviors. While it is probably unlikely that anyone can be completely congruent, the more closely the counselor approaches the state of a fully functioning person, the greater the possibility that he or she will be able to create the kind of environment necessary to the client, and the more chance there will be for success. He or she will be able to be aware of honest feelings that the client elicits in him or her. Another way of expressing this third condition is that the counselor is genuine. The counselor, in a sense, is transparent, allowing feelings and behaviors to occur within the relationship and with the client. Part of the process of counseling involves the client understanding this and sensing that if the counselor can act this way so can the client.

Unconditional Positive Regard

The fourth condition is that the counselor must experience unconditional positive regard for the client. Positive regard is an important part of the client's development. When he or she receives this from significant others, it enables him or her to function more fully and to move in a healthy way toward personality development. The added factor here is that the positive regard must have no conditions attached to it. The counselor must respect the client regardless of differences in values, differences in worldview; in short, no condition is set upon the client's behaviors and experiences.

The counselor cares for the client in the same way that a parent cares for a child. There is valuing and caring even though the parent might not like some of the child's behavior. When this condition exists, the client comes to believe that he or she is a person of worth, one capable of growing in a positive way.

Empathic Understanding

The next condition is that the counselor must experience, as closely as possible, the experience of the client. This empathic understanding means that the counselor puts himself or herself into the other person's internal frame of reference and understands it accurately. It is an attempt to understand the client from the client's point of view. It is, of course, impossible to fully understand another person's internal frame of reference, but the greater the degree to which this can occur, the greater the potential for a successful counseling outcome. Rogers suggests it is "this exclusive focus in therapy on the present phenomenal experience of the client" that is the heart and meaning of client-centered counseling (Rogers, 1959).

Client Perception

The final condition is that the client perceive, to some extent, the existence of the counselor's empathic understanding and unconditional positive regard. Simply having these as part of a counselor's makeup is not enough. They must be communicated to and perceived by the client. The more the client perceives these conditions, the more the potential for success. It is the counselor's job to insure that the conditions do exist, and he or she must show this in real terms to a client. The client will perceive any false aspects probably more quickly than he or she will sense the presence of the two conditions. One cannot play act and expect communication to occur.

To reiterate, the six conditions that are generally listed for successful client-centered counseling to occur are

1. Two persons must be in psychological contact.
2. The client must be in a state of incongruence. There must be, at least, a feeling of vulnerability and/or anxiety.
3. The therapist (counselor) must be congruent and/or genuine in the relationship.

4. The therapist (counselor) must experience unconditional positive regard for the client.
5. The therapist (counselor) must experience an empathic understanding of the client, especially the client's internal frame of reference.
6. The client must perceive, at least to a minimal degree, that conditions four and three exist and that they are actual feelings on the part of the therapist.

If the counselor provides these conditions to the client, then the process of counseling will take place, and if the process of counseling takes place, certain definable outcomes will occur. These outcomes aim at returning the individual to self-actualization. According to Rogers (1959), the greatest flaw in his statement of necessary and sufficient conditions is that they are stated in all-or-none terms. All the conditions, except possibly the first, exist on a continuum. Recent research, to be discussed in detail later, appears to indicate that these conditions exist on a continuum and that the degree to which they exist is perhaps even more crucial.

Given these six conditions, what can a counselor expect to happen in the process of counseling? What changes will occur in the transactions between client and counselor, and what changes can we expect in the client?

The Counseling Situation

One of the major tasks for the client-centered counselor is to provide the above conditions as part of the counseling setting. In this type of threat-free, accepting, and nonevaluative atmosphere, the client will sense that he or she is valued by the counselor. The tenor of the statements made, regardless of what these might be, are accepted with unconditional positive regard. Statements that would be considered socially unacceptable outside the counseling room do not engender negative reactions from the counselor. This leads the client to begin to feel more comfortable with himself or herself in the setting and, as a natural result of this, more self-referent statements are made; fewer nonself matters will be raised for discussion. The client will begin to discuss things in an I-me context. As an example, the client may be talking at the beginning of the counseling session about how difficult it must be for people to live together. As the session progresses, or perhaps in a later session, the topic may be how difficult it is to live with "my" spouse.

The movement toward more personalized communication by the client increases the possibility that insight will take place and the client will begin to see that his or her concerns must be owned. The client will see and understand experiences and feelings more realistically. He or she will be able to symbolize experiences accurately without the previously felt threat to self or increased anxiety. The client can begin to understand the incongruity between experiences and the concept of self because he or she is no longer threatened by the potential reaction of an outside person. The counselor accepts and encourages whatever unacceptable feelings the client wishes to discuss.

Many of the feelings that have been denied or distorted in the past can now be examined through expression of true feelings. The counselor encourages the client to examine these experiences objectively and, since they represent real feelings, to assimilate these feelings into the self. As this reorganization continues, experiences, feelings, and self become more congruent. Congruency leads to diminished threat and diminished need for defensiveness. Denial and distortion of experience are no longer necessary because the self-concept and most of the client's experiences are now in line—congruent.

It is important to note that as clients feel unconditional positive regard from the therapist, they begin to redevelop the ability to react to experiences based on the organismic valuing system rather than the conditions of worth that have been introjected. The client becomes his or her own person and can deal effectively with the threatening situations of the past as well as any new situations he or she is called upon to face. This rebirth of flexible and adaptive behavior leads the client toward becoming a fully functioning person.

As the reader will note, the above description is not as clearly defined in a stepwise fashion as one would like. Most counselors who adopt this method of counseling do not attempt to explain the process; they know only that it works. It is also difficult to explain what happens to the client in any scientific way. It is true that under the conditions described earlier the client is able to perceive experiences accurately, to examine them in terms of the inner locus of evaluation, the organismic valuing process, and to change behavior accordingly. People are catalytically aided to return to a more satisfying life through the client-centered counseling process.

Implementing a Process of Client-Centered Assistance

Client-centered counseling or therapy has undergone changes since it was first described in the 1940s. Currently less emphasis is given to the importance of any technique that might be associated with this school of therapy. More emphasis is given to the importance of the counselor and his or her attitude about counseling and clients. The client-centered counselor has a great deal of freedom in the interview in terms of techniques. As long as he or she creates the proper conditions, listed earlier, the belief is that the proper counseling process will occur, and the client will move in positive directions.

Certain concerns must be understood by a person wishing to implement a client-centered approach. These include such variant aspects as the amount of time given to each session and, perhaps, the number of sessions and the content of the communication. We will discuss several of these below.

Worth of the Individual

Of prime importance in implementing the process of relationship or client-centered counseling is the counselor's attitude toward the worth and integrity of the individual. The counselor attempts to implement the process of counseling by being as perceptive and sensitive as possible to the client and his or her experiences. In essence, the counselor must perceive the internal frame of reference of the person as accurately and completely as possible, and then feed these perceptions back to the client. In one sense the client-centered counselor becomes an alter ego for the client, a self out of the self. This allows the client to see and examine his or her own attitudes, feelings, and perceptions as worn by another. As a result the counselor can view clients more objectively without the complications of emotion. The counselor assumes that the client, having perceived these elements more closely in a nonthreatening and nonjudgmental atmosphere, will come to welcome her or his feelings into the structure of the self.

Nature of the Counseling Relationship

The nature of the relationship is of major importance in establishing the counseling process. This relationship has been initiated by the client's coming to the counselor to seek help. Hence, the major responsibility for the relationship is the client's, not the counselor's. In defining the nature of the relationship to the client, the counselor must make it clear that he or she does not have all the answers; it is the client who has the answers. The counselor is there to help the person find her or his own solutions. The major responsibility for the success of counseling rests with the client. The unique aspect of client-centered counseling is this emphasis on client responsibility.

Time Limit

The counselor should place a time limit on the relationship, specifying the length of each session, and perhaps also the number of sessions. There are two primary reasons for establishing these limits. The first is the obvious reality that a counselor has a limited amount of time available. But perhaps more important is the belief that, given certain time limits, the client may sense a need to make the sessions as productive as possible. Although the counselor sets this limit, it must be made clear that the client is basically responsible for what occurs within the allotted time.

Focus on the Individual

The emphasis in client-centered counseling is on the individual and his or her needs. A particular concern or problem is not considered as important as the individual. This relates to the belief that any aspect of behavior, positive or negative, is related to the entire system. Hence, the entire system—the person—requires attention. The outcome of this belief system is that the counseling or therapeutic relationship will help the client develop better ways of dealing with life in general. He or she will become a more mature, socialized, and self-enhancing person. Any problems or concerns will be resolved as the person moves toward self-actualization. The important goal is the restoration of the client's personal growth process by providing those conditions that are necessary for therapeutic change.

Here and Now

There is a need to focus emphasis on the here and now of the client's existence, inside and outside the therapeutic relationship. Although it might be interesting to know the background of the difficulties being experienced by the client, this information is unnecessary and might, in fact, inhibit the therapeutic process. The manner in which the client is operating right now is the concern of the counselor and of the client. Whatever the problem, the current feelings and how these affect behavior is what is important. It is an important part of the counselor's role to help the client focus on his or her current feelings through having the client express them verbally.

Diagnosis

This is an aspect of counseling that is not a formal part of client-centered therapy. The emphasis on the here and now and the individual in a particular situation eliminates the need for diagnosis. It is considered unnecessary, even undesirable, because the person is self-determining and is responsible for his or her own actions. Diagnosis is logically impossible, even if the counselor wanted to do it, because the client is the only one who can accurately see his or her internal frame of reference. Finally, diagnosis categorizes the person, something the client-centered counselor avoids in responding to each client as a unique person who has the potential for self-diagnosis and, more importantly, positive growth.

Emotional Content

Another emphasis in client-centered counseling is the focus on the emotional elements of the relationship. Knowledge, intellectual content, is of little or no assistance to the client because the impact and meaning of the knowledge is blocked from awareness by emotional satisfactions experienced in the here and now. The emotional responses keep the client from using knowledge, however obtained, to change behavior.

The important concern is what the client feels about the situation. These feelings are what must concern the counselor. The therapist helps the client focus on personal feelings as related to self, others, and/or events. The counselor provides feedback for the client as the client attempts to present and view his or her feelings more objectively.

Information

Information does have a part in client-centered counseling, however. It is information brought by the client not the counselor and can be obtained outside the counseling session. The counseling experience is used to help the client sort out the information with special attention given to the client's feelings about the information. Once again feelings of the client are more important than their cause.

Testing

In client-centered counseling tests occupy a minor spot. They are not completely excluded, but they are seen as a special type of information gathered and brought into the relationship by the client. His or her feelings about test information continue to be important. When tests become a real desire for the client, they may be appropriate. Even so, there is a need to discuss why test data may be desired. The focus is always on why the person feels certain needs and eventually on the feelings about the information however generated.

It is clear that the self-theory, client-centered, or relationship approach to counseling does not place much emphasis on counseling techniques. The emphasis is almost exclusively on the importance of the relationship. The focus is on the ability of the counselor to establish a relationship in which the six necessary conditions outlined earlier are present. To the degree that these conditions are present and are perceived as being present by the client, the counseling process will be effective.

The key elements in establishing these conditions are the counselor and the counselor's relationship with the client. The counselor must be a patient and expert listener who fully accepts each person by offering an atmosphere of unconditional positive regard and empathic understanding. In an attempt to help the client develop insight into her or his difficulty, the counselor encourages free expression from the client and then reflects these feelings. In a very real sense the counselor becomes an alter ego for the client. In this process no specific problem, information, or other intellectual elements are discussed; the focus is on the individual in her or his current state.

If the counselor follows this process, then the necessary and sufficient conditions for counseling will be established. The client will be able to go through the process of articulating feelings, developing insight and self-understanding, and finally developing reoriented goals and new modes of behavior. Although counseling may end at this stage, it is not the end of the process. The client has simply been returned to a state where he or she is able independently to continue the lifelong process toward self-actualization. The person is in control of his or her own behavior once again. The conditions of worth, the introjected values of others, have disappeared and the organismic valuing process has taken its proper place as the evaluator of experiences and controller of behavior.

The Process from the Client's Point of View

A client's perceptions, in any counseling relationship, are initially influenced by client expectations about counseling and, perhaps, the counselor. These, of course, vary but most often ambivalence and some trepidation seem to be present. When both people begin to perceive the relationship in a similar way progress is more likely than during times when each person has his or her own ideas about what can or may happen. In many forms of counseling, this is accomplished by some sort of structuring process usually initiated by the therapist. This may not completely solve the dilemma of differing expectations.

In client-centered counseling the process is designed to increase the similarity of perceptions. The counselor is a warm, accepting person who is trying to understand and who is placing a great deal of trust in the client. As this happens, often with initial frustration, the client begins to see the therapeutic time as supportive and accepting time that can be used to advantage by the client.

The theory suggests that people are best able to determine their needs and establish their goals. When the counselor behaves in a consistent manner throughout each session, this soon becomes part of the client's makeup. He or she senses that the counselor is concerned about his or her needs and that the progress to be made will be through efforts indicated by the client not the counselor. Once this occurs, again a process not easy to define, the client begins to experience the therapy in certain ways and begins to change toward a self-directed actualized person.

Several things happen. Often the client feels responsibility as a first reaction. This may be seen as an awesome factor since he or she may not have had to accept this in the past. Someone else took care of them. They may feel anger, and they may feel as though they are stranded and alone again. As he or she works through this, the client begins to experience his or her feelings and attitudes in a different way. These can be explored and examined without fear of threat from the counselor since he or she has not inserted this into the relationship. The client also begins to sense that what goes on outside the relationship is important to his or her actualization.

Often aspects of self that have been distorted or denied previously now reappear. The client's feelings become part of his or her awareness and, again, he or she is able to deal with these in the counselor relationship without fear of external evaluation and control. The self begins to change and feelings are experienced at a previously nonexistent level. Therapy is now seen as the experience of feelings, and the need to deal with specifics no longer holds the importance it once did.

As the person progresses through these stages, he or she begins to gain confidence in his or her own ability to explore, to experience, and to grow. Even those aspects that are upsetting or depressing are seen as growth factors since the client tapes no longer distort or deny these types of feelings.

There is usually a formal end to the therapeutic process, which the client must be prepared to accept. Even though the therapist avoided allowing any dependence to take place, there will be a reluctance to end what has turned out to be a positive growth-producing experience. It may help the client to discover that the experience can and does continue outside the relationship. The formal end of counseling need not signify the end of growth and self-actualization.

In general, the process produces certain outcomes that are related to the process itself.

1. There is a change in feelings. The person expresses feelings more easily and is not defensive about any or all of the feelings that he or she has.
2. Since the therapy is desired to provide for experiencing a wide range of emotions, the person changes his or her experiential manner. Experiences are now accepted in the existential moment, and as this occurs there is a movement from incongruence to congruence in what is experienced and how it relates to the organismic self.
3. The client's communication skills improve. He or she is able to talk about topics that were denied earlier. He or she is able to do this in a more cohesive and understandable way.
4. As the process moves toward conclusion the client experiences a change in perception of and concern over "problems." He or she is now able to experience in the present, and "problems" no longer occupy a significant spot in life.
5. Finally, the person will adopt new ways of relating to self and others. The relationship will be more open and honest, and the client will no longer be overly concerned about outside evaluations and reactions. He or she will not become a self-centered, noncaring person. He or she will, however, behave and have experiences based upon an internal locus of evaluation and will be more aware of whether or not the experience can meet innate needs and foster self-actualization.

Recent Extensions of Self-Theory

One of the outstanding contributions to the field of counseling by self-theorists has been their willingness to submit their methods of counseling to the test of research. Since the inception of self-theory, client-centered or relationship counselors, led by Rogers, have made it clear that their hypotheses should be submitted to research and then reformulated on the basis of that research; Rogers's own theory has undergone several changes since 1942. Whereas initial research consisted mainly of analyzing tapes from counseling sessions, it now covers a wide range of techniques, most of them based on client self-reports. This approach fits with the theory's basic assumption that only the client can really tell whether or not the counseling has been beneficial.

Studies on the actual process of counseling include early research by Rogers and Dymond (1954), Hogan (1948), and Raskin (1949). These studies indicate that as counseling progresses, the defensiveness of the client decreases, congruence between the self and experience increases, and the client tends to see himself or herself as the locus of evaluation. Later studies by Truax and Carkhuff (1967) and Carkhuff and Berenson (1977) demonstrate that, given the necessary and sufficient conditions, a client will move into self-exploration, which will lead to positive changes in the individual.

The research on the outcomes of counseling is perhaps both the most interesting and the most important. Theorists ask: Given the conditions and the process of counseling, what kinds of outcomes can be expected? A review of the research in this area shows that this aspect of the theory has received the least confirmation. Studies by Cowen and Combs (1950) and Grummon and John (1954) tend to support the hypothesis that individuals who have gone through client-centered counseling have better overall adjustments. A similar study, conducted by Carr (1949), found no evidence of better adjustment following counseling. Much of this research is based on self-reports and is extremely difficult to evaluate. However, more studies are now appearing that lend support to the effectiveness of counseling based on the process described above.

Perhaps the greatest amount of research and writing has come from Robert Carkhuff and Charles Truax and some of their associates. Sufficient data has come from these research efforts to merit inclusion at this point.

Carkhuff's (1969a,b) early work, *Helping and Human Relations: A Primer for Lay and Professional Helpers,* Volumes 1 and 2, sets forth a model for helping based upon the necessary and sufficient conditions that Rogers postulated earlier. Carkhuff has added several to the list. (These will be covered later.) He also prescribes three goals for the helping (counseling, or therapeutic) process.

1. *Client self-exploration.* The first goal of counseling must be to provide conditions that facilitate the client's self-exploration. Before anything else can happen, both the counselor and the client must explore all dimensions of the present difficulty.
2. *Client self-understanding.* If the client is able to explore his or her problems and feelings in depth, the client will come to understand exactly what is causing difficulty.
3. *Client action.* Once understanding is achieved, the client is ready to begin what is perhaps the most difficult part of the process—taking action. Understanding without action is generally nonproductive. In this stage, the counselor helps the client consider the available alternatives and then helps the client plan a series of steps that will lead to a successful outcome.

Carkhuff's counseling process (1971) uses six conditions or dimensions that are provided to the client. The counseling process is also seen as a two-stage process: facilitation and action. During facilitation, the primary objective is to establish a working relationship with the client so that she or he feels free to enter into self-exploration, which in turn leads to self-understanding. During this stage the dimensions of empathy, respect, concreteness, and genuineness are most important; in the action stage, confrontation and immediacy are most important.

Empathy

Carkhuff (1969a) contends that empathy is the most important element in the counseling process. According to Carkhuff and Berenson, "We must emphasize that empathy is not the client-centered mode of reflection with which it is most often confused" (1977, p. 8). In their view, it combines reflection and accurate diagnosis. Rogers (1975) noted that "the gentle and sensitive companionship of an empathic stance—provides illumination and healing" (p. 9).

Respect

"Respect is the ability to respond to the other person in such a way as to let him know that you care for him and that you believe in his ability to do something about his problem" (Carkhuff, 1971, p. 170). Respect means recognizing the uniqueness of each individual and conveying to the client the belief that he or she is a unique individual. The notion of respect goes beyond Rogers's unconditional positive regard in that it is to be conveyed throughout counseling (Carkhuff & Berenson, 1977).

Concreteness

This is the ability of the counselor to get the client to be specific about her or his concerns. "Specifically, concreteness refers to the helpee (client) pinpointing or accurately labeling his feelings and experiences" (Gazda, 1973, p. 26). The counselor helps the client accomplish this by being concrete himself or herself. An early study of Truax and Carkhuff (1967) indicates that a counselor's ability to be concrete may be even more important than empathic understanding.

Genuineness

Genuineness means that the counselor is able to be himself or herself in the relationship. The counselor does not wear a facade and is able to let personal feelings operate in counseling when appropriate. The counselor must always, however, keep in mind what will benefit the client; this will sometimes make it necessary to withhold a genuine expression (Carkhuff, 1971).

Confrontation

Often in counseling, the counselor will note discrepancies, either between things the client is saying, or between what the client is saying and doing. In such circumstances, the counselor must be able to point out these discrepancies to the client. Carkhuff (1969a) describes three general types of confrontations. They point out a discrepancy:

> between what the client says she or he wants to be and what the client is;
>
> between the client's statement about himself or herself and actual behavior;
>
> between the way the client describes herself or himself and how the counselor perceives the client.

The counselor must use confrontations of any type with caution, particularly early in the counseling process. They are action oriented and involve some risk, but often are necessary to move clients forward.

Immediacy

Immediacy is the ability of the counselor to get the client to focus on what is currently going on in the counseling relationship. This generally involves some dynamic between the counselor and the client.

Carkhuff has developed scales to measure the levels of counselor performance on each of the six dimensions. His scale contains five points, and the minimum level at which a counselor must perform on each dimension in order to be helpful is level three. Carkhuff and others have conducted a great deal of research with these scales and the dimensions. Generally, the research supports the hypothesis that the dimensions are, at the least, necessary conditions for counseling; they may not be sufficient. Because of their importance in counseling, however, they are discussed in more detail later in the book.

Summary

The recent developments in self-theory, though based on Rogers's thinking, represent a movement toward eclecticism. Rogers has contributed to an understanding of some basic requirements for effective counseling regardless of a counselor's particular theory. As a leader in the humanistic psychology movement, his ideas continue to exert a significant influence on individuals, the professions of psychology and other helping approaches, and on society in general.

References

Boy, A. V. & Pine, G. J. (1963). *Client-centered counseling in the secondary school.* Boston: Houghton Mifflin.

Carkhuff, R. (1967a). *The counselor's contribution to facilitative processes.* Urbana, IL: Parkinson.

Carkhuff, R. (1967b). Toward a comprehensive model of facilitative interpersonal processes. *Journal of Counseling Psychology, 17,* 62–72.

Carkhuff, R. (1969a). *Helping and human relations: A primer for lay and professional helpers* (Vol. 1). New York: Holt, Rinehart and Winston.

Carkhuff, R. (1969b). *Helping and human relations: A primer for lay and professional helpers* (Vol. 2). New York: Holt, Rinehart and Winston.

Carkhuff, R. (1971). Helping and human relations: A brief guide for training lay helpers. *Journal of Research and Development in Education, 4*(2), 17–27.

Carkhuff, R. R., & Berenson, B. G. (1957). *Beyond counseling and therapy.* New York: Holt, Rinehart and Winston.

Carkhuff, R. R., & Berenson, B. G. (1977). *Beyond counseling and therapy* (2nd ed.). New York: Holt, Rinehart and Winston.

Carr, A. C. (1949). An evaluation of nine nondirective psychotherapy cases by means of Rorschach. *Journal of Consulting Psychology, 13,* 196–205.

Coombs, A. W., & Snygg, D. (1959). *Individual behavior: A perceptual approach to behavior* (rev. ed.). New York: Harper & Row.

Cowen, E. L., & Combs, A. W. (1950). Follow-up study of 32 cases treated by nondirective psychotherapy. *Journal of Abnormal Social Psychology, 45,* 232–258.

Friedman, M. (1984). *Contemporary psychology: Revealing and obscuring the human.* Pittsburgh: Duquesne.

Gazda, G. M. (1973). *Human relations development: A manual for education.* Boston: Allyn and Bacon.

Grumman, D. L., & John, E. S. (1954). Changes over client-centered therapy evaluated on psycho-analytically based thematic apperception test scales. In C. R. Rogers & R. F. Dymond (Eds.), *Psychotherapy and personality change: Co-ordinated studies in the client-centered approach.* Chicago: University of Chicago Press.

Hart, J. T. (1970). The development of client-centered therapy. In J. T. Hart and T. R. Tomilerson (Eds.), *New directions in client-centered therapy.* Boston: Houghton Mifflin.

Hilgard, E. R. (1949). Human motives and the concept of self. *American Psychologist, 4,* 374–382.

Hogan, R. (1948). The development of a measure of client defensiveness in the counseling relationship. Unpublished doctoral dissertation, University of Chicago.

Holder, T., Carkhuff, R. R., & Berenson, B. G. (1967). The differential effects of the manipulation of therapeutic conditions upon high and low functioning clients. *Journal of Counseling Psychology, 16,* 139–144.

Kirschenbaum, H., and Henderson, V. L. (Eds.) (1989). *Carl Rogers: Dialogues.* Boston: Houghton Mifflin.

Meador, B. D., & Rogers, C. R. (1973). Client-centered therapy. In R. Corsini (Ed.), *Current psychotherapies.* Itasca, IL: F. E. Peacock.

Mueller, W., & Kell, B. (1973). *Coping with conflict. Supervising counselors and psychotherapists.* New York: Appleton-Century-Crofts.

Raskin, N. J. (1949). An analysis of six parallel studies of the therapeutic process. *Journal of Consulting Psychology, 13,* 106–220.

Rogers, C. R. (1942). *Counseling and psychotherapy.* Boston: Houghton Mifflin.

Rogers, C. R. (1946). Psychometric tests and client-centered counseling. *Educational Psychological Measurement, 6,* 139–144.

Rogers, C. R. (1951). *Client-centered therapy: Its current practice, implications, and theory.* Boston: Houghton Mifflin.

Rogers, C. R. (1955). *A theory of therapy, personality, and interpersonal relationships, as developed in the client-centered framework.* Unpublished manuscript.

Rogers, C. R. (1959). A theory of therapy, personality, and interpersonal relationships as developed in the client-centered framework. In S. Koch (Ed.), *Psychology—A Study of a Science* (Vol. 3). New York: McGraw-Hill.

Rogers, C. R. (1961). *On becoming a person: A therapist's view of psychotherapy.* Boston: Houghton Mifflin.

Rogers, C. R. (1969). *Freedom to learn: A view of what education might become.* Columbus, OH: Charles E. Merrill.

Rogers, C. R. (1970). *Carl Rogers on encounter groups.* New York: Harper & Row.

Rogers, C. R. (1972). *On becoming partners: Marriage and its alternatives.* New York: Delacourt.

Rogers, C. R. (1974). In retrospect: Forty-six years. *American Psychologist, 29*(2), 115–129.

Rogers, C. R. (1975). Empathic: An unappreciated way of being. *The Counseling Psychologist, 5*(2), 2–10.

Rogers, C. R. (1980). *A way of being.* Boston: Houghton Mifflin.

Rogers, C. R., & Dymond, R. F. (Eds.). (1954). *Psychotherapy and personality change: Coordinated studies in the client-centered approach.* Chicago: University of Chicago Press.

Seeman, J. (1954). Counselor judgments of therapeutic process and outcome. In C. R. Rogers & R. F. Dymond (Eds.), *Psychotherapy and personality change.* Chicago: University of Chicago Press.

Truax, C. A. (1961a). Clinical implementation of therapeutic conditions. In C. R. Rogers, *Therapeutic and research progress in a program of psychotherapy research with hospitalized schizophrenics.* Wisconsin Psychiatric Institute, University of Wisconsin.

Truax, C. A. (1961b). A scale for the measurement of accurate empathy. Discussion paper No. 20, Wisconsin Psychiatric Institute, University of Wisconsin.

Truax, C. A. (1962a). A tentative scale for the measurement of unconditional positive regard. Discussion Paper No. 26, Wisconsin Psychiatric Institute, University of Wisconsin.

Truax, C. A. (1962b). A tentative scale for the measurement of therapist genuineness of self-congruence. Discussion paper No. 35, Wisconsin Psychiatric Institute, University of Wisconsin.

Truax, C. A. (1963). Effective ingredients in psychotherapy: An approach to unraveling the patient-therapist interaction. *Journal of Counseling Psychology, 10,* 256–263.

Truax, C. B., & Carkhuff, R. R. (1965). Personality change in hospitalized mental patients during group psychotherapy as a function of the use of alternate sessions and vicarious therapy pretraining. *Journal of Clinical Psychology, 21,* 327–329.

Truax, C. B., & Carkhuff, R. R. (1967). *Toward effective counseling and psychotherapy: Training and practices.* Chicago: Aldine.

Truax, C. B., Wargo, C. G., & Silber, I. D. (1966). Effects of high accuracy empathy and nonpossessive warmth during group psychotherapy with female institutionalized delinquents. *Journal of Abnormal Psychology, 71,* 267–274.

Chapter **6**

Existential Approaches to Counseling

As the world trembled in the face of the irrational specter of the threatened destruction of Western society as we know it, there emerged on the European continent in the days preceding, during, and following the Second World War, a philosophy that crystallized as Existentialism. Its origins went back to the early and mid-nineteenth century. Schelling's series of lectures in Berlin in 1841 was followed shortly by Kierkegaard's publication of *Philosophical Fragments* in 1844 (May, 1983). As the century progressed, the philosophical movement ebbed and flowed until the emergence of Nietzsche and Bergson. Finally, the challenge to prevailing conceptions of the nature of life and the subject-object split that prevailed in Western culture was focused during the time of the First World War by the phenomenology of Edmund Husserl (May, 1983). In essence, the philosophical observations of all these men and others suggested the need "to undercut the subject-object" cleavage, which had been such a stimulating block in science as well as in philosophy. There is an obvious similarity between existentialism, in its emphasis in truth as produced in action, with the process philosophies, such as Whitehead's, and American pragmatism, particularly as in William James's (May, 1983, p. 55).

Focus on the human situation was the issue that began to emerge in the writings of those cited and in the ideas expressed during the 1930s, 1940s, and the 1950s by philosophers such as Martin Heidegger; theologians such as Gabriel Marcel and Jacques Maritain, French Roman Catholics; Paul Tillich and Nicholas Birdyaev, Protestant clergymen; and by Martin Buber, the Jewish philosopher and theologian. All over the continent, interest in this "new" philosophy developed but particularly in France where the writings of Albert Camus and Jean Paul Sartre reflected the philosophical principles of concern with the nature of existence and the pain of being free and responsible. The new philosophy appeared in art in the work of van Gogh, Cézanne, and Picasso. Rollo May notes that this was an "indigenous and spontaneous answer to crises in modern culture (and) . . . also in the fact that it emerged in art and literature (and) . . . that different philosophers in diverse parts of Europe often developed their ideas without conscious relation to each other (May, 1983, p. 56).

Existential thought in all of its aspects and in all of its variations calls into question the historicity of being. Questions arise in the literature and art of this movement pertaining to relations between human beings, between human beings and nature, and between human beings and God. Issues pertain to the unique subjectivity of men, the source and nature of fear and anxiety, and the implications of these concepts for the notion of freedom. Barclay notes that all of these issues emanate from human beings' existence in the world, "to an involvement in daily activities, looking forward or to the future, and being confused by this continual lack of personalized focus" (Barclay, 1971, p. 317). These concerns are ultimately related to death and temporality. As Barclay notes, "death is one certain event that all men face" (and) "temporality is a tendency for all individuals to look to the future, to interpret the present and even the past in relationship to a future state, goal, or plan (Barclay, 1971, p. 317).

These are the issues that existentialism addresses: concerns with being in the world and all of the contingencies implied by that phrase. More than that, existentialism is concerned with experiencing the world from the phenomenological vantage point of the experiencing one. All aspects of life, art, and science, are to be interpreted from this viewpoint. In the words of Ludwig Feuerbach, "Do not wish to be a philosopher in contrast to being a man . . . do not think as a thinker . . . this as a living, real being. Think in Existence" (May, 1983, p. 50).

The Philosophical Issues

"Nouns are for God and verbs for man," wrote Milorad Panic in the *Dictionary of the Khazurs*. The philosophical issues of existentialism relate, in large part, to resolving the issues of human existence. How shall human beings confront their situation in its totality? The philosophy may be best understood when we realize that existentialists are concerned with issues of being, doing, having, experiencing, all from the point of view of the person. The frame of reference is inside the individual and his or her experience of the "verbs" of life.

All of the writers in this complex philosophical system seem to address the same set of issues.

1. *The basic source of knowledge is the subjective self.* Human beings can be best understood from their own frame of reference. An essentially phenomenological stance prevails.

2. *Reason is only one source of understanding life.* It (rational thought) is not capable of providing all the answers. We have much to learn from emotions and even apparently irrational thoughts and behavior. Some of our affect may even have power over reason from time to time and may become a much surer means of discovering ourselves.

3. *We need continually to confront the sources of our alienation and estrangement.* As indicated earlier in our presentation, our relationships to God, nature, other human beings, and even ourselves are continually strained and tested. The existentialists are

concerned with the ramifications of these issues. Issues of helplessness and hopelessness, isolation and insulation, frustration and failure, hostility toward the self and others are all grist for the existential mill.

4. *The issue of anxiety as a constant phenomenon in life is a basic concern of existential writing.* All the points of confrontation with the sources of alienation constitute the source of our anxiety. When we deal with meaninglessness in our relations to others, when we do not understand the role of God, when natural forces such as catastrophe or illness overwhelm us, or when we question the very meaning of our lives, the overwhelming emotion we experience is anxiety and its manifestation in guilt and dread.

   As Rollo May notes, "Anxiety is the experience of the threat of imminent numbing" (May, 1983, p. 109). May continues, "Anxiety is the subjective state of the individual's becoming aware that his existence can become destroyed, that he can lose himself and his world, that he can become 'nothing'."

5. *The encounter with nothingness, the threat of ceasing to have a meaningful existence is another major area of concern for existential philosophy.* Questions abound: Is there anything else to look forward to beyond life? If there is nothing but an empty void beyond living, what are the implications for the way I live my life?

6. *Existential philosophical thought is deeply concerned about the nature and experience of freedom.* Human beings have the capacity to choose. Making a choice always implies the need to take responsibility for that choice. If we are able to exercise a choice, no matter how limited our options are, we have exercised our freedom and hence have assumed responsibility for our actions.

In a demonstration interview many years ago, the source of which is now obscure, Carl Rogers was working with a young man who professed that he had no hope, that the lights were about to go out for him. Rogers empathized and inquired if the lights were still flickering. The client indicated that they were, but just barely. Rogers inquired as to whether his client wished the light to remain on, even though it was barely flashing. The client responded that he certainly did. Rogers pointed out that he had just exercised his freedom and made a choice and that he, Carl Rogers, was prepared to participate with the client in taking responsibility for that choice.

The existential literature is concerned with issues of freedom, choice, and responsibility and the implications of the latter for human behavior. Rollo May talks about the opportunities as well as the "agonizing burden of freedom" (May, 1983, p. 34).

Merging with the "Third Force"

In some ways, the emerging "third force," a holistic conception of the human being, has a Hegelian relationship to the field of psychology. If the early influences in psychology tended to be mechanistic and reductionistic and if the initial antithesis to this approach was contained in the psychodynamic formulations of Freud and his followers, then perhaps the third force, a humanistic psychology, is the true thesis (Bugental, 1965).

Many approaches to the description of psychology are presented in a quasi-Hegelian manner as reactions one to the other. Chein's presentation of human behavior offers a contrast between *Homo Mechanicus,* passive, reacting, conditional man versus *Homo Sapiens,* knowledgeable, cognitive, self-directing man (Chein, 1972). Gordon Allport provides us with an interesting configuration that he labels similarly as having passive, reactive and active responses in depth to account for behaviorism, humanism, and psychoanalysis (Allport, 1962). Langer's disciplines of the varieties of human behavior are similarly descriptive: the *Mechanical Mirror* to represent the passive, conditioned, responding human being, and the *Organic Lamp* to represent the interacting, proactive, engaging human being (Langer, 1968). The "third force" falls into this category as a useful but not wholly accurate description of a movement in psychology.

Bugental (1965) summarizes what he perceives to be the basic postulates of humanistic psychology. Bugental believes that human beings must be understood in terms of their uniqueness as a species. He believes that this exceptional nature can only be understood in its wholeness and not as parts of the subsystems. Particularly important is the human context of this organism, namely, the interaction with other human beings. Human beings are aware of the connections between their actions and of the freedom to exercise choice, within limits. Finally, humanists believe in intentionality. Bugental notes that "man intends through having purpose, through valuing, and through creating and recognizing meaning" (Bugental, 1965, p. 12).

The belief in the uniqueness of the human organism is what connects humanistic psychology to existential thought. The issues of the existential philosophers are given life in humanistic thinking. The constructs of awareness and intentionality, in particular, strike responsively congruent chords for both humanists and existentialists. Examine, if you will, Rollo May's discussion of the phrase *human being.* For May, the concept of *being* "is a particular, a verb form implying that someone is in the process of being something" (May, 1983, p. 97). May replies that being in the existential context is really becoming, a person in the process of evolving, developing, growing. "Thus, being in the human sense is not given once and for all. It does not unfold automatically as the oak tree does from the acorn. For an intrinsic and inseparable element in being human is self-consciousness" (May, 1983, p. 97).

This unique ability of the "human becoming" to be aware of self, to make choices in the context of freedom, to be concerned about the future, to plan and intend according to a set of values and desires is at the core of the congruence between the humanistic psychology movement and existential thought. The humanists claim the existentialists as part of psychology's third force, and the existentialists claim Carl Rogers, one of humanism's most prominent spokespersons, as one of their own.

Clearly, then, existentialism is another aspect of the humanistic approach to psychology and counseling. "It represents a subject-oriented philosophy that emphasizes the existence as the transaction between subject and object rather than any essentialist point of view about the *a priori* conditions of human nature" (Barclay, 1971, p. 332).

Toward an Existential Psychology

It was their concern with the humanistic elements of existence that led existential psychologists to develop alternate psychological principles. Most of the practitioners in this field had been trained in the principles of psychoanalysis, which was the dominant psychiatric and psychological movement on the European continent. The emergence of an existential approach to the treatment of people in psychological distress was largely a reaction to prevailing modes of thought about human behavior. "These existential therapists believed drives in Freudian psychology, conditioning in behaviorism and archetypes in Jungianism all had their own significance. But where was the actual, immediate person to whom these things were happening?" (May & Yalom, 1989, p. 363). They were concerned with the impact of anxiety in the specific framework of current cultural concerns.

The existential therapists concentrated on the subjective experience of the persons with whom they were working (Maddi, 1985). They coined a phrase, *dasein,* to provide a functional and descriptive term to describe the psychological construct of their approach. Dasein is defined literally as being there (May, 1983). Some of the practitioners of this application of existential philosophy to human behavior refer to their practice as *Daseinsanalysis* (May, 1983; Boss, 1963). May points out that dasein "indicates that man is the being who *is there* and implies also that he *has* a there in the sense that he can know he is there and can take a stand with reference to that fact" (May, 1983, p. 956). Moreover, the dasein has a time dimension, which we will discuss later.

Psychological Conceptions of the World

The existential analysts distinguish three aspects of the person's world, Heidegger's *umwelt, mitwelt* and *eigenwelt.* The first of these is the *umwelt,* which means literally the world around or the environment. The *umwelt* focuses on the natural world of the individual and is the source of biological needs, drives, and instincts. It is, in effect, the biological world of the individual (May & Yalom, 1989).

The second element in the psychological world of the individual is the *mitwelt,* which means literally the with-world. It is the world of interrelationship with other human beings, what May calls one's "community" (May & Yalom, 1989). It provides the setting for contact with others and is a source of change through interpersonal relations. It is a world that is relevant to human beings in terms of the notion of mutual awareness. The latter is a potent source of change in life.

The third world of the individual is the *eigenwelt* or "own world." May feels that this aspect of the human being "has been least adequately dealt with or understood in modern psychology and depth-psychology" (May & Yalom, 1989, p. 367). *Eigenwelt* is unique to human beings. It is the source of personal meaning to the individual. The focus on the *eigenwelt* permeates much of Carl Rogers's thinking and writing (see Chapter 5), and his brilliant conceptualizations about the self have led many existentialists to claim him as one of them.

These three functional worlds are always interrelated. They operate simultaneously within the individual. In studying the psychological aspects of the person all three modes of being in the world, must be considered. The health of the *eigenwelt* is of major importance in both understanding and helping the individual because it is the *eigenwelt* that provides the individual with his or her perspective of the world. If there is a disturbance in the *eigenwelt,* there is likely to be distortion in the experience of the other two modes of existence. These distortions of perspective emerge as what other approaches to human psychology would label as symptoms. Understanding of the latter is provided by entering the *eigenwelt* of the individual.

May makes another observation about the process of studying the modes of being in the world when he points out "that it gives us a basis for understanding love . . . (because) without an adequate concept of Umwelt, love becomes empty of vitality and without Eigenwelt it lacks power and the capacity to fructify itself" (May & Yalom, 1989, p. 367). We might add that without the *mitwelt,* love lacks the context of its manifestation. The essence of existential psychology is the understanding of the interrelationship among these modes of living in the world and the need to examine their simultaneous impact from the perspective of the person.

The Significance of Time

Another aspect of the nature of existential psychology has to do with the notion of time. The uniqueness of human beings is further underscored by the capacity of the person to deal in the time framework of the past, present, and future. Time is related to the modes of being-in-the-world, in that the past is largely the domain of the *umwelt,* the *mitwelt* is largely concerned with the present, and the *eigenwelt* is generally concerned with the future. It is important to understand that these time frames are also experienced simultaneously and that the individual is constantly reshaping the past and altering the present in the context of his or her perception of the future. The past is concerned with reflection and explanation, the present with description, and the future with prediction.

Casual reviews of existential psychology and counseling frequently refer to it as an approach concerned with the here and now. This is an error, in our view, because this approach is clearly future oriented. It is the future that interprets the past and the present.

Perhaps the most brilliant of Rollo May's conceptions in existential psychology have to do with his ideas concerning time. He points out that "existential psychotherapists are struck by the fact that the most profound human experiences, such as anxiety, depression, and joy, occur more in the dimension of time than in space" (May & Yalom, 1989, p. 367). Disturbances in time are among the most profound experiences of human distress. Imagine the sense of isolation and desolation if one were unable to experience the world in terms of the past, present, and future. The individual would then be truly alienated from any meaningful intercourse with the world. As May notes, there would be no "continuity with tomorrow" (May & Yalom, 1989, p. 367).

May focuses on the future in his discussions of time rather than on the past or the present. The future in this conception reconstructs the past and defines the present. What the person is depends largely on his or her choice for the future. Approaches to intervention that concentrate on the past tend to overlook the fact that future defines past. Our aspirations and our wishes redefine our past experiences and inform our present mode of functioning. The orientation of many existential practitioners is therefore to the future. The basic objective of existential therapy may be to aid the individual to find the way to his or her future.

Existential Development and Psychodynamics

The existential psychologists conceive of human development in terms of the acquisition of the characteristics necessary for successful negotiation in the world. From early childhood on the individual is exposed to experiences that offer him or her the opportunity to master commitment, control, and challenge (Maddi, 1985). Commitment is concerned with engagement in the activities of life, control involves developing a sense of being able to influence those events, and challenge means the ability to utilize expected change and the accompanying discomfort as a stimulus to growth. Within this framework, the experiences of the developing child are incorporated to provide him or her with an ability to function within the three main elements of involvement. Positive experiences, the opportunity to experiment with these elements of development, and encouragement to refine the constructs of commitment, control, and challenge are the sources of positive development. Failure to negotiate these constructs successfully in both early and later development leave the functioning person with the need to resolve these issues later in life or perhaps permanently unfulfilled (Maddi, 1985).

With respect to existential dynamics, May and Yalom point to confrontation with four ultimate concerns, "namely death, freedom, isolation, and meaninglessness as the heart of the process." The individual's confrontation with each of these constitutes the content of the inner conflict from the existential frame of reference (May & Yalom, 1989, p. 376).

Concern with death is ever present. It is a "haunting" concern for all of our lives. Freedom, with its imperatives for choice and responsibility can be a significant source of anxiety. *Terrifying* is a word used in relation to freedom. Isolation, of course, refers to the ultimate sense of isolation from the self, from others, from the world. Meaninglessness deals with the need for a sense of purpose in our lives. Pain is an ever-present experience. The resolution of the issues implied by confrontations with death, freedom, isolation, and meaninglessness constitutes a framework for human dynamics from an existential point of view (May & Yalom, 1989).

Existential Counseling and Psychotherapy

The goal of existential counseling and psychotherapy quite simply is to provide a framework wherein individuals concerned with the issues of existential philosophy and psychology may work to resolve these conflicts. This is perhaps easier to say than to do.

Fundamentally, existential counselors and psychotherapists are concerned with clients' ability and willingness to confront the issues of life. Maurice Friedman points out that "this means the recognition that the patients' commitment, their basic decision about their lives, precedes their knowledge of themselves. In fact, they cannot even permit themselves to get insight or knowledge until they are ready to take a decisive orientation to life and have made the preliminary decisions along the way" (Friedman, 1984, p. 80).

It would appear, from this observation, that existential approaches to treatment are probably restricted to those with the capacity and disposition to make such preliminary decisions and to those who are intact enough to participate in the process. A significant degree of self-awareness is required as well as the ability to be conscious of one's self

(Friedman, 1984). Existential counseling and psychotherapy has as its basic goal to apply existential concepts to the therapeutic situation. The relationship between the counselor and the client is the heart of this process.

Existential practitioners provide a therapeutic context within the framework of a real relationship between two people. The existential counselor is totally present in the relationship in terms of her or his personhood. The focus is on the issues being faced by the human being who happens to be the client. Understanding of that human being can only take place in a context that permits the complex unfolding of all the essential conflicts and concerns in that human being's life. As May notes, "existential therapy is not a comprehensive psychotherapeutic system; it is a frame of reference—a paradigm in which one views and understands a patient's suffering in a particular manner" (May & Yalom, 1989, p. 382).

Certainly there are presuppositions about the sources of suffering. The latter are implicit in existential philosophy and psychology. However, there are no assumptions about the context of the individual's difficulties, no predisposing complexes or inevitable conflicts, no assumptions made about universal difficulties.

Nevertheless, existential therapists are not free from the expectations of the issues their clients may bring forward. As May notes, "if the therapist tunes her mental apparatus to the right channel, it is astounding how frequently patients discuss concerns emanating from existential conflicts" (May & Yalom, 1989, p. 383). However much the source of the conflict may be similar from client to client, the uniqueness of the relationship is what may make existential approaches different from other approaches to intervention.

The relationship between client and counselor is an encounter between two real people. The therapist allows herself or himself to become involved in a relationship that permits the inclusion of the client. The therapeutic relationship is powered, in part, by the counselor's ability to invest energy in the situation. In many instances, this may result in a very deep personal experience for both client and counselor. Permitting the client to experience the counselor as a real person may have the effect of providing a meaningful encounter with the world. Experiencing the counselor's real care for him or her, the client may be able to move into significant confrontation with the complex issues causing his or her suffering.

As Bugental points out from an existential perspective, "psychotherapy is not a healing process. It is a philosophic venture, the "grease" to get the relationship in motion. It is not the treatment of an illness. It is a daring to confront self-and-world. It is not a learning to adjust; it is a facing of infinite un-adjustability" (Bugental, 1965, p. 42). In an ultimate sense, this is the essence of existential intervention, namely, to help the client recognize the inevitability of his or her conflicts and their essential insolubility. The true task of this approach to treatment is the acceptance of that truth and the reality of living with pain and anxiety. More than that, it is learning to make choices and accept responsibility in the face of this truth. It is learning to function, achieve, and transcend even though certain existential truths are inevitable. It is learning to give direction and meaning to one's life. It is accepting responsibility for dealing with the future while accepting the ultimate outcome.

A Word about Techniques

Existentialists do not offer specific techniques of psychotherapy. It would undoubtedly be contrary to the underlying philosophy to prescribe techniques. Indeed, May points out that "technique follows understanding" (May, 1983, p. 151).

Techniques among existential theorists differ widely. Some may even use the couch and free association as Freud did. Some use techniques that approximate the approach of the Rogerian school. It is not inconceivable that there are those who identify themselves as existential counselors whose approaches, on occasion, may emulate the activities of cognitive behaviorists or who might utilize some techniques of behavior modification. The specific techniques are not the issue. Whatever techniques an existential counselor or therapist utilizes, the context would be clearly existential. "It would always focus on the questions of how (this technique) throws light on this particular patient's existence in his world, what it says about where he is at the moment and what he is moving toward, and so forth" (May, 1983, p. 152).

This lack of emphasis on technique does pose a problem. How can the therapeutic principles and skills be taught? The answer offered by the existential therapists is that the philosophical and psychological underpinnings provide the understanding of human behavior that leads to the appropriate procedures in counseling and therapy.

Summary

Existential approaches to counseling and psychotherapy are based on a complex system of philosophy, which has its roots in the mid-nineteenth century and was refined in the twentieth century. It is a philosophy that is essentially concerned with examining human existence in the world. It analyzes the roots of anxiety, the meaning of life, and the direction of life. It has a decidedly humanistic flavor to it. Existentialism, in part, joined forces with the humanistic psychology movement in the last quarter of the century.

Existential philosophy produced an existential psychology whose foremost proponent is Rollo May. Intervention in the form of an attempt to understand and mediate human suffering evolved as a protestation to what was viewed as more restrictive approaches in psychoanalysis and behaviorism. There are similarities in the humanistic orientation of existential approaches to treatment and the work of Carl Rogers.

Existential intervention does not advance specific techniques. Rather, it relies on providing understanding and care in the context of a real relationship to the client. The ultimate therapeutic aim of this approach is to help the client make choices and assume responsibility for his or her future while accepting the reality of living with anxiety.

References

Allport, G. (1962). Psychology models for guidance. *Harvard Educational Review, 32* (4), 373–382.
Barclay, J. R. (1971). *Foundations of counseling strategies.* New York: John Wiley.

Boss, M. (1963). *Psychoanalysis and daseinsanalysis.* New York: Basic Books.

Bugental, J. F. T. (1965). *The search for authenticity.* New York: Holt, Rinehart and Winston.

Chein, I. (1972). *The science of behavior and the image of man.* New York: Basic Books.

Friedman, M. (1984). *Contemporary psychology: Revealing and obscuring the human.* Pittsburgh: Duquesne University Press.

Langer, J. (1968). *Theories of development.* New York: Holt, Rinehart and Winston.

Maddi, S. R. (1985). Existential psychotherapy. In S. Linn and J. P. Garshe (Eds.), *Contemporary psychotherapies: Models and methods* (pp. 191–220). Columbus, OH: Merrill.

May, R. (1983). *The discovery of being.* New York: W. W. Norton.

May, R., & Yalom, I. (1989). Existential psychotherapy. In R. J. Corsini and D. Wedding, *Current psychotherapies* (4th ed.). Itasca, IL: F. E. Peacock.

Chapter *7*

Gestalt Counseling

Gestalt counseling has its roots in a hybrid combination of phenomenology, existentialism, and the waning Gestalt psychology from which it borrowed the Gestalt metaphors. The process is based on the perceptions and feelings of the client, centering on client awareness of behavior. It is largely the brainchild of Frederick (Fritz) and Laura Perls, although the latter has lamented publicly about the lack of credit she has received for her contributions. She is quoted as saying that "for some years I felt somewhat resentful that he never acknowledged my collaboration in the whole development of gestalt therapy" (Bernard, 1990, p.75). In any event, Fritz Perls with the collaboration of Laura Perls developed the early conceptions of Gestalt therapy in the 1940s.

In 1951 Fritz Perls predicted that within 20 years there would be an explosion in interest in Gestalt therapy (Perls, 1969b). The prediction was accurate: The explosion has been occurring since the 1960s. "Dynamic, dramatic, intensive, and absorbing Gestalt therapy already has exerted a powerful influence upon therapeutic counseling, encounter group therapy, marathon groups, family therapy, school counseling, psychiatric social work, and rehabilitation counseling with delinquents and drug addicts" (Belkin, 1980, p. 239). The Esalen Institute at Big Sur, California, is perhaps the best-known center for Gestalt approaches. But there are Gestalt training institutes in at least 15 cities, and more than 25 books on Gestalt procedures have been published since 1969 (Fagan, 1975). In some ways the popularization of Gestalt therapy is unfortunate. Any bookstore offers several books loosely based on Perls's writings, and "Gestalt weekends" of various kinds are widely advertised. Unfortunately, many of these publications and events tarnish the image and credibility of Gestalt counseling.

Fritz Perls was born in Berlin and began his career in Germany. In 1921 he received an M.D. from Friedrich Wilhelm University. He served in the German army during World War I and then went into psychoanalytic training in Berlin, Frankfurt, and Vienna. In the early 1930s he was with the Vienna Psychoanalytic Institute, but the rise of Nazism drove him from Germany in 1933 and from Amsterdam in 1935. From 1935 to 1946 he worked in South Africa, where he wrote his final major work: *Ego, Hunger and Aggression*. In 1946 he moved to the United States and established a private practice in New York where in the early 1950s he founded the New York Institute for Gestalt Therapy. This was followed by the publication of *Gestalt Therapy: Excitement and Growth in the Human Personality* (Perls, Hefferline, & Goodman, 1951) and *Gestalt Therapy Verbatim* (Perls, 1969b). From 1964 to 1969 Perls conducted training institutes at the Esalen Institute at Big Sur.

Perls developed the Gestalt approach to counseling and therapy from a psychological theory of perception known as Gestalt psychology, founded by Max Wertheimer, Wolfgang Kohler, and Kurt Koffka in Germany around 1910. These three psychologists formulated their ideas in opposition to a current emphasis in psychology on seeking to understand human experiences by reducing them into component parts. They argued that most often the component parts cannot be understood separately but must be considered as organized wholes. They chose the German word *gestalt,* which English and English have defined as signifying "a unified whole, properties which cannot be derived by summation from the parts and their relationships" (1958, p. 225).

Basic Concepts

Before examining the Gestalt approach to counseling and therapy, it will be helpful to understand some of the basic tenets of Gestalt psychology. Gestalt psychologists believe that human behavior is much more than a product of unrelated stimuli. A picture, for example, is a whole that has a meaning: a gestalt. Isolated, the splashes of color or shading will probably have no meaning. The parts have meaning only in relation to the whole in which they exist. Similarly, a series of musical notes tends to have meaning only in the perspective of an organized whole, a song. These examples illustrate the principle that individuals always act to organize stimuli into wholes, or gestalts.

Gestalt psychologists have developed several principles to explain how this process occurs. Three of these principles illustrate the process.

- *Principle of Closure* When people perceive a figure that is incomplete, their minds act to finish the figure and perceive it as complete. Most people would perceive the series of lines in Figure 7-1 as a house.

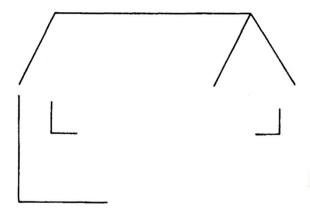

FIGURE 7-1   Principle of Closure

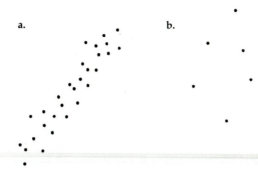

FIGURE 7-2   Principle of Proximity

- *Principle of Proximity* The relative distance of stimuli from each other within the perceptual field determines how they are seen. In part *a* of Figure 7-2 people would be most likely to perceive a series of related dots, whereas in part *b* they generally would see the dots as unrelated.
- *Principle of Similarity* The similarity of stimuli in the perceptual field causes people to group them together. Figure 7-3 would be seen as columns of squares and columns of circles, not as rows that contain both circles and squares.

Each of these principles illustrates how the mind seeks to make sense of the vast array of stimuli in the phenomenal field by pulling things together. The important point is that the stimuli have meaning only as they are organized in the mind by the individual. Out of the vast array of possibilities, what determines what people attend to in their phenomenal field? At any one time a person can be aware of only a single cluster of these stimuli that form a gestalt. The person reading this text might from time to time transfer concentration from the printed page to other gestalts in the setting, such as a couch or bed, or become aware of a favorite song on the radio. These examples illustrate the basic figure-ground principle so important in Gestalt psychology. The individual is always acting to organize

$$\square \; \bigcirc \quad \square \; \bigcirc \quad \square \; \bigcirc$$

$$\square \; \bigcirc \quad \square \; \bigcirc \quad \square \; \bigcirc$$

$$\square \; \bigcirc \quad \square \; \bigcirc \quad \square \; \bigcirc$$

$$\square \; \bigcirc \quad \square \; \bigcirc \quad \square \; \bigcirc$$

$$\square \; \bigcirc \quad \square \; \bigcirc \quad \square \; \bigcirc$$

FIGURE 7-3   Principle of Similarity

his or her phenomenal field to meet his or her needs (Coleman, 1960). The things people are focusing on in their field are referred to as the *figure;* the rest of the field is called the *ground.* Anything within the field, including bodily sensations, thoughts, pain, pleasure, or external objects, can become figures; however, two events may not be figures at the same time (Coleman, 1960).

The particular meaning the individual gives to a figure is a function of its relationship to the total ground of which it is a part. This is not as simple as it sounds, for the phenomenal field of each person depends on the individual's level of awareness. A person driving on a highway at 65 mph may casually be aware of another car at the side of the road. Her or his awareness is not acute enough to detect the fact that the car is a patrol car; the result is a ticket for speeding. Another person with a higher level of awareness in a similar situation might see the car for what it is and might change his or her behavior and not get a ticket. In both cases the patrol car is in the phenomenal field, but the two individuals gave it different meanings, depending on their levels of awareness. When people perceive clearly and sharply, their behavior is similarly efficient and accurate, but when awareness is vague, behavior is also likely to be vague, inappropriate, and disorganized (Coleman, 1960).

In summary, the major assumptions of Gestalt psychology are as follows:

1. People actively seek to form meaningful wholes out of their phenomenal fields.
2. Any event in the phenomenal field can become differentiated at any time from the ground and become the figure.
3. Whether the event does become a figure depends upon the need(s) of the individual.
4. The meaning given to the figure depends upon the perceived ground in which it exists.
5. The level of awareness of the individual in relation to his or her phenomenal field will determine the accuracy of perception and her or his behavior.

Traditional Gestalt psychology never applied these principles beyond explaining the perceptual process in humans. As Wallen indicates, original Gestalt theorists never extended these basic assumptions "to organic perceptions, to the perceptions of one's own feelings, emotions, and bodily sensations" (1970, p. 8). It was left to Perls and others to develop what has come to be known as Gestalt therapy and counseling.

Theory of Personality

Although Perls was trained as a psychoanalyst and part of Gestalt counseling is influenced by this training, the Gestalt view of people is very similar to both existential and humanistic positions with their emphasis on the interaction of the individual with the environment. "It makes no sense to speak, for instance, of an animal that breathes without considering air and oxygen as part of its definition, or to speak of eating without mentioning food. . . . There is no simple function of any animal that completes itself without objects and environment" (Perls, Hefferline, & Goodman, 1951, p. 332).

Passons's (1975b) eight assumptions about the nature of human beings act as the framework for Gestalt thinking about personality:

1. Individuals are composite wholes made up of interrelated parts. None of these parts—body, emotions, thoughts, sensations, and perceptions—can be understood outside the context of the whole person.
2. Individuals are also part of their own environment and cannot be understood apart from it.
3. People choose how they respond to external and internal stimuli; they are actors, not reactors.
4. People have the potential to be fully aware of all their sensations, thoughts, emotions, and perceptions.
5. Individuals are capable of making choices because they are aware.
6. Individuals have the capacity to govern their own lives effectively.
7. People cannot experience the past and the future; they can experience only themselves in the present.
8. People are basically neither good nor bad.

Motivating Force

It is clear from these eight assumptions that Gestalt theory views people as capable of directing their own development. In fact, Perls felt that individuals must take responsibility for their own lives. The motivation for this process, according to Perls (1969b), springs from the fact that everyone has only one inherent goal: to self-actualize. This sounds similar to the Rogerian or self-theory position, but there is a striking difference. Rogers describes the process of actualization as striving to become all that one is capable of becoming. The perspective is future oriented. The Gestalt position is much more existential and present oriented. According to Kempler, "Becoming is the process of being what one is and not a process of striving to become" (1973, p. 262). This striving to be is the basic motivating force for all behavior. All other needs are a part of this overriding need to actualize oneself. These needs include the basic biological needs that must be satisfied if the individual is to survive and what might be termed secondary needs developed through interaction with the environment. This level of needs is generally related directly to behavior, but all behaviors revert to the basic need to actualize oneself.

A person's behavior at any given time is explained by the Gestalt theorists in terms of the figure-ground relationship. As Passons indicates, "Needs move in and out of the figure and ground field. At a given moment a particular need may emerge and direct the person's behavior. The need moves from ground to figure" (1975b, p. 15). After the individual has met this need, the figure moves back into the ground and a new one captures and directs the person's behavior. This is a very flexible and flowing process, and for each person a different need may dominate (become a figure) in a particular situation. In fact, for the same individual in two apparently similar situations, a different need can dominate at various times. So it is almost impossible to predict behavior. All that can be said with certainty is that even in situations in which two or more needs are in conflict, one need will become dominant; at that time and in that situation, the meeting of that need is most important to the individual. It cannot be predicted that in a future similar situation the same need will dominate. The individual cannot deal with the past or the future, only the present.

Having examined the Gestalt view of human nature and the basic motivating force, we can now turn our attention to the process of personality development.

Personality Development

Perls conceptualizes personality development as a product of the person's interaction with his or her environment. This interacting of organism and environment is called the organism-environment field, "and let us remember that no matter how we theorize about impulses, drives, etc., it is always to such an interacting field that we are referring, and not to an isolated animal" (Perls, Hefferline, & Goodman, 1951, p. 332). At every moment the individual is confronted with either an external demand or an internal need, either one of which activates action to restore balance. This striving for balance is designed to reduce tension within the individual and the process is referred to as *organismic self-regulation* (Perls, 1969a). This inherent ability for self-regulation develops in the evolving personality in three phases: social, psychophysical, and spiritual (Kempler, 1973). Kempler describes these stages as sequential and also as representative of the person's potential level of awareness. In the social stage, the infant is aware of others without having an awareness of self. This stage is dominated by required interactions with others that simply permit the child to survive. The infant is unable to secure the food needed for survival and so must rely on those around him or her.

During the second psychophysical stage, the child develops a sense of self, or self-image. "The psychophysical stage, characterized by awareness of one's own person, is described in terms of personality and is divided into three components: self, self-image, and being" (Kempler, 1973, p. 262). Whereas being exists from birth, the other two parts of the personality develop as the person interacts with his or her environment. Generally, by the time the person reaches midadolescence these three subsystems of the personality are in full operation. According to Kempler (1973), this development occurs through three processes: adaptation, acknowledgment, and approbation.

Adaptation
Adaptation is the process whereby a person discovers the boundaries to her or his existence, becoming aware of what is self and what is nonself. No evaluative judgments are made; rather it is a becoming aware of one's world and adapting one's behavior to it. "The study of the way the human being functions in his environment is the study of what goes on at the contact boundary between the individual and his environment. It is at this boundary that psychological events take place" (Perls, 1973, p. 17). The child who touches a hot stove and burns herself or himself establishes a boundary and adapts to it. Early childhood in particular, and life in general, is replete with these encounters with the universe, and in each case the person adapts his or her behavior. This adaptation leads to a growing differentiation and appreciation of the boundaries in which the person exists (Kempler, 1973).

Acknowledgment

Through acknowledgment individuals discover themselves. "Watch me" is the child's password to the parents as he or she plays. "In his innocent wisdom he knows that he must be acknowledged" (Kempler, 1973, p. 263). Personal acknowledgment leads children to develop a sense of self and an appreciation of their own existence.

Acknowledgment is similar to adaptation in that both are processes of establishing certain truths without an accompanying judgment. Whereas adaptation defines boundaries of the universe, acknowledgment is the process of validating self and others. Children who ask a parent to watch them are asking for validation, not approval or disapproval. The proper response of the parent is a simple acknowledgment such as "OK" or "Not right now" (Kempler, 1973). In both responses there is no approval or disapproval, simply acknowledgment. Acknowledgment given in this fashion permits children to develop a personal valuing system for their own behavior. Unfortunately, most parents respond with a kind of validation that is accompanied by a notion of approval or disapproval. This process is what the Gestaltists refer to as approbation.

Approbation

Approbation is the process whereby people develop splits within their personalities. Acknowledgment leads to awareness of self, but approbation creates a self-image that is a notion of self based on external standards. As children seek acknowledgment of their existence and instead receive approbation, they soon learn to seek approval rather than acknowledgment. Instead of "Watch me," they now ask, "Didn't I do that well?" Once this process is instituted, individuals develop a polarization in their personality. On one hand there are feelings of self that represent things they want to do, and on the other hand is the self-image that represents all that individuals feel they should do because of external standards.

As Kempler (1973) points out, children must receive acknowledgment to survive, and if they cannot receive pure acknowledgment, they will seek approval. In effect, they will choose to change their own being and develop an acceptable self-image that indirectly gets them the acknowledgment they need to survive. As people move through the developmental years, they encounter myriad situations, and at each point there is possibility for the development of notions of self and notions about the proper self-image. "Life is practically nothing but an infinite number of unfinished situations . . . incomplete Gestalts. No sooner have we finished one situation than another develops" (Perls, 1969b, p. 15). Thus, the personality becomes a system with being at the center, and at the point where being encounters the external world there is potential for developing the beginnings of a continuing conflict between self and self-image—a battle between forces that want the individuals to be what they are and forces that want them to be what they should be.

From a Gestalt viewpoint, approbation interferes with the development of a sound and healthy notion of self. The self is responsible for "formulating the creative adjustment contacts within the environment. Thus, the self is active, dynamic, and changing according to emergent needs and environmental presses" (Passons, 1975b, p. 16). The self acts to move the individual to self-actualization. The self-image acts to hinder that process.

The actual development of the self occurs as the individual interacts with her or his environment. As Harman and Franklin stated, "Growth occurs when a person is willing to make contact with people, objects, and situations in the environment" (1975, p. 49). As this process takes place, the individual is bound to meet frustration, which from a Gestalt perspective is positive. "Without frustrations there is no need, no reason, to mobilize your resources, to discover that you might be able to do something on your own" (Perls, 1969b, p. 32). Frustration, which is painful, causes the infant to learn how to do things that remove the frustration. This is the process of growth as the individual learns to rely on the self rather than on others; it is the move from a dependent status to an independent one. Such an individual identifies more with the self than with the self-image, and thus is able to be creative and self-regulating. "This allows for situations to be finished, problems to be solved, and environmental contacts to be focused on those things that have interest and excitement for him" (Passons, 1975b, p.16). A person who reaches this stage of development is ready to move to the spiritual phase of personality development.

Few people achieve the spiritual stage, although most acknowledge its existence. Kempler (1973) describes this phase as the movement from "sensory-sensing" to "extra sensory-sensing" awareness. "From intellectual, physical, and emotional activity, man manifests himself as what might be called a sensitive-intuitive person" (p. 262). This is the stage of awareness many try to achieve through artificial means such as drugs. The only true way of achieving this stage, however, is through development of a fully functioning self during the second phase of development, and this does not happen very often. Most individuals lead their lives within the second phase; thus, it is the psycho-physical phase with which we should be most concerned.

Personality, then, is a product of individuals' interactions with their perceived environment from the moment of birth onward. Growth takes place through assimilating material from the environment, utilizing the processes of adaptation, acknowledgment, and approbation. Throughout the social, psychophysical, and spiritual stages of development, people strive to meet their needs by forming gestalts, the wholes that allow them to organize behavior within the environment in order to meet current needs. Because these needs are always changing, even from moment to moment, the process of gestalt formation is a continuous process. It causes an event in the environment to become a figure, which recedes into ground when that need has been met.

Each person's personality becomes a fairly rigid composite of three separate entities: self, self-image, and being. Being is the essential existence of the organism; the self is the creative process that leads the person to actualizing behaviors; the self-image is the part of personality that hinders creative growth. Whenever being comes into contact with the world, the potential exists for development of self and self-image. Thus, an internal conflict is established between what the self wants to do, and what the self-image says she or he should do. In normal growth and development people develop some balance between the self-image and the self that permits them to operate in a relatively effective way. In most cases these patterns emerge as the *character* of the individual. Unfortunately, it is the very development of character that Gestalt theorists believe keeps people from being actualized. Character leads people to play the same roles over and over again. This is the basic conflict: To be actualized the self has to be free to interact creatively with the environment (Perls, 1969a). If character is established, implying the influence of the self-image, the self is no longer free to be creative. Most people exist this way, in what amounts to basic estrangement. It is also this division within the self that leads people to experience difficulty and may eventually bring them to the counseling situation.

Maladaptive Behavior

Most people exist by maintaining some balance between the desires of the self and the "shoulds" of self-image. Perls (1973) refers to this as a state of *homeostasis*. According to Kempler (1973), however, an experience or series of experiences frequently upsets this balance. In such circumstances the self is unable to operate to maintain the homeostatic state. In effect, an internal war erupts between self and self-image that causes a person to experience anxiety and often produces ineffective behaviors. The specific nature of the difficulty will depend on the general state of a person's psychological health and the kind of experience that sets the internal war in motion. The person who is behaving in maladaptive ways is generally attempting to actualize the self-image rather than the self. Such a person is more subject to the opinions of others than to the self-control mechanisms (Ward & Rouzer, 1975). Passons (1975a) divides the kinds of problems people experience into the following six areas.

- *Lack of awareness* is usually related to rigid personality. The character people establish to maintain the delicate balance between self and self-image causes them to lose contact with the what and how of their behavior. They lack creative ability to deal with the environment: they simply exist, moving through life from day to day with an uneasy feeling of nonfulfillment.
- *Lack of self-responsibility* is related to lack of awareness, but takes the form of trying to manipulate the environment instead of the self. Instead of striving for independence or self-sufficiency, which is the hallmark of maturity, some people strive to remain in a dependency situation.
- *Loss of contact with the environment* is also related to lack of awareness. This problem can take two forms. In the first, some people become so rigid in their behavior that no input from the environment is accepted or incorporated. In effect, they withdraw from contact with the environment, including other people. Such withdrawal into self prohibits them from meeting their needs and from moving toward maturity. The other form is manifested in people who need so much approbation that they lose themselves by trying to incorporate everything from the environment. The self becomes almost totally subsumed by the self-image.
- *Inability to complete gestalts* or to complete business is another kind of problem. As Polster and Polster (1973) indicate, everyone has the capacity to tolerate internally the persistence of many unfinished situations, but if these become powerful enough they will cause difficulty. The person who gets angry with a spouse, but does not

express that anger directly, kicking the dog instead, is not completing the business. Such uncompleted business always seeks to be completed. When unfinished business becomes strong enough "the individual is beset with preoccupation, compulsive behavior, wariness, oppressive energy, and much self-defeating activity" (Polster & Polster, 1973, p. 36). The unfinished business causes the individual to continue to strive to complete it in current activities. Polster and Polster (1973) list the following examples of typical complaints representing unfinished Gestalts or business that clients bring to counseling: "I never told my father how I felt; I was humiliated when I wanted attention; I wanted to be an artist and they made me become a doctor" (p. 36). An individual who is preoccupied with unfinished business cannot bring his or her full awareness to bear on the current situation.

- *Disowning of needs* occurs when people act to deny one of their own needs. Passons (1975a) pointed out that in our society individuals commonly deny their need to be aggressive. This need is generally socially unacceptable, so individuals tend not to express it. Instead of channeling the energy into constructive behavior, people deny the existence of the need and thereby lose the energy it produces.

- *Dichotomizing dimensions of the self* takes the form of people perceiving themselves at only one end of a possible continuum such as "strong or weak, masculine or feminine, powerful or powerless" (Passons, 1975b, p. 17). Individuals who perceive themselves at only one end of the continuum never realize the full value of the continuum. As Passons (1975b) indicates, people who cannot admit any weakness cannot fully appreciate the strength they do have. The most popularly known split is what Perls (1969b) calls "top dog–underdog." The top dog is that part of the individual characterized as moralistic, perfectionistic, and authoritarian. It is the top dog who strives to get the person to behave as others expect. The underdog represents the desires of the individual and operates as the defensive and dependent part of the personality. As Perls states, "The underdog is the Mickey Mouse. The top dog is the Super Mouse" (1969b, p. 18). The resulting personality fragmentation into "controller" (top dog) and "controlled" (underdog) produces an internal conflict that is incapable of completion (Ward & Rouzer, 1975, pp. 25–26). As long as the person continues to listen to the top dog, this internal conflict will remain, for the needs of the individual will not go away.

All six categories of behavioral disturbances are directly related to the conflicts within the self. This conflict usually occurs as a direct result of dissonance between the expression of individual needs and environmental demands. Instead of relying on the self and the capacity for self-regulation, people become caught in trying to maintain an externally imposed self-image. Instead of utilizing energy to interact with and assimilate the environment, they direct energy toward playing roles. As the roles demand more and more energy, individuals have less and less energy to devote to fulfilling the needs of self. Because these needs never go away, such people experience continual anxiety, which in turn generally leads to patterns of inappropriate and unsatisfying behaviors. It is at this point that many people seek some assistance. Perls (1969a) suggests that there are potentially five levels of neurosis within each individual. These range from the very superficial day-to-day behaviors that allow people to move through life without any real investment to the total level that is the individual's inner core of being: the authentic self. The five levels of Perls are

1. *Cliché.* Here we find ways of behaving that simply help us move through the everyday exchanges required by our environment.
2. *Role-playing.* Here we find behaviors that go with the "role" the person is in rather than behaviors that relate to the "authentic self."
3. *Impasse.* Here the person feels lost for the rules of level two have been taken away. There is a feeling of being at sea without any sense of direction.
4. *Implosive/explosive.* Here the person experiences a fear of really feeling—of trusting the self. As the name implies this is a period full of emotional tension.
5. *Authentic.* Here is when we really find the true self—all else has been stripped away allowing the self to be free.

People who come to counseling may be at any of the first four levels, and determining where they are operating most of the time is important for the counseling process.

Goals of Counseling

The overriding objective of Gestalt counseling is to bring about integration of the individual. People who come to counseling suffer from the split caused by the formation of self-image concepts. This split keeps them from utilizing their energy in appropriate ways to meet personal needs and to grow, develop, and actualize. Given that the self-image is a product of the demands of others, a specific aim of counseling is to help clients discover that they do not have to depend on others, but that they can do many things for themselves (Perls, 1969b). Since a significant element of a healthy individual is the ability to regulate the self, the objective of counseling is to move the individual from dependence on others' judgments to reliance on self-regulation. This process leads to an integration of self as the need to play the roles demanded by the self-image begins to disappear. The person is encouraged to be what he or she is in the present. The ultimate goal is for the client to be true to himself or herself. As Perls suggests, this goal is never totally achieved. "Integration is never completed; maturation is never completed. It's an ongoing process forever and ever" (Perls, 1969b, p. 64). The goal of Gestalt counseling is a global one; although a client may present a specific concern to the counselor, the Gestalt counselor holds that the specific concern is only a representation of a more generalized problem, the inability to be self-regulating.

The focus of counseling is not the problem the client presents but the person's awareness of himself or herself and his or her environment. Of critical importance in the achievement of self-regulation is increasing the person's awareness. According to Perls, awareness itself is curative. Given awareness, "the organism can work on the healthy Gestalt principle: that the most important unfinished situation will always emerge and can be dealt with" (1969a, p. 51). Consistent with this belief, much of what the Gestalt counselor does is designed to help the client achieve an improved level of awareness that leads to integration and organismic self-control.

The Role of the Counselor and the Counseling Process

According to Perls (1969b), the role of the counselor is to provide an atmosphere in which the client has the opportunity to discover her or his own needs, to discover those parts of the self that the client has given up because of environmental demands, and to provide a place in which the client can experience growth. Perls has deep faith in each individual's capacity to regain the ability to use the natural adaptation process. Such an atmosphere is created as the counselor acts to facilitate the client's awareness of self in the now (Passons, 1975a). "The now is the present, is the phenomenon, is what you are aware of, is that moment in which you carry your so-called memories and your so-called expectations with you. Whether you remember or anticipate, you do it now" (Perls, 1969a, p. 44). So defined, the now is a continuous process; it is never stationary; it exists and immediately gives way to a new now. As the now moves, so does the person's awareness, for "being aware of one's now means staying aware of one's flow" (Passons, 1975b, p. 22). Being aware means being able to focus on or attend to what one is currently doing.

To facilitate this process, counselors use the most important tool they have: themselves. A counselor, fully aware of herself or himself in the now, engages the client in a here-and-now interaction. Perls (1969b) believes that Gestalt therapy rests on a two-legged principle that is "now" and "how." The counselor does not interpret, probe, preach about reality; rather, he or she interacts with the client in the now. "Gestalt counseling is active, confrontative, and concerned with what is experienced in the 'now'. The past is a memory, the future is a fantasy, and they are important only as they are experienced in the present as such" (Pietrofesa, Hoffman, Splete, & Pinto, 1978, p. 83). Perls (1969b) holds that many people do not even have the capacity to see the obvious. Thus, the Gestalt counselor must help clients learn how to use all their senses fully, to learn how they avoid things, and to become more open to the now.

The Gestalt counselor must view himself or herself as a catalyst, acting in whatever ways necessary to help the client increase his or her awareness. According to Polster and Polster (1973), the counselor above all else must be an exciting, energetic individual who brings his or her full humanity to the counseling session. Only in this way will the counselor be able to enter into the client's now and react to it. "He does not interpret behavior, but rather focuses on the 'what' and 'how' of the person's (client's) now, the assumption being that the most pressing need will eventually emerge to be dealt with" (Passons, 1975b, p. 22). As soon as the client is able to express this need the counselor can begin the process Fagan (1970) referred to as patterning, the process whereby the counselor helps the client see the ongoing pattern of her or his life. Awareness of the pattern is the first step in the move toward reintegration of the self and healthy functioning.

Techniques of Counseling

Of the many techniques that might be used by Gestalt counselors, the most common techniques employ "how" and "what" questions focusing attention on current functioning of the surface behaviors. With both types of questions the counselor is seeking to get the client to become more aware of feelings, behaviors, emotions, and sensations in the now.

At the same time, the counselor is attempting to discover what things the client is trying to avoid and in what areas of functioning he or she is suffering from internal conflicts. "Awareness is an attempt to get the patient in touch with all of himself so that he can utilize all of his potential" (Harman & Franklin, 1975, p. 50).

Frustrating the Client

People who come to counseling generally suffer from a lack of self-sufficiency and full awareness. As Perls (1969b) suggests, individuals who are experiencing difficulty cannot see the obvious; they are full of avoidances and resistances that prevent full awareness. Perls suggested also that clients are at an impasse that they really do not want to work through. "Very few people go into therapy to be cured, but rather to improve their neuroses" (1969b, p. 39). The impasse involves an unsatisfied need or some unfinished business that people believe they do not have the resources to resolve. In effect clients come to counseling hoping the counselor will provide an answer that will permit them to exist but will not require them to work through the difficulty. Instead of providing the answer, the counselor seeks to force clients to work through the impasse, first by permitting or, indeed, structuring the situation so that the impasse comes into the open, and then frustrating the clients by refusing to give them what they seek. "This is what we are again and again trying to do, to frustrate the person until he is face to face with his blocks, with his inhibitions, with his way of avoiding having eyes, having ears, having muscles, having authority, having security in himself" (Perls, 1969b, p. 38). The counselor cannot permit clients to remain unaware, to not utilize all of their senses. The counselor's goal is to help clients recognize that the impasse exists in the mind and that they have the ability to resolve their own impasse. In effect, the counselor is telling clients, You can and you must be responsible for yourself.

Experiential Techniques

The preceding general techniques are used in Gestalt counseling to establish an appropriate working environment and then to bring the impasses of clients into the open. In addition to these generalized techniques, Gestalt counselors also use a variety of experiential games, designed basically to increase individuals' awareness of themselves and their impasses and then to help them reintegrate themselves. Perls (1969b) indicated that this last step is the most crucial, for stripping the individual of all defenses and giving him or her no new ways of behaving, make the client even more vulnerable to outside forces than he or she was prior to counseling.

Levitsky and Perls (1970) and Passons (1975a) suggest a variety of these specific techniques. The following list is a summary of techniques from both lists that appear to be most appropriate for use by counselors.

- *Use of personal pronouns.* Clients are encouraged to use "I" and "thou" to personalize communication. This is one way of helping clients to acknowledge their behavior. For example, the client might be asked, "How are you feeling right now?" and the client might respond with "Fine." The counselor might then say, "What is fine?" in an attempt to get the client to respond, "*I* am fine."

- *Converting questions to statements.* Often clients use questions to keep the focus off themselves or to hide what they are really thinking. The client who asks, "Do you really believe that?" is generally saying, "I don't think you believe that." Forcing clients to use the second statement makes them declare their own belief system.

- *Assuming responsibility.* Clients are asked to end all expressions of feelings or beliefs with "and I take responsibility for it." Another way to help clients assume responsibility for their own behaviors is to have them change "can't" to "won't." Instead of saying, "I can't do _____," clients are encouraged to say, "I won't do _____." Assumption of responsibility helps clients see themselves as having internal strength rather than as relying on external control.

- *Sharing hunches.* Counselors have a tendency to interpret what they see as the meaning of a particular client's behavior or statement. A better approach is to present the material to the client as though it were a hunch. "I see you tapping your foot, and I imagine it means you are nervous." This behavior on the part of the counselor is less threatening, and it has the strong advantage of helping clients understand that all people imagine more than they know. That is, individuals see and imagine the meaning of what they see: They project meaning. Having clients use the "see-imagine" statements helps them recognize their projections.

- *Playing the projection.* Related to sharing hunches is the technique of asking clients to play their projections. When a client projects something onto another person, the counselor asks him or her to play the role of the person upon whom he or she has projected.

- *Expressing resentments and appreciations.* Many clients express strong negative feelings about people with whom they interact. The Gestalt position is that the clients would not continue to interact with these people unless some positive feelings existed. The counselor tries to get the client to express some of these feelings, believing that the client has become dominated by the negative and, to improve that relationship, should focus on some positive aspects. In this way clients can see both ends of the continuum. When a husband and wife come to counseling, for example, they generally have patterns of behavior that keep them focused at the negative end of the continuum. One of the tasks of the counselor is to get them to see, by expressing them, that there are some positive aspects of the relationship.

- *Role rehearsal and reversal.* As in the strategy for playing the projection, clients are often asked to play a role. In this case they may be asked to act out a behavior that is the opposite of the one in which they normally engage. This role reversal helps them get in touch with a part of themselves they were either unaware of or have denied existed. Clients may also be asked to rehearse in counseling a new role they are going to try outside of counseling. The rehearsal strengthens the belief that the new behavior can be carried out.

- *Game of dialogue.* When clients are caught between conflicting parts of their personalities (top dog–underdog; passive-aggressive), the counselor may instruct them to play both roles and to carry out a verbal dialogue between the two parts. Such a dialogue brings the conflict into the open so that it may be inspected and resolved.

The techniques presented here, particularly the first three generalized ones, are commonly used and are representative of many others. Techniques such as dream work and fantasy should be used only by those with extensive training in Gestalt therapy. The writings of Perls provide a fuller discussion. The book by Passons (1975b) is also very helpful for counselors.

Summary

Gestalt counseling is an outgrowth of a theory of perception known as Gestalt psychology. Its major tenets are that people behave in holistic fashion and that they have the capacity to regulate themselves. People experience difficulty because they have come to depend too much on external events rather than on their internal self-regulation mechanisms. Such a situation prohibits them from having full awareness of themselves and of the environment in which they exist. The purpose of counseling is to restore people's ability to be fully aware of themselves and their world. The process is an active, confrontative one, with an emphasis on how and what clients are experiencing. The counselor strives, through a variety of techniques, first to help clients recognize the strength they have and then to help them utilize that strength in daily experience.

References

Belkin, G. S. (1980). *Contemporary psychotherapies.* Chicago: Rand McNally.

Bernard, James, M. (1990) Laura Perls: From ground to figure. In P. Paul Happner (Ed.), *Pioneers in counseling and development.* Alexandria, VA: American Association for Counseling and Development.

Coleman, J. C. (1960). *Personality dynamics and effective behavior.* Chicago: Scott, Foresman.

English, H. D., & English, A. C. (1958). *A comprehensive dictionary of psychological and psycho-analytical terms.* New York: David McKay.

Fagan, J. (1970). The tasks of the therapist. In J. Fagan & I. L. Shepherd (Eds.), *Gestalt therapy now.* Palo Alto: Science and Behavior Books.

Fagan, J. (1975). Gestalt therapy introduction. *Counseling Psychologist, 4,* 3.

Harman, R. L., & Franklin, R. W. (1975). Gestalt, instructional groups. *Personnel and Guidance Journal, 54*(1), 49–50.

Kempler, W. (1973). Gestalt therapy. In R. Corsini (Ed.), *Current psychotherapies.* Itasca, IL: F. E. Peacock.

Levin, L. S., & Shepherd, I. L. (1975). The role of the therapist in Gestalt therapy. *Counseling Psychologist, 4,* 27–30.

Levitsky, A., & Perls, F. S. (1970). The rules and games of Gestalt therapy. In J. Fagan and I. L. Shepherd (Eds.), *Gestalt therapy now.* Palo Alto: Science and Behavior Books.

Passons, W. R. (1975a). Gestalt therapy interventions for group counseling. *Personnel and Guidance Journal, 51,* 183–189.

Passons, W. R. (1975b). *Gestalt approaches in counseling.* New York: Holt, Rinehart and Winston.

Perls, F. S. (1969a). *Ego, hunger, and aggression.* New York: Random House. (Originally published 1947.)

Perls, F. S. (1969b). *Gestalt therapy verbatim.* Lafayette, CA: Real People Press.

Perls, F. S. (1969c). *In and out of the garbage pail.* Lafayette, CA: Real People Press.

Perls, F. S. (1973). *Gestalt approach and eyewitness to therapy.* New York: Bantam.

Perls, F. S., Hefferline, R., & Goodman, P. (1951). *Gestalt therapy: Excitement and growth in the human personality.* New York: Julian Press.

Pietrofesa, J. J., Hoffman, A., Splete, H. H., & Pinto, D. V. (1978). *Counseling: Theory, research, and practice.* Chicago: Rand McNally.

Polster, E., & Polster, M. (1973). *Gestalt therapy integrated: Contours of theory and practice.* New York: Brunner/Mazel.

Wallen, R. (1970). Gestalt therapy and Gestalt psychology. In J. Fagen and I. L. Shepherd (Eds.), *Gestalt therapy now.* Palo Alto: Science and Behavior Books.

Ward, P., & Rouzer, D. L. (1975). The nature of pathological functioning from a Gestalt perspective. *Counseling Psychologist, 4,* 24–27.

Yontef, Gary M., and James S. Simkin. Gestalt therapy. In Raymond J. Corsini and Danny Wedding, *Current Psychotherapies* (4th ed.). Itasca, IL: F. E. Peacock.

_C h a p t e r_ **8**

Behavioral Approaches to Counseling

One of the exciting developments in the area of counseling theory and practice during the past three decades has been the emergence of a variety of approaches based broadly on the principles of learning theory. The domination of counseling and psychotherapy, first by psychodynamic approaches and later by humanist/existential approaches, challenged mainstream psychologists to apply learning theory to counseling practice. One of the earliest attempts to merge learning theory with psychotherapy was a seminal article by E. J. Shoben entitled "Psychotherapy as a problem in learning theory" written in 1949 (Shoben, 1949). The most important point made by Shoben was that counseling and psychotherapy are essentially a learning process and all aspects should be studied in the context of the principles of learning. According to Shoben, learning was implied in the goals and outcomes of counseling and psychotherapy. Such purposes as resolving conflicts, reducing anxiety, or modifying behavior implied learning and could be expressed in terms of behavioral objectives. Planning, goal formulation, and reliance on the "conversational content" of counseling are all part of a model that identifies desirable behavioral changes wherein positive reinforcement helps shape behavior toward the goal. The client learns to evaluate herself or himself and her or his values, learns to make choices, learns to accept responsibility for choices, and ultimately learns to initiate action consistent with these choices (Shoben, 1949).

Since these early observations at midcentury, behavioral approaches to counseling and psychotherapy have been evolving in diverse directions with a variety of viewpoints ranging from applied behavioral analysis to a "neobehavioristic mediational–stimulus response model" to social learning theory (Wilson, 1989). These approaches are incorporated in our presentation in this chapter. In addition, still further developments in cognitive behavior modification will be dealt with in Chapter 9.

Early efforts to apply learning theory principles to counseling centered largely on attempts to put the existing theories of counseling into a behavioral framework. The work of Dollard and Miller (1950) and of Pepinsky and Pepinsky (1954) are examples of this kind of effort. It was not until the Cubberley Conference at Stanford University in 1965 that behavioral counseling really gained momentum and national attention. John Krumboltz of Stanford University played a major role at that conference and has continued to play " . . . a major sustaining role in the development of the behavioral counseling approach" (Barclay, 1980, p. 457). Today "Behavioral Counseling is not simply a partisan movement, but is an integral part of counseling" (Barclay, 1980). The current trends go far beyond the early attempts of the Pepinskys, Dollard and Miller, and even Krumboltz and his associates at Stanford. "The present trends in behavioral counseling . . . recognize that behavior and perception play a reciprocal role in the process of change" (Barclay, 1980, p. 457).

The early period of development of the behavioral approach is best characterized by the now-classic debate in 1956 between B. F. Skinner and Carl Rogers. Skinner, as the leading spokesperson of behaviorism, argued that the environment was the sole determiner of behavior. He saw humans as completely reactive beings whose behavior is controlled by external events. Rogers represented the position that humans are self-determining. Although these two people would probably continue to hold opposite views, the approaches to counseling that they originally represented have changed markedly over the last quarter-century. Increasingly self-theorists are discussing the need for the counselor to use action strategies in counseling, and behaviorists are talking about people's internal feelings. Two of the most exciting recent developments in behavioral counseling have been in the areas of covert reinforcement and self-management programs. Early critics of behavioral approaches contended that it was a system for manipulating others, but the recent developments have escaped that criticism. As indicated by the title of the Mahoney and Thoresen (1974) text *Self-Control: Power to the Person,* a major emphasis in current behavioral approaches is on helping people control their own lives. It is unfortunate that many critics of behavioral counseling are still basing their arguments on behaviorism as developed in the laboratory as contrasted with that which has developed out of the research and practice of behavioral counseling over the last 30 years. The work of many individuals has greatly broadened the early behavioral approaches to counseling.

Behavioral counselors view their task as an attempt to help those who come to them learn new, more adaptive behaviors. In effect, the counselor is one kind of learning specialist (Krumboltz, 1966). This approach is not a conglomeration of techniques applied mechanically to clients but one that places a great deal of faith in the laws of learning established through scientific investigation (Michael & Meyerson, 1962). The rapidity of development and change within behaviorism and the divergences among individual theorists make it difficult to discuss all aspects of the field in a single chapter. The focus of this chapter, therefore, is on the central concepts and beliefs with which most behavioral theorists would agree.

Despite the growing emphasis on the role of the cognitive processes in human development, the laws of learning maintain their central position in the behavioral approach. Behaviorists hold to the belief that most of a person's personality can be attributed to the effects of the laws of learning as the person interacts with his or her environment. Most principles of learning fall within three general categories: (1) classical or respondent conditioning, (2) operant conditioning, and (3) imitative learning. Behavioral approaches to counseling use some combination of these models together with the principles from other branches of counseling. In many ways the behavioral approach particularly as developed by Lazarus and others is the most eclectic of all approaches.

Classical or Respondent Conditioning

Ivan Petrovich Pavlov (1849–1936) is usually credited with the founding of classical conditioning. Classical conditioning is based on the observation that some events in a person's environment are related to some human neuromuscular and glandular responses (Michael & Meyerson, 1962). The taste of a lemon, for example, causes most people to salivate. The lemon is a stimulus that causes an automatic reaction in the organism, which is a response. It is such a strong stimulus in most of us that all we need to do is to observe a lemon and our mouths begin to respond. Many such unconditioned stimulus-response connections are present at birth, and most of them are related to processes that keep our bodies functioning without conscious effort.

A neutral stimulus that has not been part of an innate stimulus-response relationship can become a conditioned stimulus that creates a response by being paired with an original unconditioned stimulus. An infant's natural response to a loud noise (unconditioned stimulus) is fear (unconditioned response). In their experiment using a small child named Albert, Watson and Rayner (1920) demonstrated that this fear response could eventually be elicited by a previously neutral stimulus in the form of a rat once the appearance of the rat (conditioned stimulus) had been paired with the loud noise several times. The response (fear) to the conditioned stimulus (rat) is called a *conditioned response.* This is the chain of learning from a classical conditioning standpoint. This new relationship will not remain as part of the organism's behavior if the conditioned stimulus is presented often enough without the introduction of the unconditioned stimulus. In the case of Albert, if the rat was presented frequently without any accompanying presentation of the loud noise, the conditioned stimulus, the rat, would lose its power to evoke a fear response. This process is termed *extinction.*

Although classical conditioning may explain the way in which some very basic simple behavior is learned, many learning theorists believe that much of a person's complex behavior cannot be explained by the classical model. To explain how most behavior is learned, these theorists turn to the assumptions of operant conditioning.

Operant Conditioning

The basic principles of operant conditioning were outlined by B. F. Skinner (1938). Skinner's contention is that most human behavior occurs at random. The critical question is: What are the environmental consequences of the behavior? This type of behavior operates on the environment, in contrast to behavior that responds to prior stimuli (Michael & Meyerson, 1962). The core of operant conditioning is a law of learning postulated originally by Skinner (1938). If a certain behavior is followed by an environmental event that brings satisfaction to a person, then the probability of the behavior's recurrence is increased. An example is the child who sucks his or her thumb. At some time the infant randomly stuck its thumb in its mouth, and the sensations generated were pleasurable, and so, rewarding. Because the behavior was rewarding, the probability of that behavior's recurring increased. In short, the child learned the behavior of thumb sucking. Thus, learning through operant conditioning is the opposite of learning through classical conditioning. Operant conditioning occurs because of what happens after a particular behavior, whereas classical conditioning occurs in response to an antedating stimulus in the environment. In operant conditioning the organism first must behave in a certain manner. This behavior is then shaped by the consequences of the environmental events that follow it.

Imitative Learning

While the classical and operant models account for a substantial part of human behavior, most learning theorists contend that some of an individual's behavior is learned through a process that does not involve directly receiving a reward. Such learning is said to take place through the process of imitation or vicarious learning: An observer learns a particular response by watching some other person (the model) perform the response. Hosford (1980) believes that most human behavior is learned through observation and that this view is substantiated by psychological and anthropological research. Miller and Dollard (1941) refer to this process as "matched dependent behavior": The person learns the response only if she or he matches the behavior of the model. Mowrer (1960) feels the observer could learn the response of the model simply by seeing the model rewarded; in this view, the reward given the model is a vicarious reward for the observer. Work by Bandura (1962, 1965, 1969) suggests that imitative learning can take place without either the model or the observer being rewarded. Bandura refers to this as a *contiguity-mediational theory,* which holds that imitative learning can take place simply through one person observing another's response. Bandura points out, however, that although the pattern of behavior may be learned simply through observation, reinforcement may be necessary in order for the observer to perform the behavior. In a sense, the behavior may lie dormant until it is called forth through reinforcement.

It is obvious how important this notion of imitative learning is to the learning theory position. Everyone has observed children modeling their behavior on someone they admire, such as holding a bat just like a famous ballplayer. Aspiring counselors also learn much of their own counseling behaviors, good or bad, through modeling based on their supervisors. Recent research indicates that this imitative learning is an extremely important factor, integral with the other laws of learning.

Classical/respondent, operant, and imitative learning are the basic models used in some combination by most behaviorists. No specific theory constitutes the one best representation of the whole field. However, some basic concepts have been developed as part of these models, upon which most behaviorists would agree. These concepts, which we will now examine, are essential to the behavioral approach to counseling.

Essential Concepts of Behaviorism

Reinforcement

Primary and Secondary Reinforcement

In general, there are two classifications of reinforcements. Primary reinforcements are such things as food, water, and air that are vital to life. Very few of the reinforcements a person seeks or receives beyond infancy are primary. As soon as a young child begins to interact with the environment, he or she begins to learn that other stimuli can be reinforcing. These secondary, or learned, reinforcers, such as money, praise, blame, and love, are stimuli that the person has learned to value. Generally, these occur as neutral stimuli until they are associated with a primary reinforcer. For example, initially the only reinforcement the infant recognizes when being held by its mother is food. The mother at this period is neutral. If the mother is warm and pleasant, however, getting attention from her soon becomes desirable, and this attention becomes a secondary reinforcement. Although the term *secondary* implies that these reinforcers are less important than primary ones, this is not true; not only do secondary reinforcements far outnumber primary ones in adult life, but many of them share equal importance with primary reinforcements and sometimes exceed them in importance, as when a person sacrifices his or her life to save others.

Positive and Negative Reinforcement

"The operation of presenting a positive reinforcer contingent upon a response is called positive reinforcement. The operation of removing an aversive stimulus contingent upon a response is called negative reinforcement" (Michael & Meyerson, 1962, p. 4). Positive and negative reinforcers are not absolutes; they are relative to the person receiving them. Although it is often assumed that most people perceive certain events (such as praise, money) as positive reinforcements and others (such as scorn, ridicule) as negative, the person's evaluation of an event as positive or negative depends on how the person receiving the reinforcement perceives the event. In positive reinforcement, the person receives something pleasurable or desirable as a consequence of behavior. "A positive reinforcer is not necessarily the same as a reward. Rewards are usually given to somebody for doing something. They [rewards] may or may not be valued by the recipient, and they may or may not increase the frequency of behavior. Positive reinforcement is probably the most widely used of the behavior theory procedures because of its compatibility with our values, its ease of application and its effectiveness" (Groden & Cautela, 1981, p. 173). In negative reinforcement, the consequence of a behavior is the removal of something undesirable or painful to the individual. Like positive reinforcement, negative reinforcement acts to increase behaviors. Negative reinforcement is not synonymous with punishment. Punishment is the *application* of an adversive event as a result of a behavior; negative reinforcement is the *removal* of the aversive event as a result of the behavior. Generally, negative reinforcement is effective in changing behavior; punishment may have short-term effects, but very few long-term ones. Negative reinforcement involves the use of aversive events, so it is not as widely used and when used should be combined with other procedures to teach appropriate behaviors (Groden & Cautela, 1981).

Many positive and negative reinforcers become generalized secondary reinforcers. Money often becomes a positive generalized secondary reinforcement because people learn that money can be used to bring many other kinds of pleasurable consequences. Similarly, the force of the negative reinforcement of social rejection may cause people to respond in certain ways in many situations.

Either positive or negative reinforcement may take place without the receiver's being consciously aware of it. Although there are many times when the person is aware of having been rewarded, there are other times when he or she will not realize that any reinforcement, positive or negative, has occurred. In the operant model, however, it makes little difference whether the person is consciously aware of the reinforcement. Groden and Cautela make a very valid point when they state: "For ethical reasons, when it appears that positive reinforcement would be as effective as alternative, less positive procedures, the former procedure should be the treatment of choice" (1981, p. 176).

Schedules of Reinforcement

Skinner and his followers have concentrated heavily on the importance of the rate and timing of reinforcement. The schedule of reinforcement is the particular pattern of reinforcement applied to a particular response. The simplest schedule is continuous reinforcement: After every response of a given nature, a reward or reinforcement is applied. This is the simplest form and is very effective in developing new behavior, but it is the least effective for the maintenance of long-term behavior. If the reward is given continuously, the effects of the reward are soon lessened. If a parent gives a child a cookie to keep the child quiet, the reinforcement will work at first, but if the parent does this every time, the cookie soon loses its effect. Reinforcement on an intermittent basis is much more effective than continuous reinforcement.

Intermittent reinforcement can be subdivided into two rather large categories: ratio reinforcement and interval reinforcement. The former involves the rate of responses: After so many correct responses, a reward is applied. An interval schedule of reinforcement is based on the passage of a given amount of time; it does not make any difference how many responses are made; the reward is delivered only after the proper amount of time has passed. Most people who have been exposed to either of the intermittent schedules will retain the learned responses longer than if they had been on a continuous schedule. The response is more difficult to extinguish. When trying to instill a particular response in a person, it is most effective to begin with a continuous reinforcement pattern and then shift to an intermittent schedule once the behavior has been acquired. The child who is rewarded for good behavior on an intermittent basis will maintain that behavior over longer periods without an additional reward.

Developing Complex Behaviors

In the behaviorist view, one of the basic models of learning—imitative learning—relates directly to the development of some complex behaviors. Other behaviors, however, are learned through the processes of extinction, generalization, discrimination, and shaping.

Extinction

"Behavior [that] has been learned through classical or operant procedures must either be reinforced on occasion or teamed with the unconditioned stimulus to continue to occur" (Groden & Cautela, 1981). If the behavior ceases to be reinforced either positively or negatively, it will eventually disappear. If, for example, a person ceased to be paid for going to work, it is doubtful that she or he would continue on the job very long. A person who had worked there only a short time would probably quit immediately; someone who had been there for some time would probably take longer to quit. The importance of this law of learning is that people's behavior is continuously able to change, and they are instrumental in changing it. Often, for example, a person learns a behavior that is appropriate to one stage of development but not at a later stage. Without the process of extinction, the behavior would persist (perseverate) and become inappropriate. Therefore, it is a useful procedure for the elimination of behaviors that are no longer useful or desirable though they might have been both at one time.

Generalization

Generalization, an extremely important principle of learning, is the assumption that a reinforcement that accompanies a stimulus increases the probability that not only will the particular stimulus elicit a particular response but that other similar stimuli will, too. Hence, a person will respond to any new situation in the environment as he or she would to a similar situation. If an infant receives satisfaction from being held by its mother and responds accordingly, the infant may generalize this satisfaction to the stimulus of being held by the father and will respond in the same manner. The same principle is involved when you walk into a new classroom. Your behavior, at least initially, will be the same as behavior that has worked in previous classrooms. The process of generalization is extremely important because no two stimulus situations are exactly the same. Having the ability to generalize allows people to move from one similar situation to the next without always having to learn completely new behaviors. People are able to carry a core of behavior with them. It is also true, however, that even similar situations may require small changes in behavior; therefore, the ability to discriminate among situations is also important.

Discrimination

It is apparent that people cannot go through life responding in the same way to related but different stimuli. For example, although the classroom situation may appear similar and although you may have been able to openly disagree with a previous instructor, it might be a personal disaster to disagree with your present instructor. To survive, people must learn the differences between given situations. The law of discrimination states that relationships between stimuli and responses that have been generated through the process of generalization may be broken down separately. This occurs through combining reinforcement with extinction. In this process the correct response to a stimulus receives reinforcement, but the incorrect response to a similar situation does not. In the case of the two instructors, in one class the student would receive positive reinforcement for disagreeing and negative reinforcement for not participating; in the other class, the opposite would be true. Because of this pattern of reinforcement a person will learn to make the correct response only in the presence of the correct stimulus; that is, he or she learns to tell the difference between two similar situations. The level of discrimination required depends in large part on how important the stimulus situation is to the person. The ability to discriminate between good and bad art is important to some but relatively unimportant to others. The fact that each person is forced to make many thousands of discriminations in everyday life proves the importance of discrimination in the learning process.

Shaping

The laws of reinforcement, extinction, generalization, and discrimination all come together in a process referred to by Skinner as shaping. Shaping is the process of moving from simple behaviors that are approximations of the final behavior to a final, complex behavior. Through this process certain behaviors that are close approximations of the final behavior are reinforced, while other behaviors are not. At each stage of the process a closer approximation of the final behavior is required before reinforcement is given.

For example, the behavior of a child who does not interact with other children in the class might be changed so that the child could interact in a positive fashion. The first step would be to help the child see the desirability of interacting with others. An environmental situation could be established in which the child was required to interact with another child. This could be accomplished by giving the child and one or two other children a common learning task to work on together. During interaction in this small group, even at minimal levels, the child would receive some form of reinforcement from the teacher or counselor. Once some interaction is developed, the degree of interaction required to receive reinforcement can be increased. Upon reaching a satisfactory level of interaction in this small group, the child could be made part of a larger group and the process used in the smaller group repeated. The final stage would be to reinforce the child's desired interaction in the context of a classroom activity. In this process a teacher or counselor may use external reinforcement to start the process, but the child's self-reinforcement will quickly become the chief motivation for the new behavior. As the child begins to interact in a controlled situation and finds that interaction pleasurable, she or he can be expected to seek out other interactions.

Shaping, then, uses situations and external reinforcement in a planned way to help people begin or learn a new behavior, but the ultimate goal is for individuals to reinforce themselves for behaviors that bring them pleasure. Someone has had to help them begin or learn any one of numerous complex behaviors, but people continue it because they find it rewarding.

Mediating Responses

The principles of learning outlined above apply to both humans and other animals. In addition, however, humans have the capacity to develop *mediating responses.* They can respond to their environment in new ways through planning and evaluation. These "higher mental processes" (Dollard & Miller, 1950) consist largely in the use of language and symbolization.

Because humans have the capacity to use symbols and language, they can label stimuli and can mediate their effects. By means of language, individuals can go through a reasoning process when confronted with a particular stimulus and can delay any immediate response to the stimulus. A person who sees a symbolization of food, despite the drive that it calls forth, is able to delay the response to that stimulus until it is time to eat. That person is mediating her or his response to a given stimulus. Much of human behavior is governed this way; indeed, most adult human behavior involves a process of mediation, and it is this process that makes humans not only different from other animals, but also more complex. Even Skinner acknowledged that individuals may have some capacity to mediate the effects of environmental events and that psychologists need to be aware of that capacity (1971).

These mediating events have received increased attention in behavioral counseling and therapy. Homme refers to them as *coverants*. "Coverants are events the laymen call mental. These include thinking, imagining, reflecting, ruminating, relaxing, day-dreaming, fantasizing, etc." (Homme, 1965, p. 502). Osgood (1953) explains these internal events in his two-stage theory of learning. Osgood's model is represented by S[r-s]R, the first S is the external stimulus, which produces a covert response (r), which in turn creates an internal stimulus (s), causing the external response (R). It is the S-R we see; the r-s occurs internally. Many behavioral counselors who place emphasis on helping people develop self-management programs use procedures that focus on these internal processes.

This overview of the basic principles underlying the behavioral approach to counseling is in no way an exhaustive treatment. Our attempt, rather, has been to provide the core principles of learning theory that form the basis for behavioral counseling. We now consider how all of these specific principles of learning come together to form a picture of what we normally refer to as personality, either normal or abnormal.

Theory of Personality

The basic assumption of the learning theory approach to personality is that behavior is learned as individuals interact with their environment. People are not innately bad or good; they are born neutral, as in the Lockian idea of a *tabula rasa* (Hosford, 1969), and how they develop their personalities depends upon interaction with the environment. From the learning theory perspective, people are reactive beings; they react to stimuli as the stimuli are presented to them. In the process, patterns of behavior and ultimately personalities are formed. Most learning theorists would concede that some behavior may be a result of the interaction of an individual's innate characteristics with the environment. However, because innate characteristics cannot be controlled or defined, behaviorists focus on things that can be controlled or explained, the observable interactions between the individual and the environment, especially in terms of the significant others in that environment.

Within the framework of learning theory, human behavior is determined by the goals that people set for themselves or, as sometimes happens, are imposed upon them by society. Behavior, even when it seems strange or bizarre, is directed toward these goals. "An individual responds with those behaviors that he has learned will lead to the greatest satisfaction in a given situation" (Rotter, 1964, p. 57). Human motives for behaving are developed through experience, and gradually people develop a set of differentiated motives or needs. The interaction between a mother and child illustrates this process. The initial stages of the infant's interaction with its mother result in satisfaction through feeding and being held. This satisfaction gradually becomes generalized to the extent that the infant receives pleasure simply by being in the presence of the mother. The infant learns to want attention from its mother, a goal or motive that is separate from the first goal of reducing feelings of hunger. Through continuing interaction with the mother, the child learns that some behaviors result in pleasurable attention from her and other behaviors do not. In order to receive this pleasurable attention, the child will strive to do things that will please the mother and gain her attention. Finally, this process may generalize to the extent that the child behaves in certain ways even when the mother is not present; the child has learned that she would approve of these behaviors, and this in itself is satisfying. Thus, motives or drives or needs are developed, not through instincts or other innate characteristics, but through the child's interaction with the environment.

Learned Needs

As a person continues to interact with the environment, he or she develops a network of motives or needs that act to guide behavior. These needs or motives will vary from being very specific, like a need for a mother's love, to very general, such as the need for good interpersonal relationships. The more specific the need, the more possible it is to predict the pattern of behavior in a given situation (Rotter, 1964). Rotter (1964) outlines three broad characteristics of these learned needs: need potential, freedom of movement, and need value.

Need Potential (Valence)

Need potential involves a set of behaviors that are directed toward a particular need, such as receiving attention from others, and the probability of their occurrence in a given situation. For example, a person who is confronted with a choice between going to class or going off with some friends has the option of responding to either the need to please friends or the need to please an instructor. If the need to please friends has a higher need potential than the need to please the instructor, then the behavior of going off with friends is the one most likely to occur.

Freedom of Movement

Freedom of movement relates to the belief a person has that certain patterns of behaviors will lead to certain satisfactions or rewards. The child learns that crying will bring attention from others, but this same behavior in a teenager will likely bring not attention but rejection. This principle accounts for the fact that people do not behave like robots. They choose behaviors that they have learned will bring them the reinforcements they desire.

Need Value

Finally, each need of a person has value. In any given situation one need or goal may have more value than some other goal. As in the preceding illustration, a student may have a need to please the instructor but also a need to be seen in a favorable light by his or her peers. The relative value the student attaches to these two needs in a given situation will in part determine what patterns of behavior she or he chooses. Thus, a type of need hierarchy develops. Each person has an innate hierarchy of needs, such as for food and water. Most needs, however, are formed through learning. The existence of a needs hierarchy serves to explain the fact that in any given situation a person may have the potential for several responses, and each of these responses has a probability for occurrence that can be ranked in order of importance. In the example of students in the classroom, one student may place more value on pleasing the instructor, and his or her response is governed by that need. To another student in the room, the need to please peers may have more value, and she or he will respond accordingly. Yet another student may value neither of these needs and may behave quite differently from the other two. Once the needs have been established, however, people actively make decisions designed to satisfy them. They become something more than simply reactors.

According to behaviorists, then, human personalities are determined largely by interaction with the environment. Once it is possible to understand a person's psychological situation, it becomes possible to understand the structure of that person's personality and to predict his or her behavior. The person learns through experience that certain situations will present certain satisfactions or dissatisfactions; through this experience, the person develops different patterns of needs that lead to different patterns of behavior. Individual differences develop because people perceive specific situations differently. The child who has received love from a parent will react to the latter's presence in certain predictable ways, and this pattern of behavior will be different from that of the child who has been rejected by a parent. In essence, each person has learned through experience to attribute a certain meaning to a given situation and reacts to the situation on that basis.

The basis for the structure of a person's personality, then, is learned patterns of behaviors. Obviously, much of this learning takes place early in the person's development. Hence, not unlike other theoretical approaches to personality, the learning theory approach recognizes the importance of early childhood experiences in the development of personality. But unlike other approaches, the learning theory approach does not attribute much of personality to innate characteristics, but ascribes a person's needs to experiences that he or she has learned would bring satisfaction.

As people interact with their environment, they are subject to the laws of learning; thus, personality is a product of learning. As people receive reinforcements from the environment, some behaviors are strengthened or learned, while others are weakened or extinguished. Many of these reinforcements are self-reinforcements, which take on increased importance as a person matures. The person who receives satisfaction from looking in a mirror after being on a diet is engaging in self-reinforcement. Reinforcement can be understood only through the eyes of the recipient; what is perceived as a positive or negative reinforcement may be quite different for each individual. Premack (1965) suggests that almost any event has the potential to be reinforcing, and to determine what is reinforcing, it is necessary to observe the activities in which a person normally engages. Behaviors that for some reason bring the person satisfaction are reinforcing. This important principle has specific use in counseling.

People may also learn some patterns of behavior through imitating others. This learning in turn leads to generalizations and discriminations and the gradual shaping of simple responses into complex behaviors. In addition, as people mature, they develop the ability to make mediating responses, largely through the use of language. These mediating responses allow people to plan and formulate responses to various stimuli or to withhold an immediate response to a particular stimulus. This is the process of personality development. Although the form of personality depends largely on the environment in which the individual develops, behaviorists are increasingly aware of the influence of the internal state on the organism.

Abnormal Personality Development

Like normal, or adaptive, patterns of behavior, abnormal or maladaptive behaviors are learned largely through the interaction of the individual and the environment. "Man's personality consists of both his positive and his negative habits. Those habits which are inappropriate (i.e., deviant) are learned in much the same way as appropriate behaviors" (Hosford, 1969, p. 2). Inappropriate behavior has been learned because it has been rewarded at various times. Children who are constantly disruptive in a classroom may behave that way because they have learned that only with such behavior can they receive attention. When the teacher shouts at them, they are receiving satisfaction or a reward for the behavior. Thus, this behavior has brought a valued reward—attention. Likewise, children who are withdrawn, who might be termed social isolates, have learned to behave in that manner. By being social isolates they may be avoiding a situation or people with whom they are uncomfortable. The reward is not having to participate in a situation that causes fear, a fear that has also been learned through experience. Because learning theory is mainly concerned with observable behavior, it does not try to take into account any inner reason for maladaptive behavior. Both the attention-seeking children and the social isolates are examples of people who have simply learned bad habits.

Maladaptive behavior is different from normal behavior, not in terms of how it was learned, but only to the degree that the behavior is atypical or maladaptive to the observers (Hosford, 1969). In other words, maladaptive behavior is behavior that either no longer brings satisfaction to the individual or that will ultimately bring the individual into conflict with the environment. In the case of a social isolate, the child is engaging in a pattern of behavior that is bringing temporary satisfaction but will ultimately cause him or her difficulty. In this case the objective of counseling would be to help the child learn to enjoy interpersonal interactions, thus helping her or him engage in behaviors that will bring both immediate and long-term rewards.

Goals of Counseling

Given that adaptive and maladaptive behaviors are learned in the same way, what do behaviorists hope to accomplish through the process of counseling? Blackham and Silberman (1971) suggest four specific steps to be followed in establishing counseling goals and methods to be used to bring about changes.

1. *Problem definition.* It is important to take the initial statement of the client and to determine where, when, and with whom the inappropriate behavior occurs. This analysis should attempt to determine the events that lead to the inappropriate behavior. If possible, the behavior of the client should be observed in the actual situation that is causing the difficulty.

2. *Development and social history.* Taking a developmental history of the client may be helpful in identifying areas of success or failure, competencies and deficiencies, interpersonal relationship patterns, adjustive behaviors, and problem areas. It is also useful in determining whether there are any physical or organic reasons for certain behaviors.

3. *Establishing specific goals of counseling.* Many counselors who adhere to other theories consider behavioral procedures helpful if a client has a very specific concern, but inappropriate for people with such feelings as inferiority, inadequacy, despair, and alienation (Marquis, 1972). Most behaviorists, however, would agree with Marquis's statement that "such highly generalized problems are usually the result of an inadequate diagnosis of the specific areas of anxiety . . . " (1972, p. 47). Thus, behaviorists' overall goals differ little from those of other counseling approaches. Behaviorists believe, however, that careful analysis of the general concern will reveal a number of specific concerns. Behaviorists would say that the general concern is too global to work with in counseling and that counselors and clients need more specific goals with which to work if counseling is to be productive.

Krumboltz (1966) contends that the goal of counseling must be stated in specific terms, that is, in terms of particular behaviors that need to be changed. People come to counseling because they have particular problems they cannot resolve by themselves, and they believe the counselor will be able to help them. The goal of counseling must be to help people resolve the problems they bring to the counseling situation. Clients will rarely come to a counselor saying they need a better self-concept; rather, a client is more inclined to say he or she feels inadequate with a group of people. Although feeling inadequate in a group of people may indicate a poor self-concept, the behavioral counselor would deal with the specific concern, not the global feeling; other aspects of the self-concept may also need some work, but the behavioral position is that the counselor needs to work on one specific concern at a time. Only in this manner can appropriate behavior changes be brought about.

The goals of counseling, then, must be stated in specific terms, and the specific short-term goal of counseling may be different for each client. The ultimate goal is always to help each client develop a system of self-management so that the person can control his or her destiny. If the client's goal is out of the counselor's realm of interest, competency, or ethical considerations, the counselor must tell her or him that this goal is personally inappropriate and uncomfortable. In essence, the counselor and the client must agree on the goal they want to achieve and concur that through counseling there is a possibility of achieving it.

4. *Determine methods to be used to bring about desired change.* The methods by which the counselor will operate are not rigid. Rather, a counselor responds within her or his own limits to the goal the client presents, and the accomplishment of that goal is of the utmost importance. The methods the counselor uses to help each client may be quite different, depending upon the client and the problem that he or she brings to the counseling situation. An article by Groden and Cautela (1981) will provide the reader with a good review of procedures that have been found effective with a variety of presenting problems.

The Process of Counseling

In the behaviorist view, the counseling process is a special type of learning situation. Both the client and the counselor should recognize the situation as such, and the counselor should view him- or herself as an aid in this learning process (Krumboltz, 1966). Any changes that come about as a result of the counseling process are a direct result of the same laws of learning that apply outside the counseling situation.

This does not entail a mechanistic approach in counseling. Wolpe (1958) emphasizes the need for the counselor to be accepting, to try to understand the client and what she or he is communicating, and to be nonjudgmental: "All that the patient says is accepted without question or criticism. He is given the feeling that the therapist is on his side" (1958, p. 106). Krumboltz likewise believes that it is essential for a counselor to be understanding and to communicate this understanding to the client. The counselor must be warm and empathic and hold each individual in high regard. Without these conditions it would not be possible to determine the client's difficulty or to gain the necessary cooperation of the client (Krumboltz, 1966). Even classic behaviorists such as Pepinsky and Pepinsky (1954) and Dollard and Miller (1950) state the need for the counselor to be personal and to establish a warm, permissive atmosphere for the client.

This phase of counseling is crucial. If the client does not perceive the counselor as a warm, caring, receptive person, it will make little difference what techniques the counselor uses. For example, a counselor might try to use praise or attention as positive reinforcement for certain behaviors. That praise or attention, however, will be effective only if the client values them from the counselor. If the client perceives the counselor as essentially noncaring, that praise or attention may not act as positive reinforcement, but may, indeed, be negative reinforcement.

A second reason for establishing a facilitative atmosphere is to give clients freedom to express their concerns. In such an atmosphere clients discover that the counselor is someone who will listen to their concerns, and perhaps for the first time in their lives, they may feel they have found someone with whom they can really talk (Dollard & Miller, 1950). Their statements are not received with a judgmental or shocked attitude, but are accepted. When this kind of atmosphere is established, clients' problems can be clarified and their feelings about the problem understood by the counselor. At this point the two participants in the relationship begin to work on resolving the client's difficulty. Unless the problem is sharply defined so that both the counselor and the client understand the problem clearly, however, counseling will not progress.

Central to the process of counseling, then, is defining the client's particular concern. From a learning theory framework it is not enough to relate a client's difficulty to having a poor self-concept. Instead, the behavioral counselor attempts to have the client define the concern in specific terms such as, "I am unable to relate to people of the opposite sex," or, "I stutter in front of a group of people." These are examples of specific behaviors and can be dealt with through counseling. This does not mean that behavioral counselors are not concerned with a person having a good self-concept or with self-actualization, but they contend that these global concepts must be translated into specific behaviors desired by the client. Only after the appropriate behaviors have been defined can the counselor and client work toward achieving them. Successful achievement of these behaviors may indeed lead the client to have a better self-concept, which is of course desirable, but it is not a workable original goal. As Bijou (1966) indicates, global attempts are doomed to failure because there is just too much behavior to deal with at one time. It is far better to work on one concern and, once that has been resolved, to move to another concern, if one exists. In this way both the counselor and the client have a clear notion of their goal and when it is accomplished.

The counselor is an active participant in the counseling process. He or she helps the client define the specific concern that has brought the latter to the counseling situation and decides whether the kind of aid she or he can offer will help the client. In addition, the counselor has the major responsibility for deciding what will be utilized in the counseling process. Once the client and the counselor have defined and agreed upon the concern, the counselor controls the process of counseling and accepts responsibility for its outcome. It is the counselor's responsibility to launch the client on a course of action that will eventually help the latter resolve his or her difficulty. To accomplish this, the counselor must control the counseling process. This is not an arbitrary manipulative control that goes against the client's wishes; it is specifically designed to meet the goals of the client and is done with her or his full consent. In the exercise of this control, the counselor may use whatever ethical techniques she or he feels will lead the client to the desired behavior. Some of these techniques will be applied in the counseling situation itself, but the counselor may also involve himself or herself in the individual's environment outside the counseling office by working with significant others in the client's life. The entire process is directed to providing each client with the necessary skills to manage his or her own life.

Techniques of Counseling

Although most behaviorists would be in general agreement about what constitutes the process of counseling, even though their emphases might differ, the differences among actual techniques of counseling are somewhat greater. The field of behavioral counseling has expanded rapidly over the last 20 years, and this growth has brought about a rich variety of techniques that have demonstrated effectiveness (Kazdin, 1978; Groden & Cautela, 1981). Some counselors follow a basically traditional model; most, however, operate from a broadly conceived behavioral base. Those who adhere to a more traditional approach, such as Wolpe, rely on techniques rooted in the basic principles of learning. Those who operate from a basic behavioral position, such as Krumboltz, Thoresen, and Lazarus, also acknowledge the importance of procedures that are not directly tied to the principles of learning. Lazarus states, "In the practical details of my day to day work with clients, I have found it necessary to broaden the base of conventional behavior therapy" (1972, p. vi). According to Krumboltz and Thoresen, "There is no 'approved list' of techniques the use of which enables one to call himself a behavioral counselor. The door must be kept open to all procedures that might be helpful" (1969, p. 3). In effect, these people are advocating behavioral eclecticism, and as pointed out earlier, it is an eclecticism that is pushing more and more people into the broadly defined behavioral camp. This section focuses on procedures that are related to the basic principles of learning designed to either increase and strengthen or to decrease and weaken certain behaviors. The procedures designed to develop new behavior or to increase some behaviors include shaping, modeling, contracting, and assertiveness training. Those designed to eliminate or weaken behaviors include desensitization, extinction, and reinforcement of incompatible behaviors. Other techniques, such as covert sensitization, can be used either to increase or to decrease behavior.

In this section, we will discuss first the techniques most directly related to traditional learning theory approach. Many of the techniques are useful both in the actual process of counseling and in client self-management programs performed outside of the actual counseling sessions. Self-management procedures have become an important addition to the field of behavioral counseling. They use the same laws of learning that the counselor uses in the counseling relationship, but the important difference is that the client is put in charge of his or her own behavioral change program. The plan is established by the counselor and the client in counseling, but the client has the chief responsibility for the implementation of the plan, with the counselor acting in a supporting role. Throughout this section we will mention specific techniques that are often used in self-management or self-control programs.

The Traditional Behavioral Counseling Model

The person originally identified with the traditional model of behavioral counseling was Joseph Wolpe. According to Wolpe's theory of reciprocal inhibition (1958), the fundamental aim of counseling must be to remove the feelings of anxiety caused by stimuli that are objectively harmless. Counseling is judged effective to the degree that it breaks down this learned response to the stimuli so that a more appropriate response may occur.

To accomplish the counseling goals, the client and counselor usually meet from one to a dozen times. During this period the counselor strives to establish a relationship in which the client feels that the counselor likes and is not judging him or her, while the client is giving the counselor all the information possible about childhood, family, school experience, vocational plans, and anything else that may relate to the client's current status as a person. This information is helpful to the counselor in attempting to understand the client in her or his state; however, it is not essential to bring a great deal of the past into the counseling situation. What is important is an understanding of how the client behaves at the current time.

After the initial interviews, the client may take some inventories designed to give information about the kinds of activities that elicit inappropriate responses. This information is used in conjunction with information from the interviews. The information is combined to establish a hierarchy of conditions that cause anxiety in the client and to which he or she responds in an inappropriate manner. The formation of this hierarchy might proceed in the following way. A person may tell the counselor that he or she is fearful or anxious when being observed by others. The counselor attempts to establish the hierarchy of needs by ascertaining what kinds of people cause the client the most anxiety. The counselor may find that the client is quite comfortable at home being observed by family, a little less comfortable in the company of friends, a little more uncomfortable in the company of strangers, and quite uncomfortable when alone with a stranger. This evidence of increasing anxiety in different situations helps the counselor form the hierarchy, which is the basis for the counseling process. The specific techniques used are assertiveness training, sexual responses training, relaxation training, and systematic desensitization.

Assertiveness Training

"In general, assertive responses are useful for anxieties evoked in the course of direct interpersonal dealings" (Wolpe, 1958, p. 113). These responses are very similar to what Salter (1949) called *excitatory responses*. A person in need of assertiveness training is one who has an inappropriate anxiety response in interpersonal relationships. This anxiety inhibits expression of assertive statements and behavior. The person internalizes the feelings generated by the situation, which can lead to the development of such symptoms as ulcers and high blood pressure. Assertiveness training simply involves trying to get the client to express these feelings during interactions with others. A person who has been hurt by something someone else has done to him or her is encouraged to tell that person her or his feelings. In effect, the client is told that there is no reason not to express these feelings and that anxiety over expressing them is groundless. Wolpe and Lazarus (1966) contend that the expression of the assertive response acts to inhibit any anxiety created by the interpersonal situation and that because the assertive behavior will be self-rewarding, the anxiety will continue to be inhibited.

The counselor first attempts to get the client to be assertive in the counseling interview, that is, to state his or her feelings to the counselor. In this initial stage the counselor uses the operant principles of reinforcement, extinction, and shaping to develop the desired assertive responses. Once this is accomplished the client is instructed to attempt the same kinds of responses outside of counseling. The principle of conditioning involved here is that in expressing assertive responses to the counselor the client finds that there is no punishment or anxiety accompanying the response. Hence, the expression of the assertive response is teamed with a relaxed situation rather than an anxiety-producing situation. The counselor must use as much pressure as is necessary to get the client to perform the assertive behavior outside the counseling situation. In some cases the counselor will be unable to motivate the client to do this and may have to resort to role playing in the interview (Wolpe, 1958).

As the client engages in assertive behaviors outside of counseling, it is to be expected that general positive feedback from others will act as positive reinforcement for the behavior. This will lead the client to feel better about herself or himself and her or his interpersonal relations, an extremely important self-reinforcement for continuing the behavior. Thus, once the behavior has been established the client engages in self-management by feeling rewarded or satisfied as he or she engages in the desired behavior.

Sexual Training

Sexual counseling, although counselors will not need to use this technique, is included here as another technique from the traditional model. This procedure is used when the client has anxiety connected with sexual situations. According to Wolpe, "the key to the problem of impaired sexual performance is the subtraction of anxiety from the sexual encounter" (1969, p. 74). The first step in the process is to define as exactly as possible the actual situation that creates the anxiety. Starting at this point, a hierarchy of increasing anxiety situations is determined. The client may simultaneously receive relaxation training. At this point the individual is instructed to engage in the activity that produces the least anxiety only when he or she is completely relaxed. Once the client can engage in that activity without any anxiety, he or she is instructed to engage in the next behavior, and so on. Thus, all this procedure involves is instructing the client to participate in sexual activities only when there is no anxiety accompanying the situation. Like the assertive technique, the critical issue is to motivate the client to follow the instructions of the counselor. In this way only pleasurable feelings are generated by sexual situations because the client avoids sexual situations that cause anxiety. Gradually, these pleasurable feelings will extend to other sexual situations.

Relaxation Training

Relaxation training is appropriate for any kind of anxiety, but it is most applicable when the stimulus causing the anxiety is an inanimate object. The technique, originally developed by Jacobsen (1938), involves instructing the client in muscle relaxation. The client is told that relaxing is a way of combating anxiety. When a person relaxes systematically, all tension in the muscular structure of the body is eliminated. This situation is incompatible with feelings of anxiety that create tension in the muscular structure. This is a form of *counterconditioning,* referred to as *reciprocal inhibition.* Relaxation of the muscles is most often used by Wolpe in conjunction with systematic desensitization. While relaxation training has been found quite effective in reducing anxiety, some authors suggest that not all individuals will respond favorably to the training.

Systematic Desensitization

"Systematic Desensitization is a form of classical conditioning in which anxiety-provoking situations are paired with inhibitory responses" (Belkin, 1980, p. 130).

The technique of systematic desensitization, based on Wolpe's theory of reciprocal inhibition, uses both the hierarchy of anxiety-producing situations developed from the initial interviews and the techniques of relaxation. An extensive analysis of the behavior of the client establishes an anxiety hierarchy. Once the hierarchy has been established, the client is trained in deep-muscle relaxation. The training sessions are roughly 20 minutes long, focusing in order on the muscles in the arms, head, neck, and shoulders, and finally the trunk and legs. At this point the actual presentation of the items from the hierarchy begins. The client, in a relaxed state, is asked to imagine the least anxiety-producing item in the hierarchy. Once the client can put herself or himself in that situation without feeling any anxiety, the next item on the list is presented. The process continues until the client can imagine the most fear-producing situation in the hierarchy without feeling anxiety. In essence, the client is being conditioned to a new response to the formerly fear-producing stimulus situations. Instead of feeling an anxiety response, he or she is being conditioned to a relaxed response, and the two are incompatible. "The essential principle of reciprocal inhibition is that an organism cannot make two contradictory responses at the same time . . . if the response that is contradictory to anxiety results in a more pleasant state or more productive behavior for the subject. The new response to anxiety-evoking stimuli will gradually reinforce the anxiety response" (Bugg, 1972, p. 823).

Each of the techniques outlined above has in common the goal of changing an old, inappropriate response to a stimulus to a response that is more appropriate. This is accomplished in large part through counterconditioning procedures in which an incompatible and more desirable response is teamed with a stimulus that previously produced an undesirable one. The list of techniques presented here is not exhaustive, but does include the ones most frequently used by therapists following the traditional model. A more detailed account of these techniques can be found in the writing of Joseph Wolpe (1958, 1969), Andrew Salter (1949), and Lazarus (1972).

Groden & Cautela (1981) suggest that a procedure known as "flooding" is related to the process of desensitization and is particularly useful in reducing anxiety and eliminating avoidance behavior. They suggest that if an individual uses avoidance behavior to continually absent themselves from anxiety, they are never in a position to learn that the event being avoided is really harmless. "In flooding, the person is exposed to an anxiety-inducing situation either in imagination or reality, while discouraging or preventing avoidance behaviors" (Groden & Cautela, 1981, p. 128). After having experienced the situation as harmless the person learns that it does not need to be avoided.

Implosive Therapy

A modified form of classical conditioning that has not been as widely known or used as other classical techniques is a procedure described by Stampfl (1961): implosive therapy. This approach combines some characteristics of classical conditioning and extinction. According to Belkin (1980), implosive therapy is unlike systematic desensitization in that " . . . the subject is not given simultaneous anxiety-inhibiting stimuli. Rather, by intensely concentrating on the fearful stimulus, the client is taught to associate 'neutral stimuli' with the anxiety-evoking ones" (p. 133). Unlike other procedures using imagination, the counselor attempts to have the client confront the "feared event that it is thought the phobic stimulus actually symbolizes" (Groden & Cautela, 1981, p. 178). The client is taught to imagine the feared thing or event in a situation in which nothing negative will or can happen. The repeated imagining in the face of a neutral response acts to extinguish the previous anxiety response. Belkin (1980) suggests that implosive procedures may be most effective when the target behavior is characterized by avoidance, such as in phobias. Seen in this way, implosive procedures are very similar to flooding.

Broad-Based Behavioral Counseling

Broad-based behavioral counseling is in reality the outgrowth of the work and research of a number of people over the last two decades. Nonetheless the single individual most often identified with this more modern approach to behavioral counseling is Arnold

Lazarus. Lazarus is the founder of the Multimodel Therapy Institute of New York. He has authored several books, most notably: *Behavior Therapy and Beyond* (1971), *Multimodel Therapy* (1976), and *The Practice of Multimodel Therapy* (1981). Originally from South Africa, he has been in the United States since 1966. His approach is eclectic despite his early work with Wolpe. Even though we do not specifically discuss his approach in the following, we believe that much of what he teaches and practices is appropriate to this section of the chapter.

Like those who generally follow the traditional model of behavioral counseling, practitioners of the broader based model place great emphasis on establishing a relationship between counselor and client. Krumboltz points out, "The client is likely not to describe the totality of his problems unless he thinks his listener will understand things from his point of view" (Krumboltz & Thoresen, 1969, p. 224). Second, "the counselor's ability to communicate his understanding of the client's problem to him establishes the counselor as an important person in the client's life and therefore one able to be an influential model and effective reinforcing agent" (Krumboltz & Thoresen, 1969, p. 224). Hence, the first goal of the behavioral counselor is to establish a relationship with the client in which the latter feels free to express herself or himself to the counselor and views the counselor as an individual genuinely interested in attempting to help with the difficulty.

Once this relationship has been established, the counselor's actual techniques will vary, depending upon the client and the nature of the concern. The techniques used will most often include shaping, extinction, contracting, time out, imitative learning, and cognitive learning. The behavioral counselors may, however, rely on more than the face-to-face meetings with clients. Because of their belief in the importance of the environment in establishing and maintaining behaviors, behavioral counselors will often attempt to make changes in the client's environment. Thus, in some cases the counselor becomes a behavioral engineer manipulating the person's environment to provide one that will aid the process of behavioral change. Although some may object to this manipulation, behaviorists point out that the manipulation is used to enhance the probability that the client will accomplish her or his desired behavior. The client, not the counselor, establishes the goals of counseling.

Shaping

The most frequently used technique of the broad-based model is that of shaping. This technique involves modifying behavior through reinforcement, helping clients acquire desired behaviors through a series of approximations of the desired behavior. If the desired behavior is present and the goal is simply to increase its occurrence, the counselor uses direct positive reinforcement of the behavior within the counseling situation. In addition, the behavioral counselor attempts to structure the real world of the client so that the latter receives positive reinforcement for the behavior in the real situation.

If, however, the desired behavior has not been a part of the client's behavioral repertoire, the counselor must reinforce initial behaviors that are approximations of the final behavior. Gradually the counselor requires the client to make finer discriminations by reinforcing behaviors that are increasingly closer to the desired behavior and not reinforcing other behaviors. The actual reinforcement used to encourage further responses in the desired direction may consist in the counselor's giving particular attention to a statement or by inattention to certain statements. The counselor may express verbal approval of certain statements and disapproval of others by not responding or by responding negatively. Through the reinforcement, whether verbal or nonverbal, positive or negative, certain responses are reinforced and certain responses extinguished. In this way the client's behavior is shaped in the direction that both he or she and the counselor have agreed upon.

Hosford (1969) outlines four crucial considerations in the use of reinforcement in counseling. First, the counselor must be sure that the reinforcement is strong enough to motivate the client to perform the desired behavior; the same kind of reinforcement does not work equally well for all clients, and the counselor must find the reinforcement that has the greatest potential for increasing the desired behavior for that particular individual. The Premack principle is of extreme importance in this process. According to this principle, the counselor must find out what the person really likes to do to determine what may be reinforcing for him or her. These highly desirable behaviors are used as reinforcers for the behavior being worked on in counseling. If a client has entered counseling in order to develop better study habits and the counselor determines that the person really enjoys certain TV programs, the counselor might establish with the parents (or directly with the client) a system in which the client is permitted to view those programs contingent upon spending a predetermined amount of time studying. If the agreement, or contract, is made directly with the client, the counselor has established a self-management program: The client is chiefly responsible for shaping her or his own behavior.

Hosford's second point is that the counselor must use reinforcement in a systematic manner. Krumboltz states, "The question is not whether the counselor should or should not use reinforcement—the question is how the counselor can time his use of reinforcement in the best interests of his client" (1966, p. 15). In the initial stages of counseling, it is important that each response indicating movement in the desired direction be reinforced; as counseling progresses, however, the reinforcement ultimately should be applied on a systematic but intermittent basis because the intermittent schedule of reinforcement tends to have the most long-lasting effect on behavior.

The third consideration is the contingency between the demonstration of the desired response and the application of the reward. For greatest effectiveness the reinforcement must follow closely the demonstrated desired response. The fourth factor is closely related to this contingency: The desired response must first be elicited by the counselor. This often involves the use of cue statements. A cue statement is a statement so designed that the client can hardly avoid responding in the desired direction. In effect, the counselor is giving a verbal prompting to the client. This prompting, or giving of cue statements, may be particularly important in the early stages of counseling; as reinforcement begins to show results, however, there should be less need for this kind of statement.

The technique of shaping in counseling, then, involves gradually molding the client's current behavior toward the desired behavior through the use of positive and negative reinforcement. This reinforcement can be verbal or nonverbal, but it must be strong enough to motivate the client, and it must be applied consistently in close proximity to the desired behavior.

Extinction

Whereas shaping is a process of increasing a desired behavior, extinction is the process of decreasing the frequency of an undesirable behavior. "When a learned response is repeated without reinforcement, the strength of the tendency to perform that response undergoes a progressive decrease" (Dollard & Miller, 1976, p. 173). Thus, extinction involves withholding any reinforcement, positive or negative. It involves ignoring a specific behavior. In counseling this means a non-response to undesirable verbal or motor behavior of the client. When trying to extinguish behavior, the counselor will often find that the target behavior of the client increases in an attempt to receive the usual previous reinforcement—perhaps attention. Gradually, if the reinforcement continues to be withheld, the behavior will decrease and eventually be eliminated. Bandura (1969) lists several factors that affect the rate of extinction:

1. the degree to which the behavior was reinforced on an irregular basis
2. the degree of effort required to engage in the behavior
3. the level of deprivation sustained during extinction
4. the degree to which changes in reinforcement conditions are distinguishable
5. the degree to which alternate modes of responding are available

Because extinction procedures are not as easy to use as it may first appear, the counselor must develop full understanding of the factors listed by Bandura in relation to each specific client before attempting the procedure with that client.

Reinforcing Incompatible Behaviors

Similar to the process of systematic desensitization, this technique involves reinforcing one response to block the appearance of the undesired behavior. For example, a client may desire to decrease the number of self-doubting thoughts. The client cannot think positively and negatively about herself or himself at the same time. Hence, the counselor uses positive reinforcement to reward the client's expression of positive self-thoughts. This in itself blocks the appearance of negative thoughts; if they do occur, the counselor uses extinction techniques. This technique is also often used in self-management programs. The client with negative self-thoughts might be instructed to carry a series of cards on which positive self-thoughts are written. As soon as the client experiences the onset of a negative thought, she or he takes out the cards and reads three of the positive statements to herself or himself. Gradually this process will reduce or eliminate the undesired negative thoughts by replacing them with positive ones. As with shaping, the client is controlling his or her own behavior change plan. The behavioral counselor's role has been to help the client develop a systematic plan for desired behavior change.

Modeling

A second technique that is receiving increasing attention from behavioral counselors is modeling, or imitative learning. Imitative or vicarious learning is one of the principal means by which people learn new behaviors. The use of imitative learning in counseling involves the presentation to the client of a model or models who demonstrate the desired behavioral outcome and with whom the client can easily identify. In the counseling situation the client may be so ignorant of ways to modify behavior or to develop new ones that reinforcement techniques may be inappropriate and ineffectual in the early stages. Instead, it may be more appropriate to present to the person some type of model that represents the desired behavior. The client may learn the new behavior simply through observing the behavior of the model. According to Bandura (1969), whether the client learns the new behavior or not will depend on four factors: (1) attention, (2) retention, (3) motor reproduction, and (4) incentive. Certainly, if a client is to learn from observing a model, his or her attention must be focused on the target behavior of the model. Second, if the client is to reproduce the modeled behavior, she or he must have the capacity to retain the behavior mentally; no amount of modeling is going to help someone who is mentally deficient learn certain complex behaviors. Third, the client must have the physical capacity to reproduce the behavior. Finally, the client must see some incentive for engaging in the behavior. Kagen addresses this last point when he states that the model's behavior must represent some desirable goal that the client would like to obtain. "The most salient of these include: (a) power over the environment . . . ; (b) competence and instrumental skills; (c) autonomy of action; and (d) the receipt of love, affection, and acceptance from others" (1963, p. 82). The model presented to the client may demonstrate more control over personal destiny than the client does; may have greater ability to deal with certain situations; may be more accepted by other individuals; and, because of these strengths, may be able to be more independent in behavior. The effectiveness of presenting a model or models to a client, then, depends upon how closely the client can identify with the behavior of the model: The closer the identification, the more incentive there will be to acquire the behavior.

Four basic types of models have been used in counseling: filmed, taped, live, and self-as-a-model. In the first three cases the model is presented to the client as an example of the desired behavior. After presenting a taped or filmed model, the counselor uses cue statements that lead the client to a discussion of the model's behavior. During this discussion the counselor can employ verbal reinforcement techniques to shape the client's behavior further in the desired direction. Seldom in counseling is imitative learning used by itself. More often, it is used in conjunction with the technique of shaping.

Live peer models who actually take part in the counseling process usually appear in group counseling. In this case the models are there to be themselves and to share the means they have used to deal with the problems confronting the clients. In this way, the clients can actually engage the models in discussion, and at the same time the counselor can use positive reinforcement in the same way as with a filmed model. In general, live peer modeling appears to be most effective with personal and social problems, and filmed and taped models with more cognitive problems.

Hosford (1980) developed a procedure he refers to as self-as-a-model. "Similar to standard modeling, it relies principally on client imitation of demonstrated examples to promote behavioral change rather than on cognitive mediation of the response contingencies, which is the stimulus for change in self-observation. During the self-as-a-model procedure, clients do not observe instances of their inappropriate behavior as is often the case in self-observation" (1980, p. 469). In the self-as-a-model procedure, the counselor takes a client through the following steps (Hosford & deVisser, 1974):

1. Clients are taught self-monitoring and self-observation skills.
2. Clients develop a list of behaviors they wish to eliminate and/or develop.
3. Clients select specific skills or knowledge they wish to change.
4. Counselor and client make a model audio- or videotape of the target behavior or hierarchy of behaviors.
5. Clients are taught positive self-imagery in order to call forth in their memory the view of themselves engaging in the behavior on the tape.

Hosford (1980) presents evidence of the effectiveness of this procedure with such problems as self-acceptance, interpersonal skills, improving teaching skills, and improving counselor attending behavior. Warner, Valine, Higgins, and McEwen (1980) have found a similar procedure effective in teaching counselor responding behavior.

Contracting

A comparatively recent development in the field of behavioral counseling, particularly in self-development programs, is the use of behavior contracts. Contracting is based on the assumption that it is helpful for a client to specify the behavioral change that is desired. Like other contracts, the behavioral contract is a negotiated agreement between two parties—in this case, between the client and the counselor—in which both parties get something out of the contract and give something to the other individual involved in the contract.

Contracting is a logical extension of behavioral principles, for it establishes reinforcement contingencies for desired behaviors in advance (Dustin & George, 1973). As Mahoney and Thoresen (1974) indicate, these consequences may be either concrete material or social rewards. In the former case, the client, as party to the contract, may deposit some amount of money or other valuables with the counselor and sign a contract that specifies how these reinforcers are to be used. For example, a client who desires to lose weight might deposit 50 dollars with the counselor and agree that for every day he or she consumes only a prescribed number of calories, 50 cents will be returned, and for every violation 50 cents will be lost. Or, a client who wishes to improve school work habits might agree that when school work is completed, her or his teacher and parents will praise the behavior, and when it is not completed, they will either ignore (extinguish) the behavior or criticize (punish) it. In either case, the response consequences of both the desired and undesirable behaviors are specified in advance and agreed to by all parties.

The following list is a summary of the desirable characteristics for effective behavioral contracts cited by Dustin and George (1973) and Mahoney and Thoresen (1974):

1. *Clear expectations.* All requirements of the contract for both parties are stated clearly and objectively. If possible, the expectations and goals should be stated in positive terms.
2. *Level of behavior and consequences.* Both parties to the contract must agree on how much of a certain behavior will lead to how much of a positive consequence. It is very important for these two elements to be in balance.

3. *Monitoring system.* The contract should specify how the parties will determine when the desired behavior has been completed so that the positive consequences can be delivered.
4. *System of sanctions.* Some procedure of penalties for failure to engage in desired behavior must be written into the contract.
5. *Reachable goals.* The contract must be written so that the goals are something the client can achieve. In some cases this means writing one contract that calls for a minimum level of performance. Once that level has been maintained for a period of time, the contract is renegotiated to require a higher level of performance. There must be a clause in the contract that will permit renegotiation downward if the goals have been set too high.
6. *Bonus systems.* Each contract should have a bonus system that rewards a long period of contract compliance by the client with extra payoffs.

Cognitive Learning

Another technique that may be used by counselors following a behavioral model is cognitive learning. In some respects cognitive learning is very similar to contracting and assertiveness training. There may be occasions when the client knows what the desired behavior is, but not how to accomplish the behavior. In such cases it may be appropriate for the counselor to suggest what to do. In essence, this technique involves an oral contract between the client and the counselor. Having agreed on the desired behavior, the client agrees to try what the counselor suggests for a certain period. This simple technique may be very effective in some cases. Like other techniques, it should not be used in a mechanical manner, but as one of several techniques in the process of counseling. The approaches developed under the cognitive/behavioral rubric will be discussed in Chapter 9.

Cover Reinforcement

Cautela and associates have developed a set of procedures "in which behavioral changes are effected by imagining specific behaviors and imagining consequences related to these behaviors" (Groden & Cautela, 1981, p. 177). This procedure involves either pairing an image of the undesired behavior with a second image that is extremely negative, or pairing an image of a desirable behavior with an image of extremely positive consequence. Used in a negative fashion, a person who wants to lose weight might first imagine eating a box of candy and then pair this with an image of getting violently ill. Used in a positive fashion with the same problem, the client might first imagine turning down the box of candy and then pair it with the positive image of receiving all kinds of attention from the opposite sex. As in the technique of desensitization, the images are first used within counseling while the client is in a state of muscle relaxation. Eventually the images will have been paired (classical conditioning) often enough so that the actual behavior outside counseling will produce the paired image. The person in the example will not eat candy either because of the image or thought of getting ill or because of the thought of getting a lot of attention. As Mahoney and Thoresen (1974) point out, the negative imagery is very adversive, although it has been shown to be effective. For this reason, the use of positive covert reinforcement is advisable whenever possible.

The behavioral counselor will probably use several techniques in combination. With some clients the counselor may employ all the techniques at various times during counseling or particular combinations of techniques. Each of the many theorists and practitioners in behavioral counseling has variations not only of the basic techniques described here, but also other techniques. All, however, find their rationale for counseling in the laws of learning discussed in this chapter.

Summary

A wide variety of approaches operate within the framework of behaviorism. This chapter has presented material that most behaviorists could support. Most, for example, have moved away from the extreme position of Skinner. They have, like practitioners of other theories, become more eclectic in their approach.

Many practitioners who do not philosophically agree with the behavioral position find that some behavioral techniques are effective aids in their own counseling. Prospective counselors should not confuse behavioral approaches with strict Skinnerian doctrine, nor should they dismiss any techniques simply because of their association with behaviorism. We believe that behavioral counseling techniques have much to offer counselors. "Considering the promise it has shown in its relatively brief history, there should be considerable optimism with regard to its potential as a tool to further alleviate human suffering" (Groden & Cautela, 1981, p. 179).

References

Bandura, A. (1962). Social learning through imitation. In M. Jones (Ed.), *Nebraska Symposium on Motivation*. Lincoln: University of Nebraska Press.

Bandura, A. (1965). Behavioral modification through modeling procedures. In L. Krasner & L. Ullmann (Eds.), *Research in behavior modification*. New York: Holt, Rinehart and Winston.

Bandura, A. (1969). *Principle of behavior modification*. New York: Holt, Rinehart and Winston.

Bandura, A. (1977). *Social learning theory*. Englewood Cliffs, NJ: Prentice-Hall.

Barclay, J. R. (1980). The revolution in counseling: Some editorial comments. *Personnel and Guidance Journal, 58,* 457.

Belkin, G. S. (1980). *Contemporary psychotherapies*. Chicago: Rand McNally.

Bijou, S. W. (1966). Implications of behavioral science for counseling and guidance. In J. D. Krumboltz (Ed.), *Revolution in counseling: Implication of behavioral science*. Boston: Houghton Mifflin.

Blackham, G. J., & Silberman, A. (1971). *Modification of child behavior*. Belmont, CA: Wadsworth.

Bugg, C. A. (1972). Systematic desensitization: A teaching worth trying. *Personnel and Guidance Journal, 50,* 823–828.

Dollard, J., & Miller, N. E. (1950). *Personality and psychotherapy*. New York: McGraw-Hill.

Dollard, J., & Miller, N. E. (1976). Learning theory psychotherapy. In William S. Sahakian (Ed.), *Psychotherapy & counseling*. Chicago: Rand McNally.

Dustin, R., & George, R. (1973). *Action counseling for behavior change*. New York: Intext.

Groden, G., & Cautela, J. R. (1981). Behavior therapy: A survey of procedures for counselors. *Personnel and Guidance Journal, 60* (3), 175–179.

Homme, L. E. (1965). Perspectives in psychology: XXIV. Control of coverants, the operants of the mind. *Psychological Record, 15,* 501–511.

Hosford, R. E. (1969). Behavioral counseling: A contemporary overview. *The Counseling Psychologist, 1,* 1–33.

Hosford, R. E. (1980). The Cubberley conference and the evolution of observational learning strategies. *Personnel and Guidance Journal,* 467–472.

Hosford, R. E., & deVisser, L. (1974). *Behavioral approaches to counseling: An introduction.* Washington, DC: APGA Press.

Jacobsen, E. (1938). *Progressive relaxation.* Chicago: University of Chicago Press.

Kagen, J. (1963). The choice of models: Conflict and continuity in human behavior. In E. Lloyd-Jones & E. M. Westervelt (Eds.), *Behavioral science and guidance: Proposals and perspectives.* New York: Columbia University Press.

Kazdin, A. E. (1978). *History of behavior modifications: Experimental foundations of contemporary research.* Baltimore: University Park Press.

Krumboltz, J. D. (Ed.). (1966). *Revolution in counseling.* Boston: Houghton Mifflin.

Krumboltz, J. D. (1967). Changing the behavior of behavior changers. *Counselor Education and Supervision, 46* (6), 222–229.

Krumboltz, J. D., & Thoresen, C. E. (1969). *Behavioral counseling: Cases and techniques.* New York: Holt, Rinehart and Winston.

Krumboltz, J. D., & Thoresen, C. E. (1976). *Counseling methods.* New York: Holt, Rinehart and Winston.

Lazarus, A. A. (1972). *Clinical behavior therapy.* New York: Brunner/Mazel.

Mahoney, N. J., & Thoresen, C. E. (1974). *Self-control: Power to the person.* Monterey, CA: Brooks-Cole.

Marquis, J. D. (1972). An expedient model for behavior therapy. In A. A. Lazarus (Ed.), *Clinical behavior therapy.* New York: Brunner/Mazel.

Michael, J., & Meyerson, L. (1962). A behavioral approach to counseling and guidance. *Harvard Educational Review,* 382–402.

Miller, N. E., & Dollard, J. (1941). *Social learning and imitation.* New Haven: Yale University Press.

Mowrer, O. H. (1960). *Learning theory and the symbolic processes.* New York: John Wiley and Sons.

Osgood, C. E. (1953). *Method and theory in experimental psychology.* New York: Oxford University Press.

Pepinsky, H. B., & Pepinsky, P. N. (1954). *Counseling: Theory and practice.* New York: Ronald Press.

Premack, D. (1965). Reinforcement theory. In D. Levine (Ed.), *Nebraska Symposium on Motivation.* Lincoln: University of Nebraska Press. (pp. 123–180).

Rotter, J. B. (1962). *Some implications of a social learning theory for the practice of psychotherapy.* Mimeographed paper.

Rotter, J. B. (1964). *Clinical psychology.* Englewood Cliffs, NJ: Prentice-Hall.

Salter, A. (1949). *Conditioned reflex therapy.* New York: Creative Age Press.

Shoben, E. J. (1949). Psychotherapy as a problem in learning theory. *Psychological Bulletin, 46,* 366–392.

Skinner, B. F. (1938). *The behavior of organisms.* New York: Appleton-Century-Crofts.

Skinner, B. F. (1953). *Science and human behavior.* New York: Macmillan.

Skinner, B. F. (1971). *Beyond freedom and dignity.* New York: Knopf.

Stampfl, T. G. (1961). Implosive therapy: A learning theory derived psychodynamic therapeutic technique. In P. Labarba & A. Devt (Eds.) *Critical issues in clinical psychology.* New York: Academic Press.

Warner, R., Valine, W., Higgins, E., & McEwen, M. (1980). An investigation of two approaches to prepracticum training for counselors. *Journal of Counseling Services, 3,* 31–36.

Watson, J. B., & Rayner, R. (1920). Conditioned emotional reaction. *Journal of Experimental Psychology, 3*(1), 1–14.

Wilson, G. Terence. (1989). Behavior therapy. In Raymond J. Corsini and Danny Wedding, *Current psychotherapies* (4th ed.). Itasca, IL: F. E. Peacock.

Wolpe, J. (1958). *Psychotherapy by reciprocal inhibition.* Stanford: Stanford University Press.

Wolpe, J. (1969). *The practice of behavior therapy.* New York: Pergamon.

Wolpe, J., & Lazarus, A. A. (1966). *Behavior therapy techniques.* New York: Pergamon.

Chapter *9*

Cognitive-Behavioral Approaches to Counseling

In the days when psychology was dominated by behaviorism as represented by B. F. Skinner and Clark Hull, the behaviorists made noncognitive learning the cornerstone of their theories (Hunt, 1988). The behaviorists rejected conscious reasoning as having anything to do with learning in a serious scientific way. The bonding of stimuli to responses was assumed to occur as a result of experiences with stimulus-response-reward sequences and not to depend on conscious reasoning. Concepts such as "planning" and "goal directed reasoning" were considered subjective and unscientific (Hunt, 1988, p. 94).

In what was his last public statement before his death, B. F. Skinner staunchly defended the behavioral position. In the keynote address to the convention of the American Psychological Association, delivered days before his death, he declared that "because of its similarity to the vernacular, cognitive psychology was easy to understand and the so-called cognitive revolution was for a time successful. . . . Cognitive psychology was left as the scientific companion of a profession and as the scientific underpinning of educational, clinical, developmental, social and many other fields of psychology. The help it has given them has not been conspicuous" (Skinner, 1990, p. 1210).

Despite Skinner's valedictory condemnation, cognitive psychology has made significant progress over the past four or five decades. In the areas of information processing, linguistics and psycholinguistics, and in the related areas of macrocognition and microcognition, progress has been made. Cognitive psychologists have studied and contributed to our understanding of schematic reasoning and memory as well as the application of cognitive factors in decision making. Strategies in the realm of noncognitive behavior have also been examined with positive results (Hunt, 1988).

Applications of cognitive psychology to the realm of intervention in human behavior is predicated on the notion that planned and purposive behavior does take place in human beings, that consciousness with respect to those goal-directed activities is relevant and that language and memory play an important part in the process of self-instruction and self-direction. In general then, psychologists interested in intervention in human behavior who were dissatisfied with the classical S-R models and who were not attracted to the psychodynamic models, turned more and more to the research which dealt with the mediation of clinically relevant constructs (Dobson, 1988). Conditioning in this context is perceived to be cognitively mediated. Conditioning also includes anticipatory responses. And if the latter is true it is possible to pause between stimulus and response and effect behavior by utilizing the cognitive realm. Out of these concepts there emerged an approach to counseling and psychotherapy that continues to evolve and thrive at the present time under the rubric of cognitive behaviorism.

Historical Antecedents of Cognitive-Behavioral Counseling

Cognitive-behavioral counseling draws upon the implications of developments in the emerging field of cognitive science. While the direct application of research data from science to practice may be sometimes difficult to demonstrate, nevertheless, the impressive developments in cognitive science provide an exciting and promising underpinning to the work of the cognitive-behavioral practitioners.

Cognitive science has been described as "a new and exciting interdisciplinary movement of paradigmatic proportions" (Mahoney & Lyddon, 1988, p. 191). It calls upon the related disciplines of cognitive psychology, linguistics, computer science, psychobiology, anthropology, and philosophy to inform its research. This pooling of ideas and efforts has led to the emergence of cognitive science "as a broad approach to studying knowing systems and processes" (Mahoney & Lyddon, 1988, p. 191). Since self-knowledge and knowledge of the context of human behavior is at the heart of cognitive-behavioral approaches to intervention, it was only natural that those practitioners linked to cognitive science and, in particular, cognitive psychology, provide the philosophical and psychological basis to their approach to treatment.

What they discovered was a philosophical base that remained squarely in the loop of naturalist, logical positivist approaches to science. The demand for experimental rigor remained at the heart of cognitive psychology. The latter was regarded as an extension of behaviorism rather than as a departure from the basic research concerns of behavioral psychology. The development of new technology and alternate ways of examining old problems led to excursions into what had long been labelled the "black box," concern with what happens inside the organism as behavior unfolds and learning takes place. "This renewed interest in cognition served to fuel a trend in behavioral psychology generally characterized as a shift from a behavioral/associationistic to a cognitive/mediational perspective" (Mahoney & Lyddon, 1988, p. 195).

While the movement to open the so-called "black box" was greeted with continued criticism by B. F. Skinner and others, it became increasingly clear that evidence was being developed, methodologies emerging, that made it possible to study and interpret the private events that occurred internal to the behaving organism.

The development of Bandura's social learning theory was a significant step forward in the departure from a strictly behavioral interpretation of learning and the approach to modify behavior. Bandura's approach took into account the involvement of cognitive-symbolic mechanisms in the acquisition of knowledge and in subsequent behavior. Bandura endorsed "an interactional reciprocity between person and environment and (this) marked a pivotal shift from exclusive environmental determinism" (Mahoney & Lyddon, 1988, p. 197).

The work of the cognitive psychologists led to a significant body of work in the area of self-control. The research on this dimension led to the acceptance of the principle inherent in social learning theory that an intrapersonal process was present which helped to determine human behavior, that this process was consistent with newer conceptions of learning, and that the introduction of more cognitive approaches to counseling and psychotherapy was the next logical step.

"In fact," as Aaron Beck notes, "there appears to be a kind of convergent evolution of concepts from the cognitive model of psychotherapy and those of cognitive psychology" (Beck, 1991, p. 369). In his article summarizing progress in cognitive therapy over the past 30 years, Beck points to the remarkable progress that has been made in this merging of theory and practice. Essentially what has occurred in this period of time has been the acceptance of the need to incorporate a mediational approach to attempt to account for some human behavior, an agreement that the psychodynamic approach was too far removed from classical psychology to provide the insights necessary to understand the mediational process, that cognitive intervention had practical applications in treating pathologies that were primarily disturbances in thought processes such as obsessional behavior on interactive cognitive and affective disorders such as depression, and that within cognitive psychology itself information-processing models were increasingly useful in understanding the mediational processes of illness (Dobson, 1988).

As Beck has observed, his call "for the admission of cognitive theory into the therapeutic arena" attracted a number of practitioners to identify with this approach to treatment including Albert Ellis, Cantela, Michael J. Mahoney, and Meichenbaum (Beck, 1991, p. 368). As a matter of fact, Albert Ellis, whose rational-emotive therapy is dealt with elsewhere in this book, lamented as only he can, that he had not been given sufficient credit for his seminal contributions to the cognitive-behavioral approach to therapy. He claimed that he was there first and perhaps he was, although the specific linkages to cognitive psychology came much later (Dryden, 1990).

General Principles of Cognitive-Behavioral Approaches

As in many efforts in applied psychology, there is sometimes difficulty in demonstrating a direct relationship between theory and application. This has always been true in dealing with various approaches to behavior modification. In that approach a relationship between the principles of learning, whether classical conditioning or Skinnerian operant conditioning, has been demonstrated, more or less. This is also true of the cognitive-behavioral approaches. Nevertheless, we shall attempt to delineate a series of general principles that describe practice in this area and which purport to derive from cognitive psychology. The following are largely derived from the writings of Aaron Beck (1976, 1991).

1. Human beings are essentially information-processing organisms. They ingest data, they generate data, and they appraise data.
2. Human beings have feelings and thoughts that are continuously influencing each other. This influence is manifested in the behavior of the individual and can be identified in the present tense.
3. The thinking of human beings may be altered by controlled intervention in their thought processes.
4. Human beings are subject to cognitive distortions through their early learning experiences. Cultural influences, feedback, and role-modeling play important parts in the acquisition of these cognitive distortions.
5. Intervention in altering the cognitive distortions utilizes the ability of the client to solve problems in the context of a collaborative process between counselor and client. The focus of the intervention is in the present.
6. Dealing with distortions in thought processes makes it unnecessary to become involved in such psychodynamic issues as transference and countertransference. Resistance is conceived of in conscious terms, rather than in terms of unconscious avoidance of the problem.
7. Clearly the emphasis in cognitive-behavioral approaches is on consciousness.
8. Cognitive counseling and psychotherapy has an active, structural focus. The ground rules are always clear, and ambiguity is minimized.
9. Cognitive counseling and therapy is goal directed and problem solving in nature. The goals are always specified as part of the process.
10. Cognitive counseling and psychotherapy are time-limited or, at least, short-term in nature.
11. The focus of cognitive counseling and therapy is on thinking. Feelings are dealt with as they are influenced by thoughts.
12. Cognitive counseling and therapy make use of outside therapeutic hour behavior. Homework assignments in the form of specific behaviors or thought processes are common.
13. Constant feedback is an integral part of cognitive-behavioral approaches to counseling and psychotherapy.

It is clear from this exposition of principles that the "cognitive approaches are based on the principle that the particular meanings which we attach to events and the thought patterns that persist in our minds determine our emotional reactions" (Weinrath, 1988). The latter, of course, affects our behavior and helps to determine the nature of discomfort, suffering, or pathology that exists. Indeed, Beck describes cognitive therapy as "based on a view of psychopathology that stipulates that people's excessive affect and dysfunctional behavior is due to excessive and inappropriate ways of interpreting their experiences" (Weinrath, 1988, p. 160).

It is in the context of these observations that the principles presented in this section merged to form the basis for the cognitive-behavioral approaches to treatment.

Variations of Cognitive-Behavioral Approaches to Treatment

The approach to treatment derived from cognitive psychology is complex and varied. Dobson (1988) presents a chronology of cognitive-behavioral therapies beginning in 1962 with Albert Ellis's rational-emotive therapy and ending with the Guidana and Liotti contribution of structural psychotherapy in 1983. Altogether Dobson presents a dozen approaches that have emerged in the 20-year period between 1962 and 1983. He classifies them as cognitive restructuring, coping skills therapies, or problem-solving therapies (Dobson, 1988).

In the cognitive restructuring group he lists Albert Ellis's rational-emotive theory, Beck's cognitive therapy, Meichenbaum's self-instructional training, Maultsby's rational behavior therapy, and Guidano and Liotti's structural psychotherapy.

In the coping skills realm, Dobson includes Meichenbaum's stress inoculation training, Goldfried's systematic rational restructuring, and Suinn and Richardson's anxiety-management training.

In the problem-solving therapies, Dobson includes D'Zurella and Goldfried's problem-solving therapy, Spivack and Shures's approach to the same name, Mahoney's personal science, and Rehms's self-control therapy (Dobson, 1988).

Mahoney and Lyddon (1988) present their own compendium of cognitive-behavioral approaches which overlaps with Dobson's but is a somewhat more extensive list of 20 approaches that add such conceptions as Kelly's personal construct therapy, Frankl's logotherapy, Lazarus's multimodal therapy, Tosi and Eshbough's rational stage directed therapy, Wessler's integrated cognitive behavior therapy, Kruglanski and Jaffe's lay epistemic therapy, Suarez's neo-cognitive therapy, Leva's Piagetian therapy, Werner's cognitive-experiential therapy, Ivey's developmental therapy, Werner's humanistic cognitive therapy, and Johnson's characterological transformation (Mahoney & Lyddon, 1988, p. 198).

Since the appearance of Ellis's work in the early 1960s, the proliferation of approaches in this arena seems monumental. In addition, there have been acknowledgments of the cognitive roots of a variety of "traditional" psychotherapies. "Refrained through the currently popular metaphors of cognitive psychology, Freud, Adler, Jung, Horney, Sullivan and others similarly appear to have anticipated many contemporary thematic developments in counseling research and theory" (Mahoney & Lyddon, 1988, p. 197). This obviously includes the current principles in cognitive psychology and cognitive behavioral approaches. Indeed, a developing academic sport is to return to Freud's original papers and attempt to discover seminal ideas that relate to current practice in a variety of modalities including the cognitive-behavioral approach.

What is also obvious in this recounting of the varieties of cognitive-behavioral approaches is the proliferation of the varieties of these conceptions of intervention. Most of them follow the rational approach to intervention and may be subsumed within the principles outlined in the previous section. However, a careful reading of the titles of the approaches will reveal a developing trend in this realm toward the incorporation of a humanist approach, partially based on the cognitive notion of anticipatory responses. Mahoney and Lyddon (1988) refer to this complex of approaches as "constructionist." We shall have more to say about this later in the chapter.

There are too many individual approaches to discuss all of them. Using Dobson's (1988) classification system we have selected two approaches from the cognitive restructuring realm, namely, Maultsby's rational behavior therapy and Beck's cognitive therapy. (We will discuss Ellis's rational-emotive therapy in Chapter 10.)

In addition, we will have a brief look at Meichenbaum's stress inoculation training under the coping skills rubric and Mahoney's personal science in the realm of problem-solving therapies.

Rational Behavior Therapy

Maxie Maultsby's book *Rational Behavior Therapy* (RBT) was published in 1984 and owes a great deal in its conception to Albert Ellis and rational-emotive therapy (RET). Maultsby credits a number of sources for the origins of his ideas. He credits his basic training in clinical psychiatry, his study of neuropsychology, and his exposure to learning theory covering the range from classical conditioning through operant conditioning to the applications of these theories to practice in behavior modification. In addition, exposure to ideas in psychosomatic medicine helped to orient him to mind-body connections. Finally, he acknowledges his debt to Albert Ellis and rational-emotive therapy (Maultsby, 1984).

His work bears a remarkable resemblance to Ellis's concepts. For example, while he does not identify as a source of difficulty "a set of basic irrational beliefs" as does Ellis, he does talk about "self-defeating cognitive habits" that Dobson describes as bearing "a remarkable resemblance to Ellis' notion of absolutistic thinking" (Dobson, 1988, p. 15). There are other examples that might be cited relative to the similarities between RET (Ellis) and RBT (Maultsby). Both RET and RBT stress the need to monitor thinking and similarly to RET approaches, RBT supports the use of *emotive imaging, behavioral practice,* and *realization* methods (Dobson, 1988).

Rational behavior therapy does offer some unique blending of theory and practice. Because of his interest in neuropsychology, Maultsby attempts to integrate knowledge about brain function and psychotherapy. Just as the attempts to accomplish this task in the realm of cognitive assessment have only been partially successful, so too with Maultsby's attempt. It is interesting, provocative, but inconclusive at the present time (Maultsby, 1984).

He does introduce a number of unique descriptive themes, which are essentially within the framework of the principles of cognitive behavior outlined earlier. For example, "camera check of perceptions" is described as a "self help maneuver in RBT that helps ensure that what seems real to people objectively fits the obvious facts of the situation" (Maultsby, 1984, p. 8).

Dobson, in an amusing observation notes that "perhaps the most notable similarity between Maultsby and Ellis' approaches is the confidence with which they are both presented" alluding to the self-congratulatory stance frequently adopted by Ellis and, apparently, emulated by Maultsby (Dobson, 1988, p. 16).

With some modest differences in philosophical and theoretical antecedents, Maultsby's RBT is clearly a derivative of Albert Ellis's rational-emotive therapy (see Chapter 10).

Aaron Beck's Cognitive Therapy

Another approach classified in the realm of cognitive restructuring is Aaron Beck's cognitive therapy. In his latest assessment of the impact of cognitive therapy, Beck concluded that this approach to treatment was "no longer fledgling and has demonstrated its capacity to fly under its own power" (Beck, 1991, p. 374). As we have indicated earlier, "cognitive therapy is based on a theory of personality which maintains that how one thinks largely determines how one feels and behaves" (Beck & Weishaar, 1989, p. 285).

Beck's approach to personality development emphasizes the role of idiosyncratic thinking in the development of individual behavior patterns. Unique cognitive structuring results in the individual approach to problem solving. Beliefs, values, and experience lead to cognitive structures labeled "schemas," which Beck notes may be either adaptive or dysfunctional. These schemas help determine the response of the individuals to stress and when they are dysfunctional or maladaptive, the process may lead to the development of pathology. When pathology occurs, "cognitive distortions" are in evidence and manifest themselves in many ways that lead the individual to make cognitive "errors" including drawing arbitrary inferences, selectively responding to events, overgeneralizing, blowing incidents out of proportion, or, conversely, ignoring important events and concerns, referential thinking, and categorizing behaviors in extremes (Beck & Weishaar, 1989).

Intervention consists of establishing a reasonable working relationship with the client, applying the principles outlined earlier in the chapter and concentrating on the three fundamental concepts in cognitive therapy, namely, collaborative empiricism, Socratic dialogue, and guided discovery (Beck & Weishaar, 1989).

Collaborative empiricism was the relationship to test the validity of the clients' own observations. Socratic dialogue is the method of questioning employed by the therapist in the process of defining problems, identifying thoughts and assumptions, discerning the meaning of events and experiences for the client, and assessment of those events and ideas (Beck & Weishaar, 1989).

Treatment involves establishing and designing specific learning experiences that teach the client "to monitor automatic thoughts," to mediate among cognitive thoughts, affect, and behavior, to be alert to and test automatic thinking, to reduce distorted cognitions, and to discern the underlying reasons for cognitive vulnerability (Dobson, 1988, p. 18).

In his latest assessment of his work Beck reports that the empirical assessment of his work, while applied fairly narrowly to depressed patients, nevertheless, provides an optimistic assessment of cognitive therapy. "Clinical studies indicate the utility of cognitive therapy as a help in a wide variety of disorders, particularly depression and the anxiety disorders" (Beck, 1991, p. 274). We concur in that assessment.

Stress Inoculation Training: Meichenbaum

Under the category of coping skills therapies is Meichenbaum's *stress inoculation training*. Meichenbaum has also developed an approach categorized under the cognitive restructuring rubric called *self-instructional training*.

Essentially, stress inoculation training is a coping skills treatment program based on a multicomponent model. It is related to other approaches to stress management and control and makes the assumption that the acquisition of coping skills in stress management leads to an "inoculation against uncontrollable stress" (Dobson, 1988, p. 23).

Meichenbaum proposed a three-stage approach that included deductive training in stage one to provide the client with a base of understanding of the issues, teaching coping skills including realization exercises and coping self-statements in stage two, and a behavioral rehearsal in stage three (Dobson, 1988). Stress inoculation training is prototypical of many programs designed to develop coping skills and is favorably regarded by those who have used it.

Personal Science: Mahoney

As an example of a problem-solving technique we turn to the personal science approach of Mahoney. This approach is designed to teach individuals approaches to resolve problem situations. Each client becomes his own personal scientist in the quest to solve problems. Mahoney describes seven basic elements in the orderly sequence SCIENCE (Dobson, 1988, p. 25).

S   Specify general problem area
C   Collect data
I   Identify patterns or sources
E   Examine options
N   Narrow and experiment
C   Compare data
E   Extend, revise, and replace

The process provides an opportunity to teach the client to be responsible for self-direction in the solution of the problem and is provided to the client during the early stages of this approach. Gradually the client assumes more responsibility. While the personal science paradigm has not generated much research interest or even enthusiasm among users, it remains a reasonable example of cognitive approaches within the problem-solving realm.

New Directions in Cognitive-Behavioral Approaches

In their seminal article in *The Counseling Psychologist,* Mahoney and Lyddon imply very clearly that cognitive-behavioral approaches have progressed far beyond the rational reaction to behavioral modification and psychodynamics. They point out that the rational reign though sovereign at the present time, may be challenged by a new trend in cognitive-behavioral thought, namely, the concept of constructivism (Mahoney & Lyddon, 1988).

Constructivism is a new trend in cognitive-behavioral thinking that challenges the rational conception of the world. "Strictly rationalist theorists—exemplified by Albert Ellis and orthodox-rational-emotive therapy—argue for the causal supremacy of explicit beliefs about self and the world . . . For the extreme rationalist, disorder and irrationality are synonymous" (Mahoney & Lyddon, 1988, p. 212). The constructivists challenge this view of realism and rationalism and have adopted a more relativistic viewpoint that incorporates emotional and behavioral components along with the cognitive domain. Constructionists place more emphasis on feeling and behavior than do the rationalists who focus on thought as the singular most important factor in human endeavors. "It is thus the rationalistic cognitivists who place themselves at the cognitive apex of a thought-feeling-behavior triangle. The constructionists, on the other hand, head for the middle ground of the triangle and suggest that these three categories—thought, feeling, and behavior, represent a questionable legacy" (Mahoney & Lyddon, 1988, p. 215).

The constructionists represent a more holistic point of view among the cognitive therapists and believe in the fusing of mind/body constructs and in the primary motivational role played by emotion. Consequently, the conception of intervention also takes on a more holistic view and goes beyond reliance on insight into the irrational and didactic instruction and direction as the primary force of the therapeutic process. Rather, the constructionists hold that insight into irrational behavior must be accompanied by emotional and behavioral integration and that the therapeutic relationship "entails a safe, caring, and intense context in and from which the client can explore and develop relationships with self and world" (Mahoney & Lyddon, 1988, p. 219).

What is most interesting is that this variation in cognitive-behavioral approaches to treatment contains elements that are consistent with the views of some existential and some ego counseling views. It may bear the fruit of providing a theoretical basis for a convergent approach to intervention that might include elements from a variety of viewpoints. At this point in the development of the constructionist view, as Mahoney and Lyddon note, the constructionists themselves constitute a group of diverse thinkers and practitioners and that "out of their diversity have emerged a host of novel techniques for assessing individual phenomenologies, life histories, self-concept relationship qualities and dynamics and a range of cognitive processes" (1988, pp. 222–233). The developments in this "new wave" of cognitive-behavioral approaches to treatment is well worth watching for future developments.

Summary

We have examined the emergence of cognitive-behavioral approaches to counseling and psychotherapy over the past quarter of a century and, particularly, in the last decade and a half. We have identified this approach to clinical services as a reaction to the strict behaviorism that preceded it, and we noted B. F. Skinner's valedictory rejection of consciousness as a valid scientific focus for psychology.

Despite Skinner's criticism, the cognitive-behaviorists have identified a complex of findings in cognitive science in general and in cognitive psychology in particular, to provide the theoretical underpinnings of their departure from behaviorism both theoretically and practically. Opening the "black box" gave rise to an acceptance of the ideas of cognitive mediation as a focus for intervention. There merged, at first, a set of rational principles of cognitive-behavioral approaches to intervention that generally were followed by practitioners in the field. Pioneers abound, but the work of Albert Ellis, Aaron Beck, and D. Meichenbaum stand out.

We described a variety of approaches to cognitive-behavioral treatment among Dobson's classification system that categorized approaches as cognitive restructuring, coping skills, and problem solving in nature. We also pointed out, after Mahoney and Lyddon, that there are, legitimately, almost two dozen approaches that may be categorized as within the cognitive-behavioral domain, ranging from the work of George Kelly, Victor Frankl, and Albert Ellis in the mid-1950s and early 1960s to the work of Weiner, Werner, and Ivey in the mid-1980s.

We presented brief summaries of a few approaches to cognitive-behavioral counseling and psychotherapy including rational behavior therapy (Maultsby), cognitive therapy (Beck), stress inoculation training (Meichenbaum), and personal science (Mahoney). We are devoting a separate chapter to the rational-emotive therapy of Albert Ellis (see Chapter 10).

Finally, we presented a brief description of new directives in cognitive-behavioral approaches and, utilizing Mahoney and Lyddon's configuration, concluded with a discussion of constructionist approaches, which have evolved from the dominant rational models to the adoption of a new set of philosophical assumptions and the beginning of a move toward a more holistic approach.

Cognitive-behavioral approaches have been demonstrated to be empirically effective in the treatment of clinical depression and anxiety disorders. There is anecdotal evidence of the effectiveness of this technique in the development of skills, decision making, stress management, and problem solving. Some adherents utilize the principles and procedures with all manner of difficulties and pathologies. There is also an admirable attempt to link cognitive-behavioral approaches with theoretical developments in cognitive psychology and, more recently, with neuropsychology, developmental psychology, and social psychology.

Cognitive-behavioral approaches are among the most promising developments in therapeutic intervention in the past 25 years. They have the potential of blending science and practice and are well worth pursuing as options in intervention.

References

Beck, A. T. (1976). *Cognitive therapy and the emotional disorders.* New York: International Universities Press.

Beck, A. T. (1991). Cognitive therapy: A 30 year retrospective. *American Psychologist, 26*(4), 368–375.

Beck, A. T., & Weishaar, M. (1989). Cognitive therapy. In R. J. Corsini & D. Wedding, *Current psychotherapies* (4th ed.). Itasca, IL: F. E. Peacock.

Dobson, K. S. (Ed.). (1988). *Handbook of cognitive-behavioral therapies.* New York: Guilford.

Dryden, W. (1990). Albert Ellis: An efficient and passionate life. In P. P. Heppner, *Pioneers in counseling and development.* Alexandria, VA: American Association for Counseling and Development.

Hunt, E. (1988). Cognitive psychology. In E. R. Hilgard (Ed.), *Fifty years of psychology: Essays in honor of Floyd Ruch.* Boston: Scott Foresman.

Mahoney, M. J., & Lyddon, W. J. (1988). Recent developments in cognitive approaches to counseling and psychotherapy. *The Counseling Psychologist, 16*(2), 190–234.

Maultsby, M. C. (1984). *Rational behavior therapy.* Englewood Cliffs, NJ: Prentice Hall.

Meichenbaum, D. (1977). *Cognitive-behavior modification.* New York: Plenum.

Skinner, B. F. (1990). Can psychology be a science of the mind? *American Psychologist, 45*(11), 1206–1210.

Weinrath, S. G. (1988). Cognitive therapist: A dialogue with Aaron Beck. *Journal of Counseling and Development, 67.*

Rational-Emotive Therapy

Albert Ellis considers himself and the approach he introduced, rational-emotive therapy (RET), as the forerunners of cognitive-behavior therapy. Indeed, he is quoted as saying that he would like people to accept the fact that he "was the main pioneering cognitive behavioral theorist and therapist, that [he] fought hard to get cognition accepted in psychotherapy, and that largely as a result of [his] efforts, it has finally been accepted, albeit a little belatedly" (Dryden, 1990, p. 70).

Coming from anyone else, the statement might be regarded as tending toward excess. Certainly, at first blush, people might be put off by the flamboyant and, sometimes, abrasive quality of the personality of Albert Ellis. His harsh-sounding flat voice and his constant repetition of his themes, while setting some of them to song and singing them in public, might make Ellis an object of derision and scorn. However, reject his ideas at your peril. He is as important as he says he is. His approach, painstakingly developed over several decades, is a legitimate approach to behavior change through counseling intervention. The elements of his system indeed reflect many of the principles of cognitive-behavioral approaches, and they also encompass many of the ideas of ego counseling approaches to therapy.

As we shall see, RET is more than cognitive-behavioral in its orientation and extends far beyond the parameters imposed by ego counseling. It includes cognitive approaches to separate the rational from the irrational. It utilizes emotive-evocative approaches to help clients highlight choices in contrast to imperatives. RET also has the option to utilize classical behavioral approaches to aid clients reduce dysfunctional behavior. Above all, it is a highly imaginative, interpretive approach to treatment that is functional, practical, and theoretically sound (Greiger & Boyd, 1980).

Rational-emotive therapy (RET), as originally developed by Albert Ellis, is an approach to counseling that is continuing to evolve. Ellis states, that "although RET did emphasize (and perhaps overemphasized) cognitive disputing in its early years, as my own experience with RET increased and as other therapists all over the world began to employ it and revise and add to its procedures, our joint efforts produced a good many other cognitive (not to mention emotive and behavioral) procedures" (1977, p. 73). This evolution has moved Ellis to refer to his approach as a cognitive-behavior approach. Roush (1984) reports that rational-emotive therapy has been shown to be effective with a wide variety of individuals including young people.

Ellis received his doctorate from Columbia University and has served on the faculties of Rutgers and New York University. Originally trained as a marriage and family therapist, he began his practice as a classic psychoanalyst in the 1940s. In the course of private practice, he began to question this approach, finding that client insight did not necessarily lead to changes in behavior. Subsequently he began to take on a more active role, incorporating into his therapy advice, homework, bibliotherapy, behavior principles, and direct confrontations. By 1955, he had rejected psychoanalytic principles entirely and was concentrating on changing clients' behaviors by confronting them with what he termed their irrational beliefs and persuading them to adopt a rational thought process. In 1959, he started the Institute for Rational Living in New York City and now operates a state-approved training program called the Institute for Advanced Study in Rational Psycho-therapy. The Institute for RET is designed primarily for the training of therapists and operates a clinic that is open to the public (Weinrach, 1980). Ellis also operates the Institute for Rational Living, which is more of a general educational operation designed to provide information to new professionals. Although others, such as Maultsby at the University of Kentucky, have developed training programs, the Ellis-operated institutes remain the major training locations for those wishing advanced training in RET procedures.

Personality Development

Ellis (1962) contends that people have an inherent capacity to act either rationally or irrationally. The former leads to effective behavior and a productive life-style; the latter leads to unhappiness and a nonproductive life-style. RET goes "back to the philosophic views of Epictegus, Marcus, Aurclins, and the Stoics, and also later Spinoza and Russell" (Ellis, 1973a, p. 155). Thus, it is largely a rational, intellectual approach. Ellis believes that thinking and emotions are closely interrelated: "among adult humans raised in a social culture, thinking and emoting are so closely interrelated that they usually accompany each other . . . (they operate in circular fashion) so that one's thinking becomes one's emotion and emoting becomes one's thought" (1958, p. 36). Because humans are largely verbal animals, this thinking and emoting take the form of self-talk, and this self-talk directs a person's behavior in either rational or irrational directions.

Because Ellis focuses on the development of maladaptive behavior, it is difficult to discuss his concepts of normal development except at a superficial level. Essentially, Ellis's position is that a person is born with the "powerful disposition to be self-preserving and pleasure-producing . . . and to actualize some of his potentials [but] he also has exceptionally potent propensities to be self-destructive, to be a short-range hedonist . . . and to avoid actualizing his potentials for growth" (1973a, p. 171). These bipolar tendencies exist in all people, but each person has inherent tendencies in one direction or the other.

Ellis also viewed people as extremely gullible and suggestible. This suggestibility is greatest during childhood. Because children are social beings with a basic need for love and attention, they quickly learn behaviors designed to elicit responses from those around them. In the course of this learning, children begin to behave in ways that are pleasing to others because that is what brings them the love and attention they need. Soon children evaluate themselves on the basis of what others say. To a certain extent this is necessary, for children have to exist in a world with other people, but Ellis maintains that "emotional disturbance is almost always associated with the individual's caring too much about what others think of him" (1973a, p. 176). Emotionally mature people are able to maintain a fine balance between caring about what they themselves feel and caring about others' evaluations. The degree to which a child's interactions with parents and significant others encourage the development of this behavior will have a direct bearing on the degree to which the child develops rational or irrational patterns of thinking. Ellis believes this process is best explained through a principle he calls ABC. He contends that whenever an event (A) occurs and is followed by some unpleasant consequence (C), people have two possible ways of thinking (B): rational or irrational. First, they generally convince themselves of a reasonable, sane, or rational belief (rB) such as "I do not like this event (A). I wish it had not occurred. I feel sorry, angry, and frustrated because it did." If people keep this rational belief they probably will do something in a realistic way that will prevent the event from recurring. This is the procedure that occurs if optimum functioning is to be obtained (Ellis, 1973a).

Most often, however, when people are upset by (C) they convince themselves of a second set of beliefs that is inappropriate and irrational (iB) such as "I can't stand this event, it is awful, it shouldn't have happened. I am worthless for letting it happen, and you are terrible for doing it to me" (Ellis, 1973a). These beliefs are inappropriate because:

1. They cannot be validated or disproven.
2. They lead to needlessly unpleasant feelings such as anxiety.
3. They prevent the person from going back to the event (A) and changing or resolving it (Ellis, 1973a).

Ellis (1973a) maintains that these irrational beliefs are magical and impossible to validate because (1) people can stand the unpleasant event (A) even though they might not like it; (2) it is not awful, for awful has no real meaning, although it may be inconvenient or unbeneficial; (3) by holding that the event should not have occurred people are playing God, in that whatever they want not to exist should not exist; and (4) by stating that they are worthless because they could not stop the event, people are stating that they should be able to control the universe and that anyone who cannot is obviously worthless.

It is this second set of beliefs (iB) that Ellis believes is most often reinforced as people develop. All the ways in which parents, schools, and other people and institutions make children feel worthless furnish proof for Ellis's contention. Being made to feel worthless reinforces children's irrational belief systems. Thus, even though "man has vast untapped resources for the growth of his potential" (Ellis, 1973a, p. 175), it is most often people's potential for irrational thinking that is reinforced.

Most people, then, develop personalities that are composed of both belief systems. Those who operate effectively do so most of the time on the basis of their rational (rB) belief system; those who experience difficulty are usually operating on the basis of their irrational (iB) belief system.

Maladaptive Behavior

"RET hypothesizes . . . that individuals suffer emotional disturbance as a result of reindoctrinating themselves over and over with certain basic irrational ideas related to absolutistic and catastrophic thinking" (Lawrence & Huber, 1982, p. 211). In Ellis's view, "human beings are the kind of animals who, when raised in any society similar to our own, tend to fall victim to several major fallacious ideas" (1972, p. 220). These irrational ideas become ingrained or imprinted at an early age before "later and more rational modes of thinking [are] given a chance to gain a foothold" (Ellis, 1972, p. 22). Once irrational ideas are part of the belief system, people continue to reindoctrinate themselves through self-talk and thereby continue to behave in inappropriate ways.

Ellis postulates that there are eleven "major illogical and irrational ideas [that] are presently ubiquitous in Western civilization and [that] would seem inevitably to lead to widespread neurosis" (1962, p. 61). These eleven ideas, originally published in 1962 in *Reason and Emotion in Psychotherapy,* "have been made into about twenty different tests of irrationality and about two hundred studies have correlated scores on these tests with various kinds of emotional disturbance" (Ellis, 1984, p. 266). The eleven ideas are as follows:

   1. *It is absolutely essential for an individual to be loved or approved by every significant person in his or her environment.* Although it is desirable for individuals to be loved, the idea is irrational because it is impossible to be loved or approved by everyone, and striving to attain the goal leads to behavior that is not self-directing.
   2. *It is necessary that each individual be completely competent, adequate, and achieving in all areas if the individual is to be worthwhile.* It is impossible for any individual to be competent in every endeavor, and an individual who feels she or he must be is doomed to a sense of failure. Such an idea also leads a person to view every situation in competitive terms. The individual strives to outdo others rather than simply enjoying the activity itself.
   3. *Some people are bad, wicked, or villainous and these people should be blamed and punished.* This idea is irrational because everyone makes mistakes. These mistakes are a result of stupidity, ignorance, or emotional unbalance, not of someone's being a certain way. Furthermore, blame and punishment are not effective ways of changing behavior. The rational idea is to admit that everyone makes mistakes and that making mistakes does not make anyone worthless. The objective should be to correct the mistake.
   4. *It is terrible and catastrophic when things are not the way an individual wants them to be.* The reality of life is such that not all situations are as people would like. This reality

may be unpleasant or bothersome, but is not a catastrophe. Treating an event as a catastrophe does not change the situation; it only makes people feel worse. If a person does not like something, she or he can try to change it. If the person cannot do anything about it, he or she should accept it.

5. *Unhappiness is a function of events outside the control of the individual.* People and events can do very little actual harm other than physically abusing an individual or depriving an individual of such things as food. This seldom happens in North American society; most events that people perceive as harmful are only psychologically harmful: It is the perception of the event that is harmful.

6. *If something may be dangerous or harmful, an individual should constantly be concerned and think about it.* This is irrational because simply thinking about it (a) doesn't change it, (b) may in fact lead to its occurrence, and (c) make it worse than it actually is. The rational person tries to evaluate the event objectively and do what he or she can to alleviate its dangerous or fearful elements.

7. *It is easier to run away from difficulties and self-responsibility than it is to face them.* This is irrational because running away does not solve the situation. Usually the situation remains and must eventually be dealt with.

8. *Individuals need to be dependent on others and have someone stronger than themselves to lean on.* Depending on others leads to insecurity and nongrowth. Such individuals never learn self-regulation and are always at the mercy of others.

9. *Past events in an individual's life determine present behavior and cannot be changed.* The past may influence the present but does not necessarily determine it. People have the capacity to change the way they now behave even though they cannot change the past.

10. *An individual should be very concerned and upset by other people's problems.* This is irrational because often those problems have nothing to do with the concerned individual, and even if they do, getting upset usually prevents someone from helping others to do anything about their problems.

11. *There is always a correct and precise answer to every problem, and it is catastrophic if it is not found.* This is irrational because there is no perfect solution to any situation. The search only produces continued anxiety. As a result the individual is never satisfied and is always searching for the one lost solution (Ellis, 1962).

Although there are many corollaries to these postulates, Ellis maintains that they are the major causes of emotional problems. McMullin and Casey (1974), Walen et al. (1980), and Roush (1984) among others have developed simplified or distilled lists of irrational ideas, but they all include the basic tenets of Ellis. In his view, once people believe these irrational ideas, they become inhibited, hostile, defensive, guilty, anxious, ineffective, inert, uncontrolled, and unhappy (Ellis, 1972). Ellis contends that most of these ideas are more or less specifically taught by parents and the culture, and that most adults in our society believe in most of them. "It must consequently be admitted that the neurotic individual we are considering is often statistically normal" (Ellis, 1972, p. 225). Ellis's contention implies that U.S. culture produces people who are to some degree emotionally disturbed. This is not necessary, but it is the current state of affairs. Hence, the task is to help people recognize their illogical thinking and to develop rational ways of thinking.

Goals of Counseling

RET counselors have one primary objective for all clients, "namely, that of finally inducing the [client] to internalize a rational philosophy of life just as he originally learned and internalized the irrational view of his parents and his community" (Ellis, 1962, p. 95). Specifically the goals of RET "are (a) to leave the client, at the end of the psychothera-peutic process, with a minimum of anxiety (or self blame) and of hostility . . . and (b) just as importantly, to give one a method of self-observation and self-assessment that will ensure that for the rest of his or her life, the person will continue to be minimally anxious and hostile" (Lawrence & Huber, 1982, p. 211). Thus, a client may come to counseling with a concern, such as getting along with peers, that is causing him or her difficulty. While dealing with this concern, the RET counselor also seeks to effect a change in the whole underlying pattern of illogical thinking. In Ellis's view, if only the symptom (the concern) is attacked, the client will probably return later with other symptoms. Therefore, the counselor must attack the "basic irrational thinking processes, which underlie all kinds of fears" (Ellis, 1962, p. 96).

The RET counselor operates from an authoritative position justified by the coun-selor's training and experience. "Even if he does not look upon himself in this manner, the members of his clientele almost invariably do. And whether he likes it or not a considerable portion of his effectiveness with patients results from his being or appear-ing to be something of an authority figure to them" (Ellis, 1962, pp. 364-365). In Ellis's view, initially clients may need to be approached in a supportive, warm fashion and be allowed to express feelings, "but the rational therapist does not delude himself that these relationship-building and expressive-emotive methods are likely to really get to the core of the (client's) illogical thinking" (Ellis, 1962, p. 95). Ellis maintains "that a therapist had better be very accepting, very forgiving, very nonjudgmental, and have uncondi-tional positive regard" (Weinrach, 1980, p. 152). These relationship techniques are, however, viewed simply as preliminary techniques, and "the rational therapist goes beyond that point to make a forthright, unequivocal attack on the client's general and specific irrational ideas and to try to induce him to adopt more rational ones in their place" (Ellis, 1962, p. 226).

The counselor needs to understand the client's world and see the client's behavior from the latter's point of view, but it is the ability to understand the client's irrational behavior "without getting involved in or believe in it that enables him to induce the 'client' to stop believing in or feeling that his behavior is necessary" (Ellis, 1962, p. 115). The counselor "must keep pounding away, time and again, at the illogical ideas that underlie the client's fears" (Ellis, 1972, p. 227). She or he must use the most direct, persuasive, suggestive, active, and logical techniques possible to help the client move from irrational to rational thinking (Ellis, 1962).

Techniques of Counseling

Over the years Ellis has continued to broaden his approach. He now maintains that RET is really multi-modal therapy, which is usually associated with Lazarus (Weinrach, 1980).

He feels he incorporates behavioral techniques such as in vivo desensitization, flooding, shame-attaching exercises, and operant conditioning. He also maintains that he incorporates Beck's cognitive therapy (Weinrach, 1980). Regardless of specific techniques, he would maintain that "all the techniques in rational-emotive therapy are designed to do more than change behavior and help the client feel better. They are also used to change basic philosophies and to give him or her specific means of restructuring these philosophies" (Ellis, 1973b, p. 62). There are essentially two ways of doing this: (1) the counselor acts as a frank counterpropagandist who directly confronts and contradicts the irrational self-talk and beliefs of the client; and (2) the counselor encourages, persuades, cajoles, and commands the client to engage in behavior that will act as a forceful counterpropaganda instrument (Ellis, 1972).

According to Ellis (1973a), these processes take place via three basic modalities: cognitive, emotive, and behavioristic. Cognitive counseling is designed to show the client "that he is an errant demander and that he had better give up his perfectionism if he wants to lead a happier, less anxiety-ridden existence" (Ellis, 1973a, p. 182). This is essentially a teaching process in which the client learns to recognize shoulds, oughts, and musts, and how to distinguish irrational beliefs from rational ones. The assumption is that the counselor is simply teaching the client how to use her or his cognitive ability more skillfully (Ellis, 1973a). During this stage all kinds of teaching devices are used, such as pamphlets, books, tape recordings, films, and filmstrips.

Emotive-cognitive counseling is designed to change the client's basic value system. During this stage various techniques are used to demonstrate to the client the differences between truths and falsehoods (Ellis, 1973a). For example, the counselor might use role playing to show the client that the latter's ideas are false; modeling to show the client more appropriate ways of behaving; unconditional acceptance and humor to show that the client is accepted even though some of her or his ideas are absurd; and exhalation to get the client to give up irrational ideas and replace them with more rational thinking (Ellis, 1973a).

The behavioral stage is basically designed to help the client develop new modes of thinking and behaving once he or she recognizes the errors in past thinking and behavior. These techniques may include homework, role playing, and operant conditioning procedures (Ellis, 1973a). Ellis has used some behavioral techniques since the early 1960s, and "there are indications of an increasing rapprochement between behavioral techniques and RET theory, which has been termed cognitive behavioral therapy" (Dolliver, 1977, p. 61). A former student of Ellis's, Maxie Maultsby (1975), describes his derivative of RET as rational behavior therapy. Ellis (1973c) himself states that there is increasing similarity between RET and behavioral techniques. In a 1977 article, Ellis raised the question whether RET really has anything that clearly distinguishes it from other cognitive-emotive-behavior therapy approaches. His answer was: "That depends on whether we consider what I now call 'general' or 'inelegant' RET and what I call 'elegant' RET" (Ellis, 1977, p. 74). He characterized his early formulations as "general" or "inelegant" RET and his current thinking as "elegant" RET. The essential difference between the two is that Ellis no longer restricts himself to the basic ABC principles of RET, but uses techniques drawn from a variety of approaches. Despite this apparently eclectic position, he has maintained that "general" RET is still the heart of his approach.

As earlier stated, the techniques used in RET counseling may come from almost every other theoretical approach; it is truly an eclectic position. "Probably fifty or sixty different kinds of cognitive procedures in therapy now exist, and more appear all the time. RET tries to use, in various ways, almost all of these methods . . . " (Ellis, 1977, p. 73). According to Ellis (1973a), the key is what can best help the client. In his view, an efficient system of counseling considers (1) economy of client and counselor time spent in counseling; (2) the rapidity with which a client can be helped with immediate concerns; (3) the ability of a counseling approach to be effective with a wide variety of clients; and (4) the depth and lasting effect of solutions. According to Ellis, RET is best able to meet all these criteria.

He maintains that the recent interest in RET is due to the fact that it is aligned with the broader cognitive behavior movement and that movement is almost the only one that has attempted to validate its ideas and test them in practice (Weinrach, 1980).

The basic assumption of the RET approach to counseling is that most people in our society develop many irrational ways of thinking. These irrational thoughts lead to irrational or inappropriate behavior. Therefore, counseling must be designed to help people recognize and change these irrational beliefs into more rational ones. The accomplishment of this goal requires an active, confrontative, and authoritative counselor who has the capacity to use a great variety of techniques.

Summary

Rational-emotive therapy is based on a complex system of theory and skills. It "hypothesizes that active-directive methods of therapy—such as confrontation, probing, or challenging or disputing irrational beliefs, teaching procedures, giving emotive exercise and assigning homework tasks—help more clients effectively than more passive and unintrusive approaches" (Greiger & Boyd, 1980, p. 21).

RET includes elements of cognitive-behavioral, ego counseling, and behavior modification approaches to treatment. It is an evolving and promising approach to human intervention, whose founder, Albert Ellis, has left a rich legacy of literature and practical approaches to training that ensure the continued evaluation of this approach to treatment.

References

Dolliver, R. H. (1977). The relationship of rational-emotive therapy to other psychotherapies and personality theories. *Counseling Psychologist, 7*(1), 57–63.

Dryden, W. (1990). Albert Ellis: An efficient and passionate life. In P. P. Heppner, *Pioneers in counseling and development.* Alexandria, VA: American Association for Counseling and Development.

Ellis, A. (1958). Rational psychotherapy. *Journal of General Psychology, 59,* 35–49.

Ellis, A. (1962). *Reason and emotion in psychotherapy.* New York: Lyle Stuart.

Ellis, A. (1972). Rational-emotive psychotherapy. In J. T. Huler & H. L. Millman (Eds.), *Goals and behavior in psychotherapy and counseling.* Columbus, OH: Charles E. Merrill.

Ellis, A. (1973a). Rational-emotive therapy. In R. Corsini (Ed.), *Current psychotherapies.* Itasca, IL: F. E. Peacock.

Ellis, A. (1973b). The no-cop-out therapy. *Psychology Today, 7,* 56–62.

Ellis, A. (1973c). Are cognitive behavior therapy and RET synonymous? *Rational Living, 8*(2), 8–11.

Ellis, A. (1977). Rejoinder: Elegant and inelegant RET. *The Counseling Psychologist, 7,* (1) 73–82.

Ellis, A. (1984). Rational-emotive therapy (RET) and pastoral counseling: A reply to Richard Wessler, *Personnel and Guidance Journal, 62*(5), 266–267.

Greiger, R., & Boyd, J. (1980). *Rational-emotive therapy: A skills band approach.* New York: Van Nostrand Reinhold.

Lawrence, C., & Huber, C. (1982). Strange bedfellows?: Rational emotive therapy and pastoral counseling. *Personnel and Guidance Journal, 61*(4), 210–212.

Maultsby, M. C. (1975). Rational behavior therapy for acting-out adolescents. *Social Casework, 56,* 35–43.

McMullin, R., & Casey, B. (1974). *Talk sense to yourself.* Denver: Creative Social Designs.

Roush, D. W. (1984). Rational-emotive therapy and youth: Some new techniques for counselors. *Personnel and Guidance Journal, 62*(7), 414–417.

Walen, S. D., Ginseppe, E., & Wessler, R. L. (1980). *A practitioner's guide to rational-emotive therapy.* New York: Oxford University Press.

Weinrach, S. (1980). Unconventional therapist: Albert Ellis. *Personnel and Guidance Journal, 59*(3), 152–160.

Chapter *11*

Toward a Theory of Counseling: Where Are We Now?

The initial chapters of this text have presented a variety of theoretical viewpoints from essentially three main points of view, namely, psychoanalytic theory and its derivatives, a humanistic point of view, and behavioral approaches and their derivatives. Specifically, we have examined the contributions of Freud, Adler, Sullivan, Horney, and the ego-counselors in the psychodynamic mode. Within the humanist context we have discussed the theories of Rogers, May, and other existentialists as well as Perls. Within the behavioral context we have examined classical behavioral theory as represented by Skinner and others, the cognitive-behavioral notions of Beck and Meichenbaum, and the rational-emotive concepts of Albert Ellis.

Many other variations could have been included, but the approaches presented are representative of the diversity of theories currently being practiced. None of these approaches has been presented in depth, and readers interested in particular areas should look at the original texts. Although the diversity in counseling perspectives causes concern to many in the field, we believe it is a strength of the profession. There is a fond hope in the hearts and minds of many practitioners that theories will move toward each other and that ultimately there will be one overarching approach to counseling theory that we may all subscribe to in the best of all possible counseling worlds. This is not likely to happen as long as individuals experience the world in unique ways and hold idiosyncratic world views. As long as values differ, we will have a variety of prevailing viewpoints.

Unravelling the similarities and differences among counseling theories is a complex process having to do, in part, with identifying the questions to ask about each one and establishing a classification system. A physicist of unknown origin once remarked that "we often think that when we have completed our study of one, we know all about two because two is one and one. We forget that we still have to make a study of "and." So too in counseling, it is the "and," the process, that often confounds us in our search for overlapping meaning. At least we have learned to ask the questions, and as Gertrude Stein has pointed out, "I suppose if there is no question, there is no answer" (Singer, 1977).

The purpose of this chapter is to examine some of the major areas of agreement and disagreement among the positions presented. This is in keeping with our belief that each counselor must develop his or her own theoretical position. As the systems model presented in Chapter 1 indicates, part of the process of developing one's own theory is synthesizing preexisting theories into a personal eclectic position. As Robinson (1965) states, the eclectic counselor examines various theories, takes from them valid and testable ideas, and molds them into a consistent approach that works for him or her. This procedure is very different from that of Robinson's syncretistic counselor, who simply uses ideas from many positions without attempting to integrate them, or that of the pragmatic counselor, who believes that theory has no place in counseling, or finally, that of the personality theorist, who advocates one single position as the answer to everyone's problems. The weight of evidence indicates that the eclectic position described by Robinson should be the choice of counselors. "As treatments useful in one area of human disturbance are found to be less valuable in another, efforts are made to arrive at better criteria for selecting patients for particular forms of therapy and for modifying existing forms. Here the stated task for the future is to achieve greater specificity concerning the effects of particular kinds of intervention" (Karasu, 1977, p. 852). The true eclectic must choose techniques based on evidence that they believe will work with a particular client with a particular problem. This chapter presents material that may help the prospective counselor move toward the kind of eclectic position described by Robinson. A conceptual model developed by Frey (1972) provides a framework for this material by showing some relationships among the various theoretical approaches.

Interrelationship of Counseling Theories: A Model

Frey (1972) indicates that several people have attempted to develop a model that would show the relationship among various theoretical approaches to counseling. Patterson (1966) used a single linear division that placed theories on a dimension ranging from rational approaches to affective approaches. More recently, others, including Karasu (1977), have studied the similarities and differences among approaches to counseling. All of these models failed to be meaningful because they were either based on a single dimension, and a single dimension could not adequately show the complexity of interrelationships among theories, or like Barclay's (1968), they were based on philosophical orientations too far removed from actual practice. The basic model developed by Frey (1972) appears to master these problems.

Frey (1972) combines the unidimensional (rational-effective) model of Patterson (1966) and the unidimensional (insight-action) model of London (1964) into a four-celled model. This model is capable of showing the relationship among theories both in terms of the actual process of counseling (Patterson) and the objectives of that process (London). Since Frey's early work in 1972, Frey and others have continued to develop systematic models that include more than one dimension. Hutchins (1979) presents a model that uses the dimensions of thinking, feeling, and acting to analyze differing approaches. Frey and Raming (1979) examine counseling goals and methods using a factor analysis of 15 theorists. L'Abate (1981) describes what he terms an E-R-A (Emotionality-Rationality-Activity) for analyzing differing approaches. More recently Gelso and Carter (1985) have examined theories by analyzing components of the counseling relationship. All of these more recent attempts share our belief first expressed in 1979 that the best way to analyze approaches to counseling is through the use of multidimensional analysis. We believe that the model we have developed is a modification of the original model proposed by Frey in 1972. In our presentation of that model we will incorporate some of the propositions put forward by L'Abate (1981) and Gelso and Carter (1985).

We will use the insight-action dimension of the Frey model to describe the objectives of each approach to counseling. Some approaches hold that counseling must deal with the totality of the individual and that insight is a prerequisite for any change in behavior. These approaches are placed in one of two cells emphasizing insight (for example, the client must develop an understanding of her or his life script). More specific and action-oriented positions will be placed in one of two cells emphasizing action (for example, the client will be able to be assertive in appropriate social situations).

The second dimension of Frey's model, the rational-affective, will be used to describe the actual process of counseling. Approaches that emphasize conative or affective expression within the counseling process will be placed in one of two cells emphasizing affect. These approaches encourage the expression of feelings about situations. Conversely, approaches that emphasize counseling as a rational learning process will be placed in one of two cells indicating an emphasis on rational thought. Here the emphasis is on clients' thinking about situations.

The basic dimensions of Frey's model (1972) are shown in Figure 11-1. The closer a particular theory is to the intersection of the four cells (such as Adlerian), the more similar it is to approaches in the other quadrants; conversely, the farther out an approach is from the intersection (such as self-theory), the more dissimilar it is from all other approaches. Those that share a quadrant may use different vocabulary to describe their approach but are similar in terms of both the process of counseling and the objectives of that process.

Figure 11-1 shows two theories in the rational-insight quadrant, three in the insight-affective quadrant, one in the affective-action quadrant, two in the action-rational quadrant, and the remaining theories, cognitive behavioral and RET, straddling the rational-insight and action-rational quadrants.

Theories in the rational-insight quadrant share a belief that a rational thought process leads clients to insight, which in turn leads to a change in emotional status, and then to actual change in behavior. Of the approaches wholly or partially in this quadrant, RET is the most rational and, together with the cognitive approaches, is very close to the axis, indicating a real balance among all four dimensions of the model. The psychoanalytic position in contrast, focuses on insight derived from past emotional expression, but it does so in a fairly intellectual way.

Approaches in the insight-affective quadrant maintain that clients develop insight into their difficulties by coming to understand their current emotions and their internal drives and motivations. As Frey (1972) indicates, emphasis is on feeling, knowing, and understanding. It should be noted how close the ego-counseling position is to the axis. In

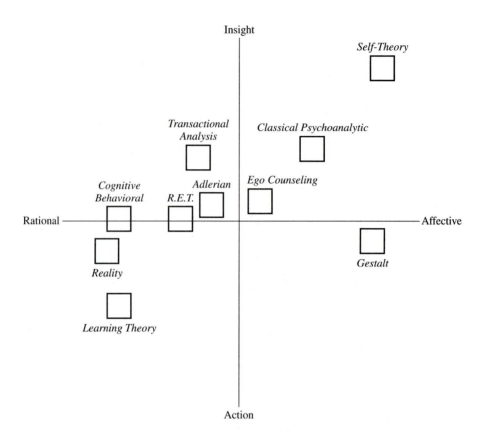

FIGURE 11-1   Modified Frey's Four-Celled Model of Counseling Theories

Source: Adapted from *Counselor Education and Supervision, 11,* 1972 p. 4. © ACA. Reprinted with permission. No further reproduction authorized without written permission of American Counseling Association.

actuality, it is closer to the Adlerian approach than to the self-theory approach. The self-theory position is the farthest from the axis. It differs not only from other approaches in the same quadrant, but also from all other approaches. This is due largely to the almost total reliance of the self-theory position on insight that comes through focusing on the here-and-now feelings of the client. Few current individual self-therapists would advocate such an extreme position. Most self-therapists would also be quite compatible using more action-oriented approaches.

The Gestalt position is the only one shown in the affective-action quadrant, and it is shown in two places to reflect a change in position from its early days under Fritz Perls. This approach is very close to the insight-affective quadrant, but it places more emphasis on feeling and its relationship to action or behavior change. Gestaltists acknowledge that insight is necessary but that it represents only half the counseling task; the other half involves planning for how this insight can change behavior. The Gestalt position is often thought to be very similar to the self-theory position, and in some ways it is, but a clear distinction exists in their respective emphases on planning for action. Gestaltists are much more concerned about actual behavior change, although Carkhuff's recent modifications in self-theory would move the latter very close to the intersection of all four quadrants.

In the last quadrant, action-rational, are the behaviorists, the reality counselors, and, to a somewhat lesser degree, the RET counselors. These approaches emphasize the role of a rational process in producing specific behavioral changes. The approaches shown in this quadrant maintain that feelings change after behavior changes, not the other way around: If people feel bad, it is because of something they are doing; if they change what they are doing, then they will feel better. Within the quadrant, behaviorists express more concern than reality counselors for specific behavior change; hence, it can be said that they are the most action oriented.

One of the most striking things about this model is that seven of the ten positions presented are grouped in close proximity to the intersection of the four quadrants. Only the behaviorists, traditional Gestaltists, and self-theorists are at any extremes, and many counselors within each of these groupings would probably appear closer to the center if their actual practices were analyzed. This indicates that even most formally stated positions are more eclectic in nature than they might initially appear. It also lends credence to our view that each person can develop his or her eclectic position as described by Robinson. It is interesting to note that the older the profession of counseling becomes and the more sophisticated its procedures, the closer toward the axis all approaches move. It is also interesting to note that it is difficult to place the existential approach anywhere in the model because of major differences within the approach.

Keeping this conceptual model in mind, we can now examine the similarities and dissimilarities among the approaches in the following areas: nature of individuals, personality development, abnormal development, the counseling process (including the goals of counseling, the counseling relationship, and the role of the counselor), and the techniques of counseling. In reading this section it must be remembered that any classification system produces generalizations. Here we are painting a picture with a large brush and some details will be lost. L'Abate (1981) stresses that the purpose of any classification system is to increase the likelihood of an optimum match between a person's desired behavior and the method used by the counselor. We believe that his basic analysis provides a useful global view to which details can be added as counseling proceeds.

Nature of Individuals

One of the most difficult questions that must be addressed by every counselor concerns the nature of human beings. Counselors must decide what human nature is before they can hope to help people. Yet, human beings are the most complex organisms known, and this complexity is reflected in the diversity of answers to the question.

In ego counseling and psychoanalytic approaches, people are reactive beings. They react to their own innate drives and needs. Those drives and needs are developed and profoundly influenced by early childhood experiences and frustrations. In these views, human nature is largely determined during the first five years of existence. During these five years, children have many emotional experiences, and these experiences form the basis for later behavior.

Behaviorists take a similar approach: They also view people as reactive. In the learning theory view, people do not react to their own innate drives, but to the world around them. In the view of behaviorists, people are biological beings who react to the stimuli in their environments. Human behavior is determined, but it is determined by the environment in which people exist. People do not control their own destinies, but are controlled by external forces. Adult behavior is a direct result of early childhood environment, for children learn patterns of behavior in reaction to their environment. These learned patterns determine later reactions to stimuli in the environment.

In contrast with these theories, the other positions presented in this text maintain that people are beings in the process of becoming, beings with potential for controlling their own behavior. In this view, human behavior is not primarily determined by forces outside of people's control, but is primarily controlled by people through a conscious and thoughtful process. People are not unthinking, controlled individuals but thinking beings who largely determine their own destinies.

Although it appears that the approaches to counseling have little in common in terms of their conception of human nature, there is one commonality that makes all the differences seem somewhat inconsequential. This commonality is implied by the fact that all these approaches to counseling were developed in order to help people bring about changes in their behavior. Hence, all the approaches acknowledge that human behavior has the capacity to change. Related to this common assumption is the common belief that certain events in a person's life can cause difficulty and that these difficulties are serious enough that the person seeks to change them. Often this brings them to counseling.

Personality Development

Virtually every approach to counseling acknowledges the importance of early childhood experiences. The approaches based on analytic principles tend to believe that what a person becomes is largely a function of internal dynamics. These internal drives move people to try to satisfy needs that for the most part exist outside awareness. Similarly, the behaviorists believe that personality is a function of people's reactions to stimuli in their environment. Those reactions (behaviors) that bring satisfaction are retained as part of the personality and those that do not are discarded. Both of these general approaches, then, hold that people acquire behaviors either in an attempt to satisfy inner drives or to bring some feeling of satisfaction. In both cases personality development is viewed as a reactive process not under thoughtful, rational control.

Conversely, the Gestalt, Adlerian, reality, RET, and self-theory positions to varying degrees share a belief in people as actors. They contend that people may have internal needs and that they are indeed subject to certain environmental constraints, but these factors do not determine entirely what people do. The emphasis is on how people perceive and evaluate their internal needs and external events. People act on the world rather than reacting to it. It is through this action, a large part of which is interpersonal interaction, that personality is formed.

In virtually all approaches, the process of personality development is a function of a person's needs being met. In the first case, this process is largely out of a person's control; in the second, the person is accorded a great deal of credit for what he or she ultimately becomes. All these approaches stress the importance of early childhood experiences. Whereas the analytic and learning theory positions both maintain that people are reactive beings, they differ to some extent about what people react to. In the analytic view, people react to both innate drives and, to a lesser degree, the environment; in the learning theory view, people basically react to stimuli in their environment. In both views, people do not have much conscious control over their own behavior. At the other extreme are approaches that attribute all of human behavior to thoughtful control: People are able to evaluate their own experiences and then to act accordingly. These approaches subscribe to the rather optimistic notion that people act on the environment and are in control of their own personality development, whereas the analytic and learning theory approaches take the comparatively pessimistic view that people react to stimuli, innate or external, and that personality development is largely outside of conscious control. Regardless of this central difference, it is clear that all approaches agree on the importance of the environment in the shaping of personality. The differences focus on how theorists view the interaction between the individual and the environment. It should also be noted once again that most theorists and even more practitioners lean toward a centralist position, believing that people have some rational control but are also subject to forces either internal or external outside of their control.

Abnormal Development

All approaches to counseling acknowledge that during early childhood a person can have experiences that lead to maladjustment or maladaptive behavior later in life. Analytic theorists maintain that this type of behavior results from a breakdown in the functioning of the ego: In some way the ego was unable to cope with some situations in a meaningful and positive fashion, and these experiences were suppressed in the unconscious. They may arise later and cause difficulty because the person never learned to deal with the experience in the first place. In contrast, self theorists believe that the memory of these events is pushed into the unconscious; the person either distorts the original experience or denies its existence because it does not fit with the conception of self. Thus, both the analytic and self-theory approaches to counseling view maladaptive behavior as stemming from experiences that have been denied awareness, and this denial in turn prevents the person from learning how to cope with them in a positive fashion. From this perspective, then, maladaptive behavior is only a symptom of some underlying cause. Gestaltists, on the other hand, while agreeing with the self-theorists about the importance of perception, believe that maladaptive behavior results from people trying to deny what they are and at the same time trying to be something they are not.

Reality therapists consider maladaptive behavior a result of a person being frustrated in the attempt to meet personal needs. This frustration leads the person to lose contact with or to misperceive the real world. Similarly, RET views maladaptive behavior as a function of the person distorting the world and continually telling himself or herself that these distortions are true. In the Adlerian view, maladaptive behavior is formed early in life, when the child perceives her or his inferiority to be so great that he or she feels rejected by others and adopts a completely self-centered life-style. Similarly, TA theorists believe that the person's perception of early events is a determiner of inappropriate behavior.

The learning theory position is quite different from the preceding approaches. In the behaviorist view, maladaptive behavior is acquired in the same manner as normal behavior. The inappropriate behavior is learned because it has been rewarded at various times. The learning theorist is concerned not with underlying causes but only with the maladaptive behavior. Maladaptive behavior differs from normal behavior, not in the manner in which it has been developed, but only to the degree that it is atypical or maladaptive to the observer. Hence, behavior is not caused by hidden motives or drives or by inaccurate perceptions, but occurs because it brings some satisfaction to the person. As we shall see, differences in opinion about the nature of maladaptive behavior are reflected in the various approaches to counseling.

The Counseling Process

Basic to the counseling relationship are the goals of counseling. Psychoanalysts, ego analysts, Adlerians, Gestaltists, and self-theorists tend to state these goals in global fashion: The goals involve reorganizing the whole structure of the individual. Adherents to these theories believe that the presenting problem is only a symptom of an underlying cause and that the cause itself must be the focus of counseling. To some extent, RET and reality counselors would agree, but they are also concerned about helping a person develop new behaviors. The behavioral counselors maintain that the goals of counseling must be stated in specific terms, and they focus directly on the presenting problem. The analysts, ego counselors, Adlerians, and Gestaltists tend to view the goals of counseling as basically the same for everyone; the reality and RET counselors occupy an intermediate position and are concerned with a global attitude that affects specific behaviors; and the behavioral counselors believe that different goals should be established for each person.

Despite these general differences, all approaches have in common the goal of facilitating changes in behavior. Some counselors view this goal holistically; others see it in terms of some combination of global and specific goals; and learning theorists see it in terms of specific behaviors. The goals move from very global to very specific, and the differences in degree affect the way in which the counseling relationship is handled.

The Counseling Relationship

As Figure 11-1 shows, self theorists, Gestaltists, psychoanalysts, and ego-counselors tend to view the counseling relationship as a basically affective or emotional process, whereas the other approaches regard the relationship as a rational one. If the analysis stopped here, however, it would do a disservice to the importance given to the counseling relationship by all the approaches. Gelso and Carter (1985) make an extensive analysis of the counseling relationship. They contend that "all therapeutic relationships consist of these [working alliance, transference relationship, real relationship] three components although the salience and importance of each part, during counseling or therapy will vary according to the theoretical perspective of the therapist and the particulars of a given therapy" (Gelso & Carter, 1985, p. 161). The working alliance as defined by Gelso and Carter "is the alignment that occurs between counselor and client or more precisely between the reasonable side of the client . . . and the counselor's working or therapizing side" (1985, p. 162). Most approaches would reflect this basic counseling relationship. A second component described by Gelso and Carter is the transference or "unreal" relationship. They maintain, and we agree, that to some extent all therapeutic relationships have at least a medium of transference and counter transference as originally defined by Freud. This is so regardless of length of treatment or type of presenting problem. Differences in degree relate to how the various approaches encourage or discourage transference as a therapeutic tool.

Although the real relationship as defined by Gelso and Carter has its foundations in humanistic approaches to counseling, they believe it is more and present it together with the working alliances and the transference relationship. "In a real relationship, one's perceptions and interpretations of another's behavior are appropriate and realistic, the feelings are genuine, and the behavior is congruent. . . . The real relationship, then, has an important effect on the process and outcomes of counseling, again of every form of counseling" (Gelso & Carter, 1985, pp. 186–187).

As stated above, Gelso and Carter's (1985) analysis suggests that all of these components are found in all approaches. The degree will vary according to the approach of the counselor and to some extent the nature of the client and the presenting problem. It is to be expected that cognitive, rational, and behaviorally oriented counselors will place emphasis on the working alliance. Self-theorists and Gestaltists will place emphasis on the "real" relationship, and those with an analytic approach will emphasize the transference relationship. We believe Gelso and Carter's analysis is a helpful addition to the model shown in Figure 11-1. Their conclusions will be dealt with in more detail in Chapter 12.

Role of the Counselor

Central to the differences among the approaches is the role of the counselor in the counseling process. The ego-analytic, analytic, RET, and learning theory positions hold that the counselor is an expert to whom the client has come with a problem that she or he cannot resolve alone. This assumption leads to the view that the counselor must take a somewhat active role in the counseling relationship. The ego analysts and classical analysts see themselves as controlling the relationship, balancing it between the affective and cognitive domains. Furthermore, they consider the counselor responsible for making a diagnosis of the problem and then presenting a plan for resolving the situation to the client. Likewise, reality, RET, and learning theorist counselors prescribe the method of treatment once a diagnosis has been determined. All approaches emphasize the need for the client to feel confidence in and be respected by the counselor. In addition all maintain that the client must agree with the diagnosis before any particular treatment will be effective. Nevertheless, these approaches tend to regard the counselor as the controlling agent in the relationship. Their model of the relationship is quite similar to the medical model.

In contrast, the self-theorists, Gestaltists, and Adlerians argue that because of man's inherent growth tendency, the client has the capacity and the motivation to solve her or his own problem if provided with a nonthreatening atmosphere. The self-theorists emphasize that the counselor's presence or behavior in the counseling relationship does not directly influence the client's behavior. In their view, then, there is no need for the counselor to make a diagnosis and, indeed, diagnosis is detrimental to the process of counseling. In self-theory, the locus of evaluation belongs with the client; moreover, diagnosis by a counselor creates dependency needs in clients, whereas they should be helped to develop their own strength. The self-theorists believe that if the counselor controls the relationship and sets the goals for the client, she or he is interfering with basic human nature. From this perspective, the counselor's role is simply to provide the conditions so that the client may reinstitute the self-actualizing tendency. The counselor controls only the conditions, not what the client does.

Neither the Gestalt or Adlerian counselors go as far as the self-theorists, although they do agree that people basically have the potential to look into themselves and change their behavior. The Adlerians do believe, however, that the counselor can provide direct assistance to the client that will facilitate insight. This assistance often takes the form of interpretation and diagnosis. Gestalt counselors are probably the most active; the action is not interpretive, but is designed to confront the client with current behavior and, particularly, inconsistencies in that behavior.

The counseling relationship is viewed somewhat differently by the various approaches, ranging from the very cognitive, action-oriented learning theory approach through the somewhat balanced ego-analytic approach to the affective, insight-oriented self-theorists. The self-theorists believe that insight, by itself, will lead the client to change, whereas the ego analysts contend that the counselor must, in effect, prescribe the necessary changes for the client. On the other hand, the learning theory approach is exclusively action oriented. To behaviorists, the client's problem needs to be dealt with directly, not as a symptom of some hidden difficulty. The degree to which an approach is insight or action oriented directly affects the degree to which the counselor assumes responsibility for the outcome of counseling. The behaviorist, action-oriented counselor is not only more active in the actual counseling relationship, but may also take an active role in the outside life of the client.

Despite these differences, there are some common factors among the approaches to the counseling relationship. All share a belief in the necessity for a good relationship. All stress the need for the client to feel accepted and understood in the relationship; for the client to feel that the counselor is concerned and able to help; and for the counselor to be genuine and honest with the client. In effect, the counselor must come across to the client as a real person, one deserving of the client's trust. This topic is so important that Chapter 12, which begins Part II of this book, is devoted exclusively to the counseling relationship.

A second element common to all approaches is the notion that the counseling process will lead to some change on the part of the client and that this change can be aided through the use of the counseling interview. Although some behavioral, reality, and RET counselors stress the need for manipulation of the outside environment of the client, they also place a great deal of importance on the counseling interview. In terms of the amount of change expected through use of the counseling process, there are differences in degree but not in expectation. Some theorists expect a complete change in personality, others want changes only in particular areas. Most theorists take the latter position.

Most counselors, then, agree on the necessity of an appropriate counseling relationship built on the assumptions that counseling can lead to behavioral change; that this change is facilitated through the interview process; that the relationship must be based on mutual trust and understanding between the counselor and the client; and that both members of the relationship have confidence in the ability of the relationship to bring about changes in the client.

Goals of Counseling

As might be expected, the different approaches to counseling place differing emphases on outcomes or goals of counseling. Certainly some of these differences are reflected in the model shown in Figure 11-1. In general, the further an approach is from the axis and the nearer to the insight end of the model, the greater the emphasis on insight and global behaviors. Frey and Raming (1979) classify counseling goals of the various approaches using the E-R-A model. They suggest that those theorists that emphasize emotionality (Rogers, Perls, Frankl) have as goals: "Awareness and acceptance—of self in conflict and of inner resources—awareness of negative feelings" (L'Abate, 1981, p. 264). Those approaches that focus on rationality (Berne, Ellis, Alexander, Kelly, Sullivan) stress the strengthening of the ego and its functions.

We believe that the reality therapists and to some extent the broad-based behaviorists would agree with these goals. Finally those who fall into the activity part of their model (Dreikurs, Wolpe, Dollard and Miller) focus on symptom removal, not behaviors, and ways to control personal environment. Frey and Raming's analysis is a helpful way to classify general goals of the various approaches and is compatible with the model presented in Figure 11-1.

Using the conceptual model presented in Figure 11-1, we will now examine how differences in the views of the counseling relationship and counseling goals are translated into the actual techniques used in counseling.

Techniques of Counseling

Rational-Insight

The approaches in the rational-insight quadrant share a belief that insight, if not necessary, is at least helpful in bringing about behavioral change and that techniques employed by the counselor facilitate this insight. Like the insight-affective counselors, they maintain that a client must understand why he or she is experiencing difficulty before any change can be expected. Unlike the insight-affective practitioners, however, they regard the process of discovering as more of a rational than an emotional one. As Figure 11-1 shows, the Adlerian counselor tends to approach a balance in emphases on rationality and affect, whereas the RET counselor, as the name implies, places much more emphasis on the importance of reason in the process and is also more concerned about behavior. In fact, the RET counselor will often try to change behavior before working on developing client insights.

RET is basically a teaching procedure that attempts to bring the client to understand both the rational and affective components of behavior. Ellis (1973) divides counseling into three separate stages: cognitive, emotive, and behavioristic. In the cognitive stage, the techniques are designed to confront the client's expressions so that he or she can distinguish rational thoughts from irrational ones. In the emotive stage, the counselor may use role-playing techniques to help the client perceive irrational beliefs, may model how the client can adopt different values, and may use exhortation to get the client to replace old thoughts with new, more appropriate ones. In the final stage, the counselor seeks to help the client establish "habits" of behavior that are based on rational thinking about events. In this stage, the counselor may use such techniques as homework and even some behavioristic reinforcement. It is apparent that RET, although it emphasizes rational thinking that leads to insight, is also concerned with the emotive aspects of client problems and with having the client take some positive action. It is very close to a true eclectic approach, as Ellis himself has often acknowledged.

The psychoanalytic counselor, believing that profound exploration of the past is necessary for understanding the present, acts to facilitate free association and transference. This procedure is designed to help the counselor develop an understanding of the client. Through interpretations, the counselor then presents this understanding to the client. Having expressed the repressed needs of the client, the sources of difficulty, the counselor assumes that the client will be able to develop new ways of behaving. It is clear that the psychoanalytic counselor places much more faith in her or his own therapeutic potential than does either the self-theory counselor or the ego counselor.

Insight-Affective

All three approaches in the insight-affective quadrant (Adlerian, ego counseling, and self-theory) consider insight a necessary prerequisite to behavior change. The Adlerian and self-theory positions are that a client must understand the total self and all the underlying dynamics of his or her behavior. The ego counselors, while believing insight is necessary, focus more on understanding parts of oneself than on the total self. All agree that a client who cannot get along with others must know the reasons before behavior can improve. They differ markedly, however, on the kinds of counselor behaviors that lead the client to this insight and the degree to which the client's total personality must be involved. The ego counselor and the Adlerian counselor are concerned with helping the client change specific behaviors. Self-theory counselors are more inclined to believe that the total personality must be the focus.

The Adlerian approach is also very close to an eclectic position. Unlike the RET counselors and like the transactional analysts, the Adlerians are interested in the effects of early life impressions on people. Thus, early recollections, memories of childhood, play an important role in Adlerian counseling. Equally important are people's perceptions of their current lives. Developing these perceptions may involve analysis of family structure, and sometimes, the work structure. This analysis is designed to determine the patterns of behavior the clients have used and are using in the attempt to reach their chosen life goal. Once these are understood, the counselor presents the patterns to the clients. The counseling process then shifts to the development of a more appropriate life goal. As with all the approaches in this quadrant, the process is counselor directed.

Of the three approaches in this quadrant, and perhaps in the whole model, the self-theory counselor uses the fewest techniques. The emphasis is on the counselor's ability to establish the proper conditions for therapeutic change. In this view the counselor, by providing the "necessary and sufficient conditions," acts to facilitate client exploration of self, which leads to self-understanding and ultimately to changes in behavior. No other techniques are needed. In contrast, the more eclectic approaches derived from Rogers's work use specific techniques to accomplish certain goals.

Ego analysts emphasize the ability of the counselor to control the dimensions of the relationship, largely by controlling the amount of ambiguity offered to the client and through the use of partial interpretations. With these techniques, the counselor first provides the structure necessary for the client to express her or his feelings and then leads the client to an understanding of the problem. In effect, the counselor, having made a diagnosis, leads the client to self-awareness through the use of interpretation. After the client achieves self-awareness, the counselor and client plan specific steps to implement new behaviors. This stage often involves role playing, role rehearsal, and sometimes homework assignments.

Affective-Action

The affective-action quadrant contains only the Gestalt approach. According to Perls (1969), the responsibility of the Gestalt counselor is simply to provide an opportunity for the client to discover what her or his needs are and then to supply an atmosphere in which the client can grow. As such, the approach is generally without techniques. The Gestalt counselor is concerned with interacting with the client in the here and now. In doing so, the counselor focuses as much on the client's nonverbal expressions and gestures as on the verbal. Perls (1969) feels that clients must be made aware of this "psychosomatic language" in order to understand the totality of their being—their Gestalt. This awareness leads to the discovery of needs and then to the process of growth.

To bring about this awareness, the counselor seeks always to keep the client in the present, by confronting the client with current behavior in the counseling relationship. For example, the client may be saying positive things and at the same time be moving around in a chair. The Gestalt counselor would focus the client's attention on this inconsistency. The use of games forces clients to deal with current feelings. Even dreams are used actively. Dreams are not interpreted or simply recalled; the Gestalt counselor makes the client act out dreams, in effect, to relive them. All these processes are designed to bring the client to full awareness of her or his total being, which includes both the client's needs and his or her resources for dealing with them. The Gestalt approach, then, is both insight and action oriented.

Unlike the approaches in the insight-affective quadrant, Gestalt counseling emphasizes achieving insight into current functioning, not into past causes. Also, unlike other insight approaches, Gestalt counselors are more concerned with the client's taking positive action. These goals require Gestalt counselors to be much more active in the relationship than the self-theory counselors, with whom they are often confused. Pure Gestaltists are difficult to find; many counselors use Gestalt techniques, but few use them exclusively.

Rational-Action

The two approaches found solely in the rational-action quadrant work for actual behavior change, the RET and cognitive-behavioral approaches. They tend to be more cognitively oriented than any other approach in the model. This does not mean that they ignore the necessity for establishing a relationship with the client, but it does mean that they work more directly with specific behaviors rather than with feelings. The client's presenting concern is the focal problem of counseling. The importance of the past and underlying dynamics are underplayed, and the counselor tries to help the client change the specific behavior. Whereas other approaches tend to maintain that changes in feelings lead to changes in behavior, the reality and behavioral approaches tend to maintain the reverse. The dichotomy is not as simple as it sounds, but it does illustrate the difference in emphasis.

The behaviorists are concerned with specific behavioral changes rather than attitudes. They place less faith in the person's rational thought process. Those of the behavioral persuasion view counseling as simply a type of learning experience. Thus, their counseling techniques rely on the same laws of learning that apply in everyday life: reinforcement, shaping, imitative learning, and cognitive learning. The counselor decides which principles of learning will be most effective with a particular client and then applies those laws to the counseling process. The counselor must help the client decide on the desired behavioral change, must help the client understand what consequences are maintaining the current behavior, and then help the client develop behaviors that will bring desired consequences.

Both approaches, then, place emphasis on behavioral changes, on counseling as a teaching process, and on the counselor as the director of the process. They differ somewhat in the techniques they use to teach the new behaviors and in their belief in people's capacity to reason for themselves.

While each of the approaches to counseling applies different techniques, they all require that some form of verbalization take place between the client and the counselor. If this kind of exchange does not occur, neither does the process of counseling. One persistent criticism of counseling is that it is basically designed, regardless of the theory used, for those who can verbalize. In fact this criticism may be valid, and more attention should be paid to how counselors can operate with potential clients who possess limited verbal skills.

This examination of the various approaches has shown that among them there are many similarities as well as differences. The differences appear to stem from different concepts about the nature of human beings and how the events around people influence their lives. Some differences are the result of different interpretations of similar events; some, of a difference in semantics. Although these differences may in some cases be extremely important, they are often magnified out of proportion. They are not so great, or indeed, so important that some type of unity cannot be achieved among the various approaches to counseling. To that end, it may be appropriate to examine some research comparing different theoretical approaches to counseling.

Research

Some of the differences among various theoretical approaches to counseling have been demonstrated in research literature. Sundland and Barker (1962), using a Therapist Orientation Scale, conducted a survey of 139 psychotherapists. The questionnaire contained sixteen subscales; on nine of them there were significant differences among the therapists classified as Freudians, Sullivanians, and Rogerians. In the development of the Therapist Orientation Scale, however, items on which therapists agreed were discarded. When the same therapists were grouped by level of experience, differences were found only on one scale.

Wallach and Strupp (1964) examined the differences among Freudian, general psychoanalytic, Sullivanian, and client-centered counselors. Using a scale of usual therapeutic practices, they found that the four groups could be differentiated on the amount of personal distance maintained in the counseling relationship.

McNair and Lorr (1964), using a scale based on the Therapist Orientation Scale, surveyed 265 therapists. Like the previous studies, the results showed differences on three separate dimensions.

Although these studies indicate that there are differences in counseling practice, it must be remembered that these researchers were looking for differences. Perhaps an even more important question concerns the *outcomes* of counseling. Did the use of different approaches produce any differences in the outcome of counseling? To a large extent this question has not been answered by the research. Hence, we really do not know whether the differences that were found have any significance.

Just as there is evidence of differences among various theories, there is a growing body of evidence that there are many similarities. Fiedler's classic studies (1950a, 1950b, 1951) demonstrate that there is little difference among various approaches to counseling. Much of the evidence has demonstrated some approximation between the self-theory and behavioral or learning theory positions. Sapolsky (1960) found that the effectiveness of reinforcement techniques is related to the success of the relationship. Ullman and Krasner (1965) also emphasize the importance of the relationship regardless of the theoretical approach of the counselor.

In one investigation of how theory affects proactive children, Truax (1966) analyzed a single, long-term, successful case handled by Carl Rogers. Truax concluded that the data from this case indicated that Rogers was quite successful in using the techniques of reinforcement. This investigation indicates that perhaps the positions of the self-theorists and the learning theorists are really not far apart, at least in actual practice. In a later study, Truax (1968) found that when three of the necessary self-theory conditions for counseling—accurate empathy, nonpossessive warmth, and genuineness—were used as reinforcers, clients increased their amount of self-exploration. Like the previous study, this investigation indicates that actual counseling may have elements of both learning theory and self-theory.

In an investigation by Anderson, Douds, and Carkhuff (1967), there was a further indication that although theories may be different, practices at the very least overlap. In listening to 40 taped counseling interviews, they found that counselors who were operating at a high level of functioning, offering high levels of the necessary conditions for counseling, were more effective in the use of confrontations with their clients. The technique of confrontation is one that is more typically associated with the action approaches to counseling (learning theory or ego counseling), yet it was found to be effective in a self-theory context.

Ellis (1977) in an extensive review of research demonstrates quite clearly that there is increasing similarity among all approaches. Analyses of L'Abate (1981) and of Gelso and Carter (1985) demonstrate the continuing interest in the relative effects of different approaches. The best that can be said at this point is that it does appear that different approaches are effective with different clients under different situations. It is difficult, however, to point to any particular pattern that is supported by the research.

Summary

One may wonder whether there will ever be one unified theory of counseling. Rogers believes the profession of counseling must develop a broader perspective if differences are to be reconciled. In a similar vein, Allport (1961) suggests that the main trouble with counseling theories is that they are partial rather than whole theories. In effect, both said that we need to develop further the theories we now have, and that as this development occurs, we may see a rapprochement among them. Some indication of basic agreement on some crucial issues already exists.

There is little question that most approaches to counseling recognize the importance of the relationship in counseling. Although some argue that it is not sufficient by itself, all agree that it is necessary. It is also clear that all approaches to counseling recognize that difficulties do arise in a person's life and that these difficulties can be overcome through the process of counseling. Given these basic agreements, perhaps differences that exist are not insurmountable. After all, a theory is only a set of assumptions that is in the process of being tested. It is not something final and static but should always be changing.

As we stated in Chapter 1, it is most important that counselors strive to develop a theory for themselves that is based on certain assumptions, which are also open to revision. After studying current theories and the research that relates to them, the counselor is ready to try these theories in his or her own practice and research and to develop a personal theory from these experiences. The counselor's development of self-understanding is crucial to the successful development of her or his own mode of counseling.

References

Allport, A. W. (1961). Psychological models for guidance. *Harvard Educational Review, 32,* 373–381.

Anderson, S., Douds, J., & Carkhuff, R. B. (1967). The effects of confrontation by high and low functioning therapists. Unpublished paper, University of Massachusetts.

Barclay, J. (1968). Counseling and philosophy: A theoretical exposition. In B. Shertzer & S. C. Stone (Eds.), *Guidance Monograph Series.* Boston: Houghton Mifflin.

Ellis, A. (1973). Rational emotive therapy. In R. Corsini (Ed.), *Current psychotherapies.* Itasca, IL: F. E. Peacock.

Ellis, A. (1977). Rational-emotive therapy: Research data that supports the clinical and personality hypotheses of RET and other modes of cognitive behavior therapy. *Counseling Psychologist, 7*(1), 2–42.

Fiedler, F. (1950a). The concept of an ideal therapeutic relationship. *Journal of Consulting Psychology, 14,* 235–245.

Fiedler, F. (1950b). A comparison of therapeutic relationships in psychoanalytic, non-directive, and Adlerian therapy. *Journal of Consulting Psychology, 14,* 436–445.

Fiedler, F. (1951). Factor analysis of psychoanalytic, non-directive, and Adlerian therapeutic relationships. *Journal of Consulting Psychology, 15,* 32–38.

Frey, D. H. (1972). Conceptualizing counseling theories: A content analysis of process and goal statements. *Counselor Education and Supervision, 11*(4), 243–250.

Frey, D. H., & Raming, H. E. (1979). A taxonomy of consulting goals and methods. *Personnel and Guidance Journal, 58,* 26–37.

Gelso, C. J., & Carter, J. A. (1985). The relationship in counseling and psychotherapy: Components, consequences, and theoretical antecedents. *The Counseling Psychologist, 13,* 155–243.

Glasser, W. (1965). *Reality therapy: A new approach to psychiatry.* New York: Harper & Row.

Hutchins, O. E. (1979). Systematic counseling: The T-F-A model for counselor intervention. *Personnel and Guidance Journal, 57,* 529–531.

Karasu, T. B. (1977). Psychotherapies: An overview. *American Journal of Psychology, 31,* 134.

L'Abate, L. (1981). Classification of counseling and therapy theorists, methods, processes, and goals: The E-R-A model. *Personnel and Guidance Journal, 59,* 263–265.

London, P. (1964). *The modes and morals of psychotherapy.* New York: Holt, Rinehart and Winston.

McNair, D. M. & Lorr, M. (1964). An analysis of professor psychotherapeutic techniques. *Journal of Consulting Psychology, 28,* 265–271.

Patterson, C. (1966). *Theories of counseling and psychotherapy.* New York: Harper & Row.

Perls, F. S. (1969). *Gestalt therapy verbatim.* Lafayette, CA: Real People Press.

Robinson, F. P. (1965). Counseling orientations and labels. *Journal of Counseling Psychology, 12,* 338.

Rogers, C. R. (1961). Divergent trends. In R. May (Ed.), *Existential psychology.* New York: Random House.

Sapolsky, A. (1960). Effect of interpersonal relationships on conditioning. *Journal of Abnormal and Social Psychology, 60,* 241–246.

Singer, M. G. (1977). *Morals and values.* New York: Charles Scribner's.

Sundland, D. M., & Barker, E. N. (1962). The orientation of psychotherapists. *Journal of Consulting Psychology, 26,* 201–212.

Truax, C. B. (1966). Reinforcement and nonreinforcement in Rogerian psychotherapy. *Journal of Abnormal Psychology, 71,* 1–9.

Truax, C. B. (1968). Therapist interpersonal reinforcement of client self-exploration and therapeutic outcome in group psychotherapy. *Journal of Counseling Psychology, 15,* 225–231.

Ullman, L. P., & Krasner, L. (1965). *Case studies in behavior modification.* New York: Holt, Rinehart and Winston.

Wallach, M. S., & Strupp, H. H. (1964). Dimensions of psychotherapists' activities. *Journal of Consulting Psychology, 28,* 120–125.

Part *II*

Counseling Process

Theory and process are closely interrelated. A counselor begins with some general assumptions about personality, moves to more specific assumptions about behavior changes, and then forms a counseling theory that indicates procedures to be implemented. A counselor may start with a theory that feels comfortable and then modify and reformulate it through experience and evaluation. Such procedures help counselors know where they are going and what they are doing with a client. Theory in the counseling process provides both a method of helping counselors understand their clients and a set of guidelines for counseling behaviors.

Part II focuses on the process of counseling. No one theory is followed; instead, concepts about the process from various positions and research are interwoven into eclectic procedures. Generally, the frame of reference is psychobehavioral, based on insight-oriented procedures that integrate broadly defined, behaviorally oriented approaches. These chapters present the general counseling process, permitting counselors to add techniques consistent with their theory.

We present the counseling process as a relationship between the counselor and the client rather than as a set of techniques. The counseling process consists of establishing a cooperative interaction and using that relationship to help clients explore themselves and their situations, gain a clearer understanding of both, and then try out appropriate actions. The counseling process can cover a wide range of client needs, from therapeutic personal changes to developmental decisions. The therapeutic process extends over a considerable period with numerous interviews that gradually produce changes in how clients view themselves and lead to overt or covert behavior change. In a more developmental process, counseling involves fewer sessions in helping comparatively self-directed clients resolve conflicting ideas, obtain information, or work through decisions. The basic processes are similar, with emphasis differing according to client needs.

This section begins with a chapter on counseling as a relationship. It focuses on the variables that contribute to the relationship and on how these variables also function as techniques to foster client self-exploration, understanding, and appropriate action. Chapter 13 presents a model of the various phases through which a counseling relationship may pass. The model discusses the goals and the behaviors between the counselor and client as the counseling process moves from the initial interview to self-exploration to working through to termination. Chapter 14 examines important social factors in the relationship including the counselor's behaviors that contribute to increased expertness, trustworthiness, and attractiveness. Special attention is given to multicultural and gender factors in counseling.

Chapter 15 discusses the role of diagnosis in the counseling process, both as a concept of classification and as a procedure in understanding the client. We present some models for using diagnosis as a procedure in understanding the client as well as classification.

Chapters 16 through 18 are concerned with decision making in counseling, using tests, and career counseling. Although these elements may appear in any counseling relationship, they are most likely to be included for clients experiencing developmental problems. The chapter on decision making reviews models and presents a step-by-step process of decision making in counseling. The chapter on testing describes the types of tests that may be used with clients and provides guidelines for test interpretation. The career counseling chapter discusses the counselor's conceptualizing the career development process and the content of career counseling.

The final chapter examines the roles of ethics, values, and legalities in counseling. It raises ethical considerations that can improve counselors' behavior and addresses the significant relationship of counselors' values to their behavior. Likewise, counselors' awareness of the legal ramifications of their role can serve as a guide for appropriate behavior in the counseling process.

Chapter 12

Counseling as a Relationship

What differentiates the counseling relationship from any other helping relationship or friendship? Several years ago Patterson (1969) stated that counseling was a special application of the principles of good human relations and described why this relationship was so significant. First, the counseling relationship is established and continues because the client feels a need for special help or assistance with a problem she or he has been unable to resolve independently or through other relationships. Thus, the emphasis is on the client's desire for special help regarding feelings of dissatisfaction. Although friendships are beneficial to people in need of special help, they are often not sufficient to enhance a person's self-esteem or resolve a particular problem. Second, the counseling relationship is formal and structured in that it is not continued on a casual social basis. It is characterized by special arrangements for a specified duration, privacy, and confidentiality. Third, the counseling relationship is limited to the therapeutic hour. Although this practice has been challenged by those who want to make the counselor an agent for social change, the counseling relationship usually does not extend beyond the professional relationship. The counselor may see the client in settings other than the office but the principle of the therapeutic hour still holds. Fourth, although the counseling relationship is limited in time, it is a closer and deeper relationship than ordinary social friendships. The relationship is carefully established as nonthreatening. This atmosphere permits client self-disclosure and self-exploration so that the counselor comes to know the client better than anyone else does. Fifth, the counseling relationship is powerful and thus effective because the principles of good human relationships are applied consciously and purposefully without the banalities of ordinary social interaction. The counseling relationship can develop rapidly and focus on the essentials.

An Overview of the Counseling Relationship

Most theoreticians and practicing counselors agree that the counseling relationship is important to the outcome of all counseling efforts. Many counselors believe that the relationship itself is the most important factor in helping clients change. Many others believe that the counseling relationship is important in that it provides the atmosphere for the counselor to use the strategies and techniques to help the client change. In a seminal article, Gelso and Carter (1985) examine the components of the counseling relationship. They acknowledge Greenson's (1967), division of the analytical relationship into the working alliance, the transference relationship, and the real relationship. Gelso and Carter (1985) go a step further in stating that "all therapeutic relationships consist of three components, although the salience and importance of each part during counseling or therapy will vary according to the theoretical perspective of the therapist and the particulars of a given therapy" (p. 161).

The Working Alliance

The working alliance has been extended beyond its psychoanalytic origin and is important in short-term counseling as well as in longer, more personal therapy. It is important for the alliance to be established early and for both the client and counselor to agree on their goals and tasks. Although the alliance stretches across all counseling approaches, it will vary according to the counselor's theory, the client's problem, the degree of counselor-client bonding, and the stage of the relationship.

Parts of the Alliance

Bordin's (1983) conceptualization of counseling attributes power for change to two factors. One is the strength of the working alliance between the client and the counselor, and the second is the tasks that are incorporated in that alliance. He describes the working alliance as a collaboration for change and has identified three aspects of the alliance: (1) the mutual agreement and understandings about the goals sought in the change process, (2) the tasks of each of the participants, and (3) the bonds between the participants that are necessary to sustain the enterprise. Although Bordin's (1975) ideas grew from psychoanalytic theory, he states that the idea of the working alliance is not merely a way of integrating the field of therapy but is a description of the change process.

It is necessary to have a basic level of understanding and agreement between the counselor and client to reach their changed goals. The level of clarity and mutual agreement contributes to the strength of the working alliance. The kind of goals that are agreed upon in terms of thoughts, feelings, and action will also contribute to different kinds of working alliances.

The strength of the working alliance also depends on a mutual understanding about the tasks that the goals impose on each person. The particular tasks are assigned by the therapist and are usually based on his or her theoretical orientation or personal style. The alliance is influenced by how well the client understands the connection between the assigned tasks and the desired goal and how well the demands of the task fit his or her ability. Therefore, it is important that the therapist be sensitive to the client's ability and skill in participating in the alliance.

Bordin (1983) believes that the bonds of the alliance center on the feelings of liking, caring, and trusting that the client and counselor share. The various combinations of goals and tasks differ in how much liking, caring, and trusting there needs to be to sustain that type of collaboration. Usually the amount of time people spend together influences the level of the bond. In a short-term vocational counseling relationship, the bonds would not develop in the same manner as in a longer personal counseling relationship. As the client shares more personal information, there is greater potential for the bond to be enhanced.

Bordin (1983) emphasizes that the building of a strong therapeutic working alliance is a major feature of the change process and that the amount of change is probably more a function of the strength than the form of the collaboration. He does believe, however, that technique and methods are important and states that the amount of change is based on both the building and repair of strong alliances.

The types of problems that stimulate a person to seek counseling often include thoughts, feelings, or behaviors that are self-defeating. As the therapeutic process taps into such self-defeating habits, breaks in the working alliance that parallel self-defeat in other experiences are likely to occur during the therapeutic collaboration. As these issues are overcome, the client is provided with a new way of thinking, feeling, and acting. Under certain circumstances these changes can generalize beyond the working alliance to other aspects of the client's life. The idea of the working alliance goes beyond the view of rapport as a relationship factor needed before treatment is begun. In fact, it is the building and repairing of the working alliance that is the treatment.

The concept of a working alliance has been extended beyond its origins in psycho-analysis and appears to have a broader acceptance within the counseling field. Gelso and Carter (1985) present several general theoretical propositions concerning the working alliance and review some research to support their propositions. (They also acknowledge that these are intended to stimulate additional research.) First, it is important that the working alliance be established as early as possible to have the counseling be successful. This appears to be important regardless of the length of the counseling. In their review of several outcome studies, they conclude that the working alliance is important early in short-term counseling and may develop more slowly if the counseling relationship is going to be of a longer duration. Eaton, Abeles, and Gutfreund (1988) report that regardless of the length of therapy, the level of the therapeutic alliance was established within the first three sessions and was largely constant throughout. More recently, Klee, Abeles, and Muller (1990) investigated the client's positive and negative contributions to the therapeutic alliance and relationship of these to the outcome. Their findings suggest that patients who demonstrate potential for establishing a therapeutic relationship in the initial session show an increase in positive contributions to the alliance from the early to the late phases of therapy. The data also supported the prediction that among clients achieving significant change in psychotherapy, the positive client contributions would be greater in the late rather than the early sessions of treatment. There was a significant increase from early treatment to late treatment in their positive contributions to the therapeutic alliance.

Second, the strength of the working alliance will vary according to the demands of the client's problems and the kind of counseling approach. The working alliance might be somewhat different in behavior therapy than in psychodynamic therapy. Other variables affecting the type of alliance would include the client's problems and the goals for treatment, whether it is an educational/vocational problem or a personality/reconstruction approach. Kokotovic and Tracey (1990) investigated the relationship of client charac-teristics to the establishment of a working relationship and report that client hostility, quality of past family relationships, and quality of current relationships were related to the establishment of the working alliance. The higher the client's level of hostility and the poorer the past and current relationships, the poorer the quality of the alliance established between the client and the counselor. The counselor's rating of the client adjustment was also related to the quality of the working alliance, but not the client's rating of their adjustment. This study provided no support for the hypothesis that the working alliance quality would be different for those relationships that terminated prematurely and those that did not.

Gaston (1990) reviewed and contrasted the diverse theoretical perspectives on the therapeutic alliance as well as the empirical results from various alliance measures. She reports the empirical evidence supports the direct relationship between the alliance and outcome. Substantial amounts of outcome variance have been accounted for by alliance measures, even after controlling for initial levels of outcome variables. Also, significant associations between the alliance and outcome have been obtained when the alliance was rated by clients, therapists, and clinical judges. Theoretical formulations continue to be refined and more operational definitions of the alliance are being developed.

Third, although there is a need for an early bonding between the counselor and client, it is important that both have an agreement about the goals for the counseling and the tasks that each of them will perform. Fourth, although it would be ideal for the working alliance to remain strong throughout counseling, it is likely to ebb and flow. As the focus in counseling changes and the client is working on his or her task, the alliance will be of less intensity. When the client experiences a stressful time, the alliance may become more central.

The Transference Relationship

Gelso and Carter (1985) indicate that transference occurs with all theories of counseling and that it occurs regardless of the length of treatment. It is, however, difficult to get a precise definition of transference. Not only are there interpretations across different theoretical concepts of counseling, there are even disagreements within the psychoanalytic school. Gelso and Carter propose that transference be perceived in a broad sense and describe it as a repetition of past conflicts with other significant individuals that includes feelings, behaviors, and attitudes that are displaced from those earlier relationships. When these are displaced onto a counselor, it is always an error even if the counselor's behavior triggers the displacement. Transference involves a misperception or misinterpretation of the counselor whether it is a positive or negative transference. Therefore, the transference and countertransference is sometimes termed an "unreal" relationship within the total counseling relationship.

The Real Relationship

The real relationship also exists in all theoretical approaches to therapy (Gelso & Carter, 1985). The counselor's perceptions and understanding of the client's behaviors are realistic, feelings are genuine, and behaviors congruent. It is suggested that the real relationship includes two parts: a non-intimate and a more personal or intimate aspect.

The non-intimate aspect of the relationship involves the general conversational interactions between the counselor and the client, while the more intimate communication involves the more personal messages. The real relationship will increase and deepen during the duration of counseling. As the two people get to know each other as individuals and not just the roles they play in counseling, a more realistic appreciation for each other will develop.

Subprocesses of Internalization

The general model of the working alliance suggests that when clients are positively disposed to counseling with a good counselor and receive sufficient gratification of their needs early in the process, the desired internalization of the alliance takes place. Numerous changes associated with the development of a favorable therapeutic relationship result from this internalization. Internalization is a process in which the representation of the counselor and the gratifying relationship between the client and the counselor become assimilated into the client's inner world. This dynamic is similar to an ordinary developmental process in which children begin to make their first internal judgments about their worth (their essential "goodness" or "badness") and about the dependability and trustworthiness of their caretakers.

Horwitz (1974) proposes four factors as subprocesses that contribute to internalization: corrective emotional experience, increased self-esteem, a transference improvement, and identification with the counselor. The subprocesses of internalization contribute to the growth of the therapeutic alliance and, in return, tend to be enhanced by the growing quality of the relationship. Part of the mutual understanding involves the counselor's accepting the client as a person while trying to help him or her behave more appropriately.

Corrective Emotional Experience

The counselor's commitment to the client and the client's capacity to perceive this relationship not only produce a heightened self-esteem but also can modify the client's special problem behaviors. In a corrective emotional experience, the counselor responds differently to certain aspects of the client's behavior than the latter had expected; that is, retaliation is not forthcoming after the client's inappropriate behavior. Such an experience contributes to the growth of the relationship, engendering trust in the counselor's intentions and fostering hope that this relationship will fare better than others in the past. The growing alliance contributes to the client's capacity to experience and perceive helpful responses, which in turn enhances the growth of a good self-other relationship. Such a relationship permits the client to feel safe enough to explore him- or herself, increase understanding, and internalize enough learning from the counselor to try new behaviors. In contrast, parents and significant others have generally responded with criticism and lack of acceptance to the client's inappropriate behaviors. The client's internalization of these feelings and denial of self-acceptance result in a reduced level of self-esteem. This earlier experience also leads the client to expect that the counselor will not accept her or him. When the client gradually learns that those expectations are unrealistic, he or she can modify misperceptions and reduce defensiveness. Although the counselor and client are trying to help the latter behave more appropriately, the counselor is accepting the client as a person.

Enhanced Self-Esteem

Horwitz's research team (1974) observed that every client who improved had more positive feelings about him- or herself and that these changes were clearly related to experiencing the counselor's interest, concern, and valuing. The effective bond between client and counselor was strengthened.

Heightened self-esteem is more intense when experienced in a context of being accepted and valued despite the expression of inappropriate wishes or behaviors. The counselor's ability to accept the "badness" of the client's behavior reduces the pressure on the client to defend her- or himself, provides an opportunity for the client to internalize the counselor's attitudes, and enhances the client's self-regard. Enhanced self-esteem and the corrective emotional experience are reciprocal processes.

Transference Improvement

Another concomitant of an internalized good relationship is the client's effort to please the counselor by engaging in improving adaptive behaviors. The concept of a transference cure is frequently deprecated by analysts as being only the demonstration of a fleeting and transitory behavior. Such changes in behavior may be temporary and unstable when they are not based on a sufficiently strong and positive internalization. However, when a client has a positive reaction to the counselor and tries new appropriate behaviors in an attempt to please the counselor, the client can receive sufficient internal and external reinforcement to stabilize the new behavior. Thus, the transference improvement that develops in the context of a trusting relationship can be expected to persist.

Identification

Another cause and product of the internalization process is identification with the counselor's attitudes. At first, the client may identify with some of the attitudes and feelings the counselor has demonstrated toward him or her. The identification is based on the counselor's sense of commitment and feelings of responsibility and concern for the client. The client assimilates the essential ingredients of the therapeutic relationship into feelings about her- or himself. The process of identification is a basic ingredient of normal development; in counseling, it represents an acquisition in an area where normal development failed either because of conflict in relationships with parents or because parents represent an inappropriate model.

The process of identifying with certain specific attitudes exemplified in the counselor is a by-product of internalization. This does not mean that the counselor imposes values on the client but that the counselor exemplifies attitudes and behaviors consistent with the client's goals for her- or himself. Identification refers to the process of becoming like an external model, in this instance, taking on certain qualities of the counselor or other significant people. Identification involves a modification of the self-representation.

Summary
The interrelationship of the working alliance, the transference relationship, and the real relationship will vary between each counselor and client. There is no specific recipe even for a particular counselor. It would seem that the working alliance is the essential component in the counseling relationship as is a working agreement outlining tasks and behaviors. Both the client and the counselor probably come to a relationship with certain transferences that are placed on each other, and new transference feelings are stimulated as the two begin their interaction. It seems reasonable that as the two people come to know each other better there would be less transference, and the variables of the real relationship would increase.

The counseling relationship is an alliance formed to help the client move toward a goal: more appropriate behavior. The client is able to try changes through an internalization of this therapeutic alliance. The internalization is made possible by the counselor's acceptance of the client as a person and by the former's help in resolving a problem. Feeling accepted despite inappropriate behavior may be a corrective emotional experience for the client. This experience helps enhance the client's self-esteem and encourages her or him to work for improvement, sometimes in an attempt to please the counselor. Although at first the client may merely identify with the counselor's attitudes, the client can eventually internalize the concepts and personalize these new attitudes and behaviors.

Skills Used in the Counseling Relationship

This chapter examines the specific variables of the relationship. To help the client feel accepted and understood, the counselor will use different levels of facilitative communication. While being genuinely her- or himself, the counselor will communicate a positive regard and empathic understanding of the client. These facilitative conditions have been found to be imperative in a counseling relationship and help to enhance the client's self-esteem.

The relationship does not develop automatically. A client may exhibit some form of resistance to the process or to an aspect of the problem. The counselor may use varying degrees of ambiguity to control the topic and process or permit the client to define the situation. The topics and the client's feelings about them will influence the degree to which the client reacts intellectually or emotionally. At times the client may transfer to the counselor attitudes or feelings that were experienced with other significant people. The counselor may experience a countertransference by having some emotional reactions and projections toward the client. The counselor should recognize all these relationship dimensions and work to help the client function in the most effective manner. The counselor recognizes these dimensions through the client's verbal and nonverbal communication and uses his or her own communication skills to help the client explore herself or himself, improve self-understanding, and begin more appropriate behaviors.

The counselor's skill in understanding these relationship dimensions and in communicating can facilitate the client's entry into the therapeutic alliance and movement through the stages of counseling that make up the counseling process. Therefore, counseling is a relationship consisting of various dimensions.

Although the relationship dimensions are presented separately in this chapter, many occur simultaneously. They are discussed independently to provide adequate coverage of each topic; however, they must be seen as an integrated process in counseling. We begin with a thorough examination of the therapeutic alliance and the general counseling process. This will be followed by discussion of the specific dimensions of the counseling relationship.

Facilitative Conditions

Since Rogers's (1957) assessment of the necessary and sufficient conditions for therapeutic personality change, the counselor attitudes and behaviors of positive regard for and empathic understanding of the client and counselor congruence have been believed important in the counseling relationship. In Rogers's view, clients change only in a relationship in which the two persons are in psychological contact; that is, both the client and counselor are truly aware of the presence of the other. Although counselors' acceptance of these facilitative conditions has varied over the years, they are still considered helpful in developing the therapeutic relationship.

The counselor must be congruent or integrated in the relationship, without any facade, role, or pretense. What the counselor says is not only honest, but also congruent with the counselor's feelings. The counselor's willingness to be genuine in words, behavior, feelings, and attitudes is the only way to guarantee reality in the relationship.

The second facilitative condition in a relationship is the counselor's experiencing an empathic understanding of the client's world and being able to communicate some of this understanding to the client. The counselor senses and experiences the client's private feelings and personal meanings as if they were his or her own. When the counselor can perceive these internally as they seem to the client and can successfully communicate some of this understanding to the client, then this condition is fulfilled.

The third condition for growth and change is the counselor's experiencing a warm, positive, accepting attitude toward the client. Although Rogers lists this condition third, it probably is the first thing the counselor is able to communicate to the client. It means that she or he likes the client as a person and cares for the latter in a nonpossessive way as a person with potential. This condition means that the counselor respects the client as an individual; this is usually termed *positive regard.*

The last condition for personal change in the relationship is called *unconditionality of regard.* Rogers hypothesizes that the relationship will be effective to the degree that the positive regard is unconditional. The counselor does not accept certain feelings in the client and disapprove of others; there is a consistently positive feeling, without reservation and without evaluations. The counselor's acceptance of the client is unconditional in the sense that it is nonjudgmental: no conditions or strings are attached. It means an acceptance of and regard for the person's current attitudes no matter how negative or positive they may be. This acceptance of fluctuating feelings in the client makes for a relationship of warmth and safety. The client does not have to conceal aspects of self, behave in certain ways, or play certain games to gain the counselor's attention or positive valuation. In recent years, the unconditionality of regard has been dropped from the core conditions as research demonstrated that clients may experience various levels of positive regard;

however, they would not consider it unconditional. Nevertheless, the less counselor conditions are communicated, the more acceptance the clients will feel and the more freedom to explore themselves.

To the core conditions of empathy, positive regard, and congruence, Carkhuff (1969) added immediacy, concreteness, and confrontation. The condition of immediacy involves the counselor asking "What are clients trying to tell me that they can't tell me directly?" The counselor's immediate behavior, then, reflects directly to clients the message he or she thinks they are trying to communicate. Concreteness is sometimes described as the specificity of expression. It involves focusing not only on the feelings and experiences the client is expressing, but also on the immediate interaction between the client and counselor. Being concrete contributes to the relationship by requiring complete, comprehensive, and relevant material about the client's problems. It also contributes to selecting a definite action to help the client resolve problems. Concreteness is important in the early stages of the relationship, when the counselor is helping the client focus on specific aspects of the problem, and then again in the later phases, when the counselor is helping the client focus on specific courses of actions. The addition of confrontation to the facilitative conditions brings more assertiveness to the counselor's role. Confrontation involves the counselor's communicating his or her observation and evaluation of clients' behavior by focusing on the discrepancies between real self and ideal self, between insight and behavior, and between self-perceptions and the perceptions of others. Effective confrontation helps clients make a change. It is more likely when the relationship contains higher degrees of empathy and positive regard. As a result, clients engage in deeper self-exploration and move toward a better understanding and, eventually, more appropriate behavior. (The use of confrontation as a therapeutic skill will be addressed in detail later in this chapter.)

Research and Evaluation

During the 1960s and early 1970s there was considerable research into the facilitative conditions. Most of the reported studies indicated that higher levels of the conditions were related to a variety of positive outcomes. Truax and Mitchell (1971), in a review of research conducted up to 1970, concluded that there was clear evidence that counselors who were accurately empathic, warm, and genuine provided the necessary and sufficient conditions for effective counseling regardless of the kind of problem or theory of counseling. They also concluded that clients who received lower levels of facilitative conditions not only tended to fail to improve but even became worse. However, Parloff, Waskow, and Wolfe (1978) stated that some of the research included in that review had been seriously questioned and that the earlier assessment had not given sufficient weight to obvious inconsistencies among the reports. They went on to challenge the idea that empathy, warmth, and genuineness were prerequisites for change. They maintained that these conditions should not be dismissed but should be considered as among a number of important factors. In a 1977 review, Mitchell, Bozarth, and Krauft concluded that there had been conflicting evidence regarding a direct relationship between facilitative conditions and outcome. Although a number of studies suggest that one or more of the conditions are related to positive outcomes, other studies report little or no evidence of such a relationship: "The recent evidence, although equivocal, does seem to suggest that empathy, warmth, and genuineness are related in some way to client change, but that their potency and generalizability are not as great as once thought" (Mitchell et al., 1977, p. 181).

From their review of the literature, Gelso and Carter (1985) conclude "The conditions originally specified by Rogers are neither necessary nor sufficient, although it seems clear that such conditions are facilitative." They go on to acknowledge that there appears to be a modest relationship between the level of facilitative conditions and the client's in-counseling behavior and outcomes. Secondly, there is support for the findings that under certain circumstances lower levels of facilitative conditions may contribute negatively to client behavior.

It is apparent that the facilitative conditions are important characteristics in establishing a counseling relationship. However, numerous other dimensions involving interpersonal skills are necessary for an effective relationship. The manner in which the counselor behaves in the relationship and uses various dimensions of interaction is related to this effectiveness.

Ambiguity

Ambiguity refers to the amount of structure the counselor provides in the counseling relationship. It is assumed that clients react to a stimulus situation in a way that communicates their needs. If the counselor provides a structure and asks questions in the interview, clients respond only in the areas established by the counselor. When the counselor presents a more vague stimulus situation, clients' responses are more likely to involve the unique aspects of their life history. A more ambiguous counseling situation leads clients to express emotional and motivational material that is usually repressed, thus allowing the counselor a deeper understanding of their behavior.

Bordin (1968) cited three areas in which the counselor communicates the degree of ambiguity: "(a) The topic he considers appropriate for the client to discuss; (b) the closeness and other characteristics of the relationship expected; and (c) the counselor's values in terms of goals he sets up toward which he and the client should work as well as his values in general" (p. 150). The degree of ambiguity when the counselor opens the interview with "What would you like to talk about today?" is very different from that when the interview starts with "How are things going on your job?" If the counselor provides the topic for the interview, he or she structures the degree of ambiguity. When the counselor permits any topic to be discussed, the greater degree of ambiguity allows clients to project the area of their interest. The selection of topic is often related to whether the counselor establishes the goal or works with the client's values.

The counselor's decision to heighten the ambiguity in the relationship should be based on the needs of the individual client. Ambiguity produces anxiety, and while anxiety is an important aspect of effective counseling, there is an optimal level of anxiety that each person can use. If anxiety exceeds this point, clients may be so overwhelmed that they will use their energy for self-protection rather than therapeutic progress. Clients with schizoid tendencies need less ambiguity, because they are working to maintain contact with reality and actually benefit from a more structured situation. The counselor does not need to introduce a high degree of anxiety in an interview with a relatively well-adjusted person who is seeking assistance for a decision-making process.

It is also important that the counselor recognize his or her tolerance level for ambiguity. A counselor who becomes more anxious when control of the interview is maintained by the client is more likely to try to maintain control. Counselors' difficulties with ambiguity are evidenced by an avoidance of self-disclosure to the client or by an expression of uncertainty and concern about making a wrong move. The counselor's self-awareness and awareness of the client's present level of stress will be important in providing the most appropriate level of ambiguity.

Resistance

Resistance probably exists to some degree in all interviews and may be viewed as the opposite of coping with emotional expression. Resistance varies from outright rejection of counseling to subtle forms of inattention. Although it is always present to some degree, the client usually does not recognize it. Therefore, it is mostly an unconscious phenomenon. It is an ambivalent attitude toward counseling: The client wants help yet resists it. Resistance is the client's tendency to defensively oppose the purposes of counseling. The counselor's skill must overcome this resistance by building and maintaining an effective relationship.

Otani (1989) reviewed three theoretical models of resistance in counseling: anxiety control, noncompliance, and negative social influence. The anxiety control model stems from Freud's conceptualization of resistance as the client's effort during therapy to repress anxiety-provoking memories and insights in the unconscious. The materials that were blocked from consciousness during the free association helped the client avoid pain and anxiety. This assumption is still held by many dynamically oriented counselors. Behaviorally oriented therapists frequently believe resistance is the client's noncompliance with the prescribed behavioral assignments. They believe that the assessment and management of individual or environmental factors contribute to the person's resistance. A negative social influence in the interpersonal relationship of the counseling process is a third model of resistance.

Kell and Mueller (1966) view resistance as both a counselor and a client activity reflecting ambivalence. The client's inappropriate behavior receives sufficient reinforcement to make the prospect of giving it up for uncertain rewards a difficult process. Therefore, many clients enter counseling with mixed feelings about wanting to change. For example, a client may project onto the counselor the attributes of significant others who were helpful or hurtful. In assessing, understanding, and reacting to the client's ambivalence, the counselor's own ambivalence may become activated if the latter uncritically believes either side of the client's projections. The client may become ambivalent and immobilized because the counselor feels confused by his or her inability to cope with the client's double messages. The client struggling with ambivalence will be particularly sensitive to any ambivalence exhibited by the counselor.

Lerner and Lerner (1983) describe a concept of resistance based on family-systems theory that they believe is relevant to individual therapy. In a family-systems perspective, one person's resistance serves as a positive and adaptive function within the context of the person's family. Often one family member attempts to protect others by not changing his or her own behavior, because the person unconsciously associates change with being disloyal to the family system. In individual counseling that person's resistance could be involved with the rest of the family system. When the counselor becomes aware of resistance in the counseling relationship, the client may be at the center of a tug of war, feeling a need to be loyal to the family and remain the same and also a need to work toward a change with the counselor. If the counselor can understand the client's predicament and view the resistance more positively, this understanding and positive behavior may help reduce the resistance impasse.

Working with resistance in the interview is one of the most taxing situations confronting counselors. It is important that they become aware of any external causes that may be contributing to the client's resistance, including the influence of their own behavior. Since resistance is a normal part of the struggle for change, they need to be aware of the client's feelings but not respond to them. They focus only on accepting and understanding the client. Should the level of resistance increase or become prolonged, they may need to become more active in reducing the client's resistance. They can move the discussion to a more intellectual level to reduce the tension and provide some support as well as clarification. Sometimes a temporary diversion can reduce the intensity of the client's feelings. If the client appears to be aware of the resistance and if a good relationship exists, counselors may offer an explanation of what they think the client is doing. Such an interpretation may help the client achieve at least an intellectual understanding of it. Empathic expression of the feelings of resistance may be helpful before even a slight interpretation.

Resistance is most prevalent during the early stages of counseling. While it may never completely disappear, the counselor needs to engage the client in the counseling process and increase the compliance to the counseling process. Reframing is one method that can be used to reduce resistance so the client and counselor can work toward the common goal. Reframing involves presenting the client with a new perspective regarding the problem. The reframe does not deny the problem. It defines a more adaptive and less painful way of seeing it. The new frame puts the problem in a perspective that there is a solution to move toward. It is important to note that reframing is not the total therapeutic treatment. It is merely the first step in the process. A change in the meaning of some part of the client's life in the early stage of therapy is an important method (LaClave & Brack, 1989). Meanings attached to certain aspects of the client's problem are changed to motivate the development of new ways of adaptation. Reframing merely shifts the focus of the client from the problem to the process. The counselors may also use reframing on themselves.

When the counselor reframes an adolescent's behavior from that of a misbehaving delinquent to that of a person who is looking for attention, the counselor's attitudes and methods can also change. Many counselors use reframing as a part of their general counseling approach. LaClave and Brack (1989) suggest that reframing-oriented counselors merely seek to make it more succinct and effective, but they design their reframes deliberately rather than just letting them happen. Successful reframing often requires an approach to clients that at first seems paradoxical, but these techniques are the most humane way of approaching clients who have presented some resistant behaviors.

Metaphors, anecdotes, and stories are additional methods that can be used in responding to client resistance (Romig and Gruenke, 1991). Resistant behaviors appear in a variety of self-protecting functions for the client, and Dolan (1985) suggests that the counselor must respect the client and these behaviors. When a counselor communicates understanding and respect for the functions served by the resistance behaviors without challenging them prematurely, a sufficient relationship may be established to begin counseling. Indirect methods can be helpful in addressing the initial resistance to begin counseling. This means meeting the client within their frame of reference rather than challenging it. Metaphors and anecdotes may be successfully used to bypass this initial resistance.

Metaphor is a nonliteral form of communication, which uses stories, myths, parables, allegories, anecdotes, and fairy tales. Towers et al. (1987) describes metaphor as a language of analogy which tends to facilitate thought processes that are more imagistic than literally verbal. In a review of research using metaphors in counseling, Towers et al. reported that metaphors arouse client interest in the counseling process. They also disrupt old thinking patterns and result in nondefensive self-exploration. The use of metaphors also increases the client's view of the counselor as a trustworthy person. Metaphorical information can be particularly helpful with resistant clients. The ambiguous nature of metaphor allows counselors to deny an attempt to convey directly any particular message to a client. This permits the client the freedom to choose the meaning he or she wishes to give to the metaphor.

Metaphors are useful, however, only if they fit the frame of reference of the client. Therefore, the counselor needs to identify the client's frame of reference by examining the pertinent childhood experiences, pastimes, occupations, and other likes or dislikes. Carefully constructing stories that fit with the experiences of the client will help ease tension and enable the counselor to establish rapport. Dolan (1985) stated that when the stories fit the client it demonstrates an understanding of the client, making it more difficult for the client to challenge or discount the counselor. Creatively constructing metaphors with resisting clients can be a useful way of establishing the counseling process.

After assessing his or her own confidence and examining the defenses of a highly resistant client, the counselor may wish to refer this person to another counselor who can remove the source of external resistance that has been inhibiting their relationship.

Transference

Transference has been identified as an important aspect of the therapeutic relationship. Psychodynamic counselors may be more interested in analyzing transference as a way of understanding other client relationships. At the other end of the continuum, behaviorally oriented counselors are more apt to regard the therapeutic relationship as a vehicle for effecting behavior change or cognitive change and are not concerned with the transference phenomenon.

Counselors, even those with a psychodynamic orientation, do not use a strictly psychoanalytic approach to therapy and therefore would not work through transference in the same way. Even though the counselor and client face each other in a relationship to resolve whatever the client's problem may be, some transference feelings may exist. Even Rogers (1951) acknowledged that transference occurred in client-centered relationships; however, he contended that this did not mean the transfer of infantile attitudes into the present relationship.

Brammer and Shostrom (1982) describe transference as a type of projection of the client's past or present unresolved and unrecognized attitudes toward authority figures and love objects. In other words, clients respond to the counselor similarly to the ways in which they respond to other significant individuals. In this transference process, clients build certain expectations of the counselor's role. The intensity of the transference depends on the type of client, the setting, the length of counseling, the extent of emotional involvement, the counselor's personality, and the counselor's techniques. The counselor does not depend on transference for effective counseling but needs to be aware that transference is present in varying degrees.

Cerney (1985) writes that transference occurs on an unconscious level and also that not all reactions or feelings toward the counselor can be labeled transference. Many behaviors are responses to reality, and counselors must be cautious in their interpretations. As an example, when a client expresses displeasure about the counselor's being late for an appointment, it may not be transference but an appropriate response to the reality of the counselor's behavior. A counselor is not really a blank screen. Through his or her personality and theoretical approach to counseling, the counselor creates an image that affects the intensity of the transference.

Gelso and Carter (1985) note that even though the client may have some conscious awareness of the feelings and perceptions that are being transferred to the counselor, the client's misperception is not conscious. They also suggest that clients have predispositions to certain distortions about other people and that certain aspects of the counselor may stimulate in clients those perceptions to which they are predisposed. Therefore, transference is actually a part of the client's inner life that may or may not ever become evident in counseling. It has been suggested that all counseling situations and counselors have what Gelso and Carter call "transference pull." A counselor is not really a blank screen. Through his or her personality and theoretical approach to the process, the counselor will create an image that will affect the type and intensity of transference.

Bauer and Mills (1989) note that work with transference in short-term psychodynamic therapies has progressed from analysis of the genesis of transference reactions to a more active interactional here-and-now approach. In recent years there has been an interest in the more active use of transference in the counseling relationship to clarify, examine, and modify the interpersonal dynamics rather than using them as a springboard to discuss the genesis of the conflicts. Bauer and Kobos (1984) reviewed the major contributors to the development of short-term dynamic therapy and reported that the crucial change agent in their techniques was an emphasis on interpretation and working through the transference relationship.

Working with transference in the here-and-now relationship includes (1) helping the client to be aware of the importance of examining his or her reactions to the counselor; (2) identifying the self-defeating aspects of the patterns; and (3) developing a more flexible and mature discussion with the counselor. It concentrates on the transference reactions or patterns of behavior that are transference based and de-emphasizes gaining access to repressed, infantile conflict. Although this approach to transference has increasing acceptance conceptually, Bauer and Mills (1989) believe it is often underutilized in practice. This difference between theory and practice involves resistances from both the client and counselor.

Bauer and Mills (1989) present several of the client-centered resistances as well as the counselor-centered resistances. Client resistance to the present relationship transference analysis includes the client's perception of the counselor as ignoring the client's "real-world" problems, client difficulties in both identifying and accepting their transference reactions, and the fears that occur when the resolution of transference difficulties result in increasing autonomy and personal responsibility.

Counselors can assist clients in becoming aware of transference patterns by responding to illusions of transference in communications unrelated to the therapy relationship. When the client is describing characteristics of other individuals in her or his life, the counselor may introduce the possibilities that the client experiences similar reactions in the therapy process. Timing is an important part of this intervention. The counselor needs to permit the client sufficient time to express the feelings and recognize some of the implications of those feelings by being patient and providing a safe environment. Such safety will enhance the therapeutic alliance and help the client risk examination in the present relationship.

Clients may refuse to consider the possibility of transference stating that their reactions are based only on the reality of the therapist and are not related to any past conflict or development. This type of resistance may be handled by examining historical parallels. By discussing similarities in earlier relationships, the client may be able to discuss and resolve the impasse in the present relationship.

Some clients' refusal to examine transference reactions with the counselor is a resistance to accepting the responsibility for how they could choose to think and feel. They are avoiding facing personal conflicts and their own roles in such conflicts, and the stress involved in giving up secure self-defeating mechanisms. If they work through the transference with this relationship they would need to relinquish much of the externalizing projective defenses as well as the level of security they furnish.

The counselor's resistances also contribute to an underemphasis of transference analysis in a here-and-now manner. The types of counselor resistances may include an avoidance of the present affect, overemphasis on investigating the genesis of the client's transference, limited counselor activity, the difficulty in differentiating the transference from nontransference behavior, presenting a posture of certainty, and prematurely interpreting the client's projections. Bauer and Mills (1989) suggest that the counselor resistances may originate in the countertransference of the counselor, deficiencies in the training and supervision experiences of the counselor, or complex interaction of those two important influences. A client's perceptions of the counselor may be insightful and threatening, thereby increasing the affect in the here-and-now process, and may stimulate the counselor's conflictual areas if the counselor has not successfully learned to manage those conflicts.

The analysis of the transference in the here-and-now requires the creation of an active give-and-take dialogue working to identify, examine, and modify patterns currently being used with the counselor.

Speculations have been made that although transference reactions increase through-out the course of successful counseling, the reactions increasingly come under the client's conscious control (Gelso & Carter, 1985; Luborsky, 1985). Therefore, clients gain insight into the transference as counseling proceeds. Kivlighan, Gelso, Wine, and Jones (1986) report supporting data for the increase of both transference and insight during the course of time-limited eclectic counseling. To extend this concept, Gelso, Hill and Kivlighan (1991) investigated the effects of transference and client insight on the quality of the session as well as the relationship between the transference and counselor intentions in a single counseling session. They report that counselors rate the counseling session to be high in quality when there is considerable transference accompanying insight by the client. Conversely, high amounts of transference without the client's insight seemed to interfere with the perceived quality of the counseling hour. Interestingly, when little transference occurs, the effects of insight were negligible. It is important to note that only a very small portion of the counselors who participated in this study were strictly psycho-analytic in orientation.

The findings indicate that the existence of strong negative transference stimulates the counselor to work at assisting clients in exploring what they are doing and feeling and how they are relating to their counselor; however, when transference is negative, counsel-ors tend to avoid structuring techniques and directing behavior changes with the clients. It seems appropriate that client's negative reactions would need to be worked through before structuring and directing methods would be effective. It appears that negative transference provides a stronger cue than positive transference for the counselor to do something in the relationship.

The development of short-term dynamic psychotherapy has brought with it variations in the techniques. Strupp and Binder (1984) state that transference is still central in short-term therapy. There is a great diversity in the way in which transference is managed. Their review of the literature reported several independent investigators concurring that the use of interpretation of transference and resistance could be successful in short-term therapy. Strupp and Binder also stated that active work with negative transference was associated with positive therapeutic outcomes. Mills, Bauer, and Miars (1989) recom-mend some techniques to use with transference reactions in short-term therapy. It was suggested that transference reactions and short-term dynamic therapy be managed ac-tively. Confronting transference reactions should generally be limited to situations in which the feelings or behaviors are resistant to the focus of the interview or when working through the feelings could yield new effectively based learning. The counselor's sensitive attention to the client's emerging experience of the counselor and the counseling setting are potential areas for working on transference. The manifestations of the transference should be addressed as they occur in the immediate counseling relationship to maximize the impact of the work. Transference feeling should be addressed quickly, not only for the element of time but also to prevent the development of more difficult and regressive transference.

Brammer and Shostrom (1982) offer several suggestions for handling and resolving transference reactions at various depths. The usual technique for resolving transference is simple acceptance, which permits the client to live out the projected feelings and feel free in the interview. The counselor may reflect the client's level of feeling or ask clarifying questions about the forms of anxiety the client seems to be manifesting. Frequently calling attention to feelings causes the client to react in the opposite manner; therefore, a counselor may want to call attention to negative feelings but not to positive. Another method is to focus on what is currently happening with the client's feelings rather than why the client is having them. A stronger method is to interpret the transference feelings directly, communicating information the client has not already stated and therefore may be rejecting. It is important to remember that counselors should seek supervision in the resolution of difficult situations or refer the client to a counselor more qualified in working with the intensity of the transference.

Countertransference

Countertransference refers to the emotional reactions and projections of the counselor toward the client. Countertransference may include conscious as well as unconscious attitudes toward real or imagined client attitudes and behavior. It may be caused by internal anxiety. The anxiety patterns may be classified into three types: unresolved personal problems, situational pressures, and the communication of the client's feelings to the counselor by empathic means. The counselor's unresolved personal problems should be worked out with another counselor. Both transference and countertransference typically refer to the interplay of irrational forces occurring when the client and counselor become intimately involved in the relationship. These phenomena operate as modes of illogical thought and a denial of reality (Kwawer, 1980).

Although the original concept of countertransference as the analyst's emotional reaction to the client's transference is still used by many people following a psychoanalytic theory, more recent conceptualizations of countertransference have been set forth. Peabody and Gelso (1982) discuss a subtle but important change in the attitude toward countertransference over the years. Earlier definitions focused on the counselor's manifest behavior, whereas a more current definition stresses the counselor's internal reactions, feelings, and attitudes. Peabody and Gelso's study indicated that the counselor's empathic ability was positively related to reports of openness to countertransference feelings. They suggest that there is a limit to how often countertransference can be expressed without spilling over into behavior. It is important for the counselor to be aware of countertransference feelings, but not necessarily to always express them. Cerney (1985) also writes about countertransference involving the feelings of empathy that develop in the counselor. When counselors become aware of growing feelings of irritation or annoyance, they might consider whether the client is communicating, even at a nonverbal level, in an attempt to get others to feel as the client feels—annoyed and irritated. If counselors can set aside their own feelings and just experience the client's feelings, the process is more similar to empathy, allowing them to sense the underlying feelings of the client. Springmann (1986) differentiated between "client-induced" and "therapist-induced" countertransferences.

Singer, Sincoff, and Kolligian (1989) discuss three uses of the term *countertransference* that have been prominent in the literature. One definition describes countertransference referring to all feelings the therapist experiences toward the client. Other writers use countertransference as the therapist's specific reactions to the transference of the specific client. A third description of countertransference refers to it as the therapist's transference toward a given client. Singer et al. (1989) preferred the third definition believing that therapists share with all human beings the potential for transference reactions to other people. It is suggested that not only do clients have experiences in their lives that lead to transferences but so do therapists. Given that therapists have transference reactions toward their clients, Singer et al. emphasize that the distortions are inherent in the therapist's cognitive processing.

A common agreement exists among therapists that therapists' internal reactions need to be noticed, understood, and managed (VanWagoner, Gelso, Hayes, & Diemer, 1991). It is important that the therapists be aware of the reactions, examine them, and use them effectively in the therapeutic process rather than having them interfere with effective therapy. In their review of the literature, VanWagoner et al. (1991) report that counter-transference behavior in the form of counselor withdrawal, antagonism, or hostility appear when client transference material is presented in an area of the therapist's unresolved conflicts and when the client's emotional negative feelings are presented. Those countertransference behaviors contribute to less successful counseling outcomes. Through a review of the theoretical and empirical literature, VanWagoner et al. developed a conceptualization of the factors believed to mediate how a therapist manages counter-transference feelings and identified five interrelated factors. The first factor was the therapists' self-insight, which referred to the extent of therapists' awareness of their own feelings and understanding their basis. Robbins and Jolkovski (1987) report that therapists' awareness of countertransference feelings was inversely related to withdrawal of involvement with a client. They suggest that counselors who are aware of their feelings are more able to do something about them before they overtly act on them.

The second factor, empathic ability, involves both effective empathy and diagnostic empathy. Effective empathy is the counselor's ability to put him- or herself in the client's shoes temporarily and experience those feelings while diagnostic empathy is the intellectual understanding of the client's experience. Self-integration, the third factor, refers to the counselor's psychological health and stable identity, including the ability to differentiate self from others and to put aside her or his own needs in working with a client. The anxiety management factor involves both the counselor's general anxiety level as well as the anxiety level experienced in the therapy sessions. It is believed that the better a counselor is able to manage personal anxiety, the less likely the counselor will manifest countertransference behavior.

Conceptualizing ability, the fifth factor important in countertransference management, refers to the ability of the counselor to conceptualize the client's dynamics in terms of the counseling situation as well as the client's past. The Robbins and Jolkovski (1987) study reported that under conditions of the counselor's low awareness of feelings, theoretical understanding resulted in emotional distancing from the client. However, when theoretical understanding was combined with a moderate level of self-awareness, use of theoretical understanding facilitated involvement.

VanWagoner et al. (1991) found that when compared to therapists in general, excellent male and female therapists were found to have more insight into their own feelings and the bases for those feelings. They also had a greater empathy to sense the client's emotional experience and an intellectual understanding of client emotions. The excellent therapists were more able to differentiate client needs from their own needs since they were more highly personally integrated. The excellent therapists were also lower in general anxiety as well as aware of the client's anxiety in the sessions and were more adept at conceptualizing client dynamics. Although countertransference may be inevitable, counselors with higher levels of these five characteristics may be more successful in managing their countertransference.

Acting out is a description that is usually applied to a client's behavior; however, Watkins (1983) suggests that counselors may also act out. Although the term *acting out* lacks a clear definition, it does involve people acting or behaving as a result of conflicts in feelings. Watkins describes five counselor acting-out behaviors: attentional failures, empathic failures, aggressiveness, sensual and seductive behaviors, and logistical failures. Attentional failures involve the counselor's "tuning out" temporarily and missing the client's communication. Empathic failures involve a misuse of empathic responses, such as indiscriminate or uncritical use of empathy that is not helpful in the therapeutic relationship. Aggressive behaviors such as verbalizing anger or sarcasm or teasing the client are more blatant examples of acting out. Inappropriate touching or sexual innuendos are categorized as sexual or seductive acting out. Being late, missing appointments, and premature termination of a session or the counseling relationship constitute logistical failures. Any of these acting-out behaviors can be defined as countertransference and are appropriate topics for supervision.

Developing an effective counseling relationship involves becoming aware of and resolving countertransference feelings. The traditional approach to dealing with countertransference is through supervisory assistance, which focuses on locating the source of the feelings and attempting to resolve them. The counselor may also be referred to another professional to resolve problem situations. The use of audio and videotape recordings has become a major source of developing awareness of one's behaviors and feelings in the counseling relationship. A more recent approach is dealing with countertransference issues by discussing them with the client. We suggest that the counselor discuss this approach in supervision before bringing countertransference issues into the counseling relationship.

The Cognitive-Conative Dimensions

The cognitive-conative balance that exists in the counseling relationship was discussed by Bordin (1968). The conative aspects of behavior include a person's feelings, strivings, and emotions: the cognitive aspects of behavior include conceptual, perceptual, and motor processes. The affective aspects of behavior are generally related to the release of energy. The infant's release of energy involves disorganized and unintegrated motor discharge. As a child develops perceptual and motor skills, energy is released in a more organized manner to express the child's needs. Therefore, the cognitive processes are particularly important in modifying and controlling most complex and meaningful behavior. Bordin suggests that the cognitive process serves two purposes in the cognitive-conative balance of behavior. "The cognitive aspects may either serve the purpose of controlling affect in the sense of leading to less or no expression, or may serve a truly instrumental function through the fullest possible successful expression of the affect" (p. 169). Therefore, cognitive processes function to control and organize energy. To understand the client fully, the counselor must understand both aspects of the client's communications by applying his or her own cognitive and conative capacities.

The counselor can control cognitive-conative balance in the counseling relationship by her or his actions and communications with the client. To do this effectively, the counselor must understand the client and know when each tactic is appropriate. For example, a client who expresses emotions through over-intellectual or over-rational examination needs to be encouraged to express feelings more freely and to relax the efforts to control them. On the other hand, a client who expresses feelings freely needs to be encouraged to introduce more conceptual aspects into her or his own communications.

A major assumption in counseling is that insight leads to changed behavior. The counselor's role is to help the client explore affective regions, to gain cognition of the relationship between feelings and actions, and with this new cognition change his or her own behavior to meet personal goals more appropriately. The counselor usually transmits cognition to the client through an interpretation by applying two considerations. First, interpretation, whether accepted or rejected, will be ineffective before defenses are loosened. Second, the amount of emphasis on cognitive aspects of the interaction should be related to the intensity of affect that the client expresses. The greater the client's affective expression, the more cognitively the counselor can respond. Interpretation can be useful only when the client is ready for it.

Cognition, or giving information and calling attention to particular behaviors, will be most effective when introduced during a period of low resistance. It is best for the client to make the final interpretation, with the counselor leading up to but not stating it. If the client is defensive and fearful, however, any effort to introduce cognitions that are not specifically related to the avoidance will be distorted by the defenses. When feelings are built up and the reasons for avoidance are near the surface, the interpretation of resistance may be made.

As a client begins to see successive examples in which her or his defenses have operated, an awareness of distorted actions develops. This process, called *working through,* refers to the repetitive process of rediscovery. The client finds in different incidents the need to defend the self and sees how these affect his or her interpersonal relationships. The number of times the counselor must work through incidents with the client depends on how well integrated the client is. Some people understand with awareness of one or two experiences; others need more examples.

The counselor must also be aware of her or his own personal needs and take care not to impose on the client interpretations and cognitions that are not relevant to the latter's problems. These interpretations may be part of the counselor's defenses against a particular conflict. Finally, counselors seem to overemphasize the use of verbal reasoning and should remember that interpretation can advance the therapeutic process only when it is relevant to the client's needs.

Self-Disclosure/Self-Involvement

It is desirable for the client to reveal personal information, because such disclosure has been positively related to personal adjustment and successful counseling. In addition, the level of counselor disclosure is important, because self-disclosure occurs in a reciprocal fashion (Jourard, 1964). In a dyadic relationship there is a high correlation between self-disclosure to a person and the amount of disclosure received from the person. Several studies reported evidence of the efficacy of reciprocal self-disclosure between the counselor and client (DeForest & Stone, 1980; Gary & Hammond, 1970; Graff, 1970; Worthy, 1969). They found a linear relation from low to medium and medium to high with counselor/client disclosures.

Although the literature strongly supports the value of counselors' self-disclosure, there is some evidence that it can be detrimental. It may cause negative reactions by the client and lead to feelings that the counselor is guilty of improper conduct by not remaining in a professional role. The self-disclosing counselor may violate the client's role expectations, and the client may view the counselor as less relaxed, strong, stable, or sensitive (Dies, 1973; Weigel, Dinges, Dyer, & Straumfjord, 1972).

Jourard (1971) suggests that the relationship between self-disclosure and mental health is nonlinear, indicating that there is an optimum level of disclosure and that when the counselor goes beyond that it may be destructive to the interpersonal relationship. We conclude that too little counselor self-disclosure may fail to produce client disclosures, and that too much may decrease the time available to the client or cause the client to have concern about the counselor.

Although there is considerable research about disclosure, there have been few attempts to identify what the client would like in terms of self-disclosure from a counselor. Hendrick (1988) developed an instrument used to ask potential clients what disclosures would be desirable from a counselor and then to assess the position of counselor disclosure in relation to those by best friends and other professional persons relevant to the client. The Counselor Disclosure Scale is a multidimensional instrument that measures desired disclosure on Personal Feelings, Interpersonal Relationships, Sexual Issues, Attitudes, Professional Issues, and Success and Failure. Later, additional versions of the scale were developed to gain the desired disclosure from other persons, such as a close friend, physician, a person who cuts hair, and a professor or teacher. The findings clearly show that the close friend is the person from whom the greatest amount of disclosure was sought by college students. However, for personal feelings, interpersonal relationships, and sexual issues more disclosure was wanted from counselors than from the other three professional people. More disclosure on the attitudes scale was desired from professors than the other three professionals. The results of the study indicate that potential clients would like the counselors to disclose information about their training, orientation to therapy, methods of coping with problems, and handling of interpersonal relationships. Hendrick points out that it is too simplistic to assume that because potential clients say they would like counselors to disclose, that counselors should always do so. Many counseling situations require little or no self-disclosure, and each counseling relationship must be individually evaluated in terms of other self-disclosure. Hendrick (1990), using actual clients to compare results with those from the undergraduate student sample, found virtually no differences in disclosure preferences between the undergraduates and the client participants.

In recent years attention has been directed toward a more specific investigation of *self-involving statements*. Whereas self-disclosing statements refer to past history or personal experiences, self-involving statements are present expressions of the counselor's feelings about or reactions to the client's statements or behaviors (Danish, D'Augelli, & Hauer, 1980). McCarthy and Betz (1978) and McCarthy (1982) report that self-involving counselors were perceived more favorably by their clients than self-disclosing counselors in terms of expertness, social attractiveness, and trustworthiness. Self-involving counselor responses elicit client responses that tend to focus on greater exploration in the present, whereas self-disclosing responses are more likely to elicit responses focusing on the counselor that do not help the client concentrate on the present. It appears that self-involving disclosures keep the focus on the client, and self-disclosing statements may provide a conversational shift to the counselor. Reynolds and Fischer (1983) confirm these findings. McCarthy (1982) reports such results across all possible counselor/client gender pairings. We can conclude that it is more effective for the counselor to use self-involving statements than self-disclosing statements in keeping the client focused on self-exploration and understanding.

In a study about the frequency and type of self-reference used by male and female counselors at varying levels of experience, Robitschek and McCarthy (1991) reported that both self-disclosure and self-involving responses occurred at least sometimes in counseling interviews. They examined the use of both positive and negative self-involving statements as well as positive and negative self-disclosing statements and found that each of the subtopics under these four areas was disclosed by at least a few counselors. However, there were differences in the frequency of certain types of information. For example, counseling style and training were both disclosed frequently while sexual experiences and beliefs were rarely disclosed. Counselors reported using mild to moderately intense positive self-involving statements more frequently than strong negative statements to their clients. Even so, at least a few counselors reported using intensely negative emotions, such as disgust with their client. It was pointed out that because self-involving statements can be either elicited by or felt by the client, the counselor could express strong negative emotions about the client's experiences, such as feeling disgust about the client's being battered. The counselors reported significantly more positive than negative self-references, indicating they provide a supporting, trusting environment. The use of positive disclosure of personal information may normalize the client's experience, thereby reassuring them, while the positive self-involving statements also demonstrate positive regard and respect. Negative self-disclosure may be used less frequently since it would probably be perceived as challenging.

Hill, Mahalik, and Thompson (1989) studied therapist self-disclosure in eight cases of brief psychotherapy (12 to 20 sessions) with anxious/depressed clients and experienced therapists. Each self-reference was rated on two dimensions: involving/disclosing and reassuring/challenging. Then both client and therapist helpfulness ratings were assessed on 89 self-references classified into one of the four types involving/reassuring, involving/challenging, disclosing/reassuring, and disclosing/challenging. Interestingly the eight therapists varied from one to thirty-seven self-disclosures through their therapy sessions indicating that the therapists differed significantly in the frequency of their self-disclosures. Also, the therapists did not use the four types equally. Some used more challenging statements, others more assuring, some more disclosing, and some more involving. In rating the helpfulness of the different self-references, the therapists rated assuring disclosures as more helpful than challenging disclosures. Clients rated the involving/reassuring disclosures as more helpful than the other three disclosure types, but they also rated reassuring disclosures as more helpful than challenging disclosures. The level of client experiencing was used as another outcome measure. The experiencing scale measured the level of the client's feelings being explored and experienced, which serves as a basic referent for problem resolution and self-understanding. The findings give evidence that clients had higher levels of experiencing following reassuring than challenging disclosures. The reassuring, supportive disclosures seem to assist clients in feeling more comfortable and helping them experience themselves at deeper levels suggesting that the disclosures led to client progress.

Hill et al. found that counselors used reassuring disclosures during three different phases of therapy. In the beginning of therapy some counselors shared their feelings about the experience, which seemed to help clients feel less alone and upset about their anxiety. This also modeled talking about feelings and was a valuable activity in therapy. Over the course of therapy counselors occasionally reassured clients. Some reinforced clients, while others reassured them that their feelings were normal. Seven of the eight counselors used "Good-bye" disclosures during the last few minutes of the final session. For several, this was their only disclosure, indicating that even therapists who believe disclosures are inappropriate use them to end therapy. They noted that while there were no significant disagreements between the therapists and clients relative to the helpfulness of the four disclosure types, therapists' ratings were always lower. They speculate that disclosures may be more threatening to therapists because they feel vulnerable in sharing part of themselves with clients.

An interesting point to consider in understanding the place of self-disclosures is that self-disclosures generally occur with other counselor behaviors, such as direct guidance, clarification, or interpretation. Counselors should attend to how these responses may moderate the effects of self-disclosure. Counselors may also want to consider why they use self-disclosure at a particular point. Actually, self-disclosure needs to be examined much more on a case specific basis, examining the contextual clues to provide information about the clinical significance of the disclosure and the impact it has on a particular client. One would assume that the nature of the problem, background of the client, and interpersonal dynamics affect when and why a therapist uses a self-disclosure as well as the impact that disclosure has on a client.

Consistent throughout the literature, counselor use of positive self-involving statements during the first interview receives the most consistently high appeals. It appears that this response relates to its supportive and encouraging characteristics. Focusing on some positive aspect of the immediate counselor and client relationship may be perceived as nonthreatening, affirming type of behavior by the counselor. Such encouragement and support by the counselor's positive self-involving statements may be particularly important in reducing the client's anxiety and putting him or her at ease about beginning counseling (Watkins & Schneider, 1989). The lack of acceptance of negative self-involving statements may relate to their nonsupportive nature. Responses that focus on some negative interaction between the counselor and client may be more threatening to clients. Although such statements may be useful sometimes during the counseling relationship, they are less likely to be effective in the initial interview. It should be remembered that the positive self-involving statements focus on the client in the present while positive self-disclosing statements focus the interview, at least temporarily, on the counselor. During the initial interview, the clients may be more interested in discussing their concerns and find the counselor's self-disclosure distracting. Hence, it may be more appropriate for counselors to use positive self-involving behaviors during the initial interview with positive self-disclosure occurring later. It would seem that negative self-involving and self-disclosing statements should be used as specific techniques to help clients confront themselves and their situations, but that these should occur only after the counseling relationship is well established.

Confrontation

The term *confrontation* all too often conjures up a hostile act. In counseling, however, confrontation challenges clients to examine, modify, and control aspects of their behavior. It helps them understand what they are doing and what the consequences may be and encourages them to assume responsibility for the change. A good confrontation promotes clients' self-examination. If a counselor fails to confront when it is needed, this failure allows clients to continue their self-deceptive behaviors. A good confrontation does not pit the counselor against the client but promotes the client's self-confrontation (Tamminen & Smaby, 1981).

Leaman (1978) identifies three purposes for confrontation. First, it helps clients recognize manipulations and ineffective communication patterns. Clients may be unaware that these patterns are an integral part of their defense mechanisms and are frustrating their fulfillment. Another purpose is to assist clients in evaluating the consequences of such maladaptive behaviors, because they may not recognize the cause/effect relationship between their patterns and the responses of other people. A third purpose is to help clients "own" their feelings and take responsibility for their actions.

Berenson (1968) described the five types of confrontation as experiential, didactic, strength, weakness, and encouragement to action. Experiential confrontation involves the counselor's response to any discrepancy between what clients say about themselves and how the counselor experiences them. A didactic confrontation is the counselor's offer of correct information when clients lack such information—for example, regarding education, vocational, or social areas. When clients talk about not being able to do anything, a counselor may confront them by stressing the strengths they have to act and move toward their goals. A confrontation of client weakness is used very seldom. It may be used when clients are unrealistic in their self-appraisal, and the counselor points out some characteristics that are interfering with their success. Encouragement involves the counselor's pressing the client to act in some constructive manner.

Tamminen and Smaby (1981) have developed a five-level response scale for confronting behaviors: acquiescing, scolding, identifying ineffective behaviors, realizing negative consequences, and committing to change. (1) If the counselor acquiesces by either ignoring the self-deceptive behavior or makes a weak attempt at confronting the client and then backs away if there is resistance, this may mean the counselor is fearful of being disliked or attacked or he or she is not committed enough to really become involved. (2) At the second level, scolding, the counselor would attempt to coerce the client into changing by shaming the client or telling him or her what a good person should do. In such a situation, the counselor would be recognizing the client's behavior but would be so emotionally involved that he or she would not be handling the situation productively. (3) At the third level of identifying effective behaviors, the counselor would describe the client's behavior as well as the probable factors that sustain the pattern. This could include communication of empathy about how difficult it is to accept one's behavior, thereby offering acceptance to the client while helping him or her to identify self-defeating behavior. (4) At the fourth level, realizing negative consequences, the counselor's responses more clearly contain empathy and a commitment to become more involved with a client. A counselor would not only identify the self-defeating pattern of the client, but would also deal with his or her feelings as well as those of the client. (5) In committing to change, level five, the counselor would incorporate the responses from levels three and four and challenge the client to accept appropriate responsibility for the behavior and make changes.

Leaman (1978) asserts that confrontation and interpretation are closely related techniques, because both are direct statements to the client that define specific behavior patterns. A major difference involves the source of meaning. Interpretation involves assigning a meaning to a behavior from the counselor's theoretical framework, whereas confrontation allows the client to assign a meaning to this behavior. Therefore, a confrontation allows greater flexibility for the client than does an interpretation.

Eagan (1976) emphasizes that the manner of the counselor's confrontation is as important as the type of confrontation and offers some guidelines on how confrontation should be done. It is important that confrontation be offered in a spirit of empathy. The confrontation should be offered tentatively, particularly in the early stages of counseling. A tentative observation gives clients an opportunity to hear and examine a different perspective without having it thrust on them. A caring confrontation presupposes the development of a working alliance, and it is another way for counselors to communicate that they care enough to help.

Communication

The counseling process is a relationship between two people, rather than a meeting dominated by the counselor. As part of this relationship, however, the counselor uses techniques to help the client understand him- or herself and the environment and reach decisions for effective behavior. These techniques affect the ways counselor and client discuss problems and the steps clients try to take between interviews. The techniques of counseling involve the counselor's sensitivity and skill, both in receiving communication from the client and in communicating to the client. Each dimension of the relationship requires communication between counselor and client.

Communication Techniques

The counseling relationship with all its social variables and relationship techniques involves verbal and nonverbal communication. The skills of counseling entail both receiving information from clients and communicating to them. Clients present their current state of behavior, organize difficulties, and begin to state more clearly what has been confusing. Clarity of language is an objective way of helping identify problem areas, interpret facts and feelings about themselves and their situation, and gain a better perspective from which to make decisions.

Degree of Leading

A specific skill in communication is the degree of leading used by the counselor in stimulating clients' exploration of their problems and development of insight. Some early research in communication indicated that counselors' verbal techniques tended to fall into definite categories (Robinson, 1950). Awareness of the different degrees of leading lets counselors enlarge their repertoire of techniques. The categories of verbal responses can be labeled and placed on a continuum. Responses with the least degree of leading include silence, acceptance, restatement, clarification, and summary clarification. The first three of these involve communicating understanding, acceptance of what the clients are saying, and encouragement for them to continue. Counselors do not communicate about themselves, but give attention to the client. Even when they clarify the client's rambling comments, they are only making a more precise statement about the situation. The focus is still on the client, and they have not communicated anything about themselves. Assuming the clarification is accurate, this is an example of empathic communication.

A greater degree of leading involves giving a general lead. When counselors would like more information about a topic, they can respond by saying "Can you tell me a little more about that?" which leads the client into further description of the topic. This is not a very strong lead, but it does encourage the client to tell more about the previous statement.

Much stronger leading techniques are tentative analysis, interpretation, and urging. Counselors go beyond communicating that they understand the client and introduce some new ideas. They may tentatively encourage the client to look at the problem or a new solution in a different way, still leaving the client free to accept, modify, or reject this communication. When they offer an interpretation, they are making an inference from what the client has said. Although an interpretation may speed up insight, it should be given at a time when the client is ready to see the relationship between what he or she has said and the insight the counselor is presenting. If the client is not ready or the interpretation is too great a lead, it may lead to the client's resisting what the counselor has said. Urging the client to reveal something or make a certain decision may not be helpful. Clearly, the verbal methods of tentative analysis, interpretation, and urging involve the counselor much more in the process than milder techniques. It is possible to see how these verbal skills are involved in aspects of transference, countertransference, resistance, and confrontation.

Methods such as depth interpretation, rejection, assurance, and introducing an unrelated aspect of the subject have the greatest degree of leading, and they may be detrimental in the counseling relationship. A depth interpretation is made from the counselor's theory of personality dynamics and, therefore, may lead far beyond the client's present thinking. Even when the counselor feels that the client's attitudes or decisions may be wrong, rejection of her or his view would only hurt the client or increase resistance. More effective communication would involve bringing the client to a self-realization with more gradual degrees of leading. Reassurance may also feel like rejection to clients, because they may feel that the counselor is belittling their problems. When counselors say "I'm sure everything will work out OK," they are also conveying a rejection of the topic that the client has been discussing. This communicates that they are not interested in understanding what the client is talking about or feeling.

Other systems have been developed to categorize counselors' responses. Hill (1978) developed such a categorization by incorporating parts of existing systems. Hill's system contains 14 types of responses: minimal encouragement, approval/reassurance, information, direct guidance, closed question, open question, restatement, reflection, nonverbal referent, interpretation, confrontation, self-disclosure, silence, and "other." This system is not based on a degree of leading, but it does define a large range of counselor responses that may be helpful in researching counselor/client communication.

Elliott (1979) conducted a content analysis of the literature on how clients and helpers perceive particular helper behavior. He reported the most typical: Advice was perceived as guiding the client; acknowledgment—for example, "uh-huh"—as reassuring the client; reflection, as communicating understanding of the client's statement; interpretation, as explaining clients to themselves; questions, as gathering information; and self-disclosures, as helpers using themselves to help the client.

Elliott, Barker, Caskey, and Pistrang (1982) used an analog sample and a counseling sample to study the helpfulness of counselor responses. Clients rated interpretations as the most helpful type of counselor response, with trained raters ranking advice and interpretation as the most helpful responses.

Several other studies focused on counselor interpretation. Strong, Wambach, Lopez, and Cooper (1979) reported that students perceived interpretations as conditional and evaluative. However, the research did indicate that interpretation motivated change by making the problem behavior more serious, more relevant, and more threatening to the client's self-esteem. The researchers suggest that when clients see problems as caused by a factor they can directly affect, such as lack of effort, they are able to exert themselves to correct the situation. However, an interpretation that identifies causes of a problem that they cannot do anything about, such as past events, does not provide them with tools they can use to change. The type of interpretation has differing effects on their motivation to change.

Although counselors using different theories may offer different opinions and descriptions of interpretation, it is counseling skill that is generally thought to be essential in the counseling relationship, not one's theoretical approach. Claiborn's (1982) review of the literature indicates that interpretations are equally effective across theoretical approaches, suggesting that no theoretical framework has been superior to any other in promoting the therapeutic process. Claiborn suggests that providing clients with a different meaningful perspective on their situation is more helpful than not doing so. In this light, interpretation is described as providing clients with a viewpoint that is discrepant with their own, with the intent to induce them to adopt a new perspective.

Claiborn, Ward, and Strong (1981) examined the extent to which the counselor's interpretation of the problem differed from the client's belief and how much that difference affected the client. They found that interpretations that were congruent with or only slightly different from the client's produced somewhat more change than interpretations that were highly discrepant. Clients who received more congruent interpretations expected to change more and tended to show greater change and greater satisfaction than those who received more discrepant interpretations. A further important finding in this study was that even though congruent interpretations were viewed more positively, they still tended to arouse resistance in the client. The resistance appeared to reflect an awareness of the counselor's discrepant opinion and intent to influence rather than a rejection of the counselor's interpretation.

Counselor Awareness and Communication

It seems reasonable that counselors' interventions would in part be dependent on their awareness of how clients respond to their interventions. Hill and O'Grady (1985) suggest that counselors would be likely to feel more comfortable continuing with their current strategy if they believed their clients feel supported by the interventions. On the other hand, counselors would be more likely to shift their strategies to meet respondents' needs if they perceived that the client felt misunderstood or worse about themselves after the counselor's intervention. This led Thompson and Hill (1991) to add that the problem may arise if the counselor is unaware of the client's reactions to interventions. If clients hide or distort their reactions or if the counselors are unaware of their reactions, counselors possibly would not plan effective interventions.

Rennie (1985), as reported in Thompson and Hill, found that when clients experienced negative reactions to their counselors or the process, they did not state them. Often they retained negative feelings out of "deference" to the counselor. Since Rennie reported that counselors were often unaware that clients intentionally hid reactions from them, Thompson and Hill continued to study counselor perceptions of client reactions and the impact of these perceptions in facilitating or hindering the counseling process. They report that counselors were able to correctly perceive client reactions to their interventions 50 percent of the time in a single counseling session. The ability of the counselors to actually perceive the client reactions seemed to influence the immediate process depending on the different types of interventions. The counselors were fairly accurate in recognizing client reactions to therapeutic work, supportive interventions, and no reaction. These reactions tend to be acceptable and therefore, may be easier for clients to acknowledge and for counselors to perceive. A better immediate outcome was reported when counselors matched clients on their reactions of therapeutic work. Therapeutic work includes such things as greater self-understanding and new ways to behave, which are frequently goals of most therapies. It is important to note that higher helpfulness ratings did not result when the counselors matched clients on no reaction, which is more apt to be a nonproductive or desired client reaction.

Challenged and negative reactions of clients were more difficult for counselors to recognize. These could be situations in which clients were attempting to hide their reactions from the counselors or just gave fewer verbal and nonverbal cues making their challenge and negative reactions more difficult for the therapists to recognize. Since this study focused on initial interviews, the counselors did not have previous experience with the clients and may have relied more heavily on their experience with clients in general.

Hill and Stephany (1990) suggested further research is needed to examine how individual clients express their reactions to counselor interventions both in their verbal and nonverbal behavior.

Nonverbal Communication

Nonverbal behaviors emphasize or accent the verbal message; such behaviors may amplify part of the message, explain a silence, add new information, or distort the verbal message. Several studies have reported on the importance of nonverbal clues. In a review of the literature regarding nonverbal involvement in social behavior, Edinger and Patterson (1983) suggest that nonverbal behaviors play an important role in changing attitudes and opinions. Gesturing, paralinguistic expressiveness, and looking at the client were generally found to increase the effectiveness of an attempt to persuade. Also, nonverbal reinforcements such as increased eye contact, smiling, and positive head nod were effective in improving learning, test performance, and applicant performance on employee interviews. Edinger and Patterson concluded that gaze and facial expression were the most prominent nonverbal behaviors contributing to social control.

In a study of verbal interventions and nonverbal behavior, Claiborn (1979) reported that clients perceived the counselor's use of responsive nonverbal behaviors such as more vocal variation, facial expressions, eye contact, and gestures as more expert, attractive, and trustworthy than the use of comparatively unresponsive nonverbal behavior. Roll, Crowley, and Rappl (1985) found that clients perceived no significant differences in effectiveness, attractiveness, trustworthiness, and helpfulness between counselors who used a high frequency of nonverbal communication and those who used a moderate frequency.

Lee and Hallberg (1982) report that nonverbal communication had no impact in an evaluation of counselor effectiveness. The counselors' frequency of nonverbal behaviors as well as their decoding and encoding skills did not determine the effectiveness of the counseling session. However, counselors' verbal and nonverbal congruence was positively related to their effectiveness. This finding indicates that nonverbal communication should be examined not in isolation but with verbal communication, because the two seem to work together. The two methods of communication may be congruent, or nonverbal communications may deny or distort part of what is being verbally communicated. Tyson and Wall (1983), using an analog study, reported that nonverbal behavior seemed to increase the impact of congruent verbal communication. When there was incongruence between the verbal and nonverbal method, however, the communication was altered in the direction of the nonverbal method. Nonverbal behaviors appeared to make the verbal message believable or unbelievable.

Although the importance of nonverbal behaviors in counseling is long-standing, only recently have there been attempts to examine the interplay between clients' verbal and nonverbal behaviors. Counselor training in nonverbal communication has emphasized the areas of body orientation, distance, eye contact, and body movement to a forward incline for purposes of increasing attention in communicating facilitative messages in the interaction. A study by Hermansson, Webster, and McFarland (1988) found the process of making a deliberate lean seemed to make some difference in the levels of intensity and respect. When counselors made a required backward lean, they were rated with higher levels of intensity and respect. The greatest effects of this were in connection with the movement away from clients by counselors who preferred to move forward and were assessed as being the more effective counselors. Hermansson et al. suggested that the sensitivity of the affected counselors might involve a low arousal threshold to subtle intimacy variations so their reactions to deliver changes in behavior might be greater. They may feel that movement away from the client would be evaluated negatively; therefore, compensatory behaviors heighten their facilitative conditions. Likewise, being required to lean forward toward clients may have been considered as too soon in the interaction or too arbitrary and therefore, compensatory efforts lowered the facilitative conditions. They are suggesting that for these male counselors with female clients that making torsal leans in the communication of facilitative conditions involves subtle adjustment toward maintaining an equilibrium of involvement appropriate to the context and stage of contact.

Analysis of client and counselor communication is particularly valuable in monitoring and understanding the client's psychological states during the counseling process. Rice and Greenberg (1984) argue that counselors continually assess the fluctuations in the process and use this information to guide their interventions. Jones, Cumming, and Horowitz (1988) demonstrated that experienced clinicians tailor their interventions to meet the needs of their clients' psychological states. For example, Mahl's (1968, 1977) research indicates that nonverbal behavior may anticipate verbal content in which the emergence of new material is preceded by a new inadvertent action or body position of the client. Davis and Hadiks (1990) extended this type of research with an intensive videotape analysis of segments from the videotapes of 62 sessions conducted by one therapist and client over a one-and-one-half year period. They focused on the body positions and gesture patterns of the client in relation to the changes in her verbal behavior. The results yielded two significant correlations between the verbal behavior on the Experiencing Scale and two of the position variables, indicating the client shifted from superficial discussion to more actively exploring her internal reactions as her body positions became increasingly more open, accessible, and oriented toward the counselor. Although the changes in position were related to changes in verbal involvement, they did not anticipate the change in the ways described by Mahl (1977). They should further the Davis and Hadiks's data suggesting that position shifts and gesture patterns that were coded were independent and related to different intropsychic phenomena. The Davis nonverbal states scales (1986) may tap into fluctuations (cognitive set) and attitude toward what is occurring at the moment. Changes in gesture quality and intensity may reflect subtle fluctuations in affect and arousal. These subtle aspects of nonverbal behavior are now quantifiable and may allow greater insight into the emotional processes during therapy.

Summary

In the relationship between the counselor and client, two people join in a therapeutic alliance to help the client resolve his or her problem. The relationship is the vehicle for exploring the situation, increasing understanding, and trying out appropriate behaviors. Through internalizing the relationship, the client can have a corrective emotional experience, try new behaviors, and enhance self-esteem. Counseling is a process rather than a set of techniques, although the counselor will have techniques for providing and maintaining the relationship. This chapter has suggested how to use the facilitative conditions of empathy, congruence, positive regard, and specificity of communication—concepts that embrace all counseling theories—as a basis for the counseling relationship; explored several other dimensions that appear in the counselor-client relationship; and presented methods for using and recognizing verbal and nonverbal communication to understand and help the client.

References

Bauer, G. P., & Kobos, J. C. (1984). Short-term psychodynamic psychotherapy: Reflections on the past and current practice. *Psychotherapy, 21,* 153–170.

Bauer, G. P., & Mills, J. A. (1989). Use of transference in the here and now: Patient and therapist resistance. *Psychotherapy, 26,* 112–119.

Berenson, B. (1968). Level of therapist functioning, patient depth of self-exploration, and type of confrontation. *Journal of Counseling Psychology, 15,* 317–321.

Bordin, E. (1968). *Psychological counseling.* New York: Appleton-Century-Crofts.

Bordin, E. (1975). The generalizability of the psychoanalytic concept of the working alliance. *Psychotherapy: Theory, Research, and Practice, 16,* 252–260.

Bordin, E. (1983). A working alliance based model of supervision. *The Counseling Psychologist, 11*(1), 35–42.

Brammer, L., & Shostrom, E. (1982). *Therapeutic psychology.* Englewood Cliffs, NJ: Prentice-Hall.

Carkhuff, R. (1969). *Helping and human relations* (Vols. 1–2). New York: Holt, Rinehart and Winston.

Cerney, M. (1985). Countertransference revisited. *Journal of Counseling and Development, 63,* 362–364.

Claiborn, C. (1979). Counselor verbal interaction, non-verbal behavior, and social power. *Journal of Counseling Psychology,* 378–383.

Claiborn, C. (1982). Interpretation and change in counseling. *Journal of Counseling Psychology, 29,* 439–453.

Claiborn, C., Ward, S. R., & Strong, S. R. (1981). Effects of congruence between counselor interpretations of client beliefs. *Journal of Counseling Psychology, 28,* 101–109.

Danish, S., D'Augelli, A., & Hauer, A. (1980). Helping skills: A basic training program (2nd ed.). New York: Human Sciences Press.

Davis, M. (1986). *Guide to the Davis Nonverbal States Scales coding method.* Available from the author, Psychiatric Institute, Division of Clinical Psychology, Box 80, 722 West 168th Street, New York, NY 10032.

Davis, M., & Hadiks, D. (1990). Nonverbal behavior in client-state changes during psychotherapy. *Journal of Clinical Psychology, 46,* 340–350.

DeForest, C., & Stone, G. (1980). Effects of sex and intimacy level on self disclosure. *Journal of Counseling Psychology, 27,* 93–96.

Dies, R. R. (1973). Group therapist self-disclosure: An evaluation by clients. *Journal of Counseling Psychology, 20*(4), 344–348.

Dolan, Y. (1985). *A path within a heart: Eriksonian utilization with resistant and chronic clients.* New York: Brunner/Mazel.

Eagan, G. (1976). Confrontation. *Group and Organizational Studies, 1,* 223, 243.

Eaton, T., Abeles, N., & Gutfreund, M. (1988). Therapeutic alliance and outcome: Impact of treatment length and pretreatment symptomotology. *Psychotherapy, 25,* 536–542.

Edinger, J., & Patterson, M. (1983). Non-verbal involvement and social control. *Psychological Bulletin, 93,* 30–56.

Elliott. R. (1979). How clients perceive helper behaviors. *Journal of Counseling Psychology, 26,* 285–294.

Elliott, R., Barker, C., Caskey, N., & Pistrang, N. (1982). Differential helpfulness of counselor response modes. *Journal of Counseling Psychology, 29,* 354–461.

Gary, A. L., & Hammond, R. (1970). Self-disclosure of alcoholics and drug addicts. *Psychotherapy: Theory, Research and Practice, 4,* 142–146.

Gaston, L. (1990). The concept of the alliance and its role in psychotherapy: Theoretical and empirical considerations. *Psychotherapy, 27,* 143–153.

Gelso, C., & Carter, J. (1985). The relationship in counseling psychotherapy: Components, consequences, and theoretical antecedents. *The Counseling Psychologist, 13,* 155–243.

Gelso, C., Hill, C., & Kivlighan, D. (1991). Transference, insight, and the counselor's intentions during a counseling hour. *Journal of Counseling and Development, 69,* 428–433.

Graff, R. W. (1970). The relationship of counselor self-disclosure to counselor effectiveness. *Journal of Experimental Education, 38*(3), 19–22.

Greenson, R. R. (1967). *The technique and practice of psychoanalysis* (Vol. 1). New York: International Universities Press.

Hendrick, S. S. (1988). Counselor self-disclosure. *Journal of Counseling and Development, 66,* 419–424.

Hendrick, S. S. (1990). A client perspective on counselor disclosure (brief report). *Journal of Counseling and Development, 69,* 184–185.

Hermansson, G., Webster, A., & McFarland, K. (1988). Counselor deliberate postural lean and communications of facilitative conditions. *Journal of Counseling Psychology, 35,* 149–153.

Hill, C. (1978). Development of a counselor verbal response category system. *Journal of Counseling Psychology, 25,* 461–468.

Hill, C., Mahalik, J., & Thompson, B. (1989). Therapist self disclosure. *Psychotherapy, 26,* 290–295.

Hill, C., & O'Grady, K. (1985). List of therapist interventions illustrated in a case study with therapists of varying theoretical orientations. *Journal of Counseling Psychology, 32,* 3–22.

Hill, C., & Stephany, A. (1990). Relation of nonverbal behavior reactions. *Journal of Counseling Psychology, 37,* 22–26.

Horwitz, L. (1974). *Clinical prediction and psychotherapy.* New York: Jason Aronson.

Jones, E., Cumming, J., & Horowitz, M. (1988). Another look at the nonspecific hypothesis of therapeutic effectiveness. *Journal of Consulting and Clinical Psychology, 56,* 48–55.

Jourard, S. (1964). *The transparent self.* Princeton: Van Nostrand.

Jourard, S. (1971). *Self-disclosure: An experimental analysis of the transparent self.* New York: John Wiley and Sons.

Kell, B., & Mueller, W. (1966). *Impact and change.* New York: Appleton-Century-Crofts.

Kivlighan, D. M., Gelso, C. J., Wine, B., & Jones, A. (1986). The development of working alliance, transference, counter-transference in time-limited psychotherapy. Paper presented at the 1986 convention of the American Psychological Association, Washington, DC.

Klee, M., Abeles, N., and Muller, R. (1990). Therapeutic alliance: Early indicators, course and outcome. *Psychotherapy, 27,* 166–174.

Kokotovic, A., & Tracey, T. (1990). Working alliance in the early phase of counseling. *Journal of Counseling Psychology, 37,* 16–21.

Kwawer, J. (1980). Transference and countertransference in homosexuality-changing psychoanalytic views. *American Journal of Psychotherapy, 34,* 72–79.

LaClave, L., & Brack, G. (1989). Reframing to deal with patient resistance: Practical applications. *American Journal of Psychotherapy, 43,* 68–76.

Leaman, D. (1978). Confrontation in counseling. *Personnel and Guidance Journal, 56,* 630–633.

Lee, D., & Hallberg, E. (1982). Nonverbal behaviors of a 'good' and 'poor' counselor. *Journal of Counseling Psychology, 29,* 414–417.

Lerner, S., & Lerner, H. (1983). A systematic approach to resistance: Theoretical and technical considerations. *American Journal of Psychotherapy, 37,* 387–399.

Luborsky, L. (1985). Psychotherapy integration is on its way. *The Counseling Psychologist, 13,* 245–249.

Mahl, G. F. (1968). Gestures and body movements in interviews. In J. M. Schlien (Ed.), *Research in psychotherapy* (pp. 295–346). Washington, DC: American Psychological Association.

Mahl, G. F. (1977). Body movement, ideation and verbalization during psychoanalysis. In N. Freedman and S. Grand (Eds.), *Communicative structures and psychic structures* (pp. 291–310). New York: Plenum Press.

McCarthy, P. (1982). Differential effects of counselor self-referent responses and counselor status. *Journal of Counseling Psychology, 29,* 125–131.

McCarthy, P., & Betz, N. (1978). Differential effects of self-disclosing versus self-involving counselor statements. *Journal of Counseling Psychology, 25,* 252–256.

Mills, J., Bauer, G., & Miars, R. (1989). Use of transference in short-term dynamic psychotherapy. *Psychotherapy, 26,* 338–343.

Mitchell, K., Bozarth, J., & Krauft, C. (1977). A reappraisal of the therapeutic effectiveness of accurate empathy, non-possessive warmth, and genuineness. In A. Gurman and A. Razain (Eds.), *Effective psychotherapy: A handbook of research.* New York: Pergamon Press.

Otani, Akira. (1989). Client resistance in counseling: Its theoretical rationale and taxomic classification. *Journal of Counseling and Development, 67,* 458–461.

Parloff, M., Waskow, I., & Wolfe, B. (1978). Research on therapist variables in relation to process and outcome. In S. Garfield and A. Bergin (Eds.), *Handbook of psychotherapy and behavior change: An empirical analysis.* New York: John Wiley and Sons.

Patterson, C. H. (1969). A current view of client-centered or relationship therapy. *School Psychologist, 1,* 2–25.

Peabody, S., & Gelso, C. (1982). Countertransference and empathy: The complex relationship between two divergent concepts in counseling. *Journal of Counseling Psychology, 29,* 240–245.

Rennie, D. (1985, June). *The inner experience of psychotherapy.* Paper presented at the annual meeting of the Society of Psychotherapy on Research, Chicago.

Reynolds, C., & Fisher, C. (1983). Personal versus professional evaluations of self-disclosing and self-involving counselors. *Journal of Counseling Psychology, 30,* 451–454.

Rice, L., & Greenberg, L. (1984). *Patterns of change.* New York: Guilford Press.

Robbins, S., & Jolkovski, M. (1987). Managing countertransference feelings: An interactional model using awareness of feelings and theoretical framework. *Journal of Counseling Psychology, 34,* 276–282.

Robinson, F. (1950). *Principles and procedures in student counseling.* New York: Harper & Brothers Publishers.

Robitschek, C. G., & McCarthy, P. R. (1991). Prevalence of counselor self reference in the therapeutic dyad. *Journal of Counseling and Development, 69,* 218–221.

Rogers, C. (1951). *Client-centered therapy.* Boston: Houghton Mifflin.

Rogers, C. (1957). The necessary and sufficient conditions of therapeutic personality change. *Journal of Counseling Psychology, 21,* 95–103.

Roll, S., Crowley, M., & Rappl, L. (1985). Client perceptions of counselors' nonverbal behavior: A reevaluation. *Counselor Education and Supervision, 24,* 234–243.

Romig, C., & Gruenke, C. (1991). The use of metaphor to overcome inmate resistance to mental health counseling. *Journal of Counseling and Development, 69,* 414–418.

Singer, J., Sincoff, J., & Kolligian, J. (1989). Countertransference and cognition: Studying the psychotherapist's distortions as consequences of normal information processing. *Psychotherapy, 26,* 344–355.

Springmann, R. (1986). Countertransference: Clarifications in supervision. *Contemporary Psychoanalysis, 22,* 252–277.

Strong, S., Wambach, C., Lopez, F., & Cooper, R. (1979). Motivational and equipping functions of interpretation in counseling. *Journal of Counseling Psychology, 25,* 98–107.

Strupp, H., & Binder, J. (1984). *Psychotherapy in a new key.* New York: Basic Books.

Tamminen, A., & Smaby, M. (1981). Helping counselors learn to confront. *Personnel and Guidance Journal, 51,* 41–45.

Thompson, E., & Hill, C. (1991). Therapist perceptions of client reactions. *Journal of Counseling and Development, 69,* 261–265.

Towers, D., Wollum, S., Dow, E., Senese, R., Ames, G., Berg, J., & McDonald, D. (1987). *Metaphor as a tool for counselor.* Paper presented at the annual convention of the American Association for Counseling and Development, New Orleans. (ERIC Documents Reproduction Service No. ED285096)

Truax, C., & Mitchell, K. (1971). Research on certain therapist interpersonal skills in relation to process and outcome. In S. Garfield and A. Bergin (Eds.) (1978), *Handbook of psychotherapy and behavior change: An empirical analysis.* New York: John Wiley and Sons.

Tyson, J., & Wall, S. (1983). Effect of inconsistency between counselor verbal and nonverbal behavior on perceptions of counselor attributes. *Journal of Counseling Psychology, 30,* 433–437.

VanWagoner, W., Gelso, C., Hayes, J., & Diemer, R. (1991). Countertransference and the reputedly excellent therapist. *Psychotherapy, 28,* 411–421.

Watkins, C. E. (1983). Counselor acting out in the counseling situation: An exploratory analysis. *Personnel and Guidance Journal, 53,* 417–422.

Watkins, C. E., & Schneider, L. J. (1989). Self-involving versus self-disclosing counselor statements during an initial interview. *Journal of Counseling and Development, 67,* 345–349.

Weigel, R. G., Dinges, N., Dyer, R., & Straumfjord, A. A. (1972). Perceived self-disclosure, mental health, and who is liked in group treatment. *Journal of Counseling Psychology, 19*(1), 47–52.

Worthy, G. (1969). Self-disclosure as an exchange process. *Journal of Personality and Social Psychology, 13,* 59–63.

C h a p t e r 13

A Continuing Process

The counseling relationship evolves through various phases as clients explore, gain understanding, and work through understanding and try new behaviors to a point of termination. This chapter presents a model of a continuing counseling relationship. Not all counseling will follow this model exactly, but we will use it to explore the developmental stages of the counseling process. Understanding these phases in the relationship can help the counselor place a single event in perspective.

This model may be more appropriate for counseling personal-social problems than for educational-vocational decision making. Nevertheless, there is some overlap since vocational decisions often involve emotions and personal problems and often include decision making. Therefore, many of the concepts presented here can be integrated with the chapters on decision-making interviews and vocational counseling.

A number of social scientists have described developmental changes in the continuing counseling relationship. Each phase of this model is a composite of the models presented in the literature. A consensus of the literature establishes phases of initiating counseling and setting up a relationship, exploration of self, deeper exploration, and working through to termination of counseling. Although the initial interview has received separate attention, aspects of that phase are reviewed to illustrate that it is an integral part of the continuing relationship. The early phases of counseling develop the relevant problem area as it is experienced by the client. The client's self-exploration leads to self-understanding. Although the client may have stated goals when he or she initially comes to counseling, clearer, behaviorally stated goals may be better defined after the client has a more thorough self-understanding. Frequently, precise goals may not be stated but the client describes only emerging and modifiable directions.

After a client has achieved a higher level of self-understanding and has more clearly stated her or his directions or behavioral goals, the client and the counselor can consider alternative courses of action to attain those goals. The client and counselor's consideration of the advantages and disadvantages of each alternative will lead to a higher probability of success. Incremental new behavior patterns can be established to ensure the success of new behavior, and the behavioristic sequence used that most effectively leads to the success of that behavior pattern.

The process presented in this model does not always move in sequence through the phases, but may move backward and forward, though with a general forward movement. The phases are not discrete and have no time limit. Some clients will move quickly into self-exploration; others will experience more difficulty in overcoming their resistances. Many clients will not require the deeper self-exploration involved in the third phase, but can move to working through aspects of the process. The process of understanding self and trying new behaviors will vary with each client.

Phase 1: Initiating Counseling and Establishing a Relationship

The first step in the counseling relationship must involve the client's recognition that he or she has a problem and motivation to work with the counselor toward a solution. The best situation exists when the client recognizes the existence of a problem and sees the counselor voluntarily. If a client is referred by someone else who recognizes a problem, it is important that the client wants to work toward a resolution. A client who is unaware or unwilling to recognize the problem area will not be sufficiently motivated to work in the counseling process.

Frequently clients come to the counselor with a rather vague feeling that something is wrong, but are unable to put the problem into words. It is not uncommon for clients to talk about "it." Rogers (1958) describes the clients' fixity and remoteness of feelings at the initial interview. In Rogers's view, a great blockage of internal communication prevents the clients from accurately describing feelings or the problem. Frequently clients do not recognize many of their feelings, and many aspects of the problem are not apparent to them. It is not unusual for clients to be unwilling to communicate about themselves at this point and instead to describe external situations that impinge upon them rather than talking about themselves. Rogers suggests that in such cases there is no desire for change—the client wants the problem solved but really does not want to risk changing.

Goals

The primary goal for this phase is to establish the working alliance. Gelso and Carter (1985) suggest that it is important that the alliance be established as early as possible. The alliance includes a mutual agreement and understanding about the goals of counseling, mutual understanding of the tasks of the counselor and client, and developing bonds of caring and trust between the two participants (Bordin, 1975).

An important feature in Phase One is to define the client's problem in terms as specific as possible. For example, if the client's stated problem is that school has lost meaning, she or he should try describing the behaviors that demonstrate that attitude. The client may be able to count the number of positive and negative thoughts regarding various aspects of school experience. The counselor and client can eventually use the specific descriptions and the number of behaviors to monitor changes and assess the effectiveness of the counseling process. Another way to determine the client's present behavior is to gather what is called a *baseline,* the information about the client's behavior before counseling actually begins. For example, the counselor might have a client count the number of inappropriate behaviors he or she exhibits during the school day. The definition of inappropriate behaviors would have to be agreed upon by both client and counselor, and the client could count behaviors for several days in an effort to establish the baseline.

One part of defining the problem is to examine the antecedents of an inappropriate behavior. In a behavioral approach to counseling, the antecedents refer to the stimuli in a situation just prior to the occurrence of the inappropriate behaviors, such as what occurred in the classroom, what the teacher did, what peers did, or what the client was thinking about. An awareness of the immediate antecedents to an inappropriate behavior gives the client and counselor some idea of the immediate causes of the inappropriate behavior. A second aspect of the behavioral exploration would be to determine which reinforcements maintain the inappropriate behavior: The counselor would ask the client to describe what happens immediately after the inappropriate behavior. This would include how other people behave toward the client as well as how the client feels about him- or herself. This would involve both external and internal reinforcements.

Defining the problem in behavioral terms is important regardless of the counselor's theoretical orientation. The counselor need not think in terms of baseline, antecedents, or reinforcements, but all counselors examine the circumstances involved in a problem behavior.

From the definition of the problem the client and counselor can discuss desired outcomes. Although they are tentative at this stage, behavioral goals give the client something tangible to work toward.

Part of defining the problem in the early phase of counseling concerns clients' expressions of feeling about their problem. The goal at this point is to have clients maintain their expression of feelings, to confront themselves with their feelings and behaviors, and thus help them clarify their problem. At this point, the counselor is able to begin formulating hypotheses about the problem area and patterns of behavior.

The other goal in the first phase of counseling is to establish a relationship with the client. Chapter 12 has already discussed the facilitative conditions of positive regard, empathy, and congruence as important in establishing this relationship. The client needs to feel accepted, to experience mutual liking, and to trust the counselor. Brammer and Shostrom (1982) describe this as building a pipeline between two individuals. The client is able to trust in the strength of the counselor and will thus feel safe enough to investigate aspects of his or her personal feelings and behavior. This does not deny the strength and potential for growth within a client, but does give him or her comfort and security with a new person.

According to May (1967), the first phase of the interview consists of establishing rapport, which exists when both the client and the counselor feel at ease. This is probably best facilitated by the counselor's being comfortable and being able to show it. This relaxation will help break the psychological tension that the client may feel. May suggests that the counselor's attitude must be a balance between sensitivity and robustness. Sensitivity is communication of understanding of the client without letting this openness appear too obvious. When the counselor's concern becomes too obvious the client may feel that he or she is not genuine and consequently withhold confidence. Robustness is the use of a hearty voice and a good sense of humor to communicate the counselor's humanness. It is not easy to establish the balance between sensitivity and robustness, and the balance will vary with different clients. As May suggests, one must be sensitive enough to know when to be robust.

The counselor's professional manner could interfere with establishing rapport by communicating a separation between client and counselor. According to Holland (1965), two kinds of relationships are apparent in this early phase of counseling: one ostensible and one hidden. The ostensible relationship is one of equality between the counselor and client in which both defend the client's inadequate self-concept. This equality demonstrates that both are equal as human beings; the counselor is not superior, because the client, too, is dealing with the problem. The counselor may have information or skills to help the client solve the problem, but this does not make the counselor a superior human being. The counselor may have car difficulty on his way home and require the services of a mechanic. The counselor is no less a person than a mechanic in needing the latter's assistance in solving the problem. The hidden aspect of the relationship is that the client does have a problem and may feel inferior because he or she has to seek help for it. Generally the client does, in fact, have a dependent position.

Process

Early communication relates to the discrepancy between the apparent and hidden aspects of the relationship (Holland, 1965). If the counselor dominates the interview, the client may retreat even more deeply into feelings of inadequacy, and if the counselor is too passive the client may feel she or he is not getting any help. Therefore, there must be an appropriate sharing of responsibility in this early phase. The counselor wants to encourage the client to talk and to permit him or her to control the interview and the depth of self-exploration. Counselor responses will generally be restricted to acceptance, reflection, and clarification. These are the least leading responses and permit the counselor to verify her or his understanding of the client. They also serve to clarify the problem area for the client.

Counseling outcomes are dependent to a significant extent on the client characteristics. From the initial meeting with the client, the counselor seeks to define the nature of the problem requiring treatment. Counselors become diagnosticians, attempting to identify a problem in order to take appropriate therapeutic steps. The diagnostic process requires understanding the vast array of individual differences among clients as well as how to deal with them. Coming to understand individual differences is very complex. Strupp (1978) states that it is hazardous for a variety of reasons to categorize or type clients on the basis of a presenting difficulty. The utility of the classical diagnostic categories is very limited for therapeutic practice. Other systems of classification such as defense mechanisms or ego functions may sometimes be useful but also have shortcomings. It has long been recognized by clinicians that clients differ on many dimensions.

Phase 2: Exploration of Self

The second phase of counseling begins when the client feels a minimal level of acceptance. Rogers (1958) describes this as the point when the client feels fully received. When the relationship is secure for the client, there will be a loosening and a flowing of expression from the client. This phase may occur in the first interview or it may take more than one. In the beginning, the client's expression starts to flow in connection with nonself topics. Describing problems as external to her- or himself requires little sense of personal responsibility for the problem. Feelings are usually talked about rather than experienced in the present. The differentiation of personal meaning and feelings is somewhat superficial. Although the client may express some contradictions, there is little recognition of them as contradictions.

Goals

The counselor wants to elicit and determine the client's self-evaluation, so that the client can be aware of various feelings about him- or herself and can see how these feelings and attitudes affect his or her behavior. The main objective of this phase of counseling is a clearer and more complete delineation of various aspects of the client's self-concept and situation. Holland (1965) suggests that three different self-concepts usually emerge. One is self-depreciation, in which the client points out bad characteristics and inferiority in certain areas. Closely related to this is a second self-concept representing compensatory fantasies, which tend to compensate for the negative self-depreciation. The third self-concept includes the client's contemporary attributes that constitute a more or less realistic image and an evaluation of self by reasonable standards.

Self-Exploration

Carkhuff (1969) proposes a five-point scale to examine self-exploration. In his view, the counselor's awareness of the client's level of self-exploration will aid in understanding the client and making more appropriate responses. At the first level a client avoids any self-description or self-exploration that would reveal personal feelings to the counselor. At this level the client probably does not trust his or her own feelings and may not like him- or herself well enough to offer inner feelings to the counselor. This lack of self-exploration is a common occurrence in beginning counseling. At the second level of self-exploration the client responds with discussion to the introduction of personally relevant material by the counselor. The response, however, is mechanical and does not demonstrate any real feeling. The client is answering questions, giving conclusions already reached about self-concept, but is not exploring her- or himself. At this level the counselor can learn much about the client's current self-concept. At the third level the client voluntarily introduces discussions of personally relevant material but does so mechanically and without demonstrating much feeling. This frequently is a volunteering of material that the client has already rehearsed or possibly has discussed with other people. There is no spontaneity and no inward probing for new feelings or experiences.

At the fourth level the client voluntarily introduces personally relevant material in a spontaneous manner. The client is dealing with the current level of feeling. This behavior may lead to the fifth level, in which the client actively and spontaneously probes into newly discovered feelings and experiences about her- or himself and her or his situation.

Process

What are some things the counselor can do to help a client in self-exploration? In addition to presenting the various levels of client self-exploration, Carkhuff (1969) suggests a number of guidelines to assist the counselor in the exploratory stage of counseling. First, the counselor must establish client exploration as the immediate goal. Without this the client will not gain new insights, gain new understanding, or be able to incorporate new behaviors into her or his pattern. Second, the counselor must initially understand the client at the presented level of self-exploration. Exploration of personal material is most likely to occur when there is understanding and a suspension of attitude or judgment by the counselor. The client will move increasingly toward initiating exploration and toward spontaneous emotions if the counselor is willing to accept him or her at each level. Third, the counselor should initially offer minimal levels of the facilitative conditions. By offering minimal levels of empathy, respect, concreteness, and genuineness, the counselor establishes a relationship that the client can explore, test, and experience. The minimal facilitative conditions provide the client with knowledge that the counselor understands the client on the latter's terms and also provides the feedback necessary for later reformulations. Fourth, the counselor should employ the client's self-sustaining level of self-exploration as a guide for moving to the next stage in the counseling process. Within a given problem or topic area, the criterion for movement to the next stage of counseling is the client's ability to deal with his or her own explorations. When the client is able to do this, the counselor can focus on the client's self-understanding or action, depending on the client's understanding. Fifth, the counselor should recognize a repetition of the cycle of self-exploration both within and between different content areas. Having worked through the process in terms of a situation with her or his parents, for example, the client may begin at the first level of self-exploration when the topic turns to relationships with peers or a teacher.

Several studies have demonstrated that differing levels of counselor-offered facilitative conditions affect the self-exploration of high- and low-functioning clients (Holder, Carkhuff, & Berenson, 1967; Piaget, Berenson, & Carkhuff, 1967). For the higher-functioning client, variance in the counselor-offered conditions has little effect on the level of self-exploration. Such a client appears to have enough self-confidence to self-explore even when the counselor is not highly facilitative. The lower-functioning client, however, or the one with a poorer self-concept, is affected considerably by the different levels of counselor-offered conditions; self-exploration is much greater when the counselor offers higher levels of facilitation.

May (1967) calls this stage of counseling the confession and assumes that two-thirds of every hour will be taken up with the client's "talking it out." It is important for the client to talk about the problem thoroughly in order to reach the essentials. In May's view, if the client does not do most of the talking in the interview, something is wrong with the counseling procedure. He assumes that every word the counselor utters must have a purpose.

The counselor may employ specific or concrete communication to ensure that his or her responses will not be too far removed from the client's current feelings and experiences. Concreteness or specificity of communication serves a function complementary to that of empathic understanding. It helps the client know that the counselor is focusing directly on the former's feelings. During later phases of counseling, specific communication focuses directly upon problem solving.

Thus, it is important for the counselor to make reflections and interpretations specific, even in response to a vague and abstract client statement. This helps the counselor sharpen the client's communication and reduces the possibility of emotional remoteness from the latter's current feelings and experiences. It also encourages the client to formulate his or her own expressions in more concrete and specific terms. Developing concrete and specific communication helps the counselor emphasize the personal relevance of the client's communications. This will keep the client's focus on personally relevant material rather than on stories that include irrelevant information and keep the counselor and client away from the real problem. At times the counselor must ask for specific details and instances: who, what, when, why, where, and how specific feelings and experiences are involved. These questions serve the function of entry and should make way for the follow-through by various reflections and interpretations.

The counselor should not express shock or offense at anything the client says. Emotional upsets must be a part of this period; clients become upset because they are expressing their ideas and fears and frequently suppressed information they may not have told anyone before. The client may cry, and the counselor must exercise skill in remaining calm and communicating empathy to the client. At this point we can clearly discriminate between empathy and sympathy. Giving sympathy at this point would augment emotional upsets; empathy is more objective and valuable.

Brammer and Shostrom (1982) call this phase of counseling a catharsis and point out that it has positive and negative aspects. First, the client experiences strong physiological relief from the burden of tension, similar to the relaxation one may feel after crying. There is also a feeling of satisfaction that comes from the control of verbalizing the material. The client feels that gaining control of the problem verbally provides a certain amount of security and control over the problem. There is also a release of emotional energy previously used for self-defense, and the client may feel considerably better.

According to May (1967), the fact that the client has talked about the problem will make her or him psychologically healthier. It will relieve some inhibitions, make possible a more ready flow of internal feelings, and help the client to see the problems with clarifying objectivity. A skillful counselor helps focus the client's confession on the core of a problem. Skill and sensitivity are required to perceive the feelings beneath the client's statements.

One of the limitations of the catharsis involves this feeling of control and exhilaration with new energy, for the client sometimes makes a "flight into health," believing the problem is solved. In many cases a client has dealt with some aspects of the problem but needs further understanding and behavior changes. Frequently a catharsis includes only material at an intellectual level that the client has already been able to think out alone while other material is being defended. Holland (1965) points out that clients feel defensive when they have communicated all that they know or are willing to tell about themselves, but are aware that this is not sufficient. These clients' defensive periods usually follow one or a combination of three patterns: avoiding discussion of themselves while directing the counselor's attention to externals; denying weaknesses and inadequacies in themselves; or exposing their own concepts and evaluations of the problem.

A Critical Point

This is a crucial point in counseling, and the client may be sufficiently threatened by lack of understanding and control to drop out of counseling. The client has made a deeper exploration of feeling and this is not a pleasant experience. He or she feels less secure and comfortable and may not be sure if the pain involved in working through the process is something he or she wishes to endure. The client may be aware of other aspects of the problem, for the defense system is open enough that the client is seeing things she or he has denied before and may recognize that things may get worse before they get better. It is important for the counselor to support and encourage the client at this point. Frequently, if the counselor is able to explain to the client that these anxieties occur in many clients, the client will be able to pass through this critical point even despite the fear of exposing too much of her- or himself (Brammer & Shostrom, 1982).

Transition

There may be a transition stage in this phase of counseling. Clients become aware that they cannot account for their behavior through what they know about themselves, and the logic of their behavior does not always lead to understanding. Therefore, the clients relax some of their defenses and the counselor becomes more actively involved, using short leading techniques.

Holland (1965) suggests that clients may strongly resist dealing with feelings about themselves. Clients will reach a point of avoiding discussion of their depreciated self. They may be reluctant to evaluate their compensatory fantasies, and their real self-concept is not strong enough to provide security. The counselor will have to fulfill several client needs during this period. Because they are unable to do so, clients need the counselor to see some of the negative aspects of the depreciated self they avoid. Clients may resolve this problem with very little help from the counselor. The counselor also wants to see how much clients can handle, and it is important to let them know that the counselor trusts them and will enter more actively only when he or she is needed.

During these early interviews the client is communicating inadequacies and wants help from the counselor. The counselor should communicate recognition of this desire to gain something from him or her, and Holland (1965) suggests the counselor may indicate that some progress is being made and that the client has been largely responsible for this progress. This communicates that the counselor regards the client as functioning adequately. The counselor may also wish to communicate to the client that they are both personally involved in the process by trying to make this evaluation. There may also be plans of action being developed, and the counselor may be able to indicate some of these to the client.

The counselor should permit clients to maintain control of themselves in the interview for as long as possible. If clients are effective in handling their problems and if the problem is not too difficult, the counselor can provide clients with labels to put on the feelings they have about themselves. For instance, it may be that a client's expression of behaviors and feelings is loosening and there is some freedom in terms of his or her internal communication, but he or she still may be having difficulties tapping spontaneous feelings. The counselor will help the client by pointing out some relationships between various self-concepts and his or her behavior pattern.

During this stage of confrontation, the counselor concentrates on tentative formulations concerning discrepant communications from the client (Carkhuff, 1969). The counselor confronts the client with the discrepancies between the client's self versus ideal, insight versus behavior, or self versus other experiences. The counselor may employ probing questions rather than direct confrontations. Tentative comparisons of contradictory communications are both natural and appropriate for the counselor at this point. A premature direct confrontation may demoralize and demobilize an inadequately prepared client. The client needs the acceptance, approval, and support of the counselor while examining various self-concepts that she or he would rather avoid.

Holland suggests that the counselor may become more active in the later part of this phase and assume a more controlling role, thus appearing more authoritarian. If the counselor is controlling more of the communication at this point in the relationship, the client will have the greatest need for the counselor's acceptance and help. Otherwise, strong feelings about being controlled would interfere with the progress of counseling. It is important for the counselor to be gentle and provide acceptance and support for the client.

In addition to reflection and clarification, the counselor will probably be sharing information and ideas and providing some interpretation for the client. Sharing involves the client's acceptance of the counselor as a real person rather than his or her projections about the counselor. The counselor does not force information upon the client but presents it for him or her to use. The interpretation is one further step in leading in which the counselor presents some hypotheses to the client.

According to May (1967), after the client has talked out the problem, interpretation will take place. Both the client and counselor survey the facts that have been brought to light and discover through them the pattern of the client's behavior. "Interpretation is a function of both the counselor and the counselee working together." It is not a matter of the counselor's diagnosing the pattern and then presenting it to the client. The counselor may make some tentative analysis or some tentative suggestions. The counselor suggests interpretations rather than stating them dogmatically.

It is important for the counselor to read the meaning of the client's reactions to the interpretations or suggestions. If the client is indifferent, and the suggestions do not seem to make any difference, the counselor may assume that the idea was not very important. If the client rejects the suggestions or interpretation violently, protesting strongly that it is untrue, the counselor may tentatively assume that the interpretation is close enough to have struck a cord. The counselor, however, must be careful not to make this assumption, for it may in fact be inaccurate and the rejection appropriate. If the client accepts the suggestion or interpretation and agrees with it, both the counselor and client can accept it for the time being. Whether or not it is accurate and meaningful may not be known until the client continues to work further on the problem and a solution. The client could have just accepted the interpretation rather than rejecting it.

Many clients will move from this point to working through the behavior problems and developing the insight that leads to behavior change. Some clients, however, will go into a deeper exploration of feelings.

Phase 3: Deeper Exploration

Some clients need more therapeutic counseling than others in order to tap feelings that will lead to better self-understanding. These clients will be involved in a deeper exploration of feelings and attitudes. Most counselors are not equipped to deal with the intense feelings and intricate problems involved in personality reorganization that may occur at this depth of counseling. Most counselors who work in agencies, schools, or colleges will probably not have sufficient time to work through this phase of counseling. Most counseling relationships will proceed instead to the working-through phase. However, the goals and process of deeper exploration are presented here to illustrate their relevance in the counseling process.

Goals

The counselor attempts to eliminate depreciated and fantasy self-concepts as determinants of client behavior and at the same time to complete the client's awareness of his or her real self-concept and establish reasonable standards to evaluate it. It is apparent that part of the depreciated self-concept may have been valid at one time, but because it is no longer true it must be reevaluated in terms of reasonable standards being developed for the self. As this occurs there will be a reduction in the client's need for fantasies to compensate. The client may find, however, that part of the compensated fantasies coincide with some of her or his actual attributes (Holland, 1965).

During this time the client's feelings will be expressed more freely in the present. Feelings will burst forth even though the person may fear and distrust what he or she feels. The client tends at first to realize that what she or he is feeling involves a direct referent. There is frequently surprise as well as fright at the feeling that bubbles up. The result is increasingly freer communication within the person and increasing ownership of the feelings as a part of the self (Rogers, 1958).

As clients become aware of themselves and their uniqueness, they should establish reasonable personal standards. Such standards can be relative standards, indicative of behaviors and achievements of other people comparable to themselves. Instead of global evaluations, clients should break down these standards and examine smaller parts of the whole. This process is one of helping to fill in the details of the self-concept and the cognitive structure.

Process

The counselor communicates, either directly or indirectly, what he or she considers inaccurate or inadequate in the client's thinking process. This means that the counselor is fairly active in the interview and exerts some control because she or he is involved with active emotional resistance. It always seems to amaze beginning counselors that when they are trying to help a client, the latter is resisting that help. Clients continue to deceive themselves in part and to attempt deception of the counselor. Holland (1965) offers four reasons for this level of resistance. There may be a generalization of hostile feelings toward people who exert some control over others' lives. There are possibly negative feelings about giving up various self-concepts and anxieties associated with depending upon a new self-concept that is not yet reliable outside the counseling situation. There may be negative feelings about the efforts and risks involved with living this new self-concept. It is this aspect that the client needs to change in order to use new behavior patterns.

Because of these feelings, the client is not a passive recipient of the counselor's communication. In order to meet the objectives of this phase, the counselor may need to use persuasion. Persuasion does not entail persuading the client to do something to meet the counselor's needs. The counselor uses persuasion when less controlling techniques have not worked to help the client meet the objectives that the latter has established. Persuasive efforts should be directed toward what the client thinks, letting the behavioral responses be her or his decision. The confrontation at this point is focusing on the client's avoidance tendencies in tying things together. The counselor tries to persuade the client to give up self-defeating and self-deceptive ways of thinking. The counselor must be careful not to be too controlling in this endeavor and not to enter into persuasion too early.

According to Carkhuff (1969), the highest level of action in the counseling process consists in interpretations of immediacy. Immediacy is the counselor's ability to understand feelings and experiences that intrude between her- or himself and the client. The client may be telling the counselor something about how he or she feels about the counselor without even knowing it. The client may not be able to tell the counselor these things directly. The counselor must be able to focus on these feelings to understand the client and communicate what is going on so that the latter can gain self-understanding. Interpretations of immediacy state what the client is trying to communicate that she or he cannot say directly. These interpretations translate the counselor's immediate experience of the client in relation to the counselor directly into action. As with confrontation, there is a transition stage into direct interpretations of immediacy. With most clients the counselor will tentatively approach interpreting what is happening in the immediate relationship, perhaps with formulations that do not define precisely the counselor's experience in the moment.

Turock (1980) offers some guidelines for immediacy. He suggests that the immediacy interpretations of the client's subverbal communication are tentative hypotheses, and he looks at the counselor's task as bringing the hypotheses to the surface and then examining the issues. First, the counselor needs to experience the influence effort of the client. Even if the client is trying to manipulate the counselor, it appears to be more productive to use the initial attempt at influence to learn about the client's manipulative style. The second step involves abstracting from the client's behavior what may be a well-practiced, recycling interaction pattern of manipulation. It is also important for the counselor to be aware of his or her own response to the client's eliciting behaviors. The third stage involves disengaging and reflecting on the experience of the immediate relationship to examine the client's eliciting behavior and the counselor's own emotional reaction. It is through this process that the counselor can identify him- or herself as the specific target of the client's statement although the client may be talking about someone else or people in general. The major part of the immediacy process comes when the counselor makes the tentative hypotheses into a tentative interpretation. The client may then agree with the interpretation but not work with further exploration, request further information about the counselor's thoughts, or reject the counselor's interpretation. For the immediacy to have any impact, the counselor must continue to examine the issues by offering additional feedback to the client, helping the client to examine whether or not this is generalized behavior, and continuing to work on these issues throughout their counseling relationship. It is important that the counselor's interpretations of the immediacy not derail a meaningful experience or sidetrack the client's movement. Therefore, when movement is somewhat halting and directionless, it is a particularly appropriate time to focus on the interaction between the counselor and the client.

Critical Point

A second critical point in the counseling relationship occurs during this deeper exploration process. The client may become aware of the inadequacy of her or his defense mechanisms. They may no longer provide protection from the awareness of deeper feelings. A sudden awareness of too many impulses, thoughts, or feelings may be quite traumatic. The counselor should control the relationship to enable the client to explore these situations slowly. A client who experiences too much pain at this point may be frightened of his or her lack of control and withdraw from counseling.

Phase 4: Working Through

A significant part of changing one's behavior to be consistent with the new insights is involved in the process of "working through." When originally used by Freud, the concept generally meant breaking down the network of resistance. Today's broader conception refers to clients' becoming aware of the meaning of past experiences and present feelings. Clients develop awareness of inner feelings as well as of the external world. A rational understanding of problems, feelings, and behaviors can lead to further behavior change.

Goals

May (1967) considered the transforming of the client's personality the final stage of the counseling process and the goal of the whole process. Although the terminology is different, the concept is very similar to working through. May assumed that during the confession-interpretation stages the client has identified the tensions involved in her or his problems and has been able to see the relationship between mistaken attitudes and behavior. He considers this phase transforming because the client now learns a new awareness of tensions and behaviors. The goals of this phase of counseling include the client's clarification and acceptance of current feelings and defense manipulations. The client will rationally understand the historical roots of the problem and will work it out in terms of the relation between past events and current experience in the relationship with the counselor. The culmination of this phase is to elicit and establish behavioral responses that are consistent with a valid self-concept (Brammer & Shostrom, 1982).

Feelings and experiences need to be worked out in all areas before the client is able to integrate feelings and behavior patterns. Working through involves resolving conflicts from many vantage points, possibly described in different words with varying degrees of insight.

Insight

The client is increasingly able to face internal contradictions and incongruencies. His or her feelings are located much more in the present instead of being postponed and thought about. The client begins to acknowledge feelings and has a freer dialogue within her- or himself. There is increasing acceptance of responsibility for the problems being faced and a concern about how he or she has contributed to the problems (Rogers, 1958).

As deeper insight occurs, feelings that have previously been inhibited are now released and experienced presently. They seem to flow within the individual. Now the client is living feelings subjectively rather than thinking about them and is gaining trust in the feelings and in their momentary changes.

In the process of self-exploration, clients develop insights or become aware of other facets of their feelings that affect their behaviors. The majority of counseling approaches are insight oriented. Counselors assume that as clients gain insight or self-knowledge, they will see alternate behaviors and this new insight will lead to behavior change. This does not mean that when insight is achieved the problem automatically disappears. Most counseling, however, is still based on the concept that it is important for clients to have insight or an understanding of themselves in order to make the behavior change. Although sometimes insight occurs suddenly, more often a series of insights is involved with slow changing of behavior during the working-through process. These insights and changed perceptions of self become integrated into a new behavior pattern. There is a deepening in clients' awareness of what is going on, both objectively and subjectively. They are able to see relationships they have not been aware of previously. They are able to give up former defensive patterns and have greater self-confidence.

Self-Understanding

When the client is able to deal with self-exploration and immediate feelings, the counselor can help draw together the fragmented insights and help the client develop self-understanding, focusing on the construction or reconstruction of the latter's communication process. The counselor can judge the level of the client's self-understanding (Carkhuff, 1969). At lower levels of self-understanding, the client's responses or statements detract noticeably from expressed feeling and content, either in her or his own expressions or in those of others involved in the problem situation. At a minimum level of understanding the client is able to make statements about self that reflect essentially interchangeable affect and meaning; this interchange adds cognition to explorations of feelings. When the client makes statements that promote self-exploration at even deeper levels, she or he is functioning at a high level of understanding and should be able to move on to appropriate action. At this point the client can sustain the search for direction independently of the counselor.

A Critical Point

A third critical point in counseling may occur in this phase of the relationship (Brammer & Shostrom, 1982). It is another type of flight into health. After a client has explored some current feelings, for example, and understands them in terms of previous experiences, she or he may have a feeling of well-being. With this newfound insight, the client may think he or she is ready to terminate counseling. It may be that the client has the insight but lacks commitment to action. In addition, as part of the working-through process, the client may run into difficulty carrying out the decision in everyday life. The fact that the client has new insights is no guarantee that other people will change in the way they relate to the client. All of this may lead to the client's terminating counseling prematurely. The client may experience a relapse. The counselor must be careful not to keep the client in counseling longer than he or she desires, but must also be careful not to terminate prematurely. It is a fine line for a decision.

Process

The working-through phase involves putting understanding into action. The client's self-understanding is an intermediate goal, as well as process, that leads to constructive action. The counselor may begin by focusing on the client's areas of greater competence. The probability of the client's understanding and acting upon the situation is greatest in areas in which she or he is functioning at the highest levels. Success in these experiences will increase the probability of understanding and action in other areas. With greater exploration and an improvement in self-understanding, the counselor can increase the level of facilitative conditions. When the client is safe enough to explore her- or himself and is gaining new insight, she or he is able to handle additive responses within the given content areas. As the client gains in self-understanding and is able to sustain the level of effective understanding, the counselor can focus attention on the next stage of counseling: action. The client must recognize that the cycle of self-exploration to understanding to action is a repetitive one. For example, a client may have achieved self-understanding in relation to school situations and start constructive behaviors there, but may not have done the same in relation to parents. The counselor and client may need to start with exploration in that area and follow the cycle of exploration leading to understanding and finally to action. The early phase of self-exploration and understanding may lead to some action, which will provide feedback that can modify the original concepts and elicit further explorations leading to a deeper level of understanding, and culminate in new action.

On the basis of what the counselor has learned from the client's exploration of the problem, the counselor tries to put the picture together. The counselor gives the counseling process direction by attempting to help the client understand himself or herself at a deeper level and finally to act upon this understanding. The conditions initiated by the counselor are called action-oriented dimensions because they involve action by the counselor and because they lead the client to initiate her or his own ideas of what is happening and to act upon these ideas.

The client gains little in the long run from an intellectual understanding of the problem unless she or he is able to try out new methods of behaving. Prior to this, the client has been behaving according to various self-concepts and giving up those behavior patterns to adjust to the new self-concept may be quite difficult. Holland (1965) points out that part of this aspect of counseling involves behavioral retraining—giving up undesirable responses and trying out some new ones. Many clients can work through the understanding, gaining insight, and adapting behaviors by themselves. With other clients, the counselors may need to play a more active role.

Gelso and Carter (1985) suggest that the working alliance is important and central in the relationship during the early stages of therapy. Once the working alliance has been established the client may take more responsibility for what is occurring in the process and should exhibit less anxiety. During this stage, the working alliance may recede more into the background although it remains a basic support for the client.

When the client is experiencing a stressful time the need for the working alliance will come to the forefront again. A strong working relationship permits the client to feel enough support and trust in the relationship to work through the stressful times. It is important to note that it is the working alliance that permits the client to come to understand that the transference reactions are really his or her issues and not an accurate perception of the counselor (Gelso & Carter, 1985).

Action

The ultimate goal for the counselor should be to help the client toward constructive action. There is an interrelationship between the client's self-understanding and action, each serving to sharpen the other. The counselor emphasizes action in the area in which the client has the best self-understanding. This offers the highest probability of successful action. As the client increases other areas of understanding and approaches action, the counselor can increase the client's level of action orientation. Carkhuff (1969) suggests that the counselor begin to initiate more activities based on her or his experience in the situation, thus serving as both a model and agent for the client to do likewise. The counselor also attempts to ensure that learning and acting in relationships become more general outside of the counseling situation. This is done most effectively when a full description of the goals of counseling has been achieved. An important aspect is the behaviorally stated objectives for the client. A behavioral objective allows the counselor to specify goals in terms of the specific extent to which a response is to be performed; thus, it provides a reliable standard for the client. The behavioral objective also specifies the criterion level—how much or how frequently the behavior is required to meet the client's objective. It should also state under what circumstances the behavior is to occur.

When the counselor and client are able to describe the dimensions desired, a plan can be put into operation to meet those goals. Based on his or her experience and abilities, the counselor should select the techniques with the greatest chance of success. In addition to insight-oriented verbal counseling, the counselor may select alternative behavior modification techniques. In any event, the counselor must tailor the techniques to each client.

When operational goals have been established, step-by-step procedures for their attainment can be developed. The more fully the goals have been described, the more fully the steps can be described and implemented. Once the client is able to employ constructive action in one area, the counselor can repeat the cycle in another problem area. When the client demonstrates increasing ability to act constructively in all the relevant problem areas, termination of the relationship may take place.

One variable that May (1967) suggests in changing the client is the utilization of his or her suffering. The counselor should channel this suffering to furnish power to bring about change. A person will not change a pattern until forced to do so by her or his own suffering. Many people prefer to endure the misery of their situation rather than risk the uncertainty of what would come with change. May believes the counselor should not relieve the client's suffering but rather redirect it into constructive channels. The client may leave the interview more courageous, strengthened with the realization that he or she must change behavior. If the counseling is more than superficial, the client may feel shaken and probably unhappy with her or his current situation. Part of what the counselor does is to show the client that he or she is suffering with inappropriate attitudes and behaviors.

To help clients confront themselves the counselor must charge them with the discrepancies in their behavior. This confrontation is most effective when the counselor concentrates on clients' verbal and nonverbal expressions. It is important for the confrontation to come when the client feels accepted and understood. The confrontation does more than communicate understanding from the client's frame of reference; it provides the experience of an external, sensitive, and accurate viewpoint of the discrepancies in behavior. At this time the counselor must focus with increasing specificity on the implications of these discrepancies. The increasing specificity will lead the client to understand the distortions in her or his assumptions and, ideally, to reconstruct both assumptions and behaviors. Directional confrontation creates a crisis that offers the client the possibility of movement to more appropriate functioning. When the counselor observes critical discrepancies, she or he confronts the client with them. The client is pressed to consider the possibility of changing and, in doing so, utilizing resources not yet employed. The client cannot avoid responsibility for choices denied so far because the counselor will not permit him or her to do so. The counselor is free to employ both a didactic and experiential form for confrontation, and may also confront the client with either deficits or assets that the client has denied. The desired outcome of the confrontation is to enable the client to confront him- or herself and to make decisions toward more appropriate behaviors.

Alternatives

At this point in counseling the client may have to look at a variety of alternative responses to a situation. Once again, concreteness or specificity becomes a critical function in the counseling process. Concreteness is the key to considering potentially preferable modes of treatment and involves weighing alternative courses of actions and the advantages and disadvantages of each. Concreteness during later stages of counseling makes a major contribution by requiring the client to consider specific material that is potentially relevant to the problem and to implement specific courses of action to resolve that difficulty.

When the client is unable to generate such alternative responses, the counselor may become involved by suggesting several alternatives. By offering more than one alternative, the counselor is not advocating a specific behavior but is continuing to help the client think through various alternatives. May (1967) claims that suggestion is often condemned as a technique because it is misconstrued to be advice. It is not. The counselor can use suggestions intelligently to lay all the constructive alternatives before the client. From these alternatives the client can select the one that will best meet her or his needs.

The counselor must maintain some evaluation of the process. Evaluation based on achievement of stated behavioral objectives makes it possible to observe client progress. This evaluation can help the counselor decide if the selected technique is moving the client toward a goal or if the approach should be discontinued or modified. The process is not static, and a change in the client's objectives also calls for a change in the technique the counselor is using. The counselor encourages the client to live out his or her insights by trying new behaviors. The success of these experiences will reinforce new behavior patterns. Setbacks are worked through in the later sessions, and the client tries out new insights and behaviors. Counselor accountability is a critical question in the process. How stable or enduring are the effects of the counseling? Prior to termination the counselor must make provisions with the client to establish a program to maintain this newly established insight and behavior.

Termination in Counseling

Termination of the counseling process may be complicated. There may be feelings of ambivalence about it. The client both desires to be free and is anxious about leaving. Frequently a client will recognize that he or she is handling a problem adequately and consider termination. The counselor can discuss the idea with the client to help him or her prepare for termination. This communicates that the counselor has confidence in the client and removes any concern the latter might have about the counselor's feeling rejected by this move toward independence. Actually the relationship is never over; it may be renewed if the client desires.

The process of terminating a counseling relationship has been inadequately covered in the literature and probably in the counseling process (Ward, 1984). Ward suggests some contributing factors. One is the strong tendency to avoid issues of loss by not acknowledging or dealing with them, which results in a lack of models for productively working with such issues. A second factor is that theoreticians and educators have primarily emphasized the establishment of the facilitative therapeutic techniques and strategies and have been less interested in closing the relationship. It is important, however, that termination be recognized as a major part of the counseling process.

Ward notes that the termination stage has three primary functions. The first function is to assess the client's readiness to end the counseling process and consolidate learning. The second function involves resolving the remaining affective issues and bringing the relationship between the client and counselor to a close. The third function is to maximize the client's transfer of learning and increase his or her self-reliance and confidence in the ability to maintain the changes.

Hoyt (1979) in emphasizing the importance of termination, points out that much of what has been accomplished in counseling can be either consolidated or compromised in the termination phase. This phase is not merely a recapitulation and nailing down of the previous work; rather, all the work of the counseling sessions may be seen as prologue to the termination. With the end of counseling imminent, the client's fears or conflicts may be restimulated, especially if they involved struggles to achieve separation or independence. The manner in which the issues are handled in the termination phase will do much to determine how closely the ultimate goal of counseling is met.

Maholick and Turner (1979) suggest that termination presents a powerful analogy to how we deal with farewells in life. In their view, termination is one of the natural pausing points that present people with the opportunity to say good-bye, and when and how to say good-bye are critical issues. Termination in counseling can be thought of as a recapitulation of the multiple preceding good-byes in life; at the same time, it is a preparation for being able to deal more adequately with future good-byes.

Maholick and Turner (1979) emphasize that power exists in the ending of any relationship. A choice exists: The person can avoid the farewell, creating a potential for destruction and continuing unhappiness, or the person can accomplish the goodby and provide for new creative experiences.

Termination is also an important aspect of the continuing process of counseling. In each counseling session and series of counseling sessions, there is a need to bring closure to what has been occurring in the counselor-client interaction. Termination can occur at three points: at the conclusion of a discussion unit within an interview, at the conclusion of each interview, and at the conclusion of the counseling process.

Terminating Discussion Units

Termination is necessary following the discussion of a specific client concern. Although some counselors seem to want the client to keep talking without clearly delineating or dealing with his or her concerns, most often the counselor-client interaction takes the form of a series of minisessions within a block of time. It is not always possible or meaningful to close off these segments, but when it is possible several techniques can be of value.

The unit or minisession can be terminated by a summary statement by either the client or counselor. The intent of the statement is to draw together what has been said during the unit and to help the client see what progress has been made. The client must then decide whether to move on to other areas or to continue the present discussion. The latter decision suggests that the summary or closure by the counselor was premature. The counselor must be sensitive to the client's needs in order to use the summary termination effectively, and must convey to the client that continuation of the topic is possible even though, in the counselor's mind, the discussion has been almost completely developed.

There is a second, more direct method of stopping discussion of a topic. The counselor suggests directly that the discussion may not be as meaningful at the particular time due to client psychological condition, counselor skill, or other inner or external factors. The counselor does not eliminate the possibility of returning to the topic, but suggests that further discussion may be inappropriate or nonrewarding and that when certain other factors are present the topic can be reintroduced. The counselor will have to explain this action at times because she or he is really interpreting something in the client, the relationship, the environment, or her- or himself that may not be as apparent to the client. The crucial variable here is communication of what is happening and why it is happening.

A third termination technique falls somewhere between these two methods. This intermediate method is designed to shut off the particular topic without stopping client progress and client involvement. Several procedures can be used. The counselor may choose to alter the subject slightly so that the direction is unaltered but the intensity of feelings exhibited by the client is reduced. This is done when a client is deep in self-exploration and the counselor wants to bring him or her up and cap that emotion for the time. Old topics or new, related topics can be introduced. In another procedure, the counselor can react to different parts of client statements, leading the client into a different topical area. Or the counselor can increase the number and direction of pauses to reduce the interview's speed and intensity of affect. It is important to understand the effect of this type of activity on the client: Any action of the counselor that shuts off the client's communication has an undesirable effect and should be avoided.

Terminating an Interview

Termination of an interview presents dilemmas to many counselors. Those beginning their professional careers, in particular, report that the client really begins to bring up important material right at the end of the allotted interview time. Counselors are understandably hesitant to terminate at what appears to be a crucial point in the counseling session. Yet time constraints and the need to keep counseling within some reasonable boundaries force the issues. In this situation it is often of considerable value to examine two factors: What, if any, aspects of the counselor's "modus operandi" precluded earlier client meaningful involvement, and what, if anything, stimulated the client to move at the end of the session? These factors require counselors to examine both their own motivations and their understanding of the client. Assuming that this particular area can be understood and any necessary corrective steps taken, the techniques of termination become important.

The counselor and client should establish a time limit in which the counseling is to take place. A client with a prearranged appointment should be aware of the specific limits, and in most situations the counselor can simply refer to the time factors to effect a termination. Simply saying, "Your time is up," however, will probably not satisfy the client. Someone must summarize what has occurred, what has been discussed during the session, and what the next steps might be. Often the counselor is likely to take responsibility for summarizing, but she or he should at least consider the possibility of including the client. Having the client suggest what might be done is also a valuable tool. Setting up the time and date for the next meeting as well as some of the potential discussion topics makes the termination of the interview smooth and does not leave the client without a sense of direction or accomplishments.

With some clients, summarizing is not enough. They still wish to sit and talk. The counselor often has to leave the situation by standing up and moving toward the door to assist the client to get her or his coat. The counselor may use some subtle devices to suggest that it is time to end the particular interview, such as moving her or his chair or placing her or his hands on the arms of the chair as if to rise. The client usually accepts these devices without any particular stress or strain. The more nervous the counselor is about using them, the more likely the client is to resist the action.

Depending upon the type of counseling approach used, there are some other fairly meaningful ways to end the interview. Assigning some task to the client is one example of a general method. The counselor can phrase the instructions so as to communicate the intent to end the session, such as, "Now that we are finished for today I would like to suggest some questions that both of us should consider for next time." A related approach is to arrange for any tests or reading that may have been determined during the session.

Two or three limitations affect the termination of an interview. First, the counselor must avoid, as much as possible, leaving the client in an ambiguous situation. The more hesitancy, unsureness, or uneasiness the counselor exhibits, the less likely the client is to be able to understand or accept what is occurring.

Second, the counselor may wish to provide extra counseling time when he or she senses there is a need for the client to continue. This simply means that the counselor should have some flexibility to provide additional assistance when necessary. Some clients, however, may use this as a manipulative device to meet their own needs, wasting the scheduled session in order to effect some control or manipulation over the counselor. This tactic calls for counselor self-examination and understanding.

Regardless of the method used, the counselor should make sure that the client leaves with the most positive feeling possible about what occurs in the session and what the future activities might be. The counselor should have in mind a tentative plan and some activities to effect termination.

Terminating the Relationship

Maholick and Turner (1979) deal with the critical issues of when and how to say goodbye. Termination is indicated when the client has progressed as far as she or he wants in gaining awareness and changing behavior patterns. This is certainly a natural and desirable time to terminate, but it is important that the client leave with a respectful and genuine goodbye, not a mechanical or cold farewell. Termination may be precipitated by an unexpected development such as a job change or a shift in working hours. When these circumstances are out of the client's power to manipulate, it is still important to experience closure even though the client may not have achieved the originally defined goals. This is obviously a time when clients and counselors may be hesitant or resistant about terminating, for they have not really completed their relationship with each other. Another time for termination is when the presenting problem has been clarified with some significant resolution and there are indications that the old patterns of behaving are not returning to the same degree. It may be tempting to continue in counseling at this point because the client is becoming increasingly enjoyable to both her- or himself and the counselor. It is wise at this point to ask what the client wants to continue working on; if no new goals can be agreed upon, it may be advisable to have the client terminate and grow independently. In another situation, the client may refuse either to deal with the issues or to say goodbye. This may be the least successful termination experience and is particularly difficult for the counselor. At this time the counselor must encourage the client to work on his or her problem independently, thereby decreasing dependence on the counseling situation. Another difficult time for termination occurs when no progress occurs or, even worse, a maladaptive behavior is accelerating. In some cases it may be necessary for the counselor to work through a termination into a process of referring a client to someone else.

Usually, termination comes when the client feels she or he has made the decision, has the information, or is coping adequately with the problem. The client may give clues that he or she does not need the counseling any longer. It is not uncommon for a feeling of friendship and goodwill to develop between the two people. After talking through some meaningful things in your life with another person, it is difficult to separate yourself suddenly.

Maholick and Turner (1979) suggest that there are checkpoints that clarify indications and reflect the appropriateness of termination. The counselor and client should examine the initial symptoms or problems and see if they have been resolved. This involves returning to the original point of counseling for a review. They can explore the extent to which resolution has been achieved and search for indications of improved coping ability. Other areas to check include the degree of increased awareness, appreciation, and acceptance of self and others.

The steps involved in closure of a series of counseling sessions are somewhat parallel to those used in unit and session termination. First some preparatory steps should be taken; this simply means that the counselor does not wait until the last minute to indicate inability to continue the relationship. Whatever the reasons for termination, they seldom wait to present themselves until the middle of the final interview. The counselor should provide or encourage the client to provide an overall summary of what has occurred. Sometimes, due to the nature of an extended series of meetings, both participants must be involved, and considerable clarification may be necessary.

It is important that the same conditions exist when case termination occurs as when session termination takes place. The counselor must avoid leaving the client in an ambiguous or defenseless position. The counselor must either be certain that the client can function outside the counseling situation or provide further assistance. In any case the counselor, regardless of orientation, must be able to understand the situation the client faces, understand her or his own situation, weigh the values, and make a decision.

Maholick and Turner (1979) discuss counseling as a transitional process. Initially the client relinquishes some of the responsibility but later reclaims it as he or she proceeds with less tension and anxiety and greater ability to define and fulfill him- or herself authentically. Therefore, if counseling is successful, termination can be implemented with the full knowledge that the client is now ready to take on responsibilities for his or her own counseling and to live it in life. Termination does not preclude future contact with the counselor. It is a closure of a unique interpersonal relationship that may be resumed or may be exchanged for real-life social relations. In some instances, this might be of considerable significance to each person.

Premature Termination

There are situations in which, despite the counselor's opinion, the client decides to withdraw from counseling. Premature termination cannot be clearly described by the number of interviews completed. The appropriateness of termination is determined by the extent to which the client's problems and ineffective behaviors remain and the degree to which these factors have a negative impact in the client's life. Hansen et al. (1980) suggest that if a client indicates or the counselor thinks the client may terminate prematurely, the topic of termination should be openly discussed. Should a client simply not return for a scheduled session and does not contact the counselor to reschedule, the counselor should make an effort to contact the client. It may be that the client is merely testing the counselor's concern or may have reached a difficult period in the counseling process and be overwhelmed with his or her ability to work through the situation. It is possible that a client may have negative feelings and be resistant to continuing the relationship. The counselor needs to help the prematurely terminating client to deal with the negative reactions. Ward (1984) lists four possible positive outcomes of a client's participation in an exit interview: (1) There may be a reduction of many negative influences before the client resumes life without counseling; (2) some critical issues may be resolved so the client may continue the counseling with another counselor; (3) the client can be prepared for benefit from a referral to another counselor; and (4) the probability is increased that the client will reenter counseling at another time.

The problem of clients terminating from counseling prior to significant improvement has been a major concern to counselors. Heilbrun (1982) has investigated the degree to which clients' early termination relates to their degree of social insight and level of defensiveness. His findings include a three-way interaction for defensiveness, social insight, and sex. Examination of these findings reveals that there is an association of men with high social insight who are also highly defended to be more likely to terminate prematurely. Heilbrun concludes that the factors governing early commitment to counseling and those contributing to success or failure in full-term counseling are interrelated and confounded in a broad sense. Researchers may confuse situations where clients terminate their counseling early without benefit with those situations where the client shows short-term improvement (Frank, 1979). Early terminating clients may have different characteristics from those who continue. The data suggest that men who drop out of counseling have cognitive attributes that allow them to participate effectively in insight treatment and to generalize the benefits from counseling through their insightfulness. Men are more independent in their problem solving and have more social insight and are more highly defended against an evaluative threat. Therefore, they may leave counseling early due to some improvement rather than because they cannot maintain a commitment to counseling. Heilbrun proposes that men who are more likely to remain in counseling may present a more difficult problem for an insight-oriented counselor. Such clients may be more dependent on others to solve their problems, with less social insight than others who maintain a defensive posture.

Women who drop out prematurely, according to Heilbrun, are likely to include those whose distress has decreased because of an immediate relief. This is a type of short-term success, though different from that proposed from early terminating men. Early terminating women are described as dependent and problem solving, with low social insight and strong defenses, suggesting limitations as participants in insight-oriented counseling and lower ability to generalize from the experience. The immediate relief from the catharsis, however, may be preferable to long-term counseling without major improvement.

Temporary Termination

Seligman (1984) presents a model for helping clients deal with temporary intervals in counseling relationships that are caused by the counselor being absent. She points out that it is important to inform clients in advance so they can anticipate the temporary break in the relationship. She uses four weekly sessions to prepare the clients. In session one, in addition to some usual business, the clients are informed of a trip or vacation and assured that a plan for their continuing growth will be developed and referrals provided if necessary. In the second session, although some time is allocated to the usual topics of the client, more extensive time is used for discussions of the client's reactions to the counselor's absence, and there is a presentation of a plan. Most of session three is used to generate goals and plans and provide the client time to discuss the separation. In the fourth session the client's plans are completed and put into writing, and time is spent in processing the client's feelings about the separation.

Barish (1980) postulates that how clients deal with interruptions in their treatment reflects their progress and reports three types of sessions occurring before breaks. In one type of session, the client may be well defended in filling time with meaningless conversation. In a second type of session the client is preoccupied with the interruption and tries to keep defenses high by masking feelings of rejection and fear of loss. In these two types of sessions, Barish suggests that the counselor and client work toward understanding the reactions to the separation. In a third type of session the separation acts as a stimulus that permits the client to deal with earlier loss and anxiety experiences and to deepen his or her self-awareness.

Seligman (1984) recommends formulating a plan with the client that includes a written outline of five variables. The client and counselor should work together to develop appropriate goals and plans for achieving them during the period they are not meeting. The counselor may recommend that the client can continue communication by writing to the counselor during the separation period. Even though clients choose not to accept a referral to another mental health professional, all clients should be given the names of two people they could contact if needed. Before the separation occurs, it is appropriate for the counselor and client to assess the accomplishments the client has made toward the established goals. Discussing the gains the client has made can serve as a reinforcement to strengthen the client's self-confidence. The remaining task for the counselor and client is to establish a date and time for their next appointment. This will provide a sense of continuity and reassure the client that the therapeutic relationship will resume.

Summary

This chapter has presented a descriptive model of a continuing counseling relationship. Not all relationships, and probably no single one, would follow this model exactly. However, it is a guide to the various stages of counseling that we have observed. Clients frequently enter counseling with apprehensions and talk about their problem, move to some exploration of themselves, gain some understanding of themselves and the problem, work through the understanding and trying of new behaviors, and then terminate counseling. The process does not move in sequence but with stops, starts, and regressions through various phases. The various aspects of termination occur through the process and provide closure of the various points. Because a counselor may not be able to help a client through the entire process, referral is a part of the continuing relationship.

References

Barish, S. (1980). On interpretations in treatment. *Clinical Social Work Journal, 8,* 3–15.

Bordin, E. (1975). The generalizability of the psychoanalytic concept of the working alliance. *Psychotherapy: Theory, Research, and Practice, 16,* 252–260.

Brammer, L., & Shostrom, E. (1982). *Therapeutic psychology.* Englewood Cliffs, NJ: Prentice Hall.

Carkhuff, R. (1969). *Helping and human relations* (Vols. 1 and 2). New York: Holt, Rinehart and Winston.

Frank, J. (1979). The present status of outcome studies. *Journal of Consulting and Clinical Psychology, 47,* 310–316.

Gelso, C., and Carter, J. (1985). The relationship in counseling psychotherapy: Components, consequences, and theoretical antecedents. *The Counseling Psychologist, 13,* 155–243.

Hansen, J., Warner, R., & Smith E. (1980). *Group counseling: Theory and process.* (2nd ed.). Chicago: Rand McNally.

Heilbrun, A. (1982). Cognitive factors in early counseling termination: Social insight and level of defensiveness. *Journal of Counseling Psychology, 29,* 29–38.

Holder, B., Carkhuff, R., & Berenson, B. (1967). The differential effects of the manipulation of therapeutic conditions upon high- and low-functioning clients. *Journal of Counseling Psychology, 14,* 63–66.

Holland, G. (1965). *Fundamentals of psychology.* New York: Holt, Rinehart and Winston.

Hoyt, M. (1979). Aspects of termination in a time-limited brief psychotherapy. *Psychiatry, 42,* 208–219.

Maholick, L., & Turner, D (1979). Termination: That difficult farewell. *American Journal of Psychotherapy, 33,* 583–591.

May, R. (1967). *The art of counseling.* New York: Abingdon.

Osipow, S. H., & Walsh, W. B. (1970). *Strategies in counseling for behavior change.* New York: Appleton-Century-Crofts.

Piaget, G., Berenson, B., & Carkhuff, R. (1967). The differential effects of the manipulation of therapeutic conditions by high- and low-functioning counselors upon high- and low-functioning clients. *Journal of Consulting Psychology, 31,* 481–486.

Rogers, C. (1958). A process conception of psychotherapy. *American Psychologist, 13,* 142–149.

Seligman, L. (1984). Termporary termination. *Journal of Counseling and Development, 63,* 43–44.

Strupp, H. (1978). Psychotherapy research and practice: An overview. In S. Garfield and A. Bergin (Eds.), *Handbook of psychotherapy and behavior change.* New York: John Wiley and Sons.

Turock, A. (1980). Immediacy in counseling: Recognizing clients' unspoken message. *Personnel and Guidance Journal, 59,* 168–172.

Ward, D. (1984). Termination of individual counseling: Concepts and strategies. *Journal of Counseling and Development, 63,* 21–25.

Social Factors in the Relationship

Several social factors affect the counseling relationship. In recent years considerable attention has been given to such variables as perceived competence, power, expertness, intimacy, attractiveness, and trustworthiness. Social factors, as perceived by a client, appear to have an impact on the early stages of the counseling relationship. When clients rate their counselors higher on the social factors, the counselors are also rated as more successful.

Concern for racial and cultural differences has become increasingly apparent in the professional literature. One's culture consists of all that one has learned to do, believe, value, and enjoy. It involves the ideals, beliefs, skills, tools, customs, and institutions into which one is born. Most, if not all, current theories of counseling have developed from a Western European, postindustrial knowledge base. Many of the philosophical assumptions inherent in modern culture contribute to difficulties in counseling individuals from other cultures. One section of the chapter will explore ethnic identity, acculturation, and the role of counselors.

After years of research into sex bias in counseling, the literature is turning to positive proposals to enhance feminine identity, encourage strength, and achieve equal power. The concepts of feminist therapy can be beneficial for men and women alike.

Counseling gay men and lesbians is a topic that has received too little attention. The values, attitudes, and behaviors of counselors are explored and some guidelines presented.

Counselor Social Personal Influence

Dixon and Glover (1984) report that counseling research has shown that counselors' influence over a client is affected by the client's perception of their expertness, attractiveness, and trustworthiness. Also, their influence is enhanced and they are more able to influence client change when they are perceived to be high in these social variables.

Egan (1985) uses the term competence to describe clients' belief that the counselor has the necessary information and ability to be helpful. Their perceptions of the counselor's competence or expertness increase their confidence in the counselor and help them accept and work with the counselor.

He lists three variables relative to clients' perception of a counselor's competence: reputation, role, and behavior. The counselor's reputation is established by other people stating that he or she is competent. Such communication comes from friends, colleagues, and former clients. When seeking a counselor, people may be referred by another professional or seek the advice of their friends. Although a reputation communicated in this manner may not always be a reliable indicator of a counselor's actual expertise, when a very positive referral is made, the client enters the relationship with an expectation of successful treatment. First indications of a counselor's role are communicated through his or her introduction, dress, demeanor, office, and diplomas. The counselor's personal demeanor in responding to clients will have an impact on their perceptions of his or her expertise. Clients also will notice office decor, including diplomas and certificates, which are interpreted as a statement of expertise. Although a counselor's reputation and role are influential, it is really the counselor's interaction with clients that has the strongest impact on their perception of competence. Effective counselors demonstrate their skills and professional knowledge by providing help to their clients. It is also through the behavior of the counselor that clients develop a sense of trust. As Egan (1985) notes, "Trust in a helper can evaporate quickly if little or nothing is accomplished" (p. 139).

Trustworthiness, like expertness, may come as part of the counselor's reputation. For a meaningful counseling relationship to occur, however, the counselor must continuously behave in a credible manner. Egan (1985) and Johnson (1981) have suggested counselor behaviors that communicate trustworthiness. It is important that the counselor provide accurate and reliable information. If clients detect errors, they may doubt other aspects of the counseling relationship. It is important to be dependable, because dependability builds trust. Dependable behaviors such as being on time, returning phone calls promptly, and living up to all the provisions of the client/counselor agreement will increase the feeling that the client can depend on the counselor. Maintaining the confidentiality of the client's communication is probably the most important aspect of trustworthiness. Learning that a counselor shared information without permission will quickly destroy the client's trust. Other counselor behaviors that enhance credibility involve being dynamic and active in the relationship, rather than passive and lethargic. Clients assume that frequent and dynamic responses indicate a sincere involvement by the counselor. Egan suggests that any evidence of ulterior motives such as voyeurism, selfishness, or superficial curiosity will certainly erode trust. Therefore, it is important that counselors communicate sincerity in their behavior in order to be trusted by clients. Clients will be more cooperative when they trust the counselor. They will also learn to trust themselves and to communicate more openly and fully what they are thinking and feeling. This learning will help them understand themselves and the situations in which they live. By trusting the counselor, clients will also trust the solutions that they and the counselor establish for them to work through.

Social-influence theory suggests that when clients perceive the counselor as attractive, the therapeutic relationship will be strengthened, and they will like and cooperate more with the counselor. Strong (1968) described interpersonal attractiveness as clients' perceived similarity to, compatibility with, and liking of the counselor. Interpersonal attractiveness involves more than physical characteristics and general appearance of the counselor. Although these variables may have some impact on clients' perceptions, the role, reputation, and behavior of the counselor are important variables. A behavior such as appropriate self-disclosure may help clients see the counselor as being compatible with them. The counselor's disclosure of similar attitudes and opinions about a situation may increase his or her perceived attractiveness to clients.

A number of variables have been used to learn about the counselor's social influence. Researchers have examined the impact of counselors' techniques, reputations, and personal characteristics on clients' perceptions of counselor expertness, trustworthiness, and attractiveness.

Reputation

Does the counselor's reputation make a difference in the client's perception? Littrell, Caffrey, and Hopper (1987) conducted two similar studies to determine if precounseling effects of reputational cues affected high school students' preferences for counselors and perceptions of the counselors' credibility and interpersonal attractiveness. Seven different experimental conditions were presented on videotape. Three tapes showed high school students delivering positive, neutral, and negative reputational cues about a male or female counselor. One videotape presented only a brief counseling session. Significantly different perceptions and preferences of the counselors were found for the positive, neutral, and negative cue conditions. Since the reputational cues strongly influenced high school students' preferences and perceptions prior to counseling, what clients and former clients say about counselors may have an impact on new clients' perceptions of their counselor.

Techniques

Several studies have been conducted to examine the importance of the counselor's behavior or techniques on clients' perception of the counselor's social influence. Krantz and Marshall (1988) studied the effects of facial expression and the use of psychological terminology on client's initial evaluations of counselor's expertness, attractiveness, trustworthiness, masculinity and femininity. They reported that smiling significantly decreased ratings of masculinity and that the use of jargon decreased ratings of attractiveness. There was also a nonsignificant trend for smiling to decrease expertness and trustworthiness.

Anderson and Anderson (1985) asked male and female undergraduate students to read transcripts of a counseling session between a male counselor and a female college student. The transcripts were identical except for the use of a positive self involving or a negative self-involving statement by the counselor. The positive self-involving statement was a personal, present tense response made by the counselor following the client's statement. The negative self-involving statement involved a negative evaluation on the client response. After reading the transcripts the subjects rated the counselor in terms of attractiveness, expertness, and trustworthiness as well as appropriateness of the counselor's behavior and their willingness to see the counselor. The findings revealed that the counselors using the positive self-involving statements were perceived more positively on all of the dimensions. Interestingly, for the male subjects differences were greater than for the female subjects.

Two studies asked subjects to listen to an audiotape of an interview and then to rate the counselor. McMillan and Johnson (1990) asked undergraduate students to listen to an audiotape of a client describing severe anxiety reactions and a counselor giving a paradoxical intervention that combined symptom description and restraining directives in which the counselor either gave an explanation or did not give an explanation for the method. Other subjects listened to a tape of the client's descriptions and a counselor using a cognitive behavioral directive. The counselor was described to the subjects as either a novice or an expert. The students who listened to the cognitive behavioral style of counseling rated the counselor as more attractive, expert, and trustworthy than the students who listened to either of the two paradoxical interventions. They also rated the expert counselor higher on expertness and trustworthiness. In another study, Jones and Gelso (1988) studied the impact of tentative and absolute interpretations of a female counselor to a female client. The women subjects were classified as resistant, intermediate, or nonresistant. The subjects listened to taped interactions of the initial phase of counseling in which the counselor gave one or the other style of interpretation and then rated the counselor's social influence in terms of expertness, attractiveness, and trustworthiness as well as the helpfulness and effectiveness of the interpretations and their own willingness to see the counselor. The tentative interpretations were generally viewed more positively than the absolute interpretations, and the subjects rated as resistant reported the counselor as more attractive than did the others.

In a study to examine the degree to which counselors' opened and closed body postures were related to client perceptions of expertness, trustworthiness, and attractiveness, undergraduate students rated three female counselors on the Counselor Rating Form. The findings suggest that an open posture communicates a sense of confidence and involvement to a significant degree; however, this had no effect on the perceptions of attractiveness as reflected by friendliness, likability, warmth, and sociability. The open posture also had no effect on the perceptions of trustworthiness as measured by honesty, sincerity, and reliability (Ridley and Asbury, 1988).

Another study examined client self-reported reliance on nonverbal cues to actual changes in counselor's nonverbal behavior. Forty high school students with high sensitivity to nonverbal behavior and forty students with low reliance on nonverbal behavior viewed two stimulus tapes. One of the tapes contained a responsive counselor and the other tape a counselor with unresponsive behaviors. The students rated the expertness, trustworthiness, and attractiveness of the counselor as well as indicating the degree to which they relied on nonverbal cues in making their judgments. The students gave their highest positive ratings to the counselor in the responsive tape for all three attributes. The students with a higher reliance on nonverbal behavior also showed a greater sensitivity to the changes in the counselor's nonverbal behaviors than the students with less reliance on nonverbal cues (Uhlemann & Lee, 1990). Uhlemann, Lee, and Hasse (1989) studied the relationship of university students in differential levels of arousal conditions to their perceptions of the counselor's nonverbal behaviors. The students rated the counselors in terms of expertness and were able to discriminate counselor positive and negative nonverbal behaviors during the early portion of an interview but this tendency deteriorated as the interview progressed. The students with a higher level of cognitive complexity were abler to tolerate higher levels of arousal without showing perceptual impairment in their discrimination of counselors' nonverbal behaviors.

A related study investigated the degree and experience of school psychologists consulting with teachers. After they watched a videotaped vignette of a consultation, they rated the psychologist's expertness, trustworthiness, and attractiveness using the Counselor Rating Form. The results show the school psychologist's degree affected the perceptions of expertness and trustworthiness, and experience as a school psychologist affected the teacher's perception of the psychologist's trustworthiness (Short, Moore, & Williams, 1991).

Client perceptions of counselor expertness, attractiveness, and trustworthiness have also been used to evaluate premature termination of clients. Kokotovic and Tracey (1987) reported that undergraduate student clients' satisfaction and perceptions of trustworthiness and expertness of the counselor were related to their returning for appointments. There were no differences in the client's perceptions of counselor attractiveness or client-counselor agreement on problem identification between the clients who continued and those who dropped out.

Personal Characteristics

Strohmer and Biggs (1983) studied the effects of counselor disability on client perceptions of the counselor's attractiveness and expertness. Actually, they studied the influence of the counselor and client both having a disability, the counselor's reputational cues, and the counselor's attending behavior on the client's perceptions of the counselor's attractiveness and expertness. Individuals with physical disabilities observed a series of vignettes showing a counselor and client interaction. Following each vignette, the subjects rated the counselor's expertness and attractiveness. There was no main effect for the counselor and client both having a disability on the disabled individual's ratings of counselor attractiveness or expertness; however, there was a significant effect for the counselor's attending behavior on the client's ratings of expertness and attractiveness. Interestingly, the results do not support the idea that a counselor and client having a disability similarity favorably influences the client's perception of the counselor's social personal influence.

A study reports the effects of cultural variables influencing the client's perception of the counselor's social influence. Sodowsky (1991) studied the effects of culturally consistent counseling tasks on American and international student subjects' perceptions of the counselor. This study included Asian Indian, South Korean, and Caucasian U.S. college students viewing videotapes of simulated counseling sessions. In the culturally consistent simulated tape, the counselor tailored tasks to be consistent with the cultural values of an international student-client. In the culturally discrepant simulation, the counselor used a counseling response demonstrating Western biases. The Asian Indian students rated the counselor significantly higher in expertness and trustworthiness when the counselor was in the culturally consistent tape. The U.S. students rated significantly greater expertness and trustworthiness in the culturally discrepant counseling video. In neither of these counseling perspectives were the counselors highly rated by the South Korean students, suggesting that the constructs may not be generalized across various cultural groups.

Multicultural Factors

Over the past decade, attention to multicultural factors and how these factors impact upon the counseling process have been apparent in the professional literature. Due to the ever-increasing population of individuals with diverse cultural and ethnic backgrounds, counselors and psychologists are challenged to provide services that are culturally relevant and appropriate. It is necessary for those providing counseling services to value, manage, and appreciate the dilemmas created by cultural diversity. This chapter will provide an overview of information to aid counseling professionals in expanding their knowledge and understanding of multicultural issues in counseling. Specifically, race and ethnicity, gender issues, and gay and lesbian diversity will be explored.

The terms multicultural and cross-cultural counseling are used interchangeably in the literature. D. W. Sue, Bernier, Durran, Feinberg, Pederson, Smith, and Vasquez-Nuttall (1982) define cross-cultural counseling as any counseling relationship in which two or more of the participants differ with respect to cultural background, values, or life-style. This includes counseling situations in which the counselor is a member of the majority group and the client a member of a minority group, the counselor is a minority group member and the client a majority group member, the counselor and client are members of different minority groups, and the counselor and client are similar in race and ethnicity but differ in terms of cultural grouping based upon gender, sexual orientation, socioeconomic status, religious affiliation, or age.

Introduction

Pederson (1991b) calls for a broad definition of culture and multicultural perspective. He explores the possibility of moving toward a generic theory of multiculturalism as a "fourth force" position, which would be complementary to the other three forces explaining human behavior: psychodynamic, behavioral, and humanistic. Multiculturalism has generally been regarded more as a method than as a theory. When it refers specifically to narrowly defined culture-specific categories such as ethnicity, multiculturalism is best considered a method of analysis. It could be applied to the encounter of specific cultural groups within another and could emphasize the specific characteristics of each group. Multiculturalism should be considered a theory if it refers to broadly defined social-system variables such as ethnographics, demographics, status, and affiliation (Pederson, 1991b).

Pederson prefers to define culture broadly so the construct of multicultural would become generic to all counseling relationships. The broad definition of culture would include demographic variables such as age, sex, and place of residence; status variables such as social, educational, and economic variables; affiliations, both formal and informal; and ethnographic variables such as nationality, ethnicity, language, and religion (Pederson, 1991b).

Even so, there are some strong arguments against the broad definition of culture. Lee (1991) argues that the term *multiculturism* is in danger of becoming so inclusive that it will be meaningless. The broad definition is ever expanding and encourages groups to perceive themselves as being disenfranchised in some manner. Locke (1990) has a similar perspective suggesting that the term has been stretched to include virtually any group that considers themselves different. As that occurs, the intent of multicultural counseling theory and practice becomes unclear. Locke believes that the broad view of multiculturalism can best serve as a prologue for a more focused perspective in counseling.

Multiculturalism should be understood in a perspective that does not replace traditional theories of counseling. Multiculturalism should complement the traditional theories of counseling; it is problematic for a counselor to be skilled according to any theory without some way of accounting for the ever-changing culture of him- or herself or the client's perspective.

Culturally Encapsulated

Although the literature regarding multiculturalism has grown dramatically in recent years, cultural encapsulation still exists in institutions, professions, and individuals. Wrenn introduced the concept of the culturally encapsulated counselor. His idea of cultural encapsulation assumes five basic features. (1) Reality is defined according to one set of cultural assumptions and stereotypes, and these become more important than the real world. (2) The culturally encapsulated counselor becomes insensitive to variations in culture among individuals and assumes that his or her view is the only legitimate one. (3) People have unreasoned assumptions, which are accepted without proof and protect them without thinking. (4) Technique-oriented job definitions contribute to encapsulation. (5) If there is no evaluation of other viewpoints, then there is no accommodation for interpretation of others' behaviors except from self-reference criteria (Wrenn, 1985).

Ponterotto and Casas (1991) report that the majority of traditionally trained counselors use a culturally encapsulated framework that results in culturally conflicting and oppressive counseling.

Ponterotto (1988) summarized the criticisms of cross-cultural research methodology: (1) A conceptual theoretical framework is lacking. (2) Important psychosocial variables are disregarded and counselor-client process variables are overemphasized. (3) Experimental analog research is overused. (4) There is little study of within group intracultural differences. (5) Most samples include student samples of convenience. (6) Culturally encapsulated measures are used. (7) Sample cultural backgrounds are not adequately defined. (8) There is a failure to describe the limits of generalizability. (9) Minority cultural input is lacking. (10) Researchers have failed to show responsibility toward minority subject pools.

Pederson (1991b) points out that there are some real functional benefits in defining culture broadly rather than narrowly. The broad definition allows counselors to be more accurate in matching the client's intended and culturally learned expectations for the client's behavior. A broad definition also helps the counselor become aware of their own culturally learned perspectives and how these influence them toward particular decision outcomes. As counselors use a broad perspective, they become more aware of the complexity in cultural identity patterns. These may or may not include indicators of ethnicity and nationality. The broad definition will assist counselors in perceiving the ever-changing nature of the client's different interchangeable cultural identities within an interview.

Several factors can impede the development of a cross-cultural counseling relationship. Language differences, class-bound values, and culture-bound values may make it difficult for a counselor to truly understand a client's situation, difficulties, or strengths.

The counselor may also experience difficulty in understanding and feeling empathy with the client's worldview. Each of these make it more important for the counselor to use culturally relevant counseling modalities (Sue et al., 1982; Ibrahim, 1985).

It is crucial to recognize that counseling is sociopolitical in nature with an inherent set of cultural values and norms at its core. The values and norms that underlie counseling are those of the white culture, which is dominant in the United States (Katz, 1985). Tables 14-1 and 14-2 outline the values and beliefs of white culture and counseling respectively. Counselors must be aware of the values and norms that exist in both the majority culture and minority cultures that they encounter and how these differing beliefs and behaviors

TABLE 14-1   The Components of White Culture: Values and Beliefs

Rugged Individualism:
  Individual is primary unit
  Indivdual has primary responsibility
  Independence and autonomy highly
    valued and rewarded
  Individual can control environment

Competition:
  Winning is everything
  Win/lose dichotomy

Action Orientation:
  Must master and control nature
  Must always do something about a
    situation
  Pragmatic/utilitarian view of life

Decision Making:
  Majority rule when Whites have power
  Hierarchical
  Pyramid structure

Communication:
  Standard English
  Written tradition
  Direct eye contact
  Limited physical contact
  Control emotions

Time:
  Adherence to rigid time schedules
  Time is viewed as a commodity

Holidays:
  Based on Christian religion
  Based on White history and male leaders

History:
  Based on European immigrants'
    experience in the United States
  Romanticize war

Protestant Work Ethic:
  Working hard brings success

Progress and Future Orientation:
  Plan for future
  Delayed gratification
  Value continual improvement and progress

Emphasis on Scientific Method:
  Objective, rational, linear thinking
  Cause and effect relationships
  Quantitative emphasis
  Dualistic thinking

Status and Power:
  Measured by economic possessions
  Credentials, titles, and positions
  Believe "own" system
  Believe better than other systems
  Owning goods, space, property

Family Structure:
  Nuclear family is the ideal social unit
  Male is breadwinner and the head of
    the household
  Female is homemaker and subordinate
    to the husband
  Patriarchal structure

Aesthetics:
  Music and art based on European cultures
  Women's beauty based on blonde,
    blue-eyed, thin, young
  Men's attractiveness based on athletic
    ability, power, economic status

Religion:
  Belief in Christianity
  No tolerance for deviation from single
    god concept

Source: J. H. Katz, The sociopolitical nature of counseling. *The Counseling Psychologist,* 1985, *13,* 615–624. Copyright 1985 by the Division of Counseling Psychology. Reprinted by permission of Sage Publications, Inc.

TABLE 14-2   The Cultural Components of Counseling: Values and Beliefs

The Individual in Counseling:
  Individual is the primary focus
  Individual has primary responsibility
  Individual independence and autonomy
    highly valued
  Individual problems are intrapsychic and
    rooted in childhood and family

Action Orientation:
  Client can master and control own life
    and environment
  Client needs to take action to resolve
    own problems
  Bias against passivity or inaction

Status and Power:
  Belief that Western counseling strategies
    are best
  Therapist is expert
  Credentials are essential
  Therapy is expensive
  Licensing used to maintain control
    of profession

Processes (communication):
  Verbal Communication or talk therapy
  Standard monocultural English
  Direct eye contact
  Reflective listening

Goals of Counseling:
  Insight, self-awareness, and personal
    growth
  Improve social and personal efficiency
  Change individual behavior
  Increase ability to cope
  Adapt to society's values

Protestant Work Ethic:
  Work hard in counseling and counseling
    works for you

Goal Orientation and Progress:
  Belief in setting goals in counseling
  Belief in reaching goals in life

Emphasis on Scientific Method:
  Therapist objective and neutral
  Rational and logical thought
  Use of linear problem solving
  Cause and effect relationships
  Childhood and family sheds light on
    present behavior
  Reliance on quantitative evaluation,
    including psychodiagnostic tests,
    intelligence tests, personal inventories,
    and career placement
  Dualism between mind and body
  Primary focus on the psychological as
    opposed to the physiological
  Label problems using DMS III

Time:
  Scheduled appointments
  Adherence to strict time schedule
    (50-minute hour)

Family Structure:
  Nuclear family is ideal

Aesthetics:
  YAVIS Client: Young, Attractive, Verbal,
    Intelligent, Successful

Source: J. H. Katz, The sociopolitical nature of counseling. *The Counseling Psychologist,* 1985, *13,* 615–624. Copyright 1985 by the Division of Counseling Psychology. Reprinted by permission of Sage Publications, Inc.

impact upon one another. Table 14-3 presents some generic characteristics of counseling that Sue and Sue (1977) summarize and compare with the values of several minority groups: Asian Americans, Blacks, Chicanos, and Native Americans.

It is important for the counselor to be aware that the client's level of acculturation, the extent to which a minority individual has assimilated the values, norms, and world-view of the dominant culture with his or her cultural patterns, has an influence on the counseling process (Ponterotto, 1987).

Counselors are encouraged to become qualified or competent regarding cross-cultural or multicultural counseling (Sue et al., 1982; Katz, 1985; Johnson, 1987). Sue et al. (1982) suggest that counselors can develop cultural competence through the exploration of beliefs/attitudes, the acquisition of knowledge regarding specific cultures, and the practice

TABLE 14-3   Generic Characteristics of Counseling

Language	Middle Class	Culture
Standard English Verbal communication	Standard English Verbal communication Adherence to time schedules (50-minute session) Long-range goals Ambiguity	Standard English Verbal communication Individual centered Verbal/emotional/behavioral expressiveness Client-counselor communication Openness and intimacy Cause-effect orientation Clear distinction between "physical" and "mental" well-being

Third-World Group Variables

Language	Lower Class	Culture
	Asian-Americans	
Bilingual background	Nonstandard English Action oriented Different time perspective Immediate, short-range goals Concrete, tangible, structured approach	Asian language Family centered Restraint of feelings One-way communications from authority figure to person Silence is respect Advice seeking Well-defined patterns of interaction (concrete structured) Private vs. public display (shame/disgrace/pride) Physical and mental well-being defined differently

of counseling skills that are culturally relevant. A culturally competent counselor is one who is sensitive to his or her own cultural heritage and that of clients. The counselor values and respects cultural differences and recognizes when referral to another counselor may be necessary due to the needs of the client or the limits of the counselor. Knowledge of the history and present status of the country's sociopolitical system in regard to minorities, information regarding the specific minority group with which the counselor is working, and an understanding of the generic characteristics of the counseling process are necessary for the counselor to practice in a culturally competent manner. The counselor must be aware of institutional barriers minorities experience in using mental health services and be able to act as an institutional advocate for clients. It is important for the

TABLE 14-3 *continued*

Language	Lower Class	Culture
	Blacks	
Black language	Nonstandard English Action oriented Different time perspective Immediate, short-range goals	Black language Sense of "peoplehood" Action oriented "Paranorm" due to oppression
	Concrete, tangible, structured approach	Importance placed on nonverbal behavior
	Chicanos	
Bilingual background	Nonstandard English Action oriented Different time perspective Immediate, short-range goals Concrete, tangible, and structured approach	Spanish speaking Group-centered cooperation Temporal difference Family orientation Different pattern of communication A religious distinction between mind/body
	Native Americans	
Bilingual background	Nonstandard English Action oriented Different time perspective Immediate, short-range goals Concrete, tangible, and structured approach	Tribal dialects Cooperative not competitive individualism Present time orientation Creative/experiential/intuitive/ nonverbal Satisfy present needs Use of folk or supernatural explanations

Source: D. W. Sue and D. Sue, Barriers to effective cross-cultural counseling. *Journal of Counseling Psychology,* 1977, *24,* pp. 420–429. Copyright 1977 by the American Psychological Association. Reprinted by permission.

counselor to be able to communicate and process a variety of verbal and nonverbal responses accurately and appropriately given the specific cultural context of the client.

White Racial Identity

Carter (1990) points out that the literature is lacking material on how white people experience themselves as racial beings and how they respond to themselves as racial beings affects their perceptions and attitudes of minorities. Since whites seldom examine the meaning of their whiteness, they may not consider how racist attitudes may be related to variations in white racial identity, a within-group variable.

Helms (1984) proposes a five-level model of white racial identity development: contact, disintegration, reintegration, pseudo-independence, and autonomy. She suggests that whites develop their racial identity corresponding to attitudes about African Americans as a racial group.

Racial identity in the contact stage has the person essentially unaware of his or her racial group membership and tending to ignore the racial identity of others. Individuals avoid African Americans or may befriend them out of curiosity. During the disintegration stage, the individual's whiteness becomes an important characteristic, and the person may experience feelings of ambivalence and conflict between his or her internal moral standards and society's norms regarding interracial interactions. Some people overidentify with African Americans and become paternalistic, while others withdraw into a white society to avoid conflicts. Those who overidentify or become paternalistic in behavior are likely to experience rejection from African Americans. Stereotypical thinking and feelings of fear and anger toward African Americans are typical in the reintegration stage. In this stage of development, individuals may remain distanced from African Americans or accept the personal implications of being white. During the pseudo-independence stage individuals are likely to intellectualize about racial issues before they develop an emotional understanding of the relations. During this time the interpersonal interactions are generally limited to a few African Americans. As individuals increase their interactions with African Americans, they move into the autonomy stage of racial identity. As they internalize a positive white identity, they can integrate an emotional and intellectual appreciation as well as respect for racial differences and similarities. When individuals are secure in their own racial identity, they can seek opportunities to become involved in interracial interactions.

Helms (1984) hypothesized that the better the personal identity adjustment, the better interracial relationships would be. She also believed that better counseling relationships might occur from the development of higher levels of racial identity. In a preliminary study Claney and Parker (1988) reported that white racial attitudes had a curvilinear relationship to perceived comfort with African Americans. The lower and higher levels of racial identity were related to comfort with African Americans.

Carter (1990) investigated the relationship between white racial identity attitudes and racism and found that white racial identity attitudes were predictive of racism; however, the findings were different for men and women. First of all, the data demonstrated that men and women in this sample differed in their level of white racial identity attitudes. The separate multiple regression analysis found men to be higher in disintegration attitudes while women were higher in pseudo-independence and autonomy attitudes. The data for all levels of white male racial identity attitudes contributed to the prediction of racism; however, reintegration attitudes were the closest to being a significant predictor of racism for white men. The overall regression was significant for women; however, contact attitudes were predictive of racism in a negative direction indicating that women with higher contact attitudes are likely to have low endorsement of racism beliefs.

Familiarity of racial identity development is an important component in the knowledge and understanding of a culturally competent counselor. Cross (1971) proposed a five-stage model of Black identity development: pre-encounter, encounter, immersion-emersion, internalization, internalization-commitment. In the pre-encounter stage, individuals are unaware and accepting of oppression and work toward assimilation into the majority culture. The encounter stage results from some profound experience or realization of discrimination and oppression. Individuals in this stage begin to reject oppression and experience feelings of guilt and anger. During immersion-emersion, individuals initially withdraw from the dominant culture and become immersed in Black culture and heritage. An emersion phase begins, and the individual develops a sense of pride about being Black. The internalization stage is characterized by a resolution of conflicts regarding Black and white and the presence of a sense of inner security and self-confidence about blackness. The final stage of internalization-commitment involves the individual's desire to integrate his or her identity into meaningful action for the benefit of the minority community (Cross, 1971; Downing and Roush, 1985; Parham, 1989).

Parham (1989) expands Cross's model to propose a model of Nigrescence that hypothesizes that changes in Black identity occur within the context of the life cycle. The five Cross (1971) stages are examined with respect to late adolescence/early adulthood, middle adulthood, and late adulthood. Several possibilities are suggested for how Black individuals progress through these stages. Stagnation occurs when the individuals' racial identity attitudes remain constant throughout the life span. A stage-wise linear progression is present when an individual's attitudes emerge in a stage-like fashion concluding in internalization. When an individual's attitudes appear to move through the stages over and over again, recycling is said to occur (Parham, 1989).

A critique of the Parham model suggests it to be creative, well developed, and an excellent conceptual base for use in empirical investigation. Beginning the Nigrescence with childhood versus late adolescence/early adulthood to examine racial identity development for children offers a more life span–oriented approach (Ponterotto, 1989).

Research has examined various cultural groups (African American, Asian American, Mexican American, Hispanic/Latino, West Indian American, Native American) and facets of the counseling process (counselor characteristics, duration satisfaction, perceived effectiveness, counseling style) (Watkins, Terrell, Miller, & Terrell, 1989; McKenzie, 1986; Atkinson et al., 1989; Ponterotto, 1987; Terell & Terell, 1984; Pomales & Williams, 1989; Kunkel, Hector, Coronado, & Vales, 1989; LaFromboise, Trimble, & Mohatt, 1990). Caution is necessary in generalizing the results of these studies to different geographic samples. It is important to recognize that while differences clearly exist between cultural groups, differences also exist within groups (racial identity development, level of acculturation) (Ponterotto, 1989). It is impossible for a counselor to know the intricacies of every culture or to not encounter literature that perpetuates stereotypes. Therefore, the counselor needs to obtain relevant cultural information from the client (Scott & Borodovsky, 1990).

Biracial Identity

Most psychological theories on identity development have focused on the white culture with some attention given to certain minority cultures. However, identity development is also important for biracial individuals. For many years the predominant model of biracial identity followed Stonequist's (1937) ideas of the biracial individual's "marginal" identity. That model postulated that individuals with biracial heritage did not establish firm identities but had marginal identities. In fact, the biracial individual has generally been ignored. There is very little research and literature that focuses on biracial individuals, and even the U.S. Bureau of the Census does not provide a space for identity as a biracial individual.

Poston (1990) describes two major reasons why racial identity development is important. First, it influences people's attitudes about themselves, as well as about individuals from other minority groups and about people from the majority group. Second, the development of a racial identity dispels the myth of cultural conformity that all individuals from the minority group are the same. Poston suggests that these two concepts indicate that there are different levels of development and specific attitudes associated with the different levels.

Poston (1990) suggests that the applications of racial identity development models designed for specific minority groups have limitations when applied to biracial individuals. Such models imply that an individual might choose one group's culture or values over another at different stages or might first reject a minority identity and culture and then reject the dominant culture. Those models do not project the integration of several group identities, but see rejecting one racial identity and accepting others rather than recognizing multiple ethnic identities. Those models require acceptance into the minority culture of origin while biracial persons have two cultures and often experience lack of acceptance by both parent cultures.

Poston (1990) proposes a new and positive model specifically for biracial identity development. He acknowledges that it is tentative and based on little research on biracial individuals. It is suggested that the stages be examined as changes in reference group orientation attitudes. Cross (1987) as quoted in Poston (1990), defines reference group orientation as including such constructs as racial identity, racial esteem, and racial ideology.

Personal Identity

In the initial stage of this model, personal identity, the individuals are often very young and children tend to have more of a sense of self that is somewhat independent of ethnic background. After membership in an ethnic group becomes salient, however, the child is aware of race and ethnicity. Phinney and Rotherham (1987) suggest that children's reference group orientations are yet to be developed and their identity is primarily based on their personal identity factors, such as self-esteem and the self-worth they learn from their families.

Choice of Group Categorization

Young people at this stage are frequently pushed to choose an identity, which is usually one ethnic group, and this may create a crisis for the individual. Hall (1980) noted that many biracial individuals feel that society forced them to make a specific choice in order to participate with peers, family, or social groups. When that experience occurs, individuals have two choices: one is to choose a multicultural position which emphasizes the racial heritage of both parents; the second is to choose one parent culture as the dominant one over the other. Hall found several factors that were influential in making this choice, and Poston focused on three. The first include the status of the parents' ethnic background, the demographics of their neighborhood, and the ethnicity and influence of their peer groups.

The second set of factors involve social support variables such as parental style, acceptance and participation in various culture groups, and parental and family acceptance. The third set of variables, personal factors, include the physical appearance, knowledge of the languages, knowledge of the culture, age, political involvement, and individual personality variables. Poston (1990) feels it would be somewhat unusual for an individual to choose a multiethnic identity at this stage because it requires some level of knowledge of multiple cultures and a level of cognitive development that he believes is not yet characteristic of this age group.

Enmeshment/Denial

Following the choice of a group is a stage of confusion and guilt due to choosing an identity that is not fully expressive of the individual's background. Also the person may experience feelings of guilt, self-hatred, and lack of acceptance from one or more groups. Sebring (1985), as quoted by Poston, suggested that a child who is unable to identify with both parents may have feelings of disloyalty and guilt over the rejection of one parent. If a child is to move beyond this level, it will be necessary to resolve the anger and guilt and learn to appreciate both parents' cultures.

Appreciation

As individuals begin to learn about their heritage and cultures, they begin to appreciate their multiple identity and can broaden their reference group orientation. They still identify more with one group, and that is likely to be influenced by the factors described in the choice stage.

Integration

As individuals tend to recognize and value their ethnic identities, they experience a wholeness and integration. Individuals at this level develop a secure and integrated identity.

Poston (1990) suggests that this model differs from others in that it focuses on the uniqueness of biracial identity development. It emphasizes that individuals need to know and integrate different cultures and specifies the personal and social factors necessary in that process. This model also notes the difficulties in identity development of a multiethnic person and emphasizes that the developmental process can progress in a healthy fashion. Poston goes on to describe several issues and assumptions that are present in this model. First, biracial individuals may have identity problems when they internalize societal prejudice so that the reference group orientation has an impact on the person's self-esteem. Secondly, several social factors, such as family and peer influences have an impact on the individual's identity choice. Third, individuals may feel some guilt or alienation during this choice phase and may make a choice even if they are not comfortable with it. Fourth, the denial involved in choosing one identity over another may be associated with feelings of disloyalty and guilt. Fifth, the integration of both cultures is important and is related to positive indicators of mental health. Sixth, the most identity confusion occurs during the choice and enmeshment/denial phases when the personal identity of the individual is most vulnerable to the reference group orientation attitudes.

Implications for Counseling

Gibbs (1987) who worked with biracial adolescents, identified several issues and problems including identity confusion, self-hatred, denial of self, suicide, alienation, gender identity confusion, substance abuse, feelings of guilt, and disloyalty. Sebring (1985) suggested that the counselor can work with clients helping them to understand how they internalized society's biased attitudes about their cultural backgrounds and assist them in moving to a more internal perspective of themselves. The counselor is providing a safe atmosphere for clients to express their feelings of anger and guilt. In addition to providing social and emotional support, the counselor may make referrals to groups that can provide specific support for biracial individuals.

The use of psycho-educational methods can be effective both with the clients and their parents. The counselor can provide resources as well as some education regarding the parents' ethnic or cultural backgrounds and stress the positive aspects of each as well as adopting a biracial identity. McRoy and Freeman (1986) identified several environmental factors that can facilitate the development of positive racial identities: (1) Encourage clients to acknowledge and discuss their racial heritage with their parents. (2) Help parents acknowledge that their child's racial/ethnic heritage is different from their own and indicate that as positive. (3) Encourage parents to give their child opportunities to develop relationships with children from many different backgrounds. This can most naturally occur by permitting them to live in integrated neighborhoods and attend integrated schools. (4) Encourage parents to allow their children to meet role models by participating in social activities held by community support groups. (5) Encourage parents to form a family identity as an interracial unit.

Counselors need to consider several issues for their personal and professional development. Counselors must recognize that the ethnic background of every client has implications for acceptance for all factions of our society. Counselors need to be aware of their own feelings and attitudes about interracial marriages, biracial individuals, and people from all cultures that differ from their own. Individuals who are having difficulty with biracial identity can benefit from counselors who are knowledgeable about this population.

Brandell (1988) stated that the racial identity of a biracial child is a complex and variable process. Historically, biracial individuals have been viewed as marginal people who had to resolve an ambiguous ethnic identity (Root, 1990). A traditional racial identity model did not encompass the people whose racial heritage involved two different groups. Root noted that biracial individuals could not reject either part of their heritage without experiencing a process of internalized oppression. They need to find a resolution permitting the diverse parts of their racial heritage to coexist.

Root described another framework of identity resolution for biracial individuals. Her model challenged the linear notions of traditional development models and outlined a process of facing the "internal conflict over a core sense of definition of self" (p. 204). Her model includes more than one acceptable outcome. Accepting the identity that society assigns is one resolution. It is a passive resolution, and the individual usually is defined as a person of color. Due to the racism in this culture, individuals with non-white heritage are often defined exclusively by the minority heritage. A second option for resolution involves the individual identifying with both racial groups. These individuals may often recognize their similarities to and differences from others around them and work to be involved with both groups. A third option for resolving a biracial identity is to identify with one of the racial groups. This is an active choice to identify with a particular group. It is a choice in which the individual may or may not deny the other part of his or her racial heritage. The final option involves identifying with a new racial group, which means the person's strongest connection would be with other biracial people. These options are not mutually exclusive, and individuals are able to move among them at different times in their lives. This framework is flexible and offers a dynamic view of identity development in a nonlinear process.

Root (1990) has identified some of the complexities of multiple identities when those identities are from oppressed groups and dominant groups. However, being biracial and a member of more than one oppressed group, such as African American and Chicano, may have different meanings than being biracial and identifying with both an oppressed and dominant group such as Japanese American and white. These complexities require further exploration and research before a better understanding will occur.

Native Americans

The Native American population is extremely varied, and it is impossible to make generalizations that will apply to all Native Americans. Thomason (1991) summarized some figures that provide a perspective on the Native American population. There are 505 federally recognized tribes plus additional state-recognized tribes and bands. There are 304 federal reservations and over 150 tribal languages. It is estimated that there are over 1.8 million Native Americans and that more than half of these live in urban areas. Most counselors are likely to have opportunities to provide counseling services to them. Thomason (1991) provides a primer on Native Americans for non-Native American counselors. He describes some aspects of their culture that are relevant to counseling and then provides some guidelines for counselors.

It is difficult to describe Native Americans because not everyone agrees on how to decide who is one. According to the Bureau of Indian Affairs (1988) as described by Thomason (1991), a Native American is a person who is an enrolled or registered member of a tribe or whose blood quantum is one-fourth or more genealogically derived. However, some tribes set lower blood quantum levels so that more individuals can receive tribal benefits, and the U.S. Bureau of the Census accepts self-identification.

Attneave (1982) points out that not only do tribes differ from each other, but individuals within a tribe vary greatly from another. An important variable in understanding an individual Native American has to do with that person's degree of traditionalism in comparison to his or her degree of acculturation into the mainstream of society. Dillard (1983) describes a continuum that stretches from the very traditional person—who was born and reared on a reservation and who speaks a tribal language—to the Native American reared in a city who speaks only English and may feel little identification with the tribe.

Significant differences may exist among people living on reservations. From an investigation of Blackfeet, Sioux, and Navaho reservations, Riner (1979) describes four types of households. An "isolated" family may live in a home isolated in a remote area of a reservation and have a strong preference for the use of the native language. In the "traditional" category, the families have bilingual homes and actively participate in tribal ceremonies. The "bi-cultural" categorized families live on a reservation and engage in the traditional ceremonies but prefer speaking English. The "acculturated" Native Americans use English as their primary language and the family activities are similar to white norms.

Native Americans who live in cities or non-reservation areas may return to the reservation for ceremonies or to visit relatives. Other Native Americans have never lived on a reservation and live lives similar to those of their neighbors in rural or urban areas.

It is important not to stereotype Native Americans based on general assumptions. Studying the culture can benefit the counselor; however, it must be recognized that the information learned will only be helpful in general understanding and that each client is unique and must be met as an individual.

Thomason (1991) describes a general model of healing that is common to many tribes. This illustrates how Native Americans' thought may differ from that of non-Native Americans and may be helpful for counselors in adapting their thinking and methods to understand and serve their clients more effectively. He points out that the model is an example of how some Native Americans think rather than a description of how all Native Americans think. One ancient idea about health is that it results from having a harmonious relationship with nature. All creation is seen as a living whole, and nature is structured and follows rules of cause and effect that are not necessarily in a manner understandable by humans. Living in harmony with nature means following the traditions of the tribe, and ignoring a tradition may result in a state of disharmony, which may be manifested in individual disability, disease, or distress (Dinges, Trimble, Manson, & Pasquale, 1981; Spector, 1985).

All life is seen as a spiritual process and nature is a whole, not separated into physical, mental, or social parts. Individuals are less important than the tribe and an individual's problem is considered a problem of the group (Attneave, 1982). Traditional healers do not specialize in physical or mental problems since these are not separate. The term *mental health* is a misnomer implying that a mental aspect of an individual could be separated from the rest of the person. The individual exhibits a problem that is assumed to be rooted in the community (LaFromboise, 1988). Traditional healers are less likely to treat an individual alone, but rather use the extended family, friends, and neighbors to support the individual and help integrate the person into the social life of the group (Lewis & Ho, 1989). The healing ceremonies are frequently held in the individual's usual surroundings rather than in a less familiar place.

The concept of helping is important to understand. When an individual sees a traditional healer, he or she presents a problem and the healer's responsibility is to diagnose the cause of the problem. Clients frequently are passive throughout the diagnosis and treatment procedures. Clients are hopeful, but understanding of the problem and the curative powers are believed to lie with the healer rather than the client (Dinges et al., 1981). Thomason points out that the healer makes a diagnosis without asking personal questions or expecting intimate self-disclosures. There might be collective discussions in which everyone involved meets together and the individual is encouraged to make a ritualized confession of being out of harmony with nature (Spector, 1985). This may be followed by an atonement ritual whereby the individual is restored into the good graces of the family and community (LaFromboise, 1988). Improvement in the individual is usually expected to occur rather quickly.

Cultural Application in Counseling

The success of cross-cultural counseling is dependent on the counselor meeting the expectations of the client. Failing to meet the expectations of Native American clients may explain why a high percentage drop out of counseling. Thomason (1991) suggests that counselors should make the first interview with the Native American client therapeutic rather than using it to collect information and make a diagnosis. The counselor may wish to provide an orientation to counseling so clients will know what is expected of them and how they can work together.

Thomason also points out that the counselor is likely to have more success when keeping in mind the general Native American model of healing. The general model suggests that clients would expect the counselor to diagnose the problem without asking deep, personal questions or intimate questions (Edwards & Edwards, 1989). Clients might expect that family members would be involved in counseling and that improvements in their state would occur rather quickly. Even less traditional Native Americans might have a tendency to expect the counselor to solve the problem for them. By being aware of such expectations by the clients, the counselor may prepare to discuss the mutual responsibilities of counselor and client.

Native Americans who have gone to college seeking an education or moved to another community for employment may experience stress in coping with the new environment. Such a situation may heighten their feelings of being pulled between the traditional tribal culture and the mainstream culture. Counselors who are sensitive to such issues may be able to help clients explore and resolve them (Trimble & Fleming, 1989). A counselor who sees clients from a nearby tribe may benefit by learning about the history of the tribe, traditional beliefs and values, and current organization. Investigating the family structure, age and gender roles, and characteristics of the nonverbal and paralinguistic behavior would also be helpful for a counselor. Factors such as the beliefs about how problems should be resolved, meanings attributed to illness or disability, and traditional healing practices are also relevant to counseling. Knowledge about the natural support systems, developmental stress points, and coping strategies can also be helpful (Trimble & LaFromboise, 1985).

The first interview should be used for the client and counselor to get to know each other and possibly to decide if their working together will be beneficial. The counselor should accept the role of structuring the session and explain to the client that they will have plenty of time to get to know each other before discussing any concerns the client may have (Attneave, 1982). Time is not rigidly structured, and it is assumed that there is never a lack of time. The counselor should use an informal, conversational style and provide an atmosphere that is relaxed, casual, and nonthreatening. More time is likely to be used in social conversation in an attempt to build acceptance and rapport. Asking questions should be avoided, and the counselor may use self-disclosures as a way to prompt self-discussion on the part of the client (Everett et al., 1983).

A traditionally oriented Native American may feel uneasy seeing a non-Native American stranger in an office to talk about personal problems. Therefore, the counselor must take time and attention to ease the client's feelings and to help the client understand that there are no demands to behave in a certain way. Having the client complete intake forms or questionnaires is likely to contribute to uncomfortable feelings and should be avoided (Everett et al., 1983). If a friend or family member comes along to the interview, he or she should be accepted also (Edwards & Edwards, 1989). Accepting and working within the Native American belief system is important if a non-Native American is to be of service in counseling.

Nonverbal behavior of both the client and counselor is an important variable in the counseling relationship. Understanding nonverbal behaviors of the client may be problematic. A non-Native American counselor should not expect direct eye contact from their clients and are advised to avoid direct eye contact, since it can be considered disrespectful. The counselor is encouraged to use a low tone of voice, refrain from touching the client other than with a handshake, and use a soft handshake rather than a firm or aggressive one (Attneave, 1982; Everett et al., 1983). These suggestions will not fit with all Native American clients. As with any client, it is appropriate to meet each as an individual and to take the lead from the client's behavior in responding.

Thomason (1991) concludes that a patient, informal exploration of the client's concerns is an appropriate course of action. A fairly active and directive problem-solving approach is likely to be effective; however, other strategies can be used as they seem appropriate with specific clients. In addition to individual counseling, the counselor may include the client's family and friends, visit the client's home, or possibly involve a traditional healer from the client's tribe as valuable activities in therapy.

Acculturation

The concept of acculturation has received considerable attention in counseling (Sodowsky, Lai, & Plake, 1991). The concept of acculturation attempts to understand the adjustment of minority groups to the dominant group culture. The level of the client's acculturation into the society has been shown to have an impact on the effectiveness of counseling (Cuellar, Harris, & Jasso, 1980; Sanchez & Atkinson, 1983).

Acculturation has been defined as a process in which a group of people selectively adapt to a value system as well as the integration with and differentiation from the majority culture (Social Science Research Council, 1954, as quoted in Sodowsky, Lai, & Plake, 1991). Although anthropologists and sociologists have not addressed acculturation at an individual level, psychological research has focused on individual differences or within-group heterogeneity. Some authors explain acculturation as a unidirectional process in which the person from the minority culture relinquishes values, customs, beliefs, and behaviors and adopts those of the majority culture (Garcia & Lega, 1979). Increasingly, however, researchers are describing acculturation as a bidirectional adjustment process in which the level of the person's acculturation can be assessed in two directions: the degree of retention of her or his own culture as well as the degree of assimilation of the majority culture (Berry, 1980; LeVine & Padilla, 1980; Mendoza & Martinez, 1981; Sanchez & Atkinson, 1983). Acculturation is a multifaceted process and individuals adopt different options of acculturation in different situations (Mendoza, 1984). Berry (1980) identified four bidirectional options of acculturation: assimilation, integration, rejection, and deculturation. A minority person could choose different options of acculturation at different times to deal with various issues; hence the acculturation of the individuals would best be described by a composite profile rather than a single score (Sodowsky, Lai, & Plake, 1991).

Acculturation and Counselor Characteristics

Research findings related to minority group members' preferences for counselor ethnicity have not been consistent. Some studies support the idea of similar counselor-client ethnicities while others have reported no support for similarity. Likewise, preferences for counseling style among minority clients have not been consistent. After reviewing the literature, Atkinson (1983) suggested that the preference for an ethnically similar counselor is not universal. He suggested that minority group members are not homogeneous and that within-group differences must be recognized in studying minority clients. It is possible, then, that the level of acculturation of the minority clients could account for the within-group variations. The degree to which clients are committed to their own minority culture or to the majority culture may have an impact on their attitudes about the counseling style and process.

In a study that controlled for the level of acculturation, Sanchez and Atkinson (1983) found that individuals with a strong Mexican-American commitment expressed a strong preference for a Mexican-American counselor, while subjects with a strong Anglo-American preference expressed the least preference for an ethnically similar counselor. However, later studies report conflicting findings. Folensbee, Draguns, and Danish (1986) reported no significant relationship between acculturation and counseling style with Puerto Rican students; Atkinson, Furlong, and Poston (1986) reported no significant relation between black students' commitment to African-American culture and preferences for counselor characteristics.

Pomales and Williams (1989) investigated the effects of the level of acculturation and counseling style on Hispanic students' perceptions of a counselor. Hispanic undergraduate students completed acculturation instruments that categorized them as Hispanic acculturated, bicultural, or Anglo acculturated. They viewed a videotape of a white female counselor conducting either a directive or nondirective type of counseling interview. The Anglo acculturated students rated the counselor higher in terms of trustworthiness than did the bicultural or Hispanic acculturated students. It was hypothesized that the Hispanic students may have been more sensitive to trustworthy and untrustworthy cues than other counselor characteristics. The Anglo acculturated students rated the counselor as more trustworthy whether the counseling style was directive or nondirective. The Hispanic acculturated students rated the nondirective counselor as more understanding than did the bicultural students; however, they were not significantly different from the Anglo acculturated students. This suggests that attitudes about counseling are different according to the client's cultural commitment. There were no significant differences in their perception of expertness. The authors note that their study did not control for cultural sensitivity but acknowledged that perceived expertness by minority clients may be linked to counselor-cultural sensitivity. The overall preference for directive counseling suggests that counseling style had a stronger influence than acculturation on the perception of certain counselor attributes such as trustworthiness, understanding, and willingness to help.

Counseling Principles

Johnson (1987) emphasizes the need for counselors to not only "know that" cultural differences exist but also to "know how" to work effectively with clients from diverse backgrounds. Ponterotto and Benesch (1988) suggest the use of five principles, as described by Torrey (1972), to facilitate successful counseling in any culture: (1) the client's problem is named; (2) the personal qualities of the counselor are extremely important; (3) the client's specific expectations must be met; (4) the counselor must establish credibility through the use of symbols, skill, or power; and (5) the counselor must apply certain techniques designed to bring relief to the troubled client.

Problem Definition
When defining the client's problem, the counselor must be aware that what is considered a problem in one culture may not be seen as a problem in another culture. For example, in the dominant United States culture, a lack of assertiveness is considered problematic but in some cultures, acting assertively in particular situations is seen as disrespectful and problematic.

Personal Qualities
Counselor characteristics that may facilitate the counseling process in a cross-cultural context are genuineness, empathy, positive regard, expertness, trustworthiness, interpersonal attractiveness (Ponterotto & Benesch, 1988), age and educational level higher than that of the client, and attitudes and personality similar to those of the client (Atkinson, Poston, Furlong, & Mercado, 1989).

Client Expectations
It is common for client's from any cultural background to terminate counseling if their expectations are not met (Atkinson et al., 1989). Research indicates that minority clients terminate counseling after one session more frequently than majority clients, and unmet expectations of the client could be a contributing factor in this finding (Sue & Zane, 1987). An illustration of how the expectations of client and counselor might conflict is found in the role the counselor takes as a helper. In the white American culture, the counselor is traditionally expected to be of help by encouraging the client to verbalize and explore feelings and to solve problems based upon what the client discovers from this process. In some American minority cultures, the client may expect and prefer the counselor to act as an expert or teacher and give the client advice or instructions on how to solve the problem.

Counselor Credibility
Counselor credibility is dependent upon the cultural experience of the client. A client of a middle-class white background may view a counselor credible based upon the counselor's degree and office decor, while a lower-class Black may view the same counselor

as incompetent due to his or her experiences with white bureaucracy (Ponterotto & Benesch, 1988).

Techniques

A counselor has available a variety of techniques to alleviate client problems. It is important for the counselor to consult with the client as to what the client would find helpful and how the client's cultural experiences and background are an influence. For some clients, approaches that are active and focus upon symptom relief and/or skill acquisition (relaxation training, biofeedback, time management, study skills training, stress management) may be more helpful than traditional feeling expression and exploration (Ponterotto & Benesch, 1988). Help-giving could include out-of-office strategies such as consultant, outreach, change agent, or ombudsman activities (Sue et al., 1982).

Scott and Borodovsky (1990) suggest that cultural boundaries or barriers in cross-counseling can be overcome by the use of cultural role taking. Cultural role taking is defined as "cognitively putting oneself in another's shoes" (p. 168). The counselor is aware of the specific cultural differences between him- or herself and the client. The counselor must acknowledge that he or she is faced with a client whom he or she must get to know; a culture that he or she must learn about; and an individual client whose thoughts, feelings, and conceptions about his or her culture must be understood as they pertain to the client specifically.

Stages of Development of Cultural Competence

To further address the issue of cultural competence, a developmental model to describe how counselors learn to consider cultural diversity in counseling can be useful (Lopez et al., 1989). At Stage 1 the counselor is unaware of cultural issues. Stage 2 is characterized by the counselor experiencing an awareness of cultural issues. During Stage 3, the burden of considering cultural issues is felt. At Stage 4, the counselor is moving toward integration of culture into clinical work (p. 370). Table 14-4 provides an overview of these stages and the consequences the counselor may experience within each stage. It is important to note that this model describes a developmental process which may be better understood as a fluid, discontinuous process than as a continuous stage-like process (Lopez et al., 1989).

Conclusion

Pederson (1991a) concluded that counselors and counseling will need to make many changes for multiculturalism to be relevant. Counselors need to be aware of their own cultural assumptions as well as those of their clients. It is clear that two people with different assumptions may disagree without either being wrong, only culturally different. Counselors need to apply the implications of a multicultural perspective to other counseling theories, not to replace them but to enhance their application to culturally different populations. The cultural differences of various populations need to be acknowledged in

TABLE 14-4   Proposed Stages and Stage-Specific Consequences in Therapists' Development of Cultural Sensitivity

Description	Consequence
Unawareness of cultural issues	
Therapist does not entertain cultural hypotheses	Does not understand the significance of the clients' cultural background to their functioning
Heightened awareness of culture	
Therapist is aware that cultural factors are important in fully understanding clients	Feels unprepared to work with culturally different clients; frequently applies therapist's perception of the client's cultural background and therefore fails to understand the cultural significance for the specific client; can at times accurately recognize the influence of the clients' cultural background on their functioning
Burden of considering culture	
Therapist is hypervigilant in identifying cultural factors and is, at times, confused in determining the cultural significance of the client's actions	Consideration of culture is perceived as detracting from clinical effectiveness
Toward cultural sensitivy	
Therapist entertains cultural hypotheses and carefully tests these hypotheses from multiple sources before accepting cultural explanations	Increased likelihood of accurately understanding the role of culture in the client's functioning

Source: S. Lopez, K. P. Grover, D. Holland, M. Johnson, C. Kain, K. Kanel, C. Mellins, & M. Rhyne, Development of culturally sensitive psychotherapists. *Professional Psychology: Research and Practice,* 1989, *20,* 369–376. Copyright 1989 by the American Psychological Association. Reprinted by permission.

counseling research. This will permit the findings to more accurately reflect the cultural perspectives of the participants. The counselors also need to modify their skills, strategies, and techniques to different cultural populations so they are able to appropriately apply methods to differing cultural populations. It is also imperative that educators incorporate multicultural perspectives into the training of counselors, who will be increasingly working in a multicultural world.

Counseling of Women

Gender is a very powerful and almost immediate determinant of experience for individuals. It is a powerful factor in identity development both at the societal and interpersonal levels. People behave and respond to others in ways that correspond to their gender (Brown, 1990).

Historically, psychology has operated from the "uniformity myth," the assumption that a particular approach will work for all (Downing & Roush, 1985). The traditional theories and approaches of psychology and counseling are based in the male experience (Miller, 1976; Lerner, 1988). In recent years, literature has emerged which suggests that men and women have crucial differences that need to be considered in the counseling arena (Gilligan, 1982; Surrey, 1985; Lerner, 1988).

American society is not sex fair. The sexism that women experience is similar to the racism that various racial/ethnic groups experience. Women are a special subgroup due to this sexism. Just as counselors should develop attitudes, skills, and methods appropriate to working with clients of diverse racial and ethnic backgrounds, counselors should also develop attitudes, skills, and methods appropriate for working with women clients.

To better understand the psychological development of women, several women (Miller, Surrey, and Stiver) from the Stone Center at Wellesley College have proposed the self-in-relation theory. Self-identity in women is thought to develop via the connectedness in relationships rather than from the separation in relationships (Surrey, 1985). The primary context for action and growth is based in connection with others. Engagement in the active process of facilitating and enhancing relationships leads women through a gradual development of a differentiated self (Kaplan, 1986). This model is in contrast to the traditional models which proposed that self-identity emerges via separation from significant others. Whereas value is placed upon autonomy, self-reliance, independence, and the fulfillment of one's own unique dream in the traditional model, the self-in-relation model values mutual empathy, mutual empowerment, and authenticity (Surrey, 1985).

Feminist Identity Development

Downing and Roush (1985) present a model of feminist identity development that parallels the Black identity development model described by Cross (1971). The feminist model consists of the following five stages: passive acceptance, revelation, embeddedness-emanation, synthesis, and active commitment.

During the passive acceptance stage, a woman is either unaware of or denies that discrimination toward women exists. The woman may consider men to be superior and believes traditional sex roles to be positive for women. Movement into the revelation stage occurs when a woman experiences a crisis or event that enlightens her to the oppression or limitations placed upon women. Passage into this stage may also be dependent upon a woman's readiness to change her frame of reference.

The third stage has two phases. In the embeddedness phase, a woman becomes or attempts to become part of the female subculture. This phase can be particularly difficult for women because of their considerable involvement with and in the dominant male culture. Many women seek out women's centers, study classes, and support groups to experience embeddedness. Emanation occurs as a woman develops a more open and relativistic perspective regarding women and men.

As a woman increasingly values femaleness and can integrate this with her personal qualities and self-concept, a synthesis takes place. At this stage, a woman is able to find a balance within the world of men and women. The active commitment stage emerges as the woman transforms her identity into meaningful and effective action.

It is assumed that women can recycle, stagnate, or regress to earlier stages of this model. These changes may be precipitated by the woman's readiness and her own unique life experiences (Downing & Roush, 1985).

Issues of Concern

Issues that appear consistently throughout the literature as specific to women are depression (Kaplan, 1986), eating disorders (Barnett, 1986; Surrey, 1985), violence/victimization (Herman, 1985; Koss, 1990), poverty (Russo, 1990; Belle, 1990), and multiple roles (Russo, 1990; McBride, 1990; Wolfman, 1985).

Kaplan (1986) uses the self-in-relation model to explain the high frequency with which women experience depression. Components of depression include experience of loss, inhibition of action or assertiveness, inhibition of anger and aggression, and low self-esteem. Depression is suggested as a distortion or exaggeration of the normative state of being female in Western society, not as an "illness."

A preoccupation with food and eating is of concern for many women. Several factors appear to be involved in the relationship between women and food. The expression of the mothering role is grounded in the woman providing food for the child. The provision of food becomes the symbol of the woman to sustain life and to provide for her child emotionally and physically. American society values thinness as the ideal in body shape for women. The normal physiological structure and changes in women's bodies that result from the capacity to bear children is devalued and treated with disdain (Surrey, 1985). Barnett (1986) suggests that bulimarexia results from the sex-role strain young women experience when their career choice conflicts with their sex-role socialization into the feminine role.

In terms of victimization, women are reported to be no more likely than men to experience criminal victimization, except in the case of rape and sexual violence. Over 90 percent of rape victims are women, and over 85 percent of the offenders arrested for or charged with rape are men (Koss, 1990). Intimate violence, which includes child abuse, incest, date rape, and battering are more often experienced by women (Russo, 1990). One out of four women will experience an incident of abuse over the course of her marriage (Straus, Gelles & Steinmetyz, 1980 as cited in Bograd, 1982).

The prevalence of poverty is increasing dramatically in the United States, especially among women. More households headed by women, concentration of most new jobs in the poorly paid service sector, inadequacies of child support payments following divorce, limited affordable and quality child care, and a decrease in governmental assistance to low-income families have contributed to poverty for women (Belle, 1990; Russo, 1990). Belle (1990) indicates that poverty is a correlate of psychological distress and mental disorder.

Women tend to function in multiple roles from childhood throughout adulthood (Wolfman, 1985). McBride (1990) summarizes research that indicates that women experience more changes than men in terms of parenting responsibilities; for those who work outside the home, they contend with occupational stress as well as the stress associated with household responsibilities; and women whose spouses are unsupportive of their multiple roles or who have not been able to find satisfactory child care arrangements, experience increased role stress.

Positive aspects of women's multiple roles do exist. The reward of one role may cancel the negative aspects of another role. Some multiple role women report superior health, increased sense of autonomy and competence, and positive life-style (McBride, 1990). Wolfman (1985) suggests that women utilize ability, flexibility, and compatibility to manage and cope with handling more than two tasks or roles at the same time.

Men and Women

Terms such as caring, dependency, and autonomy may have different meanings for women and men in U.S. society. Stiver (1986) differentiates between "caretaking" and "caring about" in therapeutic relationships. The traditional male model of psychotherapy espouses that the therapist takes care of the client by remaining objective, nonemotional, and relatively impersonal and uses medication and appropriate treatment modalities as ways to take care of the client. A caring-about position in psychotherapy suggests that the therapist is a giver of care to the client and has an investment of feelings in the client. The caring-about position does not support an emotional involvement of the therapist with the client but supports the therapist's concern for the well-being of the client. Power is viewed as unequal or parental in the caretaking relationship, whereas the power in the caring-about relationship is seen as more egalitarian (Stiver, 1986).

Men and women alike struggle with issues regarding dependency, but their struggles are different due to different life experiences and cultural expectations. Dependency is usually considered a feminine characteristic and carries a pejorative connotation. A woman's desire for close relationships is often seen negatively and is indicative of dependency. For men, recognition of dependency needs may be a threat to autonomy, masculinity, and independence. Women may present themselves as dependent as a means to engage in relationships with men. Men may support this dependency to meet needs for control and power. Viewing dependency as an interpersonal dynamic or a process of counting on others to facilitate emotional and physical coping may offer both men and women the opportunity for growth and development (Stiver, 1986).

Autonomy has traditionally been considered a male characteristic. An autonomous person is one who is independent, separate from others, distant, and has the power to make decisions based upon personal needs. With autonomy being seen as opposite of "female-ness," in women, it is frequently confused with "maleness." For women, autonomy equates selfishness, but for men it equates maturity and psychological health (Hare-Mustin & Marecek, 1986).

Lemkau and Landau (1986) examine how women have followed cultural values and norms seeking satisfaction via self-denial and fulfilling the needs of others at the expense of their own needs. Termed the "selfless syndrome" women present cognitive, affective, and behavioral symptoms that proscribe self-denial and satisfaction through vicarious means. Healthy self-centeredness is the midpoint of a continuum, with selflessness and self-absorption occupying each extreme.

Another way in which men and women differ based upon societal expectations is in the expression of anger. For men and boys, anger and aggression are encouraged and even glorified (i.e., sports, such as boxing and football; world of work competitiveness; and war). If women express anger in an open, direct manner, they are labeled unladylike, hostile, castrating, or hysterical. When a woman does express anger in an open direct manner, she may also experience tears, guilt, anxiety, and sadness. Unconsciously, women may be fearful of alienation from others if their anger is expressed (Lerner, 1977).

Interesting differences are found in the types of pathology diagnosed for men and women in the DSM-IIIR. Women are more frequently diagnosed as histrionic, dependent, or borderline personalities. These diagnoses all have characteristics that involve interactions with others and intense expressions of emotions. Men are more frequently diagnosed as paranoid and anti-social personalities, which involve symptoms that distance the individual from others (Stiver, 1986).

Feminist Therapy

Walker (1990) presents an overview of the development of feminist therapy as well as the tenants of feminist therapy theory. She points out that feminist therapy emerged from the women's movement in the late 1960s. Feminists were critical of traditional psychotherapy theories stating that they tended to keep women oppressed. The goals of the feminist movement were to empower women, emphasize their strength and uniqueness, and move toward equality between men and women. Considerable criticism was directed toward accepting and perpetuating stereotyped sex role behaviors. Another area of critique involved the issue of mental health standards for men and women. Labels of mental illness were reported to be used for political reasons and possibly as a punishment for not following traditional sex role standards (Chesler, 1972). In the often quoted study by Broverman et al. (1970), it was found that therapists described "normal" male and "normal" person with the same characteristics, being intellectual, rational, and aggressive, while describing women as more passive, nurturing, and emotional. This type of comparison indicated that women did not have the characteristics of mentally healthy individuals.

Dutton-Douglas and Walker (1988), as quoted in Walker (1990), describe three phases in feminist-therapy theory development. The first phase began in the early 1970s and lasted about 10 years. It was an activist's position, which borrowed methods from other therapies and used them with feminist philosophy. Early feminist therapy aimed to empower all women by strengthening the individual. This continues to be one of the feminist's tenets, "the personal is political."

The second phase of development involves the mainstreaming of feminism into other theories. Following the application of a political gender analysis to the mainstream theories, they began to eliminate the more sexist parts of the theory while keeping the sections that made theoretical sense.

The third phase is focusing on the development of a complete theory including developmental explanations for the common experiences of women. The theory holds that there are factors that devalue women, separate from their personal backgrounds and yet having impact on an individual woman's mental health.

Walker (1990) outlines the tenets of feminist therapy theory, which have been articulated by various therapists in different parts of the world. These tenets include:

1. Egalitarian relationships are established between the client and therapist to model women taking responsibility to develop egalitarian relationships with others. Although the therapist and client are not equal in terms of skills, the client has better knowledge of herself, which is as important as the therapist's skills.

2. Women are taught to examine power in relationships as a way of developing independence. They are encouraged to examine the consequences of taking power as well as look at gaining power and control in relationships. Enhancing the strengths of women is the focus rather than remediation of their weaknesses.

3. There is a non-victim-blaming and non-pathology-oriented bias. Feminist theory rejects the medical model frequently used by other therapists. Women's behavior is observed and analyzed in terms of coping rather than as pathology. Problems that women present are generally seen as a combination of situational factors, genetic components, and intra-psychic personality characteristics.

4. Education is seen as a method of changing some of the thoughts that are detrimental to the enhancement of strengths. Bibliotherapy is frequently used as an adjunct to therapy to help the client learn more about the condition of women. The therapist functions more as a teacher and facilitator rather than as an authoritarian. The model is more an educational orientation than a reparative model. The learning and supportive philosophy is also applied in group therapy.

5. There is an acceptance and validation of feelings. Feminist therapists are encouraged to use self-disclosure to remove the barriers between the client and counselor. This permits more empathic connections between the two individuals as issues are discussed.

Feminist therapy theory has focused on several issues that interfere with women's mental health including the "identification and expression of angry feelings; women's sexuality; self-nurturance; relationships with parents, spouse, children, and friends; and victimization experiences" (Walker, 1990, p. 82). It is important to understand the impact of social-cultural influences on the mental health of individual women. Women who have experienced racial discrimination, ethnic bias, and discrimination against age, disability, sexual orientation, or class require particular sensitivity.

Although considerable variability is found in the literature regarding the number and types of feminist counseling skills, Russell (1986) identified four central skills that were commonly endorsed, specific counselor behaviors. One of the skills involves social analysis, which provides an assessment of sex-related social and cultural restraints that impinge both internally and externally on women's behavior. A second skill involved androgyny encouragement, which involves supporting the integration of male and female traits. The third skill, self-disclosure, involves the use of evaluative or emotionally expressive self-references. The fourth skill involves behavior feedback in which the therapist provides accurate and concise feedback about behavior or behavioral manifestations of affect.

DeVoe (1990) concluded that feminist therapy can benefit men. It can increase their awareness of the damaging impact of sexist values on relationships. Men can initiate change toward an appropriate sharing of power. DeVoe stated that men can develop behaviors that reflect a more feminist or nonsexist orientation. Feminist values have had an effect on families, schools, and other social institutions, and they are having an impact on counseling.

Counseling Lesbians and Gay Men

Even though gays and lesbians comprise 10 to 15 percent of the overall population, little attention has been given to this "hidden minority" in the psychological literature. The complexity of negative societal attitudes and stigmatization, fear on the part of gay and lesbian students/clients, and lack of awareness of knowledge on the part of researchers and clinicians are at the core of this "blind spot" in the literature (Fassinger, 1991).

Historically, homosexuality was viewed as deviant and an individual engaged in homosexual behavior was in need of a "cure" to return to heterosexuality. Research and the voices of gay and lesbian individuals have led to homosexuality being seen as nonpathological. During the mid-1970s, the American Psychiatric Association and the American Psychological Association declassified homosexuality as a mental illness (Fassinger, 1991).

Even with this change toward a positive outlook on homosexuality, tremendous discrimination and hostility exist in U.S. society. Homophobia, or the fear and hatred exhibited toward homosexuals by family, friends, and society, is all too frequently encountered by gay and lesbian individuals throughout society and even in the psychological community.

Counseling professionals need to address their attitudes, values, and biases regarding homosexuality. As with other minority groups, counselors need to sensitize themselves with the issues faced by homosexual clients and develop a knowledge base and skills relevant for gay and lesbian clientele. Heterosexism is an ideology that values non-gay norms and experiences and considers heterosexuality to be inherently natural. This ideology devalues the gay experience and precludes a true appreciation of gay life-style and choices (Fassinger, 1991).

Identity Development

Fassinger (1991) outlines Cass's (1979) model of gay identity development. Stage one is termed identity confusion and is characterized by turmoil and questioning regarding one's assumptions about one's sexual orientation. The second stage is identity comparison. An individual in this stage feels alienation and accepts the possibility of being gay and becomes isolated from non-gay individuals. Identity tolerance, the third stage, is characterized by ambivalence, in which one seeks out other gays, but maintains separate public and private images. During stage four, identity acceptance, the individual selectively discloses and legitimizes his or her sexual orientation. Identity pride is characterized by anger, pride, activism, and emersion in gay subculture. The final stage, identity synthesis, is characterized by clarity, acceptance, and an incorporation of one's sexuality into an integrated identity. Caution is necessary in the use of this model due to the linear nature of the process described and the lack of attention to racial, ethnic, class, locale, occupation, and gender issues.

Clark (1987, as cited in Fassinger, 1991) gives specific guidelines for counseling with gay and lesbian clients.

1. It is essential that you feel comfortable with and appreciate your own sexuality before you can work successfully with gay and lesbian clients. Whether you consider yourself gay or non-gay, seek to rid yourself of homophobic feelings or they will act as blind spots with your gay clients.
2. Consider very carefully before entering into a contract to eliminate gay feelings and behaviors in your client. Willingness to enter into such a contract implies that homosexuality is pathological and undesirable. Many clients who ask for change are really asking for acceptance.
3. Encourage your clients to establish a gay support system. Support consciousness-raising efforts such as joining gay rap groups, reading pro-gay literature, and getting involved in gay community activities. Know resources and make them available.
4. Help your clients become aware of how oppression (internal and external) affects them. Help clients free themselves of stereotypes and negative conditioning. Encourage your clients to question basic assumptions about being gay (in both the gay subculture and in society) and to develop a personally relevant value system.
5. Desensitize shame and guilt surrounding homosexual thoughts, feelings, and behaviors by encouraging discussion of gay experiences and showing your approval and affirmation. (Clark, 1987, as cited in Fassinger, 1991, pp. 170-171)

In addition to the guidelines offered by Clark (1987), Fassinger added five additional guidelines for researchers and practitioners:

1. Work to develop the attitudes, knowledge, and skills necessary for effective scientific and therapeutic work with lesbian women and gay men. Educate yourself about gay life-styles and concerns, and be familiar with gender-specific socialization and therapeutic issues as well.
2. Understand the interaction of other kinds of diversity (e.g., racial/ethnic, gender, age, (dis)ability, socioeconomic, religious, geographical) with the development and maintenance of a positive gay identity. Be aware that the coming-out process and preservation of a healthy life-style differ widely within the gay and lesbian population, and adjust your research questions and therapeutic interventions accordingly.
3. Be familiar with the treatment of addictive behaviors such as alcohol abuse and eating disorders, fairly common in the gay and/or lesbian community and often masked by other presenting issues.
4. Acquire knowledge and training in AIDS-related issues and in death and dying.

5. Be particularly sensitive to ethical issues such as confidentiality and, for gay and lesbian therapists, the difficulties inherent in providing mental health services within one's own community of social support. (Fassinger, 1991, p. 171)

Browning, Reynolds, and Dworkin (1991) suggest the following issues be addressed in the counseling of lesbian women: identity management (coming out, occupational issues, race, ethnicity, class, locale, age), interpersonal issues (coupling), special issues (substance abuse, sexual abuse, domestic violence), and spiritual and existential issues. Gartrell (1985) suggests that the coming out process for lesbians, a breaking of the silence, marks an improvement in an individual's psychological well-being. It is important for counseling or therapy to focus on the risks and benefits of coming out. Lesbian clients frequently need information about community resources, literature, women's activities, and support groups.

Issues needing attention in the counseling and therapy for gay men are identity development and management, occupational/career concerns, race, ethnicity, class, locale, isolation, coupling, aging, anti-gay violence, AIDS, and spiritual and existential issues (Shannon & Woods, 1991; Carl, 1990).

Barret (1989) offers a perspective on emotional aspects of counseling of gay men with AIDS. Denial, anger, rage, guilt, and shame are common reactions experienced by these clients. The clients may also be adjusting to being gay at the same time they are confronting AIDS. Barret suggests the most powerful contribution a counselor can make is to be present with and for the person with AIDS.

A task force of the APA Committee on Lesbian and Gay Concerns surveyed a large sample of psychologists to elicit specific reports of biased and sensitive responses in therapy with lesbians and gay men. Their report contains examples of biased, inadequate, or inappropriate practice as well as exemplary practice. They also add a rich list of references for lesbian and gay male affirmative models of therapy (Garnets, Hancock, Cochran, Goodchilds, & Peplau, 1991).

References

Anderson, B., & Anderson, W. (1985). Client perceptions of counselors using positive and negative self-involving statements. *Journal of Counseling Psychology, 32,* 462–465.

Atkinson, D. R. (1983). Ethnic similarity in counseling psychology: A review of the literature. *The Counseling Psychologist, 11,* 79–92.

Atkinson, D. R., Furlong, M. J., & Poston, W. C. (1986). Afro-American preferences for counselor characteristics. *Journal of Counseling Psychology, 33,* 326–330.

Atkinson, D. R., Poston, W. C., Furlong, M. J., & Mercado, P. (1989). Ethnic group preferences for counselor characteristics. *Journal of Counseling Psychology, 36,* 68–70.

Attneave, C. L. (1982). American Indians and Alaska native families: Emigrants in their own homeland. In M. McGoldrick, J. Pearce, & J. Giordano (Eds.), *Ethnicity and family therapy* (pp. 55–83). New York: Guilford.

Barnett, L. R. (1986). Bulimarexia as symptom of sex-role strain in professional women. *Psychotherapy, 23,* 311–315.

Barret, R. L. (1989). Counseling gay men with AIDS: Human dimensions. *Journal of Counseling and Development, 67,* 573–575.

Belle, D. (1990). Poverty and women's mental health. *American Psychologist, 45,* 385–389.

Berry, J. (1980). Acculturation as varieties of adaptation. In A. M. Padilla (Ed)., *Acculturation: Theory, model, and some new findings* (pp. 9–25). Boulder, CO: Westview.

Bograd, M. (1982). Battered women, cultural myths and clinical interventions: A feminist analysis. In New England Association for Women in Psychology (Eds.), *Current feminist issues in psychotherapy* (pp. 61–78). New York: Haworth Press.

Brandell, J. (1988). Treatment of the bi-racial child: Theoretical and clinical issues. *Journal of Multicultural Counseling and Development, 16,* 176–187.

Broverman, I., Broverman, D., Clarkson, R., Rosencrantz, P., & Vogel, S. (1970). Sex role stereotypes and clinical judgments of mental health. *Journal of Consulting and Clinical Psychology, 34,* 1–7.

Brown, L. S. (1990). Taking account of gender in the clinical assessment interview. *Professional Psychology: Research and Practice, 21,* 12–17.

Browning, C., Reynolds, A., & Dworkin, S. (1991). Affirmative psychotherapy for lesbian women. *The Counseling Psychologist, 19,* 177–196.

Bureau of Indian Affairs. (1988). *American Indians today.* Washington, DC: Author.

Carl, D. (1990). Counseling same-sex couples. New York: W. W. Norton.

Carter, R. (1990). The relationship between racism and racial identity among White Americans: An exploratory investigation. *Journal of Counseling and Development, 69,* 46–50.

Cass, V. C. (1979). Homosexual identify formation: A theoretical model. *Journal of Homosexuality, 4,* 219–235.

Chesler, P. (1972). *Women and madness.* New York: Doubleday.

Claney, D., & Parker, W. (1988). Assessing white racial consciousness and perceived comfort with Black individuals: A preliminary study. *Journal of Counseling and Development, 67,* 449–451.

Clark, D. (1987). *The new loving someone gay.* Berkeley, CA: Celestial Arts.

Committee on Lesbian and Gay Concerns. (1991). Avoiding heterosexual bias in language. *American Psychologist, 46,* 973–974.

Conarton, S., & Silverman, L. (1988). Feminine development through the life cycle. In M. A. Dutton-Douglas & L. E. Walker (Eds.), *Feminist psychotherapies: Integration of therapeutic and feminist systems.* Norwood, NJ: Ablex.

Conoley, J., & Bonner, M. (1991). The effects of counselor fee and title on perceptions of counselor behavior. *Journal of Counseling and Development, 69,* 356–358.

Cross, W. E. (1971). The Negro-to-Black conversion experience. *Black World, 7,* 13–27.

Cross, W. E. (1987). A two-factor theory of Black identity: Implications for the study of identity development in minority children. In J. S. Phinney & M. J. Rotherham (Eds.), *Children's ethnic socialization: Pluralism and development* (pp. 117–133). Newbury Park, CA: Sage.

Cuellar, I., Harris, L., & Jasson, R. (1980). An acculturation scale for Mexican American normal and clinical populations. *Hispanic Journal of Behavioral Sciences, 2,* 199–217.

Denmark, F., Russo, N. F., Frieze, I., & Sechzer, J. (1988). Guidelines for avoiding sexism in psychological research. *American Psychologist, 43,* 582–585.

DeVoe, D. (1990). Feminist and nonsexist counseling: Implications for the male counselor. *Journal of Counseling Development, 69,* 33–36.

Dillard, J. M. (1983). *Multicultural counseling.* Chicago: Nelson-Hall.

Dinges, N. G., Trimble, J. E., Manson, S. M., & Pasquale, F. P. (1981). Counseling and psychotherapy with American Indians and Alaskan-Natives. In A. J. Marsella & P. B. Pedersen (Eds.), *Cross-cultural counseling and psychotherapy* (pp. 243–276). New York: Pergamon.

Dixon, D., & Glover, J. (1984). *Counseling: A problem-solving approach.* New York: Wiley.

Downing, N. E., & Roush, K. L. (1985). From passive acceptance to active commitment: A model of feminist identity development for women. *The Counseling Psychologist, 13,* 695–709.

Dutton-Douglas, M., & Walker, L. (Eds.). (1988). *Feminist psychotherapies: Integration of therapeutic and feminist systems.* Norwood, NJ: Ablex.

Edwards, E. D., & Edwards, M. E. (1989). American Indians: Working with individuals and groups. In D. R. Atkinson, G. Morten, & D. W. Sue (Eds.), *Counseling American minorities* (pp. 72–84). Dubuque, IA: William C. Brown.

Egan, G. (1985). *The skilled helper: Model, skills and methods for effective helping* (3rd ed.). Pacific Grove, CA: Brooks/Cole.

Everett, F., Proctor, N., & Cartmell, B. (1983). Providing psychological services to American Indian children and families. *Professional Psychology, 14,* 588–603.

Fassinger, R. (1991). The hidden minority: Issues and challenges in working with lesbians and gay men. *The Counseling Psychologist, 19,* 157–176.

Folensbee, J. R., Draguns, J., & Danish, S. (1986). Impact of two types of counselor intervention on Black American, Puerto Rican, and Anglo-American analog clients. *Journal of Counseling Psychology, 33,* 446–453.

Garcia, M., & Lega, L. (1979). Development of a Cuban ethnic identity questionnaire. *Hispanic Journal of Behavioral Sciences, 1,* 246–261.

Garnets, L., Hancock, K. A., Cochran, S. D., Goodchilds, J., & Peplau, L. A. (1991). Issues in psychotherapy with lesbians and gay men: A survey of psychologists. *American Psychologist, 46,* 964–972.

Gartrell, N. (1985). Issues in psychotherapy with lesbian women. *Work in Progress* 83:04. Wellesley, MA: Stone Center Working Series.

Gibbs, J. R. (1987). Identity and marginality: Issues in the treatment of biracial adolescents. *American Journal of Orthopsychiatry, 57,* 265–278.

Gilligan, C. (1982). *In a different voice: Psychological theory and women's development.* Cambridge, MA: Harvard University Press.

Hall, C. C. I. (1980). *The ethnic identity of racially mixed people: A study of Black-Japanese.* Unpublished doctoral dissertation. University of California, Los Angeles.

Hare-Mustin, R. T., & Marecek, J. (1986). Autonomy and gender: Some questions for therapists. *Psychotherapy, 23,* 205–212.

Helms, J. (1984). Toward a theoretical explanation of the effects of race on counseling: A Black and White model. *The Counseling Psychologist, 12,* 153–165.

Herman, J. (1984) Sexual violence. *Work in Progress* 83:05. Wellesley, MA. Stone Center Working Series.

Ibrahim, F. (1991). Contribution of cultural world view to generic counseling and development. *Journal of Counseling and Development, 70,* 13–19.

Ibrahim, F. A. (1985). Effective cross-cultural counseling and psychotherapy: A framework. *The Counseling Psychologist, 13,* 625–683.

Ibrahim, F., & Kahn, H. (1987). Assessment of world views. *Psychological Reports, 60,* 163–176.

Jackson, B. W. (1975). Black identity development. *Journal of Educational Diversity, 2,* 19–25.

Johnson, D. W. (1981). *Reaching out: Interpersonal effectiveness and self-actualization* (2nd ed.). Englewood Cliffs, NJ: Prentice-Hall.

Johnson, S. D. (1987). "Knowing that" versus "knowing how": Toward achieving expertise through multicultural training for counseling. *The Counseling Psychologist, 15,* 320–331.

Jones, A., & Gelso, C. (1988). Differential effects of style of interpretation: Another look. *Journal of Counseling Psychology, 35,* 363–369.

Kaplan, A. (1986). The "self-in-relation": Implications for depression in women. *Psychotherapy, 23,* 234–242.

Katz, J. H. (1985). The socio-political nature of counseling. *The Counseling Psychologist, 13,* 615–624.

Kokotovic, A., & Tracey, T. (1987). Premature termination at a university counseling center. *Journal of Counseling Psychology, 34,* 80–82.

Koss, M. P. (1990). Violence against women. *American Psychologist, 45,* 374–380.

Krantz, N., & Marshall, L. (1988). First impressions: Analog experiment on counselor behavior and gender. *Representative Research in Social Psychology, 18,* 41–50.

Kunkel, M. A., Hector, M. A., Coronado, E. G., & Vales, V. C. (1989). Expectations about counseling in Yucatan, Mexico: Toward a "Mexican psychology." *Journal of Counseling Psychology, 35,* 322–330.

LaFromboise, T. D. (1988). American Indian mental health policy. *American Psychologist, 43,* 388–397.

LaFromboise, T. D., & Dixon, D. N. (1981). American Indian perception of trustworthiness in a counseling interview. *Journal of Counseling Psychology, 28,* 135–139.

LaFromboise, T. D., Trimble, J. E., & Mohatt, G. V. (1990). Counseling intervention and American Indian tradition: An integrative approach. *The Counseling Psychologist, 18,* 628–654.

Lee, C. C. (1991). Promise and pitfalls of multicultural counseling. In C. C. Lee & B. L. Richardson (Eds.), *Multicultural issues in counseling: New approaches to diversity* (pp. 1–13). Alexandria, VA: American Association for Counseling and Development.

Lemkau, J. P., & Landau, C. (1986). The "selfless syndrome": Assessment and treatment considerations. *Psychotherapy, 23,* 227–233.

Lerner, G. H. (1977). The taboos against female anger. *Menninger Perspective,* Winter, 5–11.

Lerner, H. G. (1988). *Women in therapy.* Northvale, NJ: Jason Aronson.

LeVine, E., & Padilla, A. (1980). *Crossing cultures in therapy: Pluralistic counseling for the Hispanic.* Belmont, CA: Wadsworth.

Lewis, R., & Ho, M. (1989). Social work with Native Americans. In D. Atkinson, G. Morten, & D. Sue (Eds.), *Counseling American minorities* (pp. 51–58). Dubuque, IA: William C. Brown.

Littrell, J., Caffrey, P., & Hopper, G. (1987). Counselor's reputation: An important precounseling variable for adolescents. *Journal of Counseling Psychology, 34,* 228–231.

Locke, D. C. (1990). A not so provinicial view of multicultural counseling. *Counselor Education and Supervision, 30,* 18–25.

Lopez, S. R., Grover, K. P., Holland, H., Johnson, M. J., Kain, C. D., Kanel, K., Mellins, C. A., & Rhyne, M. C. (1989). Development of culturally sensitive psychotherapists. *Professional Psychology: Research and Practice, 29,* 369–376.

McBride, A. B. (1990). Mental health effects of women's multiple roles. *American Psychologist, 45,* 381–384.

McKenzie, V. M. (1986). Ethnographic findings on West Indian-American clients. *Journal of Counseling and Development, 65*(9), 40–44.

McMillan, D., & Johnson, M. (1990). Paradoxical versus cognitive-behavioral interventions: Effects on perceptions of counselor characteristics. *Journal of Mental Health Counseling, 12,* 67.

McRoy, R., & Freeman, E. (1986). Racial identity issues among mixed-race children. *Social Work in Education, 8,* 164–175.

Mendoza, R. (1984). Acculturation and sociocultural variability. In J. L. Martinez, Jr. & R. H. Mendoza (Eds.), *Chicago psychology* (2nd ed.), (pp. 61–75). Orlando: Academic Press.

Mendoza, R., & Martinez, J. (1981). The measurement of acculturation. In A. Baron, Jr., (Ed.), *Exploration in Chicanos Psychology* (pp. 71–82). New York: Praeger.

Miller, J. B. (1976). *Toward a new psychology of women.* Boston: Beacon.

Olmedo, E. (1979). Acculturation, a psychometric perspective. *American Psychologist, 34,* 1061–1070.

Parham, T. A. (1989). Cycles of psychological nigrescence. *The Counseling Psychologist, 17,* 187–226.

Pederson, P. (1991a). Concluding comments to the special issue. *Journal of Counseling and Development, 70,* 250.

Pederson, P. (1991b). Multiculturalism as a generic approach to counseling. *Journal of Counseling and Development, 7,* 6–12.

Phinney, J. S., & Rotherham, J. J. (Eds.). (1987). *Children's ethnic socialization: Pluralism and development.* Newbury Park, CA: Sage.

Pomales, J., & Williams, V. (1989). Effects of level of acculturation and counseling style on Hispanic students' perceptions of the counselor. *Journal of Counseling Psychology, 36,* 79–83.

Ponterotto, J. G. (1987). Counseling Mexican Americans: A multimodal approach. *Journal of Counseling and Development, 65*(2), 308–311.

Ponterotto, J. G. (1988). Racial consciousness development among White counselor trainees: A stage model. *Journal of Multicultural Counseling and Development, 16,* 146–156.

Ponterotto, J. G. (1989). Expanding directions for racial identity research. *The Counseling Psychologist, 17,* 264–272.

Ponterotto, J. G., Anderson, W. H., Jr., & Grieger, I. (1986). Black students' attitudes toward counseling as a function of racial identity. *Journal of Multicultural Counseling and Development, 14,* 50–59.

Ponterotto, J. G., & Benesch, K. F. (1988). An organizational framework for understanding the role of culture in counseling. *Journal of Counseling and Development, 66,* 237–241.

Ponterotto, J. G., & Casa, J. M. (1991). *Handbook of racial/ethnic minority counseling research.* Springfield, IL: Charles C. Thomas.

Poston, W. S. C. (1990). The biracial identity development model: A needed addition. *Journal of Counseling and Development, 69,* 152–155.

Reynolds, S. A., & Pode, R. (1991). The complexities of diversity: Exploring multiple oppressions. *Journal of Counseling and Development, 70,* 174–180.

Ridley, N., & Asbury, F. (1988). Does the counselor body posture make a difference? *School Counselor, 35,* 253–258.

Riner, R. D. (1979). American Indian education: A rite that fails. *Anthropology and Education Quarterly, 10,* 236–253.

Root, M. (1990). Resolving "other" status: Identity development of bi-racial individuals. In L. S. Brown & M. P. P. Root (Eds.), *Complexity and Diversity in Feminist Theory and Therapy* (pp. 185–205). New York: Haworth Press.

Russell, M. (1986). Teaching feminist counseling skills: An evaluation. *Counselor Education and Supervision,* 320–332.

Russo, N. F. (1990). Forging research priorities for women's mental health. *American Psychologist, 45,* 368–374.

Sanchez, A., & Atkinson, D. (1983). Mexican-American cultural commitment, preference for counselor ethnicity, and willingness to use counseling. *Journal of Counseling Psychology, 30,* 215–220.

Scott, N. E., & Borodovsky, L. G. (1990). Effective use of cultural role taking. *Professional Psychology: Research and Practice, 21,* 167–170.

Sebring, D. L. (1985). Considerations in counseling interracial children. *The Personnel and Guidance Journal, 13,* 3–9.

Shannon, J., & Woods, W. (1991). Affirmative psychotherapy for gay men. *The Counseling Psychologist, 19,* 197–215.

Short, R., Moore, S., & Williams, C. (1991). Social influence in consultation: Effect of degree and expereince on consultees' perceptions. *Psychological Reports, 68,* 131–137.

Social Science Research Council Summer Seminar on Acculturation. (1954). Acculturation: An exploratory formulation. *American Anthropologist, 56,* 973–1002.

Sodowsky, G., Lai, E., & Plake, B. (1991). Moderating effects of socio-cultural variables on acculturation attitudes of Hispanics and Asian-Americans. *Journal of Counseling and Development, 70,* 194–204.

Sodowsky, R. (1991). Effects of culturally consistent counseling tasks on American and international student observers' perception of counselor credibility: Preliminary investigation. *Journal of Counseling and Development, 69,* 253–356.

Spector, R. (1985). *Cultural diversity in health and illness.* Norwalk, CT: Appleton Century Crofts.

Stiver, I. P. (1986). The meaning of care: Reframing treatment models for women. *Psychotherapy, 23,* 221–226.

Stonequist, E. V. (1937). *The marginal man: A study in personality and culture conflict.* New York: Russell & Russell.

Strohmer, D., & Biggs, D. (1983). Effects of counselor disability status on disabled subjects' perceptions of counselor attractiveness and expertness. *Journal of Counseling Psychology, 30,* 202–208.

Strong, S. (1968). Counseling: An interpersonal influence process. *Journal of Counseling Psychology, 15,* 215–224.

Sue, D., & Sue, D. (1977). Barriers to effective cross-cultural counseling. *Journal of Counseling Psychology, 24,* 420–429.

Sue, D. W., Bernier, J. E., Durran, A., Feinberg, L., Pederson, P., Smith, E. J., & Vasquez-Nuttall, E. (1982). Position paper: Cross-cultural competencies. *The Counseling Psychologist, 10,* 1–8.

Sue, S., & Zane, N. (1987). The role of culture and cultural techniques in psychotherapy: A critique and reformulation. *American Psychologist, 42,* 37–45.

Surrey, J. (1985). *Self-in-relation: A theory of women's development.* Wellesley, MA: Stone Center for Developmental Studies and Services.

Terrell, F., & Terrell. S. (1984). Race of counselor, client sex, cultural mistrust level, and premature termination from counseling among Black clients. *Journal of Counseling Psychology, 31,* 371–375.

Thomason, T. (1991). Counseling Native Americans: An introduction for non-Native American Counselors. *Journal of Counseling and Development, 69,* 321–327.

Torrey, E. F. (1972). *The mindgame: Witch doctors and psychiatrists.* New York: Emerson Hall.

Trimble, J. E., & Fleming, C. M. (1989). Providing counseling services for Native American Indians: Client, counselor, and community characteristics. In P. B. Pederson, J. G. Draguns, W. J. Lonner, & J. E. Trimble (Eds.), *Counseling across cultures* (3rd ed.), (pp. 177–204). Honolulu: University Press of Hawaii.

Trimble, J. E., & LaFromboise, T. D. (1985). American Indians and the counseling process: Culture, adaptation, and style. In P. Pederson (Ed.), *Handbook of cross-cultural counseling and therapy* (pp. 127–134). Westport, CT: Greenwood Press.

Uhlemann, M., & Lee, D. (1990). Self-reported reliance on non-verbal behavior. *Canadian Journal of Counseling, 24,* 92–97.

Uhlemann, M., Lee, D., & Hasse, R. (1989). The effects of cognitive complexities and arousal on client perceptions of counselor nonverbal behavior. *Journal of Clinical Psychology, 45,* 661–665.

Walker, L. (1990). A feminist therapist views the case. In D. Cantor (Ed.), *Women as therapists: A multi-theoretical casebook* (pp. 78–95). New York: Springer.

Watkins, C. E., Terrell, F., Miller, F. S., & Terrell, S. (1989). Cultural mistrust and its effects on expectational variables in black client–white counselor relationships. *Journal of Counseling Psychology, 36,* 447–450.

Wolfman, B. R. (1984). Women and their many roles. *Work in Progress* 83:03. Wellesley, MA: Stone Center Working Series.

Wrenn, C. G. (1985). Afterword: The culturally encapsulated counselor revisited. In P. Pederson (Ed.), *Handbook of cross-cultural counseling and therapy* (pp. 323–329). Westport, CT: Greenwood Press.

Chapter *15*

Diagnosis and Treatment Planning

Counselors must first be diagnosticians before they can engage in some activity they consider therapeutic. Strupp (1978) contends that whatever the counselor's background or level of training, it is unlikely he or she will escape the necessity of forming some hypothesis about the client's problem or difficulty and deciding what needs to be done to improve the client's situation.

The concept of diagnosis has its origin in medicine, where it is defined as distinguishing an illness or disease and identifying its symptoms. Diagnosis is the attempt to classify illness or disease in discrete, mutually exclusive categories, each of which is characterized by a common origin or cause, a common course, and a common prognosis or outcome.

The concept of diagnosis was brought into counseling through the influence of psychiatry, a branch of medicine that deals with social and emotional problems. Classification of disease and treatment, however, does not seem to apply to counseling with normal people. This has caused some controversy about the function of diagnosis in counseling. Advocates of diagnosis suggest that it plays a central role in counseling; opponents claim that problems are not sufficiently discrete nor techniques specific enough to be effective. Diagnosis for classification is still used, particularly with more severe problems, however, the concept of diagnosis as understanding the client is more useful in the counseling process. This chapter discusses some of the major concepts of diagnosis in counseling and some ideas regarding the process of diagnosis.

The purpose of diagnosis in counseling is to identify the client's life-style of functioning or more specifically, the disruptions of the life-style. By identifying the problem area, the counselor and client can establish the goals of the counseling process. Diagnosis can serve three different functions in the counseling process. First, it can be used to categorize the problem of the client and therefore to label the problem area. This is a carryover from the medical model in which the first step is to diagnose the problem in order to prescribe appropriate treatment. Because most of the labels in counseling are not sufficiently discrete to suggest differential treatment, a diagnosis that gives a comprehensive picture is frequently used. Secondly, drawing together all the information about a client in his or her situation as a basis for decision making is an important part of the counseling process. Another use of diagnosis is the working process to understand the client. The counselor develops a model of the client or an individual theory that changes as the counselor learns more about the client. This moment-to-moment understanding is particularly important for both personal and social problems. The model is usually based on the counselor's counseling theory as it is applied to the individual client.

In some clinical settings, the counselor may hold a diagnostic interview in which he or she evaluates the current psychological status of the client and the causal factors of behavior, which leads to suggesting treatment and a prognosis of future adjustment. Such an interview is used only for evaluation; the counseling process begins later, frequently with a different counselor. In most settings, however, diagnosis and counseling are interwoven as the counselor begins the process with an initial interview and continues working with the client. With this approach, diagnosis is not a judgment at a specific time, but an intricate part of the continuing process of counseling.

Proponents of diagnostic evaluation base their support on the assumption that diagnosis brings clarity and order into a very complex field. They contend that diagnosis enables the counselor to fit many diverse items of information into a pattern, which then allows the counselor to make a prediction about the client's behavior. This procedure gives the counselor a firm basis on which to construct a plan for counseling. Another factor in support of diagnostic evaluation is the assumption that it will aid in the selection of clients for treatment. The counselor must accept only those clients for which he or she is able to provide appropriate treatment and refer other clients to another clinic, hospital, or mental health professional. Another reason for using diagnosis is to aid the counselor in determining what the client seems to need most. Is the client's stated reason for seeking counseling the real problem or is it a facade? Does the client lack information or insight? Is the client in need of clarification or support or a combination of these?

The existing diagnostic schemes are helpful but often inexact. The same can be said for the theoretical formulations of client problems in terms of presenting symptoms. Diagnosis is a process that calls for an exercise of keen clinical skills. It should be systematic and lead to prognostic judgments that are translated into a plan for treatment. The personality and behavior pattern of the individual client is the single most important aspect of understanding for the counselor in formulating an individual treatment plan for counseling.

Because diagnosis and treatment often remain nonspecific, many counselors have not regarded diagnosis as an essential part of counseling. Diagnosis was considered one of the most important skills for the counselor until the rise of the nondirective or client-centered movement. Since then, the proponents of diagnosis in counseling have done much research and writing in an attempt to demonstrate the positive contributions of counselor diagnosis. Two major concepts of diagnosis approach it as either classification or as a process of understanding.

Diagnosis as Classification

A diagnostic or assessment system is useful when it produces information that relates to some desired set of counseling outcomes that is the object of treatment or intervention. A system for assessing behavior needs to be broad and objective to minimize a counselor's misunderstanding of the client. Therefore, a good diagnostic and assessment system is designed to facilitate the understanding of the client's behavior for both an internal and external perspective and to lead to the specific interventions (Osipow, Walsh, & Tosi, 1984).

Category Systems

Several categorization systems of diagnosis have been proposed over the years. Most of them have been established for education, vocational, and personal problems in school or university settings. Although these systems may be appropriate for many community clinical settings, some clinics and most hospitals use a psychiatric classification.

Educational/Vocational/Personal Constructs

Numerous diagnostic category systems have evolved that are still appropriate for record keeping in schools and some community clinics. In 1937, Williamson and Darley identified the diagnostic categories that they felt would encompass all problems dealt with by the counselor: vocational, educational, personal-social-emotional, financial, health, and family. Bordin (1946) views the Williamson-Darley diagnostic constructs as sociologically oriented and as excluding psychological dynamics, describing the difficulty but ignoring the source. He suggests that these categories overlap and do not lead to differential treatment. Bordin proposes instead a "psychological description" that starts with the individual describing the organization of his behavioral characteristics and predicting what his or her reactions will be to his or her social environment (1946, p. 169). Bordin's set of constructs involve the common course and suggested treatment. His constructs include dependence, lack of information, self-conflict, choice anxiety, and no problem. In evaluating Bordin's constructs, Robinson (1963) contends that the categories do not give any diagnostic indication of the specific cause of the frustration and, therefore, little indication of the treatment to be used.

Pepinsky (1948) makes another attempt to define and to differentiate empirically among the causal categories of client problems. Pepinsky bases his diagnostic categories on Bordin's set of constructs but expands the construct of self-conflict to include three subcategories: cultural, interpersonal, and intrapersonal self-conflict. Pepinsky replaces Bordin's no-problem category, which did not explain the reason the client sought counseling, with lack of assurance, and adds a sixth category, lack of skill.

Pepinsky evaluated his system by studying intercounselor agreement in applying the constructs to 115 cases. Each counselor based his or her diagnosis on an analysis of the client's record blanks, test scores, and other available reports. There were three important findings; (1) the constructs of interpersonal self-conflict, intrapersonal self-conflict, lack of assurance, lack of information, and lack of skill, which were used with consistency by the counselor, were relatively mutually exclusive and seemed to identify important cause factors; (2) counselors were unable to distinguish clearly between cultural self-conflict and dependence; and (3) choice anxiety was not studied systematically because problems of this type were rarely observed in the cases used.

Byrne (1958) replaces the construct of self-conflict and its subcategories with two categories: lack of insight and lack of information. Byrne also replaces the category of dependence with that of immaturity, believing dependence to be only one expression of immaturity. He drops choice anxiety because anxiety is a symptom, not a cause, but retains the category lack of assurance. The construct lack of skill was altered to lack of problem-solving skill. Byrne adds a new category, domination by authority, persons, or situations, to include clients who are unable to make a choice or plan for the future because of pressures from the environment to do something other than what they want to do.

Robinson (1963) revises the Bordin, Pepinsky, Byrne, and Callis (1960) systems of classification and proposes the following categories: (1) personal maladjustment, (2) conflict with significant others, (3) discussing plans, (4) lack of information about the environment, (5) immaturity, and (6) skill deficiency.

Callis (1965) subsequently describes a departure in diagnostic divisions with a two-dimensional diagnostic classification plan. Along one dimension are three of the Williamson-Darley categories: (1) vocational (VOC); (2) emotional (EM); and (3) educational (ED). This dimension is labeled *problem-goal.* Along the cause dimension are (1) lack of information or understanding of self (LIS); (2) lack of information or understanding of the environment (LIE); (3) motivational conflict within self (CS); (4) conflict with significant others (CO); and (5) lack of skill (LS), such as poor reading skills or poor study habits. The cause dimension attempts to focus on what is lacking in the client's personal resources that causes the inability to solve the problem.

This system of classification makes 15 diagnostic hypotheses possible. The counselor places a client into one category from each dimension and can record a diagnostic hypothesis by using the symbols from each dimension. The problem-goal dimension is written first, with the cause dimension second. Callis's system of classification has been successfully used in record keeping.

Diagnostic and Statistical Manual of Mental Disorders

In many clinical settings the counselor may need to make a diagnosis of mental disorder or may receive a client's case history with psychiatric diagnostic nomenclature. The American Psychiatric Association's most recent effort to categorize mental disorders, the *Diagnostic and Statistical Manual of Mental Disorders* (DSM-III-R) is generally used for this purpose (APA, 1987). The DSM-III-R is a revision of the 1980 DSM-III. It contains more than 30 new diagnostic categories that were added to the DSM-III (Spitzer et al, 1989).

The Work Group to Revise DSM-III-R note that although the manual provides a classification of mental disorders, no definition adequately specifies precise boundaries for the concept *mental disorder.* Nevertheless, they present a definition of mental disorder that influenced the decision to include certain conditions in the DSM-III-R as mental disorders and to exclude others. Each of the mental disorders in the DSM-III-R "is conceptualized as a clinically significant behavior or psychological syndrome or pattern that occurs in a person and that is associated with the present distress (a painful symptom) or disability (impairment in one or more important areas of functioning), or with a significant increased risk of suffering death, pain, disability, or an important loss of freedom." They go on to say "Whatever its original cause, it must currently be considered a manifestation of behavioral, psychological, or biological dysfunction of the person." There is also no assumption in the DSM-III-R that each mental disorder is a discrete entity with distinct boundaries (discontinuity) between it and other disorders or between it and no mental disorder (APA, 1987, p. xxii).

The Work Group clarifies a common misconception that a classification of mental disorder classifies people by stating that what is classified are the disorders that people have. Therefore, the text of DSM-III-R avoids the use of such expressions as "a schizophrenic" or "an alcoholic," but uses a more accurate description "a person with schizophrenia" or "a person with alcohol dependence." They also clarify that all people described as having the same mental disorder have the defining features of the disorder; however, they may well differ in other important respects that may affect the clinical treatment and outcome (APA, 1987, p. xxiii).

The DSM-III-R is basically "descriptive" and definitions of the disorders are generally atheoretical in regard to ideology because the inclusion of ideologic theories would be an obstacle to use of the manual by clinicians of varying theoretical orientations. It would not be possible to present all reasonable ideologic theories for each disorder.

Each of the disorders is systematically described according to essential features, associated features, age at onset, course, impairment, complications, predisposing factors, prevalence, familial pattern, sex-ratio, and differential diagnosis. It is descriptively comprehensive but it does not include information about theories of ideology, management, or treatment. In addition, it does not classify disturbed diadic, family, or other interpersonal relationships.

Diagnosis in the DSM-III-R takes a multiaxial form. This is particularly helpful because the evaluation insures that certain information which may be of value in planning treatment and predictable outcome for each person is recorded on the different axes. Axes I and II include the mental disorders; Axis III the physical disorders and conditions; and Axes IV and V describe the severity of psychosocial stressors and the global assessment of functioning. This system provides a bio-psychological approach to assessment and diagnosis.

Three cautionary statements are made regarding the use of the DSM-III-R. First, specialized clinical training is required for proper use of the DSM-III-R. Second, other conditions that are not included in the DSM-III-R classification may be appropriate subjects of treatment or research efforts. Third, the clinical and scientific basis of the DSM-III-R classification criteria may not be relevant for consideration outside the research setting, such as in legal determinations.

It is important to use caution when applying the DSM-III-R classification to a person from an ethnic or cultural group that differs from that of the clinician. It is important that the counselor is sensitive to the differences in language, values, behavioral norms, and idiomatic expressions of distress. Counselors must apply this system with open-mindedness in the presence of distinctive cultural patterns and be sensitive to the possibility of unintended bias because of such differences.

Frequently counselors leave diagnostic interviews open-ended and diagnosis has been based on his or her sense or general impression of the client. Using the DSM-III-R counselors have specific criteria for each disorder so that both they and other persons that may read the report will be able to know the criteria used for the diagnosis. To gain specific information to compare with specific criteria, counselors need to interview in an exploratory but focused manner as a part of the diagnostic process. To gain an awareness of a client's life events the counselor needs to explore the background of the symptoms as well as present stresses.

The Work Group to Revise the DSM-III (APA, 1987) outlined the process to use the multiaxial evaluation. Diagnosis begins by observing the client, and observational skills of the counselor are critical in the diagnostic process. Counselors need to be familiar with the terminology used in the manual and need to use standard, technical language when describing their clients. A glossary of technological terms is provided so there will be no confusion. The manual aids in differential diagnosis by providing decision trees. When a counselor has determined a general category, he or she starts at the top of the decision tree and goes down the tree through a series of questions requiring yes or no answers. This directs the counselor toward a tentative diagnosis by sorting out the possible alternatives. It is important to remember that this is only a tentative diagnosis.

Although diagnostic category systems are necessary in many settings, several professionals have commented on the shortcomings and suggested alternatives. Beutler (1989) reviewed the literature to conclude that psychiatric diagnosis has proven to be of little value in the development of individual psychotherapy plans or to the differential prediction of therapy outcomes. He concludes that the dimensions that underlie diagnosis appear to be different from those that govern the therapeutic process and suggests that complex relationships among nondiagnostic and situational variables are involved in the development of differential treatment indications and plans. He points out that in medical diagnosis the question of what constitutes a clinical pattern of symptoms has been answered by whether or not a diagnosis differentiates the ideology of the disorder, provides information about the course of the disease, and/or promotes differential assignment of specific treatment (Katz et al., 1965; Sharma, 1970). However, some psychiatric diagnoses specify the nature of the ideology and some define a course of the disorder, but they have not achieved the same degree of consistency in these areas as medical diagnoses have.

The committees that developed the DSM-III and DSM-III-R used a descriptive system for categorizing behavioral and psychological symptoms. With this system, diagnosis has become more specific in defining what characteristics constitute various syndromes. The procedures have become more reliable and can be consistently applied across individuals and settings. However, even these descriptive dimensions provide little direction in selecting a mode of therapeutic intervention such as group, family, marital, or individual therapy. In addition, none of them suggest implications for any theoretical approach that would be more appropriate. Therefore, clients are likely to receive the type of therapy in which the counselor is most experienced.

Beutler (1989) points out that little attention has been given to methods of selectively using different methods of therapy for clients based on characteristics other than diagnosis. He goes on to suggest that nondiagnostic dimensions should be sought that allow therapists to apply different therapeutic models and formats. He uses previous research in suggesting that it may be possible to develop a disposition-based diagnostic system. A disposition-based assessment would see diagnosis as a dynamic process delineating the probability that an identified client would respond to a given treatment or setting. The assessment procedure would involve "a sequential common, multistep process of defining the treatment propensities, needs, settings, enabling factors, and social context through which effective treatment occurs" (p. 276). It is believed that today's knowledge could be used to develop a system to assign clients to different treatments, which could provide an alternative to the present diagnostic systems.

Persons (1986) advocates studying individual symptoms rather than studying the diagnostic categories. She uses the category of schizophrenia to describe six advantages. First, using the diagnostic category in studying a thought disorder may result in misclassification of subjects. Second, studying symptoms will identify important phenomena that are ignored by the diagnostic category approach. Third, the use of symptoms will contribute to the development of psychological theory, specifically in developing coherent hypotheses linking phenomena to the underlying mechanisms. Fourth, using the symptom approach one can isolate the single elements of pathology. Fifth, the symptoms method recognizes the continuity of clinical phenomena and mechanisms with normal phenomena and mechanisms. Sixth, the study of symptoms will contribute to the refinement of systems of diagnostic classification.

The Diagnostic Interview

Most professionals believe it is necessary to become knowledgeable about the client prior to establishing the treatment plan. Clients enter counseling with a variety of problems, goals, strengths, and abilities for change. The primary purpose of the interview is to gather information about the client (Choca, 1988).

Separate Diagnostic Interview

The large number of people seen in some agencies necessitates some form of diagnostic workup. Many agencies use a separate diagnostic interview, separating the diagnostic from the counseling process. Shectman, De La Torre, and Garza (1979) discuss some of the advantages and disadvantages of a system in which intake interviews are separate from the counseling process.

A particular advantage to the client is that, theoretically, she or he can obtain the best person the institution has to offer. Through the diagnostic interview, the client may be placed with the staff counselor most likely to be able to help. It is possible to match the client with the appropriate counselor and treatment modality.

The referral of a client to another counselor after the diagnostic interview has the potential disadvantage of interrupting a relationship that has just begun. The client could feel rejected by the diagnostician or by the institutional machinery. It is therefore important when using a diagnostic interview to prepare the client to give information to the diagnostician and to begin counseling with another counselor.

Another possible disadvantage of conducting the diagnostic interview separately occurs when the client is aware that the relationship is limited by time and might consciously or unconsciously stall in order to save more important information for the "real" counselor. In other cases, the client might try to cram long-term counseling into a short period of time. In some cases the client may resort to premature closure as a way of easing the transfer from one person to another, dealing with an issue only intellectually rather than with feeling.

A diagnostician who has a short-lived diagnostic involvement with clients before referring them to a counselor may feel drained or threatened and may avoid the openness required to help the clients optimally and to perform the diagnostic task. It is obviously important for the diagnostician to balance diagnostic interviews with counseling clients on a longer-term basis. In most agencies there is a rotation system whereby all counselors perform some diagnostic interviewing as a part of their regular case load.

A diagnostician can serve an excellent role by preparing the client for counseling. Some counselors, however, experience a disadvantage when they begin counseling a client in the middle of an experience between the client and the diagnostician, particularly if the counselor has begun with a client in a different way or has suggested a different procedure. The counselor also relies on the diagnostician for a type of testing out of how the client may respond to or deal with the counselor's mode of counseling.

The Interview Process

The beginning of a diagnostic interview is similar to most others in that the counselor attempts to put the client at ease and to establish rapport. There is a clear intent to clarify the purpose of the interview and to answer questions that the client may have about the procedure. Choca (1988) describes several areas of information that should be gathered from the client. The first area to explore is the client's presenting problem. What problems are occurring presently, and how long have these been seen as problems? Why has the client sought counseling at this time rather than previously? It is appropriate for the counselor to follow up with questions to gain more specific and accurate descriptions from the client. The counselor continues in gathering information about the client's present life situation. The counselor needs to know where the client lives and with whom and how the relationships between the different members are seen by the client.

The mental health and medical histories are both important. Any major medical illness or accidents could have an impact on the client's life situation. Any emotional problems that have occurred in the past or any treatment received is particularly important information. How much alcohol an individual has used or any other substance abuse is particularly important information.

A brief description of the individual's family of origin is important information. Has any relative suffered major emotional problems? Descriptions of the client's perception of major family events and of the person's earlier life are important. Information is sought regarding any marriages and children the client has had. The relationships the client has outside the family and sexual experiences of the past are also important variables. The extent of the client's education and training as well as the types of jobs the person has held will add to the total picture of the client.

Choca (1988) suggests that the usual strategy in diagnostic interviews is to use open-ended statements and questions, such as "Tell me about your family," which will permit the client to describe the information they think is most important and that they are willing to share. This permits the client to maintain control of the interview and the information that they provide. If a client stops talking before the counselor believes adequate information has been gathered, it is appropriate to use further promptings, e.g., silence, a nod, a comment like "yes," or "go on, please." Counselors occasionally use self-disclosure in a diagnostic interview in the belief that self-disclosure may help the client feel less vulnerable.

There are times when the counselor must switch from an open-ended question to more specific ones. This occurs when the client has handled the general questions by giving more irrelevant answers or has left out details that seem important to the counselor. The counselor may then ask specific questions in a direct and clear manner suggesting answers for the client. After a specific topic has been adequately covered, the counselor may switch to a different area, using the general, more open-ended questions.

The clinical observations made by the counselor during the interview together with the information obtained are used to evaluate many aspects of the client's functioning. The counselor should be paying attention to the nonverbal behavior and what the behaviors may be communicating. Such variables as eye contact, physical distance, gestures, facial expressions, and body movement have been covered in Chapter 12.

An advantage of the separate diagnostic interview is that it allows the counselor to circumscribe the task and separate diagnosis from treatment. Therefore, issues can be clarified before treatment begins. It is often easier to clarify issues in advance; neutrality can be much more difficult to maintain once the client-counselor relationship is under way. Menninger, Mayman, and Pruyser (1963) claim that diagnosis "is not a search for a proper name by which one can refer to this affliction in this or other patients. It is diagnosis in a sense of understanding just how a patient is ill and how ill the patient is, how he became ill and how his illness serves him. . . . It is still necessary to know in advance, to plan logically as we can, what kind of interference with a human life we propose to make" (1963, p. 103).

A major function of a diagnostic study is to improve the accuracy of clinical prediction about the client's probable response to possible treatment situations. The diagnostician, then, focuses on assessing the variables about the client and makes predictive statements that will help in deciding the treatment procedure. Therefore, the counselor has an opportunity to use the diagnostician to help in planning. The way in which the client responds to the diagnostician can provide good information in predicting behavior and issues in counseling. The diagnostic interview, therefore, is a brief experiment, a kind of trial counseling, and a preview of what will occur with the counselor.

Diagnosis as Understanding

Client-centered theory challenges the concept of diagnosis by classification. Diagnosis, however, may also be viewed as a process of understanding and entailing a very different approach: "In a very meaningful and accurate sense, therapy 'is' diagnosis, and diagnosis is a process which goes on in the experience of the client, rather than in the intellect of the clinician" (Rogers, 1951, p. 223). We suggest that diagnosis is a process that involves both the counselor and the client. Diagnosis as understanding uses working hypotheses that are constantly subject to revision by any new cognitive and affective factors introduced in the interview by the client and by other sources.

How does the counselor establish the working hypothesis? In a statement challenging the use of categories, Bordin advocates understanding the client, suggesting that it seems more fruitful to rely on a well-differentiated theory of personality as a basis for trying to understand a particular person (1955). This concept bases diagnosis on the counselor's understanding of the client in accordance with the counselor's philosophy of human nature, personality theory, and counseling theory.

The concept of the counselor as hypothesis maker and model builder has received wide support. Pepinsky and Pepinsky (1954) propose that the counselor be a model builder by forming a "microtheory" of the client's behavior. They contend that the counselor must distinguish between observation and inference; state testable hypotheses; test them; and reconstruct the microtheory in light of new information. It is clear that the counselor's responses in the interview result from her or his understanding of the client.

Similarly, Meehl (1954) views the process as one in which the counselor brings events and immediate circumstances together into a "conception of this person." Wrenn (1951) characterizes it as "process diagnosis," while Super (1957) talks about the counselor's "picture of the client." These early writers embraced the idea of diagnosis as understanding. The counselor maintains continuing understanding by formulating a personal theory for the client. That personal theory is generally based on some larger theory of personality development, maladjustment, and counseling theory.

Diagnostic Process

To use diagnoses effectively as understanding, the counselor remains open to him- or herself and to new information. The process of diagnosis is complex and calls for understanding as many facets of the client as possible.

Robinson (1963) contends that at least four aspects of client analysis are needed in formulating a diagnosis that is to serve as a basis in selecting appropriate counseling methods. The first aspect follows the traditional concept of looking for the cause of difficulty to determine the treatment. An intensive case study is necessary to understand the complex pattern of causal factors as well as the client's previous dynamics of adjusting to his or her situation. Much of this will be gathered in the counseling interview; however, testing may contribute valuable information.

Psychological tests present problems to be solved by the client under specified interactional conditions. Compared with usual interview procedures, most psychological tests provide greater standardization of stimulus conditions. Test results should represent objective material; the subjective element consists in the client's interpretation of the factual results. Psychological tests are an objective aid in the diagnostic process.

All too frequently, testing is conducted in a separate interview and the results of the tests communicated to the counselor for implementation of the diagnosis. However, there is much to be gained from having the counselor making the diagnosis administer a test during the interview. In addition to the specific answers given in the test, the counselor can thereby obtain a behavioral sample of the patient's reaction to a problem situation in a relatively stressful interpersonal situation. The use of tests in the interview can be considered a miniature life experience, yielding information about the patient's interpersonal behavior and variations in behavior as a function of the stimulus conditions (Kanfer & Saslow, 1965).

The client's modes of achieving adjustment reflect a range of responses, from reliance on particular defense mechanisms and selective responses to stimulation associated with those defenses. Responses to various test items are verbalized end products of thought processes initiated by the items. A test response, then, is more than just a score, although scores may be helpful in making comparisons with other individuals or with the same client after therapy. Because it represents the client's characteristic style of thinking, a test response allows inferences concerning the client's predominant behavior pattern. Hence, the person administering the test may learn more from the client than just the test score. The use of tests in counseling is covered more comprehensively in Chapter 17.

The client must be made to think in a variety of problem situations so that the counselor can distinguish the pervasive aspects of her or his efforts at adjustment. It is important for the counselor to learn about the client's past adjustment efforts (including his application of assets and liabilities) to new problems. Usually there is considerable continuity between past and present adjustment behavior, but it is possible to have a discrepancy. From the test responses, the counselor can form a picture of the characteristic efforts at adjustment. It is imperative that the counselor check the implications of any one response or pattern against the implications of all others. When enough patterns have one or two major implications in common, a hypothesis is possible. The counselor seeks as few general conclusions as possible to embrace all the significant patterns. A hypothesis is a prediction that certain behavior or thinking will be found by direct observation to characterize the client. The hypothesis applies to thinking or behavior that can be immediately apprehended and does not commit the counselor to any diagnosis. The counselor incorporates test data, case experience, and observations into a set of diagnostic hypotheses about the patient.

The second focus of client analysis looks for the client's positive characteristics. It emphasizes describing the goals involved in building the strengths of a client, thus giving direction to counseling. The diagnosis is focused on identifying the positive areas of the client's life that he or she would like to strengthen.

A third focus of the process involves discovering the manner in which the client responds to stimuli so that the counselor can select appropriate counseling methods. The counselor looks for the client's adjustment techniques so that they can be reinforced. The counselor studies how the client responds to certain situations and why certain responses make it possible to develop a model of the client. This is helpful in understanding the client and determining which methods will be effective.

The fourth aspect involves the moment-by-moment responses of the counselor to aid the client in learning more appropriate behaviors. With the conceptualization of the client—the problem area, the client's dynamics of adjustment, and the counseling goals—the counselor selects the techniques that best suit the goal being worked on at the time.

Thought Process

In the counseling interview the counselor's thought processes can involve various diagnostic styles. Gauron and Dickinson (1966) investigated diagnostic decision making in psychiatric interviews and then described six approaches. Their illustrations seem appropriate to the processes that might be found in counseling. In the intuitive-adversary approach, the counselor commits him- or herself to a diagnosis on an intuitive basis early in the interview and then challenges the information to disprove the diagnosis. This approach, dependent as it is on intuition, is vulnerable to attitude. bias, or distortion.

In another approach, the overinclusive-indecisive, a counselor starts in one direction and drifts into a different one when information that suggests another potential direction is presented. The final result is a decision maker in conflict with no apparent confidence in his or her ability to form conclusions. Diagnosis is then impulsive and probably arbitrary.

The textbook approach is used by a counselor who follows a rigid format, asking for information as it appears in written records and case history write-ups. This counselor has no concept of the relative value of the information and ignores information with potential diagnostic clues in favor of a predetermined course. The bibliography approach is closely related, though not as structured. Information is not requested in any predetermined order but apparently on the basis of whim. A counselor using the bibliography approach is compulsive in obtaining all the information, but impulsive in getting it.

Two other approaches result in more meaningful processes. In a diagnosis-by-exclusion approach, the counselor lists several broad diagnostic possibilities. As the counselor gathers information, she or he excludes these possibilities one by one until the most meaningful one remains. This approach is inductive in nature: The counselor infers conclusions on the basis of information and functions as a data gatherer and excluder. This approach might be an effective process if a counselor has to diagnose for classification.

In the flexible-adaptable approach, the counselor has no preconceived ideas about the order in which information is requested but goes where the information leads, modifying ideas as he or she receives data. The counselor's current thinking, derived from the impact of the combined information, determines what she or he responds to next with the client.

If diagnosis is viewed as a continuous process to understand clients—where they are at the moment as well as where they have been—the last approach would be most helpful. It seems that a relatively unstructured method of gathering information would permit clients more freedom to explore themselves and their environmental situation. This will yield more meaningful information and help clients gain self-insight. The thought process of the counselor could extend from the inductive-logical to the intuitive-alogical. The inductive thinking would probably be more productive. The logic might follow the inductive process rather than a prescribed set of questions.

Used in the capacity of a working hypothesis, diagnosis seems valuable. The following excerpt from Kell and Mueller (1966) describes how to make the best use of diagnosis:

> Diagnosis . . . is an interpersonal process in which the sole purpose of the diagnosis is to understand the relationship well enough to be able to help the client to change. . . . The initial diagnosis is only one of the means that the counselor has

of setting the counseling relationship into motion. As the counseling process continues to progress appropriately, the process of diagnosis becomes a more intimate, idiosyncratic one. . . . Whether the counselor's diagnosis changes will be a function of whether the relationship becomes closer, because only in an intimate relationship is it safe for the client to talk about the meaning that his behavior has for him. . . . As the relationship grows stronger, the diagnosis necessarily becomes more specific to this person, and the counselor leaves the generic ideas farther and farther behind him as he and the client delve more deeply into the meanings of his experiences. (pp. 16–17)

Impediments in Diagnosis

The counselor's clinical judgment is a major part of the diagnostic process, and there are a number of factors that make clinical judgment a difficult task. Arkes (1981) outlines five impediments to accurate clinical judgment: inability to assess covariation, influence of perceived notions, lack of awareness of the counselor's judgmental process, overconfidence, and the hindsight bias.

Covariation Misjudgment

The inability to assess covariation accurately is the first impediment to diagnostic judgment. Arkes demonstrates the problem through an example of a counselor, noting that some people have symptom X while others do not. The counselor attempts to determine if the presence of symptom X is diagnostic of a future problem. Arkes believes that most counselors would base their assessment of covariance largely on the number of instances in which symptom X led to the specific problem outcome. It is, however, important to know the numbers of people who have the symptom, but do not have the eventual problem outcome. Likewise, the diagnostician needs to consider the number of people who do not have the symptom, but do have the problem outcome as well as the people who have neither the symptom nor the outcome. At best most counselors would only deal with people who show the symptom. They would then determine the ratio of those who do and do not have the problem outcome. Arkes notes that if counselors use tests as a diagnostic tool to predict an outcome behavior, they should not only keep track of those clients who have a specific profile and later had or did not have the problem outcome, but they should also record the instances of clients who have the profile and did not have the symptom and those who did not have the symptom and those who did not have the profile but did have the problem outcome.

Preconceived Ideas

The second impediment to accurate diagnostic judgment is the influence of preconceived notions. Arkes proposes that the personality theory a counselor uses guides his or her recall of a client's behavior and the theory may serve as a preconceived set of assumptions that are more powerful than the data the counselor collects. Arkes also provides supportive evidence that judgments may be in error due to previous influences about the topic rather than the specific information presented. It is possible that as a case develops the counselor is consistent with the tentative hypotheses and does not add new data that would change his or her concept of the client and possibly the treatment plan.

Lack of Awareness

Arkes proposes that many counselors are not aware of the factors that influence their judgment. The counselor may end up with a diagnostic judgment, but not truly understand the process and the variables that are involved in reaching that outcome.

Overconfidence

The overconfidence of a diagnostician in his or her diagnosis could impede him or her from improving his or her judgment. In many ways the impediment of overconfidence is closely linked with a lack of awareness. Early research has indicated that as people are given more information, they may become more confident without being more accurate, and also that the most confident judges tend to be the least accurate. Snyder (1981) reports that people selectively seek data that confirm their current ideas. The manner in which a counselor asks questions will be more apt to provide information supporting his or her opinions. Closely related to this is that people tend to disregard data that contradict their judgment (Koriat, Lichtenstein, & Fischhoff, 1980). If counselors lack awareness of the process and variables they consider and become overconfident, their accuracy will certainly be impeded.

Hindsight

After the case is concluded or at least after enough data has been gathered, the probability of the counselor making the proper diagnosis is increased. All of us are more accurate through hindsight.

Treatment Planning

Treatment planning bridges the gap between diagnosis and treatment. Very little is written on the process of treatment planning for counseling. Most of the material in the field reflects a medical model of treatment with minimal emphasis on the counseling process and procedures. However, Seligman (1986) provides an excellent overview of the stages of treatment planning.

Goal Setting

Certainly the first aspect in treatment planning involves understanding and diagnosing the individual client. Whether the counselor uses a separate diagnostic interview, a classification process, or an ongoing understanding diagnostic process, the counselor needs to gather information from the client and to use his or her own conceptual skills in describing the client and the client's life situation.

Early in the counseling process, even if there are separate diagnostic or initial counseling interviews, the counselor should begin the treatment planning process. It is important that the goals for counseling are established early in the process. It is also beneficial to establish the goals with the client. Mutual goals are more likely to motivate the client as well as to provide a more cooperative situation.

Whenever possible, clear and measurable goals should be defined. This means putting things in behavioral terms so that both the counselor and client will know when improvement is being made. One method of doing this involves discussion of what will be different in the client's life when the goals are achieved. Through this method the client can describe both behaviors and situations that occur in her or his life, and these can be used to determine if progress is being made. As progress is made, the goals will change; therefore, establishing goals is not a one-time event in counseling, but an ongoing process.

It is often beneficial to set short-term goals as well as long-term goals. The client is looking for the ultimate goal that should occur near the conclusion of counseling. Some clients become discouraged when that is not achieved. If they understand that progress is a process and that short-term goals will be achieved along the way, their motivation will be enhanced and they are more likely to remain involved in the counseling process.

Counselors should also set process goals for their work. The process goals are linked to the outcome goals but are really designed to look at what sort of process needs to be occurring during this therapeutic stage. There are times when the counselor will be working to overcome a period of resistance with a client so that the process goal will be focused more on working through that particular period in the counseling rather than on the specific outcome goal.

The goals should be stated in terms of objectives that the client wants to achieve. The counselor and client can list "my objective is to . . . " for as many items as the counselor deems appropriate. This method will help make a larger goal of a set of specific objectives that are attainable.

Methods

In developing a treatment plan we need to be more specific than just say "individual counseling." What are we going to do and how do we select that technique? Seligman (1986) suggests that we look at the duration and frequency of counseling, the level of directiveness, and the specific methods that the counselor may use.

The frequency of counseling contact and the duration of the counseling relationship may be determined by the agency in which you work. Some schools, counseling centers, and agencies set a limit on the number of interviews that are granted to clients. In most of those situations when the counselor can present a need for continuing a relationship, extensions are available. Often the counselor has a general idea about the amount of time it will take to assist the client in resolving the situation and can estimate the number of interviews per week or month that will be necessary for the client. In many situations it is helpful to discuss the possible length with the client to give him or her an idea of the amount of time available to work. This again may motivate the client.

The level of directness or the amount of activity that the counselor assumes in the relationship may vary according to the theoretical preference of the counselor, but can be modified to meet the specific needs of the client. If differential treatment is truly provided, the counselor would not provide the same style of interview for each client seen. There is a continuum in terms of counselor activity or directness in the counseling process. With a highly motivated client, the counselor may be less active and permit the client to lead in self-exploration, thereby permitting the counselor to help clarify aspects of that exploration so the client better understands him- or herself as well as the life situation. Better understanding should lead, then, to the client's selection of more appropriate action to resolve that situation. If a counselor likes a behavior modification approach to counseling, the client can still do much of the work in terms of the self-exploration and understanding and can be an important part in setting up a reinforcement schedule for dealing with other parts of the environment in which to receive reinforcements for appropriate changes in behavior. When a client is more disorganized, overwhelmed, or possibly has weaker coping skills, the counselor may need to be a more active interventionist in the process. By setting a structure in the interview, the counselor can help the client focus attention on specific aspects of his or her attitudes, feelings, and behaviors and be more involved in helping the client come to understand him- or herself, perhaps even choosing behaviors the client may want to try. All of this suggests how important it is for the counselor to understand the characteristics of a particular client.

Another continuum in counseling methods involves the range from supportive to exploratory approaches. Supportive counseling focuses more on clients' strengths, while their defenses and past experiences receive little attention. A supportive approach in counseling is usually offered to more action-oriented clients who can profit from help in coping with the everyday demands of their lives. Exploratory methods encourage clients to look beyond the presenting problems and focus on the antecedents and earlier difficulties in their lives. This methodology involves weakening some client defenses and increasing their anxiety levels to increase their concerns that have previously been denied or suppressed. This methodology has been used with clients who have emotional resources to look at their developmental concerns and life patterns as well as adequate time and motivation to engage in resolving issues beyond their presenting problems. Once again it is important to consider the knowledge of the individual client in selecting methods along this particular continuum.

Another methodological decision to be made in the counseling process is the attention given to the cognitive, affective, and behavioral areas. Obviously, this is not an all-or-none type of decision since nearly all counseling involves some affective and cognitive components, and at some point the client's behavior is involved in that process. Frequently the counselor will use some methods of all three, but is likely to have a personal style that focuses more on one of the areas. It is important to focus part of this methodology to meet the needs of the specific client. Cognitive methods focus on the client's thoughts and seek to evaluate and change her or his thoughts that are inaccurate or self-destructing. Often clients think negative things about themselves or situations and this interferes with how they feel about themselves or the kind of behaviors that they are able to carry out. The counselor listens for such descriptions in a client's discussions, points them out and helps the client to assess the merits and accuracy of these thoughts. They may assist the client to replace these thoughts with more constructive thoughts that can lead to the client both feeling differently and behaving appropriately. Behavioral methods are often preferred with clients who manifest phobias or habit disorders. The demonstrated effectiveness of behavioral approaches in resolving disorders has led many counselors to use these techniques. Even with behavioral disorders, however, clients have strong affective and cognitive components. Strong affective approaches in counseling are often used with clients suffering from anxiety or low self-esteem or having difficulty in controlling their feelings. This is a more slow-paced methodology than the other two; however, the pace can be accelerated by combining it with one of the other approaches. The affective methodology typically involves an exploration of the antecedents and nature of the client's problem in the context of the supportive relationship. Such exploration will contribute to the client's self-understanding before behavior changes are made.

It is apparent that each one of these topics in the method of counseling selected by the counselor for the treatment plan can be considered on a continuum. In most cases, counseling may be optimal as an integrated approach. How the counselor determines the balance of ingredients is an important and difficult decision. Taking into account the methodologies with the particular characteristics of the client and the counselor leads to a more effective treatment plan.

Evaluating the Treatment Plan

Although developed early, a treatment plan goes through several phases and needs evaluation (Seligman, 1986). As clients' needs shift and the counselor moves from one phase of treatment to another, there must be a conscious evaluation of what has occurred both in the counseling process and with the individual client. The treatment plan is not a one-time thing nor is its evaluation. The evaluation will help take into account the client's readiness for change and help pace that process. A more gradual approach in counseling may be used with a more fragile client while a more direct approach may be useful with a stronger functioning client. Therefore, pacing and sequencing are two additional aspects of the counseling process that the counselor must consider in treatment planning.

Adjunct Services

Although individual counseling is generally the core service in the counselor's treatment plan, there are other types of services that may be appropriate or necessary for some clients. Many clients can profit from group counseling with others who are experiencing similar problem situations. If there is a relationship problem, couples counseling would be more appropriate than just seeing one of the individuals. In resolving many problems for children and some for adolescents, family counseling brings the whole system to bear on the solution.

Seligman (1986) points out that the information obtained from the diagnostic procedures may indicate that the client's need may not be met exclusively through counseling, and supplemental services are required. When adjunct services are indicated, it is important that they are established in the treatment plan. The counselor needs to address several questions in this process. What additional services are needed? The counselor usually suggests the nature of the services and frequently makes the referral.

Another important question involves the timing of the adjunct services. Is it more appropriate to provide additional services concurrently or, in fact, can they be integrated? At times it may be more appropriate to have the adjunct services before focusing on individual counseling. If the counselor remains the primary service provider, he or she needs to establish the communication relationship with the adjunct service provider. Sometimes the counselor merely makes a referral to an agency or a specific service provider without follow-up. At other times the counselor will receive some follow-up periodically from the adjunct service provider. At times they maintain frequent communication when both services are being provided. They are then able to discuss the sequence of the different aspects of the treatment plan (Seligman, 1986).

Referral

When the counselor recognizes the client needs a service that he or she is unable to provide, a referral is made. The counselor may provide the client with names of agencies or individuals who can provide that service. Sometimes the referral process can be facilitated by the counselor's involvement in calling to assist the client in establishing an appointment. Following most referrals the counselor and the new service provider generally have little communication.

In situations where the client needs additional services but will still be seen by the counselor, it is important that the counselor and other professionals are able to work in collaboration. Each of the professionals will be in charge of an important component of the client's treatment plan, but agree upon who is overseeing the total process. An example might be the counselor who sees a young adolescent for individual counseling but who believes the client could also profit from family therapy. In such a situation, the counselor would continue seeing the individual client while another counselor would see the entire family. It is important that no struggle exists between the collaborating professionals in which one or both believe that his or her mode of treatment is more important or more appropriate for the client. The two must understand how each technique is facilitative to the overall growth of the client.

Consultation

There are times when a counselor will encounter a client with a specific type of problem or situation in which he or she could profit from consultation with another professional. An outside expert can be used by the counselor to assist in understanding the client and possibly in helping to describe an appropriate approach to treatment. At times the consultant may interview, observe, and assist the client; however, the consultant does not actually provide treatment for the client. The consultant's role is to communicate expert information to the counselor who would then continue treatment. Another type of consultation service may also be used as part of the treatment plan: The counselor may provide consultation to parents, teachers, or employers to assist the client to more successful changes. Before the counselor would enter into such a consultation process, it would be discussed with the client and an agreement on the procedure would be made.

Monitoring, Evaluation, and Progress Notes

As the counselor initiates the treatment, he or she must monitor the progress of the client. A variety of things can happen as the treatment plan is implemented, and the counselor uses progress notes to verify client movement in terms of established goals. Once counseling is under way, the client may present new or other concerns that did not arise during the intake process. Such concerns may require modification of the treatment plan in terms of the process of counseling or even necessitate a consultation or referral. There are times when the counselor may feel stuck or confused regarding the case. In this situation consultation may be indicated, and, at times, the counselor may want to refer the client to a different professional. In most situations, progress in counseling will lead to changing regular goals. The movement that the client makes in achieving short-term goals will move him or her toward achievement of long-term goals and will have some impact on what happens in the treatment process. It is important to remember that the treatment plan is not a one-time thing but is modified throughout the process of therapy. Such progress ultimately leads to termination of the counseling relationship.

As counseling continues, the client may show little progress or even regress. If the counselor is monitoring the treatment, he or she will be able to identify what is occurring and possibly have a better idea of what is interfering with the client's progress. Treatment may be affected when something in the client's life situation is changed. For example, if the client or the parents of a client file for divorce, the filing would have an impact on the client and quite possibly the process of treatment.

A discussion between the counselor and client regarding the progress being made will help reinforce the client in terms of the change he or she has achieved. It also permits the counselor and client to clarify where they are in goal achievement and may help them change or make changes in the objectives for the upcoming sessions. The counselor can plan to have these types of collaborative evaluations either spontaneously or at appropriate scheduled intervals. The goals that were established in the first treatment plan can be used to establish a list of accomplishments made by the client, and this can lead to developing new goals and objectives for the continuing counseling relationship.

Progress notes are a part of the counselor's responsibility in most mental health situations. Progress notes are made in the client's chart each time the counselor has an interaction with the client. It is important that the progress notes relate to the goals and methods that were established in the treatment plan. If the sessions are not related to the goals and the counselor is not using the methods, there is a need to reexamine the treatment plan. Counselors typically write notes after each session with the client, and it is advisable to periodically write a summary of the progress that is made.

Having a framework for the progress notes will make them more useful than unstructured comments that are quickly written after the session. An often-used guideline is the acronym SOAP to identify four categories covered in progress notes. Progress notes should briefly summarize the *subjective* reactions to the session, noting the degree of progress made, the client's mood, and the interaction in that session. *Objective* information, which provides specific and factual information on the progress and behavior noted in the session, should be included. The counselor then *analyzes* the implications of the subjective and objective material commenting on the relationship of this session to the treatment goals. The progress notes conclude with *plans* for the future in which the counselor lists tasks that the client agreed to undertake, anything the counselor needs to prepare for the next session, and the areas to be explored or considered in the next session.

Counselors have limited time between interviews and therefore, progress notes tend to be fairly brief. Informative notes can be written briefly, but they provide the basis for the counselor to monitor and refine the treatment process. Counselors should also consider that their progress notes are able to be subpoenaed by courts and may be open to review by the client. Therefore, they should avoid labeling, judging, and using terminology that may be stigmatizing of the client.

Conclusion

Although many systems of diagnosis have been formulated, revised, or modified, no one has met all four of the desired characteristics mentioned earlier. Diagnosis by classification has received considerable criticism. It usually focuses only on the client's weaknesses and fails to look at the strengths that can be used. There is a preoccupation with the client's history. The classification oversimplifies the client, creating the possibility that the counselor may conceptualize and treat the client as a stereotype of the label and miss the client's individuality. The classification systems are not reliable enough to lead to differential counseling plans, and the label suggests a final judgment indicating that diagnosis is an act that is not tentative.

Classification systems have failed to relate the label to differential counseling procedures, and it seems clear that a classification bearing no relation to counseling procedures is of little value in the process. It has been assumed that there should be different counseling methods associated with the various categories of client problems. The attempt to look at the diagnostic categories with this in mind has led to persistence in attempts at classification. Although the classification system does not establish guidelines for treatment, knowledge of the descriptions provided in the DSM-III-R is helpful for counselors in clarifying the symptoms of the client.

Over the years, the opponents of diagnosis, frequently client-centered theorists, have not stressed structure of any sort, including diagnosis or assessment. In their view, diagnosis is palliative and superficial and is sometimes restrictive and negative to the counseling relationship. The basic reason for humanistic theorists' rejection of diagnosis has been their position that the client is the only one who can fully understand the dynamics of her or his own behavior. Diagnosis places evaluation in the hands of someone else, which may foster feelings of dependency and interfere with the empathic relationship.

Actually counselors of nearly all approaches use a process to understand their clients. For many, the process of understanding is used in gathering information that also is helpful in developing the classification aspect of diagnosis. The methods in the diagnostic process can assist the counselor and client to establish common goals, thereby fostering the working alliance. This will also help the counselor develop a treatment plan including the specific methods to help the client achieve the goal.

References

American Psychiatric Association. (1987). *Diagnostic and statistical manual of mental disorders* (3rd ed., rev.). Washington, DC: American Psychiatric Association.

Arkes, H. (1981). Impediments to accurate clinical judgments and possible ways to minimize their impact. *Journal of Consulting and Clinical Psychology, 49,* 323–333.

Beutler, L. E. (1989). Differential treatment selection: The role of diagnosis in psychotherapy. *Psychotherapy, 26,* 271–281.

Bordin, E. S. (1946). Diagnosis in counseling and psychotherapy. *Educational and Psychological Measurement, 6,* 169–184.

Bordin, E. S. (1955). *Psychological counseling.* New York: Appleton-Century-Crofts.

Byrne, R. H. (1958). Proposed revisions of the Bordin-Pepinsky diagnostic constructs. *Journal of Counseling Psychology, 5,* 184–188.

Callis, R. (1960). Toward an integrated theory of counseling. *Journal of College Student Personnel, 1,* 2–9.

Callis, R. (1965). Diagnostic classification as a research tool. *Journal of Counseling Psychology, 12,* 238–243.

Choca, J. (1988). *Manual for clinical psychology trainees.* New York: Brunner/Mazel.

Gauron, E., & Dickinson, J. (1966). Diagnostic decision making in psychiatry. *Archives of General Psychiatry, 14,* 233–237.

Kanfer, F., & Saslow, G. (1965). Behavioral analysis: An alternative to diagnostic classification. *Archives of General Psychiatry, 12,* 529–538.

Katz, M. M., Cole, J. O., & Barton, W. E. (1965). *The role and methodology of classification in psychiatry and psychopathology.* (Publication No. 1584). Washington, DC: U.S. Department of Health, Education, and Welfare.

Kell, B. L., & Mueller, W. J. (1966). *Impact and change: A study of counseling relationships.* New York: Appleton-Century-Crofts.

Koriat, A., Lichtenstein, S., and Fischhoff, B. (1980) Reasons for confidence. *Journal of Experimental Psychology: Human Learning and Memory, 6,* 107–118.

Meehl, P. E. (1954). *Clinical versus statistical prediction.* Minneapolis: University of Minnesota Press.

Menninger, K., Ellenberger, H., Pruyser, P., & Mayman, M. (1958). The unitary concept of mental illness. *Bulletin of the Menninger Clinic, 22,* 4–12.

Menninger, K., Mayman, M., & Pruyser, P. (1963). *The vital balance.* New York: Viking Press.

Osipow, S., Walsh, W. B., & Tosi, D. (1984). *A survey of counseling methods.* Homewood, IL: Dorsey.

Pepinsky, H. B. (1948). The selection and use of diagnostic categories in clinical counseling. *Applied Psychological Monographs, 15.*

Pepinsky, H. B., & Pepinsky, P. (1954). *Counseling: Theory and practice.* New York: Ronald Press.

Persons, J. (1986). The advantages of studying psychological phenomena rather than psychiatric diagnosis. *American Psychologist, 41,* 1252–1260.

Robinson, F. P. (1963). Modern approaches to counseling diagnosis. *Journal of Counseling Psychology, 10,* 325–333.

Rogers, C. R. (1951). *Client-centered therapy.* Boston: Houghton Mifflin.

Schacht, T., & Nathan, P. (1977). But is it good for psychologists? *American Psychologist, 32,* 1017–1025.

Seligman, L. (1986). *Diagnosis and treatment planning in counseling.* New York: Human Sciences Press.

Sharma, S. L. (1970). A historical background of the development of nosology in psychiatry and psychology. *American Psychologist, 25,* 248–253.

Shectman, F., De La Torre, J., & Garza. A. C. (1979). Diagnosis separate from psychotherapy: Pros and cons. *American Journal of Psychotherapy, 33,* 291–302.

Snyder, M. (1981). Seek, and ye shall find: Testing hypotheses about other people. In E. T. Higgins, C. P. Herman, and M. P. Zanna (Eds.), *Social Cognition: The Ontario Symposium* (vol. 1, pp. 277–303). Hillsdale, NJ: Earlbaum.

Spitzer, R., Gibbon, M., Skodol, A., Williams, J., & First, M. (1989). *DSM-III-R Casebook.* Washington, DC: American Psychiatric Association.

Strupp, H. (1978). Psychotherapy research and practice: An overview. In S. Garfield and A. Bergin (Eds.), *Handbook of Psychotherapy and Behavior Change.* New York: John Wiley and Sons.

Super, D. E. (1957). The preliminary appraisal in vocational counseling. *Personnel and Guidance Journal, 36,* 154–161.

Williamson, E. G., & Darley, J. G. (1937). *Student personnel work.* New York: McGraw-Hill.

Wrenn, G. G. (1951). *Student personnel work in college.* New York: Ronald Press.

16

Counseling for Decision Making/Problem Solving

Should I go to college? Which school should I attend? Is marriage at this point a reasonable alternative for me? Should I quit my job? What is the right occupation for me? As a dual career couple, how should we job hunt: his first or mine first? Shall I get a divorce? Should we have children? Should we vacation at the shore or in the mountains? If we have children, should I return to work? Should I retire? Should I "come out of the closet" and live an open homosexual life-style? These are but a few examples of the types of decisions with which people are confronted each day. Many of us both need and want assistance with these types of decisions. They bring individuals to counseling; they arise as a focus of counseling for clients already in a counseling relationship.

Despite the fact that we all daily make decisions of varying importance, an alarming number of people have no idea of how or why they make decisions; consequently, the decisions that they make are less wise than they otherwise might be. When the decisions to be made are relatively trivial, the consequences of faulty decision making are benign; however, when the decisions are vital, the consequences can be psychologically devastating. As a result, counseling that focuses on decision making or problem solving has become a popular area of study and application for counselors in diverse settings.

Some Basics of Decision Making

There are many ways of viewing the study of decision making. Almost two decades ago, Jepsen and Dilley (1974) proposed that decision making or problem solving could be conceived of as occurring along two dimensions: short-range changes versus long-range changes and high understanding versus low understanding on the part of the decider. Although their paradigm is meant for vocational decision making, they concluded that it is applicable to different types of decisions as well. If one dimension (amount of understanding) is placed on a vertical axis and the other dimension (distance in time) is placed on a horizontal axis, the result is a representation of decision types as depicted in Figure 16-1. Each quadrant consists of a combination of time and understanding elements.

Herr and Cramer (1992) reviewed the decision-making literature and reached several conclusions. Among these were the following: (1) Many factors in decision making will not be controlled by the person making the decision (e.g., the state of the economy). (2) Deciders are not likely to be able to get and to use all possible information in making a decision. Consequently, they use what they have and then rationalize the result. (3) The evaluation of decision making is frequently more a question of process than of outcome. In long-range decisions, the result of a decision can be years away, so an outcome is too far removed from the counseling process to be judged. The result is that we turn to process evaluations, and we say that a decision is "good" if it was made logically and consistently and in accordance with "good" procedures and an accepted model of decision making. (4) Individuals can be taught a procedure not only to make a decision in the counseling

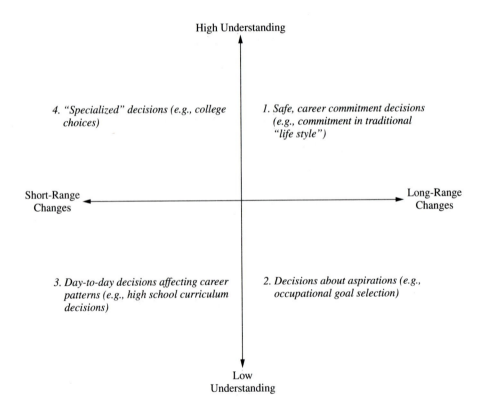

FIGURE 16-1   Theoretical Vocational Decision Types

Source: D. A. Jepsen and J. S. Dilley, Vocational decision-making models: A review and comparative analysis. *Review of Educational Research,* 1974, *44* (3), 334. Copyright 1974 by the American Educational Research Association. Reprinted by permission of the publisher.

process, but also to generalize that skill in order to make decisions throughout life. (5) Many moderators, mediators, and correlates affect people's ability to make decisions. Some of these factors are values, propensity for risk, achievement motivation (e.g., fear of failure, fear of success), coping style, and age. Not quite so clearly related are such factors as gender, anxiety, and ego identity status, among others. (6) We do not currently understand why decision makers emphasize specific factors or information in their decisions or how they use these data. Later in this chapter, we shall describe some of the external and internal variables that impinge on decision making and lead to decision-making *styles*. (7) All models of decision making assume motivation on the part of the chooser (or seek to establish a readiness). (8) The effects of information on decision making are complex and not completely clear. All in all, Herr and Cramer state:

> In summary, all of these decision-making models for use in individual counseling are action-oriented. By whatever terminology they are called, they address choice in a staged, systematic manner. They are intended to assist individuals in filtering objective data through subjective systems of risk-taking, emotionality, utility determination, and so on. Again, no single model has been determined to be superior to any other; yet each implies its unique success. They suggest to counselors that virtually any model of assisting an individual in . . . decision-making—extant or yet to be invented—can be successful if based on sound theoretical or research findings, and if operationalized in logical, consistent ways. (1992, p. 426)

The remainder of this chapter discusses counseling stages in decision making and problem solving, styles of decision making, and three types of intervention to enhance client proficiencies: counseling, groups, and self-directed methods.

Stages in Decision Making/Problem Solving

Decision making and problem solving are predominantly left-brain types of activities. Consequently, the most common decision-making strategies are step-by-step, rational, logical, and by-the-numbers sorts of procedures. They will differ in the variables that clients are encouraged to examine (e.g., values, self-concept, motivation) and in terms of the degree to which environmental factors are considered (i.e., the extent to which clients are regarded as captains of their fates and masters of their souls). They also depart from each other in judging how much information and of what type the client needs to consider and how closely probabilities need to be determined and adhered to in the decision-making process.

Given all of these potential differences, however, theoreticians and researchers have evolved various stage models to describe prescriptively how clients should make decisions. These stage models, in our judgment, are more similar than different. Consequently, we present only a relatively small number of them in order to provide the reader with a flavor of their content.

Janis and Mann (1977) offer a five-stage process of decision making; each stage is accompanied by key questions (p. 172).

Stage	*Key Questions*
1. Appraising the Challenge	Are the risks serious if I don't change?
2. Surveying Alternatives	Is this alternative an acceptable means of dealing with the challenge? Have I sufficiently surveyed the available alternatives?
3. Weighing Alternatives	Which alternative is best? Could the best alternative meet the essential requirements?
4. Deliberating about Commitment	Shall I implement the best alternative and allow others to know?
5. Adhering despite Negative Feedback	Are the risks serious if I *don't* change? Are the risks serious if I *do* change?

Social problem solving is a frequent type of decisional focus in counseling. Cognitive/behavioral therapists refer to problem-orientation cognitions in this regard and argue that training clients in problem-solving skills will increase social competence and help to prevent the development of new maladaptive behaviors. Virtually every theoretical counseling orientation addresses problem solving. One of the more well-known approaches is D'Zurilla's (1988) problem-solving training (PST). In this model, the problem is first defined and formulated by gathering information, clarifying the nature of the problem, setting a realistic problem-solving goal, and determining the significance of the problem for personal-social well-being. Secondly, counseling helps the client to generate as many alternative solutions as possible. Third comes the actual decision-making phase of PST when the client is assisted to judge and to compare the available alternatives and to select the best from among them. The client does this by eliminating obviously unacceptable solutions, by anticipating solution outcomes for each remaining alternative, and by evaluating each solution in terms of emotional well-being, amount of time and effort required, and a comparison of psychological benefits and costs. Finally, the client implements the solution and verifies its "goodness." There is an obvious temptation to consider PST and all similar decision-making systems as entirely rational, but even though it has a huge element of rationality, it is psychological as well in the sense that it is an active coping process and the client brings more than simply cognition to the act. Behavioral and emotional components also interact to lead to effective problem solving and decision making.

A third illustrative stage model is that of Van Hoose and Worth (1982). Their incorporation of problem-solving techniques in the counseling process includes the following stages.

1. *Exploration*: the problem is defined; potential solutions are generated and reviewed.
2. *Commitment*: both counselor and client commit to a course of action chosen from among the alternative solutions.

3. *Intervention*: the choice is actually implemented and counselors intervene at this stage, essentially to teach the client what he or she needs to effect the choice.
4. *Evaluation*: the client and counselor jointly determine the outcomes of the problem-solving process.

Another problem-solving/decision-making approach is described by Martin and Hiebert (1985) in their concept of *instructional counseling*. They propose a goal-setting stage during which the client and counselor determine what the client wants to achieve, and clients are introduced to problem solving/decision making as viewed from the orientation of an instructional counselor. When the problem has been operationally defined in concrete terms and the client's feelings about it have been explored, the counselor makes some determination of the client's current problem-solving and decision-making skills. Based on this preassessment, objectives are formed so that the client knows exactly what must be done to address the problem (e.g., formulating and evaluating alternatives, choosing the most desirable alternative). These objectives are implemented through counseling activities and homework. Finally, evaluation takes place.

Blocher (1987) expands the number of steps to 11 in a comprehensive, rational decision-making process. He suggests (1) identifying the decision to be made; (2) listing the alternative courses of action; (3) listing the desired outcomes and establishing priorities; (4) listing and weighing the probable costs; (5) reviewing the lists of alternatives, outcomes, and costs and specifying the kinds of information needed to reduce uncertainty as much as possible; (6) searching widely and extensively for needed information; (7) organizing and summarizing needed information; (8) reviewing each alternative; (9) choosing from among the alternatives; (10) implementing a decision; and (11) evaluating and reviewing decisions.

Finally, Gati (1986, 1990) proposes another 11-step process for decision making. In what he calls the Sequential Elimination Approach (SEM), he advocates a continual ranking of alternatives, progressively eliminating those that fail to measure up to others. Once the counselor has identified the client's specific decision problem (e.g., lack of information, inability to deal with uncertainty, etc.) and the client's decision-making style, SEM becomes a possible intervention mode. Here is Gati's sequence of stages:

1. Identify the client's problem.
2. Help the client define and structure the decision problem.
3. Present the SEM as a framework for decision making.
4. Help the client to identify the aspects that are important to him or her and relevant to the elimination process.
5. Help the client to clarify the relative importance of the aspects enumerated in Stage 4.
6. Help the client to identify the range of levels considered as acceptable or satisfying with respect to each of the more important aspects.
7. Help the client to organize the alternatives into meaningful clusters in order to reduce the complexity of the elimination process.
8. Provide feedback to the client regarding the available alternatives that remain after each additional aspect has been considered.

9. Help the client to check the relative insensitivity of the results to any particular judgment.

10. Help the client rank the alternatives that survive the elimination by identifying relations of dominance.

11. Help the client to outline the steps to be taken to actualize the preferred alternative(s).

All of these staged procedures, then, call for clients to invest themselves cognitively, emotionally, and behaviorally in a systematic effort to make a decision or to solve a problem. Once the system is effected, it is presumed that clients will be able to apply it in any future decision-making or problem-solving situation.

Styles of Decision Making

We have just reviewed prescriptive writing about decision making/problem solving that tells us how people *ought* to make decisions. Since we do not live in the best of all possible worlds, individuals often do not make decisions as we would prescribe their being made. Instead, clients rely on one or more of a variety of styles, many of which are countertherapeutic and counterproductive. Research into these often maladaptive behaviors has produced a body of descriptive literature. That research is summarized below.

Much of the literature on effective and ineffective styles of decision making emanates from the field of vocational psychology. For example, a study by Larson, Heppner, Ham, and Dugan (1988) revealed four types of career-undecided college students. One type was termed *planless avoiders* (about one-quarter of the sample). These people were the least informed about career-planning activities, had engaged in minimum problem-solving activity, and rated their problem-solving ability negatively (indicating a lack of confidence and avoidant problem-solving attitudes and behaviors). Thus, they lacked information and perceived themselves as poor problem solvers. The second type was called *informed decisives* (a very small group) who possessed a great deal of career information, but nevertheless reported a lack of confidence and the avoidance of problems. Thus, they had more than adequate information but appraised themselves negatively. A third group (one-quarter of the sample) were designated *confident but uninformed*. These students offered a positive appraisal of their ability to solve problems, but were deficient in information about the career planning process. The final group, and by far the largest of the types (almost one-half), were the *uninformed*. These individuals had some self-perceived ability to solve problems and possessed some career information, but obviously did not have enough information to make a decision. Research such as this suggests that counselors need to appraise their clients' status in terms of their self-perceptions of problem-solving abilities, their past experience in decision making, and the amount and quality of the knowledge they possess.

One other example from career decision making is provided by Lucas and Epperson (1990). Using male and female undergraduates, they determined that five clusters of undecideds emerged. Cluster 1 (21.4 percent) were high anxious, low self-esteem, external locus of control, dependent decision-making style, and needful of occupational information, among other factors. Cluster 2 (19.9 percent) exhibited some anxiety, below-average self-esteem, somewhat external locus of control, and some need for vocational information. Cluster 3 (29.6 percent) had little anxiety, high self-esteem, internal locus of control, but still needed occupational information. Cluster 4 (18.4 percent) showed some anxiety, slightly depressed self-esteem, strong internal locus of control, and no need for occupational information. Cluster 5 (10.7 percent) demonstrated little or no anxiety, high self-esteem, external locus of control, a nondependent style, and no need for occupational information. It is clear that clients will differ in terms of a variety of variables, not the least of which are decision-making styles and anxiety. The curvilinear relationship between anxiety and decisiveness is also confirmed by Fuqua, Blum, and Hartman (1988). Whether one causes the other or they simply covary is moot at this point.

Lunneborg (1978) offers an additional paradigm of styles in decision making based on the Career Decision-Making Questionnaire (CDMQ). A *planful* style is one much like those described previously in prescriptive methods; that is, one characterized by a logical and systematic approach to the task. An *intuitive* style is one in which the decider relies on internal affective states to make decisions (e.g., "It feels right"). A *dependent* style is one in which a person's decisions are very much determined by the responses of others—family, friends, peers, and so on. In general, those who have a dependent style are people who are considerably less decisive.

Some evidence (at least in terms of career decision making) supports the belief that style is related to ego identity status. Blustein and Phillips (1990) found that individuals who are defined as possessing a stable ego identity (i.e., people who have experienced some exploration and have come out with a clear commitment to their ego identity) tend to employ rational and systematic decision-making strategies. On the other hand, subjects whose identity status is foreclosed (i.e., people who have a firm level of commitment only by taking on the attitudes of their parents without thinking or exploring) tend to rely on dependent strategies. Those with a diffused ego identity status (i.e., no exploration or commitment) primarily rely on intuitive or dependent styles or demonstrate an absence of systematic and internal styles.

Arroba (1977) has offered six empirically derived styles of decision making. A person who uses a *logical* approach appraises a situation coldly and objectively and makes a choice on the basis of what is "best." Another style of decision making involves *no thought*—no objective consideration occurs. The *hesitant* style is one in which a decider keeps postponing a final commitment to an alternative and is unable to make a decision. This type may reflect the so-called indecisive personality. The *emotional* style of decision making is based on what an individual subjectively wants or likes. In the *compliant* style, decisions are made in accordance with others' expectations. It is a passive sort of decision making. Finally, *intuitive* decision makers base their choices only on personal feelings of rightness or availability. There is clearly overlap between the Arroba and Lunneborg classifications.

Janis and Mann (1977), as well as speaking to the question of an effective, prescriptive approach to decision making, also identify four defective decision-making styles. In *unconflicted adherence*, an individual just denies any serious risks from a current course of action. Denial is always a dysfunctional defense mechanism. With *unconflicted change to a new course of action* the person simply denies any serious risks in making a decision or change. Again, a different form of harmful denial is in effect. In *defense avoidance* the person in a decision situation avoids anything that might stimulate choice anxiety or painful feelings and gives up trying to find a solution. Lastly, in *hypervigilance*, the decider becomes very emotionally excited as the time of the decision becomes more pressing.

These examples of decision-making styles should be sufficient to alert the counselor to the fact that clients will bring with them distinct individual differences in their approach to problem solving as well as in their ability to use developed or undeveloped personal resources. They will differ in terms of their motivation to make decisions and their perceptions of impeding external barriers that may make it difficult for clients to exercise the free and unencumbered choice that we all should have. They will vary in terms of the values that they place on various choices and of the amount and type of information that they perceive is necessary or that they are willing to acquire. They will present with all sorts of dysfunctional and idiosyncratic styles of decision making, ranging from fatalistic ("Que sera sera") to compliant ("Whatever you say, Dr. Smith") to delaying (As Scarlett O'Hara said, "I'll think about it tomorrow") to paralytic ("I just can't do it").

Interventions for Decision Making/Problem Solving

In general, interventions to enhance clients' abilities to solve problems effectively or to make "good" decisions can take three forms: one is counseling (usually one-to-one, but sometimes group); a second is the use of structured groups; and a third is the application of self-directed programs. Each of these is discussed in the following sections.

Counseling

For many theorists, counseling itself is nothing more nor less than a problem-solving process (Dixon & Glover, 1984). Starting phenomenologically, they postulate that all counseling relationships focus on the perception of clients that they have problems, either generalized or specifically stated. If these theoreticians are accurate, then evaluation is made comparatively easy, for the "proof" of successful counseling is the degree to which clients' problems are solved.

Some regard decision making as a part of problem-solving training (PST). In all cases of problem-solving counseling, the problem is defined, goals are selected, and a strategy is chosen and implemented. In almost every case, that strategy is one or another of the decision-making models. We are generally using the terms interchangeably. As a rule, the outcomes of decision making can be viewed in terms of their effects on the personal/social/occupational/educational development of the decider as well as in terms of both long-term and short-term consequences.

Sometimes clients will consistently make poor decisions or will be unable to make decisions, not because of skill deficiencies or lack of "know-how," but because of internal states that prevent them from deciding. The so-called indecisive individual is one such example. Indecisiveness is a construct that describes people who have a generalized trait predisposition that renders them incapable of making any type of decision. They bring this deficit to all sorts of specific decision situations. While these individuals are very few in number, they do exist and must be dealt with. Most people who are undecided and who experience indecision, however, are state rather than trait deficient. Another example is seen in individuals who have thought disorders and are out of touch with reality or otherwise incapable of rationally generating and processing information.

All decisions involve judgment. People tend to make common errors of judgment; counselors need to be alert to these errors in the judgment process. Rachlin (1989) delineates examples of such errors, including not having sufficient and appropriate information, poor cognition (biases), perception mistakes, misunderstanding of probabilities, and judgments made in a social context (ascribing "right" and "wrong" values).

All decisions are made under conditions of *uncertainty* to one degree or another. Many researchers (see, for example, Yates, 1990) suggest mathematical modeling as a way to deal with uncertainty, but few of us have either the sophisticated knowledge or the patience to formalize mathematically a determination of risk for each decision that we make. What is clear is that some of us have an aversion to risk and others of us have a high propensity for risk. Yet, even then, many people are not consistent in their behavior even if they appraise risk correctly; that is, clients are sometimes risk-averse for decisions that will surely give them gains and risk-seeking for other events that have a high probability of loss. It is, then, the counselor's focus to point out the incongruities and to help the client to understand what is happening.

Hogarth (1987) presents a conflict model of choice, postulating that individuals make choices to satisfy needs (physiological, social, psychological, and so on). Different types of conflict are entailed in any choice. Conflict is defined as incompatibility, or the fact that an end cannot be obtained without giving up something else. Conflicts are resolved by balancing the costs and benefits of alternative actions.

The perception of what causes the problem for which the client seeks a solution frequently differs among theorists. Psychodynamically oriented counselors believe that problems lie within the person and that we should consequently examine a person's needs, drives, and so on. Other theoretical orientations combine internal and external factors in looking at the etiology of problems and for their solution. It is also possible for the cause of a problem and its solution to be completely external to the individual; it is unlikely, however, that such conditions would bring the person to counseling.

One of the best summaries of the literature in decision-making counseling is provided by Olson, McWhirter, and Horan (1989). Their précis of assessment questions and intervention strategies in decision-making counseling is reproduced in Table 16-1.

Most individual counseling orientations related to problem solving/decision making begin with evolving a statement of the problem and the desired solution (goal identification). The client is encouraged to "own" the problem or the responsibility for making the decision. Usually, the counselor and the client will cooperatively define the problem and generate a statement of desired outcome. The more concretely the goals can be stated, the better. Once this aim is accomplished, most counseling interventions will engage in an inventory of both the resources of the client to solve the problem or to make the decision and the necessary skills and information that are lacking. Based on these client resources and needs and in terms of the problem and the hoped-for solution, the remaining course of the counseling is plotted and can take the form of any of the stages of decision

TABLE 16-1   Assessment Questions and Intervention Strategies in Decision-Making Counseling

Summary Model	Assessment Questions	Intervention Strategies (when the answer is no)
Conceptualization	(1) Is affective arousal low?	listening (extinction) relaxation training desensitization and variations cognitive restructuring
	(2) Can client correctly define problem as one of choice?	paraphrasing probe (cuing and reinforcing) socratic dialoguing
	(3) Can client explain the decision-making paradigm?	cognitive restructuring emotional role playing cognitive modeling verbal reinforcement
Enlargement of response repertoire	(4) Has client avoided an impulsive response?	thought stopping-substitution covert sensitization outcome psychodrama emotional role playing cognitive restructuring skill-building interventions
	(5) Has client identified all alternatives known to counselor?	creative instructional set originality training brainstorming metaphorical thinking modeling
	(6) Will client search for additional alternatives?	verbal cuing and reinforcement modeling
Identification of discriminative stimuli	(7) Has client identified all discriminative stimuli known to counselor?	outcome psychodrama modeling
	(8) Will client search for additional discriminative stimuli?	verbal cuing and reinforcement modeling simulation strategies
Response selection	(9) Does client report adaptive utilities and probability estimates?	cognitive restructuring emotional role playing outcome psychodrama induced cognitive dissonance awareness of rationalizations peer modeling
	(10) Can client explain a response-selection paradigm?	modeling variations
	(11) Are client's skills sufficient to implement the selected response?	comprehensive behavioral programming stress inoculation emotional inoculation

Source: C. Olson, E. McWhirter, and J. J. Horan, A decision-making model applied to career counseling. *Journal of Career Development,* 1989, *16,* 114–115. Reprinted by permission.

making/problem solving identified earlier in this chapter. The chosen solution or decision is then implemented and, in so far as possible, evaluated.

By way of illustration, we may consider the case of a couple who present in marriage counseling as disillusioned with their marriage and unsure of whether or not to continue the relationship. They are first assisted to state the problem in very concrete terms and to verbalize a desired solution. First, they must be able to verbalize whether they want the union dissolved or maintained or some point in between, such as separation. For the sake of example, let us assume that maintenance is the goal. They next must be helped to identify all of the behaviors that are leading to the difficulty—extended family, sexual dysfunction, relationship issues, household management, child rearing, values, budgeting, and so on. Current coping patterns and resources are identified, and the couple is helped to generate alternative behavioral possibilities that could assuage sources of tension. The couple next weighs each alternative in terms of its psychological costs and benefits. One or more alternatives are selected and implemented. With continuing monitoring of the choice(s) by the couple and the counselor, an evaluation is made to determine if the process needs to be recycled. This type of intervention should not be confused with the semantically similar orientation to family therapy known as problem-solving therapy (Haley, 1976). The only commonality is that a problem is clearly identified and defined. The differences are that the problem is thought to arise and be maintained because of an interactional sequence in the family. Interventions take the form of the therapist's giving directives, either straight or paradoxical.

Gazda, Childers, and Brooks (1987) propose that decision-making/problem-solving skills are really a part of life-skills training. As such, they are equally applicable in the school, at work, in the family, or in the community in both prevention and remediation modes. There are many life-skills training models, all of which are directed at helping clients develop the skills necessary for effective living. Problem solving/decision making becomes one of four generic life skills, along with interpersonal communications/human relations, physical fitness/health maintenance, and identity development/purpose in life. The specific form of the problem-solving/decision-making life skill is very much like all of those previously discussed: recognize a problem, define it (in terms of both situational and personal elements), generate alternatives, decide (on the basis of desirability of outcome and probability of outcome), implement the decision, and assess feedback.

Groups

Systems such as problem-solving training (PST) and life-skills training (LST) can be effected in groups as well as with individuals. Indeed, problem solving/decision making is particularly effective in structured groups of one type or another. This result is especially the case, for example, with career decision making, wherein the use of structured groups has produced outcomes just about as effective as those achieved through individual counseling (see, for example, Oliver & Spokane, 1988). A few examples of decision-making workshops, courses, and other structured groups will serve to illustrate the types of decision-making/problem-solving interventions possible in groups.

Savickas (1990) reports the results of implementing a career decision-making course with tenth grade students. Using principles of Crites's (1978) Career Maturity Inventory

(CMI), these students were provided didactic career counseling by means of a career decision-making course that aimed to enhance necessary attitudes and competencies for readiness to make career choices. Twenty sessions were effected in six classes, using a different teacher in each class in an urban, midwestern high school. Four other classes served as controls. The results suggest that compared to the controls, the participating students "improved their foresight and reduced their decisional difficulties" (p. 275).

Mann et al. (1989) conducted a workshop to teach generic decision-making skills based on Janis and Mann's (1977) conflict theory and the five types of decision strategies outlined earlier. Participants fell into two groups: *Problem clients* were those who had specific decision-making problems and who rated themselves as poor decision makers; *learners* were clients who appraised themselves as competent decision makers but who simply wanted to improve their abilities. These two groups reacted differently to the intervention, causing the investigators to conclude that the more homogeneous the group, the more a general, "all-purpose" decision-making workshop will succeed; the more disparate the decision-making competencies of the group and the more varied their reasons for attending, the more likely that the counselor will be confronted with difficulties.

One final example utilizing very small groups (N=2) is presented by Mitchell and Krumboltz (1987) who provided an intervention to reduce anxiety about career decision making and to stimulate career exploratory behaviors. They compared subjects given a cognitive restructuring intervention with subjects exposed to decision-making training and those who served as controls and determined that cognitive restructuring produced superior decision-making outcomes, including client satisfaction with the decisions made. In this study, clients were seen in groups of two for treatment purposes. The cognitive restructuring interventions were applied over five sessions (one per week) and included "(a) didactic instruction about the role of maladaptive beliefs and generalizations in career indecision, (b) training in the monitoring of personal beliefs and their effect on behavior, (c) modeling by the counselor of the rational evaluation of beliefs and identification based on that evaluation, (d) feedback to the clients on attempted modification of generalizations and beliefs, and (e) performance (homework) assignments designed to test new beliefs for their accuracy and usefulness" (p. 172). The decision-making skills program utilized is one known as DECIDES (Hamel, 1980) an acronym in which D=define, E=establish an action plan, C=clarify values, I=identify alternatives, D=discover probable outcomes, E=eliminate alternatives systematically, and S=start action.

Self-Directed Methods

Because decision making/problem solving has such a large cognitive component, many researchers believe that choices can be enhanced by self-directed programs delivered via workbooks, computers, gaming and simulation, and other interactive media. We present a few examples.

The shelves of any large bookstore are crammed full of workbooks that take individuals through a decision-making system related to career-planning, life-planning, or some combination (see, for example, Mitchell & Young, 1982; Hecklinger & Curtain, 1987).

What all of these fill-in-the blank workbooks have in common is that they are self-paced, claim to be "practical," and take the user through a series of decision-making/problem-solving steps such as those identified earlier. What is typically missing is the opportunity to process with a counselor.

Examples of more sophisticated decision-making systems are Holland's (1985) Self-Directed Search (SDS) and Harrington and O'Shea's (1982) Career Decision-Making System (CDM). The SDS is a self-administered, self-scored, and self-interpreted instrument designed to help high school students through adults to plan careers. Self-assessments of interests, abilities, and competencies are used to produce a modal personality type code that then can be related to about 1,200 occupations similarly coded. The usual caveats in employing such instruments are present here: mistakes in self-correcting, inaccurate self-estimates, lack of psychological processing of the results, and so on. As a stimulus to decision making, however, we believe that instruments such as the SDS serve a very useful purpose.

The CDM is also intended for both youths and adults and is focused specifically on career decision making. Self-assessments of interests, occupational and school subject preferences, work values, and estimated abilities are related to potentially appropriate occupational groups, and then the user is helped to explore specific occupations within these groups. Self-scoring and self-interpretation are hallmarks (although for this instrument and most similar ones, computerized versions are available for administration, scoring, and reporting). Again, we view such instruments as preludes to and aids in decision making/problem solving and not as be-all's and end-all's.

Computerized programs exist and continue to proliferate. Almost all extant paper-and-pencil decision-making systems have a computerized version. For instance, *Decision-Making: A Methodical Approach* (Career Aids) helps the user to analyze options and provides practice in solving problems. *The Idea Generator* (Experience in Software, Inc.) helps clients to deal with academic, personal, and career problems by defining them, generating ideas, and determining the best ones. *MAPS: Methodical Aid to Problem Solving* (Educational Media Corp.) is based on social learning theory and is intended as an adjunct to counseling. It focuses on client motivation to solve the problem and the skills and knowledge required to do so. These are but a few of many problem-solving programs available. All of these programs and others designed for different counseling purposes (e.g., self-concept exploration) may be found annotated in Walz and Bleuer, 1989.

Summary

Although decision-making/problem-solving counseling is usually viewed as a cognitively oriented, systematic type of activity, it requires psychological investment on the part of the client. Decision making is invariably more complex than it appears on the surface; consequently, clients will often exhibit dysfunctional decision-making styles. Interventions may take the form of individual counseling, groups, and self-directed programs.

References

Arroba, T. (1977). Styles of decision-making and their use: An empirical study. *British Journal of Guidance and Counseling, 5,* 149–158.

Blocher, D. H. (1987). *The professional counselor.* New York: Macmillan Publishing Company.

Blustein, D. L., & Phillips, S. D. (1990). Relation between ego identity statuses and decision-making styles. *Journal of Counseling Psychology, 37,* 160–168.

Crites, J. O. (1978). *Career maturity inventory.* Monterey, CA: CTB/McGraw-Hill.

Dixon, D. N., & Glover, J. A. (1984). *Counseling: A problem-solving approach.* New York: John Wiley & Sons.

D'Zurilla, T. J. (1988). The problem solving therapies. In K. S. Dobson (Ed.). *Handbook of cognitive-behavioral therapies* (pp. 85–135). New York: Guilford.

Fuqua, D. R., Blum, C. R., & Hartman, B. W. (1988). Empirical support for the differential diagnosis of career indecision. *The Career Development Quarterly, 36,* 364–373.

Gati, I. (1986). Making career decisions—A sequential elimination approach. *Journal of Counseling Psychology, 33,* 408–417.

Gati, I. (1990). Why, when, and how to take into account the uncertainty involved in career decisions. *Journal of Counseling Psychology, 37,* 277–280.

Gazda, G. M., Childers, W. C., & Brooks, D. K., Jr. (1987). *Foundations of counseling and human services.* New York: McGraw-Hill Book Company.

Haley, J. (1976). *Problem solving therapy.* San Francisco: Jossey-Bass.

Hamel, D. A. (1980). *The effect of decision training on selected measures of career decision making competence.* Unpublished doctoral dissertation, Stanford University.

Harrington, T. J., & O'Shea, A. J. (1982). *Career decision-making system.* Circle Pines, MN: American Guidance Service.

Hecklinger, F. J., & Curtain, B. M. (1987). *Training for life: A practical guide to career and life planning.* Dubuque, IA: Kendall/Hunt.

Herr, E. L., & Cramer, S. H. (1992). *Career guidance and counseling through the lifespan: Systematic approaches.* New York: Harper/Collins.

Hogarth, R. (1987). *Judgment and choice: The psychology of decision* (2nd ed.). New York: John Wiley & Sons.

Holland, J. L. (1985). *Self-directed search: A guide to educational and vocational planning.* Odessa, FL: PAR (Psychological Assessment Resources, Inc.).

Janis, I. L., & Mann, L. (1977). *Decision-making: A psychological analysis on conflict, choice, and commitment.* New York: The Free Press.

Jepsen, D. A., & Dilley, J. S. (1974). Vocational decision-making models: A review and comparative analysis. *Review of Educational Research, 44* (3), 331–349.

Larson, L. M., Heppner, P. P., Ham, T., & Dugan, K. (1988). Investigating multiple subtypes of career indecision through cluster analysis. *Journal of Counseling Psychology, 35,* 439–446.

Lucas, M. S., & Epperson, D. L. (1990). Types of vocational undecidedness: A replication and refinement. *Journal of Counseling Psychology, 37,* 383–388.

Lunneborg, P. M. (1978). Sex and career decision-making styles. *Journal of Counseling Psychology, 25,* 299–305.

Mann, L., Beswick, G., Allouache, P., & Ivey, M. (1989). Decision workshops for the improvement of decision making skills and confidence. *Journal of Counseling and Development, 67,* 478–481.

Martin, J., & Hiebert, B. A. (1985). *Instructional counseling.* Pittsburgh: University of Pittsburgh Press.

Mitchell, C., & Young, W. (1982). *Career exploration: A self-paced approach*. Dubuque, IA: Kendall/Hunt.

Mitchell, L. K., & Krumboltz, J. D. (1987). Cognitive restructuring and decision-making training on career indecision. *Journal of Counseling and Development, 66*, 171–174.

Oliver, L. W., & Spokane, A. R. (1988). Career intervention outcome: What contributes to client gain? *Journal of Counseling Psychology, 35*, 447–462.

Olson, C., McWhirter, E., & Horan, J. J. (1989). A decision-making model applied to career counseling. *Journal of Career Development, 16*, 107–117.

Rachlin, H. (1989). *Judgment, decision, and choice: A cognitive/behavioral synthesis*. New York: W. H. Freeman.

Savickas, M. L. (1990). The career decision-making course: Description and field test. *The Career Development Quarterly, 38*, 275–284.

Van Hoose, W. H., & Worth, M. R. (1982). *Counseling adults: A developmental approach*. Belmont, CA: Brooks/Cole.

Walz, G. R., & Bleuer, J. C. (1989). *Counseling software guide*. Washington, DC: American Association for Counseling and Development.

Yates, J. R. (1990). *Judgment and decision-making*. Englewood Cliffs, NJ: Prentice Hall.

Chapter *17*

Testing and Counseling

Testing is a flash word that evokes in people all sorts of negative images and reactions. The first image called up is one of the use of tests to make institutional decisions about persons. These decisions typically involve some sort of gatekeeping purpose; that is, they are utilized in deciding who will or will not be given opportunity to engage in some sort of behavior—schooling, training, a job, a promotion, tracking, and so on. These uses of tests for personnel selection, classification, and placement are thought by many to be undemocratic, nonegalitarian, discriminatory, and not based on sufficiently sound empirical findings to justify their widespread application.

While it is moot whether tests should be employed in the above fashion, it is less of an issue whether or not tests should be utilized in counseling. If assessment is applied in counseling, the purpose always is *to inform*. On the one hand, some tests and inventories primarily inform the *counselor*; on the other hand, some assessment devices mainly inform the *client*. Table 17-1 displays examples of these two different types of informational assessment. While there is certainly some overlap of purpose, the distinction serves a heuristic purpose.

It is important to recognize the limitations of this chapter. Because of space considerations, we have limited our discussion to the use of tests in counseling as the counselor and the client cooperatively sort through the results of assessment. We are *not* dealing with psychodiagnostics in the sense of classifying or identifying problem behaviors or intra-psychic states or in the sense of trying to determine the etiology of these conditions. Further, we are *not* here concerned with the use of these types of tests to instruct clinicians on possible appropriate treatments or for evaluating the results of the application of treatments. For example, the standard psychological assessment battery for adult "patients" consists of the Rorschach, Thematic Apperception Test (TAT), and Wechsler Adult Intelligence Scale—Revised (WAIS-R) (Wetzler, 1989). The use of these types of tests for purposes only to inform the counselor is not dealt with here. We concentrate in this chapter chiefly on the use of tests to inform clients.

Any assessment instrument given to inform the client must be interpreted. It is essentially this activity—one of helping clients to translate test results into meaningful

TABLE 17-1   Examples of Tests to Inform the Client and Tests to Inform the Counselor

Primarily Client	Primarily Counselor

1. Aptitude Tests
   a. Differential Aptitude Test (DAT)
   b. Armed Services Vocational Aptitude Battery (ASVAB)
   c. Career Ability Placement Survey (CAPS)
   d. Preliminary Scholastic Aptitude Test (PSAT), Scholastic Aptitude Test (SAT) or American College Test (ACT)
	1. Projective Personality Measures
	   a. Rorschach
	   b. Thematic Apperception Test (TAT) or Children's Apperception Test (CAT)
	   c. Draw a Person
	   d. Rotter Incomplete Sentences Blank

2. Interest Inventories
   a. Strong Interest Inventory
   b. Various Kuder Instruments
   c. Ohio Vocational Interest Survey (OVIS)
   d. Self-Directed Search (SDS) or Vocational Preference Inventory (VPI)
   e. Jackson Vocational Interest Survey (JVIS)
	2. Diagnostic Personality Inventories
	   a. Minnesota Multiphasic Personality Inventory (MMPI)
	   b. California Psychological Inventory (CPI)
	   c. Manifest Anxiety Scale or Children's Manifest Anxiety Scale

3. Values Inventories
   a. The Values Scale (VS)
   b. The Rokeach Values Survey
   c. Hall Occupational Orientation Inventory (HOOI)
   d. Minnesota Importance Questionnaire (MIQ)
   e. Allport-Lindsey Study of Values
	3. Intelligence
	   a. Wechsler Scales, Revised
	   b. Stanford-Binet, Revised
	   c. Kaufman Assessment Battery for Children (K-ABC)

4. Measures of "Normal" Personality Characteristics or "Style"
   a. Edwards Personal Preference Schedule (EPPS)
   b. Myers-Briggs Type Indicator (MBTI)
   c. NEO Five Factor Inventory (NEO-FFI)
   d. Gordon Personal Profile-Inventory (GPP-I)
	4. Instruments Related to Specific Disorders
	   a. Eating Disorder Inventory-2 (EDI-2)
	   b. Suicidal Ideation Questionnaire (SIQ)
	   c. Comprehensive Drinker Profile (CDP)
	   d. Beck Depression Inventory (BDI)

5. Miscellaneous Career Instruments
   a. Adult Career Concerns Inventory (ACCI)
   b. The Salience Inventory (SI)
   c. Harrington-O'Shea Decision-Making System
6. Achievement Measures
   a. Comprehensive Test of Basic Skills (CTBS)
   b. Wide Range Achievement Test (WRAT)
   c. Woodcock-Johnson Psychoeducational Battery (WJPEB)
   d. Stanford Achievement Tests (SAT)
	5. Psychoneurological Assessment
	   a. Halstead-Reitan Battery
	   b. Wisconsin Card Sorting Test (WCST)
	   c. Dementia Rating Scale (DRS)
	   d. Frostig Development Test of Visual Perception (FDTVP)
	   e. Bender Visual Motor Gestalt Test
	   f. Luria-Nebraska Neuropsychological Inventory

information and then to help them to internalize these data—that is the focus of the use of assessment in counseling. There are some who argue that the use of tests in counseling is a "marriage that failed," (Goldman, 1972) in that tests seem to be used too often in a round-peg in the holes, square-peg in the squares, trait-and-factor, narrowly myopic manner that approximates a mechanistic ritual. If, however, they are used in an integrated manner to stimulate self-exploration and to enhance self-understanding, then they come closer to being an exemplary mate for counseling.

The remainder of this chapter focuses on principles of test selection and test interpretation in counseling.

Test Selection

The experience of most clients with tests will be one of evaluation; thus, it is important they understand that the use of tests in counseling is for purposes of providing them with an enhanced knowledge of self and that the results do not imply value judgments of "good" or "bad." Clients' negative attitudes toward tests can obviously affect the vigor and conscientiousness with which they approach the task, so building a positive mind-set toward assessment in counseling is a *sine qua non* of good practice. And since assessment ought to be an integrated aspect of counseling, the tests that are selected should obviously have high content validity in that the client ought to perceive readily that the instruments will bear on the focus of counseling.

There is some debate in the literature about how active clients should be in selecting the sorts of tests to be administered and interpreted. Some believe that clients should actively participate in the process of selecting the *types* of tests, largely based on the assumption that the clients' psychological investment in choice will cause them more readily to accept and to internalize the results. Further, it is thought that by participating in the selection, clients will reduce their dependency on the counselor. The counselor, however, would still be responsible for the choice of specific tests (Healy, 1990). Others believe that clients have no idea of what they need; if they did, they would not be in counseling. Those who adopt this stance feel that the counselor is the expert and should choose both the type of test and the specific form of that assessment domain, carefully explaining to the client why the testing is important. There is absolutely no research evidence, compelling or otherwise, to instruct either view of the selection of tests in counseling.

As counselors select specific tests, they are guided by standards regarding assessment developed by professional associations (American Educational Research Association, 1985; Association for Measurement and Evaluation in Counseling and Development, 1989). These guidelines suggest that tests must possess the typically desired psychometric characteristics, such as adequate and appropriate reliability, validity, and norms. Further, they maintain that any test selected be one for which the user is qualified in terms of educational preparation and experience. Once the specific test is chosen, counselors will need to determine if they are going to administer it in paper-and-pencil form or via computer. The latter mode requires adherence to still other guidelines (American Psychological Association, 1986), for there is certainly potential for mischief and abuse when tests come with handy-dandy printed-out interpretations, and neither the counselor nor the client has enough sophisticated knowledge to know when and how to build on the interpretation and to integrate it with counseling.

Practical considerations frequently intrude in the test selection process as it relates to counseling. For example, cost is one factor. Will the outcome of the assessment justify the financial outlay necessary? Secondly, will the time required for administration, scoring, and/or interpretation warrant the use of the test? Thirdly, can the information yielded by the test results be obtained more easily from nontesting procedures (e.g., extant records, interview data, and so on)?

Drummond (1988) has summarized the criteria for test selection in counseling in the form of 10 questions (pp. 76–79).

1. Was the test designed to measure the behavior under consideration?
2. Do the test items appear to be measuring traits, objectives, or behaviors that are to be assessed?
3. Does the test have validity information?
4. Is the test reliable?
5. Does the test provide sufficient information for the psychologist or counselor to interpret the results?
6. Does the test provide interpretive feedback for the examinee?
7. Is the test appropriate for the examinee?
8. Is the test free from bias?
9. What level of competency is needed to administer the tests?
10. Is the test a practical one to select?

Finally, in terms of test selection, the counselor will want to consider alternative methods of gathering data independent of standardized tests. For instance, self-observation by the client and observation by the counselor (with or without rating scales) are methods that yield information to be interpreted in counseling. Another technique is simply to structure an interview to glean information. The data from this structured interview are then used for diagnosis, research, treatment decisions, and feedback to the client (Friedman, 1989).

Test Interpretation

We should recognize at the outset that the interpretation of tests in counseling is a decidedly under-researched area—perhaps as ill-informed by the findings of empirical research as any other single aspect of the counseling enterprise. What little research we do have is relatively outdated and not particularly instructive. Both Herr and Cramer (1992) and Goodyear (1990) lament the sorry state of the research in this regard.

One of the inescapable conclusions that stems from this sparse research literature is that no single method of test interpretation appears to be superior for all clients. Clients seem differentially to recall their test results and to accept them depending on the type of presentation and the characteristics of the client (e.g., whether the counselor or the client is dominant in the test interpretation session; whether or not a "learning set" is first established; whether the client has high or low scholastic aptitude; how much the clients know about themselves prior to the interpretation; whether the client is disabled, a minority, an older person, or is otherwise distinguishable from a typical normative population; whether different modes of interpretation are used, such as a computer or group versus individual or audio-visual aids; what language is used to convey the interpretation—sophisticated or otherwise; and so on).

Some also argue that the "Barnum effect" may be operative in test interpretations. This is the name given to the phenomenon that suggests clients will accept test results if they are presented convincingly (despite the fact that they may not be accurate) or if they contain universal truths. Psychics, graphologists, astrologers, and others of this ilk have long recognized the potency of this principle of essentially telling people what they want to be told. This phenomenon would suggest to counselors, for example, that for the best effect they should word their interpretations in positive rather than negative terms.

Beyond these basically simplistic conclusions, however, there is little in the research on which to draw profitably as we seek to provide clients with useful interpretations of appraisal data. Consequently, we have had to rely on the logic of those who think deeply and frequently about the process. No shortage of literature exists about how theoreticians and practitioners *believe* tests ought to be used and interpreted in counseling. A sampling of some of these rationally derived models follows: first, several examples of general test interpretation principles and then examples of test interpretation suggestions relating to specific tests.

Generic Test Interpretation

Recall that earlier it was noted that there is disagreement regarding how active a role clients should assume in choosing and interpreting their appraisal data. The view at one pole of the continuum is exemplified by such individuals as Bozarth (1991) and Healy (1990). The latter maintains that among the obstacles to the effective use of appraisal data in counseling is the counselors' perception that clients are subordinates rather than collaborators and that clients' self-assessments are discounted while counselors' assessments are favored. Clients should therefore be assisted to develop self-assessment skills. Bozarth, drawing on Rogerian theory, argues that a therapeutic counseling relationship is typically antithetical to the systematic use of testing and assessment. This is thought to be true because in so-called person-centered counseling, the clients—not the therapists—are presumed to be the authorities in their own lives. The more the clients are so perceived, it is assumed, the greater the likelihood of personality change and/or problem resolution. Hence, tests should never be mandatory for clients, and the clients themselves should be the instigators of testing by requesting it. Further, they should assist in selecting the tests and have the results reported to them in a nonjudgmental fashion. Especially in career counseling, only information that the client needs and wants (as the *client* states that need) is appropriate in person-centered assessment. In terms of the use of tests to inform the counselor rather than the client (psychodiagnostics), the person-centered approach generally considers such use inconsistent with its theoretical orientation. (Since client-centered therapy provides basically only one treatment for all cases, why diagnose?)

Bozarth maintains that person-centered assessment will be relatively rare. "Testing and other forms of activity (e.g., dispensation of medicine, behavior modification, homework) are consistent with the theory in that they may occur as unsystematic actions that are decided on by the client from the client's frame of reference in interaction with the therapist" (p. 459). Only in three conditions would person-centered theory permit testing: (1) The client wants to take a test and verbalizes that desire; (2) the institutional setting requires that tests be given (e.g., for insurance or forensic purposes); and/or (3) in career counseling, assessment may be used as a kind of "reality testing" (external referents) as long as the client, and not the counselor, remains the authority and all decisions emanate from the client's frame of reference.

Most counselors would find the person-centered view extreme, and, indeed, there are relatively few "pure" client-centered counselors in practice. The vast majority of counselors believe that as long as appraisal data are appropriate and not misused or abused, they provide the client with valuable self-knowledge that can be effectively employed in decision making, problem solving, self-exploration, and so on. Given that stance, the remainder of this chapter deals with the interpretation of such tests in counseling. The reader is again reminded that the use of tests primarily to inform the counselor (e.g., psychodiagnostics, selection or placement decisions such as institutionalization or release) are not covered in this chapter.

Zunker (1986) has written extensively about the use of assessment results in career counseling. His model has four essential stages. (1) The first is *analyzing client needs*. In order to do so, the counselor must establish the counseling relationship (trust and mutual respect); accept and adopt the client's views (i.e., the uniqueness of persons and their right to own their own viewpoints); establish life-style dimensions (elements of importance in a desired style of life); and specify the needs (from the general to the detailed). (2) The second stage of using assessment results is *establishing a purpose for testing*. The client should understand the reasons for administering each assessment instrument in light of the client's expressed needs. (3) The third stage is *determining the instrument*. Obviously, the counselor will need to be familiar with what instruments are extant in each of several possible domains: aptitudes, interests, personality, work values, personal style, and so on. (4) Finally, the fourth stage consists of trying to *relate identified personal characteristics to career and self-exploration*.

Hood and Johnson (1991) offer nine general guidelines for communicating test results.

1. The first step in interpreting a test is to know and understand the test manual. In this way the validity of a test can be related to the purpose for which the test is used. The manual is also likely to contain information regarding the limits to which the test can be used and suggestions for interpreting the results.
2. In interpreting test results it is important to review the purposes for which the client took the test and the strengths and limitations of the test.
3. In interpreting results, the procedure by which the test is scored should be explained, along with an explanation of percentile ranks or standard scores if they are to be included in the interpretation.
4. Where possible, the results should be presented in terms of probabilities rather than certainties or specific predictions.

5. The emphasis should be on increasing client understanding and, where appropriate, encouraging clients to make their own interpretations.
6. The test results should be presented as they relate to other available information about the client.
7. The counselor should ensure that the interpretation of the test information is understood by the clients and that clients are encouraged to express their reactions to the information.
8. Any relevant information or background characteristics, such as gender or handicapping conditions, should be examined, along with any apparent discrepancies or inconsistencies that appear.
9. Both strengths and weaknesses revealed by the tests results should be discussed objectively. (p. 221)

Power (1991) echoes many of these suggestions, while focusing specifically on rehabilitation clients who manifest physical, mental, or emotional disabilities. He suggests, for example, that communication of appraisal results should be at a level that clients understand and that alternatives should always be presented to clients so that they can make choices. Further, clients should be active in the interpretation and helped to sort through their reactions to the results. Finally, clients should never be confronted with negative information about which they previously had no cognizance. Within this context, Power suggests a four-phase interpretation as displayed in Table 17-2. While related specifically to vocational appraisal, the paradigm would seem equally useful for interpreting other types of appraisal data.

Tinsley and Bradley (1988) offer some practical suggestions for test interpretation, especially as it relates to career counseling. They urge that counselors relate the results to the questions that clients have about themselves and to the goals that they have in mind. Secondly, they advocate that counselors constantly remind themselves about the instrument's degree of precision; that is, they should interpret data with clients in terms of confidence or probability band parameters rather than trying to pinpoint success. Thirdly, they suggest that counselors do everything they can in terms of minimizing clients' defensive reactions. Fourth, they maintain that counselors should avoid jargon and technical terms that may serve only to confuse clients. Finally, they assert that counselors should encourage clients' feedback. Again, the emphasis is on client participation.

Comprehensive guidelines for test interpretation are also provided by Garfield and Prediger (1982). Their listing of counselor competencies and responsibilities relates specifically to vocational counseling, but it could apply equally as well to any type of testing to encourage client self-exploration and/or self-understanding. The following key pertains:

1 = I do this routinely—as a regular practice.
2 = I have done on occasion.
3 = I do not do—but ought to consider doing.
4 = Not applicable to the instrument(s) I am using.

TABLE 17-2 Summary of Actual Interpretation Session

Phase	Tasks
First phase (Introduction)	1. Know about measures to be interpreted to client. 2. Establish a relationship. 3. Review goals of evaluation for the client.
Second phase	1. Give the client an opportunity to talk about the assessment experience. 2. Summarize in a general manner the overall results of evaluation, emphasizing positive test results. 3. Solicit feedback from the client.
Third phase	1. Interpret carefully each evaluation measure—Interest, Aptitude/Ability, Intelligence, and Personality. Use such guidelines as norms, percentiles, etc. 2. Solicit feedback about the client's feelings concerning the results. 3. Deal with such problems as contradictory test scores, reluctance, and unrealistic vocational aspirations. 4. Suggest particular interest areas, the respective occupations, and the qualifications for each in the physical, emotional, and intellectual areas.
Fourth phase (Conclusion)	1. Summarize results for the client and discuss how this information can relate to rehabilitation planning. 2. Ask the client for further feedback, especially about what has been learned from the evaluation experience. 3. Develop rehabilitation plans.

Source: P. W. Power, *A guide to vocational assessment,* 2nd ed. (Austin, TX: Pro-Ed, 1991), Table 13-1.

Their list of interpretation responsibilities/competencies is as follows:

1. Study suggestions for interpretation provided by the test manual (and/or score report form) and determine which of them are supported by the psychometric data provided for the test.

2. Review, with the counselee, the purpose and nature of the test. Topics include:
    ____ a. Why the test was given; what the test can and cannot do.
    ____ b. Who will receive the test results.
    ____ c. What the test results cover and how they will be used.

3. Interpret test results in the context of the testing experience, the counselee's background, and other assessments (if any) of the same characteristics by:
    ____ a. Encouraging a discussion of how the counselee felt about the testing experience, in general; his/her performance, in particular; and any difficulties or problems (e.g., nervousness, fatigue, distractions) encountered.
    ____ b. Examining the possibility that the counselee's background (race, sex, handicap, age, etc.) may have influenced the test results.
    ____ c. Seeking additional information to explain any inconsistencies that become evident.

4. Apply good counseling techniques to test interpretation by:

_____ a. Emphasizing "strengths" while objectively discussing "weaknesses."

_____ b. Allowing sufficient time for the counselee to assimilate information and respond.

_____ c. Listening attentively to the counselee's responses (i.e., attending to the counselee first and test results second).

_____ d. Checking the counselee's understanding of the test results from time to time; correcting misconceptions.

5. Help the counselee begin (or continue) the career (educational and vocational) planning process by:

_____ a. Identifying, with the counselee, career options and steps for exploring each.

_____ b. Providing assistance to the counselee through ongoing career guidance activities such as field trips, career conferences, film strips, library resources, etc.

_____ c. Monitoring and encouraging career planning efforts through progress reports, follow-through counseling sessions, etc. (pp. 460–461)

No matter how carefully counselors prepare for test interpretations within counseling sessions, there are inevitably problems that arise and recur from client to client. Drummond (1988) cites some of these as *acceptance* (appraisal data that are contrary to what a client desires not infrequently provoke resistance); *readiness* (those who feel a need for the information may be more ready to accept results and to explore the personal meaning of the data); *negative results* (can often threaten a client's sense of self and security); *flat profiles* (results that yield no peaks and valleys of performance are much more difficult to interpret); and *motivation and attitude* (essential for peak performance and willingness to integrate the results in counseling). To this formidable listing of problems in interpretation we might well add those that may emanate from a client's atypicality. In this regard, such variables as gender, race or ethnicity, and age may require special attention.

For example, in terms of gender, a debate has long taken place regarding whether to norm test data (especially interest data) by gender or independent of gender. Which method would eliminate sex bias in assessment instruments? Which method would produce a sex-fair instrument? Many tests and inventories now provide both same-sex and opposite-sex norms so that clients can better understand the ramifications of a test score (Tittle & Zytowski, 1980). Race and ethnicity also pose issues related to test fairness. Cultural differences may, in some cases, militate against the indiscriminant application of test data. This is certainly the case when the purpose of testing is selection, classification, and/or placement, and it may even be the case when appraisal data are generated to help the client to gain self-knowledge and self-understanding (Brescio & Fortune, 1989; Lonner & Sundberg, 1987). Lastly, by way of illustration of differences, older adults pose unique appraisal problems (Teri & Lewinsohn, 1986; Hunt & Lindey, 1989). It has long been known, for instance, that the Minnesota Multiphasic Personality Inventory (MMPI) profile of the "average" male adolescent very closely resembles that of the adult institutionalized psychopathic deviate. Age clearly makes a difference. In every case of utilizing appraisal data, the basic question that both counselors and clients must address is the *meaning* of a test score. It is difficult (if not impossible) to determine that meaning without considering cultural, gender, and age contexts. Counselors must ask, "With this client, using this test, am I sure that the data before us are truly representative? If not, how must we alter our interpretation?"

Schuerger and Watterson (1977) have also proposed a test interpretation paradigm to assist clients in their decision making. They suggest that the four general principles for interpreting test results to a client are "(1) know the test, (2) supply information relevant to the client's situation, (3) tune in to the client's values, and (4) follow the client's needs and reactions to the information" (p. 97).

Specific Test Interpretation

We have thus far discussed generic or general suggestions for interpreting tests in counseling. The developers of certain assessment instruments also provide in their test manuals models for using their specific tests or inventories within the counseling experience. Three such examples follow.

Hansen (1985) takes the counselor step-by-step through a pre-interpretation preparation for the Strong Interest Inventory (SVIB-SII). The 12-step process is reproduced in Figure 17-1.

This preparation is followed by the actual career counseling sequence in which the counselor is urged to involve the client in all aspects of the interpretation. This sequence is reproduced in Figure 17-2.

A second example is provided by Nevill and Super (1986) in their manual for the Values Scale. Their developmental assessment model for career counseling focuses on "the relative importance of work, the centrality of values sought in work, and the level of career maturity including a sense of autonomy and self-esteem" (p. 6). Figure 17-3 reproduces their four-step model.

Finally, in terms of examples of counseling utilizing specific instruments, we may look to the case of the Myers-Briggs Type Indicator (MBTI) (Myers & McCaulley, 1985). The manual provides many suggestions for using the MBTI in both a teaching mode and a counseling mode. Not surprisingly, since we are dealing with an instrument that purports to measure "basic preferences" of individuals in interacting with life, the developers suggest that interpretations be geared to "type" in that clients will presumably respond differentially to various modes of test interpretation depending on their type. The tailoring of counseling style to client characteristics has long been suggested in counseling. Unfortunately, in the case of the MBTI, we have little evidence thus far that such an *a priori* attractive proposal does, in fact, yield expected results. Nevertheless, the authors—citing Yeakley (1983)—suggest the following for counselors.

Listening in the sensing style means *interpreting* at a very practical level and asking questions such as:
- What is the speaker saying?
- How should the words be decoded?
- How should the message be perceived?

Steps 1 to 3	Determine profile validity • Total Response Index • Infrequent Response Index • LP, IP, and DP Indexes CHAPTERS 14 AND 15
Step 4	Identify high scores on the General Occupational Themes and Basic Interest Scales CHAPTERS 4, 5, 6
Step 5	Note "Moderately Similar" or higher Occupational Scale scores CHAPTERS 8 AND 9
Step 6	Look for scale-score consistencies and inconsistencies CHAPTER 11
Step 7	Identify potential nonoccupational interests CHAPTERS 7 AND 11
Step 8	Check scores on the opposite-sex Occupational Scales CHAPTER 10
Step 9	Check the AC Score CHAPTER 12
Step 10	Check the IE Score CHAPTER 13
Step 11	Develop hypotheses CHAPTERS 7 AND 19
Step 12	Generalize beyond the profile CHAPTERS 9 AND 20, APPENDIXES A AND B

FIGURE 17-1   Flow Chart for SVIB-SII Pre-Interpretation Preparation

Source: Reproduced by special permission from the *User's Guide for the Strong Interest Inventory,* Revised Edition 1992 of the *Strong Interest Inventory of the Strong Vocational Interest Blanks®*, Form T325. Copyright 1933, 1938, 1945, 1946, 1966, 1968, 1974, 1981, 1985, 1992 by The Board of Trustees of the Leland Stanford Junior University. All rights reserved. Printed under license from Stanford University Press, Stanford, California 94305. Reproduced by special permission of the Publisher, Consulting Psychologists Press, Inc., Palo Alto, CA 94303. Further reproduction is prohibited without the Publisher's consent.

Step 1	Review the purpose of the SCII to measure interests, not abilities
	CHAPTERS 1 AND 2
Step 2	Emphasize lifestyle exploration, not just occupational interests
	CHAPTER 7
Step 3	Discuss the client's reaction to the SCII
	CHAPTERS 14 AND 15
Step 4	Give the client an overview of the interpretation process
	CHAPTERS 1, 2, AND 19
Step 5	Briefly explain Holland's theory
	CHAPTER 4
Step 6	Explain each Theme and its related Basic Interest Scales
	CHAPTERS 4, 5, 6, AND 7
Step 7	Diagram the profile
	CHAPTER 9
Step 8	Identify diametrically opposed interests
	CHAPTER 4
Step 9	Interpret the Occupational Scales and integrate them with the Themes and Basic Interest Scales
	CHAPTERS 8, 9, AND 11
Step 10	Review low scores on all three main scale types
	CHAPTER 7
Step 11	Integrate opposite-sex scores into the emerging interest pattern
	CHAPTER 10
Step 12	Discuss the ACADEMIC COMFORT score
	CHAPTER 12

FIGURE 17-2   Flow Chart for SVIB-SII Interpretation

Source: Reproduced by special permission from the *User's Guide for the Strong Interest Inventory,* Revised Edition 1992 of the *Strong Interest Inventory of the Strong Vocational Interest Blanks*®, Form T325. Copyright 1933, 1938, 1945, 1946, 1966, 1968, 1974, 1981, 1985, 1992 by The Board of Trustees of the Leland Stanford Junior University. All rights reserved. Printed under license from Stanford University Press, Stanford, California 94305. Reproduced by special permission of the Publisher, Consulting Psychologists Press, Inc., Palo Alto, CA 94303. Further reproduction is prohibited without the Publisher's consent.

FIGURE 17-2 *Continued*

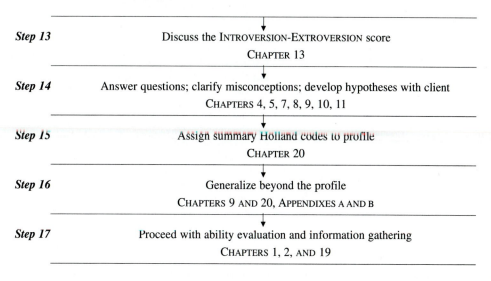

Step 13	Discuss the INTROVERSION-EXTROVERSION score CHAPTER 13
Step 14	Answer questions; clarify misconceptions; develop hypotheses with client CHAPTERS 4, 5, 7, 8, 9, 10, 11
Step 15	Assign summary Holland codes to profile CHAPTER 20
Step 16	Generalize beyond the profile CHAPTERS 9 AND 20, APPENDIXES A AND B
Step 17	Proceed with ability evaluation and information gathering CHAPTERS 1, 2, AND 19

Listening in the intuitive style means *understanding* at a much deeper level and asking questions such as:

- What does the speaker really mean?
- What are the assumptions underlying the message?
- What are the implications of the message?
- What are the possibilities suggested by the message?

Listening in the thinking style means *analyzing* and *organizing* while asking questions such as:

- What is the structure of the message?
- What is the central idea?
- What are the main points?
- What are the subpoints?
- How are the various points related?
- Is there adequate evidence to justify each claim?
- Is the reasoning logical?
- Are the claims true or false?

Listening in the feeling style means *evaluating* and *appreciating* while asking questions such as:

- What are the values suggested by the message?
- Should these values be accepted or rejected?
- How do I feel about the message?
- How do I feel about the speaker? (pp. 70–71)

Step I. Preview
- A. Assembly of data on hand
- B. Intake interview
- C. Preliminary assessment

Step II. Depth-view: further testing?
- A. Work salience
  - 1. Relative importance of diverse roles
    - a. Study
    - b. Work and career
    - c. Home and family
    - d. Community service
    - e. Leisure activities
  - 2. Participation in each role
  - 3. Commitment to each role
  - 4. Knowledge of each role
- B. Values sought in each role
- C. Career maturity
  - 1. Planfulness
  - 2. Exploratory attitudes
  - 3. Decision-making skills
  - 4. Information
    - a. World of work
    - b. Preferred occupational group
    - c. Other life-career roles
  - 5. Realism
- D. Level of abilities and potential functioning
- E. Field of interest and probable activity

Step III. Assessment of all data
- A. Review of all data
- B. Work salience
- C. Values
- D. Career maturity
  - 1. Individual and occupations
  - 2. Individual and nonoccupational roles
- E. Planning communication with counselee, family, etc.

Step IV. Counseling
- A. Joint review and discussion
- B. Revision or acceptance of assessment
- C. Assimilation by the counselee
  - 1. Understanding the present
  - 2. Understanding the meaning of work and other life roles

FIGURE 17-3 A Developmental Assessment Model for Career Counseling

Source: Modified and reproduced by special permission of the Publisher, Consulting Psychologists Press, Inc., Palo Alto, CA 94303 from *The Values Scale: Theory, Application, and Research Manual,* Research Edition by Dorothy D. Nevill, Ph.D. and Donald E. Super, Ph.D. Copyright 1986 by Consulting Psychologists Press, Inc. All rights reserved. Further reproduction is prohibited without the Publisher's written consent.

FIGURE 17-3 *Continued*

      3. Exploration for maturing?
      4. Exploration in breadth for crystallization?
      5. Exploration in depth for specification?
      6. Choice of preparation, training, or jobs?
      7. Searches for job and other outlets?
      8. Exploring self and situation for self-realization?
  D. Discussion of action implications and planning
      1. Planning
      2. Monitored execution
      3. Follow-up for support and evaluation

Recommendations for Test Interpretation

Given the paucity of empirical research regarding the effective use of assessment data in counseling, while at the same time recognizing the large body of "suggestions" and "guidelines" that pervades the professional literature, what recommendations emerge to instruct counselors? We can offer several; again, however, we caution that what appears to be logically sound may not stand up to empirical scrutiny.

1. We are speaking only of tests to inform the client. Testing should be an organic or internal part of the counseling experience and not a disjointed throw-in that seems independent of the business at hand.
2. Tests should never be used without counselors working to establish motivation and readiness in clients and helping them to understand the purpose of the assessment.
3. While the counselor selects specific tests, the client may aid in defining some of the domains in which assessment may occur (e.g., aptitudes, interests, values, personal style, etc.). The client does this by articulating the questions to which he wants answers. It is also acceptable for the counselor to suggest assessment in domains for which the client has not verbalized a need and for both client and counselor to discuss the wisdom of additional assessment. In all cases, it is the counselor's duty carefully to explain what domain is being measured and for what purpose.
4. No tests or inventories should be utilized if there is a more valid, reliable, and timely way to get the same data.
5. The test score itself is relatively unimportant. The *personal meaning* of that score to the client is the *raison d'etre* of testing. Therefore, all interpretation of assessment data should be directed toward determining that meaning. Clients must be given opportunity to reflect and to explore the meaning of the data.
6. The criteria for effective test interpretation are both nebulous and arguable. In our opinion, however, clients at the very least should be able accurately to recall their test performance and to accept the results.

7. Absent any definitive research, we recommend that counselors adhere to the test interpretation procedures described in manuals (if available) for specific tests. If no such descriptions exist, we suggest that counselors follow any and all of the step-by-step generic guidelines in this chapter.
8. It is a *sine qua non* that clients actively participate in the interpretation of assessment data, not only in terms of determining personal meaning as described in Item 5 above, but also in terms of taking necessary action steps suggested by the data and by the content of counseling.

Summary

The use of assessment data can be informative for clients as they seek self-understanding and engage in self-exploration. Clients must be motivated, however, to produce such information with integrity and then helped to sort through the personal relevance of the data. Because there are almost no useful research findings in regard to test interpretation, we must rely on suggestions of experts for rational use. These suggestions have been delineated and synthesized in this chapter.

References

American Educational Research Association, American Psychological Association, & National Council on Measurement in Education. (1985). *Standards for educational and psychological testing*. Washington, DC: American Psychological Association.

American Psychological Association. (1986). *Guidelines for computer-based tests and interpretations*. Washington, DC: Author.

Association for Measurement and Evaluation in Counseling and Development. (1989, May). *The responsibilities of test users. AACD Guidepost*, 12–28.

Bozarth, J. D. (1991). Person-centered assessment. *Journal of Counseling and Development, 69,* 458–461.

Brescio, W., & Fortune, J. C. (1989). Standardized testing of American Indian students. *The College Student Journal, 23,* 98–1104.

Drummond, J. R. (1988). *Appraisal procedures for counselors and helping professionals*. Columbus, OH: Merrill.

Friedman, J. M. H. (1989). Structured interviews: The expert's vantage. In S. Wetzler & M. M. Katz (Eds.). *Contemporary approaches to psychological assessment* (pp. 83–97). New York: Brunner/Mazel.

Garfield, N. J., & Prediger, D. J. (1982). Testing competencies and responsibilities: A checklist for vocational counselors. In J. T. Kapes and M. M. Mastie (Eds.), *A counselor's guide to vocational guidance instruments*. Washington, DC: National Vocational Guidance Association.

Goldman, L. (1972). Tests and counseling: The marriage that failed. *Measurement and Evaluation in Guidance, 4*(4), 213–220.

Goodyear, R. K. (1990). Research on the effects of test interpretation: A review. *The Counseling Psychologist, 18,* 240–257.

Hansen, J. I. C. (1985). *User's guide for the SVIB-SII*. Palo Alto, CA: Consulting Psychologists Press.

Healy, C. C. (1990). Reforming career appraisals to meet the needs of clients in the 1990s. *The Counseling Psychologist, 18,* 214–226.

Herr, E. L., & Cramer, S. H. (1992). *Career guidance and counseling through the lifespan: Systematic approaches* (4th ed.). New York: Harper/Collins.

Hood, A. B., & Johnson, R. W. (1991). *Assessment in counseling: A guide to the use of psychological assessment procedures.* Washington, DC: American Association for Counseling and Development.

Hunt, T., & Lindey, C. J. (1989). *Testing older adults.* Austin, TX: Pro-Ed.

Lonner, W. J., & Sundberg, N. D. (1987). Assessment in cross-cultural counseling and therapy. In P. Pederson, *Handbook of cross-cultural counseling and therapy* (pp. 199–205). New York: Praeger.

Myers, I. B., & McCaulley, M. H. (1985). *Manual: A guide to the development and use of the Myers-Briggs Type Indicator.* Palo Alto, CA: Consulting Psychologists Press.

Nevill, D. D., & Super, D. E. (1986). *The Values Scale: Theory application and research manual* (Research ed.). Palo Alto, CA: Consulting Psychologists Press.

Power, P. W. (1991). *A guide to vocational assessment* (2nd ed.). Austin, TX: Pro-Ed.

Schuerger, J., & Watterson, D. (1977). *Using tests and other information in counseling: A decision model for practitioners.* Champaign, IL: Institute for Personality and Ability Testing.

Teri, L., & Lewinsohn, P. M. (1986). *Geropsychological assessment and treatment.* New York: Springer.

Tinsley, H. E. A., & Bradley, R. W. (1988). Interpretation of psychometric instruments in career counseling. In J. T. Kapes & M. M. Mastie (Eds.). *A counselor's guide to career assessment instruments* (2nd ed.) (pp. 39–54). Washington, DC: American Association for Counseling and Development.

Tittle, C. K., & Zytowski, D. G. (Eds.). (1980). *Sex-fair interest measurement: Research and implications.* Washington, DC: National Institute of Education, U.S. Government Printing Office.

Wetzler, S. (1989). Parameters of psychological assessment. In S. Wetzler & M. M. Katz (Eds.). *Contemporary approaches to psychological assessment* (pp. 3–15). New York: Brunner/Mazel.

Yeakley, F. R. (1983). Implications of communication style research for psychological type theory. *Research in Psychological Type, 6,* 5–23.

Zunker, V. G. (1986). *Using assessment results in career counseling* (2nd ed.). Monterey, CA: Brooks/Cole.

Chapter 18

Career Counseling

When most people think of career counseling, they focus on the counseling of individuals to assist them in making an initial occupational choice. If clients do not know "what they want to be when they grow up," they are urged to get "vocational counseling." Indeed, such an emphasis was common several decades ago, when a mechanistic trait and factor approach was prevalent. Vocational counseling in this orientation was disparagingly referred to as "three sessions and a cloud of dust" or "test 'em and tell 'em." Vocational counseling for initial choice, however, has undergone a substantial change in emphasis from trait and factor to what has been termed person-environment fit; and it has been supplanted by the much broader notion of career counseling, wherein total life-style concerns, career-family issues, leisure, and a host of other foci are addressed.

At one time, career counseling was solely the province of school counselors, rehabilitation counselors, employment counselors, and counseling psychologists. More recently, clinical psychologists have become more active in the discipline, and occupational clinical psychology and career counseling in industry are fast-growing specialties. It is not surprising that this interest has evolved, since there is a growing recognition of both the potentially healthful and the potentially inimical effects of work in people's lives. For example, longevity may be closely tied to job satisfaction; stress measurements (ranging from major life event approaches to daily hassle orientations) always assess aspects of work life; and it is clear that work affects all other phases of a person's life. Expanding Freud's well-known aphorism of life being composed of love and work, Neff (1985) added play and the trichotomy of love-work-play does indeed broadly describe the major facets of life. Counseling regarding career development issues, encompassing as they do all aspects of work and leisure, is therefore an honorable and important type of counseling. The field of career counseling is thus extremely comprehensive and consequently requires specialized training. Counselors need to study vocational psychology, occupational sociology, vocational assessment, career development and career choice, career decision making, and a variety of other topics.

In the past, career counseling was dominated by a trait and factor focus. Trait and factor vocational counseling is based on an occupational model; that is, at a single point in time (e.g., prior to entry into the labor market or after dislocation), the client's aptitudes were profiled via tests, and these were subsequently matched with existing occupational options. The closer the match, the better the counseling was presumed to be. Little attention was paid to a client's values and preferences, and practitioners tended to minimize the more psychological aspects of vocational choice. In other words, vocational dimensions of choice were accentuated; psychological aspects were ignored or treated as discrete from the decision-making process. In the last 40 years, thanks to the stimulus provided by the great vocational psychologist, Donald Super, and others, the vocational and personal aspects of career choice have been blended, and foci other than initial choice of an occupation have been incorporated into counseling related to aspects of work life and the quality of work life. Concepts such as self-understanding and self-acceptance became important; a static, point-in-time orientation gave way to a more dynamic process; and counseling replaced the mechanistic ritual of narrowly matching person and occupation. Further, interventions in an occupational model presume a deficit in the client and thus a need for treatment. Treatment implies a problem; and a problem orientation suggests that interventions are appropriate only when clients are vulnerable to crises and discontinuities.

In contrast, a career model does more than simply react to existing problems, although it will do that also. It helps clients to develop a psychological set composed of knowledge and attitudes by which they can respond in any future decision points. It assists them to develop an occupational identity and to gain career maturity. It has a future-oriented, developmental focus and does not require a problem to stimulate an intervention. In many respects, a career model of intervention is educative as well as responsive to problems. Rather than concentrating solely on fixing something that is broken, however, it seeks to facilitate growth. There is thus an equilibrium between treatment and the enhancement of career development throughout the life span.

Although a number of heuristics are possible for describing the field, we choose to present an overview of career counseling by utilizing career development stages to describe the types of emphases addressed by career counselors within each stage. Secondly, we present techniques and typical counseling life cycles that are appropriate to career counseling. Thirdly, we discuss theoretical orientations. Finally, we offer a summary of outcome studies in career counseling.

Career Development Stages and Counseling Emphases

Over half a century ago, the German psychologist Charlotte Buehler was among the first to propose developmental stages throughout one's life. This life cycle perspective influenced Donald Super (1957) who adapted Buehler's stages to describe the career life cycle. This model postulates five major developmental career stages, from postinfancy to death, with many of the stages having substages. We present each of the stages and discuss some of the more common counseling emphases within each.

Growth

The growth stage of career development begins after infancy (about age 4) and extends through the age of approximately 14. Each stage requires the mastery of a number of career-related developmental tasks. The growth stage has attendant to it the necessity for individuals to begin to develop a self-concept—a picture of the kind of person they are. In addition, they need to orient themselves to the world of work and to understand the meaning of work in people's lives. The growth stage is composed of three substages. The *fantasy* substage exists from about ages 4 through 10. It should be noted that as with any developmental stage model, age ranges will be approximate, since some individuals will achieve the developmental tasks of the stage earlier (and be vocationally precocious), while others will achieve the tasks later or never achieve them (and thus be vocationally disabled). During the fantasy substage, children will simply imagine themselves being what they see as dramatic, beautiful, exhilarating, or simply what they can comprehend from their limited experience. Hence, despite efforts to prevent stereotyping on the basis of gender, girls will generally want to be ballerinas, for example, and boys will want to be ball players. In other words, no consideration is given to abilities or real interests, for they have not yet emerged; the response of these youngsters is visceral and little or no cognition is involved. About ages 11 and 12, the *interest* substage evolves from fantasy. Here what people like becomes dominant and determines their aspirations and career-related activities. The final substage of growth occurs from ages 13 and 14, when *abilities* begin to be given more weight.

Given this developmental stage of growth, counseling interventions are primarily directed toward establishing in young people an awareness of both themselves and the world of work and a beginning exploration of these dimensions at a depth appropriate to their age. Counseling interventions are not so much one to one as they are group-oriented; and they are certainly more facilitating and enhancing of career development than they are involved in the treatment of deficits. This is not to say that treatment of deficits is ignored. For example, early intervention in the lives of the very poor is necessary if their career horizons are to be expanded and their aspirations made congruent with those of the more privileged segments of society. Illustrations of some of the more common developmental tasks to be achieved during the growth stage are developing an awareness of self and a positive self-concept, acquiring rudimentary aspects of the discipline of work, acquiring knowledge about work, developing interpersonal skills, presenting oneself appropriately, and showing respect for others and their work. While these examples are not all-encompassing, they should provide a flavor of the types of tasks that need to be mastered in the growth stage if individuals are to be designated as career mature.

It is clear that children in more advantaged circumstances achieve these types of outcomes as a matter of course much more frequently than those children who are exposed to fewer role models and other vocational resources. Consequently, intentional interventions with all children, but especially those who are less advantaged (e.g., children in barrios, ghettos, reservations, and farms; the children of immigrants; children of non-intact families; etc.) are necessary. Almost all of these interventions will occur within the formal educational enterprise. Some will take the form of *infusion*; that is, regular classroom teachers dealing consciously and deliberately with career relevant subject matter, attitudes, and so on. Instances might be an English teacher having students read and discuss a vocational biography or math teachers talking about a career in mathematics. Other interventions in the school will come through formal courses. For example, all students in grade 8 in New York State must take a course called "Home and Career Skills."

Counselors conducting structured groups constitutes a third type of school intervention designed to enhance self and career awareness and beginning exploration. For instance, field trips to work sites might be arranged; tests might be given and interpreted; worker role models might be brought into the school to speak and/or demonstrate the tools of their trade. Finally, school counselors can and do provide remedial vocational experiences for those students who have not mastered the appropriate developmental tasks. All of these educational activities should be designed and coordinated within a systematic approach that assures an articulated, integrated, sequenced, and developmental set of experiences at each grade level (Herr & Cramer, 1992). External to the school, this early awareness and exploration counseling takes place in a limited way in church-related groups, Boy Scout and Girl Scout activities, community centers, and specially funded federal and state programs.

Exploration

The second major stage of the career life cycle is the exploration stage, extending from about age 15 to age 24. It begins typically with a *tentative* substage (ages 15–17) in which choice is quite generalized and not at all certain. This substage precedes that of *transition* (ages 18–21) during which reality considerations intrude—sometimes harshly—in the career choice process, necessitating more specific planning. The third and final substage of exploration is *trial–little commitment* (ages 22–24) in which a provisional choice is made and implemented. Some people may skip exploration entirely, having made a definite choice during the growth stage. Such people are said to have a career "passion," but they are relatively few in number. Other people, largely because of economic circumstances, may not even perceive that they have a choice; they feel that they are buffeted by life forces over which they have no control. During the exploration stage, individuals enhance their knowledge of self, acquire a more sophisticated understanding of the world of work, and develop decision-making skills. They reality test their self-concepts and get to understand the relationship between education and training and occupational choice, among other insights. In short, by the end of the stage they implement a vocational preference.

Most career counseling at this stage is directed toward broadening exploration along a variety of dimensions (e.g., aptitudes, interests, work values, personality characteristics, achievements, the worlds of education and training, occupational alternatives, desired life-style, and so on). In its later stages, it seeks to help individuals to narrow their perspectives in the sense of channeling their exploration energies into increasingly delimited parameters. It is the typical type of counseling that most people think of when they conjure up images of career counseling. As such, it is counseling for decision making (discussed in detail in Chapter 16).

Such counseling usually takes place in high schools, two-year colleges, four-year colleges, and universities, and is effected in school counseling offices, career planning and placement offices, and counseling centers. Specialized schools within institutions may have their own resources for providing help in career choice (e.g., engineering, law, management, and so on). Institutions other than educational, ranging from private practice entrepreneurs to the military to social service agencies and rehabilitation agencies to government employment offices also provide considerable assistance at this stage. Vocational rehabilitation is a large industry devoted to helping the physically, mentally, and emotionally disabled to enter and adjust to the work force. An example of a private agency that provides career choice assistance would be B'nai B'rith Vocational Guidance Service. Individual entrepreneurs—for fees ranging from reasonable to outrageous—also offer career choice counseling.

Some counselors at this stage adhere more to John Holland's (1985a) model of career choice than to Super's developmental model. Holland postulates six modal personality types—realistic, investigative, artistic, social, enterprising, and conventional—and suggests that both individuals and occupations can be described as having characteristics of one or more of these six types. People with an artistic personality type should choose artistic occupations, for instance. Whether one subscribes to self-concept theory or to the idea of personality types or to sociological theories or to psychoanalytic theories of career development might well determine what specific assessment instruments are utilized but will not appreciably affect the aim of career choice counseling, which is to help individuals acquire this relatively sophisticated self-knowledge, knowledge of the world of work, and decision-making skills.

Establishment

At approximately age 24, the establishment stage begins. A choice has been made, presumably in an appropriate field, and the person now makes an effort to establish his or her place in that field. There are two substages during establishment. The first extends from about ages 25 to 30 and is called *trial-commitment and stabilization*; the second is *advancement*, from 31 to 44 or so. Clearly, the primary task of career development in the establishment stage is for workers to secure their place in a chosen occupation.

For some individuals, however, an initial choice of occupation will prove to be inappropriate; either the person is not satisfied or the person's work is judged to be unsatisfactory. Rather than advancement, these individuals may experience frustration; others may simply consolidate what they have obtained. At this stage, as well as in later stages, the concept of *renewal* is frequently observed as individuals seek to make career shifts. Whether occurring early in one's career or in mid-career or, indeed, after retirement, such shifts typically require considerable economic and social support.

In the establishment stage people begin to grapple with a variety of work and life-style concerns that can persist throughout their remaining work-life cycle. For example, working mothers will need to deal with the guilt that sometimes arises from the conflict between societal or family expectations regarding child rearing and the demands of work life. Dual-career couples are a special type of two-worker family that has three primary distinguishing characteristics: Both spouses have high career salience (i.e., a career is very important to both spouses); the career progression of each is continuous with little or no discontinuity for either spouse; and both work at professional or managerial level occupations. The problems inherent in dual-career marriages are significant, and couples frequently need assistance in working through potential and real concerns. Special minority issues persist from the exploratory stage and through subsequent stages (e.g., immigrants, people with disabilities, African Americans, Hispanics, Native Americans,

Asian Americans, homosexuals, and so on). Another population that frequently requires career assistance during this stage is reentry women. These are women who have been removed from the labor force for a protracted period of time because of child bearing and child rearing and who—perhaps because of the alleged "empty nest syndrome" or because of a change in marital status—seek to reenter the world of work. Typically, they have little self-confidence and few up-to-date skills and need help in negotiating the reentry. Finally, by way of examples of the types of career-related concerns addressed in the establishment stage, there are issues of career ladders within organizations. How can individuals achieve upward mobility within organizational structures? How can "rust-out," "plateauing," and other dysfunctional work behaviors be avoided? Certainly, these examples are not complete, but they should provide a sense of the need for career interventions and counseling during the establishment stage.

During this stage and the preceding exploration stage counselors address with their clients the development of job-finding and job-seeking behaviors. While these skills are regarded by many counselors as prosaic and less interesting than other aspects of career counseling, they are nevertheless important. Helping clients to develop résumés and affording them practice in interviewing, for example, are worthwhile pursuits.

Since most individuals are out of school by this stage of the career life cycle, counseling will usually occur in the workplace itself (as in employee assistance programs that encompass career planning activities), in community agencies (displaced homemakers programs, rehabilitation agencies, VA hospitals, etc.), employment service offices, federal and state funded programs, private counseling organizations, the military, and university-related services to the community. In the latter case, for instance, many colleges and universities have programs for reentry women.

Maintenance

During the long maintenance stage (ages 44 to approximately 65), individuals try to hold on to or preserve the status and gains that they have achieved. For most, it is a holding action that can be characterized by innovation and constant updating; for others, it is a time of stagnation.

Midcareer shifts continue during this stage. Older workers (defined by the U.S. Department of Labor as workers 45 years of age and older) are particularly vulnerable at this stage. If they are out-of-work, they tend to be unemployed for longer periods than their younger counterparts; they lose the ability to continue to perform certain physical and speeded tasks; and they are subject to potentially debilitating psychological consequences of work. Unemployment, especially in the form of dislocation, can also take a tremendous toll at this stage. If an individual works most of his or her life for a single industry or organization and that institution closes permanently or relocates, the consequent dislocation or involuntary unemployment results in client symptoms similar to those characterizing anyone experiencing the psychology of loss. Ultimately it may lead to discouraged workers—those who no longer even bother to look for work.

Further, at this stage, what has been facilely but confusingly dubbed as "burnout" may surface. Unfortunately, the term is nebulous and, in fact, when people use the term they may be speaking of any one of several possibilities. One is that occupational stress is operative to such an extent that it affects work performance and/or general life functioning. If work has the potential to meet all sorts of psychological needs in positive ways, then the obverse is also potentially true—that work can provide strains that result in symptoms of stress. These strains may emanate from multiple roles, conflicting roles, poor supervision, lack of challenge, too much challenge, dangerous work, and other factors; and the stress symptoms may include substance abuse, sleeplessness, high blood pressure, depression and anxiety, job dissatisfaction, and so on. Counseling to blunt the effects of occupational stress and to assist individuals to cope is very common. In addition to referring to occupational stress, however, the term burnout may also be employed to mean aspects of job dissatisfaction—unpleasant work, inability to use one's skills, repetitive tasks, lack of mobility in an organization, and so on. Finally, burnout may simply refer to the long stage of maintenance in career development that for some is characterized by frustration and boredom rather than by advancement.

Frequently, leisure problems emerge during this period as well as in earlier or later periods. Some individuals have difficulty engaging in the productive use of leisure. At one extreme we observe the so-called "workaholics"; at the other extreme, we see the "couch potatoes" or the "cocooned" individuals who spend hour upon hour in passive, mindless leisure activity (or nonactivity). For some who do not find personal fulfillment in work, leisure will serve a compensatory function. Assistance in balancing the complementary nature of leisure and work is thus a necessary and helpful career counseling intervention.

Counseling in the maintenance stage will occur in most of the same settings as pertained with the establishment stage. In addition, outplacement counseling (helping dislocated workers find work) constitutes another focus.

Decline

The last stage of the career life cycle is designated as decline. Two substages are *deceleration* (65–70) and *retirement* (70+). Clearly, people can retire earlier or later. If work meets psychological needs, then the loss of work through involuntary or voluntary retirement has potential for psychological mischief. Many individuals will need and want assistance in the segue from work to nonwork as they reengage society on different terms from those of the previous 40 to 50 years.

Preretirement counseling takes place within organizations, in senior citizen centers, and through continuing education programs of one type or another. Gerontologically related counseling, in general, is still in its infancy and only a small percentage of older people ever see a psychologist, psychiatric social worker, or counselor. As the population profile in the United States changes to include a greater proportion of elderly citizens, this situation will obviously change.

These career life stages, then, contain by their very nature a comprehensive and significant set of concerns that frequently require the intervention of a skilled counselor. Clients need assistance in handling a gamut of career-related issues, from establishing a readiness for career decision making to gathering and using appropriate information, to actually making decisions and implementing their plans. Counselors will need to be alert for various problems that may emerge, whether they be generated from within the individual or externally from economic, social, cultural, familial, or institutional impediments to development. Complete career-related diagnostic systems may be found in Campbell and Cellini (1981) or Rounds and Tinsley (1984). Because the field of career counseling is so extensive, we shall limit our remaining discussion to career choice counseling and the particular content, process, and theory that research suggests is appropriate in working with clients.

The Content of Career Counseling

What goes on in typical career counseling sessions in which career choice is the focus? First of all, it should be recognized that career counseling is usually not open-ended; rather, it is time-limited and clearly focused. Counselors and clients are able to state outcomes of the counseling in behavioral terms and to demonstrate comparatively easily whether or not these outcomes have been achieved. Consequently, both client and counselor know "up-front" how long the experience will last and what reasonable expectations may be held in terms of results.

Even in relatively "pure" career choice counseling, however, there will inevitably be elements of mental health that arise and with which counselors will have to deal. Niles and Pate (1989), for example, argue that a symbiotic relationship exists between work and mental health; therefore, any counselor who offers career services to clients ought to be able also to offer mental health counseling. Hence, they propose that any career counselor should have expertise in understanding psychopathology, the effects of medications, and assessment techniques as they are useful in determining mental status and career-related concerns, to cite just a few mental health counseling competencies. We certainly cannot conceive of a career issue that does not have psychological content. All decisions involve affect, whether verbalized or not. Any attempt, then, to separate career counseling into a discrete category and suggest that it is affect-free is both inaccurate and naive. For heuristic reasons, we offer a separate discussion in this chapter, but the discussion does not imply a distinct separation.

In fact, however, the content of career counseling sessions and other career interventions is likely to be more structured than is the case with many other types of counseling. One study (Taylor, 1985), for example, sought to determine what career counselors actually do in a typical series of career choice sessions. Ten counselors working in a counseling unit in a Department of Technology and Further Education in New South Wales, Australia, were studied as they worked with 81 clients. Basically, their counseling was found to be trait and factor oriented. The typical interview was primarily focused on presenting, reviewing, and clarifying information and subsequently evaluating that information in the light of a client's interests, values, abilities, and the effects of any institutional barriers. Some time was also devoted to discussing the client's vocational self-concept. Rarely were issues of the client's general adjustment addressed, and seldom were tests utilized. Cognitive aspects of decision making were accentuated. The counselors tended initially to be collaborative and then to be more directive. In summary, the typical interview strayed very little from the specific vocational-educational concerns presented by the client. The common strategy was systematic review and evaluation of alternatives on the basis of information. Clearly, this sample of career counselors used a trait and factor, "thinking man's" approach to career choice.

This type of study is descriptive. Although cross-cultural in nature, this investigation coincides with our observations regarding the nature of typical career counseling sessions when the goal is generating occupational alternatives and choosing from among them. Prescriptive writing—outlining what *ought* to occur—would suggest a much broader approach to the task. Concentration on a specific decision is indeed one type of career counseling. More prescriptive approaches would argue for assisting individuals to go beyond the use of information and the discussion of issues in order to make a specific decision. They would urge that the focus be on providing the client with the psychological wherewithal to make decisions in the future and generally to assume responsibility for the direction of her or his life.

In a very real sense, career counseling for choice would include elements of life-style counseling and identity counseling. The counselor would facilitate the client's responses to such questions as Who am I? What do I want out of life? What do I value? What is my purpose in life? What are my primary strengths and limitations? What major influences in my life have shaped my attitudes toward work? How do my personal attributes, values, opportunities, and cultural factors come together in my life? How do I see myself 5, 10, 15, 20 years into the future? How committed, how ego-involved am I in relation to work? These are but a few of the types of questions that should be dealt with in a series of career counseling sessions.

In any case, both the client and the counselor will bring to career counseling needs, values, feelings, expectations, self-perceptions, and so on. These variables will clearly affect the course of career counseling, just as they affect the tenor of all counseling. Consequently, traditional types of counselor self-awareness are necessary to guard against abuses in the counseling process. Issues of transference, countertransference, the working alliance, self-disclosure, and so forth are real in career counseling and require no less skill of the career counselor than they do of more generic counselors.

The typical career counseling sequence has been discussed in detail in several volumes (see, for example, Yost & Corbishley, 1987; Raskin, 1987; Peterson, Sampson, & Reardon, 1991; Spokane, 1991; Brown & Brooks, 1991). We do not have the space here to delineate completely the subtleties of the process. We do, however, present a general description of the career counseling cycle—again, as it relates to career choice. In general, there will be a data-gathering phase, followed by an emphasis on self-understanding, the generation and evaluation of alternatives, and the implementation of plans.

Gathering Information

In the data-gathering stage, formal and informal assessment resources are employed. Formal aptitude assessment batteries or individual aptitude tests may be utilized; interest inventories and work values inventories may be administered; personality variables may be assessed; job satisfaction may be determined; and past achievements may be catalogued, to cite just a few possibilities. Decision-making systems, such as the Self-Directed Search (Holland, 1985b), the Harrington-O'Shea (1982) Career Decision-Making

System, or various computerized programs, such as Guidance Information System, DIS-COVER (Harris-Bowlsbey & Rayman, 1978), or SIGI (Katz, 1975), may be utilized at this initial stage of career counseling in order to obtain information. The use of assessment in counseling is more fully discussed in Chapter 17. In general, career assessment will cover one or more of four purposes: prediction, discrimination, monitoring, and evaluation (Herr & Cramer, 1992). The use of tests for *prediction* usually involves aptitude results (although it can entail the use of interest data) to forecast how well someone is likely to perform some future career-relevant behavior, such as success in training or success on the job. *Discrimination* refers to the use of interest, values, or other data to tell people how similar they are to individuals in various occupational groups. *Monitoring* is nothing more than the use of instruments to evaluate an individual's career progress. If we wanted to see what career development tasks a person has already accomplished and what tasks remain to be achieved, for example, we might administer a career maturity inventory. *Evaluation* is simply the use of assessment instruments to determine how closely goals of interventions have been achieved.

All of these types of assessment devices are available to the career counselor. In conjunction with data gathered in the counseling situation, they permit the counselor to accomplish what is, in effect, a needs assessment. A recommended resource for evaluating appropriate assessment instruments is Kapes and Mastie (1988).

The first interview of a career counseling sequence is very much like an intake interview. It involves the gathering of pertinent data, such as demographics (e.g., client age, name, address, telephone number, marital status, etc.); present family configuration and/or family of origin make-up, if different; education; occupational history; general mental and physical health (e.g., any history of major and significant problems that would affect the career counseling experience). The counselor will want to get some idea in the words of the client of the nature of the presenting problem. The counselor might simply ask: "Why are you coming for career counseling?" As a follow-up, the counselor may encourage the client to speak in detail about what assertive efforts have been made in the past to address the problem. Clearly, the presenting problem—as is always the case in counseling—may or may not be an accurate depiction of the real problem. At this stage, the counselor is beginning to form a picture of the client's status in order to determine the goals and the direction of the counseling experience. The counselor will later test these perceptions against those of the client.

During information gathering, many career counselors will do a developmental work history. They will try to determine the occupations of the client's parents and siblings in order to gauge family occupational expectations, to determine the client's aspiration level, and to achieve some sense of work salience in the client's life. Some counselors will even want to know about fantasy choices and, indeed, any early career choices that were considered and rejected.

At any rate, the client and counselor will reach some agreement by the end of this stage regarding where they both want to go and how they are likely to get there. It is important that the goals be attainable (i.e., that they are realistic and sufficiently few in number to be achieved). Usually, any broad goal will be translated into behavioral objectives so that both the counselor and the client will know whether or not the desired end results have been reached. For instance, rather than merely deciding with the client that she ought to understand her vocational interests as a result of career counseling, that goal will be transformed into behavioral outcomes (e.g., She will be able to state her three highest Holland codes and her three highest basic interest scales).

The logistics of the sessions should be made explicit. *When* will assessments be given and *where*? *Why* are they being administered? *How* will the results fit into the counseling experience? *How many* sessions will there likely be? *What* will be the length of each session? Will homework (some sort of extracounseling assignments) be necessary? If there are costs, this is the time to speak about fees.

Self-Understanding

Once goals have been agreed upon, they will inevitably include the necessity for the client to enhance self-understanding—to clarify and accept a vocational self-concept. The counselor will assist the client to explore and understand aspects of the self that are important in career planning and decision making. These aspects will include values, interests, experiences, and abilities, among other factors. At this stage the career counselor will want to confirm if there are any special impeding or facilitating psychological issues that may affect career counseling. If some psychological characteristics are thought to be seriously dysfunctional or debilitating, the counselor may make a recommendation during the course of counseling that the client engage in subsequent counseling to address these issues. In no case should the career counseling sessions be turned into an attempt to alter a person's basic personality structure or general mode of engaging the world. There is enough to do in career counseling. Again, however, this recommendation should not be construed to mean that psychological aspects of self should be disassociated from career counseling; that is impossible. It simply means that if the client does not have the psychological strength to choose, enter, and succeed in an occupation, remedial interventions are necessary, or at least desirable. Rehabilitation of those who are psychiatrically disabled is a specialty within career counseling.

What sorts of psychological issues should be addressed in the course of career counseling? Here are some examples. If a person is unable to make a decision because of dependency on a significant other, the counselor may choose to try to make the person counterdependent. If the client has difficulty with assertiveness or other aspects of self-presentation, the counselor may elect to focus on these issues. If the client is unaware of how he or she affects other people and is affected by them, the counselor may want to help develop the client's self-awareness. If the client has no clear interests or values, the counselor may opt to delve into why.

The counselor will help the client to synthesize all relevant aspects of self-knowledge. As well as psychological barriers to choice and implementation of a career, the counselor and client will together discuss any environmental, social, or cultural barriers that might prevent the client from attaining a career in a chosen field and at the level desired. What environmental constraints are in operation? Are necessary resources attainable? Do important other people (family, friends, spouses, and so on) have ideas that are in opposition to those of the client? Does the client have a plan to deal with any specific societal barriers (i.e., age, sex, disability, religion, and so on)?

As this synthesis occurs, the counselor will draw from the client some notion of preferred life-style. What is desired? Is it realistic? Is the client's aspiration level appropriate or is it overly ambitious or too modest? These are questions that may bring into play a counselor's own values. Consequently, the counselor will want to be sure that these values are conscious and that they do not interfere with the working alliance.

Generating and Evaluating Alternatives

On the basis of a vocationally well-developed self-concept and a consideration of environmental constraints, the client will now determine—with the assistance of the counselor—a range of possible career alternatives. At this stage occupational and educational information is necessary.

Frankly, not a great deal is known about the use of educational and occupational information in career-related decisions. Research is relatively sparse. Perhaps the best source on the effective use of career information in counseling is Peterson, Sampson, and Reardon (1991). They maintain that the use of information in counseling represents a learning event. As such, it should be treated the same as any learning event; that is, there should be an objective (what should be acquired), an intervention to bring about the desired capability, and an evaluation to see if the objective was obtained. When information is used in decision making, Peterson et al. recommend a CASVE cycle, where C is *communication* (identifying a need), A is *analysis* (interrelating problem components), S is *synthesis* (creating likely alternatives), V is *valuing* (prioritizing alternatives), and E is *execution* (forming means-ends strategies). These types of decision-making systems are discussed more fully in Chapter 16.

Some occupational and educational information will be good, in the sense that it is recent, valid, and applicable; while other information will be bad, in the sense that it is outdated, designed simply for proselytizing, or very difficult to use. Guidelines for the evaluation of occupational information are available from the National Career Development Association (NVGA, 1980). In general, the need for information will vary from client to client. The more vocationally ingenuous the client, the greater the need for information and, consequently, the longer the time frame required for counseling; the more vocationally sophisticated the client, the less the need for information and the shorter the duration of counseling.

There are numerous sources of educational and occupational information. We do not have the space here to discuss these sources, but they range from printed materials to computer programs, from media approaches (films, videotapes, audio cassettes and filmstrips) to interview techniques, from card sorts to simulation and gaming, from visits to work sites to formal workshops, from exploratory work experiences to part-time work, among others. Some media are interactive; some are noninteractive. Some will require that the client have the assistance of a counselor in negotiating the information system; others can be accessed and utilized by the client with no assistance at all. One source for locating and evaluating educational and occupational information is Zunker (1986).

Clients will probably need assistance in determining what information is available to explore each alternative. At this stage of the career counseling cycle, homework is typically utilized, and the client is required to seek out and use information outside of the counseling session. Time in the counseling session is reserved for helping the client to understand the personal relevance of the information and to help the client to process the information.

If the self-understanding phase has been completed successfully, there should be little difficulty in the client and the counselor together generating many reasonable occupational alternatives. For example, a client's Holland code alone will send them to the *Holland Occupational Finder* in which scores of occupations at various occupational levels are listed for each code. Clients will need to gather information for each option that they judge to be viable. It is very important at this stage to get the client sufficiently motivated so that he or she accepts and internalizes the fact that securing and evaluating educational and occupational information is an assertive, active process, not one that is static and passive. At this stage, the counselor may want to have the client access any one of a number of computer interactive systems in order to facilitate the processing of information. Care should be taken, however, to remember that the computer is an aid to the counselor, not a substitute for a counselor.

After broad research, the usual procedure is to encourage the client to narrow alternatives to a workable number, usually no more than a half dozen. The procedure is not dissimilar to the way some of the more popular interest inventories are organized: They provide a broad Holland category description, a narrowed overview of basic interest scales, and then evolve down to specific occupational scales. The few chosen alternatives are then explored along a variety of parameters in terms of their "fit" with the client's self-characteristics and any potentially limiting environmental conditions.

One consideration at this point in career counseling concerns the nature of the time frame. Is the career choice being made now but implemented at a relatively far point in the future? If so, planning must project education and training. For example, a college freshman who decides that she wants to become a clinical psychologist must first decide on a major. Although psychology is the obvious selection for focus of baccalaureate level study, there are attendant questions of minor, exploratory work experiences, the universe of graduate study (e.g., Psy.D. versus Ph.D.), and so on. The eight or nine years of education and training necessary for entry into the profession allow for a relatively leisurely contemplation of some of these issues. If however, the choice is immediate, that luxury is not afforded. Time is more of a press, and the urgency compels that the process be accelerated and intensified. In the former case, counseling would provide the client with a "future file" of things to accomplish; in the latter case, the focus is on the here and now.

The counselor and client comparatively evaluate the narrowed options in terms of the economic and psychological costs entailed in each, the probability and desirability of each, and so on. There are many aids designed to assist clients at this stage of decision making, such as "balance sheets" (Janis & Mann, 1977). Chapter 16 discusses some of these in more detail. The client is encouraged to consider how keen he or she is about each option, how significant others feel about each possibility, the short- and long-term implications of each decision, the risk-taking probability of achieving each goal, and the time frame. Some choices require a client to have a capacity for delayed gratification during long training and professional socialization, while others do not.

Implementing Plans

It is certainly possible that even after all the work that went into the career counseling cycle up to this point, a client will not reach a decision. Readiness and maturity that have not developed over the course of a quarter-century or so may not always be compressed into a few weeks. Persistent client fears, dysfunctional coping behaviors, indecisiveness, lack of risk-taking propensity, and so on may prevent the individual from deciding. Equally vocationally hobbled is the person who is multipotentialed and for whom many choices are not only possible but also probable. Choice anxiety for the multipotentialed person can be intense. In cases where the career counseling experience does not seem to lead to the prospect of a satisfying, reasonable choice, the counselor and the client should try to agree on what aspects of the person or the environment need to be altered in order for choice to occur and then outline necessary steps for action to remedy these handicapping conditions.

For most people at this point, the counselor and the client will collaboratively determine what specific actions need to be effected to make the choice a reality. Time lines for various milestones to be accomplished will be calculated. If additional abilities are required (e.g., résumé preparation, interviewing, job seeking and job finding), they can be developed.

Termination in career counseling is little different from termination in any other type of counseling. The sessions can carry through to "term," or either the counselor or the client can terminate prematurely if either has the perception that the experience is not fruitful. At any rate, termination typically includes an evaluation of the counseling in terms of the degree to which goals have been met and an expression of the feelings of both counselor and client. Behavioral insights gained will be summarized; next steps will be reinforced. While dependency and separation anxiety and other termination problems are possible at this stage, they are not common in career counseling.

Theoretical Counseling Orientations

Within the career counseling cycle, virtually any theoretical counseling orientation can and has been utilized. The likelihood is that bits and pieces of many relatively distinct theories will be employed, but there are career counselors who lean more or less heavily on one or another orientation. For example, there are those who urge that career counseling be client centered, rational-emotive, behavioral, and even psychodynamic, among other possibilities.

In general, we are inclined to view career counseling as employing a variety of theoretical counseling foundations. As with all counseling, the career counselor will establish therapeutic conditions in the counseling relationship that are facilitative, regardless of the theoretical orientation. He or she will utilize "pet" techniques from several theories to accomplish various phases of the career counseling cycle. For instance, when nondirective encouragement is required in the process of client self-exploration, the counselor will act accordingly. When the client's seeking of information is the aim, the counselor will want to use various reinforcement techniques.

All in all, however, because much of career counseling rests on a cognitive base, career counselors can profit greatly, in our experience, from using cognitive restructuring techniques. The emphasis that these techniques place on cognitive processing of causal attributions and other internal monologues strike us as appropriate for most career counseling interventions. These theories, such as those of Beck (Scott, Williams, & Beck, 1989), Ellis (1962), and Meichenbaum (1977), have been reviewed earlier in this volume. Simply stated, Ellis reminds us that maladaptive or irrational beliefs about events, not the events themselves, are what cause difficulties. In career counseling, examples of irrational beliefs might include the following: "There is only one occupation that is good for me" or "My career decision must please significant others in my life." The "cure" is to teach clients to think rationally rather than irrationally. Beck urges that counselors help clients to recognize their distortions in thinking about reality, since a client's emotional response is consistent with the distortion and not with the reality. Hence, the counselor points out conclusions based on little evidence ("Accountants are all anal"), reasoning from single instances ("My lawyer is a jerk; I wouldn't want to be a lawyer"), or magnifying consequences, for example ("If I make the wrong career decision, my life is ruined forever"). Meichenbaum points out the complex relationship between cognitions and emotions and advocates that counselors help clients to alter their internal dialogues—their inner speech. The client's cognitions are, in fact, the behaviors that need to be altered. So, through such counseling techniques as conditioning, modeling, and behavioral rehearsal, the client is helped to change thoughts, feelings, and behaviors related to career choice.

All of these theoreticians are really directing counseling toward the goal of helping people to "think straight," in the sense of thinking realistically. The goal is not for counselors to change clients' beliefs for them. Rather, it is to help clients to acquire the skills so that they can identify and change their self-defeating thoughts. To do so requires that both the client and the counselor be active in the counseling relationship and that they collaborate in the resolution of career problems.

Career Counseling Outcomes

The outcomes of career counseling are much more measurable than those for many other foci of counseling, since objectives are typically delimited and made explicitly behavioral. Consequently, it is easier to determine if they have been achieved. Career literature is characterized by a plethora of outcome studies that compare the effectiveness of various types of interventions with various types of clients.

Meta-analyses and other types of review studies of the effectiveness of career counseling interventions are reasonably clear in pointing to the overwhelming efficacy of career interventions (Holland, Magoon, & Spokane, 1981; Fretz, 1981; Spokane & Oliver, 1983; Rounds & Tinsley, 1984; Oliver & Spokane, 1988). Specifically, what they demonstrate is that generally almost all career interventions are successful (upwards of 80 percent, on average), perhaps because typical clients bring to the interventions so few positive career skills, knowledges, and attitudes. All types of interventions have been found effective—group, individual, computer mediated, self-directed, and so on. In general, there is no clear evidence that one type of intervention is any more effective than any other or that specific types of clients benefit more from one type of intervention than from another.

All in all, the evidence for the effectiveness of career counseling is robust and suggests that this type of counseling is an appropriate specialization for counselors who feel a strong need for closure and who require relatively immediate feedback that tells them they did somebody some good.

Summary

Career counseling is a comprehensive, psychologically oriented type of counseling that extends throughout the life span. Counseling for initial occupational choice is but one aspect of this specialization. This chapter focused on delineating career-related concerns for elementary school through retirement. It described the typical career decision-making counseling cycle and the content of career counseling. It offered theoretical orientations and presented the research on the outcomes of career counseling. In general, career counseling is seen as far from a simple, mechanistic type of counseling; rather, it requires considerable skill and knowledge.

References

Brown, D., & Brooks, L. (1991). *Career counseling techniques*. Boston, MA: Allyn & Bacon.

Campbell, R. E., & Cellini, J. V. (1981). A diagnostic taxonomy of adult career problems. *Journal of Vocational Behavior, 19*(2), 175–190.

Ellis, A. (1962). *Reason and emotion in psychotherapy*. Secaucus, NJ: Lyle Stuart.

Fretz, B. R. (1981). Evaluating the effectiveness of career interventions. *Journal of Counseling Psychology, 28*, 77–90.

Harrington, T. F., & O'Shea, A. J. (1982). *Technical manual for the Harrington-O'Shea Career Decision-Making System*. Circle Pines, MN: American Guidance Service.

Harris-Bowlsbey, J., & Rayman, J. R. (1978). *DISCOVER: The Career Guidance System: System description and counselor guide*. Baltimore, MD: IBM Corporation.

Herr, E. L., & Cramer, S. H. (1992). *Career guidance and counseling through the lifespan: Systematic approaches* (4th ed.). New York: Harper/Collins.

Holland, J. L. (1985a). *Making vocational choices: A theory of vocational personalities and work environments*. Englewood Cliffs, NJ: Prentice-Hall.

Holland, J. L. (1985b). *Professional manual Self-Directed Search*. Odessa, FL: Psychological Assessment Resources.

Holland, J. L., Magoon, T. M., & Spokane, A. R. (1981). Counseling psychology: Career interventions, research, and theory. *Annual Review of Psychology, 32*, 279–300.

Janis, I., & Mann, L. (1977). *Decision-making: A psychological analysis of conflict, choice, and commitment*. New York: Free Press.

Kapes, J. T., & Mastie, M. M. (Eds.). (1988). *A counselor's guide to career assessment instruments* (2nd ed.). Washington, DC: National Career Development Association.

Katz, M. R. (1975). *A computer-based system for interactive guidance and information*. Princeton, NJ: Educational Testing Service.

Meichenbaum, D. (Ed.). (1977). *Cognitive behavior modification: An integrative approach.* New York: Plenum.

Neff, W. S. (1985). *Work and human behavior* (3rd ed.). New York: Aldine.

Nevo, O. (1987). Irrational expectations in career counseling and their confronting arguments. *The Career Development Quarterly, 35,* 239–250.

Niles, S. G., & Pate, R. H., Jr. (1989). Competency and training issues related to the integration of career counseling and mental health counseling. *Journal of Career Development, 16,* 63–71.

NVGA. (1980). Guidelines for the preparation and evaluation of career information literature. *Vocational Guidance Quarterly, 28*(4), 291–296.

Oliver, L. W. & Spokane, A. R. (1988). Career-intervention outcome: What contributes to client gain? *Journal of Counseling Psychology, 35,* 447–462.

Peterson, G. W., Sampson, J. P., & Reardon, R. C. (1991). *Career development and services: A cognitive approach.* Belmont, CA: Brooks/Cole.

Raskin, P. M. (1987). *Vocational counseling: A guide for the practitioner.* New York Teachers College Press.

Rounds, J. B., Jr., & Tinsley, H. E. A. (1984). Diagnosis and treatment of vocational problems. In S. Brown & R. Lent (Eds.), *Handbook of counseling psychology* (pp. 137–177). New York: Wiley.

Scott, J., Williams, M. G., & Beck, A. T. (1989). *Cognitive therapy in clinical practice.* London: Routledge.

Spokane, A. R. (1991). *Career intervention.* Boston, MA: Allyn & Bacon.

Spokane, A. R., & Oliver, L. W. (1983). The outcomes of vocational intervention. In S. H. Osipow & W. B. Walsh, (Eds.), *Handbook of vocational psychology,* Vol. 2. Hillsdale, NJ: Erlbaum.

Super, D. E. (1957). *The psychology of careers.* New York: Harper & Row.

Taylor, N. B. (1985). How do career counselors counsel? *British Journal of Guidance and Counseling, 13*(2), 166–177.

Yost, E. B., & Corbishley, M. A. (1987). *Career counseling: A psychological approach.* San Francisco: Jossey-Bass.

Zunker, V. G. (1986). *Career counseling: Applied concepts of life planning* (2nd ed.). Monterey, CA: Brooks/Cole.

Ethics, Legalities, and Values in Counseling

Counselors must be concerned with the moral, ethical, legal, and other axiological aspects of counseling whether on a group or individual basis. Counselors throughout their training and within their practices must accept the responsibility of understanding and integrating these aspects into the counseling process.

Ethics is a moral philosophy that deals with making judgments—good or bad, proper or improper, approval or disapproval, right or wrong, and so on. Professional ethics in counseling thus pertains to which counseling actions or behaviors are right and which are wrong. Professional ethics are set up as an ideal or standard of professional conduct. Consequently, certain actions are deemed to be desirable while others are deemed undesirable; certain actions are thought to be wise while others are judged to be foolish; certain behaviors are thought to be laudable while others are judged reprehensible. The primary determiners of what actions are ethically acceptable and what behaviors are not are the professional organizations that encompass the counseling specialties. Each of these groups has its own code of ethical conduct (American Association for Counseling and Development, 1988; American Association for Marriage and Family Therapy, 1988; American Psychiatric Association, 1989; American Psychological Association, 1981, 1982, 1987, 1990a, 1990b; National Association of Social Workers, 1990). Thus, rightful and wrongful practices in counseling are consensually derived on the basis of peer judgment, and the ethical dicta of the various mental health specialties are much more alike than they are different.

The general area of values and the interrelationship of client, counselor, and societal values are receiving increased attention in the literature and in the preparation programs for potential professionals in this field. Counselors have been encouraged traditionally to know their own values, even though sharing these values was often discouraged. In recent times, it has become clear that clients bring value concerns to counselors and expect counselors to help them identify, shape, and sometimes change their values. They often want a counselor to, at least, aid in the development of new behaviors that will allow them to act more in line with their value system. Value-free counseling, although once practiced, may be a contradiction in terms. Counselors must understand their own values, those of their clients, and those of their society, as well as determine how these affect the lives of their clients. Counseling almost always is affected by the values of one or more of the participants. It cannot be value free.

Legal concerns in counseling are receiving increased attention. Much of what the counselor does has legal implications, especially in cases where data may be used for or against the client, where selection decisions are related to counselor activities, or where the counselor is expected by the client or by society to develop a plan of action for the client to follow. The counselor's awareness of the legal implications will promote better client assistance and better protection for the counselor.

Counselors will find that situations related to ethics, values, and the law may not fit neatly into categories. The statements of ethics by the various professional associations, although valuable, do not always provide a clear-cut direction for counselors. The law is dynamic, and as new situations arise in the legal realm, counselors must be prepared to integrate new information into their practice. Values tend to change, and in today's world, they may change faster than ever. What a person believes today about him- or herself, other people, and society may change by tomorrow.

It is a given that counselors must act ethically and legally with clients. This requires constant awareness of existing standards of professional ethics. Counselors must understand the legal responsibilities and obligations in their professional involvement with clients and the client's rights.

Counselors should be aware of how values affect their interaction with clients, especially those clients with different backgrounds. Counselors must be able to help clients identify their values or value systems. Although most people behave consistently in relation to a value system, some may not be able to articulate the values that influence their behavior. A counselor may be called upon to help clarify a client's values. Some clients know a little about their values but find the need to clarify and perhaps change them. If the client needs to develop a method for changing his or her values, a counselor can help identify a process and work through it with the client. In this way a counselor can help a client identify, clarify, and change values and develop a continuing process that he or she can use throughout life.

The literature of ethical and legal issues in counseling is indeed very large and the focus of a great deal of attention. In a single chapter, we simply provide an introduction. A number of excellent texts are devoted solely to the topic.

Ethical Considerations

Ethics are suggested standards of conduct based on an agreed-upon set of values. A profession attempts to translate as many values as possible into structured expectations of behavior as its members relate to one another, their clientele, and the public. These standards usually take the form of statements that constitute complete codes of ethics.

Knowledge of these standards can provide the counselor with a method of dealing with various difficult situations. But many situations arise for which no ethical statement has been developed or for which only a tangential relationship exists to current statements.

In most cases, ethical statements relate to several key areas of concern. In general these areas are identified as follows:

1. General concerns and responsibilities of the professional
2. The relationship between counselor and client
3. Methods used for obtaining information about the client
4. Methods of evaluating the counselor's own activity
5. Research and publication as regards human subjects
6. Publication of materials or research resulting from the counseling process
7. Outside activity of the counselor as a consultant or specialized counselor
8. Administrative concerns
9. Preparation concerns

One of the most comprehensive studies of the types of ethical dilemmas encountered by practicing psychologists is reported by Pope and Vetter (1992). They tallied the responses of 545 psychologists who reported 703 ethically troubling critical incidents. These incidents organized into 23 general categories as revealed in Table 19-1. The majority of these categories are discussed within this chapter.

General Concerns

In this area professionals are provided guidelines for their commitment to the counseling profession. Responsibility to the client, the agency, and society is the primary focus of the guidelines. In addition, the degree of responsibility of counselors for their activities and the positive and negative consequences that might occur are discussed. Counselors are exhorted to make every effort to insure the appropriateness of the services provided to and used by their clients. Finally, the interrelationship of the counselor and other professionals is considered. In short, the general area of ethics presents a broad picture of the profession: working with clients, being an employee of an agency, and relating to the general public as well as to professional colleagues.

Counselor–Client Relationships

The heart of counselors' work is interacting ethically with clients as individuals or in group settings. This second area of ethical behavior spells out a number of issues that relate to the counseling process. It provides guidelines for counselors to examine themselves, their clients, and the interrelationships that exist. The ethical statements in this area reflect a concern for the counseling relationship and the integrity of the client. In all actions a counselor is expected to keep the client uppermost in his or her mind, and to

TABLE 19-1   Categories of 703 Ethically Troubling Incidents

Category	*n*	%
Confidentiality	128	18
Blurred, dual, or conflictual relationships	116	17
Payment sources, plans, settings, and methods	97	14
Academic settings, teaching dilemmas, and concerns about training	57	8
Forensic psychology	35	5
Research	29	4
Conduct of colleagues	29	4
Sexual issues	28	4
Assessment	25	4
Questionable or harmful interventions	20	3
Competence	20	3
Ethics (and related) codes and committees	17	2
School psychology	15	2
Publishing	14	2
Helping the financially stricken	13	2
Supervision	13	2
Advertising and (mis)representation	13	2
Industrial–organizational psychology	9	1
Medical issues	5	1
Termination	5	1
Ethnicity	4	1
Treatment records	4	1
Miscellaneous	7	1

Source: K. S. Pope and V. A. Vetter, Ethical dilemmas encountered by members of the American Psychological Association. *American Psychologist,* 1992, *47*(3), pp. 397–411. Copyright 1992 by the American Psychological Association. Reprinted by permission.

insure that, to the greatest degree possible, the confidential nature of the relationship is maintained. This pertains to all methods of communicating with the client.

Counselors also need to communicate the conditions of the counseling relationship. Such factors as fees, times for the sessions, purposes, goals, procedures, and counselor limits are among the topics for discussion. There is usually a discussion of the process for selection of group members and how sessions are to be monitored to insure that clients are moving forward, no matter how slowly it may be. Counselors are expected to monitor their own process as they provide assistance to clients. Referral of clients who may be outside the professional competence level of a counselor is also a consideration.

Methods for Obtaining Information in Counseling

Generally this area of the ethical standards is concerned with the use of assessment instruments, such as tests, questionnaires, or checklists and observational approaches. It provides a guideline for the selection of tests and the uses of the results. The prerequisite competence of counselors in administering and interpreting the tests receives considerable attention. The standards also suggest that communication with clients and others is an important part of the assessment process.

In general, the guidelines maintain that clients have the right to know about the testing process, test results, and the uses made of tests as part of the counseling process. Informed consent also implies that they have a right to know the basis for decisions related to selection of tests and the decisions that result from testing.

Methods for Evaluation

It has become more critical that objective evaluations of counseling and counselors occur. Ethical statements provide guidelines for assisting counselors in accomplishing this task. Their own evaluative efforts and the use of outside personnel are part of the standards. The ability to present objective, verifiable data on the process, the interaction, and the outcomes of counseling is essential.

Research and Publication

Since counselors deal with human beings and human behavior, it is essential that care be exercised in insuring that any research that is attempted be as clear-cut and definable as possible. There is a need to produce information that can be shared with other professionals and be used to benefit clients, but research should not harm people. In the last analysis, a person's integrity far outweighs any benefit research can offer.

There are several safeguards against the misuse of research. One is communication; that is, it is essential that there is a clear understanding between the researcher and his or her subjects. Also most agencies and organizations have rules and regulations that define how research should be carried out. The counselor-researcher has an obligation to know and to follow these rules. Lastly, proper publication should state the conditions of the research and a reasonable description of the process and outcomes. It is incumbent on researchers to ensure client welfare as much as possible.

Outside Activities

Counselors and psychologists normally have opportunities to provide a variety of services outside the normal areas of their counseling activity. Consultation to others, supervisory activities, public relations, and professional commentary are examples. It is essential, from an ethical point of view, that counselors act and speak in a manner consonant with professional guidelines. It is necessary for counselors to realize that they may be seen as speaking for the whole profession and, therefore, have a duty to act and speak in a professional manner.

It is incumbent upon counselors to know their level of expertise and to avoid going beyond this level, either as consultants or in public statements. The counselor should exhibit restraint when offering services as a consultant or advisor, even though regulations regarding advertising allow more leeway than was once the case.

Administration

Counselors are sometimes part of an administrative structure. They have people to whom they report, and they may have staff for whom they have responsibility. It is essential that counselors understand the lines of communication and operate within this parameter.

The line of authority may not be perfect; many times people obtain positions for which they may have little or no competence. It is important, however, for counselors to temper their attempts to change bad administrative personnel and practices. It is a good idea to try to determine an organization's hierarchy before taking a position with it. Although changing jobs may be an American way of life, it does raise some ethical issues when people accept jobs knowing that the administrative arrangements are not in line with their beliefs or how they function.

Preparation

Counselors should try to insure that the preparation they receive is of the highest possible caliber. This can be done by checking professional groups' accreditation lists and by carefully examining the program they are considering.

Making ethical decisions when specific conflicts occur is often difficult because the codes furnish only broad guidelines. Counselors must base their actions on their perceptions of the counseling relationship and the society in which the client lives. Unethical behavior sometimes occurs when the counselor's communication to the client establishes a particular set of expectations for the latter that are inconsistent with the counselor's actual behavior.

Ethics impinge upon the lives of counselor and client. Each is faced with certain issues that relate to ethical and moral choices. The counselor, as stated earlier, has a code of ethics to follow as he or she interacts with the client. The client's expected behavior will be less clearly defined but is still an important variable in the counselor-client interactions. Some of the concerns and questions related to ethics follow.

Moral Rules

Society provides certain rules that relate to each citizen's life. These rules, explicit and implicit, are brought into counseling relationships as people attempt to develop or define their moral and ethical positions.

In the majority society, honesty is considered better than cheating. Honesty leads to positive outcomes; cheating leads to punishment. Honest people are considered more mentally healthy than people who cheat. Yet many clients enter counseling with conflicts about these concerns. What society says is not always completely true, and clients often seek clarifications or justification of society's rules, wishing to order their lives according to the "real" rules of society. One counselor task, therefore, is to help clients sort out these rules and integrate them into their behavior and value systems. The greater the understanding of the rules, the greater the possibility that clients will be able to resolve these value dilemmas and come to terms with societal ascriptions.

Counselors' words and actions often influence clients' perceptions. By word or action counselors may communicate a number of moral positions to clients. It is incumbent upon counselors to understand their own positions and to insure clients clearly understand the choices that they make in an ethical/moral realm.

The counselor has some important areas with which to be concerned as he or she functions as a professional. His or her personal goals must be understood and clarified. His or her professional behavior must be monitored. The methods that counselors may use to effect behavioral change must be carefully considered. Any experimental actions must be weighed and evaluated. Finally, the counselor must deal with ethical and legal aspects of confidentiality.

Personal Goals

Professionals need to examine their positions in terms of their qualifications for the counseling activity and any possible violation of standards as they relate to the good of the client, society, and the profession. During the course of any counselor's professional life, she or he must inevitably assess her or his qualifications to handle a particular client. Even though the client may be willing to continue, the counselor may feel a lack of sufficient skill to continue and may need to refer the client to another professional. The counselor may be forced to decide if presenting objective data at this time is helpful to a client. The decision and the process of decision making will provide the counselor with a better understanding of ethical and personal goals.

One of the primary ethical mandates of virtually all codes of professional ethics is that counselors should not provide services beyond their levels of training. This area becomes arguable when counselors feel that they are capable of working with certain types of clients, but some professional organizations believe that they are not properly trained. A case in point is masters-level counselors working without supervision with individuals who manifest a considerable degree of psychological disturbance. The argument manifests what some believe is a form of professional racism. Psychiatrists believe they should provide services and that others should be denied (e.g., medication, hospital privileges, etc.). Licensed psychologists feel that they are more professionally adept than psychiatric social workers or professional counselors (i.e., NBCC certified). Many feel that they are at least as well qualified as the genre above them in the "pecking order."

Another example of personal goals clashing with the welfare of the client may be found in the case of certain media psychologists. This represents a type of "long distance education" that has become increasingly visible. The bounds of what constitutes reasonable advice dispensed via television, radio, or print and potentially harmful meddling can easily become obfuscated. A television producer sometimes cares more about the television attractiveness of a counselor than about his or her credentials.

A third instance occurs when religious beliefs of the counselor are either imposed on the client or conflict with those of the client. When religious ardor and deeply felt beliefs transcend professional objectivity, there is some reason to believe that professional ethics have been compromised. On the other hand, viewing the situation from the point of view of religious ethics, it is possible to argue that these canons of behavior would be violated by following recommended professional practice (e.g., abortion counseling under certain circumstances). More discussion about the potential values conflict inherent in religion and psychology is presented later in this chapter. All of these and other conflicts between personal goals and client welfare are sources of potential mischief.

Behavior

Sometimes counselors must monitor their own activities and those of other professionals in the counseling relationship. How does one react to and deal with a colleague's incompetency? How does one deal with one's own mistakes in the counseling interaction? To what extent does one use the counseling relationship for personal gratification? This is a crucial area, for it is the basis for potential legal action against the counselor. Some self-monitoring of personal behavior is essential to all counselors to ensure awareness of what is going on and of its effect on the needs of the client.

Semi-pejorative terms, such as "whistle-blower," are sometimes applied to professionals who call to the attention of disciplining bodies the unethical behavior of their colleagues. Such should not be the case, for professionals indeed have an obligation to monitor not only their own ethical behavior but also that of their colleagues. In terms of self-monitoring, counselors might ask themselves such questions as: Am I providing the solutions for this person's problems by giving advice and thus increasing the client's dependency on me? Am I "stringing out" the client and seeing her more than is necessary, either for financial gain, for increased dependency on me, or for some other reason? Am I self-disclosing only because it is gratifying my own needs? Am I setting myself up as an expert because it massages my own ego to do so?

Change of Behavior and Experimentation

Professional counselors should be alert to and involved with new ideas in counseling. They should be aware of the activities of a variety of professional groups and of the interactions of each counseling contact so that evaluation and change can occur when appropriate. This process must be continuous to ensure that assistance offered to the client is appropriate to the latter's needs. Experimentation for its own sake is of questionable value and is sometimes unethical. Counselors should study professional associations' statements of ethics and continue to examine and reevaluate their ethical position as revealed within the counseling dyad in terms of its effects on clients.

Confidentiality

Confidentiality involves the retention of information received in a personal interaction with a client. A dilemma exists because not all such information or data can be treated as completely confidential. Understanding what information is confidential and what is not is crucial.

Both confidentiality and privileged communication relate to the issue of privacy—the freedom of individuals to choose what, when, and to whom information will be revealed.

The counseling profession has taken as one of its basic tenets that confidentiality must be assured for clients—in so far as possible—if the therapeutic relationship is to thrive.

Some issues of confidentiality can be especially irksome. For example, more and more counseling services are reimbursed by third-party insurers (private or government) who want detailed diagnostic and treatment information that they subsequently enter into their electronic data banks (e.g., a Medicaid audit). Also nettlesome is the issue of when confidentiality ought to be breached, either ethically or to comply with the law. Child abuse is one such instance where there are few options for a professional. Other instances of mandated reporting cited by Popiel (1980) are matters of criminal action, certain court actions, expert report to an attorney, litigation between client and clinician, when the therapist is court-appointed, and when danger is perceived that clients will harm themselves or others. Many of these issues are discussed later in this chapter.

Fischer and Sorenson (1991) have concluded that neither common law, the U.S. Constitution, nor the Federal Rules of Procedure guarantee the counselor–client relationship the aegis of privileged communication. Some states do so, but only under certain circumstances. Therefore, assurance of confidentiality, while ethically sound in most cases, is not always legally possible. Hence, sensitive issues such as tapes of client contacts, case notes and records, and release of information present opportunities for a counselor to exercise ethical choice. These issues are discussed in greater detail later in the chapter.

Dual Relationships

A dual role relationship exists when a counselor and client (or counselor-in-training and supervisor) have conflicts of interest that extend beyond the professional relationship. The most easily recognized of such relationships is that of sexual intimacy between a therapist and a client. This issue will be discussed later in this chapter because it has legal as well as ethical implications. Less dramatic dual relationships are, however, no less ethically questionable in most—although not all—cases.

When a therapist is simultaneously both counselor and something else with a client (e.g., friend, relative, business associate, teacher, supervisor, researcher, and so on), there is potential for exploitation. Kitchener (1988) suggests three reasons why dual relationships can cause problems: (1) incompatibility of expectations between roles; (2) divergence of the obligations inherent in each role; and (3) the power and prestige of the professional. Kitchener and Harding (1990) cite several potential problem dual relationships in addition to sexual intimacy. These include counseling those for whom one has evaluative responsibilities; bartering therapy services for other goods or services; and working with friends or relatives.

Counselors thus need to ask themselves if they are free of a dual relationship or, at the very least, if one does exist whether there is potential for harm and violation of the trust and nonexploitative nature of the counseling relationship. The basic question is one that centers around whether or not the dual relationship interferes with or has the possibility of interfering with the progress of the working alliance.

Legal Aspects

The legal aspects of counseling, although not as clearly defined and understood as one would like, are becoming more clearly defined. Court actions and verdicts are beginning to provide a greater insight into the legal responsibilities and liabilities of counseling. It is necessary for counselors to understand the implications of the law on various levels.

Although there is a great deal of concern in the mental health professions about legal aspects of practice, it should be remembered that clients file *relatively* few law suits against their therapists. There are several possible reasons for this relative lack of legal activity. One is that clients frequently must prove "emotional damage," a very difficult construct to substantiate. A second reason may be that because of the nature of the client–therapist relationship, the client is often psychologically unable to engage in assertively aggressive acts against the counselor. Another reason may be the fear of societal exposure and consequent stigma because a person is "in treatment." Whatever the reasons, the number of cases is relatively few and the monetary awards are typically not large.

The Counseling Relationship and Informed Consent

Counselors have a legal responsibility to inform clients what their skills are and what types of activities will be a part of the normal counseling interaction. Counselors should be certain that the client knows the conditions under which counseling will occur. Such aspects as fees, scheduling, client obligations, and counselor responsibilities should be discussed. It is probably wise to have a written description of the counseling service and the people involved for the client's perusal. This suggests there is a kind of contract between counselor and client that whether written or oral, more clearly defines the counseling relationship.

It may seem to some counselors that this explicit agreement is unnecessary. Clients "know" why they are there and what they hope will occur. And in most cases, this is probably true, but in today's society, where legal recourse is quickly undertaken, it is very helpful to have a contract, preferably a written one.

Informed consent is clearly necessary, but how specific it needs to be and in what form it is given are moot. The client surely needs to understand the nature of the counseling experience and its potential pitfalls. Clients, after all, may or may not have the right either to refuse treatment or to get treatment. In any case, through informed consent, clients must have the right to accept or to reject a particular treatment. If this is indeed their right, they must be provided with accurate information and have the capacity to process it rationally to make a decision.

Some individuals suggest that in voluntary treatment, clients need to be apprised in clear language of the nature of the counseling and possible risks. The client, many believe, needs to be told the counselor's perception of the nature of the difficulty and the proposed treatment, some probability statement regarding successful outcome, and any available alternatives. Everstine et al. (1980) recommend providing clients with a written statement such as the following: "Psychotherapy may involve the risk of remembering unpleasant events and can arouse intense emotions of fear and anger."

This approach may indeed frighten some clients to the point that they reject much needed counseling. In the same vein, some recommend that clients be told that not only may therapy not work, but also that it may make things worse. In addition, costs should be made clear "up front." Finally, clients should know that at any time during the course of counseling, they are free to rescind their informed consent.

Making certain that supervision is available for each case is another way to insure the counseling relationship is clearly understood. This may be done by sharing tapes with a colleague or in staffing meetings. Wherever it happens, supervision insures there is a check on the counselor's activities within the counseling relationship. Many times what one believes is occurring may not be. A counselor may develop a particular pattern of behavior that strays from what was originally described to the client. Supervision helps to focus on the counselor's behavior. Supervision also provides a method for diagnosing a client's needs. Regardless of the diagnostic pattern, it is essential that the diagnosis occur and that some verification of the process take place. Whether individually or in a case conference, supervision will help counselors perform better and will afford them greater protection should there be a legal action.

The emphasis upon clearly defining what counseling will be is necessary so that clients understand what help the counselor can provide and the form under which this assistance will be given. It also insures that the client knows what will be expected within the counseling framework.

Liability

Malpractice insurance is a common and increasingly high-priced necessary expense for many counselors, especially those not covered by umbrella protection provided for public employees. The sources of liability for malpractice are many. There are both sins of omission (failing to act when one should do so) and sins of commission (acting wrongfully toward a client). A few illustrations follow.

No ethical or legal issue receives more attention in the media than sexual activity within the therapeutic encounter. Sexual misconduct is both an ethical and a legal issue. It becomes the latter when clients seek legal redress of grievances for inappropriate therapist sexual behaviors. Few client-therapist sexual interactions actually eventuate in legal action, but surveys indicate that as many as four to seven percent of clinicians have had sexual relations with clients (Sadoff & Showell, 1981). Clients are obviously vulnerable, and sexual relationships are both countertherapeutic and exploitative. Consequently, sexual activity by a counselor that exploits the client's vulnerability usually results in legal findings in favor of the client when clients press the issue in court.

Counselors should realize that the definition of sexual activity is much broader than intercourse. It can include touching, fondling, caressing, petting, kissing, masturbation, talking about intercourse, exhibition, and so on. One major study has demonstrated the deleterious nature of sexual activity in therapy. Bouhoutsos et al. (1983) conducted a study in California that clearly showed, "When sexual intercourse begins, therapy ends." About 90 percent of current clients of therapists who described sexual activity with former therapists exhibited ill effects. The results of thus abusing clients and violating the intimacy of the therapeutic relationship may range from professional censure, to loss of license, to civil liability for money damages. In fact, any type of exploitation of clients is not only ethically reprehensible but also potentially leaves the counselor vulnerable to legal recourse by the client.

A second type of potential liability is failing to act when one should. A case in point is the so-called duty to warn or inform third parties of potential harm or danger. The now well-known case of Tarasoff v. Regents of the University of California (1976) determined that counselors must take action to warn others or the counselee themselves if there is a clear and imminent danger. In the case in point, an outpatient at the UCal/Berkeley Counseling Center in the summer told his counselor that he intended to murder his former girlfriend, Titiana Tarasoff, when she returned to school in the fall. The counselor informed both campus security and his superior of the threat and recommended commitment of his client, Prosenjit Poddar. Both the campus police and the supervising psychiatrist ordered that Poddar not be detained. When Ms. Tarasoff returned from the summer hiatus, Poddar killed her. Ms. Tarasoff's parents then sued, claiming that their daughter should have been warned of the danger. The court ruled in their favor, stating:

> When a therapist determines, or pursuant to the standards of his profession should determine that his patient presents a serious danger of violence to another, he incurs an obligation to use reasonable care to protect the intended victim against such danger. The discharge of this duty may require the therapist to take one or more various steps, depending on the nature of the case. Thus it may call for him to warn the intended victim or others, to apprise the victim of the danger, to notify the police, or to take whatever steps are necessary under the circumstances.

Thus, a dilemma is created by the desire to protect the confidential nature of the counseling relationship and the legal duty or moral obligation to warn of potential or real danger. Other clear cases in point relate to reporting child abuse, promiscuous AIDS carriers, and so on.

Failure to provide proper care for an obvious suicide risk could also have possible legal implications. Therapists may reasonably be expected to conduct competent lethality assessments, when appropriate, and to recommend sound procedures, if warranted (e.g., hospitalization). Further, if treatment and management of cases of those who may do harm to themselves are therapeutic and according to best accepted practice, it is unlikely that counselors will be held legally responsible for any resulting suicide.

One final example: Dealing with minors can also cause problems of liability. Child abuse is one obvious area of potential difficulty, and much of the problem may involve a counselor's failure to understand the difference between privileged communication and confidentiality. Privileged communication laws vary from state to state (in some states only M.D.'s have it, in other states psychologists are also given the privilege, and so on). Basically, privileged communication permits a litigant the right not to give in a court of law information that was originally communicated in confidence. Depending on where in the country one is, privileged communication may exist between client-attorney, husband-wife, priest-penitent, doctor-patient, and therapist-client. The idea is to protect those relationships that require mutual trust. Privileged communication is a legally bestowed condition. On the other hand, confidentiality is based on ethical rather than legal mandates. Unless there is a specific state law to the contrary, counselors cannot technically promise minors confidentiality. Hence, child abuse and neglect laws take precedence over confidentiality as children's rights issues come to prominence. A parent, in fact, may be able to force a counselor to disclose information about the child in a court of law. Rinas and Clyne-Jackson (1988) cite several instances where confidentiality can (and in some cases must) be violated: public safety as mandated by law, legitimate societal interest, involuntary commitment procedures, certain research procedures, third-party disclosures, court proceedings, and intra-agency personnel.

Defamation

Both libel and slander are usually treated as one action—defamation, an attack on a person's reputation by false accusations.

According to Hopkins and Anderson (1990), the key elements in any defamation suit are "(1) the information must be defamatory, that is, the party must be exposed to hatred, ridicule, contempt, or pecuniary loss; (2) the defamatory information must have been communicated to another person other than the person defamed; (3) the party defamed must be a living person; and (4) the person defamed must have suffered some type of injury or loss" (p. 40).

Libel is a false written or printed statement that injures the reputation of a living person. With the advent of the open records law in some states, the potential for defamation action has increased. Such documents as letters of recommendation for school or employment may be negatively interpreted by a client. He or she may see the letter of recommendation or have portions of it quoted during a job interview and feel that the comments made by the counselor have caused him or her injury. Slander is more tenuous than libel due to the less permanent nature of spoken statements, but it is just as serious. In each case malice is an element. Malice is personal ill will or reckless disregard for the rights of others. If the counselor makes remarks or prepares statements that contain malice, the likelihood of legal action is increased.

There are defenses against action in either area. If the statements are true or if the individual has consented to the statement, then no libel or slander would take place. There is also a possibility of qualified privilege. This implies that the statement or communication was made in good faith by one person who has an interest in or obligation for a client to another person with similar interest or duty. This tends to decrease or eliminate the presumption of malice. Some simpler defensive measures are also possible. Hummel, Talbutt, and Alexander (1985), for example, recommend that no information should ever be revealed over the telephone (and, by extension, perhaps, faxed).

Because counselors must prepare written statements about clients for required records or for subsequent educational or vocational opportunities, they will be faced with the possibility of action for defamation. In addition, because feedback to other persons who have some relationship to the client is essential, counselors may also find that action for slander is possible. The obvious way to avoid losing a court case in either area is to use the guidelines of truth and good faith. Increased communication with the client may also deter potential libel or slander charges.

Defamation can also be a professionally internecine issue. For example, many suits have been filed by one professional against another. Most common are cases of counselors who serve as gatekeepers—that is, who serve on certification or licensure boards, who make tenure or other types of employment decisions, and so on. Charges of impairment by one professional against another may also end up in court.

Sometimes the counselor may have to put him- or herself on the line and take a chance that court action may ensue. If the counselor has well-established data about a client's physical, mental, moral, or psychological health, he or she is obligated to report this information to various significant people in the client's life even though in the process some statement might be construed to be slanderous. Thus, if the counselor has good evidence that a female client is pregnant, he or she should attempt to ensure that her health is protected by examination and medical care. If the minor client will not see the doctor voluntarily, the counselor may have to involve her parents even though this means that the counselor is violating the girl's confidence and revealing information about her sexual activities. Because the counselor and parents share an interest in the client, this is an area of qualified privilege.

Counselors have a grave professional and moral responsibility not to defame and injure the reputation of others. This is true whether the individuals are students, parents, or other associates. Counselors must take care that communications are related to the needs of the client and that they accurately reflect the truth.

Rights of Clients

Clients have a number of implied and explicit rights. This issue centers on due process. Due process is guaranteed to everyone and is the right of an individual to have certain legal procedures followed whenever any complaint or action is taken against him or her. Due process is also applied to the rules and regulations social and various governmental agencies have had to develop. Even though many service and assistance programs are available to citizens today, in this diversity there is the possibility that some people may be denied assistance when they merit it or that services may be discontinued when they should be continued.

There are two separate types of due process: substantive and procedural. Substantive due process takes place when there has been a deprivation of a person's constitutional rights. Any rule that arbitrarily limits the freedom of an individual is a violation of substantive due process. Procedural due process applies when some rule is broken. Thus, the client may know the rule, but is often uninformed about the process necessary to initiate or complete any action.

The counselor's first task may be to ensure that the client knows both substantive and procedural material. The counselor may be called upon to be an advocate for the client to see that his or her rights are upheld. The counselor must know the rights of clients, know what constitutes due process, and be prepared to work with the proper personnel to ensure the application of due process to any action that may be instituted against the client.

Confidentiality of records also relates to the client's legal rights. The legal aspects of this change rapidly, but in general the counselor should avoid revealing data in client records unless he or she has the client's permission. Within this legal area the counselor may use the following guidelines:

1. Avoid revealing any data from client records without the client's specific permission.
2. When it is no longer possible to avoid revealing data, present the data with appropriate interpretative material.
3. Under extreme pressure, release the data if the law so states.

Counselors should seldom be forced into the final step if they ensure that their records are accurate and if they present material so that misinterpretation is minimal.

Research Use of Clients

Both ethical and legal issues can intrude whenever clients or nonclients are used in research. When there is a possible risk for research participants, the problem is exacerbated. Whenever research is conducted, counselors must deal with many of the issues discussed in this chapter: subjects' rights, informed consent, competency, confidentiality, dual relationships, and so on. Most institutions have some sort of human subjects review procedure that serves a watchdog function, but the private practitioner lacks this safeguard.

The major critical issues are those of subject autonomy (What can researchers do with a subject's mind and body?), undue risk, and truth (e.g., How much can a researcher disguise the purpose of an experiment or manipulate the conditions?). These issues become even more troublesome when psychiatric patients are used as subjects. Further, since the various standard therapies have not yet been conclusively demonstrated to have effectiveness, it is difficult to deny the legitimacy of many nontraditional therapies that are applied in research. On the basis of research, then, some rather esoteric therapy modes have been effected and justified (e.g., nude encounter groups).

Some Recommendations for Counselors

The legal aspects of counseling change relatively rapidly. As new issues are raised and dealt with in or out of court, more information will be available for developing strategies for insuring that the legal aspects are taken into consideration and at the same time the best possible service is available to clients.

The following are guidelines for counselors as they deal with clients:

• **Know what you can do as a counselor and communicate this to the client.** Although this seems to be a given for any counselor, it is true that many clients receive a faulty notion of what counselors can or will do for them. If misinterpretation is allowed to persist, the chances are increased that some dissatisfaction will occur. Communication, orally and written, will decrease the possibilities.

• **As part of the counseling interaction be sure that there is a definable diagnostic system.** Counselors must have a basis for providing services that focus upon clients' needs. They should have a method for determining the needs of clients and a way of relating their counseling activities to these client needs. (See Chapter 15 on diagnosis.) It is essential that counselors develop methods of diagnosis and be able to present the diagnosis, as well as the treatment, to appropriate personnel.

• **Counselors should clearly define their theory of counseling and personality development.** Many people attempt to counsel others with sincere intentions of helping them, but they may not spend the appropriate amount of time developing the methods by which this help may be best provided. It is important that a counseling theory be defensible and consistent. This is not to suggest that counselors select one specific theory and try to emulate the theorist. Counselors can use a combination of theories in their counseling practice, but they should have a clear, overall notion of what their practice will consist of and what their methods will be.

• **Counselors should understand their liability and the extent of the employing agent's liability.** In many cases counselors work under the aegis of a larger political or social entity. Many work in schools, colleges, community agencies, or state or federally funded institutions. Most of these do support the counselor whenever any legal problem arises, but there are always limits. There are usually some specific guidelines that spell out the employer's liability and responsibility.

• **Counselors should be sure to have regular supervision.** Supervision, in whatever form, provides the necessary link between counselors' training and growth and how they function in practice. Whether done on an individual basis or on a case conferencing basis, the supervision helps counselors clarify their perceptions of clients and their needs. It focuses on the counseling activity and the skills of counselors. Supervision assists counselors in altering those skills that may not be effective. It also provides feedback for counselors in terms of examining whether they actually counsel the way they profess to do. Many counselors get into a rut, tending to routinize their approach. When this happens the needs of individual counselees are sometimes ignored. Supervision can help counselors avoid this problem. Finally, supervision is a very sound way of preventing many legal problems.

Again, these suggestions are not given to limit counselors' activities but rather to suggest ways counselors can make better decisions about interactions with a variety of clients. The more these limits are defined, the better and more effective professionals will be because they can function without constantly looking over their shoulders.

Values in Counseling

It is essential that the counselor's and the client's value systems are as clearly understood as possible. If both parties have this reciprocal kind of understanding, the counseling outcome may be more relevant and helpful. Counseling may be defined as a search for values. The process can help the individual develop new values or reshape old ones to better function in society.

Values include ideals, goals, normative action, and group standards of behavior. A well-defined and understood value system allows a person to develop criteria for more effective behavior. As suggested earlier, values and the quest for purpose and identity are major concerns for many people. It is also essential for counselors to be aware of and concerned with their own values and with client and societal values and how these two interact.

Values, among other things, provide a definition of what is right, good, beautiful, or genuine. A person's value system aids in the process of decision making and in differentiating between those things that may be helpful and good for him or her and those things that may be harmful and bad.

A recognition of the importance of values to human development is essential to the counselor. It also is necessary to understand that values cannot be handed to or imposed upon clients. Individuals, including clients, must choose their own values. They must find them meaningful enough to act upon them to create a better life for themselves. Or they must believe strongly enough to begin to change themselves or the society in which value conflict occurs.

Two specific aspects of values and valuing are important to the counseling process. The first relates to the counselor's values and the degree to which these are known and have an effect upon the counseling process. The second relates to the values of the client: How were these developed? How might the client's values change? And how will these values affect the counseling process and, more importantly, outcomes?

The Counselor's Values

In the professional literature, there has been little disagreement concerning the need for counselors to understand their value systems. The counselor's value system has influenced the important decisions of her or his life. Some counselors seem unaware of the values they espouse, but observation indicates a consistent reflection of values. Counselors' value systems are critically important to their interaction with clients. But success in counseling may be related less to the nature of a counselor's personal and professional values than to the degree of control he or she has over them and to her or his ability to use them in a systematic way.

Values are the inferred criteria by which choices of objects or goals are justified. There is a distinction between the desired and the desirable: The desired is tied closely to physiological needs; the desirable seems to transcend mere physiological needs. Values are related to imitations of action and to setting directions for action.

From where do values emanate? Some counselors' values stem from their religious beliefs, usually based on some hermeneutic interpretation of one scripture or another. Other counselors take their value systems from a humanistic, altruistic desire to do good for the sake of others. Some counselors simply believe that it is logical to make appropriate moral choices, although they may disagree with the "correct" moral choice in a given situation or in general. Still others believe that one's self-interest is a sufficient justification to make moral choices and thus express one's values. In counseling, some values have become generally accepted as governing principles of practice. Blocher (1987) calls these second-order principles, and lists them as

1. Respect for human life.
2. Respect for truth.

3. Respect for privacy.
4. Respect for freedom and autonomy.
5. Respect for promises and commitments.
6. Concern for the weak, vulnerable, and helpless.
7. Concern for the growth and development of people.
8. Concern lest others be harmed.
9. Concern for human dignity and equality.
10. Concern for gratitude and reparation.
11. Concern for human freedom. (p. 36)

Values serve as reference points. They provide a basis for deciding which course of action to take. People have always needed these guidelines in order to continue their existence. However, values change, and what was prescribed as absolute and final at one time becomes tenuous at another. People may not be able to adjust to rapidly changing value systems; the result is shame, guilt, and/or anxiety. Although some may question a counselor's involvement in developing value systems, few would suggest that counselors can avoid values, either their own or their clients'. Values are the core of the counseling relationship. They are reflected by the content and the interaction. Thus counseling, which promotes modification of behavior, also provides a basis for the client to change attitudes and values.

The Role of Counselor Values

A counselor's value system may serve any of several roles. A counselor may know her or his own value system but avoid introducing it into the counseling interview. This counselor will not indicate his or her own position in any of the moral or value questions raised. The goal is to provide a situation in which the client can move from a position of external evaluation and valuing to an internalized locus of evaluation. Any value input by the counselor would work against the objective.

Another role makes it impossible for the counselor to remain neutral or not have an influence on the client. A client comes to a counselor for assistance. This assistance will have value questions associated with it. The question raised here is If, in fact, values and a moral stance are inherent in any relationship, to what degree are they used or abused by the counselor? Most people who adopt this role want to avoid manipulating values. They suggest that a person's philosophy is and must remain his or her own. Another question is whether the counselor ought to provide instruction to the client in developing a value system, clarifying personal values, or any of several related value-learning activities. Some counselors reject this teaching function in the counseling session, contending that there are more appropriate things to do and more appropriate ways to learn whatever might be taught in the counseling session. Others suggest the opposite: For some clients the first and most appropriate objective of counseling is learning or developing a more comprehensive and acceptable value system.

Given that various types of values or morals are introduced into the counseling setting, there may be some areas in which the counselor's own thoughts or development of an acceptable system are incomplete. This counselor cannot help the client in the realm of values because the latter may already be beyond the reach of the counselor, say, in the area of religious values.

The third role entails the active imposition of values upon the client. In this role the counselor must intervene. This intervention should be an identifiable part of counseling. The counselor must first deal with the values of the client: values about him- or herself, about the various prospects available, and about life and its interrelationships. Until these are known and accepted, the client will not be able to make a decision, move in meaningful directions, escape therapy, or whatever the more cognitive objectives of counseling might be.

This role tends to suggest that the counselor has greater intelligence, skills, or knowledge than anyone else and is entitled to a superior position toward others. This is not acceptable to some counselors, who would characterize this as a dehumanizing process. Regardless of criticism, however, there is some evidence that many clients want and will readily accept this more directive assistance without regard to the topic or area of concern. In effect, the client comes seeking help and wants the counselor to provide the assistance. More cynical observers suggest that these clients are only seeking justification from someone else for what they have already done or are contemplating. As long as someone agrees with them, the action is more acceptable to their own value system.

It is difficult to believe that the values and moral attitudes of the counselor can be hidden from the client. The counselor is better advised to recognize and accept his or her values, using them to promote greater awareness in the counseling relationship and expressing them when it appears that doing so will improve or further the relationship. When this occurs the client will feel less coerced into defending his or her own values and will be able to examine them in the privacy of the counseling session. This openness in sharing values will shift the emphasis to the act of valuing instead of evaluating the content of values. The client will be able to mature or function more effectively when the emphasis is on decision making. Valuing can thus help the client relate to a situation and then form a commitment to a course of action.

The Client's Values

Perhaps the most important part of counseling deals with client values and the relationship of these to the client's life. Several important facets of values need to be considered.

First, there is a need to understand the client's values and how these were developed. Obviously, value development relates to the social environment in which a person lives and the significant persons surrounding that person. Even though the environment is not the sole determining factor, it does weigh heavily on the forming of values.

Numerous studies and articles chronicle the fact that various groups of people hold certain beliefs that motivate their actions. The focal point of concern over values is that values influence behavior that may, at some point in a person's life, be inappropriate. Whether "society," however defined, determines that a person's behavior is not adequate or the person finds that his or her life is not as meaningful as he or she would like, the person's values will need to be examined.

Another concern over values relates to how people understand and accept their own values. In some cases, clarifying values helps a person to know what values are meaningful and valuable. Interestingly, people often behave according to a set of values they may not understand. But knowing what one's values are may not lead to a change of behavior, which is a major goal in counseling. It is usually easier to identify values than to change behavior. Almost everyone has something that they would like to change but find difficult to. The counselor's job includes finding ways of helping clients change behavior.

Differences between client and counselor values is also a concern. The literature on values raises such issues as minority clients and majority counselors, women clients and men counselors, specific ethnic groups and counselors with completely different backgrounds. Some suggest that there is a need to better match client and counselor values. Others take the position that this "fitting" is too great a limitation and that counselors need only work harder or be trained differently to be effective with a variety of clients. It is probably true that this issue is more clearly in the hands of the client. If a person wants to change, alter his or her values, or learn more appropriate behavior, any number of counselors can be helpful. If, however, a counselor bases her or his belief system upon the overt characteristics of the individual client or the setting, then such aspects as stereotype could be a factor.

It is clear that counselors and their agencies or organizations should be sensitive to clients' values. Counselors should be open to adjusting their counseling to fit clients' needs. This does not mean, however, that counselors should accept everything that clients say. On the contrary, counselors might feel it is necessary to use such techniques as value clarification, instructional methods, or confrontation to stimulate change in clients' behavior.

Value Concerns

Regardless of the method by which the above dilemma is solved, clients tend to have several types of concerns that relate to values and that are raised in counseling sessions with counselors. Sometimes the categories are vague and some time may need to be spent in actually identifying the need. In general, however, the following categorization seems to have some relevance.

The Meaning of Life

Many people at certain points in their lives have questions about themselves and the meaning of life. They may wonder where they fit in life. Events such as the loss of a job, the death of someone close, or divorce often cause people to ponder more closely their goals in life and the directions their lives are taking. This reassessment may occur at various ages, but often it will be a time of personal, professional, or social upheaval. Many people solve these problems on their own or with the help of a friend. Many others turn to a counselor hoping to find a way to resolve their problems.

Certain age groups often have greater difficulty understanding life than others. Adolescents, for instance, struggle with what they have been told and what they observe in society. They may face a dilemma of what is right defined by a new set of significant people and how to handle the guilt that accompanies the rejection of a previously accepted set of values. Students often have conflicts during their years at college. Their sudden freedom often poses difficulties in maintaining a stable way of life or understanding the life they are living.

Adults at certain ages are also subject to this pressure. As people grow older, they may find less and less meaning to life and begin to search for some other meaning. A woman who has devoted her life to raising a family and maintaining a home may feel a void in her life when her children leave home. The death of someone near often triggers feelings of uncertainty about life. New experiences often lead people to examine the meaning of life. In contemporary society, the drug culture provides a potent reinforcer for all types of people to reexamine what life is all about.

The counselor's first job in working with this problem is to help the client become aware of his or her current value system, to provide a situation in which clarification can occur. The counselor should avoid assuming an expert's role in this process: The client needs to develop a personal system and this is more important than some system suggested by another. Eventually, the counselor should help the client deal with his or her beliefs and how they can be most effectively implemented in life. Finally, the client should move into a period of more acceptable understanding of her or his own life and the meaning attached to it.

Many factors are interrelated within this area of counseling, including forces of a physical, psychological, or familial nature that affect a person's freedom. Although it is probably true that people can do most of what they want to do in life, these factors play an important role and must be recognized by the counselor and the client. In all cases the counselor should be alert to the possibility that other, more competent assistance, might be necessary.

Problems of Interrelatedness

A second area of value counseling involves the relationships people have with others. People are basically social animals and need to feel wanted and needed by others. When this does not occur, they develop all kinds of methods for handling the social void.

Satisfaction is often achieved by belonging to identifiable groups in society. Political groups, work groups, and family units all can be helpful in meeting individual social needs, but in certain situations these groups may pose problems for people. For example, people who devote time and energy to getting ahead in business may, upon reaching certain levels, find that they are just a "product" and not the significant people they thought they were. If these people did not have a relationship in the most important aspect of their life, where does this occur? How do they handle this, especially if future achievements do not seem as meaningful or available as they were in the past?

In most such cases, clients need to develop a balance in their relationships. They must begin to learn to invest in other activities that provide a broader base for generating relationships. They must learn where other potential relationships exist and how to take advantage of them. The counselor can help these clients by simply creating a counseling relationship in which the latter see themselves as meaningful people who can change and who can be more effective in relating to others. They are helped to see how their own behavior or personality may be related to the problem and that once they change this behavior, others will tend to respond more favorably.

Life Traumas

Various life traumas, such as loss of job, retirement, death, some physical problem or change of geographic location, can bring the individual into a counseling relationship. Sometimes the crisis is not as bad as the thoughts the client has about it. In all of life many things occur or statements are made that are misinterpreted by the hearer. For example, many students hear about a change in the curriculum in which they are involved and, without checking for the truth, become quite anxious about their own situation. Eventually learning the truth does not automatically and completely relieve that anxiety.

The counselor tries to resolve the dilemmas in both the trauma itself and the words that accompany the trauma. Often people use earlier experiences with lesser traumas to cope with the greater ones in life. Sometimes, though, the person either has not faced the lesser trauma or has not learned from the experience. This person enters counseling with a need to learn how to cope with the specific problem he or she is presently facing.

The counselor provides a relationship in which to deal with the doubts and inadequacies facing the client. The client begins to examine his or her own life and begins to learn strategies for dealing with the particular event that led to counseling. In this case, the counselor may not know whether he or she was instrumental in helping the client change or whether the passage of time was sufficient to block out whatever was related to the dilemma. The counselor should still strive to help the client work through self-understanding and learning effective strategies for dealing with future situations. The counselor's goal is to help alleviate the present condition and to provide assistance for generalizing to other situations in the future.

Moral Problems

Whenever individuals behave in ways contradictory to the mores of society, they may eventually seek assistance in reconciling these differences. Sometimes the client is only searching for someone who will support his or her action, in effect saying, I think what you are doing is all right, keep on behaving that way. This person is then no longer alone in his or her conflict and can use the opinion of the expert, the counselor, as justification to those who may be pressuring him or her. In this instance, change of behavior is less a goal than finding an important ally.

It is more often true that a person is really seeking to understand the differences and to work toward a solution that may well include changing behavior. The rapid change in society creates a conflict between some values that are acceptable in today's world with values that have been developed over a significant period of time and have been quite potent in shaping a person's life and behavior.

Two types of difficulties may exist. First, clients may feel that they are not doing as well as they would like to. Often this feeling is generated by outside forces, parents or friends, for example. Frequently, a person sees only negative factors in his or her life because people who are meaningful and relevant tend to point them out. The translation of these outside reactions is I am bad in some way. This tends to become a way of life because the person does not really know any other way to react.

A second concern is when someone breaks a specific rule, law, or moral precept. Most people are aware of the rules and the goodness inherent in following the rules. People who break the rules are seen by society as being not as good as people who somehow live by the basic rules. A person who breaks the rules often turns inward, and instead of talking about the problem allows negative feelings to increase and control his or her life, leading, of course, to personal problems at several levels.

Guilt, as described above, is of considerable importance in the counseling relationship. The counselor may have to go through a number of preliminary steps before even beginning to deal with the actual problem. First, the client's tensions and anxieties should be lessened. The relationship that is created and exists between counselor and client must be such that the client can freely express her or his feelings. This expression, regardless of how it may be generated, allows the client to begin to understand the reasons behind her or his actions. The client is able to examine needs and values and how these are related to the problem at hand. Such factors as responsibility, self-esteem, and self-understanding as well as new and more acceptable ways of acting can then follow.

This potential new and more effective way of acting may entail a change of behavior(s) on the part of the client. It may, however, simply mean learning to accept the feelings that exist. Sometimes it simply is not possible to change the things that have occurred. In this case, a person must find ways to accept his or her "bad" behavior and learn to live with it. Ideally, any future behavior would reflect a change in understanding and, perhaps, values on the part of the client. It is probably easier to work toward a behavioral change. Often the client can do this by him- or herself. Living with the undesirable behavior may cause a number of problems, not least of which is that society, family, and friends may find it unacceptable.

Religion and Counseling

Frequently, the implicit or explicit religious values of a counselor come into conflict with those of a client. Religiosity is a well-researched aspect of human behavior. Yet few definitive findings have resulted. Sevensky (1984) reviewed the research on the beliefs of mental health workers concerning certain religious principles (e.g., contact with the dead, life after death, personal immortality, and so on) and the existence of God. Compared with the general population, he concluded that the mental health workers had decidedly different views of the world. He states:

> In short, many people hold beliefs which most doctors and scientists (and presumably most psychiatrists, psychologists, and other mental health workers) regard as impossible; they organize and make sense of their lives around meanings and goals which a majority of the scientific-medical establishment consider mistaken. And unless these differences are recognized, the possibilities of professional bias, misinterpretation or error in the psychotherapeutic process remain quite real. (p. 75)

Depending on the therapist's orientation, then, certain religious practices may be viewed as either healthful or pathological. Various studies have compared the mental health of religious and nonreligious individuals. In meta-analysis, the result is that neither positive nor negative group effects can be linked to religiosity (Bergin, 1983). Clearly, in individual cases religiosity can be good (mentally healthful) or bad (mentally unhealthful). And even in cases where the beliefs are clearly unhealthy for a person, there are those who argue that any effort to change those religious beliefs is a violation of the client's civil liberties.

Some religious symptom patterns may be countertherapeutic. For example, clients may believe that their problems are the result of a lack of faith or that the therapist must be of the same faith. In the extreme, some clients may identify with religious figures such as Jesus or the Virgin Mary. Other clients may believe that demons possess them or that they have been abandoned by God.

In non-extreme cases, it is unclear when religiosity is healthy and when it is unhealthy. Much will depend on the values of the counselor and issues of countertransference. Probably all of us should keep in mind that the holiest, most revered and respected figures in most religions—the saints and the prophets—exhibited behavior that psychohistorians could easily describe as psychotic, asocial, neurotic, or, at the very least, bizarre.

Providing Assistance in Value Situations

Helping clients in the area of values may well be the most difficult task most counselors undertake. Even though the definition of problems may occur in a reasonable way, the process leading to understanding, accepting, and/or changing is much more difficult. One thing the counselor can and should do is to promote an environment in the counseling relationship that allows the client the freedom to explore, in some detail and depth, the value concerns she or he has.

Glaser and Kirschenbaum (1980) suggest some areas and questions that might be helpful as the counselor engages the client in a value-oriented session.

Topic: Choosing from Alternatives
Questions: **1.** Have you considered any alternatives to that?
                2. How long did you look around before you decided?
Comment: The general intent here is to identify the decision-making process, if any,
                which the client undertook. The client is helped to become aware of the
                fact that there may have been or may be alternatives to the action. He or
                she also becomes aware that there is usually a process, however
                tentative, that is undertaken by people regardless of the behavior. Of
                course the counselor can learn something about the client and his or her
                method of deciding, as well as the range of behaviors that might be part
                of the person's repertoire.

Topic: Choosing after Considering Consequences
Questions: **1.** What is the best thing you like about that idea?
                2. What would happen if everyone had your belief?

Comment: Again the client is helped to see that various alternatives may have more positive values attached to them than others. Although no alternative may be completely positive or negative, one that contains the greatest positiveness may lead to more positive outcomes and less negative consequences. Secondly, the client is helped to see the potential magnitude of the action and consequences if significant numbers of people were to adopt a particular position that might be out of step with the general society.

The counselor, in posing these types of questions, is helping the client to express a way of behaving. The counselor also gains additional insight into the client and her or his way of constructing her or his world, as well as the greater society.

Topic: Choosing Freely
Questions: **1.** Is that really your own choice?
2. Where do you suppose you first got that idea?
Comment: The client looks at the degree to which outside influences may affect decisions. Although he or she may generally believe that his or her decision was his or hers alone, this topic area introduces the idea that others often have subtle, as well as direct, input into decisions. Both types of questions can be aimed at helping to establish this fact.

The counselor learns more about the client and the significant people in his or her life. This information will be helpful when action is necessary and when the client and counselor need to work together to develop it.

Topic: Prizing and Cherishing
Questions: **1.** Is that something that is important to you?
2. Are you proud of how you handled that?
Comment: The client learns that people frequently behave on the basis of how important an activity and behavior may be. She or he also learns that it is all right to have some beliefs and parts of life that are important even though they may be seen by others as selfish. She or he sees that the value of the task is important and that the actual process of moving toward and completing activities is meaningful. For some clients this may bring about an important revelation: It is all right to prize something or someone and to feel good about it.

The counselor adds more information to his or her understanding of the client's method of operation. The data gleaned from the discussion of prizing and cherishing adds to the counselor's diagnostic understanding of the client and this should eventually be helpful in formulating a new and different behavior pattern.

Topic: Publicly Affirming
Questions: **1.** Is this something that you'd like to share with others?
2. Who would you be willing to tell that to?

Comment: It is generally necessary for the client to share his or her understandings and values with others. Sometimes this may be done in a direct manner, but often it is done through actions and behaviors that reflect the values. Obviously, it is usually important for the client to share this material with the counselor. If, however, this is as far as the client is willing to go, then there is probably more work to be done.

The counselor is given additional data that allows him or her to understand the client's value and person hierarchy. Through discussions, the counselor knows more of what is important to the client and who if anyone, the significant people in his or her life may be.

Topic: Acting
Questions: **1.** Is that something you'd be willing to try?
2. What would your next step be if you choose to pursue that direction?
Comment: As in most cases values counseling should lead to a change of behavior or at least a better understanding and acceptance of behavior. The questions suggested here should lead to the generation of several alternatives of behavior, which the client can examine. The questions also suggest that some decision needs to be made and some action taken so that the client can begin to move toward whatever goals she or he may have. By concentrating on these types of questions and levels, the counselor is helping the client to establish new ways of coping with her or his dilemmas.

The counselor should consider the degree of skill the client has for developing strategies for action. Depending, of course, on the counselor's own notion of counseling, this may afford her or him an opportunity to introduce some new ideas into the action stage. In this crucial stage of counseling, it would give both counselor and client a chance to develop ways of assessing how the client acts upon her or his knowledge and decision.

Topic: Acting Repeatedly
Questions: **1.** Is this typical of you?
2. Will you do it again?
Comment: One of the goals of counseling is to aid the client in learning new behaviors and in including these appropriate behaviors into his or her life. Frequently, the generation of ideas and the implementation of these ideas in action do not work out as much as is desirable. The client may find that he or she cannot behave in the way that has been agreed upon. He or she may need to alter the behavior again. It is eventually necessary that new behavior becomes part of the life-style. It is the counselor's job to insure that the new behavior is included in the client's life and that the behavior works.

From the counselor's point of view, this is the time where counseling is successful and helpful or falls short. The counselor, again depending upon personal philosophy, monitors the progress of the client and helps him or her adjust the activity or better understand the outcomes of the change. It should be noted here that most of the behavior we have discussed takes place outside the counseling dyad. The counselor needs to develop some ways of dealing with this detachment of the behavior from counseling while still monitoring and supporting the person.

The use of this model, or one like it, can be helpful in the process of identifying value concerns and developing ways to deal with them. Each counselor will probably modify any model; the important point is that the counselor understand the potency of values to behavior and life. He or she must understand his or her own values and must have a way to help the client identify his or her own values as well. When conflict occurs, the counselor is largely responsible for any modifications within the relationship that might take place. Finally, the counselor and client need to develop ways that will assist the client to move through the process from problems with values, identification of personal value systems, and modification of values to action based upon a reasoned decision-making process.

Summary

Counselors need to know about and take into account the ethical and legal ramifications of the counseling profession. Ethics, as an internal control mechanism, are provided by the major professional organizations to aid counselors in offering services to clients in a reasoned and proper fashion. Breaches of ethical behavior are dealt with by professional groups at local, state, and national levels.

The law, through court actions, provides an external control for counselors. This will continue to have greater importance to practicing counselors. Court actions taken by clients will provide more direction and added dimensions to the counselor's interaction with clientele, their families, and the society at large. The more knowledge the counselor has in this area, the greater the probability that his or her services will be effective and valuable to the client.

Values, long a relevant part of counseling, continue to have importance as counseling services are offered to an expanding range of clients by a much more diverse group of counselors. The greater the degree to which counselors can understand their own and their clients' value systems and integrate this knowledge into the relationship with clients, the greater the positive effect upon the outcomes of counseling. Clients may be bringing more value concerns to counseling and will be looking for someone who understands them and their values. They are searching for someone who shows potential for dealing with these types of problems. Counselors, throughout their training and experience, should continue to be aware of the meaningfulness of values in the life of each client. This should lead to better assistance for the client or to a referral that puts the client in touch with a counselor who can provide the help the client needs.

References

American Association for Counseling and Development. (1988). *Ethical standards* (rev. ed.). Alexandria, VA: Author.

American Association for Marriage and Family Therapy. (1988). *Code of professional ethics for marriage and family therapists* (rev. ed.). Washington, DC: Author.

American Psychiatric Association. (1989). *The principles of medical ethics with annotations especially applicable to psychiatry* (rev. ed.). Washington, DC: Author.

American Psychological Association. (1981). *Specialty guidelines for the delivery of services: Clinical psychologists, counseling psychologists, industrial/organizational psychologists, school psychologists.* Washington, DC: Author.

American Psychological Association. (1982). *Ethical principles in the conduct of research with human participants.* Washington, DC: Author.

American Psychological Association. (1987). General guidelines for providers of psychological services. *American Psychologist, 42*, 712–723.

American Psychological Association. (1990a). Ethical principles of psychologists. *American Psychologist, 45*, 390–395.

American Psychological Association. (1990b). *Guidelines for providers of services to ethnically and culturally diverse populations.* Washington, DC: Author.

Bergin, A. E. (1983). Religiosity and mental health: A critical reevaluation and metaanalysis. *Professional Psychology: Research and Practice, 14*, 170–184.

Blocher, D. H. (1987). *The professional counselor.* New York: Macmillan.

Bouhoutsos, J., Holroyd, J., Lerman, H., Forer, B. R., & Greenberg, M. (1983). Sexual intimacy between psychotherapists and patients. *Professional Psychology, 14* (2), 185–196.

Everstine, L., Everstine, D. S., Heymann, G. M., True, R. H., Frey, D. H., Johnson, H. G., & Seiden, R. H. (1980). Privacy and confidentiality in psychotherapy. *American Psychologist, 35*(9), 828–840.

Fischer, L., & Sorenson, G. P. (1991). *School law for counselors, psychologists, and social workers* (2nd ed.). New York: Longman.

Glaser, B., & Kirschenbaum, H. (1980). Using values clarification in counseling settings. *Personnel and Guidance Journal, 58*, 569–574.

Hummel, D. L., Talbutt, L. C., & Alexander, M. D. (1985). *Law and ethics in counseling.* New York: Van Nostrand Reinhold.

Hopkins, B. R., & Anderson, R. S. (1990). *The counselor and the law.* Alexandria, VA: American Association for Counseling and Development.

Kitchener, K. S. (1988). Dual role relationships: What makes them so problematic? *Journal of Counseling and Development, 67*, 217–221.

Kitchener, K. S., & Harding, S. S. (1990). Dual role relationships. In B. Herlihy & L. B. Golden (Eds.), *Ethical standards casebook* (pp. 146–154). Alexandria, VA: American Association for Counseling and Development.

National Association of Social Workers (1990). *Code of ethics* (rev. ed.). Silver Springs, MD: Author.

Pope, K. S., & Vetter, V. A. (1992). Ethical dilemmas encountered by members of the American Psychological Association. *American Psychologist, 47*(3), 397–411.

Popiel, D. J. (1980). Confidentiality in the context of court referrals to mental health professionals. *American Journal of Orthopsychiatry, 50*, 678–685.

Rinas, J., & Clyne-Jackson, S. (1988). *Professional conduct and legal concerns in mental health practice.* Norwalk, CT: Appleton & Lange.

Sadoff, R. I., & Showell, R. (1981). *Sex and therapy: A survey of female psychiatrists.* Paper presented at the annual meeting of the American Psychiatric Association, New Orleans, LA.

Sevensky, R. L. (1984). Religion, psychology, and mental health. *American Journal of Psychotherapy, 38*, 73–86.

Tarasoff v. Regents of University of California, 528 P.2d, 553 (Cal. 1974); modified, 551, P.2d 334 (Cal. 1976).

Author Index

Subject Index